Series Editors:
David R. Beukelman, Ph.D.
Joe Reichle, Ph.D.

**Augmentative and Alternative
Communication for Adults with
Acquired Neurologic Disorders**

AAC
Series

Augmentative and Alternative Communication for Adults with Acquired Neurologic Disorders

edited by

David R. Beukelman, Ph.D.
University of Nebraska–Lincoln

Kathryn M. Yorkston, Ph.D.
University of Washington–Seattle

and

Joe Reichle, Ph.D.
University of Minnesota–Minneapolis

·PAUL·H·
BROOKES
PUBLISHING C°

Baltimore • London • Toronto • Sydney

Paul H. Brookes Publishing Co.
Post Office Box 10624
Baltimore, Maryland 21285-0624

www.brookespublishing.com

Typeset by Argosy, West Newton, Massachusetts.
Manufactured in the United States of America by
The Maple Press Co., York, Pennsylvania.

This volume contains some information about drugs frequently used to treat neurologic disorders. The information here is in no way meant to substitute for a physician's advice or expert opinion; readers should consult a medical practitioner if they are interested in more information.

Library of Congress Cataloging-in-Publication data
Augmentative and alternative communication for adults with acquired neurologic disorders / edited by David R. Beukelman, Kathryn M. Yorkston, and Joe Reichle.
    p. cm.
Includes bibliographical references and index.
ISBN 1-55766-473-0 (alk. paper)
  I. Communicative disorders—Patients—Rehabilitation.   2. Communication devices for the disabled.   3. Nervous system—Diseases—Complications.   I. Beukelman, David R., 1943–   II. Yorkston, Kathryn M., 1948–
III. Reichle, Joe, 1951–
  [DNLM: I. Communication Disorders—rehabilitation.   2. Nervous System Diseases—rehabilitation.   3. Nonverbal Communication.   WL 340.2
A9213 2000]
RC423 .A929 2000
616.85′503—dc21

                        00-042942

British Library Cataloguing in Publication data are available from the British Library.

Contents

Series Preface vii

Editorial Advisory Board ix

Volume Preface xi

About the Editors xiii

About the Contributors xv

Acknowledgments xxi

Part One

1   Meaningful Communication Roles
     Lynn E. Fox and McKay Moore Sohlberg 3

2   AAC Message Management
     Sheela Stuart, Joanne P. Lasker, and
     David R. Beukelman 25

3   Decision Making in AAC Intervention
     Kathryn M. Yorkston and David R. Beukelman 55

4   Integrating AAC Strategies with
     Natural Speech in Adults
     Katherine C. Hustad and David R. Beukelman 83

5   Acceptance of AAC by Adults with
     Acquired Disorders
     Joanne P. Lasker and Jan L. Bedrosian 107

6   Rebuilding Communicative Competence
     and Self-Determination
     Janice C. Light and Maija Gulens 137

Part Two

7   AAC for Individuals with
     Amyotrophic Lateral Sclerosis
     *Pamela Mathy, Kathryn M. Yorkston,
     and Michelle L. Gutmann* 183

8   AAC for Huntington Disease and
     Parkinson's Disease: Planning for
     Change
     Estelle R. Klasner and Kathryn M. Yorkston 233

9   AAC and Traumatic Brain Injury:
     Influence of Cognition on
     System Design and Use
     *Molly Doyle, Mary R.T. Kennedy,
     Ginta Jausalaitis, and Barbara Phillips*..271

10   Proactive Management of
     Primary Progressive Aphasia
     *Margaret A. Rogers, Julia M. King,
     and Nancy B. Alarcon*...305

11   AAC and Aphasia: Cognitive-Linguistic
     Considerations
     Kathryn L. Garrett and Mikael D.Z. Kimelman 339

12   AAC and Dementia
     *Melanie Fried-Oken, Marie T. Rau, and
     Barry S. Oken*..375

Index 407

Series Preface

The purpose of the *Augmentative and Alternative Communication Series* is to address advances in the field as they relate to issues experienced across the life span. Each volume will be research-based and practical, providing up-to-date and groundbreaking information on recent social, medical, and technical developments. Each chapter is designed to be a detailed account of a specific issue. To help ensure a diverse examination of augmentative and alternative communication (AAC) issues, an editorial advisory board will assist in selecting topics, volume editors, and authors. Prominent scholars, representing a range of perspectives, will serve on the editorial board so that the most poignant advances in the study of AAC are sure to be explored.

In the broadest sense, the concept of AAC is quite old. Gestural communication and other types of body language have been widely addressed in literature about communication for hundreds of years. Only recently, though, has the field of AAC emerged as an academic discipline that incorporates graphic, auditory, and gestural modes of communicating. This series will concentrate on achieving specific goals. Each volume will detail the empirical methods used to design AAC systems for both descriptive groups and for individuals. By tracking the advances in methods, current research, practice, and theory, we will also develop a broad and evolutionary definition of this new discipline.

Many reasons for establishing this series exist, but foremost has been the number and diversity of the people who are affected by AAC issues. AAC consumers and their families, speech-language pathologists, occupational therapists, physical therapists, early childhood educators, general and special educators, school psychologists, neurologists, and professionals in rehabilitative medicine and engineering all benefit from research and advancements in the field. Likewise AAC needs are not delineated by specific age parameters; people of all ages who have developmental and acquired disabilities rely on AAC. Appropriate interventions for individuals across a wide range of disabilities and levels of severity must be considered.

Fundamentally, the field of AAC is problem driven. We, the members of the editorial advisory board, and all professionals in the field are dedicated to solving those problems in order to improve the lives of people with disabilities. The inability to communicate effectively is devastating. As we chronicle the advances in the field of AAC, we hope to systematically dismantle the barriers that prevent effective communication for all individuals.

Editorial Advisory Board

Volume Preface

The lives of people with acquired neurologic disorders and conditions changed considerably during the 20th century. At the beginning of the century, the medical community primarily emphasized diagnosis. Over the years, a variety of types of therapeutic interventions have been developed and implemented. These interventions involve surgery, pharmacology, behavioral rehabilitation, and technology and continue to change the ways in which adults with acquired disabilities manage their life activities, such as nutrition, breathing, mobility, and communication. This volume focuses on the communication options of people with the most severe communication disorders, yet it also deals with the societal, medical, and technical changes that affect the lives of these individuals.

This volume is written for those who are interested in the social consequences of neurogenic and neuromuscular disabilities. We anticipate the people with advanced interests in neurology, neurorehabilitation, and speech-language pathology, as well as AAC, will be interested in the contents of this book. The volume is divided into two parts. The chapters of Part One focus on issues related to all adults with severe communication disorders caused by acquired neurogenic and neuromuscular disabilities. These issues are relevant to adults with acquired disabilities, regardless of underlying etiology. Fox and Sohlberg (Chapter 1) discuss the meaningful communication roles of adults with severe acquired communication disorders. Stuart, Lasker, and Beukelman (Chapter 2) describe strategies to capture the messages that adults need to maintain their communication roles and to participate effectively. Yorkston and Beukelman (Chapter 3) review clinical decision-making strategies for adults with neurogenic and neuromuscular communication disorders. Hustad and Beukelman (Chapter 4) focus on how combining natural speech and AAC strategies affects the communication effectiveness of people with some residual speaking ability. Lasker and Bedrosian (Chapter 5) deal with the acceptance of AAC strategies by adult AAC users and members of their social networks. Finally, Light and Gulens (Chapter 6) articulate ways of rebuilding communicative competence and self-determination for adults after the onset of severe communication disorders.

The chapters in Part Two of this volume cover issues that pertain to people with specific neurologic and neuromuscular conditions. Mathy, Yorkston, and Gutmann (Chapter 7) review the characteristics of people with amyotrophic lateral sclerosis and its affect on AAC interventions. Klasner and Yorkston (Chapter 8) focus on the capabilities of people with the movement disorders Huntington disease and Parkinson's disease, and they describe AAC options. Doyle, Kennedy, Jausalaitis, and Phillips (Chapter 9) examine the linguistic and cognitive limitations of adults with traumatic brain injury and the effect of these limitations on AAC intervention and device design. Rogers, King, and Alarcon (Chapter 10) describe the communication and cognitive impairments of people with progressive primary aphasia and outline AAC strategies that are useful for this population. Garrett and Kimelman (Chapter 11) consider the unique language and cognitive issues that affect AAC intervention for people with nonprogressive aphasia. Finally, Fried-Oken, Rau, and Oken (Chapter 12) outline AAC issues for people with dementia.

About the Editors

David R. Beukelman, Ph.D., Director of Research and Education, Munroe/Meyer Institute for Genetics and Rehabilitation, University of Nebraska, Lincoln, Nebraska 68583. Dr. Beukelman is the Barkley Professor of Communication Disorders at the University of Nebraska. He is also Director of Research and Education at the Munroe/Meyer Institute for Genetics and Rehabilitation at the University of Nebraska Medical Center. He specializes in motor speech disorders and AAC for adults with acquired communication disorders.

Kathryn M. Yorkston, Ph.D., BC-NCD, Head, Division of Speech Pathology, University of Washington, Box 356490, Seattle, Washington 98195. Dr. Yorkston is Head of the Division of Speech Pathology and Professor in the Department of Rehabilitation Medicine at the University of Washington. She also holds an adjunct appointment in the Department of Speech and Hearing Sciences. Dr. Yorkston has a long history of clinical research and publication in acquired neurologic communication disorders in adults. She is a past president of the Academy of Neurologic Communication Disorders and Sciences.

Joe Reichle, Ph.D., Associate Chair, Department of Communication Disorders, University of Minnesota, Minneapolis, Minnesota 55495. Dr. Reichle is Professor and Associate Chair of the Department of Communication Disorders at the University of Minnesota. He has worked for 20 years in general and special education programs serving school-age children with moderate to severe developmental disabilities, families, teachers, and paraprofessionals. Dr. Reichle is currently responsible for master's, doctoral, and postdoctoral personnel preparation programs in the area of AAC. Dr. Reichle has served as Co-Principal Investigator of a number of model in-service projects in the areas of AAC and proactive approaches to challenging behavior. He has published numerous articles in the area of AAC and challenging behavior. Along with Dr. Steven Warren of Vanderbilt University, Dr. Reichle served as Co-Editor of the *Communication and Language Intervention Series* (Paul H. Brookes Publishing Co.).

About the Contributors

Nancy B. Alarcon, M.S., CCC-SLP, BC-NCD, Senior Lecturer and Clinical Director, Department of Speech and Hearing, University of Washington, 1417 N.E. 42nd Street, Seattle, Washington 98105. Ms. Alarcon is a speech-language pathologist with extensive experience in the area of adult neurogenic communication disorders. She is Senior Lecturer and Clinical Director in the Department of Speech and Hearing at the University of Washington. Her clinical research with colleagues focuses on family-based intervention in aphasia and a longitudinal investigation of primary progressive aphasia. In addition, her work emphasizes functional integration of treatment objectives in individual and group intervention, maximization of multimodality communication skills, and inclusion of communication partners in the intervention process.

Jan L. Bedrosian, Ph.D., Professor, Department of Speech Pathology and Audiology, Western Michigan University, 1201 Oliver Street, Kalamazoo, Michigan 49008. Dr. Bedrosian is Professor in the Department of Speech Pathology and Audiology at Western Michigan University. She is currently Associate Editor for the journal *Augmentative and Alternative Communication.* Her presentations and publications focus on research design issues in AAC, variables influencing perceptions of communicative competence of adult AAC system users, and literacy development in children who use AAC systems.

Molly Doyle, M.S., CCC-SLP, Program Director, Las Floristas Center for Applied Rehabilitation Technology, Rancho Los Amigos National Rehabilitation Center, 7601 E. Imperial Highway, Downey, California 90242. Ms. Doyle is currently Program Director of the Las Floristas Center for Applied Rehabilitation Technology at Rancho Los Amigos National Rehabilitation Center. She has more than 12 years of experience in providing AAC services and has both published and presented in the area of AAC for adults with acquired disabilities.

Lynn E. Fox, Ph.D., Assistant Professor, Speech and Hearing Sciences Program, Portland State University, 85A Neuberger Hall, Portland, Oregon 91207. Dr. Fox is Assistant Professor in the Speech and Hearing

Sciences Program at Portland State University in Portland, Oregon. She was Clinical Training Coordinator and a staff speech-language pathologist at the Portland Veterans Affairs Medical Center prior to accepting her current academic appointment. Dr. Fox's clinical practice and teaching focus on adults with acquired speech and language disorders.

Melanie Fried-Oken, Ph.D., CCC-SLP, Associate Professor of Neurology and Pediatrics, Oregon Health Sciences University, 3181 S.W. Sam Jackson Park Road, L226, Portland, Oregon 97201. Dr. Fried-Oken is Associate Professor of Neurology and Pediatrics at Oregon Health Sciences University. Dr. Fried-Oken has spent more than 20 years specializing in AAC. She works at an AAC clinic in the Neurology Department at Oregon Health Sciences University and manages the Assistive Technology Program at the Child Development and Rehabilitation Center. She recently co-edited *Speaking Up and Spelling It Out*, a book of essays written by augmented speakers (co-edited with Hank A. Bersani, 2000, Paul H. Brookes Publishing Co).

Kathryn L. Garrett, Ph.D., CCC-SLP, Assistant Professor, Department of Speech-Language Pathology, Duquesne University, 410 Fisher Hall, 600 Forbes Avenue, Pittsburgh, Pennsylvania 15282-2231. Dr. Garrett is Assistant Professor of Speech-Language Pathology at Duquesne University. She obtained her doctorate at the University of Nebraska–Lincoln in 1993. She teaches and directs a clinical program for individuals with aphasia, other adult neurogenic communication disorders, and AAC needs. Her research focuses on the effect of contextual strategies on the communication interactions of adults with aphasia. She has published and presented numerous chapters and articles in the areas of aphasia and AAC strategies.

Maija Gulens, B.A., Department of Communication Disorders, Pennsylvania State University, 110 Moore Building, University Park, Pennsylvania 16802. Ms. Gulens is a graduate student completing her master's degree in communication disorders at Pennsylvania State University. Ms. Gulens' research interests include AAC, language development, and literacy. Ms. Gulens is working on a research grant directed by Dr. Janice C. Light and Dr. David McNaughton at Pennsylvania State University that focuses on an Internet-based training program to teach individuals who use AAC effective communication skills, collaborative problem-solving and goal-setting skills, and information on disability-related resources in preparation for their role as mentors.

Michelle L. Gutmann, M.S., CCC-SLP, Speech-Language Pathologist, Department of Special Education and Communication Disorders, University of Nebraska, 253 Barkley Memorial Center, Box 830731,

Lincoln, Nebraska 68583-0731. Ms. Gutmann is a speech-language pathologist with 9 years of experience in the area of AAC. She has worked with both adults and children who have severe communication impairments in a variety of settings, including a mobile adult AAC service, a pediatric rehabilitation center, and a clinic for amyotrophic lateral sclerosis. Ms. Gutmann is currently pursuing her doctorate degree.

Katherine C. Hustad, Ph.D., CCC-SLP, Assistant Professor, Department of Communication Disorders, Pennsylvania State University, 110 Moore Building, University Park, Pennsylvania 16802. Dr. Hustad is Assistant Professor in the Department of Communication Disorders at Pennsylvania State University. Her areas of research and clinical interest include speech intelligibility, motor speech disorders, and AAC.

Ginta Jausalaitis, M.D., Chief, Adult Brain Injury Service, Rancho Los Amigos National Rehabilitation Center, 7601 E. Imperial Highway, Downey, California 90242. Dr. Jausalaitis is Chief of the Adult Brain Injury Service at Rancho Los Amigos National Rehabilitation Center and Assistant Professor of Neurology at the University of Southern California. She completed a fellowship in neurorehabilitation and has several years of experience in providing acute rehabilitation to adults with acquired brain injuries.

Mary R.T. Kennedy, Ph.D., CCC-SLP, Assistant Professor, Department of Communication Disorders, University of Minnesota, 115 Shevlin Hall, 164 Pillsbury Drive, Minneapolis, Minnesota 55455. Dr. Kennedy is currently Assistant Professor at the University of Minnesota and worked clinically for 17 years with adults who have neurogenic disorders. She has published and presented on cognitive-communication disorders in adult survivors of traumatic brain injury and right-hemisphere stroke.

Mikael D.Z. Kimelman, Ph.D., Chair, Department of Speech-Language Pathology, Duquesne University, 403 Fisher Hall, 711 Forbes Avenue, Pittsburgh, Pennsylvania 15282-2231. Dr. Kimelman is Chair of the Department of Speech-Language Pathology in the John G. Rangos, Sr., School of Health Sciences at Duquesne University. He teaches and conducts research in the areas of neurogenic communication disorders and speech production. His research focuses on auditory information processing in aphasia and on the production of prosody.

Julia M. King, Ph.D., CCC-SLP, Assistant Professor, Department of Communication, University of Wisconsin, Oshkosh, Wisconsin 54901. Dr. King received her doctorate at the University of Nebraska–Lincoln. She is currently Assistant Professor in the Department of Communication at the University of Wisconsin–Oshkosh. Previously, she was Assistant Professor at the University of Nevada–Reno.

Estelle R. Klasner, Department of Speech and Hearing Sciences, Department of Rehabilitation Medicine, University of Washington, Seattle, Washington 98195-6490. Ms. Klasner is currently a doctoral candidate in the Department of Speech and Hearing Sciences at the University of Washington–Seattle. Ms. Klasner has had extensive clinical experience with individuals with Huntington disease. She worked with the Huntington Society of Canada, conducting research and developing educational materials concerning the speech and communication difficulties associated with Huntington disease.

Joanne P. Lasker, Ph.D., CCC-SLP, Assistant Professor, Department of Speech Pathology and Audiology, Western Michigan University, 1201 Oliver Street, Kalamazoo, Michigan 16802. Dr. Lasker is Assistant Professor in the Department of Speech Pathology and Audiology at Western Michigan University. She specializes in the study of adult neurogenic communication disorders and AAC. She has been involved in the assessment and treatment of adults with severe communication disorders for the past 10 years. Her presentations and publications focus on acceptance and implementation of AAC by adults with acquired disorders and their communication partners.

Janice C. Light, Ph.D., Associate Professor, Department of Communication Disorders, Pennsylvania State University, 217 Moore Building, University Park, Pennsylvania 16802. Dr. Light is Associate Professor in the Department of Communication Disorders at Pennsylvania State University. She is involved in research, personnel preparation, and service delivery in the area of AAC. Dr. Light is currently Principal Investigator on a project funded by the U.S. government that supports graduate students in developing specialized competencies in rehabilitation practice and research in AAC. She is Project Director in the Rehabilitation Engineering Research Center (RERC) in Augmentative and Alternative Communication, a "virtual" research consortium that is funded by the National Institute on Disability and Rehabilitation Research. Dr. Light teaches courses in AAC at the undergraduate and graduate level and provides consultation to individuals who require AAC and their families. In 1999 she received the Dorothy Jones Barnes Outstanding Teaching Award.

Pamela Mathy, Ph.D., Clinical Professor and Director of Clinical Services, Speech and Hearing Clinic, Department of Speech and Hearing Science, Arizona State University, Post Office Box 870102, Tempe,

Arizona 85287-0102. Dr. Mathy is Director of Clinical Services in the Department of Speech and Hearing Sciences at Arizona State University. In addition to her administrative duties, she engages in clinical teaching with a focus on adults and children with neurogenic and neuromuscular disorders, and she teaches the graduate courses on AAC. Before moving to Arizona, Dr. Mathy directed the AAC clinical program at the Munroe/Meyer Institute for Genetics and Rehabilitation at the University of Nebraska Medical Center.

Barry S. Oken, M.D., Professor, Department of Neurology and Behavioral Neuroscience, Oregon Health Sciences University, 3181 S.W. Sam Jackson Park Road, Portland, Oregon 97201. Dr. Oken is Professor in the Department of Neurology and Behavioral Neuroscience at Oregon Health Sciences University (OHSU). He is a neurologist and clinical neurophysiologist and directs the Clinical Neurophysiology Department at OHSU hospital. He runs a cognitive neuroscience laboratory that has a major focus on cognitive changes associated with aging that is supported primarily by National Institutes of Health funding.

Barbara Phillips, M.S., OTR, ATP, Occupational Therapist, Las Floristas Center for Applied Rehabilitation Technology, Rancho Los Amigos National Rehabilitation Center, 7601 E. Imperial Highway, Downey, California 90242. Ms. Phillips is an occupational therapist with more than 11 years of rehabilitation experience. She provides technology assessments to individuals with physical disabilities, acts as a consultant to care providers in the community, and presents to professional groups on a regular basis.

Marie T. Rau, Ph.D., Program Director, Department of Speech Pathology, Veterans Administration Medical Center, Post Office Box 1034, Portland, Oregon 97207. Dr. Rau has 30 years of experience in working in a medical setting with people who have dementia and their families and caregivers. She has presented numerous papers and workshops at state and national meetings on such topics as the effects of dementia and other neurogenic communication disorders on individuals and caregivers. She has published several book chapters on treatment issues related to progressive communication disorders associated with dementia and has written a book for family caregivers of people with dementia.

Margaret A. Rogers, Ph.D., CCC-SLP, BC-NCD, Associate Professor, Department of Speech and Hearing Sciences, University of Washington, 1417 N.E. 42nd Street, Seattle, Washington 981005. Dr. Rogers is Associate Professor of Speech and Hearing Sciences at the University of Washington–Seattle. Her research includes investigation of spoken language production in typical adults and individuals with aphasia and apraxia of speech, the dissolution of spoken language in primary progressive aphasia, and the efficacy of treatments directed toward decreasing the activity limitations and participation restrictions of individuals with neurogenic communication disorders.

McKay Moore Sohlberg, Ph.D., Assistant Professor, Communication Disorders and Sciences Program, University of Oregon, Box 5251, Eugene, Oregon 97403. Dr. Sohlberg is Assistant Professor in the Communication Disorders and Sciences Program at the University of Oregon. Dr. Sohlberg is well known in the field of cognitive rehabilitation for the development of treatment programs designed to remediate impairments in attention, memory, and executive functions following acquired brain injury. Her research also extends to the development and evaluation of methods to facilitate effective partnerships of clinicians and families affected by neurogenic disorders.

Sheela Stuart, Ph.D., Director of Speech-Language Pathology Services, Children's National Medical Center, 111 Michigan Avenue NW, Washington, DC 20010. Dr. Stuart earned her doctorate from the University of Nebraska, with special emphasis in the area of AAC. She has worked in this area providing clinical service and teaching in South Dakota and New Mexico. She currently is Director of Speech-Language Pathology Services at Children's National Medical Center, and she also is Associate Professor in Pediatrics at George Washington University.

Acknowledgments

The editors wish to thank Paul H. Brookes Publishing Co. for its support of the AAC field through the years. Publication of this volume is just one more indication of their commitment to those with severe communication disabilities. We also wish to acknowledge the support that we have received through the years to develop the AAC capacities in our own institutions. In particular, the Barkley Trust, the Hattie B. Munroe Foundation, the AAC Leadership Personnel Preparation Grants (U.S. Department of Education [USDE]), the Muscular Dystrophy Association, and the Rehabilitation Engineering and Rehabilitation Center funded by the National Institute on Disability and Rehabilitation Research (NIDRR) of the U.S. Department of Education have supported the AAC program at the University of Nebraska. We also appreciate the Leadership Personnel Preparation grants (USDE) and the Research and Training Institute on Community Integration (NIDRR) at the University of Minnesota. The Muscular Dystrophy Association, in support of the Neuromuscular Clinic for Speech and Swallowing Disorders, and the Research and Training Centers in Traumatic Brain Injury and Multiple Sclerosis from the National Institute on Disability and Rehabilitation Research (USDE) have supported the AAC program at the University of Washington. Finally, we wish to thank Nancy Brown and Laura Hayes for providing organizational support for the preparation of this volume.

Part One

1

Meaningful Communication Roles

Lynn E. Fox
McKay Moore Sohlberg

When a communication disorder shatters the long-established social roles of an individual, the augmentative and alternative communication (AAC) interventionist is challenged to find an approach that will provide the augmented communicator with strategies to achieve meaningful social interaction. The multitude of considerations that confront the interventionist might best be characterized in three salient questions:

1. What social roles does the individual desire to perform?
2. How will personal factors, such as motivation, influence role performance?
3. How will environmental factors alter role performance?

To answer these questions and thereby discover an approach that permits meaningful communicative interaction among communicators who use AAC and their environments, this chapter explores research in social psychology, family systems theory, and psychosocial outcomes of communication disorders. Another rich resource, the stories of individuals who have persisted in actively fulfilling some social roles despite the onset of acquired communication disorders, are also included.

Derrel is a 50-year-old man who suffered a stroke 2 years ago. Since his stroke, he communicates only fragments of ideas using speech, gestures, written words, drawings, and a few symbols in his communication book. Recently, Derrel and his wife, Gail, had an especially frustrating interaction. Derrel and Gail were sitting in the living room of their home. Derrel pointed toward the front of the house, opened his palms, and shrugged his shoulders to indicate that he wanted to know something. Gail began to play 20 Questions. Was there something outside? Was it about the neighbors? Derrel finally drew a small rectangle and showed it to Gail. Gail thought a bit and asked a few more questions. Was it about the yard? Was it about the car? "Yes," Derrel nodded enthusiastically. It was about the car! Gail felt frustrated. She knew that the message was about the car, but she couldn't decipher the meaning of the small rectangle. To each of the next questions that Gail asked, Derrel shook his head "no." Finally, in frustration, Gail asked, "Is this really important?" Derrel shrugged and indicated that it wasn't that important.

Later that day, as he was sitting in his den, Derrel glanced at a family picture and saw that his daughter-in-law was wearing a beautiful blue dress. The next time Gail came into the room, Derrel pointed to the blue dress and pointed outside. Again, Gail asked a series of questions, to which Derrel shook his head "no." Suddenly Gail thought, *car ... blue ... rectangle.* She asked, "Derrel, is it about the handicapped parking pass?" "Yes!" Derrel nodded. That was exactly it! It took only a few more questions to determine that Derrel wanted to know when the car's handicapped parking pass expired.

George is a 60-year-old man with quadriplegia who experienced a severe illness that resulted in long-term use of a mechanical ventilator. George now spends most of his time alone in his bedroom. His wife and his grown son and daughter are his caregivers. Although George has a computer, he doesn't use it. He doesn't often even agree to get up in his wheelchair, and when he does, he quickly asks to be put back to bed. Yet, when George was asked what one thing he would most like to discuss with his family, he used head nods to spell out "home repairs" as his wife pointed to letters on an alphabet board.

Jim, a man with aphasia, is 55 years old and is working on perfecting drawing to communicate stories and other complex ideas. His wife likes to tell about Jim's instructing her to change the oil in their old Chevy by drawing a picture of the car with the hood up, and a figure bending over the car and pulling out of the engine what appeared to be a dipstick. She said, "I can't believe he's still nagging me about how I take care of the car. He used to do that all of the time before his stroke."

Derrel's, Jim's, and George's stories are woven with the threads of common themes. Each of these AAC users persisted in communicating concerns related to social roles they played prior to the onset of their communication disorders. In these three examples, home or automobile maintenance was the focus of the communicative interaction. According to their wives, they were not inspired by other communication topics to the same degree of persistence. Gail has mentioned that Derrel doesn't use his communication book when she attempts to talk with him about his feelings. George refuses to use a simple call bell to alert his wife when he needs help and would not use AAC tools to communicate with nursing staff when he was hospitalized. Jim often prefers to sit in his easy chair watching football while his daughters make small talk with his wife. All three augmented communicators appear to use their communicative abilities selectively. They communicate to perform some social roles, yet other roles that appear to be of equal or greater importance to their caregivers often are neglected.

Current disablement models recognize that the social consequences of disabling conditions, including alterations in social roles, are dependent on the interplay of both personal and environmental factors (World Health Organization [WHO], 1993, 1999). These models conceptually link underlying anatomical, physiological, or psychological impairments with the functional changes experienced by individuals and the consequences they encounter in their social or cultural environments. The implication of such linkages is that the social roles that a person performs will be influenced by an underlying impairment, by the functional changes that one experiences, and by the social consequences of the disabling condition. According to Peters (1996), one must consider personal and environmental factors that mediate, amplify, or reduce the social consequences of disablement in addition to the context in which disablement occurs.

This chapter focuses on the personal and environmental factors that influence the social role performance of five individuals with acquired neurogenic or neuromuscular diseases (see Table 1). This chapter reviews literature from the fields of psychology and sociology that identifies categories of social roles performed by adults in American culture and that points to the importance of some roles in compensating for disability. Theoretical constructs are introduced to explore possible explanations for the communicative persistence seen in the stories. Finally, this chapter introduces a model for understanding the impact that role change may have on a family's interactions and characteristics.

SOCIAL ROLES

David is a 48-year-old man who was diagnosed with amyotrophic lateral sclerosis (ALS) while on active duty as a communications specialist in the Navy. Following his diagnosis, he retired from the Navy and returned to his hometown in order to be near his family. In the early stages of his disease, David struggled to maintain his independence,

Table 1. Summary of examples

Augmented communicator	Age	Etiology	Preferred social role
Derrel	50	Aphasia	Family member/advisor worker
George	60	Ventilator-dependent quadriplegia	Family member/handyman
Jim	55	Aphasia	Family member/advisor
David	48	Amyotrophic lateral sclerosis	Volunteer/peer counselor
Frank	55	Aphasia	Husband/financial manager

often, according to his parents, taking great risks. For instance, a year after his diagnosis, he attempted to climb a ladder to take care of a minor home repair, and he fell and broke a hip. After a lengthy hospitalization and recovery in a skilled nursing facility, David returned home in a wheelchair.

Bulbar and spinal involvement associated with his disease progressed rapidly. David soon required 24-hour care, and he began using a computer with an adapted keyboard and Words+EZ Keys software for writing and for telephone communication. Yet, despite the limitations imposed by his disease, David remained active in life. He married his caregiver and became a parent to his wife's two biological children. David remained active in church, joined a wheelchair square dancing club, and continued to learn about computers and computer software. David also willingly spent days at the hospital acting as a peer counselor, training another man diagnosed with ALS in the use of EZ Keys software. Ten years later, David is dependent on a ventilator and communicates by accessing his computer with a single soft-touch switch. He has become a biological parent, he remains active in church, he counsels friends via the Internet regarding computer and software issues, and he still attends an ALS support group in which he and his wife share their knowledge and experience with families of individuals who have been newly diagnosed with the disease.

David's case illustrates the variety of social roles that some augmented communicators choose to perform following the onset of a neurogenic or neuromuscular disease. Research has identified five broad categories of roles that adults often perform in their daily lives: student, worker, citizen, homemaker/family member, and leisurite (i.e., roles performed during recreation and leisure activities) (Super & Nevill, 1986). Although prior to being diagnosed with ALS much of David's life was focused on performing the worker role, after his diagnosis a rich balance of many roles has characterized his life.

David's story illustrates the experience of one man with an acquired communication disorder. Research conducted in the United States and Canada indicates that role participation levels are relatively similar for working men and women (Madill, Brintnell, Macnab, Stewin, & Fitzsimmons, 1989). Often both men and women devote the greatest amount of time to the role of worker, although women typically participate at higher levels within the homemaker role. It is interesting that although the role of worker is important to most adults, research findings suggest that it is often not an adult's primary or central life role (Niles & Goodnough, 1996). The roles of homemaker, family member, or leisurite often are rated as more important for self-esteem. Moreover, the importance of balance among life roles is illustrated by Crist-Houran's (1996) finding that excessive commitment to one role may be detrimental to feelings of well-being. In fact, self-esteem is enhanced when individuals have multiple roles (Crist-Houran, 1996).

Few studies have looked at the impact of injury or disability on participation in social roles. Brintnell, Madill, Montgomerie, and Stewin (1992) found that men and women with injuries or disabilities (with a mean age of 33–36 years) reported decreased participation in the worker role, and women's participation in student and leisurite roles also decreased. They concluded that learning and recreation are closely tied to work activities for many women, whereas student and leisurite roles are more independent of the worker role for men.

Some research findings suggest that the homemaker/family role is most affected by an acquired disability. For example, families of both men and women with visual impairment reported reduced participation in decision making in their family member's homemaker/family member role (Gill-Williamson, 1991). Research on the psychosocial impact of aphasia suggests that communicative loss produces a lasting impact on the roles that people within a family play. Moreover, this research points to role change wherein children assume roles that had been performed by parents and roles once performed by husbands or wives are assumed by their partners following the onset of their aphasia (Artes & Hoopes, 1978; LeDorze & Brassard, 1995; Malone, 1969).

Although research findings tend to point to significant role changes for many individuals with disabilities and their families, Brintnell and colleagues (1992) found that individuals who were injured maintained preinjury levels of commitment to life roles despite a reduction in their postinjury performance levels. This discrepancy between role performance and role commitment may lead to the personal dissonance that is experienced by many individuals with disabilities. Crist-Houran (1996) suggested that one method for resolving this dissonance is through volunteerism. Formal or informal volunteer work has the potential to address a person's continued commitment to worker and homemaker roles when disability limits that person's ability to perform those roles. Crist-Houran proposed that volunteerism may achieve that end by providing opportunities for people with disabilities to perform the nurturing and caregiving roles experienced by parents and by providing an opportunity for functioning in multiple roles in which social supports are fostered.

David's story illustrates how volunteerism and assuming new social roles may mitigate the effects of social role loss and lessen the burden experienced by a person with a communicative disability. David's commitment to volunteerism as a computer consultant also illustrates the potential for the volunteer role to enhance the perceived self-worth of a person with an acquired communication disorder. As Crist-Houran (1996) suggested, David appears to gain fulfillment and to enhance his self-esteem by functioning as the expert in his capacity as a volunteer computer consultant. In addition, both his e-mail interactions and support group contacts provide David and his wife with a broader social network than would be the case without their participation as volunteers.

PERSONAL AND ENVIRONMENTAL FACTORS INFLUENCING SOCIAL ROLE PERFORMANCE

During each day in the lives of individuals with severe acquired communication disorders, choices are made regarding when, how, and with whom to engage in social interactions. Unlike those who communicate typically, by using speech, people with severe acquired communication disorders often must expend great effort to communicate. Such high-energy demands result in selective use of communication for many individuals. The following section explores some of the personal and environmental factors that may influence choices that individuals make about social role performance.

Influence of Motivation on Social Role Performance

In order to understand the factors that influence role choices, this section summarizes a conceptual framework for motivation that describes how motivation influences behavior patterns and that describes the processes that lead to communicative persistence (Ford, 1992). This framework gives a historical perspective to theories of motivation. Three areas in motivational theory are reviewed: 1) expectancy and incentive theories; 2) theories of volition; and 3) an integrated theory of motivation that considers both individual and environmental factors.

Expectancy and Incentive Theories   Expectancy and incentive theories attempt to explain how individuals make choices in life. Both theories propose that behavior is guided by the anticipation of future events and by the achievement of goals (Rotter, 1954; Tolman, 1959). In the case of people with severe acquired communication disorders, one might say that an individual's behavior is guided by the rewards that he or she expects to receive as a result of engaging in communication. Expectancy theory proposes a paradigm whereby internal cognitive maps, or expectations, guide and direct an individual toward a goal (Tolman, 1959). For example, expectancy theory would suggest that David uses e-mail to teach others about computers because he has an image of himself acting as a teacher. It is this image that inspires David to expend the energy needed to sit for long periods of time at his computer, activating a single switch in order to compose messages about how his friends should deal with their computer problems.

Incentive theory (Bindra, 1974; Bolles, 1972) proposes that motivation is determined by both internal needs and anticipated external incentives. In order for an individual to initiate action, Bindra (1974) proposed, first there is the need for a state of readiness and then for the creation of a motive state, which is produced by a combination of internal need and anticipated external incentives. The motive state triggers approach behavior that initiates action or avoidance behavior that inhibits action. According to Bolles (1972), the incentive to initiate action is enhanced by the expectation of a reward during creation of the internal motive state. Incentive theory may be viewed in a more concrete manner by understanding that it is David's desire to teach and to be viewed as a teacher that encourages him to expend the energy to communicate. David's performance as a teacher is dependent on both his internal motivation and the external reward that he anticipates he will receive from others in his environment.

Theories of Volition   Theories of volition make the distinction between the formation of intentions (motivation) and the actual carrying out of actions necessary to achieve the intention (volition) (Heckhausen, 1991). In order to understand volition, one must consider three separate but related phenomena: 1) action initiation, 2) perseverance, and 3) overcoming obstacles to action. For action to be initiated, one must overcome tendencies to delay initiation and to attend to other competing desires. Intentions that are ultimately activated have the strongest expectancy for a positive outcome and are present at the most favorable times for their implementation.

To achieve mastery of multicomponent or complex goals, a person must implement an action and then must persevere. For an action to be implemented, it must be given a high priority. For action to be sustained, incentives must be apparent, and obstacles must be overcome. When an obstacle exists, a discrepancy also exists between the present state of action and the standard, or expectation, of what should be taking place.

Self-reinforcement results if the initiator of the action concludes that the standard has been met. If there is a small negative discrepancy, a program for solving the problem is initiated. If there is a large negative discrepancy, strong self-criticism will ensue that is likely to halt movement toward action (Heckhausen, 1991). To persevere, an action must be guided by a consistent underlying desire. It must be maintained despite interruptions and must be given a high priority, despite other competing desires.

The principles of volition theory are exemplified by Derrel's persistence in telling Gail about the handicapped parking pass. Derrel was apparently guided by a consistent underlying desire to communicate his message to Gail. He continued moving toward his goal despite interruptions and despite other competing desires. Clearly, for Derrel, performing the role of advisor to Gail held a high priority, and his willingness to persist was supported by his confidence that Gail would act upon his concern. It is also likely that Gail's use of multiple follow-up questions promoted Derrel's confidence that he would ultimately communicate his message successfully. Such confidence is necessary in order to minimize the negative discrepancy he experiences when temporarily halted in his communicative attempts.

The interplay of factors illustrated in Derrel's story of communicative success is further explained by intrinsic and extrinsic theories of motivation. Underlying concepts of behavior initiation and volition are the incentives that drive and sustain behavior. As the early theorists pointed out, behavior is motivated by internal (intrinsic) and external (extrinsic) factors. Heckhausen suggested that in order for intrinsic motivation to exist, the goal must be "thematically identical with the action so that it is carried out for the sake of its own objectives" (1991, p. 406). Behavior that is intrinsically motivated implies an enjoyment and absorption in the activity (Csikszentmihalyi, 1975) and results in feelings of competence and autonomy (Deci & Ryan, 1985). Extrinsic motivation exists when behavior represents a means to an end that is thematically different from the original behavior (Heckhausen, 1991).

Heckhausen (1991) suggested that the strongest desire to act results from internal (intrinsic) motivation and that extrinsic incentives have the potential to undermine actions initially triggered by intrinsic motivation. Such a theoretical orientation contrasts with operant conditioning theories, such as matching theory (Herrnstein, 1961), which emphasize external reinforcement for teaching new behaviors. In fact, a series of experiments that examined participation in activities first with, then without, and then with external reinforcement showed a decline in performance in the third experimental phase, when external rewards were provided for preferred activities (Heckhausen, 1991). The same experiments showed improved performance when nonpreferred activities were rewarded, suggesting that operant conditioning theories may be most relevant in such conditions.

Consistent with Heckhausen's perspective, social-cognitive theory proposes that individuals sustain interest in activities in which they perceive themselves as competent and that provide self-satisfaction (Bandura, 1986). In order to maximize intrinsic motivation, individuals must achieve an awareness of their competence (self-efficacy). To improve their sense of competence, they must aim for and master goals that are achieved by meeting measurable subgoals. The subgoals and their incentives must provide information about task mastery that the individual perceives as meaningful and relevant. Through improved self-efficacy, individuals experience mastery, which results in satisfaction and growth of interest.

According to social cognitive theory, if David and Derrel did not have an awareness of their competence in their attempts to communicate, they might experience a reduction in their motivation to sustain the actions necessary for communication. David must have confidence in his ability to scan accurately to create his messages, and Derrel must know that if he continues to give Gail bits of information, she will eventually combine them to decipher his message. The implication of Bandura's (1986) concept of self-efficacy is that it is dependent on a receptive environment that provides feedback to the individual. Without environmental feedback, one's perception of self-efficacy becomes uncertain.

Integrated Theory of Motivation   Motivational systems theory (MST) integrates many of the concepts introduced by earlier theorists and also takes into account the impact of factors beyond an individual's control (Ford, 1992). According to MST, four prerequisites are necessary for effective functioning of an individual in a given context. They are 1) the motivation necessary to initiate and to maintain goal-directed activity, 2) the skill necessary to produce the desired consequences, 3) biological functioning necessary to support the activity, and 4) the cooperation of a responsive environment. The relationship of these prerequisites is expressed in Figure 1. Ford (1992) defined *personal agency beliefs* as beliefs that individuals have regarding their capabilities to achieve goals and their expectations regarding the support for goal attainment that is available in the environment.

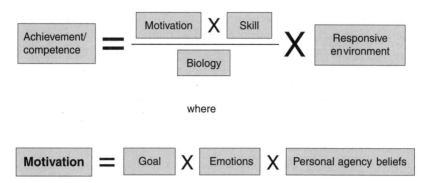

Figure 1.   Motivational systems theory equation.

The principles of MST are illustrated by Derrel's experiences as a participant in a research study (Fox, Sohlberg, & Fried-Oken, 1999). The purpose of the project was to determine whether choice of conversational topic by research participants would influence outcomes of a conversational communication aid intervention. As a participant in the study, Derrel completed a sorting task to rank topics of conversation. Of the topics he identified as preferred, he chose one topic for intervention, and the lowest-ranked preferred topic was identified as his nonchoice topic. Derrel chose to have a communication aid developed for conversing about the construction jobs that he had performed during his working years. His nonchoice topic was landscaping. Derrel and Gail were landscaping their new home, and Derrel wanted to be able to offer advice and share in decision making about the work that would be done. In terms of life roles, Derrel chose to communicate about his worker role, and his nonchoice communication aid focused on his role as homemaker/family member. Communication aids were developed for each topic using comparable syntactic classes of vocabulary depicted by 36 Boardmaker symbols or photographs.

Throughout a 6-week training period, dependent variables were measured in clinical and natural environments. In the clinic, the number of nonambiguous symbols used to respond to questions were measured (see Figures 2 and 3). During training and a 4-week maintenance period, Gail recorded the total number of minutes that Derrel used his communication aids in conversations at home and in other natural environments (see Figure 4). When the data in Figures 2 and 3 were examined, it was clear that Derrel consistently used the communication aid designed to discuss his worker role with greater success in the clinic. However, at home and in other natural environments, Derrel used the communication aid designed to discuss his homemaker/family member role more frequently. In fact, Figure 4 shows that he used

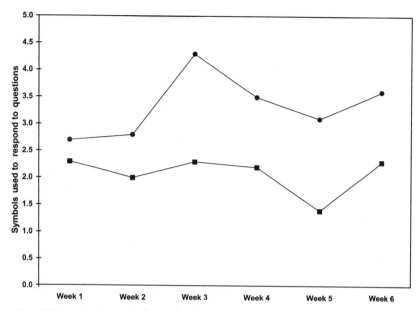

Figure 2.   Number of unambiguous communication aid symbols Derrel used to respond to questions posed by a familiar conversational partner in clinical probes. (Key: —●—, choice topic = construction; —■—, nonchoice topic = landscaping.)

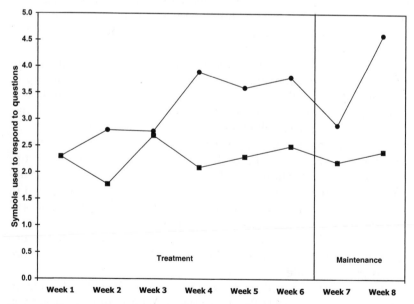

Figure 3.   Number of unambiguous communication aid symbols Derrel used to respond to questions posed by unfamiliar conversational partners in clinical probes. (Key: —●—, choice topic = construction; —■—, nonchoice topic = landscaping.)

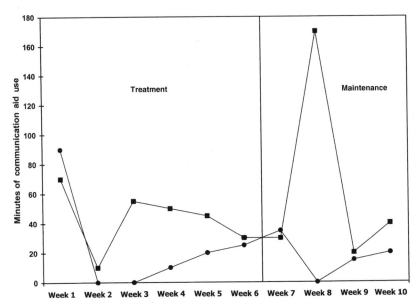

Figure 4.   Number of minutes Derrel used communication aids in natural environment conversations. (Key: —●—, choice topic = construction; —■—, nonchoice topic = landscaping.)

his landscaping communication aid more frequently in 7 of 10 data collection weeks. Overall he used his construction communication aid for an average of 21.5 minutes per week and his landscaping communication aid for an average of 51.5 minutes per week.

Guided by MST (Ford, 1992), one might attribute Derrel's use of his two conversational communication aids to an interplay of important internal, external, and environmental factors. By choosing to talk about construction, Derrel selected a meaningful or relevant goal. Collaborative feedback following each session allowed Derrel to view his goal as attainable and supported his belief that he could communicate effectively about his topics. In natural environments, Gail's support compensated for limits that Derrel's stroke imposed on his ability to initiate communication aid use. The success that he experienced in communicating information about the two topics lent emotional salience to the experience and further supported his personal agency beliefs. However, the environments in which Derrel attempted to use his communication aids gave different levels of support to the two topics and their associated roles.

The relationship of these factors may best be visualized using an adaptation of the formula that was introduced previously. For Derrel, the elements critical to his competence in communicating with his

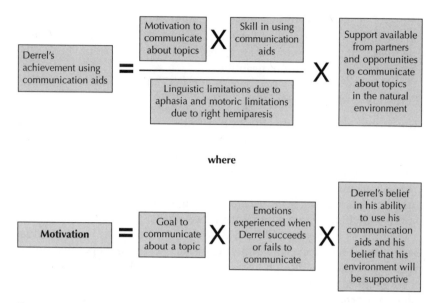

Figure 5.   Motivational systems theory (MST) equation applied to Derrel's communication aid use.

landscaping and construction communication aids are depicted in Figure 5.

In the clinic, where Derrel had equal opportunities to use the communication aids, he was more successful in communicating about his worker role. At home and when he spent time with family and friends, talking about his role as a worker received less support. Derrel experienced greater support when talking about the homemaker/family member role. As predicted (Crist-Houran, 1996), Derrel's life roles had shifted from an emphasis on work to home and family concerns. MST assigns a greater relative value to the environment, allowing it to overshadow the combined effect of motivation, skill, and biology. Such a theoretical framework provides an explanation for why Derrel used his construction communication aid less to discuss his worker role in natural environments, despite the fact that his use of the aid was clearly superior in all clinical interactions.

If one considers the life roles that people with severe communicative impairments choose to perform from the perspective of MST (Ford, 1992), one can see the complex set of factors that influence role performance. Achievement or competence in communicating to perform a life role is influenced by a person's motivation to communicate, which in turn is influenced by that person's goals, emotional readiness, and confidence in his or her ability to succeed. Yet, the opportunities for communication afforded in the environment must also be considered.

For AAC users with chronic communication disabilities, environmental opportunities are more likely to support communication about current life roles than about dominant roles enjoyed by an individual before the onset of a communication disability.

Families and Social Roles

The review of motivational theory illustrates a dynamic interplay among personal and environmental factors in determining the roles AAC users assume. The environmental context for interaction for many people with communicative disabilities is the family. The social roles that individuals assume and how those roles affect family functioning is the focus of this section. To illustrate the impact that social roles have on family functioning, we begin with a case study.

Frank is a 55-year-old man who survived a stroke with residual severe nonfluent aphasia. Following his stroke, Frank depended on his wife for his care. Although he had supported the family and managed their financial affairs prior to his stroke, his wife assumed those and other important family roles after his stroke. Frank's wife functioned as the family driver, banker, and planner for most family activities.

His wife's dominance in homemaker/family member roles continued until Frank was given the opportunity to choose his treatment goals in an aphasia intervention group. In treatment, Frank sorted pictures representing topics of interest to other adults (Stuart, Vanderhoof-Bilyeu, & Beukelman, 1994) to identify his preferred areas of communication (Fox & Fried-Oken, 1996). In repeated sortings, Frank identified finances as the area that he wanted to emphasize. His clinician posed questions in order to narrow and specify Frank's interest in communicating about finances. The clinician discovered that Frank wanted to resume his role as financial manager for the family. His wife agreed, and treatment was initiated that helped Frank learn to use a set of AAC tools to write checks for the family's rent and utility bills and to communicate with his wife about financial matters. As Frank increased in his ability to perform his role as family financial manager, he and his wife showed increased optimism in his ability to improve other communicative abilities according to the Code-Muller Protocols for psychosocial change (Code & Muller, 1992). Ultimately, Frank's wife returned to full-time employment, and Frank undertook some of the homemaker/family member roles that had been assumed by his wife.

The role reversal experienced by Frank and his wife is characteristic of many families in which a member experiences acquired aphasia (Artes & Hoopes, 1978; LeDorze & Brassard, 1995; Malone, 1969). Because psychosocial issues have not been explored in the same depth for other acquired communicative disorders, this review focuses on role change as described in the aphasia literature. The discussion begins with a review of the family systems model (Turnbull & Turnbull, 1991).

The psychosocial impact of communicative loss is the "social context of the emotional experience" of that loss (Code & Muller, 1992, p. 6). Turnbull and Turnbull (1991) synthesized four core areas of family functioning that are affected when a member develops a communication impairment. These areas include family characteristics, interactions, roles or functions, and the life cycle. With family cohesion and adaptability influencing each of the core areas, the model illustrates the interconnectedness of communication patterns of the family and the roles played by family members. The family systems model provides a framework for examining the changes in roles and interactions experienced by families coping with aphasia, as depicted in Figure 6.

A systems model fosters understanding of the effects of communicative loss by illustrating the interconnectedness of family characteristics, functions, and interactions. The adoption of coping strategies by families may be seen as the outcome of this relationship under the influence of a family's innate adaptability and cohesion, two factors that influence a family's ability to cope with change. *Adaptability* is defined as a family's ability to change in response to situational stress (Turnbull & Turnbull, 1991). A family's adaptability ranges from rigid (families who require a high degree of control) to chaotic (families with little control or structure). Flexible families are midway on a scale of adaptability and are likely to adjust roles when necessary.

Cohesion influences the ease with which families adapt to change. *Cohesion* is defined as the balance of a family's emotional bonds with the independence or autonomy its members are allowed (Turnbull & Turnbull, 1991). Just as family adaptability may be viewed on a continuum, family cohesion also varies from low to high. Cohesion may range from disengaged, a state in which members feel little bond to each other, to enmeshed, a state in which members have little individuality and may have difficulty separating from the family. Optimal levels of family cohesion are identified as connected. At the connected level, members are bonded to the family but are able to function independently. Families that make adjustments more quickly and with less disruption are likely to function at the connected level.

Figure 6 portrays the complex nature of acquired aphasia and the effect it has on individuals and families. Family characteristics may be altered by the stress experienced due to long periods of rehabilitation (Artes & Hoopes, 1976) and the increased fatigue experienced by many people with aphasia (LaDorze & Brassard, 1993). Family characteristics also change if spouses' attitudes or behavior changes (Kinsella & Duffy,

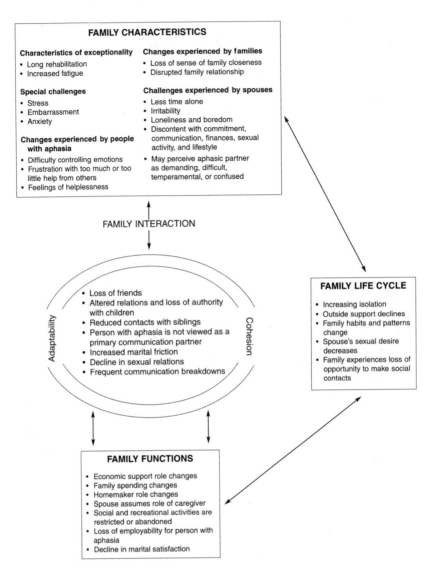

Figure 6.   Family Systems Model interpretation of research findings on the psychosocial impact of aphasia. (Adapted from Turnbull & Turnbull [1991].)

1979; Malone, 1969; Williams, 1993; Zraick & Boone, 1991). When spouses experience irritability, loneliness, or boredom, those feelings ultimately alter family interaction, affect family functions, and potentially change the life cycle of the family.

As a result of changes in individual or family characteristics, family functions often change. If the primary wage earner was affected by aphasia, economic support roles may change, and family spending is likely to be adjusted (Artes & Hoopes, 1978; Malone 1969). Often, families modify the homemaker role as spouses assume the role of caregiver (Malone, 1969). Family functions of socialization and affection may also change if social activities are restricted or if spouses experience a decline in marital satisfaction (Artes & Hoopes, 1978; Malone 1969).

Changes in family characteristics and family functions affect the family life cycle. Even young families may experience increased isolation, with reduced opportunities for social contact (LeDorze & Brassard, 1993; Malone, 1969). Many spouses report reduced sexual desire and increased health problems as they attempt to cope with the changes imposed by aphasia (Williams, 1993). Such life cycle changes are likely to create strain in other areas of the family system.

At the center of the model is family interaction, which is influenced by and in turn influences all other components of the family system. Common alterations in family interaction include frequent communication breakdowns; altered relationships with children, friends, and spouses; and changes in communication patterns with siblings (Artes & Hoopes, 1978; LeDorze & Brassard, 1993; Malone, 1969).

The family systems model illustrates the synergistic nature of family functioning. It emphasizes the potential for a communication disorder, such as aphasia, and the coping strategies that families employ to alter other components of the system. As with other coping strategies adopted by families, successful AAC interventions may affect all aspects of a family system. As Frank's story illustrates, a simple AAC intervention has the potential to alter family roles significantly. A role change or role normalization such as Frank's may have far-reaching effects on a family's characteristics, interaction, and life cycle.

EDUCATIONAL AND CLINICAL IMPLICATIONS

This section introduces three concepts relevant to specialists who develop and implement AAC interventions for adults with acquired neurogenic communication disorders. First, successful AAC use demands consideration of the social roles that individuals desire to perform. Although attention to participation patterns and communication needs is accepted as an integral part of AAC assessment (Beukelman & Mirenda, 1998), current assessment practices most often do not take social role preferences into account. We have reviewed social role research and have explored theories related to motivation and learning that underscore the importance of extending assessment practices to include role preference. As MST suggests, motivation is equal in importance to skill in the equation of factors likely to lead to achievement and competence (Ford, 1992).

On a personal level, individuals' stories repeatedly support the potential for preferred social roles to enhance communicative motivation. David endures discomfort and fatigue to attend an ALS support group at which he can guide and counsel others who are coping with the disease. Derrel and Jim persist in advising their wives about care for their automobiles, despite the limitations aphasia imposes on their ability to communicate. George laboriously spells out *home repairs* when asked what he wants to talk about with his wife. The intrinsic motivation experienced by these individuals when they perform social roles that they perceive as important appears to outweigh some of the negative influences imposed by their communicative disorders. Directed by MST, interventionists may find that by tapping the motivation inherent in preferred social roles, reducing the emphasis given to teaching new skills is possible, thereby achieving an equal or superior outcome with less clinical effort.

Second is the notion that social role performance changes with the onset of an acquired disability. As Derrel's use of his construction and landscaping communication aids illustrates, clinicians should explore carefully the environmental factors that influence an individual's opportunities to perform preferred communicative roles. When disability is of sudden onset, AAC assessment may precede adjustment of an individual's communicative role preferences. Roles of interest immediately after the sudden onset of a communication disorder may be more closely tied to a predisorder lifestyle. New roles may not yet be identified. To promote adjustment to an acquired communication disorder, clinicians may want to explore alternative roles with their clients. Some individuals desire AAC interventions that let them reassume roles performed prior to their illness. Others may want to explore how AAC may facilitate performance of new or expanded roles.

The potential for AAC to enhance role performance increases as more people with acquired communication disorders become active Internet users. E-mail communication with friends and family members can allow today's AAC users to fulfill communicative roles that were limited or impossible for them to attain even in the early 1990s. Augmented communicators, interventionists, and family members benefit from discussing the range of role performance options provided by AAC and computer technology. Discussion of the potential for clients to assume new roles, an examination of those roles for their potential to achieve a high level of satisfaction, and exploration of their applicability in the individual's current environment will guide the AAC team to appropriate and satisfying interventions.

Finally, this review points to a need for AAC specialists to consider the effects their interventions may have on the balance of current and future social roles assumed within a family and the impact the family may have on the outcomes of their interventions. The family systems model (Turnbull & Turnbull, 1991) illustrates the dynamic nature of family relationships. AAC specialists must understand that all aspects of a family system are altered by the onset of a disability. Regardless of the social roles AAC intervention addresses, it is likely that the family system will require a period of adjustment before reaching stability again. Without an awareness of the potential impact of AAC interventions on a family's social roles, barriers to successful intervention may confront unsuspecting clinicians. Barriers related to family role adjustment may appear in the form of negative attitudes or inability to implement AAC strategies. Understanding the dynamics of role change within the family system will help clinicians gain a valuable tool for achieving successful AAC interventions.

IMPLICATIONS FOR FUTURE RESEARCH

In-depth study of social roles and role change among individuals with acquired communication disorders has been limited to aphasia research. Although aphasia literature may have the potential to inform the AAC community about the impact of other communication disorders, it is characterized by at least two limitations. The first limitation relates to the ability to generalize aphasia study findings to individuals with other acquired communication disorders. It is likely that the typical course of other acquired neurogenic disorders and the functional outcomes of those disorders will result in different patterns of role adaptation than is typical of aphasia. Whereas aphasia is usually of sudden onset, many acquired neurogenic communication disorders are either rapidly or slowly progressive. It is likely that variations in the typical course of other illnesses or diseases result in significant differences in the development of coping strategies and in role adaptation and change.

Moreover, the linguistic disability of aphasia results in entirely different limitations on role performance than do motor and sensory impairments that typically accompany other diseases. These differences imply a need to explore psychosocial change following the onset of disorders of other etiologies. It may be useful to examine these questions within at least three different groups of individuals with acquired neurogenic communication disorders: 1) those with progressive disease who typically do not experience cognitive change; 2) those with progressive disease who do experience cognitive change; and 3) those who experience a sudden loss of communication because of illness, injury, or disease.

The aphasia literature also illustrates a need for researchers to examine role performance and role change from the perspectives of all members of a family unit. Early psychosocial research on aphasia was conducted with only spouses and family members acting as informants (Artes & Hoopes, 1978; Chwat, 1980; Kinsella & Duffy, 1979; Malone, 1969; Williams & Freer, 1986). Only recently have aphasia researchers begun to ask people with aphasia about their own experiences (LeDorze & Brassard, 1995; Parr, 1994; Parr, Byng, Gilpin, & Ireland, 1997). The richness and pertinence of recent aphasia psychosocial research suggests a need to collect data from all informants within the individual's family system. Such an inclusive approach may be a natural extension of current AAC clinical practices in which clinicians have traditionally emphasized consumer participation in intervention and outcomes measurement.

CONCLUSIONS

Successful AAC interventions acknowledge the biological or physiological limitations imposed by an impairment. They holistically address functional changes, and they strive to lessen the social consequences of communicative disorders (WHO, 1993, 1999). This chapter argues that exploring an individual's historical and current social role preferences may be of considerable value in reducing the social consequences of an acquired communication disorder. We propose that the most effective AAC interventions consider each of the factors identified by MST (Ford, 1992): an individual's underlying biological or physiological capabilities, skills, motivation, and support offered in the environment. We suggest that incorporating the motivation inherent in activities related to an adult's meaningful social roles most efficiently and effectively lessens the social consequences of acquired neurogenic communication disorders.

We hope that this review of social role research and research in the field of social psychology motivates AAC clinicians and researchers to engage in study, discussion, and collaboration with researchers and professionals from other fields. Just as theories of human motivation may guide interventionists in developing productive research endeavors that address preferred communicative roles, it is likely that other theoretical perspectives will broaden and enrich the understanding of communicative disorders and their impact on individuals and their families.

REFERENCES

Artes, R., & Hoopes, R. (1978). Problems of aphasic and non-aphasic stroke patients as identified and evaluated by patients' wives. In Y. Lebrun & R. Hoopes (Eds.), *Recovery in aphasics* (pp. 31–45). Amsterdam: Swets and Zeitlinger.

Bandura, A. (1986). *Social foundations of thought and action: A social cognitive theory.* Upper Saddle River, NJ: Prentice-Hall.

Beukelman, D.R., & Mirenda, P. (1998). *Augmentative and alternative communication: Management of severe communication disorders in children and adults* (2nd ed.). Baltimore: Paul H. Brookes Publishing Co.

Bindra, D. (1974). A motivational view of learning, performance, and behavior. *Psychological Review, 81,* 199–213.

Bolles, R.C. (1972). Reinforcement, expectancy and learning. *Psychological Review, 79,* 394–409.

Brintnell, E.S., Madill, H.M., Montgomerie, T.C., & Stewin, L.L. (1992). Work and family after injury: Do female and male client perspectives differ? *Career Development Quarterly, 41,* 145–160.

Chwat, S. (1980). Environmental impact of aphasia: The child's perspective. In R. Brookshire (Ed.), *Clinical aphasiology conference proceedings* (pp. 127–138). Minneapolis, MN: BRK Publishers.

Code, C., & Muller, D. (1992). *The Code-Muller protocols: Assessing perceptions of psychosocial adjustment to aphasia and related disorders.* Kibworth, England: Far Communications.

Crist-Houran, M. (1996). Efficacy of volunteerism for role-loss depression: A complement to Weinstein, et al. *Psychological Reports, 79,* 736–738.

Csikszentmihalyi, M. (1975). *Beyond boredom and anxiety.* San Francisco: Jossey-Bass.

Deci, E.L., & Ryan, R.M. (1985). *Intrinsic motivation and self-determination in human behavior.* New York: Plenum.

Ford, M.E. (1992). *Motivating humans.* Newbury Park, CA: Sage Publications.

Fox, L.E., & Fried-Oken, M. (1996). Interactive group treatment for aphasia: An AAC alternative [Abstract]. In *ISAAC 1996 proceedings: The 7th Biennial Conference of the International Society for Augmentative and Alternative Communication* (pp. 390–391). Vancouver, British Columbia, Canada: Author.

Fox, L., Sohlberg, M.M., & Fried-Oken, M. (1999, June). *Effects of conversational topic self-selection on augmentative communication intervention for adults with aphasia.* Paper presented at the Clinical Aphasiology Conference, Key West, FL.

Gill-Williamson, L. (1991, June). The impact of a visually impaired parent on a family's decision making. *Journal of Visual Impairment and Blindness,* 246–248.

Heckhausen, H. (1991). *Motivation and action.* New York: Springer-Verlag.

Herrnstein, R.J. (1961). Relative and absolute strength of response as a function of frequency of reinforcement. *Journal of the Experimental Analysis of Behavior, 4,* 267–272.

Kinsella, G., & Duffy, F. (1979). Psychosocial readjustment in the spouses of aphasic patients. *Scandinavian Journal of Rehabilitation Medicine, 11,* 129–132.

LeDorze, G., & Brassard, C. (1995). A description of the consequences of aphasia on aphasic persons and their relatives and friends, based on the WHO model of chronic diseases. *Aphasiology, 9,* 239–255.

Madill, H.M., Brintnell, E.S.G., Macnab, D., Stewin, L.L., & Fitzsimmons, G.W. (1989). The delicate balance: Working and family roles. *International Journal for the Advancement of Counseling, 11,* 219–230.

Malone, R. (1969). Expressed attitudes of families of aphasics. *Journal of Speech and Hearing Disorders, 24,* 146–151.

Niles, S.G., & Goodnough, G.E. (1996). Life-role salience and values: A review of recent research. *Career Development Quarterly, 45,* 65–86.

Parr, S. (1994). Coping with aphasia: Conversations with 20 aphasic people. *Aphasiology, 8,* 457–455.

Parr, S., Byng, S., Gilpin, S., & Ireland, C. (1997). *Talking about aphasia: Living with loss of language after stroke.* Philadelphia: Taylor & Francis.

Peters, D.J. (1996). Disablement observed, addressed, and experienced: Integrating subjective experience into disablement models. *Disability and Rehabilitation, 18,* 593–603.

Rotter, J.B. (1954). *Social learning and clinical psychology.* Upper Saddle River, NJ: Prentice-Hall.

Stuart, S., Vanderhoof-Bilyeu, D., & Beukelman, D.R. (1994). Difference in topic reference of elderly men and women. *Journal of Medical Speech-Language Pathology, 2,* 89–104.

Super, D.E., & Nevill, D.D. (1986). *The Salience Inventory.* Palo Alto, CA: Consulting Psychologists Press.

Tolman, E.C. (1959). Principles of purposive behavior. In S. Koch (Ed.), *Psychology: A study of a science* (Vol. 2, pp. 92–157). New York: McGraw-Hill.

Turnbull, A.P., & Turnbull, H.R. (1991). Understanding families from a systems perspective. In J.M. Williams &. T. Kay (Eds.), *Head injury: A family matter* (pp. 37–63). Baltimore: Paul H. Brookes Publishing Co.

World Health Organization (WHO). (1993). *International classification of impairments, disabilities, and handicaps: A manual of classification relating to the consequences of diseases.* Geneva: Author.

World Health Organization (WHO). (1999). *International classification of impairments, activities and participation: A manual of dimensions of disablement and health* [On-line]. Available: http://www.who.int.msa/mnh/ems/icidh/introduction.htm

Williams, S. (1993). The impact of aphasia on marital satisfaction. *Archives of Physical Medicine and Rehabiliation, 74,* 361–367.

Williams, S., & Freer, C. (1986). Aphasia: Its effect on marital relationships. *Archives of Physical Medicine and Rehabilitation, 67,* 250–251.

Zraick, R., & Boone, D. (1991). Spuse attitudes toward the person with aphasia. *Journal of Speech and Hearing Research, 34,* 123–128.

2

AAC Message Management

Sheela Stuart
Joanne P. Lasker
David R. Beukelman

Message management is the formulation, storage, and retrieval of messages in augmentative and alternative communication (AAC) applications. It has occupied the attention of AAC users and their facilitators since the first AAC strategies were employed with individuals who experienced severe communication disorders. As the 21st century begins, debates over the "best" way to manage messages in AAC devices continue. For example, at the 1999 Rehabilitation Engineering and Assistive Technology Society of North America (RESNA) Conference, discussions regarding the relative merits of word-based versus phrase-based message formulation were recurring themes throughout many of the AAC presentations. Those who supported word-based strategies stressed the generative flexibility of this approach as compared with the phrase-based approach. Those who supported phrase-based strategies cited improved communication rate and timing as compared with the word-based approach.

AAC device designers have responded to this debate by developing a range of AAC products that utilize a variety of message management strategies. Some focus on an orthographic approach using letter-based spelling to formulate messages and alpha-encoding to store and to retrieve messages. Others combine letter-based spelling with iconic and/or alpha-encoding of messages using dynamic screen technology to achieve storage of a large number of messages. Still others choose iconic encoding strategies that focus primarily on formulation of phrase-length messages. Finally, some preprogram an extensive number of phrases that are retrieved in their entirety according to conversational pragmatics.

It is our impression that these arguments changed little in the 1990s. Unfortunately, the debate tends to focus on the overall "best" way to design AAC devices rather than on approaches that adjust message management in response to specific factors influencing AAC users as they participate in all avenues of life. The purpose of this chapter is to develop the position that message management varies depending on factors external to the AAC user, the capabilities and preferences of AAC users and their facilitators and the communication function being expressed. The following sections discuss each of these in turn.

TECHNICAL FACTORS THAT INFLUENCE MESSAGE MANAGEMENT

Initially, the primary task of AAC users and their facilitators was to select a small set of messages and to represent them in such a way that AAC users could communicate as effectively as possible. They struggled to fit photographs, drawings, or printed messages (i.e., symbols) onto low-technology communication boards and books in an effort to represent the messages that users desired. These limitations were externally imposed on AAC users by the characteristics of the technology available to them and by inclusion practices. In those days, the societal opportunities for people with severe disabilities were limited to a few restrictive contexts, and the messages included in AAC systems were often tailored to those specific contexts. For example, individual communication boards were often developed for personal care, eating, watching television, and visiting with family members.

During the 1970s, early electronic communication systems were developed. Typically, these devices supported letter-based message formulation only or letter-based formulation accompanied by a limited number of whole words, phrases, or sentences. Once again, the intervention goal of AAC users and their facilitators was to optimize vocabulary that would meet their communication needs and "fit" into the memory limitations of their devices.

During the 1990s, three technological innovations have occurred that have fundamentally affected message formulation, storage, and retrieval strategies. First, dramatic increases in computer memory capacity and reductions in computer memory costs have resulted in the inclusion of extensive storage capability in electronic AAC systems. At the end of the 20th century, the limitation is no longer the memory of the electronic AAC devices but the memory, organizational capacity, and new learning capability of the AAC user. Second, during the 1990s, high-quality speech output has enabled AAC users to talk in a wide variety of contexts. Individual interactions with strangers, small groups, and large-group public speaking can be supported by modern AAC systems. Only in the most adverse listening conditions do AAC users with modern AAC devices experience difficulty in being understood. Third, dynamic screen technology has allowed messages to be represented and organized using a variety of strategies such as semantic association, conversational scripts, spatial relationships, episodic relationships, and so forth.

SOCIETAL FACTORS THAT INFLUENCE MESSAGE MANAGEMENT

During the 1980s and 1990s, the social roles of people with disabilities have expanded dramatically to include attendance in general education classrooms, community activities, community-based living arrangements, the Internet, and, to some extent, employment. Thus, the message requirements of AAC systems are much more complex than they were during earlier eras. In addition, individuals with a wider range of severe communication disorders are now attempting to meet their communication needs through the use of AAC technology.

This book focuses on the communication needs of people who have lost their communication skills completely or partially after having learned to communicate according to typical developmental sequences. Such people communicated for years before experiencing injuries, genetic conditions, or illnesses that abruptly or gradually caused severe communication disorders. In many cases, the communication disorders were associated with life-changing events or processes. Their acquired condition often causes these individuals to undergo major life adjustments as they attempt to adapt to their new impairments. Typically, AAC strategies are required to support them through the many phases of this adjustment, and message management decisions must support these communication activities. Thus, message management for individuals with acquired disabilities involves dimensions that are not considered for people with developmental disabilities. The following section includes an extended discussion of the adjustment to acquired severe disabilities. At the conclusion of this discussion, implications for message management are discussed.

PERSONAL FACTORS: PRESERVING THE SELF: A NEW CHALLENGE IN AAC MESSAGE MANAGEMENT

The process of adjusting to a disability presents a new challenge to the AAC system designer. We propose that not only the end product—the actual AAC system—but also its design and implementation contribute to the AAC system user's ability to achieve new roles, to define a new self, to survive the disabling event, or to maintain communication in the face of an increasing degree of impairment.

As the AAC system designer goes about the business of presenting message choices and offering options, the person with a newly acquired disability views new life possibilities. Successful AAC intervention requires understanding not only the nuts and bolts of which messages to make available and in what manner but also the process of achieving a new sense of self and surviving an acquired disability so that appropriate messages can be offered to AAC users and their facilitators.

The literature addressing experiences of people who face disabling illness emphasizes inescapable changes in sense of self (Hanna & Rogovsky, 1991; Langer, 1994; Morse, 1997; Morse & O'Brien, 1995; Toombs, 1994). A review of this information as it appears pertinent to AAC system design leads to three categories: 1) personal consequences of disability; 2) stages of preserving self; and 3) implications for AAC service delivery.

Personal Consequences of Disability

In her article entitled "Disability and the Self," Toombs (1994) discussed several areas of fundamental change experienced by a person with significant and permanent disability. The first area deals with the sense of self experienced through changes in body identity.

Disability Transforms Identity   Prior to the disabling event, an individual engages with the world in an easy manner, reflecting his or her familiarity with the steps required to complete certain functional activities. For example, placing a telephone call to invite a friend to lunch requires simple-to-use, readily available equipment, familiar skills, and a brief amount of time. After the disabling event, talking on the telephone may be impossible or may require a great deal of prior planning. An individual may be forced to rely on assistive technology or on another individual. In addition to changing the manner in which one engages the world, disability demands an increase in the amount of effort expended to participate. Due to the effort and complexity involved in task completion, disability may lead individuals to focus on fulfillment of present needs rather than on projecting and planning for the future.

These functional changes may alter an individual's perspective of what has been, what is, and what will be. The transformation of bodily identity contributes to changes in the individual's life narrative. A sense of self-identity is typically constructed through the collection of stories or personal biographies that we build about ourselves. A personal biography incorporates references to the past, the present, and the future. For example, before a disability occurs, a statement taken from an individual's personal life narrative might read as follows:

> I got my bachelor's degree in 1983, taught for a while, and started working on my master's degree last summer. I plan to finish my master's in May and move to Tucson next summer.

After disability occurs, this statement might be altered to read:

> Now that this [disabling event] has happened, I don't think I could ever finish my master's degree, and moving to Tucson is out of the question. I have no idea what I will be doing 1 year from now, and all of the uncertainty scares me.

Disability has the power to change life narratives in drastic ways. It can undermine an individual's will to stay involved in the outside world and can cause him or her to relinquish future goals. In addition, it may make the individual afraid about the multiple "unknowns" in the future.

Disability Alters Self-Presentation to Others   Patterns of walking, talking, gesturing, and moving within the world help individuals represent themselves to others. When disability interrupts these patterns, there is a change in physical and personal style. People with acquired disability, family, friends, acquaintances, and strangers may experience this change as negative. In a culture in which bodily integrity, physical adroitness, and conversational acumen are equated with attractiveness, disabilities have the potential to result in a diminution of the self (Asch & Fine, 1988; Toombs, 1994).

Disability Disrupts Personal Goals and the Social Self   In everyday life, each person is involved in a network of relationships with others. One person functions within several roles. For example, a single individual may be a family member, spouse, friend, professional, colleague, associate, neighbor, and student. Change brought about by disability disturbs this web of interactions. Roles and duties formerly fulfilled with ease can no longer be performed. These roles may need to be abandoned or greatly modified.

The disabling event presents choices both to the individual with a disability and to those sharing the relationship. Individuals with disabilities may need to fashion involvement in new ways. In some cases, the individual with a disability must find totally new roles within old relationships. For example, a husband who was previously employed outside the home may assume the homemaker role in the marriage after the disability occurs. People with whom the individual was previously involved also have choices after disability. They may readjust to the individual they knew who now has a disability, or they may terminate the relationship.

Stages of Preserving Self

For the individual who has experienced a disabling event, the changes from being an able individual to victim to patient to recovering individual with a disability represent an evolutionary journey. Morse and O'Brien (1995) set forth four stages of this process: vigilance, relinquishing to caregivers, enduring the self, and striving to regain the self. Each of these stages has implications for AAC messaging. Although these stages focus on illnesses and conditions with abrupt onset, people with gradual degenerative diseases also experience a journey of adjustment.

Stage I of the model, *vigilance*, is described as beginning at the moment the disabling event is perceived and ending when the individual relinquishes the self to caregivers. This stage includes a heightened sense of thought, expansion of time, and protection of self while at the same time a distancing of subjective from objective body begins. Details of the disabling event are recalled, and people often describe time as slowing and an increasing awareness that their lives are in peril. As the disabling event manifests and medical help is provided, the hypervigilance is relinquished, and the individual enters Stage II.

Stage II of the model, known as *relinquishing to caregivers*, begins when the individual determines that a competent caregiver is handling the situation and that he or she is in good hands. Individuals with acquired disabilities describe surrendering to the care they are being provided. Accounts of this stage describe an initial sense of calmness and acceptance of the plight, followed by a feeling of uncertainty about reality and "being in a fog." This is a period during which there is no long-term recollection, perhaps because of administration of analgesics or fluctuations in consciousness. Reports of experiences during this phase describe a need for the presence of relatives who serve to remind them who they were and give them a sense of self. Release from this stage occurs when the physical condition improves and individuals enter the stage of confronting and regrouping.

Stage III of the model, *enduring the self*, occurs as people recognize the meaning of their injuries and what they have lost. In cases of acquired communication disorders, they may begin to mourn the loss of who they once were and what they were able to do. They struggle to retain control over their immediate environment but find they indeed are reliant on other people for specific things. At this stage, positive feedback and encouragement from therapists and others is crucial in ensuring that, despite the losses, the person with a disability initiates the work of healing. Small incremental changes in performance are registered and may help the individual progress to larger milestones; hope serves as powerful inspiration for continued effort. One significant contribution the therapist can make is to assume a partnership role in the struggle so that the person experiencing the disability is not abandoned to the disability.

Stage IV of the model, *striving to regain the self*, involves the process of merging the old self with the new reality. During this stage, people become more familiar with their new abilities and limitations. They may begin to appreciate that their situation could be worse. For people with acquired communication disorders such as aphasia, this is a stage during which group aphasia therapy could demonstrate how others are coping with even more severe aphasia. As people in Stage IV become familiar with their new strengths and limitations, they may begin to revise their life goals. Thoughts of the future and the consideration of life alternatives return. They recognize that, given their disability, they may always require the assistance of others or of technology to some extent, but they will continue to function as "new and intact selves." They begin to redefine who they are from this point forward.

Future research in message management for people with acquired communication disorders will need to address several issues related to their adjustment to acquired disability. Some of these might include

1. What are the communication forms (small talk, storytelling, unique information sharing, and so forth) that occur frequently in interactions related to "preserving the self?"

2. What unique messages appear to be frequently associated with the four stages of "preserving the self?"

3. What is the impact of providing these unique messages in an AAC system on the user's participation in support groups, counseling, and general discussions related to "preserving the self"?

4. How do AAC users with acquired disabilities prefer to be supported, from a message management perspective, during their involvement in interactions that entail "preserving the self"?

Implications for AAC Service Delivery

The goal of AAC system designers is to provide effective ways to enable the individual to communicate as independently as possible. Incorporating the stages involved in the transformation of self after acquired disability has significant implications for present therapeutic approaches. Historically, the medical and rehabilitation model has provided services by analyzing disorders and designing treatment from a mechanistic paradigm. The traditional model separates the body into systems (e.g., skeletal, muscular, neurological) and addresses needs in quantitative terms. Expanding on this model, AAC assessments have focused on identifying sensory, cognitive, and movement capabilities with great specificity (Lloyd, Fuller, & Arvidson, 1997) to enable an AAC system to be designed that matches current skill levels. In designing messages for an AAC system, researchers analyze multiple factors related to language appropriateness and communication situations. But these approaches frequently fail to consider the experience of fundamental changes that occur in an individual's life after acquired communication disability.

Literature that focuses on the individual's illness or disability experience and responses to recovery (Langer, 1994; Morse, 1997; Morse & O'Brien, 1995; Toombs, 1994) clearly suggests that disability is much more than the dysfunction of specific areas of the body. Individuals experience disability as a total disruption of the self (Toombs, 1994). With this in mind, we propose that a conceptual framework of AAC system design must include the following.

Awareness of Change   It is important that all people assisting in the recovery process remember that disability represents a fundamental change in the individual's life (Toombs, 1994). This must be discussed openly by AAC facilitators with AAC users and their families. This awareness helps facilitators address and plan for the changes in how the individual experiences the world after a disabling event. Discussions should tactfully and factually acknowledge the changes that the individual experiences in relationships among body and environment, temporal perceptions, a sense of future possibilities, daily activities, and social roles. In selecting vocabulary and arranging messages on an AAC system, it is important to provide new ways for the individual to participate in conversations and to communicate new needs. For example, for an individual with moderately unintelligible speech, it might be important to get the attention of communication partners through a specific message prior to speaking (e.g., "I have something to say") or to add messages detailing instructions for a home health aide regarding personal care needs.

Supporting a Positive Image Through Prosthetic Devices   AAC users, partners, and strangers may view aids designed for regaining or supplementing function as visible signs of disability. AAC facilitators should view these tools (e.g., eyeglasses, white cane, laptop computer) as extensions of an individual's bodily space (Toombs, 1994). The underlying goal must be to extend the individual's range of possible actions and to restore, to the extent possible, the capacity to participate without sacrificing attractiveness and cleanliness. This requires vigilance with regard to details of the construction of systems so that there is a minimum of dangling cords, odd attached items, and obtrusive switch access sites. It also requires sensitivity to message components that will be viewed by everyone. For example, some adults may be reluctant to use devices that display picture icons out of fear that these systems appear childish. Words, pictures, and colors must be selected and organized in ways that are cognitively and physically accessible as well as aesthetically acceptable. For a more extensive discussion regarding acceptance of AAC, please see Chapter 5. How the system *looks* is part of the individual's emerging sense of self. The need for awareness and sensitivity from this perspective also obviously reflects discussions about choosing words and phrases appropriate to the individual's gender, age, culture, and newly developing roles.

Validating the Grief and Difficulty Involved   Although it is crucial to present approaches for coping with disability positively, validating the difficulty of the experience of disability is also important (Toombs, 1994). During the process of choosing messages, words, and symbols, facilitators should expect to encounter grief that may be expressed through tears, anger, or withdrawal. By recognizing and verbally acknowledging these responses as natural parts of the total process, AAC clinicians can facilitate the individual's journey through these times. As partners in the process of surviving this disabling event, AAC system designers may want to include ways for the individual to "save face" as well as appropriate messages to encourage the expression of emotion during the recovery process.

Including Therapy Goals That Facilitate a New Sense of Self   During the onset of a disabling disease, events occur rapidly, leaving the individual with a feeling of powerlessness (Toombs, 1994). Initial purposes of AAC systems may be to provide ways to keep the individual informed about his or her medical status or to enable the individual to respond to questions requesting information, opinions, and comments. These efforts may take the form of low technology or computer systems. For example, AAC systems for an individual who cannot speak may include ways for the user to pose specific questions to medical staff (e.g.,

"What are you doing?"). Also, systems may include replies to medical questions about pain status, responses to questions about daily schedules, or indications of user fatigue level. Collectively, these goals help provide a means of returning control to the patient.

As previously discussed, narratives (stories) perform extremely important communicative functions in everyone's life. Early therapy goals should focus on assisting the individual in developing clinical narratives in addition to the medical history. Although medical histories focus exclusively on the facts (e.g., symptoms, etiology, modes of treatment), the clinical narrative or evolving theme story relates the meaning of this disability to the individual's life situation (e.g., expressing losses, changes, sudden insights).

Using storytelling in AAC systems may accomplish many goals. It influences the design process so that components of storytelling (e.g., cores, expansions) are incorporated into the system and enables the individual to practice the act of storytelling with an AAC system. The process of writing the narrative provides acknowledgment of many issues individuals with acquired disability face and may provide a chronicle of progress. At times, narratives also provide the individual and the therapist with an exercise in imaginative development. It is necessary to supply a lengthy list of words from which to choose in order to adequately describe the current situation, caregiver/physician behavior, and new social relationships.

Finally, accepting responsibility for assisting in the fundamental transformation of an individual requires developing goals and AAC systems that incorporate the new way of being (Toombs, 1994). Communication systems should not suggest that the individual can resume life as it was before the disabling event, ignoring the disabling event. Rather, systems should target ways to help the individual to incorporate disability into a newly defined self, acknowledging disability to be an important part of who he or she is. AAC facilitators may wish to include details regarding an individual's former job in addition to comments, hopes, and desires about seeking new employment after the disabling event. For example, an individual with aphasia may have on his or her AAC device an extensive description of the job he or she performed and where he or she worked prior to a stroke as well as pages designed to facilitate his or her current job search.

LINGUISTIC-COGNITIVE CAPABILITIES AND IMPAIRMENTS OF THE AAC USERS

The linguistic-cognitive capabilities of people with acquired communication disorders have an important impact on their message management preferences. These capabilities affect message management in several ways that are introduced here but are discussed in more detail later in this chapter as well as in other chapters. Linguistic and cognitive capabilities influence message formulation. For example, adult AAC users with intact or nearly intact linguistic skills retain the ability to formulate messages on a letter-by-letter or word-by-word basis. However, people with the most severe linguistic impairments usually do not formulate their own messages independently and therefore require the assistance of their listeners or facilitators to co-construct messages and, with the assistance of a facilitator, store a whole message for use at other times. Linguistic and cognitive capabilities also affect message encoding and retrieval. For example, people with cognitive impairments find it difficult, if not impossible, to learn and to remember retrieval codes. As a result, many of these individuals experience difficulty in using message retrieval strategies functionally. The following sections highlight the impact of cognitive and linguistic capabilities on message management for people with acquired communication disorders.

No Linguistic-Cognitive Impairments

The linguistic-cognitive capabilities of adults with acquired severe communication disorders vary greatly. Some, such as most people with amyotrophic lateral sclerosis (ALS), retain sophisticated cognitive and linguistic capabilities. Therefore, from a linguistic-cognitive perspective, most are able to formulate their messages by using many different strategies. For example, they are able to spell messages on a letter-by-letter basis; formulate messages word-by-word; formulate messages by combining phrases, words, and letters; or retrieve whole messages. From a linguistic-cognitive perspective, these individuals appear to have extensive message management options. However, their physical endurance, interface access capability, and personal care needs typically influence their message management choices. For example, individuals with primarily bulbar ALS symptoms may demonstrate the following characteristics: 1) they may be unable to speak, 2) they can access their AAC technology through direct selection, 3) they may not experience fatigue or experience reductions in endurance associated with AAC use, and 4) they are able to care for many of their personal and health care needs independently. Such individuals often prefer to formulate their messages on a letter-by-letter or word-by-word basis. However, individuals with mixed bulbar and spinal symptoms usually prefer a different message management strategy because they access their system by scanning or by head pointing. They experience considerable fatigue while communicating and have extensive personal and health care needs. They often use whole-message strategies that enhance communication timing for small talk and personal care communication and that reduce the activations necessary to communicate. However, for novel information sharing, they may use letter- or word-based strategies.

Given their cognitive-linguistic abilities, AAC users can make use of a range of message storage and retrieval strategies, also known as *encoding strategies*. *Encoding* refers to any technique in which a user produces multiple signals that together specify a particular message. Encoding strategies may employ salient letters of words, contractions, truncations, arbitrary alpha-numeric codes, colors, Morse code, and icons. Abbreviation expansion is a form of encoding in which a brief code is entered and an entire word or message is produced. Such codes may be automatically terminated, or they may be *key terminated*, in which a special key is pressed to indicate that an encoding combination has been used. With all encoding methods, recall and overall efficiency are crucial factors that determine effectiveness.

AAC users with intact cognitive and linguistics capabilities also make extensive use of *lexical prediction*. This is a process in which AAC users type in a portion of the word and the system offers options for what the word or message might be. Prediction can occur on a number of different levels according to different algorithms: single-letter prediction (based on probable letter combinations), word-level prediction (based on the most likely word given the letter already typed), word-pattern prediction (based on patterns of word combinations), linguistic prediction (based on syntactic organization of the language), and phrase- or sentence-level prediction (based on message type). Researchers have proposed several factors that interact in examining the efficacy of prediction strategies (Beukelman & Mirenda, 1998): linguistic cost (the number of selections required to communicate a word), the number of keystrokes required to produce a message, how long it takes to produce a message, the visual processing time required to synthesize the information displayed, and the cognitive processing time needed to decide on the next key activation. In addition, researchers have considered differences between simulations and actual system trials. These factors may combine in ways that influence results of research studies and clinical interventions. For example, if an individual has a primary motor impairment, prediction may save on message preparation time. If the user's impairment is primarily perceptual (e.g., as a result of multiple sclerosis) or is related to fatigue (e.g., as a result of ALS) or causes slight inaccuracies in cognitive processing (e.g., as a result of traumatic brain injury [TBI]), lexical prediction may increase selection time because of its visual and processing demands.

Linguistic Impairments

Adults with acquired severe communication disorders have extensive linguistic impairments (e.g., aphasia following stroke) and therefore are limited in their ability to independently formulate messages through spelling or through word-by-word retrieval. Rather, these individuals frequently adopt a variety of different strategies, depending on the type of message they wish to convey, who the communication partner is, and the communication context. Frequently, people with severe linguistic impairments engage in co-construction of messages with their communication partners. Four of these strategies are introduced here to support the discussion of message management. Each of these strategies is discussed in greater detail in Chapters 11 and 12, which deal with AAC strategies for people with aphasia and dementia.

When sharing new information, many people with severe aphasia communicate a portion of a message (a word or a phrase) to convey an idea, enhance it with gestures, and encourage communication partners to expand their partial message. For example, Beukelman, Yorkston, and Dowden (1985) described a man with aphasia who preferred not to have complete messages programmed into his AAC system. Instead, he included salient words. For example, he initiated an interaction by activating the word LUNCH on his system. Other communicators with aphasia use a variety of modalities in succession to convey a single message to a partner, who may facilitate the communication process by asking directed questions during an interaction. Although such strategies to co-construct a message may appear to be quite inefficient, they are eventually effective as means to communicate novel messages that are difficult to anticipate and store in advance. For example, when trying to communicate the fact that her grandson dressed up as a spider for Halloween, one woman with aphasia used multiple modalities that changed in response to her partner's degree of understanding. Not finding the word *spider* in her communication book, she first made the sound /spi/. When her partner did not understand her, the woman then tried pointing to letters on an alphabet board. When she was still not understood, the woman gesturally indicated the act of trick-or-treating to establish the topic of Halloween with her partner. The partner then verbally stated the topic and asked about the woman's grandson. At her partner's suggestion, the woman then drew a picture of a spider. Through a series of questions and a variety of communicative behaviors, the woman's partner eventually understood the message.

Jon Lyon (1995) and his colleagues have developed the use of interactive drawing to support the communication interaction of people with aphasia. The person with aphasia begins with a partial drawing that is enhanced with residual speech or gestures. Meanwhile, the listener co-constructs the message by drawing and offering words and phrases that complete the intended message. Bauer and Kaiser (1995), Lyon (1995), Rao (1995), and Ward-Lonergan and Nicholas (1995) provided successful case reports supporting the use of interactive drawing as a means of communication.

Kathryn Garrett has developed the Written Choice Communication Strategy (Garrett, 1993; Garrett & Beukelman, 1995) to facilitate communication interaction with people with severe aphasia. Written Choice is a conversational technique in which communication partners provide written word choices to people with severe aphasia and then allow them to choose appropriate responses from a written array; the partner then offers message options as the conversation progresses. In the standard written choice strategy, a partner asks a question, waits for a response, and, if the person with severe aphasia does not respond, writes down three possible answers. The partner then presents these by pointing to each written word and saying it aloud. The person with aphasia indicates his or her choice, and the partner circles the selected word. Then the partner asks another question from the same topic or switches to a different topic to continue the conversation.

Garrett (1993) and Garrett and Beukelman (1995) documented global treatment effects of the Written Choice Communication Strategy across three individuals, demonstrating that it improves the quality of communicative interactions between a person with aphasia and a partner by increasing the length of time and proportion of conversational turns spent discussing a certain topic. In this technique, the messages are words provided by the partner and selected by the AAC user. In addition, many users often retrieve previously used Written Choice pages to indicate words and initiate new messages. These strategies can be used to communicate brief stories; however, more extended story retelling can by supported with phrase- or sentence-based strategies of message management. People with severe aphasia usually require the assistance of a facilitator to enter and store their stories for retelling. The initial development of the story usually occurs through the co-construction strategies described previously. Then the facilitator stores the story in a communication notebook or an AAC device with speech output (Garrett & Beukelman, 1992), so it can be retold on a sentence-by-sentence basis.

Cognitive Impairments

People with cognitive impairments in addition to severe communication disorders manage messages in a variety of ways, depending on the nature of their cognitive impairment. For example, people with cognitive impairments that are due to TBI often retain intact spelling skills but experience difficulty with the new learning and recall memory required to learn encoding strategies. Even when they do learn some encoded messages, they typically report difficulty in code shifting from spelling to word, phrase, or sentence retrieval strategies. Therefore, many spell their entire messages even when encoded messages are available in their AAC systems, and they learn to retrieve them through instruction.

Some individuals with linguistic and cognitive impairments require the assistance of their communication partner to co-construct messages similar to people with aphasia. This occurs frequently in individuals with linguistic as well as cognitive impairments, including Huntington disease, dementia, and in some cases severe TBI. It is beyond the scope of this chapter to review each of the groups of individuals involved; however, Chapters 7–12 provide a great deal of information in this area.

COMMUNICATION FUNCTION REQUIREMENTS ON COMMUNICATION ACCURACY, RATE, AND TIMING

In addition to external and societal factors, message management is also influenced by the communication function of a message. Because they have different timing, rate, and accuracy requirements, communication functions may be facilitated by a variety of message formulation and retrieval strategies. In this chapter, the accuracy, rate, and timing profile of several communication functions are highlighted. For example, urgent messages dealing with self-care, health care, small talk, and social etiquette must be communicated promptly if they are to be effective. In addition, they must be communicated accurately to achieve the desired result. Considering that most AAC system users communicate quite slowly when they formulate messages via letter- or word-based strategies, AAC users typically find that urgent messages can be communicated more effectively if they are stored in whole-message format. Yet, information sharing has different requirements than urgent messages. For interactions that involve sharing novel information, the ability to generatively produce a unique message is the most important characteristic. Letter- or word-based message preparation allows formulation of unique messages that precisely communicate the user's intent. In this situation, word-based formulation typically allows speed enhancement over letter-based formulation yet may fail to preserve the generative quality of this type of interaction.

Generic social exchanges (i.e., small talk) are essential to engage new listeners, to determine whether familiar listeners are interested in conversing, and to interact in situations that are largely social in nature.

The characteristics of small talk messaging are discussed in much greater detail later in this chapter; however, AAC users typically find that small talk messages need to be communicated rapidly and with appropriate timing if they are to be effective in engaging others and initiating more extensive conversational interactions. The accuracy of these small talk messages is less important than for novel information sharing or urgent messages. If individuals require an extended period of time to formulate small talk, their communication loses its effectiveness. Therefore, many AAC users use whole message techniques to retrieve at least some of their more frequently used generic small talk messages.

Narration and storytelling appear to require a variety of different message retrieval strategies. Initially, narratives must be produced in a generative manner by the AAC user or, if they are not capable of doing so independently, by a facilitator. It is useful for the AAC device to capture narratives as they are being formulated for the first time, so that they can be stored, refined, and retold in a single version or in several different versions. Then, of course, they may be retold numerous times. Finally, it is useful for the AAC user to be able to retrieve and release the message or the narrative on a segment-by-segment or sentence-by-sentence basis. It helps the conversation when the user can produce generative messages while the overall narrative is presented. In this way, conversations can be individualized and enriched by generative interactions. However, the overall presentation of a narrative is very time consuming if the entire story is told generatively using letter- or word-based strategies.

RESEARCH REVIEWS OF SPECIFIC COMMUNICATION FUNCTIONS

In the following sections, the research related to a variety of communication functions is reviewed, including small talk, storytelling, information sharing, communication repairs, and communication registers. It is clear that currently available AAC systems have the capability to perform a number of these functions quite effectively. We identify areas for further research and technical development.

Social Closeness Through Small Talk

Locke (1998) described two broad purposes for human language: propositional speaking and intimate talking. Propositional speaking emphasizes transfer of information, whereas intimate talking focuses on the construction and enjoyment of relationships with others. Intimate talking includes gossip, self-disclosure, and expression of personal thoughts and feelings. Locke suggested that individuals have been "devoiced" by information overload in American society. The overemphasis on obtaining and sharing information has occurred at the expense of facilitating and nurturing human relationships. Locke's discussion of intimate talk is similar to what researchers in the field of AAC describe as "small talk," or the components of conversation that bridge the gap between greetings and information sharing. Generic small talk can be used with a variety of conversational partners in a number of different settings; it does not refer directly to specific information. For example, the comment "That's great!" is generic small talk, whereas the comment "That's a great shirt you're wearing!" is specific.

By studying the small-talk patterns of typical adult speakers of various ages, researchers have begun to understand the prevalence and importance of small talk for people with acquired communication disorders. Researchers recorded the daily conversations of typical speakers using portable, voice-activated tape recorders. King, Spoenemen, Stuart, and Beukelman (1995) found that among adults 20–30 years of age, 39% of all spoken utterances consisted of generic small talk. Older adult speakers used slightly less small talk; small talk composed 31% of the utterances of 65- to 74-year-olds and 26% of the utterances of 75- to 85-year-olds (Lasker, Ball, Bringewatt, Stuart, & Marvin, 1996). Researchers tallied the types of generic small talk utterances and found that, for the two older adult groups, *continuers* were the most frequently used type of generic small talk utterance. For the younger adults, continuers ranked second in frequency, whereas *comments* are the most frequently used type of small talk. Researchers defined *continuers* as statements or questions that keep a conversation going by indicating engagement, such as "hmm" or "really." Other frequently used types of small talk included *confirmations* and *negations* (all variations of "yes" or "no") and *comments* (statements that indicated the speaker's personal position). These findings suggest that small talk messages should be included in AAC systems of adults. AAC users might benefit from a variety of messages that enable them to indicate "yes" and "no," to indicate to their communication partner that they are listening, and to express personal opinions.

Most AAC users make rather limited use of small-talk strategies, a fact that has received little research attention. Perhaps some of the reasons for this phenomenon reflect personal attitudes. For example, Michael Williams, an experienced AAC user, reported in a personal communication that he did not understand the importance of small talk until he was about 45 years of age. It did not make much sense to him to work so hard to communicate in order to say something that contained little, if any, novel content. Because many AAC users did not have small talk available to them in earlier AAC systems, they have had little experience with this communication form.

Although there has been research into how typical speakers utilize small talk, the use of small talk by AAC users has not been extensively studied. The following issues should be addressed in future research: How does the use of small talk by AAC users influence

- Their acceptance in social (conversational) groups?
- Their personal perceptions of their own communicative competence and effectiveness?
- Unfamiliar listeners' perceptions of their communicative competence and effectiveness?
- The willingness of unfamiliar listeners to engage in more extended information-sharing interactions with them?

Social Closeness through Storytelling

In everyday conversation, in formal presentations, and in written form, people tell stories to others in their social networks. Because storytelling is such an important communication form for adults, it is emphasized in this chapter. At this point, much of what is known about storytelling has been learned from the experiences of typical adult speakers who do not require AAC technology to communicate. Obviously, it is essential to study the storytelling characteristics of experienced AAC users in order to more fully understand how storytelling can be effectively accomplished by all people who rely on AAC.

Often the act of telling the story to another person helps the teller understand and remember the events as well as sort out elements and relationships. Stories illustrate points, persuade, give life to past experiences, and allow a special sharing of events. People trade stories at times to emphasize their common experiences and at other times to emphasize the unusual (Schank, 1990). Storytelling is a distinctive mode of communication characterized by an intrinsic multiplicity of meanings; the knowledge of both the storyteller and the story listener is enhanced by the act of storytelling (Carter, 1994).

Although the stories told by adults of all ages are highly individualized (and as such can make the idea of providing for this function in an AAC system very intimidating), viewed from a larger perspective stories can be categorized into five types (Schank, 1990):

1. *Official stories:* Stories that have been carefully constructed by one or more people to tell a version of events that is sanitized and presumed to be unlikely to get anyone in trouble.

2. *Invented stories:* Stories that expand on an experience for the purpose of entertainment, sometimes leaving the original experience unrecognizable in the process.

3. *Firsthand stories:* Stories that embody a person's own experiences but that are told differently in a way that is appropriate to a specific listener.

4. *Secondhand stories:* Stories that are firsthand stories of others that the teller has heard and remembered.

5. *Culturally common stories:* Stories that come out of agreed-upon common information from the environment.

Using these definitions can guide AAC practitioners when soliciting information about the specific stories most appropriate for an adult AAC system user. Most long-term AAC users eventually need a means by which to tell at least one story from each of the preceding categories. Immediately after a disabling event, they may need only to tell official stories (e.g., how the accident happened).

With the advancement of technological elements such as rate enhancement, greater capacity for storage of preprogrammed phrases, and improved ways to control synthesized voice output, the possibility of including storytelling as a viable communicative style for AAC system users is currently a reality. A simplistic approach for including stories within a voice output communication aid (VOCA) might involve nothing more than storing an entire story for retrieval using a single encoded sequence. However, this approach is not sufficient for the complex, interactive multiplicity of storytelling forms often needed by the AAC system user.

Although research reveals that adults tell the same stories repeatedly, there are some specific ways in which the repetition of the same story occurs. Stories are comprised of basic segments and expansion segments. Basic segments supply the repeated element and tell the core story conveying information about the general topic. Stuart gave the example of a story told three times by a research participant named Russell. The core story was as follows:

> Russell and his wife went on a weekend trip to Chicago. They visited a woman who was his wife's roommate in college; they have known her for over 50 years. She has suffered many tribulations over the past 50 years. Now she has recently lost her husband. While they were visiting, this friend gave Russell the collection of long playing albums of 1940s dance music that originally belonged to her husband. (2000, p. 5)

In each of the three instances of telling this story, all of the previous information was provided, thus making it the repeated core story. The sentences used were termed *basic segments* and occurred within the body of the story in the same position (i.e., beginning, middle, and end of the story). It should be noted that, although the basic segments occurred in the same positions, storytellers may formulate these segments using different vocabulary and syntax. Stuart (2000) presented data that demonstrated this phenomenon. In some repeated stories, vocabulary items and phrasing for basic segments were exactly the same. In other repeated stories, vocabulary and sentence structure conveyed the same information but were changed in terms of level of formality or details provided. For example, in the first retelling of a story, a speaker said, "My mother passed away in 1936," and in another retelling he said, "My mom died, '36."

Stuart (2000) also noted the use of *expansion segments* to provide explanations for core story elements over the course of Russell's three story retellings. Expansions were found to occur in relation to key topic areas within the story to emphasize a particular area of information. Their use appeared to be related to the context of the telling (i.e., listener, time, and environment). For example, in Story 2 about Russell's weekend trip to Chicago, he included some additional information that was not included in the first telling, Story 1. After explaining that the friend in Chicago was his wife's roommate in college, he told the following:

> Jo [his wife] and she always got along great. They had a lot of fun playing tricks on other girls in the dorm. (p. 5)

He also expanded on the tribulations of his friend, as follows:

> In 1950 she had polio and survived it and 2 years later lost her brother in an accident. But she always managed to keep her dopper up. (p. 5)

In another retelling, he did not include the expansions used above but included an expansion about her recently deceased husband and his hobby of collecting, as follows:

> She married a guy who was a traveling salesman and went all over the country. While he was between sales meetings, he started looking in record shops and began picking up records for bands they liked to dance to, you know, and then brought these home as a little gift for her. Over the years, man, they just added up. (p. 6)

In a third retelling, he made several changes. He did not include the expansions used in the first retelling, he included a shortened version of the expansion used in Story 2, and he included a new expansion describing the collection:

> There were literally hundreds of records. She said I could have any of them I wanted. I went through them all and decided I'd just take the ones that were in the best shape (no scratches or anything). You know those

things are heavy. I've got lots of Tommy Dorsey, Guy Lombardo, and guys I bet you never heard of. (p. 6)

Stuart (2000) found that repeated stories were also told in sequential order. That is, if a specific first story was told, it might be immediately followed by the telling of a specific second story. The researchers hypothesized that the telling of these back-to-back stories might be based on the idea that the essential themes are the same in each story and can be emphasized by using two different narratives. For example, Russell frequently told a story about using "extreme measures" to kill mountain rats that had cost him "10,000 Christmas trees." He immediately followed this with a story of his use of "extreme measures" to eliminate gophers that had caused mounds and holes all over his pastureland. Although the extreme measures were different in each situation, both attempts to correct these problems resulted in some unexpected side effects. He presented these side effects as jokes on himself for not having thoroughly considered all the possibilities before taking action.

Research has revealed another type of story repetition in which the core story is repeated but continually expanded with new information about the most recent occurrence related to the topic of the story. For example, every day during lunch at the senior citizens' center, Jean would tell others about her dog (Stuart, 2000). She would always introduce the subject with the core story and then follow with one of the evolving theme expansions. The core story was as follows:

> You know, Corky has diabetes, he's on two shots a day. But he's a good old boy, and he's doing pretty good, considering. But we've got to watch him closely. (p. 7)

The story evolved over the course of 4 days as Jean expanded the core segments in the following ways:

> Day 1: The neighbors all line up to give him his shots, this one, that one. And there's old Cork right in the middle—thinks it's all so fun.

> Day 2: We got a schedule now—one neighbor comes in the morning, one in the evening. Corky better stay cute and friendly, those people are being so helpful.

> Day 3: My sister called, she wanted to know how Corky was doing. I said, "Well, I think he's gonna make it through this. Actually, he's doing better with his diabetes than his mom is with her emphysema."

> Day 4: Corky went to the vet today. We got some special fiber cookies from the vet. They come in this fancy box, I said, "Cork, maybe this diabetes thing isn't all bad—your own cookies even." (p. 7)

Another commonality demonstrated in storytelling research relates to the use of introductions and closings. People use a consistent introductory phrase at the beginning of their stories and often use some type of summation phrase at the end of their stories. Stating time and place to orient the listener is a frequent introductory technique (e.g., "I was in Presho in 1936; I had a chance to come home at Christmas time, 1944") or use of more general introductions (e.g., "You know when I was in high school," "I've got one for you"). In closing, storytellers often use a repetition of a basic segment in the story as a summation, such as, "So anyway, he was finally able to get through to his mother," or "Even though it's been frustrating, I've learned a lot."

Referencing time in story content is a sophisticated process during which older adults may select, introduce, expand, and elaborate past experience and events and intermingle these with events of the present in an overarching topical framework. Often topics of shared historical life events, shared time periods, and shared social experiences are used to contrast "the way it was" with "the way it is." For example, a discussion of some unique art items displayed in a hospital lobby elicited the following story:

> Amy, a new employee, asked, "Is there some special reason for those things [rugs] to be in the lobby? I don't get the connection." Bob, who had been employed there [for] 30 years, replied, "Those are very exclusive rugs made by the [Indians] in Central America. Back in the '50s several of the doctors got together and held clinics down there, they were given these rugs. Nobody had a place to display them so they decided to hang them in the lobby. They not only are pretty but they came to be here out of caring and giving. A lot of us see them as a symbol of that." (S.L. Stuart, personal communication, December 18, 1998)

One obvious challenge to AAC practitioners is finding ways to make each of these storytelling patterns available to AAC system users without unduly increasing the physical and cognitive burdens of communication. Although multiple ways of addressing this challenge exist, one way of incorporating the patterns of storytelling into AAC systems is described in the paragraphs that follow.

First, stories need to be chosen for inclusion in AAC systems by considering the purposes of storytelling for the user. Another consideration for the choice of stories is to determine how a story is to be delivered. It can be a single repeated story, a story that can be sequentially ordered (chained) with another, or one that includes a series of evolving expansions.

Obviously, choosing personally meaningful stories requires input from those familiar with the individual who will use the AAC system.

The informants (e.g., family members, friends) can compose stories appropriate for the target functions, being reminded to use vocabulary similar to what the individual might use if he or she were able to speak. A starting place for choosing specific stories might be to select stories that the individual shared on a regular basis prior to the onset of his or her acquired communication disorder and evolving theme stories that reflect topics that are known to be of high interest.

Once a story is identified, it needs to be transcribed and the basic segments and expansions identified. One suggestion is to write the stories including references to past and present and repeated phrases for emphasis. Variations of basic segments and expansions for each specific story should also be developed and presented in combination with an associated symbol, photograph, or remnant. This helps to support the AAC user in choosing which type of register (i.e., formal or informal) is to be used in any given rendition of the story. Choices of introductory phrases, closing or summation phrases, and general conversational segues to stories should also be identified and made easily accessible for general use across stories.

Storytelling can be available through either low-technology AAC systems or VOCAs. A story may be provided in a low-technology format by constructing a storytelling album that includes basic typewritten segments beneath pictures representing the major segments of each story. Choices of the types of basic segments (i.e., for formal and informal registers) could be provided with supplemental pictures that are color or alpha encoded. Expansions might be placed on postcards in an envelope positioned at the bottom of each story page for possible use as the story develops.

Storytelling patterns may also be incorporated into VOCAs, using codes that easily identify the formal/informal basic segments for each specific story. VOCAs that have dynamic displays can be used to link expansions, and pop-up windows can enable the AAC user to choose openers, closers, or variations in the commentary. The use of different synthesized voices, speaking rates, and volumes (e.g., whispering, speaking voice) or of a line repeat function could also provide for greater emphasis and more dramatic effects.

Of course, including the AAC system user's input during the construction of the stories within an AAC system is crucial. This not only allows the stories to be as personal as possible, but it also makes recall of the available choices easier. As use of the system continues, stories can be altered, removed, or replaced as the AAC system user deems appropriate.

The need for future research in storytelling by AAC users is extensive. A few areas of inquiry might include the following:

1. What is the attitude of peers and family members toward storytelling by people using AAC systems?

2. Are there stylistic issues that must be considered by AAC users when they prepare stories to enhance their acceptance by their social networks and the public?

3. How should stories be formulated, stored, and retrieved by AAC users? How acceptable is word-based formulation of stories by AAC user's social networks and the public? How acceptable is the use of multiple synthesized voices during storytelling?

4. How should stories be indexed, or stored, so that they can be efficiently and accurately retrieved by AAC users?

5. How can AAC systems be modified so that stories can be captured during the initial telling when they are formulated word-by-word or letter-by-letter? (Too many current AAC systems erase the speech buffer after each utterance is spoken, so that the user cannot communicate the story as it is initially formulated and save it for refinement later.)

6. What type of experiences or training do AAC users require to become effective storytellers?

7. What is the effect of story formulation, refinement, and retelling on an AAC user's memory of an event or an experience?

Information Sharing Through Unique (Novel) Messages

Novel information refers to those unique messages that are communicated through verbal expression, writing, or e-mail. Typically, these messages contain information that is communicated for the first time or for the first time in a given format. If possible, novel messages are typically produced generatively using letter- or word-based strategies. In this way, the AAC user is able to produce the messages as accurately as possible within the style (or speech register) that he or she prefers for the moment. Typically, unique messages are shared after the interactants are already engaged in conversation. Therefore, rate and timing issues are not as important as are accuracy and style.

Information Sharing Through Public Speaking

As people with severe communication disorders participate in educational, vocational, and community activities, they may be requested to give formal presentations. Modern AAC systems support formal presentations very effectively. In fact, many of the narration and story-telling strategies outlined previously are excellent for supporting formal talks and speeches. Typically, these speeches are released segment by segment (sentence by sentence) so that the AAC user can control the overall rate of presentation and can pause to allow discussion and questions. Generally, it is necessary for these individuals to have the capability of producing generative messages between the segments of the formal presentation. Although numerous AAC users are very effective public speakers, no research has been reported that identifies and documents the characteristics of effective AAC presenters.

Urgent Messages to Communicate
Personal Care and Health Care Needs

AAC practitioners often include personal and health care needs messages on the very first AAC system provided to new users. It is not uncommon for people in acute care facilities to have communication boards that include such messages. The challenge comes in delivering these messages to unfamiliar caregivers with clarity and efficiency. Over time, such messages may need to be minimized in the system or abbreviated so that other communication functions, such as small talk, storytelling, and novel information sharing, take precedence.

Speech Supplementation:
Integrating Natural Speech and AAC

Some individuals with severe communication disorders are able to use their residual natural speech if it is supplemented with messages delivered through an AAC system. Typically, two types of speech supplementation are used. *Topic supplementation* refers to the presentation of the topic of a message or a series of messages prior to communication of these messages with natural speech. To prepare individuals to use topic supplementation, appropriate topics need to be stored in their AAC systems and often need to be identified as topics. Therefore, the message might include the following statement: "The topic is sports." Typically, these messages are stored as whole messages so that they can be retrieved efficiently and not interrupt the flow of natural speech more than necessary. *Alphabet supplementation* is the communication of the first letter of each word as the word is spoken. Therefore, the AAC user identifies the first letter of each word on an alphabet board or through a spelling-based communication system (e.g., LightWriter) as the word is spoken. In order for this to be an effective mode of communication, the user must be able to access the letters of the alphabet accurately and efficiently in a timely way. The reader is referred to

Chapter 4 for an extended discussion of the roles of AAC strategies in supplemented speech. Generally, supplemented speech strategies are used by people whose speech is difficult to understand. Therefore, with or without supplemented speech strategies, communication breakdowns are likely to occur, and the AAC system is commonly used to resolve these breakdowns.

Communication Breakdown Resolution

Regardless of whether a person with a severe communication disorder communicates by using natural speech, an AAC system, or a combination of the two, communication breakdowns occur. AAC systems are frequently used to resolve communication breakdowns (Yorkston, Beukelman, Strand, & Bell, 1999). Typically, breakdown resolution messages are of three different types. First, descriptions of the AAC user's strategy to resolve the breakdown might include the following: "One more time." "I will try that again." "Let me say that in a different way." A second way of resolving a breakdown involves iterating the content of the misunderstood message through either restatements or revisions of the original message. Because messages are commonly stored in the "output" buffer of AAC devices, it is often easiest for the message to be repeated verbatim. Clinical observations suggest that, in situations in which the communication breakdown has occurred because the listener was inattentive or distracted, a reiteration of the original message is often successful. However, verbatim iterations of the original message usually do not resolve the breakdown if the message is poorly constructed in the first place or if the listener is confused as to the overall intent of a conversation. In a third communication breakdown strategy, the AAC system can be used to instruct listeners as to how to resolve the breakdown. For example, such messages might be programmed as follows: "I'll say it again. Repeat back to me what you hear, so I can figure this out," "Let's forget it for now (it wasn't important)," "Please read the message from the screen on my communication system."

Obviously, communication breakdown resolution messages must be accurate if they are to be effective; for these sorts of messages, timing, communication rate, and style do not appear to be as important as accuracy. The use of AAC systems to resolve communication breakdowns appears to be very common. However, there has been little research documenting its effectiveness, investigating the dynamics of this process by expert AAC users, or studying its impact on AAC user or their listeners.

Communication Registers

This section identifies two types of communication registers. *Speech registers* are well understood by most natural speakers but must be considered for message management of AAC users. *Internet registers* are a new and welcome addition to the communication considerations of AAC users.

Speech Registers   Each of us incorporates acrolect (i.e., formal language), mesolect (i.e., informational or ordinary language), and basolect (i.e., slang, argot, dialect, suprasegmental sounds) into everyday communication. Every conversation has a lexicon pitch. Speakers alter their language in response to situational variables, and word choice is determined by the audience who will receive the message (Haynes, 1988; Warren & McCloskey, 1993). Speakers also adapt their word choice to project a concept of self.

A high-technology AAC device has the memory capacity to store many different words and phrases. This makes it possible to provide several different types of messages related to any single topic. Unlike core vocabulary and many fringe vocabulary items such as proper nouns, slang words are not immediately considered for AAC systems. However, there is an identified expressive value in the use of different speech registers that must be understood and considered during the vocabulary selection process.

The use of slang is an "alternative idiom to be chosen rather than required" (Chapman, 1986, p. 12). It has some personal, communicative advantages that make it useful and popular with people of all ages. It is more concise, forceful, unique and colorful than ordinary word use. The use of slang often indicates an individual's age to listeners and reminds them of where the speaker comes from. It advertises biographical, mental, and psychological background, which inherently includes age-group membership.

Slang items may be included with the more formal topic-related words and phrases related when preprogramming vocabulary. However, especially for adolescents or young adults, some AAC system designers designate a special category and area just for slang commentary. The manner of inclusion is obviously a decision for the system user, but providing choice in vocabulary type is important. When making decisions about including words and phrases that fit the slang/colloquial category, considering sources and communicative functions related to age and culture is important.

At this point, AAC systems provide users with very little assistance in changing speech register. If individuals use a word-based formulation approach, they can select words that appropriately reflect register if these words have been stored in their systems. However, to store similar messages with different registers places demands on the memory and new learning of AAC users. Future research and development should consider approaches that inform the AAC system of the social context or the identity of the individual(s) with whom the AAC user is interacting. "Smart" AAC systems then could offer versions of small talk and narratives that incorporate register shifts. Future research should also investigate what is required for AAC users to develop awareness and preferences regarding vocal register so that they can implement the changes that they prefer.

Internet Registers   Dowden (1996) offered several reasons to promote Internet usage among AAC users. In particular, the asynchronous interaction characteristics of the Internet are particularly beneficial to AAC users. E-mail allows for communication with significant others who are not present and with partners who do not have to wait for a message to be generated in "real time." An example of this information is reported in Chapter 7 for AAC users with ALS.

Through the Internet, AAC users can expand their participation in a community even if they are isolated physically; they can choose when or whether to reveal their disability; they can use chat groups and listservs to share information with other AAC users, to solve problems, and to advocate (e.g., ACCOLOG). The Internet facilitates independent transactions in the real world (e.g., banking, shopping, making travel arrangements) and offers opportunities for AAC users to read and write.

In addition, the Internet provides a nearly limitless opportunity to gain access to information that supports informal learning about a wide range of topics. Increasingly, opportunities for formal education through distance education are available to people who use AAC systems. Although the future of Internet services and opportunities for people with disabilities, their families, and their facilitators is not clear, there is little doubt that the impact on the lives of AAC users is and will continue to be very important.

Successful interaction with the Internet requires the AAC community to study electronic communication to understand its requirements from the perspective of AAC users and their facilitators. From an alternative access perspective, to use the Internet AAC users require a system that enables them to use a mouse and access browser menus. Such equipment might include alternative keyboards, single-switch scanning programs, screen readers, and visual enhancement tools (Blackstone, 1996.) From a message management perspective, researchers need to research Internet interactions to learn about 1) the register of Internet interactions, 2) its etiquette, and 3) its command and control features.

With this knowledge, AAC users can enhance the effectiveness and enjoyment of this new communication and information medium.

CLOSING COMMENTS

At the beginning of this chapter, we suggest that viewing message management from either a word-based strategy or a phrase-based strategy was overly simplistic when designing or individualizing AAC devices. This is certainly true for adults with acquired communication disorders. The knowledge base in this area is very incomplete. In addition to knowledge about the message patterns of adults without disabilities, it is important for the AAC community to learn about the impact of acquired conditions on communication interaction needs and preferences as well as the impact of AAC system use on communication patterns. There is much yet to learn, and we will all benefit from the contributions from many AAC stakeholders, including users, members of their social network, AAC specialists, and AAC researchers.

REFERENCES

Asch, A., & Fine, M. (1988). Introduction: Beyond pedestals. In M. Fine & A. Asch (Eds.), *Women with disabilities* (pp. 25–26). Philadelphia: Temple University Press.

Bauer, A., & Kaiser, G. (1995). Drawings on drawings. *Aphasiology, 9*(1), 68–78.

Beukelman, D., & Mirenda, P. (1998). *Augmentative and alternative communication: Management of severe communication disorders in children and adults* (2nd ed.). Baltimore: Paul H. Brookes Publishing Co.

Beukelman, D., Yorkston, K., & Dowden, P. (1985). *Communication augmentation: A casebook of clinical management.* San Diego: College-Hill Press.

Blackstone, S. (1996). The challenge of getting online. *Augmentative Communication News, 9*(6), 4–5.

Carter, B. (1994). Surviving breast cancer. *CANCER PRACTICE: A Multidisciplinary Journal of Cancer Care, 2,* 135–140.

Chapman, R. (1986). *American slang.* New York: HarperCollins.

Dowden, P. (1996, August). *Top ten reasons to use the Internet/WWW.* Paper presented at the 7th Biennial Conference of the International Society of Augmentative and Alternative Communication, Vancouver, British Columbia, Canada.

Garrett, K. (1993). *Changes in the conversational participation of individuals with severe aphasia given three types of partner support.* Unpublished doctoral dissertation, University of Nebraska–Lincoln.

Garrett, K., & Beukelman, D. (1992). Augmentative communication approaches for persons with severe aphasia. In K. Yorkston (Ed.), *Augmentative communication in the medical setting* (pp. 245–338). Tucson, AZ: Communication Skill Builders.

Garrett, K., & Beukelman, D. (1995). Changes in the interaction patterns of an individual with severe aphasia given three types of partner support. In M. Lemme (Ed.), *Clinical Aphasiology, 23,* (pp. 237–251). Austin, TX: PRO-ED.

Hanna, W., & Rogovsky, B. (1991). Women with disabilities: Two handicaps plus. *Disability, Handicap & Society, 6*(1), 49–63.

Haynes, D. (1988). Speaking and writing: Distinct patterns of word choice. *Journal of Memory and Language, 27,* 572–585.

King, J., Spoeneman, T., Stuart, S., & Beukelman, D. (1995). Small talk in adult conversations. *Augmentative and Alternative Communication, 11,* 244–248.

Langer, K. (1994). Depression and denial in psychotherapy of persons with disabilities. *American Journal of Psychotherapy 48*(2), 181–194.

Lasker, J., Ball, L., Bringewatt, J., Stuart, S., & Marvin, C. (1996, November). *Small talk across the lifespan: AAC vocabulary selection.* Paper presented at the annual convention of the American Speech-Language-Hearing Association, Seattle.

Lloyd, L., Fuller, D., & Arvidson, H. (1997). *Augmentative and alternative communication: A handbook of principles and practices.* Needham Heights, MA: Allyn & Bacon.

Locke, J. (1998). Where did all the gossip go? Casual conversation in the information age. *Asha, 40*(30), 26–31.

Lyon, J. (1995). Drawing: Its value as a communication aid for adults with aphasia. *Aphasiology, 9,* 33–94.

Morse, J. (1997). Responding to threats to integrity of self. *Advanced Nursing Science, 19*(4), 21–36.

Morse, J., & O'Brien, B. (1995). Preserving self: From victim to patient to disabled person. *Journal of Advanced Nursing, 21,* 886–891.

Rao, P. (1995). Drawing and gesture as communication options in a person with severe aphasia. *Topics in Stroke Rehabilitation, 2,* 49–56.

Schank, R. (1990) *Tell me a story: A new look at real and artificial memory.* New York: Scribner.

Stuart, S. (2000). Understanding the storytelling of older age adults for AAC system design. *Augmentative and Alternative Communication, 6,* 1–12.

Toombs, S. (1994). Disability and the self. In T.M. Brinthaupt & R.P. Lipka (Eds.), *Changing the self: Philosophies, techniques, and experiences* (pp. 337–357). Albany: State University of New York Press.

Yorkston, K., Beukelman, D., Strand, E., & Bell, K. (1999). *Management of motor speech disorders in children and adults.* Austin, TX: PRO-ED.

Ward-Lonergan, J., & Nicholas, M. (1995). Drawing to communication: A case report of an adult with global aphasia. *European Journal of Disorders of Communication, 30,* 475–491.

Warren, A.R., & McCloskey, L.A. (1993). Pragmatics: Language in social context. In J. Berko Gleason (Ed.), *The development of language* (3rd ed., pp. 27–208). New York: Macmillan.

3

Decision Making
in AAC Intervention

Kathryn M. Yorkston
David R. Beukelman

Service providers in the field of augmentative and alternative communication (AAC) must work with each of their clients to make many
decisions: Which device is appropriate? What are the advantages of
one device over another? What means of access is best? What vocabulary or messages should be programmed into the system's memory? Is
voice output needed? What type and intensity of training is needed
before my client can use the system in a natural environment? The list
of clinical questions could go on. Clinical decision making involves
taking the information at hand and developing a plan of action. The
process can be described as the process that happens between knowing
and doing. In a lecture to a group of faculty members in University of
Washington's School of Medicine, Arthur Elstein (1999) suggested that
medical students do the wrong things in a clinical setting not because
of a deficiency in knowledge but because they do not make good decisions. They know a lot, but they do not think systematically.

The field of clinical reasoning or medical decision making began in
the 1960s. The trend represents a move toward reasoning (i.e., clinical
decision making) based on evidence. It arises out of the observations
that there are large variations in practice. If medicine is an applied *science*, then there should be a right, or at least a reasonable, way to do

things, and health care practitioners should be able to agree on that way of doing things. The heightened interest in decision making emerges out of the history of medical education. The 19th century is referred to as the era of diagnosis, as a great deal of energy was focused on describing and diagnosing diseases, illnesses, and syndromes. To illustrate, multiple sclerosis, Parkinson's disease, and amyotrophic lateral sclerosis (ALS) were all initially described in the 1800s. The 20th century has been referred to as the era of intervention. During the course of that century, surgical, pharmacological, behavioral, and prosthodontic interventions were developed for individuals with a wide variety of conditions. To illustrate, antibiotics and anti-parkinsonian medication, along with many other drugs, were developed in the 20th century. By the close of the 20th century, considerable attention was paid to the measurement of outcomes and the effectiveness of specific interventions.

Many think that the 21st century will be designated as the era of clinical decision making. The early work focusing on intervention outcomes and effectiveness outcomes is evolving into an effort by interventionists to move toward evidence-based intervention (DeJong, 1999). That is, increasingly, clinical decisions need to be based on empirical support rather than on tradition, conventional wisdom, or authoritative statements and documents. According to DeJong, evidence-based practice embraces a variety of research approaches in ascertaining recommended practices. Evidence-based practice is a commitment to a constant reexamination of practices through research and outcome analyses. DeJong also pointed out that for individuals with long-term (i.e., chronic) disabilities, recommended practices are determined from multiple perspectives (i.e., stakeholder groups), including individuals with disabilities, members of their social networks, intervention providers, reimbursement providers, and society at large. These various stakeholder groups often view a chronic condition from different perspectives. The notion of clinical decision making is not new to the field of AAC. In fact, some of the earliest articles related to this topic involved the construction of decision trees for selection of systems for particular clients (Alpert, 1980; Cook, Coleman, Praszler, & Dahlquist, 1983; Shane, 1980; Shane & Bashir, 1980).

This chapter reviews approaches to clinical decision making in the field of AAC from both the perspective of the knowledge base that must be used to make the decisions and how judgments or decisions can be made. This chapter also describes factors outside this field, such as shifts in health care services that influence clinical practice.

KNOWLEDGE BASE

This discussion of clinical decision making starts by attempting to describe the body of knowledge from which clinicians can draw in making clinical judgements. As in any branch of science, the knowledge base is continually growing and always incomplete. The following section describes 1) a model of disablement that gives a systematic way of understanding the consequences of health conditions, including chronic disease and trauma, 2) the outcome measurement movement that encourages clinicians to understand the consequences of interventions, and 3) the field of treatment efficacy research that provides evidence that interventions work and that changes are not due to other possible alternative explanations.

Models of Disablement

Models of disablement provide a useful framework for understanding the broad range of consequences that are associated with health conditions. No single model has yet been universally accepted (Frattali, 1998b; see Frattali, 1998a, for a description of various models). The World Health Organization (WHO), a leader in developing models of disablement, has proposed two influential models. The first model, described in 1980, was called the International Classification of Impairment, Disability, and Handicap (ICIDH). A reclassification was completed in 1999 and is called the International Classification of Impairment Activity and Participation (ICIAP; see WHO, 1999, for a complete description).

Before the WHO models, two quite different models of the disablement process were used: the medical model and the social model of disablement. The medical model viewed disablement as a personal problem directly caused by the disease, trauma, or health condition. Under this model, medical care was provided in the form of individual treatment by professionals, and intervention was aimed at reducing the impairment, improving the person's adjustment, and changing behavior. The social model of disablement viewed the problem as being societal. In this model, disablement is not an attribute of a person but a complex collection of conditions, many of which are created by the social environment.

The WHO models represent a true advancement in that they integrate the various dimensions of disablement into a biopsychosocial approach. Thus, these models provide a common language or set of terms to describe the entire spectrum of consequence of health conditions.

Because the original ICIDH model has been applied extensively to adults with acquired communication disorders (Beukelman & Mirenda, 1998; Yorkston, Beukelman, Strand, & Bell, 1999), it is described here in some detail along with the more recent ICIAP model.

International Classification of Impairment, Disability, and Handicap   The ICIDH model has five levels of classification: the pathophysiology level, the impairment level, the functional limitation level, the disability or context level, and the social limitation level.

Pathophysiology Level   The pathophysiology level relates to the underlying pathology of a disease or health condition. This deficit is at the cellular or the tissue level. For example, individuals with ALS have a degeneration of the upper and lower motor neurons. Instruments used to document intervention outcomes from the pathophysiology perspective involve measures of cellular or tissue function and health. These deficits are assessed during a clinical neurological evaluation and can be observed by a variety of objective techniques, such as electromyography. Medical interventions may or may not be available for targeting the cellular or the tissue level of a disorder. In Chapter 7, Mathy, Yorkston, and Gutmann review new medical interventions for ALS, and in Chapter 8, pharmacological interventions are described that have been successful for individuals with Parkinson's disease in compensating for abnormally low levels of the neurotransmitter dopamine.

Impairment Level   The impairment level refers to deficits at the subsystem level. For example, for individuals with neuromotor speech disorders, the respiratory, phonatory, articulatory, or velopharyngeal subsystems are assessed to determine the extent to which they contribute to the speech disorder. For individuals with language disorders, the subsystems of language, such as semantics, syntax, and phonology, are assessed to determine their contributions to an overall language disorder. Traditionally, behavioral and prosthodontic interventions have been focused at the subsystem level for individuals with neurospeech disorders and language disorders. However, toward the end of the 20th century, some were questioning whether or not these subsystem interventions resulted in overall increases in functional performance by people with disabilities. As is clear later in this chapter, for some individuals such interventions appear to be effective if they are scheduled at the appropriate time during the course of a disease or condition. However, such interventions appear to be quite ineffective when they are scheduled at an inappropriate time in the course of the disease or condition. Measures of intervention outcomes from the impairment perspective include respiratory, phonatory, or velopharyngeal performance during speech.

Functional Limitation Level   The functional limitation level of a disorder refers to the overall measures of personal performance. Typically, these measures are taken in clinical or educational rather than in functional settings. The concern at this level is determined by how well an individual is able to perform certain functions, such as speaking, walking, or eating, given the level of pathophysiology and the impairment of their subsystems. Typically, functional limitation is measured with overall performance measures such as ability to walk if the impairment involves leg weakness. If the impairment involves speech movements, then performance is measured using speech intelligibility, speaking rate, or the naturalness of speech. Reduction or stabilization of an individual's functional limitation is often the primary goal of a speech intervention for individuals with speech disorders. The relationship between impairment and functional limitation is not always simple or straightforward (Yorkston, Strand, & Hume, 1998). Therefore, it is necessary to assess both of these levels when determining the impact of an intervention.

Disability or Context Level   The disability (or context) level refers to a person's performance in social contexts. Although speech may be understandable in clinical or educational settings, it may not support effective communication in social contexts or in adverse listening conditions. In our work, we have assessed the disability level as a combination of information that comes from the speech signal as well as information that comes in addition to the speech signals, such as information about the topic, the first letter of a word, or the environment in which the message is communicated (see Chapter 4). Although speech may be understood by familiar individuals in familiar contexts, it may be ineffective with strangers. Instruments to measure intervention outcomes from a disability perspective include ratings of communication effectiveness completed by the speaker as well as those in his or her social context (Yorkston et al., 1999).

Social Limitation Level   Finally, the social limitation (i.e., societal) level refers to the difficulty that a person might experience in participating in a desired role because of the biases and attitudes of people in the larger society. For example, an individual speaker may be excluded from a social group because of the negative attitudes of the group. A potential employer may not hire an individual because of disability. Many quality-of-life assessment tools measure outcomes from a social limitation perspective.

A physician is obliged to consider more than a diseased organ, more even than the whole man—he must view the man in his world.
    —Harvey Cushing as cited in Kirby, 1998, p. 55

International Classification of Impairment Activity and Partici-pation   In 1999, a simplified version of the disablement model was proposed. This model contains many of the elements of activity and participation that Beukelman and Mirenda (1998) included in their Participation Model, which has been used in the AAC field for more than a decade. This model focuses on three levels of disorder: impairments that occur at the level of the body, activities that occur at the level of the person, and participation that occurs at the societal level.

Impairments (The Body)   In this model, impairment refers to body systems and their functions. Impairments may be structural or functional in origin. Biological norms are the basis for evaluation. Impairments may be 1) temporary or permanent; 2) progressive, regressive, or stable; or 3) intermittent or continuous. Impairments are categorized by body system, not by disease or illness. For example, a condition such as ALS produces many different impairments, and a variety of body systems may be affected. Chapters 7–13 focus on the impairments associated with a range of conditions that are associated with severe communication disorders. The impairment and interventions that influence the impairment are described in detail in these chapters.

Activities (The Person)   In the disablement model, activities refer to overall functions that are performed by a person, such as speaking, walking, eating, and writing. Activity limitations are evaluated on functional norms. For example, speech performance might be evaluated in terms of overall measures, such as speech intelligibility, speaking rate, or speaking naturalness.

Participation (Society)   In this model, participation refers to a person's *lived* condition. In other words, how well do individuals with disability participate in societal contexts? It considers both the performance of individuals in society as well as the response of the society to the individuals in terms of facilitation or stigmatization. Society in this context refers to the social group in which an individual attempts to participate. Depending upon one's age and interests, these societies can include family, school, work, community, religious group, and so forth.

Outcomes Measures

The knowledge base is also enhanced by understanding what interventions do. Outcomes simply reflect the result of intervention (Frattali, 1998b). Most typically, the plural term is used because of the many types of outcomes that can be applied to a single intervention. They are used to determine the merit of interventions, including the dimensions of quality and cost. Outcome research in chronic disability is organized in such a way that it is sensitive to the various perspectives and levels of performance outlined by the various models of disablement (Frattali, 1998a; Fuhrer, 1997). Outcomes may reflect changes in the communication impairment, functional limitation, and disability (Beukelman, Mathy, & Yorkston, 1998). They can also reflect administrative issues (e.g., client referral patterns), financial issues (e.g., average length of hospital stays), and individual-defined issues (e.g., satisfaction with services).

Although it is common sense to believe that clinicians need to know the outcomes of their interventions, the history of outcomes measurement has been marked by considerable disagreement (Frattali, 1998b). Originally, outcomes were measured only with information about rates of death. The story of Florence Nightingale and her zealous campaign to reform British hospitals led to the beginning of outcomes measurements, a controversial field of study (Iezzoni, 1996). In 1863, after returning home from the Crimean War, Nightingale sought to change the configuration, location, and operation of hospitals. She supplied statistics suggesting that London hospitals had a staggering 90.8% mortality rate, yet the average mortality rate of rural hospitals was 13%. A debate erupted in the London medical press over how best to calculate hospital mortality rates. Critics claimed that Nightingale and her colleagues had not adjusted for differences in severity of illness among urban and rural hospitals and that the figures were designed to mislead the public. Thus began a debate about risk adjustments (needed because some hospitals take higher-risk patients than others) that has continued for more than 130 years. If outcomes measures are to be used to compare one facility to another in health care planning, then issues of comparability of client mix must be addressed. Developing possible indicators of caseload severity is especially difficult for the field of AAC, in which patient diversity is high and the number of patients is relatively low.

Any comparison which ignores the difference between the apple-cheeked farm-laborers who seek relief at Soke Pogis (probably for rheumatism and sore legs), and the wizzened [sic], red-herring-like mechanics of Soho and Southwark, who come from a London Hospital, is fallacious.
—1864 as cited in Iezzoni, 1997

Although the need for outcomes measures seems obvious, the hazards of such measures have also received considerable attention in the medical community. The debates continue about which measures to employ. For example, it is much more straightforward to measure dimensions related to cost of services than it is to find a valid and general measure of quality of services. However, it is clear that both types of information are necessary. If outcomes are to be used to compare facilities, then adjustments must be made to reflect differences in the severity of patients' conditions. Patient privacy rights are also becoming a critical issue, as outcomes are to be measured using a comprehensive system by which access is granted to individual patients' records.

Outcomes measurement has come to the field of communication disorders. Professional organizations, including the American Speech-Language-Hearing Association (ASHA), have become involved in outcomes measurement at least in part because of managed care and regulatory agency demands for data. They have also become involved because of the perceived limitations of some of the widely used measures of functional outcome that include general ratings of communication status. The Functional Independence Measure (FIM[SM]; Keith, Granger, Hamilton, & Sherwin, 1987) is the most commonly used measure in medical rehabilitation (Johnston, Maney, & Wilkerson, 1998). It is part of the Uniform Data System for Medical Rehabilitation in the United States (Hamilton, Granger, Sherwin, Zielezny, & Tashman, 1987). Outcomes measures are also being used internationally. It has been estimated that 77% of rehabilitation centers in the United Kingdom use at least one standardized outcomes measure (Turner-Stokes & Turner-Stokes, 1997). The FIM is meant to be so general that it can be applied to many populations. For example, it has been used to study outcomes in stroke (O'Donnell & Hamilton, 1997), traumatic brain injury (TBI; Semlyen, Summers, & Barnes, 1998), multiple sclerosis (Granger, Cotter, Hamilton, Fiedler, & Hens, 1990), and residents of nursing homes (Kosasih, Borca, Wenninger, & Duthie, 1998). The FIM is a seven-level rating scale for the degree of independence in self-care, mobility, continence, communication (i.e., expressive and receptive), social cognition, and psychosocial function. Although use of the dimension of independence to measure level of function seems quite reasonable, its use poses problems in populations that depend on assistive technology, such as augmentative communication devices. Scales have been criticized for failing to capture good outcomes such as the proficient use of augmentative communication devices, because they penalize individuals who use assistive devices for not being "independent."

A number of outcome scales for communication disorders have been developed including the National Outcomes Measure System (NOMS; ASHA, 1995) and the ASHA Functional Assessment of Communication

Skills in Adults (ASHA FACS; Frattali, Thompson, Holland, Wohl, & Ferketic, 1995). Although there clearly is no shortage of scales or measurement tools, Frattali offered this note of caution, "The problem easily could shift from one of 'too little evidence' to one of 'too much weak evidence'" (1998b, p. 8). In the following section, efficacy research, a somewhat different approach to documenting the benefits of intervention, is described.

Efficacy Research

Olswang (1998) drew the distinction between efficacy research and outcomes research. She suggested that, although they exist on a continuum with some overlap in the middle, they represent different approaches to examining the influence of treatment on individuals with communication disorders. "Treatment efficacy research proves treatment benefits; treatment outcome research identifies treatment benefits" (p. 135). Efficacy research provides evidence for the benefits of intervention by carefully controlled studies that rule out possible alternative explanations for individuals' changes. They can use either group or single-subject experimental designs to ask questions about treatment effectiveness (e.g., Does treatment work?) and about treatment efficiency (e.g., Does one treatment work better than another?).

In 1996, ASHA published in the *Journal of Speech and Hearing Research* a series of review articles documenting treatment efficacy literature in a variety of populations, including people with aphasia (Holland, Fromm, DeRuyter, & Stein, 1996), TBI (Coelho, DeRuyter, & Stein, 1996), and dysarthria (Yorkston, 1996). From these reviews, it is clear that efforts are being made to document the efficacy of AAC interventions. Research on the effectiveness of AAC systems such as alphabet boards to supplement the speech of individuals with severe dysarthria associated with TBI or stroke was reviewed (Yorkston, 1996). AAC intervention for individuals with cerebral palsy was also discussed, including 1) features of augmentative communication systems (particularly identifying those system features that are most beneficial), 2) training of individuals with severe physical disability to use the systems, and 3) training of partners of system users.

JUDGMENTS AND DECISION MAKING

"We do not know nearly as much about the effectiveness of treatment as we should" (Duffy, 1995, p. 386). The field of communication disorders or AAC is not alone in this matter. Somewhat surprisingly, most medical services are not supported by strong evidence or consensus regarding efficacy. The Institute of Medicine (IOM) guidelines committee found that for perhaps 4% of all health services, the scientific evidence is strong; for perhaps 45% of patient care, the evidence is at least modest; and for another 51%, the evidence is very weak or nonexistent. Table 1 contains a hypothetical distribution of evidence and consensus for all health services and patient management strategies (IOM, U.S. Committee on Clinical Practice Guidelines, 1992). Even though "we do not know enough," clinicians who work in the field of AAC must make the best of the knowledge that is currently on hand to make decisions about the type, timing, and intensity of interventions. In the following section, strategies for more clinical judgments are reviewed, including models for staging intervention, evidence-based practice, and practice guidelines.

Decisions Based on Staging of Intervention

Staging is a term common in medical practice that refers to the notion that interventions are different depending on the level or the severity of the disorder. In a sense, it can be described as doing the right things for the right people at the right time. The cancer treatment community has made extensive use of a staging system to develop intervention protocols that involve a variety of treatment modalities, such as surgery, radiation therapy, drugs, and so forth. Efforts are currently underway to develop systems to stage interventions for individuals with acquired communication disorders. See Chapters 7 and 8 for examples of staging systems for individuals with dysarthria associated with ALS,

Table 1.   Hypothetical distribution of the strength of evidence and consensus for all health services and patient management strategies

Strength of evidence	Strength of concensus	Percentage of all service
+ +	+ +	2
+ +	+	2
+ +	−	0
+	+ +	20
+	+	25
+	−	0
−	+ +	20
−	+	25
−	−	6

From Institute of Medicine, U.S. Committee on Clinical Practicef Guidelines. (1992). Guidelines for clinical practice: From development to use. In M.J. Field & K.N. Lohr (Eds.), *Guidelines for clinical practice: From development to use* (p. 426); reprinted by permission.
(Key: ++ = 90% or more; + = 75%–90%; − = weak or no).

Huntington disease, and Parkinson's disease. The AAC field also has a variety of interventions at its disposal; however, researchers are just beginning to develop models to guide intervention decision making at various stages of the condition.

In the following section, we discuss staging of intervention as it relates to individuals who have severe acquired communication disorders and may benefit from AAC services. We introduce a rationale for staging interventions and then discuss various staging criteria associated with a variety of diseases and conditions.

A Rationale for Staging Intervention   The rationale for staging interventions is to sequence management so that current problems are addressed and future problems are anticipated. Although this rationale seems obvious, it touches upon some of the clinical errors that are made in the AAC field. One such error is the failure to deal with current problems because the intervention team is too busy focusing on the future. For example, when older adults are unable to communicate because of aphasia, traditionally the intervention has focused on the restoration of natural speech and language while ignoring the current communication problem of the individual. When intervention is successful and functional natural speech is restored, the person with aphasia experiences a very frustrating interval between the time of the stroke and the recovery of speech. However, when functional speech cannot be restored, these individuals are often dismissed from active rehabilitation with no communication system in place to meet their current communication needs.

A similar pattern has been seen with TBI. Because many individuals who are unable to speak following TBI eventually become functional speakers, there has been a reluctance to provide them with communication alternatives. Therefore, it is not uncommon that individuals with TBI must 1) participate in active rehabilitation, 2) begin their initial adjustment to their long-term disability, and 3) relate to their world in new ways without the benefit of a communication system. Yet, the decision has been made to wait before AAC services are provided in order to be sure that they are not going to recover natural speech. A review of the literature reveals that individuals with TBI have been reported to use AAC systems for many years before developing natural speech (Aten, 1988; Beukelman & Garrett, 1988; Enderby & Crow, 1990; Harris & Murry, 1984; Keatley & Wirz, 1994; Light, Beesley, & Collier, 1988; Workinger & Netsell, 1992). It is not uncommon for individuals with TBI to recover their natural speech 3–5 years following injury.

A second error in AAC intervention is to focus primarily on current communication problems and to ignore future needs or problems.

Perhaps the most apparent of these errors is routinely made with individuals who experience ALS. It is not uncommon for these individuals to be referred for AAC services only after their natural speech is no longer understandable. This is a poor clinical decision for many reasons. ALS has a rapidly progressive course, and approximately 80% of individuals with ALS are expected to need augmentative communication systems at some point in their lives. Furthermore, providing services in a crisis, when the needs are urgent and the time and ability to learn the systems are limited, is far from ideal.

Staging of Communication Interventions in Degenerative Disease
The staging of interventions is based on three types of knowledge about 1) the body's response to the natural course of the disease or condition, 2) an individual's communication activities, and 3) the society in which she or he wishes to participate. First, the knowledge of the specific disease process provides the intervention team with information about the underlying pathophysiology, the problems that are typically associated with the disease or condition, and the natural course of the condition. For example, knowledge of the processes involved in ALS identifies the pathophysiology as the degeneration of upper and lower motor neuron cell bodies. This results in a depletion of motor neurons with the accompanying spasticity and weakness. The pattern of pathophysiology may vary from individual to individual. For example, some have primary degeneration of cell bodies in the brain stem. The problems associated with this pattern are the impairment of speech subsystems, swallowing subsystems, and breathing subsystems. Other individuals with ALS experience an initial degeneration in the spinal cord. The associated problems for these individuals will be the spasticity and eventual weakness of the limbs, and, therefore, these individuals experience initial problems with mobility, posture, and so on. The natural course of ALS is quite distinct. Individuals with primary brain stem symptoms have a life expectancy of approximately 2 years following diagnosis, but individuals with primarily spinal symptoms have a life expectancy of approximately 6 years following diagnosis. As is apparent in Chapter 7, which deals with ALS, co-management decisions are increasingly beginning to affect the life expectancy and, thus, the natural course of individuals with ALS. For example, current developments in alternative ventilation, alternative feeding, medications, and nutritional supplements appear to be extending the life expectancy of individuals with ALS and, thereby, changing its natural course. In addition to knowledge of the disease process, knowledge of activity requirements and participation goals of the individual are important.

Based on the knowledge of the disease process and the model of disablement, we have suggested staging strategies for individuals with acquired communication disorders who require AAC services (Beukelman & Mirenda, 1998; Yorkston et al., 1999). The first of these strategies involves individuals with a degenerative natural course. This five-stage model is outlined in the paragraphs that follow.

Stage 1: No Detectable Communication Disorder   For individuals with a degenerative disease, the first stage is no detectable communication disorder. In many individuals with progressive diseases and conditions, speech, language, reading, and writing may not be affected for a period of time after the disease or condition has been diagnosed. Generally, the intervention during this stage focuses on a confirmation that communication is not affected and on the provision of information about the possible impact of the disease on speech, language, and communication. In particular, these individuals and their family members should be provided with clinical decision-making information so that they are aware of the critical indicators that suggest a change in their treatment strategy. In addition, they should be provided with information about where services can be obtained at each critical stage. For example, Chapter 7, which reviews staging for individuals with ALS, will indicate the need to identify the point at which speaking rate has slowed to half of a typical speaking rate. At this point, AAC intervention can be initiated in a timely manner so that their future communication activity needs can be met, and they can continue to participate in appropriate social contexts.

Stage 2: Obvious Communication Disorder with Intelligible Speech, Writing, and Functional Reading   The second stage for individuals with degenerative communication conditions involves an obvious communication disorder that does not extensively interfere with their speech, language, reading, and writing. That is, their speech may be slow, distorted, or variable, but they are still able to be understood and meet most of their communication needs. Intervention in this stage focuses on managing communication effectiveness by compensating for impairment (e.g., by practicing appropriate energy conservation techniques), by assisting their communication partner using contextual information, by simplifying syntax and using standard communication forms, and by modifying the environment to remove adverse conditions such as noise.

Stage 3: Reduction in Intelligibility   In this stage, the communication disorder becomes so severe that speakers are no longer understood. During this stage, interventions continue to focus on optimizing performance and the use of compensations. In addition, intervention may include the teaching of techniques to resolve communication break-downs by providing partners with contextual information, by monitoring partners to determine when communication breakdowns have occurred, by speaking in short, standard grammatical units, and by learning to assist partners to understand effectively an individual's written and verbal communication.

Stage 4: Natural Communication Strategies Supplemented by Augmentative Techniques   During this stage, when speech, language, writing, and reading alone are no longer effective to meet an individual's communication activity needs, it becomes necessary to provide additional information through augmentative communication techniques. AAC systems might be used to provide information about the topic, the first letter of each word, or difficult or unusual words that are included in a discourse. Although the person with a communication disorder continues to speak using residual speech, during this stage the transition to AAC techniques is completed.

Stage 5: No Functional Speech   During this stage, the individual is unable to engage in functional communication that meets his or her communication needs. Therefore, he or she increasingly depends upon augmentative communication system strategies. Typically, these individuals use a variety of strategies, some of which do not require equipment, others that require low-tech picture boards and alphabet boards, and still others that require extensive electronic multi-dimensional communication systems.

Stable or Recovering from Communication Disorders   The staging of individuals with stable, recovering, or improving communication disorders is quite similar to those described previously for individuals with degenerative disorders, except the order is reversed. Typically, these individuals experience some type of episode, such as a stroke or TBI, that leaves them with no useful speech or with speech that needs to be supplemented by AAC techniques. These interventions are often coupled with interventions to restore natural speech. For example, for individuals with severe neuromotor speech disorders resulting from TBI, requiring an AAC system for many years is not uncommon. Simultaneous with that intervention is an effort to reestablish the subsystems for speech (Yorkston et al., 1999). During this time, efforts are made to assist the individual to regain voluntary control over the respiratory system, the phonatory system, and the articulatory system (e.g., prosthodontic intervention needed in the form of a palatal lift to improve velopharyngeal function). It is not uncommon for these interventions to take many months or years, during which individuals rely primarily on the AAC system for daily interaction. As natural speech begins to be reestablished, the interventions are modified in such a way that natural speech and augmentative communication techniques are combined. In this way, part of the information is provided through speech and the remainder is provided through the augmentative communication system. In time, these individuals are able to carry their communication load increasingly through natural speech. Their use of augmentative communication techniques is restricted to communicating with individuals who have a particularly difficult time understanding them or speaking in adverse situations, such as speaking before large groups. As they continue to recover, their speech may become intelligible, although their speech disorder may still be obvious. Some recover to a stage in which they have no detectable communication disorder. After reviewing the chapters in the book, the reader may realize that this is uncommon for individuals with brain stem stroke or TBI; however, it occurs frequently for individuals with Guillain-Barré syndrome (Yorkston et al., 1999).

Practice Guidelines

Clinical practice guidelines are explicit descriptions of how patients should be evaluated and treated. The explicit purpose of guidelines is to improve the quality of care and to ensure it by reducing variation in care provided (Johnston et al., 1998). Practice guidelines or parameters that reflect management strategies are believed to have a moderate clinical certainty; that is, the benefits of a particular strategy exceed its risks by a sufficiently wide margin that the service is worth performing (Lohr, 1995). Practice guidelines are different from care paths or critical pathways, which are simpler and more administratively oriented (Johnston et al., 1998). For example, a critical path might specify that a swallowing evaluation for a stroke patient occur no later than the second day of admission. A practice guideline should go further and specify the nature of the evaluation, how different interventions depend on patients' differing characteristics, and how patients' responses (clinical outcomes) are to be measured and evaluated.

Practice guidelines are developed by panels of experts on the basis of research evidence and consensus opinion. Ideal practice guidelines should be rigorous and scientific; should allow for decision making about health care that involves both clinicians and patients; should cover the full range of clinical conditions and problems; and should be practical, explicit, working documents, not just lengthy compilations of the literature (Lohr, 1994). Practice guidelines are being published in most fields of medicine (e.g., ALS; see Miller et al., 1999). Although these parameters address some important issues such as nutrition and management of respiratory problems, they do not deal with issues related to the maintenance of communication.

Rationale for Practice Guidelines   The need for practice guidelines can be justified in a number of ways. First, practice guidelines are a means of ensuring equality of service. Variation in the practice suggests that individuals in some areas are not receiving all needed services, yet others are receiving unnecessary services (Hays et al., 1994). This variability in service has been documented in stroke rehabilitation (Forbes, Duncan, & Zimmerman, 1997). Chart reviews suggest considerable variation on a number of criteria such as rehabilitation goals, treatment plans, secondary stroke prevention, and client/family education across nursing facilities, inpatient rehabilitation facilities, and home health settings. This variability of practice no doubt also occurs in augmentative communication practice.

The second reason for practice guidelines is improved quality of services. Generally, services are judged along two dimensions: the strength of direct evidence in support of the service or management strategy and the degree of expert consensus on the benefits of the intervention. The field of AAC must first develop and then document the effectiveness of the comprehensive intervention protocols for individual (or small groups of) system users. If the protocols appear to be effective for a limited number of individuals, there is justification to engage in and to receive funding for larger clinical trials.

The third reason for practice guidelines is financial. Despite the rather weak evidence for most medical interventions, health plans are beginning to use practice guidelines. Specialists in disciplines such as neurology feel that they "cannot postpone defining appropriate care for patients even if existing treatment data are incomplete or ambiguous" (Ringel & Hughes, 1996, p. 869). Although there are differences of opinion about whether cost-effectiveness should be a part of practice guidelines, there are strong arguments for *not* including them. For example, the IOM committee concluded that

> Guidelines need not be based on formal judgments of cost-effectiveness and can stand on rigorous assessments of clinical evidence and carefully derived expert judgment. In view of the enormous gap in our understanding of the true costs of care and thus the cost-effectiveness of most of what we do today, this is probably the only sensible, practical stance that can be taken at this time. (Lohr, 1994, p. 23)

A fourth reason for guidelines is to prevent unfounded practices. The following example is taken from the Post-Stroke Rehabilitation Practice Guidelines developed by the Agency for Health Care Policy and Research (AHCPR; Gresham et al., 1995). The guidelines said this about the issue of neuromuscular facilitation techniques: "Neither research evidence nor expert consensus adequately supports the superiority of one type of exercise regimen over another (p. 243). Furthermore, the guidelines offered this opinion: "There is no evidence supporting the superiority of neuromuscular facilitation over traditional physical therapy. Since the former is more labor intensive and more expensive, objective proof of greater effectiveness is needed to justify the greater costs" (p. 243).

The final argument in favor of developing practice guidelines is that they would stimulate needed research (Stason, 1997). Practice guidelines place the burden of proof on clinicians and researchers to demonstrate that an intervention results in more good than harm (Woolf, DiGuiseppi, Atkins, & Kamerow, 1996). In summary, although the knowledge base from which to develop practice guidelines is certainly imperfect, such guidelines have several important and worthy goals, including improving quality of care, reducing unfounded intervention, and spurring treatment efficacy and outcomes research.

Development of Practice Guidelines   The way guidelines are developed can strongly affect their potential for effective use. Development can be viewed as a process of translating evidence into recommendations. The procedures for developing guidelines typically follow a sequence similar to the following:

1. A panel of experts is convened. It represents personnel who are responsible for the care of the particular condition and consumers.

2. An intensive literature search is conducted, and pertinent articles are retrieved.

3. Research is analyzed for validity.

4. An open forum is convened to obtain public opinion concerning aspects of care to be included.

5. Recommendations are drafted, reviewed, and revised. (Trombly, 1995)

The development of practice guidelines is based on evidence of treatment effectiveness. "It is still far from clear, however, exactly what counts as evidence and, even murkier, what weight to assign to different types of evidence (Hadorn, Baker, Hodges, & Hicks, 1996, p. 749). This section describes three types of evidence: direct evident (Hadorn et al., 1996), indirect evidence (Owens & Nease, 1993), and expert opinion. Many practice guidelines in medical literature are based on the following classification of direct evidence.

Class I evidence: Prospective randomized controlled trials (PRCT)—the gold standard of clinical trials. However, some may be poorly designed, lack sufficient patient numbers, or suffer from other methodologic inadequacies.

Class II evidence: Clinical studies in which the data were collected prospectively and retrospective analyses that were based on clearly reliable data. Types of studies classified in this category include observational studies, cohort studies, prevalence studies, and case–control studies.

Class III evidence: Most studies based on retrospectively collected data. Evidence used in this class indicates clinical series, databases or registries, case reviews, care reports, and expert opinion.

In many areas, including AAC, direct evidence, such as is outlined in the previous classification system, is simply not available. When this is the case, an approach that allows appropriate structuring of the relationship between the intervention and the outcome will identify indirect evidence that must be synthesized to estimate the effect of an intervention on a health outcome. Decision models have been suggested in order to provide a mechanism for linking interventions to outcomes when direct evidence is not available (Owens & Nease, 1993).

Another approach for evaluating the quality of empirical evidence regarding intervention has developed from the work of the American Psychology Association's Task Force on Promotion and Dissemination of Psychological Procedure. Chambless and Hollon (1998) proposed a scheme for determining the efficacy of psychological treatment. They asked questions such as the following:

1. Has the treatment been shown to be beneficial in controlled research?
2. Is the treatment useful in an applied clinical setting
   - With which patients?
   - Under what circumstances?
3. Is the treatment cost-effective relative to other alternative interventions?

In their scheme, a variety of factors, including the rigor of the research design, are weighed. For example, they asked, Has the population being treated been well described? Have the appropriate outcome measures been employed? Is the treatment itself well described? Are treatment manuals available? Is the therapist's training described? Are the analysis procedures adequate? Has the treatment been replicated independently? The list of factors that should be weighed is a long one. Despite the magnitude of the evaluation task, the scheme proposed seems an appropriate one for evaluating the level of evidence that supports behavioral interventions such as those in the AAC field.

The final type of evidence is expert opinion. This type of evidence can also be classified according to its strength (Trombly, 1995). *Strong consensus* is defined as agreement among 90% or more of the panel member and expert reviewers, and *simple consensus* is defined as agreement among 75%–90% of panel members and expert reviewers.

The Academy of Neurologic Communication Disorders and Sciences is developing a series of practice guidelines including the areas of dysarthria and aphasia. Questions being addressed in the dysarthria practice guidelines include the following: What consequences of dysarthria are appropriate focal points of intervention? How is intervention for dysarthria different in pediatric versus adult populations? How should the principles of motor learning be incorporated in intervention programs? And what is the role and timing of AAC intervention in dysarthria management?

Evidence-Based Practice

Evidence-based practice is the conscientious, explicit, and judicious use of current best evidence in making decisions about the care of individual patients (Sackett, Richardons, Rosenberg, & Haynes, 1997). It is different from practice guidelines in that it assumes that the questions being asked and the evidence being evaluated pertain to the management of a particular patient and not a more general population. Sackett and colleagues believed that both clinical expertise and evidence must be brought to bear in making clinical decisions. They stated,

> Good doctors use both individual clinical expertise and the best available external evidence, and neither alone is enough. Without clinical expertise, practice risks becoming tyrannized by external evidence, for even excellent external evidence may be inapplicable to or inappropriate for an individual patient. Without current best external evidence, practice risks becoming rapidly out of date, to the detriment of patients. (Sackett et al., 1997, p. 2)

In many ways, the steps involved in evidence-based practice are similar to those involved in the development of practice guidelines. The difference is one of scale. With evidence-based practice, one would proceed through the following steps with each client:

1. Convert information needed into answerable questions.

2. Track down, with maximum efficiency, the best evidence with which to answer them (whether from the clinical examination, the diagnostic laboratory, from research evidence or other sources).

3. Critically appraise the evidence for its validity (i.e., closeness to the truth) and usefulness (i.e., clinical applicability).

4. Apply the results of this appraisal in clinical practice.

5. Evaluate performance.

The field of evidence-based practice is obviously dependent on
rapid and easy access to large databases of literature. Such access is
becoming increasingly available. The web has emerged as the common
interface for desktop access to a wide range of resources, including bib-
liographic databases and full-text electronic journals. Examples of
databases that are available through the web include Medline (containing 3,900 medical journals), PsycINFO (containing indexes and
abstracts articles from more than 1,300 journals), and Cumulative
Index to Nursing & Allied Health Literature (CINAHL), covering more
than 600 journals. The full texts of a growing number journals are available on-line as well. At this time, these include some that have been
used in the preparation of this volume such as *JAMA: Journal of the
American Medical Association, Journal of Speech, Language, and Hearing
Research, Brain and Language, Dysphagia, Journal of Neuroscience Nursing,*
and the *Archives of Neurology.* The full text of the journal *Augmentative
and Alternative Communication* is available on CD-ROM.

The future is already here; it just isn't evenly distributed yet.
—Sackett et al., 1997, p. 16

Although the field of evidence-based medicine certainly has its proponents who believe that it allows clinicians to become life-long learners
and to continually update their knowledge, words of caution are also
warranted because such practice exposes the gaps in clinical knowledge
(Rosenberg & Donald, 1995). When applied to the field of dentistry,

> The results can be both exhilarating and sobering. They can indicate the
> depth or limits of available information and suggest gaps in the knowl-
> edge-base that require further study. Most importantly, however, the
> results allow practitioners to communicate incisively and truthfully with
> patients and make more informed clinical decisions. (Niederman et al.,
> 1998, p. 229)

DeLisa summarized the debate over the merits of evidence-based medicine (EBM) in a lecture to the Academy of Physical Medicine and
Rehabilitation:

> Proponents claim that EBM offers support for practice decisions, improves
> quality of care, serves as a educational tool, reduces costs, reduces

inappropriate care, and creates a research platform. Critics of EBM claim that it was introduced by insurance companies and managed care organizations rather than physicians, that it promotes "cookbook" medicine, that it is slanted to the average patient, that it has serious ethical implications, including rationing of care. (1999, p. 7)

Despite its potential pitfalls, the concepts that provide the framework for evidence-based medicine would seem to be essential for the field of AAC. This is a field in which technology and information changes so rapidly that practitioners must have a mechanism for continually updating their knowledge. Evidence-based practice may be one route to such a learning style. Of course, the successful application of the techniques of evidence-based medicine is dependence on the quality of the evidence that it provided in the literature. Clearly, the field needs to frame its research questions and to describe its interventions and candidates for those interventions with the needs of practicing clinicians in mind.

CHANGING HEALTH CARE DELIVERY

Thus far in the chapter, we have reviewed some aspects of clinical decision making for adults with severe communication disorders. We have described that knowledge base from which we work and some strategies for applying that knowledge to make decisions. Clinical decisions are not made in isolation. Rather, practice is dependent upon the health care delivery environment in which clinicians work. In the concluding pages of this chapter, we place the notion of clinical decision making within the context of change in the health care environment.

This chapter could not have been written in the mid 1970s. This statement is not particularly surprising, given all of the technical innovations in the field of AAC that have occurred since then. Clinicians have access to an array of devices that are both more powerful and more flexible than could have been imagined in the mid-1970s. Also, much more is known about adults with severe communication disorders than was known in the 1970s. In the following series of chapters, readers are introduced to various clinical populations including people with stroke, TBI, and degenerative neurologic diseases. These chapters suggest that the knowledge base (i.e., understanding of the trajectory of the disease, the problems associated with the disease, and the communication needs of these groups) is rapidly expanding.

Notwithstanding this growth, there are other reasons why practice in the area of AAC is fundamentally different from the way it was in the 1970s. In the following section, we attempt to place AAC practice within a broad context of health care delivery and to suggest that our practice has been changed fundamentally by trends and pressures from outside the field of AAC.

You cannot direct the wind but you can adjust the sails.
—Rabkin, 1998, p. 131

In a 1998 editorial, Dr. Mitchell Rabkin, then–immediate past chair of the American Academy of Academic Medicine, suggested that, although the core mission of academic medicine (i.e., patient care, teaching, research) has not changed, the core business of academic medicine may be undergoing a paradigm shift. Rabkin commented on more than 20 changes that are under way in academic medicine. We have selected four of them for discussion of how these changes may pertain to the field of AAC.

Subjective, individualized clinical judgment has changed to evidence-based decision making. In the past, many medical decisions were based on highly personal judgments based on the clinician's own experience. Today, physicians have much more systematic information, patients are followed for a longer period; outcomes are more systematically evaluated; and sophisticated, controlled studies of treatment efficacy are frequently available. The following is a personal example from the field of AAC. In 1985 we were co-authors of a textbook entitled *Communication Augmentation: A Casebook of Clinical Management* (Beukelman, Yorkston, & Dowden, 1985). That book described our clinical experience via a series of case studies in a hospital-based clinic that was established in the late 1970s. In the preface we stated,

> The need for printed material to support the continuing education efforts of professionals and the training of students is an important need in the communication augmentation field. However, we found that the task of writing a general textbook was extremely difficult.... The knowledge base of the field is derived largely from clinical experience. (1985, p. xi)

Thus, cases were presented and formed the bases upon which issues were discussed. Later, as the field developed, a number of general textbooks became available to integrate various aspects in assessment and intervention for individuals with severe communication disorders (Beukelman & Mirenda, 1992, 1998; Glennen & DeCoste, 1997; Lloyd, Fuller, & Arvidson, 1997). Today, we are involved in drafting evidence-based practice guidelines that address questions (e.g., What is the role of augmentative communication for individuals with severe and profound communication disorders?) The point to be made here is that the field has moved from being dependent on a small number of case reports to the development practice parameters based on research evidence that has accumulated since the 1970s.

Involvement of consumers in the development of practice guidelines. When medical decisions are based primarily on personal judgments based on the clinician's own experience, consumers and members of their social networks are often involved in individual intervention decisions. However, in the era of practice guidelines, the roles of consumers will expand. They will increasingly be invited to bring their unique expertise to the development of practice guidelines and standards.

The *volume-equals-revenue* equation is changing to a *volume-equals-expense* equation. In a fee-for-service health care environment, providing more services translated into more revenue. Thus, new services such as augmentative communication programs were often viewed positively by hospital administrators. Because of the move from fee-for-service health care in the United States to an increasing number of managed care arrangements, increasing the volume of services no longer translates into more revenue. Just the opposite: More services may be viewed as a drain on the system, depleting the overall resources. For the field of augmentative communication, this may translate into the need to find a different and more cost-effective service delivery model, perhaps involving different levels of staff, including speech pathology aids (Pietranton, 1998).

Quality **defined as *most* in technical terms has changed to *quality* defined as *value*, encompassing not only technical quality objectively defined but also the patient's subjective response, cost efficacy, and appropriateness.** For the field of AAC, this means developing better ways to measure the outcomes of intervention. These measures need to reflect the broadest spectrum possible: not only measures that reflect the users' ability to operate the devices but also measures that would reflect users' increased ability to participate in communication roles and the changes in perceived quality of life that increased participation may bring about.

Focus on episodic care of individuals with acute illnesses has changed to clinical and fiscal responsibility for the health of a population. For the field of AAC, we need to move from a service delivery model that includes the components of assessment, intervention, and discharge to one that provides long-term follow-up and a prompt, brief, and responsive period of intervention. Perhaps this would involve a move from freestanding assistive technology centers to services that are integrated into the primary health care service delivery system.

THE FUTURE

As medical decision making becomes increasingly evidence-based, the field of AAC will need to work steadily to develop an empirical knowledge base. The chapters in Part Two of this volume document the current state of the empirical knowledge base for individuals with severe, acquired communication disorders. A review of these chapters reveals that the extent of the knowledge base varies widely across these disability groups. In the past, AAC interventions have been numerous; however, outcome research reports have been limited. Perhaps this situation exists for a couple of reasons. The financial pressures on health care providers are such that they do not have the time to complete and publish outcome research. Meanwhile, many AAC researchers have not participated in this type of research, because they are located in university environments and are not actively involved in the delivery of services to adults with acquired communication disorders. In the future, AAC stakeholders—consumers, clinical service providers, and researchers—will need to collaborate to develop this knowledge base, which is necessary to justify and to fund AAC services for adults with acquired communication disorders.

REFERENCES

Alpert, C. (1980). Procedures for determining the optimal nonspeech mode with the autistic child. In R.L. Schiefelbusch (Ed.), *Nonspeech language and communication: Analysis and intervention* (pp. 394–420). Baltimore: University Park Press.

American Speech-Language-Hearing Association (ASHA). (1995). *ASHA Task Force on Treatment Outcomes and Cost Effectiveness: Project overview and status.* Rockville, MD: Author.

Aten, J.L. (1988). Spastic dysarthria: Revising understanding of the disorder and speech treatment procedures. *Journal of Head Trauma Rehabilitation, 3,* 63–73.

Beukelman, D.R., & Garrett, K. (1988). Augmentative communication for adults with acquired severe communication disorders. *Augmentative and Alternative Communication, 4,* 104–121.

Beukelman, D.R., Mathy, P., & Yorkston, K.M. (1998). Outcomes measurements of motor speech disorders. In C. Frattali (Ed.), *Measuring outcomes in speech-language pathology* (pp. 334–353). New York: Thieme Medical Publishers.

Beukelman, D.R., & Mirenda, P. (1992). *Augmentative and alternative communication: Management of severe communication disorders in children and adults.* Baltimore: Paul H. Brookes Publishing Co.

Beukelman, D.R., & Mirenda, P. (1998). *Augmentative and alternative communication: Management of severe communication disorders in children and adults* (2nd ed.). Baltimore: Paul H. Brookes Publishing Co.

Beukelman, D.R., Yorkston, K.M., & Dowden, P.A. (1985). *Communication augmentation: A casebook of clinical management.* Austin, TX: PRO-ED.

Chambless, D.L., & Hollon, S.D. (1998). Defining empirically supported therapies. *Journal of Consulting and Clinical Psychology, 66*(1), 7–18.

Coelho, C.A., DeRuyter, F., & Stein, M. (1996). Treatment efficacy: Cognitive-communication disorders resulting from traumatic brain injury. *Journal of Speech & Hearing Research, 39*(5), S5–S17.

Cook, A., Coleman, C., Praszler, A., & Dahlquist, D. (1983). A hierarchy of augmentative communication system characteristics useful for matching devices to clients needs and skills. In *Proceedings from the Sixth Annual Conference on Rehabilitation Engineering* (pp. 185–186). Bethesda, MD: Rehabilitation Engineering Society of North America.

DeJong, G. (1999). Toward an evidence-based rehabilitation culture: The role of values, outcomes, disclosure, and stakeholder groups. *Rehabilitation Outlook, 4,* 9–11.

DeLisa, J.A. (1999). Issues and challenges for psychiatry in the coming decade. *Archives of Physical Medicine and Rehabilitation, 80,* 1–12.

Duffy, J.R. (1995). *Motor speech disorders: Substrates, differential diagnosis, and management.* St. Louis: Mosby.

Elstein, A. (1999, April 27). Lecture presented at University of Washington, Seattle.

Enderby, P., & Crow, E. (1990). Long-term recovery patterns of severe dysarthria following head injury. *British Journal of Disorders of Communication, 25*(3), 341–354.

Forbes, S.A., Duncan, P.W., & Zimmerman, M.K. (1997). Review criteria for stroke rehabilitation outcomes. *Archives of Physical Medicine and Rehabilitation, 78*(10), 1112–1116.

Frattali, C.M. (Ed.), (1998a). *Measuring outcomes in speech-language pathology.* New York: Thieme Medical Publishers.

Frattali, C.M. (1998b). Outcomes measurement: Definitions, dimensions, and perspectives. In C. Frattali (Ed.), *Measuring outcomes in speech-language pathology* (pp. 1–27). New York: Thieme Medical Publishers.

Frattali, C.M., Thompson, C.K., Holland, A.L., Wohl, C.B., & Ferketic, M.M. (1995). *The American Speech-Language-Hearing Association Functional Assessment of Communication Skills for Adults (ASHA FACS).* Rockville, MD: ASHA.

Fuhrer, M.J. (ED.), (1997). *Assessing medical rehabilitation practices: The promise of outcomes research.* Baltimore: Paul H. Brookes Publishing Co.

Glennen, S.L., & DeCoste, D. (1997). *The handbook of augmentative and alternative communication.* San Diego: Singular Publishing Group.

Granger, C.V., Cotter, A.C., Hamilton, B.B., Fiedler, R.C., & Hens, M.M. (1990). Functional assessment scales: A study of persons with multiple sclerosis. *Archives of Physical Medicine & Rehabilitation, 71,* 870–875.

Gresham, G.E., Duncan, P.W., Statson, W.B., Adams, H.P., Adelman, A.M., Alexander, D.N., Bishop, D.S., Diller, L., Donaldson, N.E., Granger, C.V., Holland, A.L., Kelly-Hayes, M., McDowell, F.H., Myers, L., Phipps, M.A., Roth, E.J., Siebens, H.C., Tarvin, G.A., & Trombly, C.A. (1995). *Post-stroke rehabilitation. Clinical practice guidelines: Number 16* (AHCRP Publication No 95–0662). Rockville, MD: U.S. Department of Health and Human Services, Public Health Service, Agency for Health Care Policy and Research.

Hadorn, D.C., Baker, D., Hodges, J.S., & Hicks, N. (1996). Rating the quality of evidence for clinical practice guidelines. *Journal of Clinical Epidemiology, 49*(7), 749–754.

Hamilton, B.B., Granger, C.V., Sherwin, F.S., Zielezny, M., & Tashman, J.S. (1987). A uniform national data system for medical rehabilitation. In M.J. Fuhrer (Ed.), *Rehabilitation outcomes: Analysis and measurement* (pp. 137–147). Baltimore: Paul H. Brookes Publishing Co.

Harris, B., & Murry, T. (1984). Dysarthria and aphagia: A case study of neuromuscular treatment. *Archives of Physical Medicine & Rehabilitation, 65,* 408–412.

Hays, R.M., Berni, R., Guthrie, M., Dudgeon, B., Yorkston, K., & Kimura-Van Zandt, K. (1994). The team approach to rehabilitation. In G.H. Kraft & R.M. Hays (Eds.), *Chronic disease and disability: A contemporary rehabilitation approach to medical practice* (pp. 55–64). New York: Demos Medical Publishers.

Holland, A.L., Fromm, D.S., DeRuyter, F., & Stein, M. (1996). Treatment efficacy: Aphasia. *Journal of Speech and Hearing Research, 39*(5), S27–S36.

Iezzoni, L.I. (1996). 100 apples divided by 15 red herrings: A cautionary tale from the mid-19th century on comparing hospital mortality rates. *Annals of Internal Medicine, 124*(12), 1079–1085.

Iezzoni, L.I. (1997). The risks of risk adjustment. *JAMA: Journal of the American Medical Association, 278*(19), 1600–1607.

Institute of Medicine (IOM), U.S. Committee on Clinical Practice Guidelines. (1992). Guidelines for clinical practice: From development to use. In M.J. Field & K.N. Lohr (Eds.), *Guidelines for clinical practice: From development to use* (p. 426). Washington, DC: National Academy Press.

Johnston, M.V., Maney, M., & Wilkerson, D.L. (1998). Systematically assuring and improving the quality and outcomes of medical rehabilitation programs. In J.A. DeLisa (Ed.), *Rehabilitation medicine: Principles and practice* (pp. 287–320). Philadelphia: Lippincott, Williams & Wilkins.

Keatley, A., & Wirz, S. (1994). Is 20 years too long?: Improving intelligibility in longstanding dysarthria—a single case treatment study. *European Journal of Disorders of Communication, 29*(2), 183–201.

Keith, R.A., Granger, C.V., Hamilton, B.B., & Sherwin, F.S. (1987). The Functional Independence Measure: A new tool for rehabilitation. In M.G. Eisenberg & R.C. Grzesiak (Eds.), *Advances in clinical rehabilitation* (Vol. I, pp. 6–18). New York: Springer.

Kirby, R.L. (1998). Impairment, disability and handicap. In J.A. DeLisa (Ed.), *Rehabilitation medicine: Principles and practice* (pp. 55–60). Philadelphia: Lippincott, Williams & Wilkins.

Kosasih, J.B., Borca, H.H., Wenninger, J.W., & Duthie, E. (1998). Nursing home rehabilitation after acute rehabilitation: Predictors and outcomes. *Archives of Physical Medicine and Rehabilitation, 79*(6), 670–673.

Light, J., Beesley, M., & Collier, B. (1988). Transition through multiple augmentative and alternative communication systems: A three-year case study of a head injury adolescent. *Augmentative & Alternative Communication, 4,* 2–14.

Lloyd, L., Fuller, D., & Arvidson, H. (1997). *Augmentative and alternative communication: A handbook of principles and practices.* Needham Heights, MA: Allyn & Bacon.

Lohr, K.N. (1994). Guidelines for clinical practice: Applications for primary care. *International Journal for Quality in Health Care, 6*(1), 17–25.

Lohr, K.N. (1995). Guidelines for clinical practice: What they are and why they count. *Journal of Law, Medicine and Ethics, 23*(1), 49–56.

Miller, R.G., Rosenberg, J.A., Gelinas, D.F., Mitsumoto, H., Newman, D., Dufit, R., Borasio, G.D., Bradley, W.G., Bromberg, M.B., Brooks, B.R., Kasarskis, E.J.,

Munsat, T.L., Oppenheimer, E.A., & the ALS Practice Parameters Task Force. (1999). Practice parameter: The care of the patient with amyotrophic lateral sclerosis (an evidence-based review): Report of the Quality Standards Subcommittee of the American Academy of Neurology. *Neurology, 52,* 1311–1323.

Niederman, R., Ferguson, M., Urdaneta, R., Badovinac, R., Christie, D., Tantraphol, M., & Rasool, F. (1998). Evidence-based esthetic dentistry. *Journal of Esthetic Dentistry, 10*(5), 229–234.

O'Donnell, J.C., & Hamilton, B.B. (1997). Stroke rehabilitation management in the Department of Veterans Affairs: Impact of patient referral source on outcomes. *Archives of Physical Medicine and Rehabilitation, 78*(9), 929–937.

Olswang, L.B. (1998). Treatment efficacy research. In C.M. Frattali (Ed.), *Measuring outcomes in speech-language pathology* (pp. 134–150). New York: Thieme Medical Publishers.

Owens, D.K., & Nease, R.F. (1993). Development of outcome-based practice guidelines: A method for structuring problems and synthesizing evidence. *Joint Commission Journal on Quality Improvement, 19*(7), 248–263.

Pietranton, A. (1998). Clinical service delivery reform. In A.F. Johnson & B.H. Jacobson (Eds.), *Medical speech-language pathology: A practitioner's guide* (pp. 669–684). New York: Thieme Medical Publishers.

Rabkin, M.T. (1998). A paradigm shift in academic medicine? *Academic Medicine, 73*(2), 127–131.

Ringel, S.P., & Hughes, R.L. (1996). Evidence-based medicine, critical pathways, practice guidelines, and managed care. Reflections on the prevention and care of stroke. *Archives of Neurology, 53*(9), 867–871.

Rosenberg, W., & Donald, A. (1995). Evidence based medicine: An approach to clinical problem-solving. *British Medical Journal, 310*(6987), 1122–1126.

Sackett, D.L., Richardson, W.S., Rosenberg, W., & Haynes, R.B. (1997). *Evidence-based medicine.* New York: Churchill Livingstone.

Semlyen, J.K., Summers, S.J., & Barnes, M.P. (1998). Traumatic brain injury: Efficacy of multidisciplinary rehabilitation. *Archives of Physical Medicine and Rehabilitation, 79*(6), 678–683.

Shane, H.C. (1980). Early decision making in augmentative communication use. In R.L. Schiefelbusch & D. Brinker (Eds.), *Early language: Acquisition and intervention.* Baltimore: University Park Press.

Shane, H.C., & Bashir, A.S. (1980). Election criteria for the adoption of an augmentative communication system: Preliminary considerations. *Journal of Speech and Hearing Disorders, 45,* 408–414.

Stason, W.B. (1997). Can clinical practice guidelines increase the cost-effectiveness of geriatric rehabilitation? *Medical Care, 35*(Suppl. 6), JS68–JS77; JS78–JS83.

Trombly, C. (1995). Clinical practice guidelines for post-stroke rehabilitation and occupational therapy practice. *American Journal of Occupational Therapy, 49*(7), 711–714.

Turner-Stokes, L., & Turner-Stokes, T. (1997). The use of standardized outcome measures in rehabilitation centres in the UK. *Clinical Rehabilitation, 11*(4), 306–313.

Woolf, S.H., DiGuiseppi, C.G., Atkins, D., & Kamerow, D.B. (1996). Developing evidence-based clinical practice guidelines: Lessons learned by the US Preventive Services Task Force. *Annual Review of Public Health, 17,* 511–538.

Workinger, M.S., & Netsell, R. (1992). Restoration of intelligible speech 13 years post-head injury. *Brain Injury, 6*(2), 183–187.

World Health Organization (WHO). (1999, June 24). *International classification of impairment, activity, and participation: Beta-1 draft for field trials, Beginner's guide* [On-line]. Available: http://www.who.int/msa/mnh/ems/icidh/

Yorkston, K.M. (1996). Treatment efficacy: Dysarthria. *Journal of Speech & Hearing Research, 39*(5), S46–S57.

Yorkston, K.M., Beukelman, D.R., Strand, E.A., & Bell, K.R. (1999). *Management of motor speech disorders in children and adults.* Austin, TX: PRO-ED.

Yorkston, K.M., Strand, E.A., & Hume, J. (1998). The relationship between motor function and speech function in amyotrophic lateral sclerosis. In M. Cannito, K.M. Yorkston, & D.R. Beukelman (Eds.), *Neuromotor speech disorders: Nature, assessment, and management* (pp. 85–98). Baltimore: Paul H. Brookes Publishing Co.

4

Integrating AAC Strategies with Natural Speech in Adults

Katherine C. Hustad
David R. Beukelman

Communication is a multimodal process for most speakers. Communicators typically incorporate speech, gestures, facial expression, and body language into almost all communication interchanges. The simultaneous use of multiple modes of communication adds redundancy to the communicative interaction, thus increasing the listener's chance of understanding the message in the way it was intended by the speaker. Similarly, multimodal communication adds supplemental information that may enhance or clarify the intent of the message.

Multimodal communication is perhaps even more important for adults who have reduced speech intelligibility secondary to neurogenic communication disorders than it is for speakers without disabilities. For these individuals, at least one and typically more than one communication modality is compromised because of motor control problems. Augmentative and alternative communication (AAC) strategies and systems can become important components of a multimodal communication system to enhance the effectiveness of natural speech. For adults with acquired communication disorders, natural speech and multimodal communication strategies that include AAC should not be mutually exclusive choices.

For those who have the ability to use natural speech, it is unquestionably the most time-efficient and linguistically flexible mode of communication. Many individuals who have moderate to severe speech intelligibility challenges still choose to use speech as their primary mode of communication. However, when speech is too unintelligible for listeners to understand fully, the use of speech supplementation strategies can greatly enhance listeners' contextual knowledge regarding the content of the message (Beliveau, Hodge, & Hagler, 1995; Beukelman & Yorkston, 1977; Carter, Yorkston, Strand, & Hammen, 1996; Crow & Enderby, 1989; Dongilli, 1994; Garcia & Cannito, 1996a). Examples of AAC strategies that can be used to enhance natural speech include alphabet supplementation and topic supplementation. It is important to emphasize that these strategies are used in conjunction with natural speech and are not intended to replace natural speech.

ALPHABET SUPPLEMENTATION DEFINED

Alphabet supplementation strategies combine the use of natural speech with an alphabet board. To use alphabet supplementation, the speaker points to the first letter of each word in the message as he or she speaks it (e.g., pointing to the letter *r* as the target word "rainbow" is spoken). The rationale for this strategy is that the first letter of each word provides orthographic-phonetic context supporting the individual's speech production, thereby improving the listener's ability to understand (Yorkston, Beukelman, Strand, & Bell, 1999). Alphabet supplementation strategies can be employed using a low-technology alphabet board (see Yorkston et al., 1999, pp. 509–510) or a high-technology AAC system with a display that faces the interactant, such as the LightWriter.

TOPIC SUPPLEMENTATION DEFINED

Topic supplementation strategies combine the use of natural speech with communication boards containing topic words or pictures. Typically, when a speaker uses topic supplementation strategies, he or she will indicate the topic of the message on a communication board prior to producing the message using natural speech (Yorkston et al., 1999). The rationale for use of this strategy is that the topic words or pictures provide contextual information that serves as a frame of reference for the listener, preparing him or her for the forthcoming message or messages related to the topic. Consequently, listeners should understand natural speech with a higher degree of accuracy. Like alphabet supplementation, both low- and high-technology tools can be used to provide topics to listeners.

LISTENER PROCESSING OF DYSARTHRIC SPEECH

When a speaker has reduced intelligibility, the listener must process an acoustic speech signal that may be distorted in a variety of ways. This makes the task of parsing phonetic information into lexical and sentential units different and more difficult than the same task given a typical acoustic speech signal. When intelligibility is diminished, variables in addition to the listener's acoustic phonetic knowledge and decoding ability contribute to processing of speech (Kent, 1993; Kent, Weismer, Kent, & Rosenbek, 1989). The role of skills that the listener brings to the task of decoding and understanding dysarthric speech has received little attention. Examples of listener variables include linguistic knowledge, world knowledge, and disability knowledge (Hustad, Beukelman, & Yorkston, 1998).

Mutuality Model of Communication:
Intrinsic Sources of Information

In his mutuality model of communication, Lindblom (1990) dichotomized mutual understanding between speaker and listener into two components: the speech signal itself and information that is independent of the speech signal. Lindblom's model is illustrated in Figure 1.

On the vertical plane, the acoustic signal is represented as a continuum ranging from poor to rich. This dimension refers to the listener's ability to decode the speech signal in isolation, as measured by traditional intelligibility measures. The horizontal plane represents signal-independent information. Lindblom described signal-independent information as "what is in the listener's brain" (1990, p. 225), or all of the skills and characteristics that the listener brings to the communication task.

Mutuality or successful communication is conceptualized as a complementary relationship between information provided by the speech signal (i.e., signal-dependent) and information or knowledge possessed by the listener that is used to decode the speech signal (signal-independent). Lindblom emphasized that:

> Our perception of speech and other communicative events is not determined by the signal alone. It is shaped by an interaction between the signal on the one hand and information stored in our brains on the other. In fact, in communication the signal is only the tip of the iceberg. Communication is built around shared knowledge. (1990, p. 228)

Generally, Lindblom's (1990) mutuality model posited that, as the speaker's acoustic signal becomes more distorted, the listener's reliance on signal-independent or top-down intrinsic linguistic knowledge

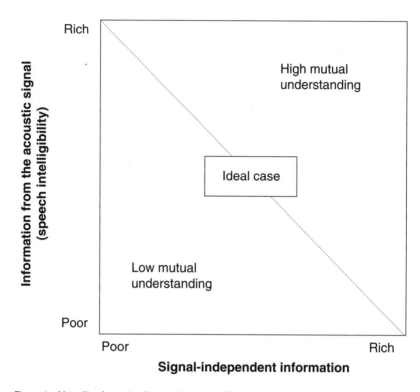

Figure 1.   Mutuality of speaker–listener interaction. (From Lindblom, B. [1990]. On the communication process: Speaker–listener interaction and the development of speech. *Augmentative and
Alternative Communication, 6,* 220; adapted by permission.)

becomes increasingly important. Conversely, as the speaker's acoustic
signal approaches normal, the listener's reliance on acoustic phonetic
information alone becomes increasingly sufficient to ensure mutual
understanding between speaker and listener.

Similarly, Vogel and Miller (1991) discussed a top-down approach
to dysarthria intervention. They referred to knowledge of the language
that listeners possess as top-down deductive knowledge. This includes
an understanding of and expectations for syntax, semantics, and pragmatics. Top-down deductive knowledge allows listeners to take available information, which may be incomplete, and construct or infer a
whole.

In addition to top-down deductive knowledge, listeners possess
bottom-up inductive acoustic-phonetic processing capabilities. These
capabilities enable listeners to parse acoustic information into phonetic
units and reconstruct the message by decoding and putting together all
of the information within the acoustic signal.

Extending the Model of Mutuality to Multiple Linguistic Levels
Communication occurs at a variety of linguistic levels including words, sentences, and connected discourse. Research on speech intelligibility has shown differential effects of stimulus length. For example, words tend to be less intelligible than sentences (Crow & Enderby, 1989; Miller, Heise, & Lichten, 1951; O'Neill, 1957; Sitler, Schiavetti, & Metz, 1983). One reason for this phenomenon may be that listeners are able to apply top-down knowledge more readily to a sentence transcription task than to a word transcription task. In sentence transcription, listeners have expectations for semantic relations and syntactic structure that may enable them to decode what they hear in an interactive or parallel fashion, employing both top-down and bottom-up knowledge simultaneously. In contrast, when listeners transcribe words in isolation, they are forced to rely more heavily on acoustic phonetic information present in the stimulus word to decode because there is reduced linguistic context and therefore reduced opportunity to apply linguistic knowledge.

Little is known about discourse intelligibility compared with word and sentence intelligibility. Narrative discourse differs from isolated sentences in that meaning is cumulative, building from sentence to sentence in a cohesive, sequential fashion. As such, listeners may be able to apply top-down linguistic knowledge even more readily with discourse than with sentences. Therefore, it might be expected that discourse would be more intelligible than both sentences and words. This hypothesis is supported by preliminary studies that have examined intelligibility differences according to stimulus length.

For a speaker with severe dysarthria, Hustad (1999b) found that listeners were able to transcribe a 10-sentence narrative discourse sample with a mean intelligibility of 27%. The same listeners transcribed unrelated sentences with mean intelligibility of 6%. Finally, word intelligibility was 3%. It is interesting to note that the difference between discourse and sentential contexts was much larger than that observed for isolated word intelligibility and sentential context in this study. Figure 2 illustrates these data.

Using DECTalk synthesized speech (available from Digital Equipment Corporation), Drager (1999) compared the intelligibility of target sentences preceded by story context with sentences presented in isolation. She found that listeners were able to repeat sentences with significantly greater accuracy when story context preceded target sentences. These results support the hypothesis that listeners are more readily able to apply top-down linguistic knowledge in discourse contexts compared with sentence contexts.

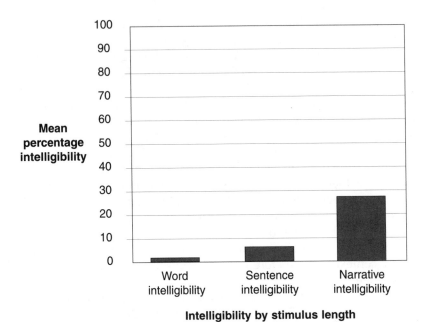

Intelligibility by stimulus length

Figure 2.   Effects of stimulus length on intelligibility of a speaker with severe dysarthria. (From Hustad, K.C., & Beukelman, D.R. [1998]. *Integrating residual natural speech and AAC.* Paper presented at the American Speech-Language-hearing Association (ASHA) Annual Convention, San Antonio, TX; reprinted by permission.)

Speech Supplementation Strategies: Extrinsic Sources of Information

Several studies have investigated the effects of different types of extrinsic information, such as alphabetic and topic cues, on speech intelligibility. This research has focused primarily on word- and sentence-level stimulus materials. Generally, findings have been consistent across studies, suggesting that when speech is less intelligible, listeners benefit more from extrinsic linguistic cues. There are several kinds of extrinsic linguistic cues: alphabetic cues, topic/semantic cues, combined alphabetic and topic cues, and visual and gestural cues.

Alphabetic Cues   Alphabetic cues have differential effects on intelligibility according to linguistic level. This section reviews literature examining words, sentences, and discourse.

Word Intelligibility   Research has demonstrated that alphabetic cues have similar effects on the word intelligibility of different adult speakers with dysarthria. Beliveau, Hodge, and Hagler (1995) obtained recordings of isolated words from speakers with moderate, severe, and profound dysarthria. Extrinsic linguistic cues were imposed on the speech samples via a videotape. Results showed that a speaker with moderately severe speech impairment showed a 14% improvement in word-level intelligibility when alphabetic cues were provided to listeners. (Mean intelligibility was 12% with no cues and 26% with alphabetic cues.) One speaker with a profound impairment showed an 11% improvement when listeners were given alphabetic cues. (Mean intelligibility was 6% with no cues and 17% with alphabetic cues.) Finally, Beliveau and colleagues found that the speaker with a severe impairment showed a 5% increase in intelligibility when listeners were presented with alphabetic cues. (Mean intelligibility was 1% with no cues and 6% when alphabetic cues were provided.)

Crow and Enderby (1989) employed a different methodology to examine the difference between alphabetic cues and no cues for word intelligibility. In their study, listeners were not provided with extrinsic information regarding the first letter of each word. Rather, recordings of speakers were obtained while each speaker used an alphabet board to point to the first letter of each word employed in the study, thus modifying the acoustic signal to increase intelligibility. Results showed that an alphabet board used concurrently with speech production modified the acoustic signal itself, resulting in increased speech intelligibility. Overall, their results showed that the use of an alphabet board increased word intelligibility by an average of 11% (with a range of 5%–25%) across speakers with dysarthria who had mild to severe impairments. Results showed that the speaker with a moderate impairment benefited most. (Intelligibility without the use of an alphabet board during production was 44%; intelligibility with an alphabet board during production was 69%.) One in three speakers with a profound impairments benefited least. (Intelligibility without the use of an alphabet board during production was 11%; intelligibility with alphabet board during production was 16%.) Overall, these results demonstrate that the use of an alphabet board enhances speech intelligibility through both provision of additional information to the listener as well as modification of the acoustic signal itself.

Sentence Intelligibility   Generally, research has demonstrated that provision of alphabetic cues for each word of a sentence produced by speakers with dysarthria enhances the listener's ability to transcribe disordered speech correctly. The magnitude of the improvement, however, has varied markedly among studies, ranging from 5% to 52% compared with intelligibility when listeners are given no cues. There are a number of variables that may affect the magnitude of improvement observed. These include the severity of the speaker's dysarthria, rate of speech, interword pauses, and whether listeners are able to see the alphabet cues.

Early research by Beukelman and Yorkston (1977) demonstrated that the use of alphabet supplementation resulted in a 33% increase in sentence intelligibility for one speaker (intelligibility without alphabet supplementation was 33%; intelligibility with alphabet supplementation was 66%) and 52% for another speaker (intelligibility without alphabet supplementation was 16%; intelligibility with alphabet supplementation was 68%). Beukelman and Yorkston observed that when adults with dysarthria employed alphabet supplementation, their rate of speech was reduced. This may have provided listeners with additional processing time. In addition, Beukelman and Yorkston observed that speakers often inserted extended interword pauses when using alphabet supplementation. This may have served to help listeners identify word boundaries more clearly. In this study, increases in intelligibility could be attributed both to changes in the speech signal itself as well as to provision of extrinsic alphabetic information to listeners in this study. To confirm this finding, Beukelman and Yorkston examined sentence intelligibility of the same two speakers when sentences were produced using alphabet supplementation, and listeners were not provided with alphabetic cues during transcription. Results demonstrated that intelligibility gains for one speaker were based almost exclusively on the provision of extrinsic alphabet cues to listeners. (Habitual speech intelligibility was 16%; speech intelligibility using alphabet supplementation when listeners did not receive extrinsic alphabet cues was 19%.) However, for another speaker who had less severe communication challenges, results demonstrated that intelligibility gains were due to provision of both extrinsic alphabet cues to listeners and changes in the acoustic speech signal associated with the simultaneous activities of speaking and pointing to the first letter of each word as it was spoken. (Habitual speech intelligibility was 33%; speech intelligibility using alphabet supplementation when listeners did not receive extrinsic alphabet cues was 52%.)

Crow and Enderby (1989) demonstrated a similar effect with speakers who had dysarthria of varying severity. Their results demonstrated that sentences produced while simultaneously pointing to an alphabet board showed an average increase in intelligibility of 15% (within a range of 5%–25%), compared with speech produced in a habitual fashion. Gains shown in Crow and Enderby's study do not reflect the effects of extrinsic information provided to the listener in the form of alphabetic cues. That is, listeners did not receive any alphabetic information in this study; rather, they only *heard* speech produced while alphabet supplementation was being employed by the speaker.

Hustad and Beukelman (1998) examined the effects of extrinsic alphabetic cues on sentence intelligibility for a speaker with severe dysarthria. For this experiment, sentences were produced using habitual speech, and extrinsic alphabetic cues were superimposed on the signal during presentation to listeners. Results showed a 10% improvement for this speaker when extrinsic alphabet cues were provided (9% intelligibility without cues and 19% intelligibility when alphabet cues were provided).

Overall, it is clear that extrinsic cues provided to listeners and signal-dependent acoustic adjustments made in the speech of individuals using alphabet supplementation both contribute to increased speech intelligibility when alphabet supplementation strategies are employed. However, the independent contribution of each is unclear.

Discourse Intelligibility   The effects of alphabetic cues on discourse intelligibility have received only preliminary attention. Hustad (1999) conducted a pilot study involving a speaker with severe dysarthria in which the speaker produced stimulus material using habitual speech and alphabet cues were imposed on the speech signal after the speech sample was collected. Results showed that extrinsic alphabetic cues provided to listeners increased speech intelligibility by approximately 40% compared with discourse intelligibility scores for the same stimulus material when no alphabetic cues were provided. This finding was statistically significant. See Figure 3 for a graphic illustration of these data. Research to further explore this finding is underway.

Taken together, results of alphabet supplementation studies suggest that listeners benefit from provision of additional phonetic information provided by alphabetic cues at word, sentence, and discourse levels. Comparison across studies discussed previously suggests that listeners may benefit to a somewhat greater extent when the acoustic signal is modified to increase word segmentation and to decrease rate of production concurrently with presentation of alphabetic cues (Beukelman & Yorkston, 1977). However, listeners benefit from a modified speech signal in which word segmentation is increased and rate is decreased even without the provision of alphabetic cues (Beukelman & Yorkston, 1977; Crow & Enderby, 1989). Conversely, listeners benefit from provision of extrinsic alphabetic cues when the speech signal is not modified (Hustad, 1999; Hustad & Beukelman, 1998). Clearly, provision of alphabetic cues has the potential to increase intelligibility markedly; however, additional research is necessary to determine more conclusively the relative contribution of the speech signal itself and signal-independent information.

Topic/Semantic Cues   Like alphabetic cues, topic cues have differential effects on intelligibility according to linguistic level. The section reviews literature examining words, sentences, and discourse.

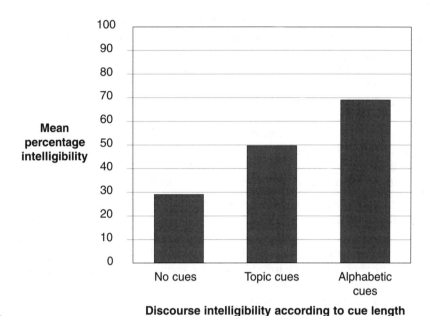

Discourse intelligibility according to cue length

Figure 3.   Effects of cues on speech intelligibility of discourse for a speaker with severe dysarthria. (From Hustad, K.C. [1999]. *Effects of context on intelligibility and comprehensibility of severely dysarthric speech* [p. 42]. Unpublished doctoral dissertation, University of Nebraska–Lincoln.)

Word Intelligibility   Research examining the effects of topic cues on speech intelligibility of single words has clearly demonstrated that when listeners are provided with topic cues, intelligibility improves. Hammen, Yorkston, and Dowden (1991) studied the effects of topic cues on word-level intelligibility of adult speakers with moderate, severe, and profound dysarthria. Results showed that all speakers had increased intelligibility scores when topic context was provided to listeners. However, differential effects based on severity of speech impairment were noted. Hammen and colleagues found that topic cues benefited speakers with severe dysarthria the most. (Average intelligibility was approximately 25% when listeners did not have topic cues and 65% when listeners were provided with topic cues.) Speakers with moderate dysarthria benefited less from the provision of topic cues to their listeners. (Average intelligibility was approximately 65% when listeners did not have topic cues and 94% when listeners were provided with topic cues.) Speakers with profound dysarthria experienced the least benefit from provision of topic cues. (Average intelligibility was approximately 4% when listeners did not have topic cues and 23% when listeners were provided with topic cues.)

Dongilli (1994) examined speakers who had flaccid dysarthria of varying severity. Provision of topic cues for words resulted in increased speech intelligibility ranging in magnitude from 29% to 40% across all speakers. Results were consistent with those found by Hammen and colleagues (1991). Topic cues increased word-level intelligibility the most for speakers with severe dysarthria, followed by speakers with moderate dysarthria, and speakers with profound dysarthria experienced the least benefit from provision of topic cues.

Research by Beliveau and colleagues (1995) also revealed gains in word intelligibility when topic cues were provided to listeners for a speaker with severe dysarthria. However, their gains were of reduced magnitude compared with other research (average improvements were between 5% and 18% across all speakers). Beliveau and colleagues found that intelligibility was increased more for one speaker with severe dysarthria than for two other speakers with profound dysarthria.

Sentence Intelligibility   The effects of topic cues on sentence intelligibility have received considerable attention with different populations of speakers and with different types of topic cues. Monsen (1983) examined the effects of topic setting on the sentence intelligibility of speakers with hearing impairments representing a range of severity levels. Topic cues provided for sentences were very broad in nature and consisted of the physical setting where the sentence may have been uttered (e.g., "outside"). Monsen's results showed that, overall, intelligibility of sentences increased by an average of 14% when they were prefaced with topic cues. This was significantly better than intelligibility of sentences presented without topic cues.

Dongilli (1994) examined the effects of topic cues on sentence intelligibility of adult speakers with dysarthria. Results showed that topic cues increased intelligibility for moderate, severe, and profound groups. However, the magnitude of improvement was considerably less than that noted for single-word intelligibility. Speakers with moderate challenges benefited the most from topic cues (75% intelligibility without topic cues; 92% intelligibility with topic cues). Speakers with severe challenges showed a 7% benefit (70% intelligibility without topic cues; 77% intelligibility with topic cues), and speakers with profound dysarthria showed a 4% benefit (0% intelligibility without topic cues, 4% intelligibility with topic cues).

Carter and colleagues (1996) examined sentence intelligibility among six speakers with dysarthria. Half of the speakers had moderate dysarthria, and half had severe dysarthria. Results showed that topic cues did not significantly improve the intelligibility of speakers who had moderate dysarthria. However, topic cues significantly improved the intelligibility of speakers who had severe dysarthria by an average of 9%. Similarly, Hustad and Beukelman (1998) found that sentence intelligibility was improved by 10% for a speaker with profound dysarthria when topic cues were provided to listeners.

Garcia and Cannito (1996b) found that the sentence intelligibility of a speaker with severe dysarthria was improved only marginally when listeners were given one of two general locational cues for each utterance (e.g., "in the house," "in the yard"). They found a statistically significant improvement (5%) when contextual cues were provided compared with no cues. Two important factors may contribute to the reduced magnitude of improvement demonstrated by Garcia and Cannito (1996b) compared with other similar sentence-level intelligibility studies. First, this study examined only one speaker with severe dysarthria, thus making results somewhat less generalizable than studies examining groups of speakers. Second, the topic cues provided to listeners consisted of broad situational information that would appear to be more ambiguous in nature, thus providing listeners with less contextual information.

Several factors may affect the magnitude of improvement observed when topic cues are provided to listeners for sentence-level material. These include severity of the speech impairment and specificity of the topic cues. Clearly, additional experimental and clinical research is necessary to better understand the effects of topic cues.

Discourse Intelligibility   The effects of topic cues on discourse intelligibility were examined in a pilot study by Hustad (1999a). In the same study discussed previously involving a speaker with severe dysarthria, Hustad found that the use of topic supplementation increased listeners' transcription accuracy by approximately 20% compared with discourse intelligibility scores when no alphabetic cues were provided. This finding was statistically significant. It is interesting to note that alphabet supplementation had a significantly greater effect on the speech intelligibility of this speaker than topic supplementation. These data are illustrated in Figure 3. Research to further explore this finding is underway.

Overall, research has demonstrated that the use of topic cues increases speech intelligibility at the word, sentence, and discourse level. Possible causes of discrepancies in findings may be attributed to severity of speech impairment and nature of the topic cues provided. In general, results seem to suggest that speakers with severe (Carter et al., 1996) or moderate (Dongilli, 1994) intelligibility problems benefit most from topic cues, and speakers with profound dysarthria benefit least (Dongilli, 1994).

Alphabetic and Topic Cues   Little research has examined the effects of simultaneous presentation of topic and alphabetic cues on speech intelligibility. However, it might be expected that differential effects are present by linguistic level.

Word Intelligibility   Only one study to date has examined the effects of simultaneous presentation of topic and alphabetic cues at the word level. Beliveau and colleagues (1995) found that the speech intelligibility of adult speakers with severe and profound dysarthria improved by an average of 18% when both topic and alphabetic cues were provided to listeners. Their results showed a differential benefit based on severity. The speaker with severe dysarthria benefited more than two speakers with profound dysarthria; however, the benefit shown for each speaker was statistically significant.

Sentence Intelligibility   Few studies have examined the effects of simultaneous presentation of alphabetic and topic cues on sentence intelligibility. Hunter, Pring, and Martin (1991) attempted to study the effects of alphabetic cues on the sentence intelligibility of individuals with moderate and severe dysarthria. However, the authors provided listeners with a single context-setting word prior to presentation of each sentence in order to more closely approximate the context available in real communicative interchanges. Consequently, their results for alphabetic cues actually reflect intelligibility when both topic and alphabetic cues are provided. Overall, results showed that listeners were able to transcribe sentences in the presence of alphabetic and topic cues significantly better than when given topic cues alone. Specifically, for speakers with moderate dysarthria, the provision of topic and alphabetic cues increased intelligibility by 13% compared with intelligibility when only topic cues were provided. Speakers with severe dysarthria showed an advantage of 18% for topic and alphabetic cues.

Discourse Intelligibility   No reported research has examined the effects of simultaneous cue presentation on speech intelligibility at the discourse level. Conclusions regarding the effectiveness of simultaneous presentation of alphabetic and topic cues are difficult to draw because of the paucity of research available. However, the two studies reviewed here seem to suggest that provision of two types of cues enhances speech intelligibility more than one type of cue alone. Additional research is needed to verify this conclusion.

Visual and Gestural Cues   In both clinical and experimental speech intelligibility research, assessment paradigms have tended to employ the auditory signal in isolation. For questions addressing bottom-up processing of the acoustic signal, this seems appropriate. However, when top-down contributions to intelligibility are of interest, provision of visual information may be important.

The effects of visual information on the decoding of typical speech are particularly striking in a phenomenon known as the *McGurk effect*

(MacDonald & McGurk, 1978; McGurk & MacDonald, 1976). Goldinger, Pisoni, and Luce (1996) described the McGurk effect as a perceptual illusion whereby an individual is presented with incongruous visual and auditory information from a speaker. The integration of auditory and visual information results in the perception of neither the visual nor the auditory production but rather something in between.

Published studies examining the effects of visual information, gestural information, or both on word-level and discourse-level intelligibility are not available at the present time. Systematic investigation of the effects of visual-gestural cues on speech intelligibility at the sentence level have demonstrated that visual-gestural information enhances the intelligibility of speakers with dysarthria to varying extents (Garcia & Cannito, 1996a, 1996b; Garcia & Dagenais, 1998). For example, Garcia and Cannito (1996a) found that the speech intelligibility of one speaker with severe dysarthria was enhanced by an average of 25% when listeners were presented with both auditory and visual information, including illustrative gestures produced concurrently with speech. In a subsequent study, Garcia and Cannito (1998a) demonstrated individual differences among speakers for effects of gestures on speech intelligibility. Improvements in intelligibility when visual-gestural information was provided concurrently with speech ranged from 14% to 45%, with a mean increase of 27%. For the speaker with the most severe intelligibility challenges, listeners showed the greatest benefit (45% increase) from multimodal presentation. Conversely, for the speaker with the least severe intelligibility challenges, listeners benefited the least from multimodal presentation including gestures (14% increase).

The effects of visual information derived from the face of the speaker without use of illustrative body gestures are less clear. Intelligibility findings for the same speakers when listeners were presented with multimodal information in the form of simultaneous video and audio signals compared with the audio signal only yielded diverse results. Generally, intelligibility is higher when audio and video signals are presented simultaneously. However, the effects of severity of the speech impairment are inconclusive. One can manipulate the summary data presented by Garcia and Dagenais (1998) to examine the difference between speech intelligibility scores obtained through audio-only transcription and scores obtained through transcription of a simultaneous audio-video signal where speakers were not producing gestures in either condition. Data suggest that listeners benefited from multimodal presentation by an average of 12% with a range of 9%–18% across four speakers who have impairments of varying severity. Garcia and Cannito (1996b) showed that the difference between simultaneous presentation of audio and video signals for a speaker with severe dysarthria and audio-only presentation for the same speaker were not significantly different. Although the observed difference was in favor of the multimodal signal presentation, it was only 2%.

Hunter and colleagues (1991) showed that for speakers with moderate dysarthria, multimodal presentation of speech stimuli resulted in a significant increase (17%) in intelligibility scores, compared with auditory presentation only. However, for speakers with severe dysarthria, the difference between audio presentation and multimodal (i.e., simultaneous audio and video) presentation was not significant (1% difference in favor of audio-only presentation).

Monsen (1983) examined the intelligibility of speakers with a diverse range of severity of hearing impairments. His results showed that when listeners were able to see speakers, sentence transcription scores increased by an average of 14%, compared with presentation of the audio signal alone. Although Monsen examined a range of speakers, summary data for individuals were not available, so differential effects of visual context on speech intelligibility by severity could not be determined.

Overall, results seem to indicate that gestures presented visually enhance speech intelligibility, and this effect was particularly salient for speakers with severe intelligibility challenges (25%–45% improvement). When gestural information was not provided but listeners were presented with multimodal information (i.e., they viewed the speaker producing speech), on average listeners benefit by approximately 15%. However, benefits according to severity of the dysarthria are contradictory and inconclusive. Individual differences among speakers would seem to play an important role in the presence or absence of this effect.

COMBINING INTRINSIC AND EXTRINSIC INFORMATION: AN INTEGRATED MODEL FOR AUGMENTED COMMUNICATION

Integration of AAC speech-supplementation strategies presented in the previous section along with Lindblom's (1990) model of mutuality led Hustad (1999) to develop a new model for considering the joint effects of intrinsic and extrinsic information. This model is illustrated in Figure 4. To iterate, intrinsic information includes bottom-up acoustic phonetic processing capability and top-down linguistic knowledge. Extrinsic information includes the acoustic signal provided by a speaker and any supplemental or contextual compensatory cues provided by the speaker to assist listeners.

Hustad's (1999) model can be characterized in a two-by-two matrix. Each of the four cells within this model represents different types of information that may contribute to the communication process. On the vertical axis, two types of information are represented. The first is extrinsic information available to the listener, such as the speech signal itself (also called *signal-dependent acoustic information*). The second type is explicit cues, or information that is independent of the speech signal, such as visual information conveyed by facial expressions and explicit compensatory cues (e.g., topic cues suggesting a context for the message, alphabetic cues suggesting word-initial phonemic information).

On the horizontal axis, two types of information are represented. The first is information intrinsic to the listener, such as bottom-up or phonetic decoding skills, that allow the listener to parse acoustic information into phonetic units. The second is top-down knowledge of the language, including its meaning (i.e., semantics), rules and expectations for how words are combined (i.e., syntax), and the rules for its use in social contexts (i.e., pragmatics).

Meaningful communication requires that at least two cells of this matrix be active. For example, the first cell represents availability of

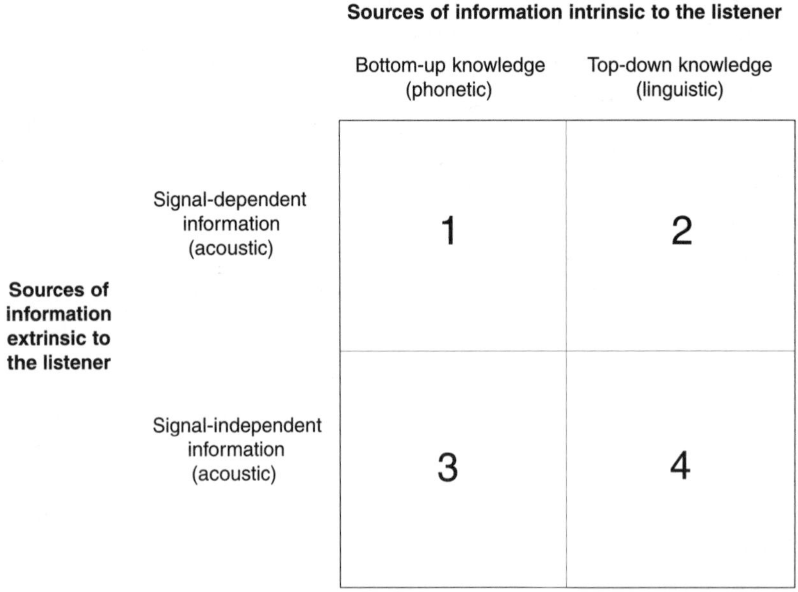

Sources of information intrinsic to the listener

	Bottom-up knowledge (phonetic)	Top-down knowledge (linguistic)
Signal-dependent information (acoustic)	1	2
Signal-independent information (acoustic)	3	4

Sources of information extrinsic to the listener

Figure 4.   A hybrid model of supplemented communication. (From Hustad, K.C. [1999]. *Effects of context on intelligibility and comprehensibility of severely dysarthric speech* [p. 13]. Unpublished doctoral dissertation, University of Nebraska–Lincoln.)

only the speech signal itself and the listener's bottom-up phonetic knowledge/decoding skills. This situation is unlikely to occur in communicative situations but may occur in the case of decoding nonsense syllables or in syntactically or semantically irregular utterances. The second cell represents availability of only the speech signal from the speaker and top-down linguistic knowledge from the listener. This situation is not likely to occur in a real interaction because listeners are never entirely without their inherent phonetic decoding ability. The third cell represents the availability of only signal-independent information from the speaker with no acoustic phonetic information and only bottom-up phonetic processing from the listener. The fourth cell represents the availability of only signal-independent information from the speaker and only top-down linguistic knowledge from the listener. Clearly, individual cells within this model do not adequately represent typical verbal communication.

When mutually understood, meaningful units that follow standard conventions of the shared language between speaker and listener are employed, listeners rely on both phonetic decoding skills and language knowledge in order to obtain meaning from the speech signal. According to this model, during spoken communication interchanges among adult speakers of the same language, the first cell must always be active. That is, there is always an acoustic speech signal provided by the speaker, and the listener always has access to his or her inherent phonetic decoding or bottom-up knowledge of speech. The listener's ability to employ his or her bottom-up knowledge successfully will vary according to the quality of the speech signal.

Furthermore, in meaningful communicative situations among adult speakers of the same language, the second cell of this model is always be active to some extent. That is, there is always an acoustic speech signal provided by the speaker, and the listener always has access to his or her knowledge of the language to assist in obtaining meaning from the speech signal. However, the extent to which the listener is able to apply his or her top-down linguistic knowledge may vary with the length of the speech material. For example, in narrative discourse, listeners have greater opportunity to apply linguistic knowledge; therefore, greater intelligibility and comprehensibility would be expected compared with sentence-length and word-length material.

The relationship between top-down linguistic knowledge and bottom-up phonetic knowledge in decoding and comprehending spoken language is a topic of considerable debate in the speech perception literature. Separating the contribution of the two sources of knowledge is inferential in nature because spoken language processing is a private event that cannot be directly observed within the mind of the listener.

The third cell of this model represents the contribution of signal-independent information in the form of explicit cues that support the intended message. The cues provided in this condition are developed to enhance the listener's bottom-up phonetic knowledge of the speech signal. When cells 1, 2, and 3 are active, signal-independent cues provide phonetic information in combination with the speech signal. This type of communication strategy is known as *alphabet supplementation*, whereby the listener is given the first letter of each word of the speaker's message (Beukelman & Yorkston, 1977). In this signal-independent cue condition, bottom-up phonetic processing is considered primary and top-down linguistic knowledge secondary.

The fourth cell of this model also represents the contribution of signal-independent information in the form of explicit cues that support the intended message. The cues provided in this condition are developed to enhance the listener's top-down linguistic knowledge of the intended message. When cells 1, 2, and 4 are active, signal-independent cues provide linguistic information in combination with the speech signal. This type of communication strategy is known as *topic supplementation*, whereby the listener is given a topical word or phrase that provides context for the entire message (Dongilli, 1994). In this signal-independent cue condition, top-down linguistic knowledge is considered primary and bottom-up phonetic knowledge secondary.

Finally, when all four cells of this model are considered together, signal-independent cues are provided along with the speech signal to enhance both top-down and bottom-up processing of the message. The relative contribution of each source of information in this condition is assumed to be equal. Research testing the hypotheses posited by this model is underway.

There is clearly a growing body of evidence derived from case studies as well as experimental investigations that support the conclusion that speech supplementation procedures are associated with improvements in speech intelligibility. Additional investigations are needed to further the knowledge base regarding the clinical usefulness of these strategies to bridge research results with clinical practice.

PATTERNS OF SPEECH SUPPLEMENTATION USE

The patterns of the use and acceptance of speech-supplementation procedures by individuals with chronic communication disorders has received very little research attention. Clinical reports indicate that individuals with dysarthria due to a variety of different etiologies have used speech-supplementation strategies. These include Parkinson's disease (Crow & Enderby, 1989; Schumacker & Rosenbek, 1986), brainstem stroke (Beukelman & Yorkston, 1977), traumatic brain injury (TBI) (Beukelman & Yorkston, 1977), motor neuron disease (Crow & Enderby, 1989; Yorkston et al., 1999), and cerebral palsy (Hustad & Beukelman, 1998). However, there is little published information about speakers who are *able* to use these strategies but choose *not* to do so. In the following sections, factors that need to be investigated to enhance understanding of acceptance and rejection of supplemented speech strategies are discussed.

Perceptions of Communication Effectiveness

For speakers who have typical speech ability for many years, the effects of a gradual- or sudden-onset severe speech disorder on communication effectiveness can be difficult to assess. Some individuals appear to overestimate the impact of their speech disorder on communication effectiveness, some underestimate the impact, and others estimate quite accurately.

Sullivan, Brune, and Beukelman (1996) studied the outcomes of group speech intervention for speakers with dysarthria due to Parkinson's disease. Although it was not the primary focus of this investigation, the variability in self-perceptions of communication difficulty reported by these individuals was remarkable. For example, one of the participants demonstrated relatively high intelligibility scores (97.7%) but estimated that more than 80% of all communication situations were difficult for him. His wife's perceptions were quite different in that she estimated that far fewer situations were difficult for him. Following eight group intervention sessions, his speech intelligibility had not changed; however, he had reduced his speaking rate somewhat. At that point, he estimated approximately 60% of all communication situations as difficult, but his wife continued to estimate the impact of his speech disorder to be less severe than he did.

An example from clinical practice provides another illustration of very different self-perceptions of communicative competence. An individual, who also had Parkinson's disease, was largely unaware of his limited communication effectiveness. He spoke at an excessively rapid rate (240 words per minute as compared with an average rate for adult speakers of 190 words per minute). His habitual speech was largely unintelligible. He learned alphabet supplementation and reduced his speaking rate to approximately 40 words per minute. At this rate, his speech was intelligible in all conversational situations. When he spoke over the telephone with his grandchildren, who lived in another state, they would demand that he use alphabet supplementation to control his speaking rate and improve his intelligibility. On several occasions, he commented that he wondered how they knew that he was not using his alphabet board when he talked over the telephone, because they obviously could not see him. He revealed little awareness of his limited communication effectiveness; therefore, he resisted using alphabet supplementation. His communication partners had to require him to use it.

In a study by Ball and Beukelman (1999), speakers with severe dysarthria due to amyotrophic lateral sclerosis (ALS) and their spouses were asked to rate the speakers' communication effectiveness using a rating scale provided by Yorkston and colleagues (1999). The results revealed that speakers and their spouses rated their communication effectiveness very similarly. Additional information about the acceptance and rejection of AAC technology by individuals with ALS can be found in Chapter 7.

Hustad and Beukelman (1998) reported a case illustration demonstrating diverse perceptions of situational communication effectiveness. In this example, a variety of adult communication partners were asked to estimate the speech intelligibility of a 6-year-old child with severe speech intelligibility challenges. Results showed that the parents and close family members estimated that the child was 85% intelligible at home. School personnel estimated the child's intelligibility at school to be between 20% and 30%. Objective measures of intelligibility, obtained from the same listeners who provided the previous estimates, revealed intelligibility scores ranging between 15% and 35% for this child. When the intelligibility of speakers is rated to be very different across situations and partners, it is not uncommon that conflicts about the need for AAC or supplemented speech strategies occur. There has been little similar research for adults with acquired communication disorders.

Differing perceptions of communication effectiveness across situations may also contribute to attitudes toward AAC use by individuals with speech disorders. Hustad and Beukelman (1998) described a 26-year-old man with cerebral palsy. Results of the Sentence Intelligibility Test (Yorkston, Beukelman, & Tice, 1996) revealed that this man's intelligibility was 21%. However, through the years, he had resisted using an AAC system in any situation. When asked to rate his communication effectiveness, his mean rating was 5.2 on a 7-point scale, indicating that he felt quite effective across communicative situations. The mean rating by his mother was 5.0. However, the mean rating by young adults who did not know him well but had encountered him in casual interaction was 2.2. The reasons that this young man was unwilling to use an AAC system may be suggested by these discrepant ratings. Because his parents evaluated his communication effectiveness so highly and because they were such important people in his life, perhaps he accepted their evaluation rather than that of peers and strangers. He apparently was so convinced of his communication effectiveness that he rejected AAC in any social situation, even though it seemed quite obvious that peers and strangers had difficulty understanding him. Because he had rejected the use of an AAC system, he did not have the strategies available to shift from his speaking mode to supplemented speech or an augmented communication mode in times of communication difficulty or breakdown.

Metacognitive Ability of the Speaker to Switch Modes

Given that communication effectiveness varies across social situations and listeners, it is important that individuals who use natural speech, speech-supplementation, and AAC strategies learn to switch communication modes depending on the situation and the listener. In the previous example, the young man did not have an AAC system available to switch to when the need arose.

The metacognitive ability to assess communication success or failure in a communication interaction is necessary for successful use of a multimodal communication system. In some individuals, metacognitive skills can be improved with coaching and practice. Hustad and Beukelman (1998) provided an illustration of the successful use of metacognitive skills for mode switching according to the communicative situation and partners. When interacting with familiar listeners, this speaker used natural speech as her primary mode of communication. If, after two repetitions of a message, listeners were unable to understand her, she used alphabet supplementation to support her natural speech. When alphabet supplementation failed, she used a voice output communication device as an alternative to her natural speech. When interacting with unfamiliar listeners, this woman's primary mode of communication was through her voice output communication device. Interestingly, this woman's average rate of successful communication was approximately 3.5 words per minute when using her voice output communication device to generate unique messages. However, when she used her natural speech with alphabet supplementation, her average rate of successful communication was between 12 and 15 words per minute, depending on the context.

The information reported in this section consists of primarily clinical reports and case illustrations. Future research is needed to identify the metacognitive skills required to determine whether to use residual speech, supplemented speech, or AAC methods. Development of protocols as well as efficacy research regarding how to teach these skills is necessary. Obviously, an enormous amount of investigation is needed in this area.

Functional Change in Performance

Chapter 3 discusses strategies to develop empirically supported interventions for individuals with disabilities. In that chapter, the chronic disabilities model and the disablement model are reviewed, both of which view chronic disabilities at social and functional levels as well as anatomic and physiologic levels. For interventionists who serve people with chronic disabilities, a central question is whether a change in performance in response to an intervention results in a functional change in the important social situations of the individual's lives. At this point, the motor speech disorders field has limited tools with which to address this question. To date, researchers and clinicians have relied extensively on speech intelligibility measures. A few measures of communication effectiveness, communication effort, and communication difficulty have been proposed; however, these measures are still in their infancy. Future research needs to address multiple issues related to the impact of intervention on communication effectiveness in social situations.

CLOSING COMMENTS

For adults with severe, acquired communication disorders, the integration of speech and AAC is an important intervention issue. As is clear from the staging discussion in Chapter 7, speakers with either degenerative or recovering conditions often make use of AAC, supplemented speech, natural speech, or a combination of these only at some stage in the course of their illness or condition. There is preliminary evidence to suggest the beneficial impact of supplemented speech strategies. However, the level of empirical support for these interventions is still very low. Chapters 3, 8, and 10 review several models (mutuality, chronic disability, and disablement) that have guided and will guide the inquiries of intervention researchers. At the beginning of the 21st century, both the speech disorders and AAC fields view AAC and natural speech as aspects of a multimodal communication system rather than as dichotomous intervention choices. It appears that the climate is conducive for extensive inquiry into the relations among natural speech, supplemented speech, and AAC for adults with acquired communication disorders.

REFERENCES

Ball, L., & Beukelman, D. (1999, November). *Communication effectiveness of individuals with ALS.* Poster session presented at the American Speech-Language-Hearing Association [ASHA] annual convention, San Francisco.

Beliveau, C., Hodge, M., & Hagler, P. (1995). Effect of supplemental linguistic cues on the intelligibility of severely dysarthric speakers. *Augmentative and Alternative Communication, 11*, 176–186.

Beukelman, D., & Yorkston, K. (1977). A communication system for the severely dysarthric speaker with an intact language system. *Journal of Speech and Hearing Disorders, 42*, 265–270.

Carter, C., Yorkston, K., Strand, E., & Hammen, V. (1996). Effects of semantic and syntactic context on actual and estimated sentence intelligibility of dysarthric speakers. In D.A. Robin, K. Yorkston, & D.R. Beukelman (Eds.), *Disorders of motor speech: Assessment, treatment, and clinical characterization* (pp. 67–87). Baltimore: Paul H. Brookes Publishing Co.

Crow, E., & Enderby, P. (1989). The effects of an alphabet chart on the speaking rate and intelligibility of speakers with dysarthria. In K. Yorkston & D. Beukelman (Eds.), *Recent advances in clinical dysarthria* (pp. 99–108). Austin, TX: PRO-ED.

Dongilli, P. (1994). Semantic context and speech intelligibility. In J. Till, K. Yorkston, & D. Beukelman (Eds.), *Motor speech disorders: Advances in assessment and treatment* (pp. 175–191). Baltimore: Paul H. Brookes Publishing Co.

Drager, K.D.R. (1999). *Intelligibility and comprehensibility of synthetic speech: Effects of age, linguistic context, and attention.* Unpublished doctoral dissertation, University of Minnesota, Minneapolis.

Garcia, J., & Cannito, M. (1996a). Influence of verbal and nonverbal contexts on the sentence intelligibility of a speaker with dysarthria. *Journal of Speech and Hearing Research, 39*, 750–760.

Garcia, J., & Cannito, M. (1996b). Top-down influences on the intelligibility of a dysarthric speaker: Addition of natural gestures and situational context. In D. Robin, K. Yorkston, & D. Beukelman (Eds.), *Disorders of motor speech: Assessment, treatment, and clinical characterization* (pp. 89–103). Baltimore: Paul H. Brookes Publishing Co.

Garcia, J.M., & Dagenais, P.A. (1998). Dysarthric sentence intelligibility: Contribution of iconic gestures and message predictiveness. *Journal of Speech, Language, and Hearing Research, 41*, 1282–1293.

Goldinger, S., Pisoni, D., & Luce, P. (1996). Speech perception and spoken word recognition: Research and theory. In N.J. Lass (Ed.), *Principles of experimental phonetics* (pp. 277–327). St. Louis: Mosby–Year Book.

Hammen, V., Yorkston, K., & Dowden, P. (1991). Index of contextual intelligibility: Impact of semantic context in dysarthria. In C. Moore, K. Yorkston, & D. Beukelman (Eds.), *Dysarthria and apraxia of speech: Perspectives on management* (pp. 43–53). Baltimore: Paul H. Brookes Publishing Co.

Hunter, L., Pring, T., & Martin, S. (1991). The use of strategies to increase speech intelligibility in cerebral palsy: An experimental evaluation. *British Journal of Disorders of Communication, 26*, 163–174.

Hustad, K.C. (1999). *Effects of context on intelligibility and comprehensibility of severely dysarthric speech.* Unpublished doctoral dissertation, University of Nebraska–Lincoln.

Hustad, K.C., & Beukelman, D.R. (1998, November). *Integrating residual natural speech and AAC.* Paper presented at the American Speech-Language-Hearing [ASHA] annual convention, San Antonio, TX.

Hustad, K.C., Beukelman, D.R., & Yorkston, K.M. (1998). Functional outcome assessment in dysarthria. *Seminars in Speech and Language, 19*(3), 291–302.

Hustad, K.C., & Morehouse, T.B. (1998, November). *An integrated approach to improving communication effectiveness in unintelligible children.* Paper presented at the ASHA annual convention, San Antonio, TX.

Kent, R. (1993). Speech intelligibility and communicative competence in children. In A.P. Kaiser & D.B. Gray (Eds.) & S.F. Warren & J. Reichle (Series Ed.), *Communication and language intervention series: Vol. 2 Enhancing children's communication: Research foundations for intervention* (pp. 223–239). Baltimore: Paul H. Brookes Publishing Co.

Kent, R., Weismer, G., Kent, J., & Rosenbek, J. (1989). Toward phonetic intelligibility testing in dysarthria. *Journal of Speech and Hearing Disorders, 54,* 482–499.

Lindblom, B. (1990). On the communication process: Speaker-listener interaction and the development of speech. *Augmentative and Alternative Communication, 6,* 220–230.

MacDonald, J., & McGurk, H. (1978). Visual influences on speech perception. *Perception & Psychophysics, 24,* 253–257.

McGurk, H., & MacDonald, J. (1976). Hearing lips and seeing voices. *Nature, 264,* 746–748.

Miller, G.A., Heise, G.A., & Lichten, W. (1951). The intelligibility of speech as a function of the context of the test materials. *Journal of Experimental Psychology, 41,* 329–335.

Monsen, R.B. (1983). The oral speech intelligibility of hearing-impaired talkers. *Journal of Speech and Hearing Disorders, 43,* 286–296.

O'Neill, J. (1957). Recognition of intelligibility test materials in context and isolation. *Journal of Speech and Hearing Disorders, 22,* 87–90.

Schumacker, J., & Rosenbek, J. (1986). Behavioral treatment of hypokinetic dysarthria: Further investigation of aided speech. *Asha, 28,* 145.

Sitler, R.W., Schiavetti, N., & Metz, D.E. (1983). Contextual effects in the measurement of hearing-impaired speakers' intelligibility. *Journal of Communication Disorders, 11,* 22–30.

Sullivan, M., Brune, P., & Beukelman, D. (1996). Maintenance of speech changes following group treatment for hypokinetic dysarthria of Parkinson's disease. In D. Robin, K. Yorkston, & D. Beukelman (Eds.). *Disorders of motor speech: Assessment, treatment and clinical characterization* (pp. 287–310). Baltimore: Paul H. Brookes Publishing Co.

Vogel, D., & Miller, L. (1991). A top-down approach to treatment of dysarthric speech. In D. Vogel & M.P. Cannito (Eds.), *Treating disordered speech motor control: For clinicians by clinicians* (pp. 87–109). Austin, TX: PRO-ED.

Yorkston, K.M., & Beukelman, D.R. (1981). *Assessment of intelligibility of dysarthric speech.* Austin, TX: PRO-ED.

Yorkston, K.M., Beukelman, D.R., Strand, E.A., & Bell, K.R. (1999). *Management of motor speech disorders in children and adults* (2nd ed.). Austin, TX: PRO-ED.

Yorkston, K.M., Beukelman, D.R., & Tice, R. (1996). *Sentence intelligibility test.* Lincoln, NE: Communication Disorders Software.

5

Acceptance of AAC by Adults with Acquired Disorders

Joanne P. Lasker
Jan L. Bedrosian

Adults with acquired communication disorders are a unique clinical population. Many of them experience life-threatening health issues as a result of sudden or gradual disease processes. These individuals face a number of challenges. They may be unable to return to their jobs, which often results in financial stress. Roles and responsibilities within the family shift. Many of the activities of daily living, such as dressing, eating, walking, or driving, become difficult or impossible. In addition to these challenges, severe expressive communication disorders, such as aphasia, motor speech disorders, and dementia, may result in dramatic lifestyle changes. Often, adults with acquired communication disorders can no longer communicate in the manner to which they are accustomed. As a result, they may avoid participating in many of their former daily activities. They may remember the nature of their relationships with others and may now be aware that people respond to them differently. For people who once had typical speech ability, the loss of spoken communication signifies an enormous life change. (See Chapter 1 for a detailed discussion of communication role changes.)

In order to address the severe communication disorders of these adults, augmentative and alternative communication (AAC) strategies and systems have been developed. These tools have been shown to enhance communication effectiveness, communication repertoire, and turn taking in conversation (Fox & Fried-Oken, 1996; Fried-Oken, Howard, & Stewart, 1991; Garrett & Beukelman, 1995; Garrett, Beukelman, & Low-Morrow, 1989). However, clinical experience suggests that not everyone who can benefit from AAC chooses to use it; some individuals do not accept AAC devices or systems.

For the purposes of this chapter, we define the acceptance of an AAC system in terms of how and to what degree it is integrated into the life of the user. Acceptance may be considered along a continuum, moving from partial usage to full usage. Such a model was proposed by Scherer (1993), who focused on potential patterns of use and nonuse for all types of assistive technology, including AAC. With respect to technology use or acceptance, she describes two patterns—optimal and partial/reluctant. Scherer defined *optimal use* as the condition in which the technology is used willingly and at every opportunity. Some adults with acquired disorders may be impressed by the benefits that AAC offers and may eagerly choose to use a system whenever possible. Partial/reluctant use occurs when the system is used in one environment but not another or when the system is used only with great encouragement. Some adults with acquired disorders may accept AAC as a tool in certain communication contexts but not in others. They may decide, selectively, when to incorporate it into their activities. For example, individuals with severe expressive aphasia may decide to use a voice output device at a weekly card game with peers but to rely primarily on residual speech at home with their spouse.

Scherer also described two categories of nonuse or rejection—avoidance and abandonment. *Avoidance* occurs when a person is unwilling to pursue the acquisition of the system or to participate in the training required for system use. For example, some individuals with aphasia may be reluctant to work on communicating using strategies other than speech. They may find it difficult to accept that they will need to use a communication book with pictures or on drawing to convey messages. These individuals will probably not agree to explore AAC options at all; they may refuse an AAC evaluation or refuse to investigate funding options. The other pattern of technology nonuse, *abandonment*, occurs when a system has been obtained but is no longer used. Some adults with acquired disorders may acquire AAC systems or devices, attempt to use them, find them to be unacceptable for one or a variety of reasons, and leave them to gather dust in a closet.

A number of other researchers in the field of assistive technology describe nonuse of technology as abandonment. Examination of the assistive technology literature, outside the specific area of AAC, reveals that few researchers investigate factors leading to acceptance; they primarily investigate technology abandonment. Depending on the type of assistive technology, abandonment has been reported as low as 8% or as high as 75%; an average of one third of all assistive devices are abandoned, usually within the first 3 months after they were obtained (Scherer & Galvin, 1994; Wessels, Willems, & de White, 1996). Caudrey and Seeger (1983) found that 13.5% of orthopedic devices were not used when assessed at 4-month follow-up. Geiger (1990) followed 500 individuals who were given assistive devices during a hospital rehabilitation program and found that 50% of devices were abandoned after discharge.

Phillips and Zhao (1993) surveyed noncommunication assistive device use in 227 adults with various disabilities at 3 months to more than 5 years after onset. They found that 29.3% of all assistive devices were abandoned. Most of these were mobility aids. They reported that the highest rate of abandonment occurred within the first year and after 5 years. A change in user needs or priorities was the factor most strongly associated with abandonment. Devices that were easily obtained or that failed to meet the user's expectations were more likely to be abandoned. In addition, retention was greater when the users believed that their opinions were considered during the selection process.

Similar abandonment results were presented by Cushman and Scherer (1996), who used telephone interviews to investigate the use of mobility and daily living devices by 47 people with mixed diagnoses who were discharged from acute rehabilitation units. They found that 33% of all prescribed devices were not in use by the 3-month follow-up. The most frequently abandoned devices included grooming aids and quad canes. The most frequent reason given for nonuse was that the device was no longer needed. The researchers also assessed actual functional improvement at the time of the survey and found that functional gains corresponded with nonuse for half of the devices that had been abandoned. In other words, half of the time, the users' skills had actually improved enough to merit abandonment of assistive technology.

Research that examines AAC system abandonment is limited. Researchers do not have an accurate estimate of how many prescribed communication devices lie unused. More important, the AAC field lacks a complete understanding of the factors involved in the acceptance of an AAC system. If the factors contributing to acceptance were better understood, researchers and clinicians might be able to optimize communication approaches and quality of life. A variety of psychosocial and circumstantial factors may influence whether users will ultimately accept AAC. In this chapter, we delineate several factors that, as a group, have not been described previously in the AAC literature:

1. A model of factors pertaining to acceptance is proposed.
2. Research incorporating systematic investigation of some of these factors is reviewed.
3. Combined user and partner profiles, illustrating aspects of the model that may lead to acceptance or rejection of AAC, are presented.
4. Future research needs are discussed.

PROPOSED MODEL FOR ACCEPTANCE OF AAC

Scherer (1993) developed a valuable model for organizing the multiple influences on the use (i.e., acceptance) or nonuse (i.e., rejection) of a particular assistive technology by a person. The Matching Person and Technology (MPT) model considers the following areas: 1) the characteristics of the *milieu* in which the assistive technology is used, 2) pertinent features of the *person* and his or her temperament, and 3) the salient characteristics of the *technology* itself. This system provides the organizational framework for discussing the factors related to AAC acceptance that we propose in the AAC Acceptance Model. An overview of these factors is presented in Table 1.

Factors Related to the Milieu

The first branch of the AAC Acceptance Model discusses factors related to the milieu, or communication context, which includes partners and environments.

Communication Partners Many researchers have addressed the topic of partners in AAC interactions (Dowden, 1999; Kraat, 1985; Light, Binger, Agate, & Ramsay, 1999; McNaughton & Light, 1989). Partners are critical to the daily use of AAC by adults with acquired

Table 1. The AAC Acceptance Model

Milieu	Person	Technology
Partner	Time since onset/course/ potential for recovery	Durability/reliability
Environment	Attitude	Customizing/programming
Funding options	Personality/emotional state	Service delivery
	Age and age cohort	Ease of use
	Skills	Appearance
	Needs	Compatibility
	Intervention history	Size/weight
		Cost
		Voice quality

disorders. Partners can facilitate AAC implementation by providing emotional, conversational, and technological support to potential AAC users. Without partners' acceptance of AAC, it is unlikely that AAC users will experience success.

For certain partners, acceptance of an AAC system may result in new responsibilities in terms of the acquisition, maintenance, and programming of an AAC device. Partners who accept AAC may choose to support the user in his or her efforts at social participation because they believe that AAC will make life better, both for themselves and for the user. Office employers, for example, may fund a computer system with voice output that would enable a user to converse over the telephone and to consult with colleagues, because it enables them to retain a valuable employee. Conversation partners may be required to mount the AAC device on a wheelchair, change the paper, program messages, or recharge the device. If a partner is unwilling to perform these tasks, the AAC device may not be used to its full advantage.

The expectations and understandings that partners hold may also contribute to their acceptance of AAC. Scherer (1993) suggested that partners who have realistic expectations are more likely to promote acceptance of assistive technology. For example, if a wife believes that a voice output communication aid (VOCA) will restore all of the conversational skills that her husband with aphasia has lost, she may be disappointed by the outcome. However, if she understands prior to acquisition of the device that considerable effort may be required to make the device optimally functional for her husband, she may be more likely to encourage him to use it.

The partner's attitudes toward AAC may influence the ultimate acceptance of a system by a user. A more detailed discussion of attitude is provided in the section of the AAC Acceptance Model that is entitled "Factors Related to the Person"; however, it should be noted that for the partner as well as for the user, attitude comprises three separate components—affective, behavioral, and cognitive. A partner who feels positively about AAC, is willing to support its use, and believes that AAC will make everyone's life better will likely have a more positive attitude toward AAC, thereby leading to a greater likelihood of acceptance. Most of the research in the AAC field discussed in later sections of this chapter has focused on partner attitude toward AAC and the AAC user; however, the precise relationship between partner attitude and eventual acceptance of AAC by a potential user is not completely understood.

Communication Environment   The environment related to the communication event may affect acceptance by influencing how the user experiences the AAC system. This factor includes aspects of communication such as setting and time of day. These variables may either support or restrict AAC use, thereby leading to acceptance or rejection of a system. For example, in a noisy environment such as a cocktail party, communicating with an AAC voice output system may be difficult if partners cannot hear or understand the synthesized speech. Time of day may affect the user's stamina and the success of AAC use. For example, if potential users in an acute care hospital participate in device trials at the time of day when they are most fatigued, they may be less likely to consider adopting a system permanently.

Factors Related to the Person

The second branch of the AAC Acceptance Model discusses factors related to the person and includes the following: features of the user's disease; attitude, personality, and emotional state; age and age cohort; skills; needs; and intervention history.

Features of the Disease   Central features of the acquired disease resulting in communication disorders may have a significant impact on AAC acceptance. These are 1) time since the onset of the disease, 2) the course of the disease, and 3) the degree of certainty about recovery. The onset of disease may be sudden, as in the case of a stroke, or gradual, as in the case of amyotrophic lateral sclerosis (ALS). After onset, the process of grief (i.e., denial, anger, bargaining, depression, and acceptance) can influence emotional adjustment and acceptance of AAC. For some adults, the fact that they have survived a traumatic event, such as stroke or traumatic brain injury (TBI), may influence attitudes toward recovery. Some people may have difficulty with accepting the sudden loss of communication skills and may reject AAC because of its unfamiliarity or artificiality. Given a gradual loss of communication skills and the time to become accustomed to their disability, some people may accept AAC more readily. It is also possible that the gradual loss of communication may offer people time to contemplate future status and may reinforce a resolve not to rely on AAC. Research is limited regarding how sudden or gradual onset affects subsequent acceptance of AAC. Further research into this topic is required.

Among people whose condition is stable or who are recovering, their level of acceptance of AAC may change as speech skills improve or degenerate. Some individuals firmly believe that they will speak as they once did and are unlikely to ever accept an AAC system. Other adults who have struggled with residual speech for a significant period of time may be willing to consider AAC options. Adults who have just received a diagnosis of a degenerative disease such as ALS may be unprepared to receive detailed information about communication options. However, after a period of time living with unintelligible speech, they may be willing to explore AAC augmentation. (The staging of intervention in degenerative disease and the transition from natural speech to AAC options are discussed in Chapter 3.)

In summary, acceptance may change at certain points in the progression of disease or in the recovery process. Individuals may move from the acute care hospital to a rehabilitation facility to home. As physical abilities change and speech deteriorates or improves, AAC may seem more or less helpful to the individual. The severity of a disease, its course, and the potential for recovery may also affect users' attitudes, emotional adjustment, and skills and may influence communication needs.

Attitudes Toward Using AAC   *Attitude* is defined as a "learned predisposition to respond in a consistent evaluative manner" toward an object, idea, or person (Greenwald, Brock, & Ostrom, 1968, p. 12). Evaluation occurs along a continuum of positive to negative responses and comprises three components: 1) an affective component, consisting of emotional and physiological reactions; 2) a behavioral component, consisting of "past action, future intentions, and predicted behavior in hypothetical situations" (Greenwald et al., 1968, p. 16); and 3) a cognitive component, consisting of beliefs and perceptions. Each evaluative component contributes to a user's attitudes toward AAC, which in turn may influence acceptance.

The three components of attitude vary in many ways. The affective component may consist of numerous emotions regarding the use of AAC, such as comfort level, frustration, excitement, satisfaction, fear, or shame. Potential users of AAC may experience some or all of these emotions when facing the prospect of using an AAC system. The behavioral component of attitude relates to the willingness to use AAC. As stated previously in this chapter, AAC use may occur along a continuum. Potential AAC users may choose to use AAC only in certain situations or only with certain partners. Finally, the cognitive component of attitude concerns beliefs about AAC itself as well as how users perceive themselves as communicators. Potential users may require proof that AAC can improve their communication effectiveness. Also, personal judgments about independence may affect acceptance. Some individuals prefer to use another person rather than a machine to function. Others resent any tool (i.e., person or machine) that diminishes their independence. Thus, a person is more likely to accept AAC when he or she feels positively about it, is willing to use it in a variety of communicative contexts, and believes that it will make him or her a better communicator.

Personality and Emotional State   Personality "represents characteristics that account for consistent patterns of feeling, thinking, and behaving" (Pervin & John, 1997, p. 4). From this definition, it is evident that aspects of personality influence attitudes. Psychologists frequently use trait theories of personality to define different personality types. One such theory was proposed by Eysenck (1967) who defined three basic bipolar factors underlying personality: 1) extroversion, the tendency toward "an outgoing nature and a high level of activity" versus introversion, the tendency "to avoid the company of others"; 2) neuroticism, the tendency "to be anxious, worried, and full of guilt" versus emotional stability, "the tendency to be relaxed and at peace with oneself"; and 3) psychoticism, "the tendency to be aggressive, egocentric, and antisocial" versus self-control, "the tendency to be kind, considerate, and obedient" (Carlson & Buskist, 1997, pp. 451–452). Although it may seem logical to assume that a person who is shy, afraid of new experiences, and highly anxious would be less likely to accept AAC, empirical support for such an assumption is lacking. Scherer (1993) suggested that people who use devices successfully are not easily discouraged and enjoy challenges. An empirical investigation of the relationship between personality type and AAC use may be warranted.

Personality poses an interesting problem to clinicians in that the user's personality may appear to alter after the onset of disease. Most theorists believe that personality remains relatively consistent throughout the life span unless there has been a traumatic event (Starratt & Peterson, 1997). A disease or accident resulting in loss of communication certainly constitutes a traumatic event. However, the relationship between personality and emotional adjustment needs to be explored more fully.

Several researchers have documented emotional shifts that may occur with changes in brain physiology in acquired diseases such as stroke and ALS. For example, Code, Hemsley, and Herrmann (1999) suggested three types of depression following stroke. Primary depression may have an organic basis, but secondary and tertiary depression may occur in response to physical, communicative, and social changes. Secondary depression may occur when individuals perceive the extent of their disabilities. Tertiary depression may occur when individuals attempt and fail to reassume former life roles, resulting in long-term psychosocial changes. The question remains as to how emotional changes relate to the potential AAC user's premorbid personality and how both influence acceptance of AAC.

Certain emotional qualities may promote technology acceptance. Vash (1983) suggested that acceptance of disability and goal-directedness are related to positive attitudes toward assistive technology. A similar concept is introduced by Wright (1983), who stated that individuals who recognize difficulties but focus on managing them are more likely to accept assistive technology. Scherer wrote that optimal users of assistive devices "say they have goals they want to pursue, believe obstacles to their independence can be overcome, tend to focus on expanding their capabilities, see opportunities rather than limitations, and believe they control their quality of life" (1993, p. 125). The partner's personality and emotional status should also be considered. Clinicians need to be sensitive to the emotional status of both users and partners in order to determine when it is best to introduce AAC options as this may affect acceptance.

Age and Age Cohort   It has been acknowledged that people of various ages and age cohorts have different responses to assistive technology (Higginbotham & Scally, 1997). The term *age* refers to the person's chronological age. Many of the physiological, sensory, and cognitive changes that typically occur with age (e.g., changes in visual acuity, auditory acuity, tactile and sensory skills, physical strength, ambulation) can influence acceptance of AAC. Individuals may adapt to these age-related changes differently. If, for example, a potential user has poor balance due to age-related changes, he or she might be reluctant to carry an AAC device that could further impair ambulation.

The term *age cohort* refers to a group who was born at the same time in history and experiences the same set of historical and social events. For example, those individuals who grew up during the Great Depression may hold similar attitudes about self-sufficiency and privacy. They may be unwilling to use a machine for voice output or may be unwilling to ask others to compile messages to be placed in a communication notebook. Anyone younger than age 30 in 2000 who eventually acquires a communication disorder may respond more favorably to technology-based AAC systems.

In a qualitative study using a social phenomenological approach, Pippin and Fernie (1997) explored the widely held belief that older people are unwilling to use noncommunication assistive technology because of its unappealing appearance. Appearance entailed how the user perceived the device, how other people viewed the device, and how they viewed the person using the device. The researchers suggested that an assistive device advertises the user's disability and influences the construction of public identity. Based on their findings, they postulated the existence of a dynamic relationship between the person's perception of individual autonomy and device appearance. Each individual finds his or her own balance between device function and appearance. According to the researchers, this is an individually determined construct; there was no evidence of a general trend that device appearance discouraged older users. They also found that social context plays a role in acceptance. When older people were living in age-specific residences, an outward sign of disability, such as a device used to enhance independence, was positively valued.

Skills   The skills of the user help AAC interventionists determine which AAC devices/systems are appropriate and also influence acceptability. Such skills may change as recovery or degeneration occurs. The first of these skills involves the user's overall communication status. This includes the quality and intelligibility of residual speech, the available communication modes (e.g., gesture, pantomime, writing, eye gaze), and the effectiveness and efficiency of communication. For example, if a user is able to communicate somewhat effectively through the use of limited speech and gestures, he or she may be less likely to accept AAC systems, such as electronic communication devices.

The language comprehension and production abilities of the user may also have an impact on acceptance. Impaired language comprehension, such as that exhibited in a person with receptive aphasia, may negatively affect the user's ability to understand how to program and use an AAC device, thus leading to rejection. In addition, people with impaired comprehension are often less strategic in their communication attempts and may fail to recognize the need for AAC to improve message clarity. In other situations, impaired language production may lend itself more favorably to acceptance of AAC. For example, a person exhibiting syntactic and word-finding difficulties, such as those associated with expressive aphasia, may be more likely to desire a system with preprogrammed phrases and sentences.

The cognitive status of the user must also be considered and can function either to facilitate or to hinder acceptance. Scherer (1993) reported that cognitive aptitude and learning styles can affect the user's ability to participate in the training process. In addition, she suggested that individuals with divergent rather than convergent approaches to problem solving may accept assistive technology more readily, given their predisposition to seeing multiple solutions to problems.

Literacy skills should be considered not only in selecting appropriate devices but also in predicting acceptance. For adults with acquired disorders who retain some orthographic skill, certain aided symbol systems that pair picture icons with written words may be offensive, thus leading to rejection of AAC. For users who are literate and have severe physical limitations, AAC systems with word-prediction capabilities may be looked upon favorably as a means to reduce fatigue and enhance communication rate.

Technology skills are a major consideration in determining acceptance, as so many aided AAC systems rely on computer knowledge and abilities. Users and partners who are accustomed to and comfortable with computers may be willing to program a dynamic screen device. Devices and systems that provide access to electronic mail and the Internet may also promote acceptance for those who are accustomed to such communication/information systems. For others, however, the technological skills required to use AAC systems may seem overwhelming and frustrating, thus leading to rejection.

Needs   This factor involves both communication and life needs. With respect to communication needs, Light (1988) identified four purposes of communication interactions: 1) expression of basic wants and needs, 2) information transfer, 3) social closeness, and 4) social etiquette. These basic communication purposes may translate to specific communication tasks, such as communicating in a medical emergency, requesting that the television be turned on, talking with friends at a party, and thanking someone for bringing flowers. If it is very important for a person to maintain social closeness with old classmates, an AAC device that enables the user to reminisce may be considered acceptable.

Life needs pertain to current and future goals, such as returning to work, meeting family responsibilities, being cared for medically according to one's wishes, or planning financial estates. If AAC can facilitate meeting these life needs, it may more likely be accepted by users. For example, people who are strongly committed to returning to work in their office after a stroke may be more accepting of an AAC device that could facilitate business transactions.

Intervention History   This factor relates to the intervention process and consists of several components that have yet to be empirically studied. These components include 1) the latency between onset of the disorder and intervention implementation, 2) the approach used during treatment, 3) the success of the approach selected, and 4) the extent to which alternative approaches were considered if the original intervention was not successful. The timing of the introduction of AAC, for example, may be different for a person with aphasia than for a person with ALS. It may be best to suggest the use of multimodal techniques for clients with recovering aphasia early in the treatment process so that they continue to view themselves as effective communicators despite their impairment. Clinical experience suggests that exposure to AAC early in the aphasia treatment process may enhance ultimate acceptance of nonspeech communication methods. Alternatively, people with ALS may do best when given a brief mention of AAC early on with gradually increasing exposure as speech skills deteriorate (Yorkston, Miller, & Strand, 1995).

Studies in the assistive technology literature emphasize the importance of initial exposure. Gitlin, Luborsky, and Schemm (1998) used a structured qualitative approach to describe the perceptions of mobility devices by stroke patients in rehabilitation. They suggested that early introduction and initial training may significantly affect how technology is eventually viewed by the user. Pippin and Fernie (1997) studied noncommunication assistive technology and found that the first major mobility device caused more concern about self-image than the second device for many adult users. They stated that it is especially important for older consumers of assistive technology to see the benefits during their first experience with an assistive device.

For people with acquired communication disorders, treatment may consist of goals focusing exclusively on speech recovery, on developing AAC strategies, or on a combination of the two. Clinicians must use their judgment in terms of the user's personality, emotional response, and disease course in designing appropriate treatment goals. For some potential users, it may be especially important for their first experience with AAC to be highly successful. If this is the case, the interventionist may need to make certain that the user works on the device to communicate at least one message successfully. When users are exposed to a number of different devices or systems without experiencing successful communication, they may come to believe that they are unable to use technology effectively. It may be important for the user to see the device or system working successfully in settings outside the clinic or with certain communication partners. Over the course of time, both users and significant partners may benefit from witnessing highly successful AAC users participating in conversations and discussing with them how AAC has affected their lives.

Several authors have suggested that user input in the selection process can be critical to ensuring later acceptance of technology. A common reason for nonuse may be that the device was forced on a person by family members or therapists (Scherer, 1993). The user needs to be actively involved in the decision-making process. Wessels and colleagues (1996) examined several methods to evaluate assistive device use. They concluded that asking users to provide opinions of their own devices is the most suitable method for conducting further research into device acceptability.

Factors Related to Technology

The third branch of the AAC Acceptance Model discusses factors related to technology. Not surprisingly, these are often the parameters used during the selection process to determine whether a device is appropriate for the user. Each user has particular needs and desires in terms of device features. It is possible that a user may accept a device with a certain set of features and reject another device without those features. For AAC devices/systems, these features may include the following:

1. Durability and reliability

2. Customizing or programming capacity: capacity for customization to meet the user's needs (e.g., personal words in word-prediction programs)

3. Service delivery: the availability of technical assistance, parts, repairs, and maintenance

4. Ease of use: learnability, clear visual display, nonfatiguing

5. Appearance

6. Compatibility: ability to work with computer, printer, and Internet

7. Size, weight, and portability

8. Cost: Concerns about funding may influence acceptance of AAC. Adults with acquired disorders may have difficulty obtaining funding though Medicare or private insurance. Scherer (1993) suggested that when devices are considered too expensive, users may avoid assistive technology.

9. Voice quality

The acceptability of synthesized or digitized voice can influence user acceptance of an AAC system. Many studies have explored the preferences for synthesized speech output by typical speakers (Crabtree, Mirenda, & Beukelman, 1990; Gorenflo, Gorenflo, & Santer, 1994; Mirenda, Eicher, & Beukelman, 1989). Only one study (Carlson, Hux, & Beukelman, 1994) examined AAC system voice quality with subjects who had acquired communication disorders. Carlson and colleagues (1994) had people with aphasia follow commands delivered in natural voice and in three types of synthesized speech. They noted a trend for people with aphasia to understand natural speech best. In addition, they found that the acceptability of the synthesized speech strongly influenced subjects' performance. Not only did the subjects in their study perform poorly when following commands delivered using poor-quality synthesized speech, but they also indicated that they rejected this type of speech. The researchers concluded that high-quality synthesized speech in combination with sufficient exposure and practice positively affected intelligibility. However, further studies that vary types of communication tasks, types of communicators, types of synthesized speech output, linguistic variables (e.g., rate, prosody), the practice effects are required to fully explore the relationship between intelligibility and acceptability for both synthesized and digitized speech output.

How the AAC Acceptance Model Works

By considering the broad areas of milieu, person, and technology, a profile of a particular user's attitude toward AAC use may be obtained and a treatment direction may be suggested. We have offered characteristics for each of the factors that might make a particular user likely to accept AAC. For example, a person may appear to be an optimal user according to the characteristics listed for person and technology, but may be a partial or reluctant user in terms of milieu characteristics. In this case, the milieu may require some modification for the person to use an AAC device with optimal effectiveness. This may entail overcoming environmental barriers to communication. Also, the categories of milieu, person, and technology are interactive. When one is altered, the other areas may be affected. For example, optimal use of one assistive device may lead to enthusiasm for trying another device, improved self-esteem, and a wider social milieu.

RELEVANT RESEARCH RELATED TO ATTITUDES

To date, there has been limited research with respect to systematic investigation of factors described in the AAC Acceptance Model as it applies to AAC. Of the factors that have been studied, partner attitude has received the most attention. Researchers have investigated attitudes toward AAC users and the ways in which they communicate. Although these studies have not specifically addressed the issue of acceptance of AAC, they shed light on one of the factors contributing to this topic: attitude. Some of these studies (Gorenflo & Gorenflo, 1991; Lasker & Beukelman, 1999) dealt with attitude as a global construct, and others (Bedrosian, Hoag, Calculator, & Molineux, 1992; Bedrosian, Hoag, Johnson, & Calculator, 1998; Hoag, Bedrosian, Johnson, & Molineux, 1994; Light & Binger, 1998) dealt primarily with a single aspect of attitude, that is, perceptions of communicative competence. Only one of these studies (Lasker & Beukelman, 1999) dealt specifically with adults who have severe acquired communication disorders, and the others pertained either to adults or to adolescents with congenital disorders. These studies shared methodologies for data collection in that subjects viewed videotapes of scripted interactions among AAC users and partners with typical speech and provided judgments through the use of written questionnaires. The content of these questionnaires is summarized in Table 2.

Gorenflo and Gorenflo (1991) studied the effects of AAC techniques (i.e., natural speech/gestures, alphabet board, and VOCA) and printed factual information about the user (i.e., presence versus absence of information pertaining to user's physical disability, social activities, and academic or employment status) on attitudes of college undergraduates who do not have disabilities toward an adult without speaking ability. For this study, they designed the Attitudes Toward Nonspeaking Persons Scale, which included questionnaire items pertaining to cognitive, affective, and behavioral components of attitudes (see Table 2). With respect to AAC technique, results indicated that subjects viewed the user more favorably as AAC techniques became more sophisticated. The user was also rated more favorably in conditions when factual information was given.

Lasker (1997) examined the effect of communication mode on observers' attitudes toward an adult with aphasia. Videotapes in which an actor with aphasia communicated autobiographical stories to a partner using natural speech, an AAC notebook, and an AAC digitized speech device were created. Peers with typical speaking ability, family members, and speech-language pathologists viewed these videotapes and completed ratings on five global attitude measures (see Table 2). Participants also completed a forced-choice ranking task in which they ranked the three storytelling modes in order of their personal preference for communicating with individuals with aphasia. Results demonstrated that peers, speech-language pathologists, and family members all rated the AAC digitized speech mode favorably. Significant between–observer-group differences, however, were found in the forced-choice ranking task, with peers choosing AAC digitized speech as most preferred and speech-language pathologists choosing natural speech as their most preferred method of storytelling. Family members selected natural speech as their most preferred method.

Bedrosian, Hoag, and colleagues conducted a series of studies (Bedrosian et al., 1992; Bedrosian et al., 1998; Hoag et al., 1994) that systematically explored the impact of three variables on perceptions of communicative competence of an adult AAC system user: 1) a user variable involving aided message length (i.e., single-word versus phrase messages); 2) a partner variable involving partner feedback (i.e., presence versus absence of expanded repetitions of the user's aided messages); and 3) an observer variable involving familiarity with users (i.e., speech-language pathologists with experience in AAC, adults with no experience with AAC, and adults with severe speech impairments associated with cerebral palsy). Four videotaped conversational conditions involving an AAC system user and a partner with typical speaking ability in an informal interaction were employed to manipulate

Table 2. Topics addressed in augmentative and alternative communication (AAC)–related questionnaires employed in relevant attitude/perception studies

Study	Affective ("I feel _____ with respect to the user.")	Behavioral ("I would be willing to _____ the user.")	Cognitive ("I think that the user is/was _____.")
		Attitude component	
Gorenflo and Gorenflo (1991)	Comfortable Pity/sympathy Respectful Inhibited Comfortable Trust	Study with Help	Intelligent Easy to talk to Trustworthy Understands Self-confident Successful
Lasker and Beukelman (1998)	Comfortable	Talk to	Competent Communicates effectively Understandable
Bedrosian, Hoag, Calculator, and Molineux (1992)		"The user _____." Expressed needs Communicated appropriately/ successfully/ reflectively in a variety of contents Was easy to understand Understands and relates well to partner Was easy to communicate with Was at ease	Accomplished goals Participated Communicated easily Wanted to communicate Communicated at a proper rate Flexible Managed breakdowns Interested in partner Kept partner's attention Sensitive to partner's feelings Responsive Satisfied with conversation
Light and Binger (1998)	Comfortable		Expressed needs Communicated appropriately/ successfully/ reflectively in a variety of contexts Easy to understand Understands and relates well to partner Easy to communicate with At ease

Note: This table represents a summary of information included in these questionnaires.

aided message length and partner feedback. A questionnaire was designed to assess the communicative competence of the user. Results indicated a significant interaction effect involving observer group and aided message length. Only the speech-language pathologists' ratings were affected by aided message length (i.e., the user was rated higher in competence when using phrase messages as opposed to single-word messages). No such impact was seen on the ratings by adults who had no experience with AAC, with the exception of certain questionnaire items related to social competence (i.e., amount of user participation, social ease), or by the ratings of adults with severe speech impairments. Partner feedback had no effect on observers' perceptions of communicative competence. In a follow-up study, Hoag and Bedrosian (1992) explored an additional variable involving AAC speech output type (i.e., digitized versus synthesized speech). Results indicated that this particular variable had no effect on observers' ratings of communicative competence.

Light and her colleagues conducted a series of investigations to examine the effect of several variables on perceptions of communicative competence of adolescent AAC users (Light, Beer, et al., 1995; Light & Binger, 1998; Light, Binger, et al., 1995; Light, Binger, Dilg, & Livelsberger, 1996; Light, Corbett, Gullapalli, & Lepkowski, 1995). Each investigation examined the impact of an observer variable (i.e., adults with no prior experience in AAC, adolescents with no prior experience in AAC, and professionals in AAC) and an AAC user variable related to gender. In addition, user communication variables involving the presence or absence of brief nonobligatory comments, partner-focused questions, an introductory strategy, and grammatical completeness were individually examined. A communicative competence scale was specifically designed (see Table 2). Across the studies, results indicated that regardless of the gender of the user, there was a significant interaction effect involving the observer group for each of the four user communication variables. The nature of the effect, however, varied depending on the specific user communication variable involved. Of interest were the findings that the communicative competence ratings by the adults with no prior experience with AAC were positively influenced by the use of brief comments, partner-focused questions, and an introductory strategy.

An important contribution from the majority of these investigations is the finding that observers' familiarity with AAC influences perceptions of user competence and attitudes toward AAC users. Judgments vary as a function of the observer involved. For this reason future investigations dealing with attitudes pertaining to acceptance must incorporate both users and potential partners.

A study by Culp and Carlisle (1988) offered a potential model for future research with adults who have acquired disorders by considering the attitudes of both the AAC users and their primary caregivers. Culp and Carlisle conducted a pilot study with children without speaking ability and their primary caregivers entitled *Partners in Augmentative Communication Training*. The researchers tested the outcomes of intervention at a day camp that provided individualized communication facilitation for all participants, all of whom had cerebral palsy and used some form of AAC. As part of the assessment, the children and their caregivers completed attitude scales before intervention, on the final day of intervention, and 3 months after completion of the intervention. These questionnaires measured attitudes regarding oral speech and AAC techniques. Results revealed a discrepancy between the attitudes of AAC users and their caregivers. Prior to the intervention, the children perceived their parents to be more positive about AAC than the parents actually reported they were. That is, the children believed that their parents wanted them to use AAC more than the parents actually did. Although the parents' attitudes toward AAC did not change significantly after the intervention, the children's perceptions of their parents' attitudes were significantly more positive after the intervention (both immediately and after a delay). Such a finding suggests that user and partner acceptance of AAC is connected. This relationship is explored further in the case profiles discussed in the next section of this chapter.

Partner and User Profiles for Acceptance or Rejection of AAC

In this section, we present three user/partner profiles, illustrating aspects of the AAC Acceptance Model that may lead to acceptance or rejection of AAC. Narrative descriptions as well as tables specifying acceptance and rejection factors are included in this section. These profiles have been compiled for this chapter based on our clinical experiences working with adults with acquired disorders and their families. The profiles do not represent any single client or family; they are intended to illustrate important factors underlying the issue of acceptance. For that reason, the most salient factors of the AAC Acceptance Model are listed for each case. Profile 1 demonstrates acceptance of AAC by both the potential user and the primary partner (i.e., his wife); Profile 2 illustrates rejection of AAC by both the potential user and the partner; and Profile 3 describes changes in AAC acceptance over time. The first two profiles present individuals with stable, chronic aphasia. In Profile 3, we discuss an individual with degenerative disease whose acceptance of AAC changes over time as her physical condition deteriorates and her life circumstances alter.

Profile 1   The first profile concerns Matt, a 45-year-old man, with stable moderate aphasia and severe apraxia of speech. He was previously employed as a mechanical press operator and has 2 years of college education. At the time of this analysis, it has been 15 months since Matt's cerebral vascular accident (CVA; i.e., stroke). His wife, Donna, is employed as an elementary school teacher. Table 3 lists factors pertaining to the acceptance of AAC by both parties. It is clear from the table that Matt and Donna are predisposed to the acceptance of AAC. Both have very positive attitudes about communication modes other than speech and believe that AAC is critical in helping Matt return to work.

Although their emotional status has been negatively affected by Matt's stroke and its sequelae, they are predisposed to dealing well with problems in their lives. Matt is acutely aware of his expressive and receptive communication impairments and has decided that AAC provides a solution to his communication difficulties. His primary life need is to return to gainful employment, and he believes that AAC is the tool that will enable him to do so. Both he and his wife are experienced and comfortable with technology, and he, in fact, enjoys computers. Despite the limited treatment and vocational support services Matt receives, he has a strong social network consisting of his family and church members.

In addition, Matt was introduced to AAC at a time when he was frustrated with his lack of progress in speech therapy and was actively looking for other options. When AAC was introduced, Matt experienced almost immediate success using the system in conversation with an unfamiliar partner. After a year spent pursuing funding, Matt acquired a DynaMyte and is attending treatment sessions weekly. Treatment at this time focuses on helping Matt accomplish his personal goals; he is planning to take his driver's license test and is looking for a job.

Profile 2   The second profile is of Carla, a 43-year-old woman with stable, moderate aphasia and severe apraxia of speech. She was previously employed in public relations at a hotel and has a college degree. At the time of this analysis, Carla is 4 years post-CVA. Her husband, Andy, is employed as a commission salesman. Table 4 lists factors pertaining to the rejection of AAC by both parties.

Carla has not fully accepted the extent of her communication deficit and still believes that some "magic pill" will enable her to speak as she used to. Although she expresses sympathy for people with disabilities, she believes that she is fundamentally different from them. She views AAC as unnatural, slow, and effortful. She is clinically depressed, perhaps because of her social isolation, but does not acknowledge that AAC could facilitate social interactions. Unlike Matt,

Table 3.   Profile 1: User and partner acceptance of augmentative and alternative communication (AAC)
Potential user: Matt, previously employed as mechanical press operator
Partner: Donna, his wife, employed as an elementary school teacher
Disease course and severity: stable, moderate aphasia and severe apraxia of speech
Time postonset: 15 months post-cerebral vascular accident

Factors related to milieu	Potential user	Spouse
Partners	Family constellation includes supportive wife, two older children, and a 2-year-old grandchild	Willing to help with AAC device programming and setup
	Supportive church community but limited communication effectiveness with unfamiliar partners	
Environment	About 80% effective communicating in highly structured contexts	
Funding	Private insurance State jobs commission	Active advocate for funding and employment options

Factors related to person	Potential user	Spouse
Attitude	Demonstrates understanding of people with disabilities Excited by AAC Expresses that he is willing to use AAC in a variety of settings Believes AAC will enable him to return to work	Demonstrates understanding of people with disabilities Is comfortable with the idea of Matt using AAC Expresses willingness to support Matt's use of AAC Believes AAC will enable Matt to return to work
Personality	Independent A perfectionist A problem-solver A hard worker	Flexible Patient Hard worker Optimistic
Age	45 years old	43 years old
Communication status	Uses variety of modes (e.g., writing, speech, gesture)	
Language	Spoken output limited to four single words per utterance Comprehension adequate for basic conversation but benefits from slowed rate and written augmentation	

(continued)

Table 3.   (*continued*)

Factors related to person	Potential user	Spouse
	Demonstrates comprehension-monitoring by frequently asking for repetition from conversation partners	
Cognition	Basically unimpaired	
Literacy	Reading comprehension at sentence level Written expression at the word level	
Technology	Experienced and comfortable with computers for employment purposes Enjoys working with technology	Is experienced and comfortable with computers for personal and employment purposes
Needs	Wants to return to work and social activities Wants to interact with family, particularly his grandchild Wants to resume family responsibilities	
Intervention history	Initial outpatient treatment discontinued because of lack of progress in speech over a 9-month period Subsequent treatment provided exposure to various voice-output AAC systems Successful use of an AAC loaner device over a 6-month period in a variety of communication settings	

Factors related to technology	User priorities	Partner priorities
	Adjustable speaking rate Good voice quality Multiple messages organized according to relevant topic	Portability Service delivery Can be used in addition to other communication modalities (e.g., writing)

Table 4.   Profile 2: User and partner rejection of augmentative and alternative communication (AAC)
Potential user: Carla, previously employed in public relations at hotel
Partner: Andy, her husband, employed as a salesman (on commission)
Course and severity of disease: stable, severe apraxia of speech and moderate aphasia
Time postonset: 4 years post-cerebral vascular accident

Factors related to milieu	Potential user	Spouse
Partners	Family constellation includes nonsupportive husband, two children (6 and 8 years old)	Not involved in therapy Believes her communication skills are adequate
Environment	Uses multiple communication modalities only in highly structured settings Occupational therapy twice per week Speech therapy twice per week Swimming once per week	
Funding	No external sources of funding	
Attitude	Demonstrates sympathy for people with disabilities Is embarrassed by her disabilities Believes she is not like others who have disabilities Believes voice-output devices are slow and effortful Believes AAC devices are not "natural"	Feels uncomfortable talking with people who have disabilities Is unwilling to take time to explore communication options Believes people with disabilities should be self-sufficient Believes his wife's communication is adequate
Personality	Uncompromising Resistant to change Diagnosed with clinical depression Currently takes anti-depressants	Workaholic Socially outgoing Uncomfortable dealing with feelings Feels stressed financially
Age	43 years old	46 years old
Communication status	Uses variety of modes (e.g., writing, speech, drawing) Limited overall effectiveness	
Language	Spoken output limited to five single words per utterance Comprehension impaired for basic conversation but benefits from slowed rate and written augmentation demonstrates limited comprehension-monitoring	

(continued)

Table 4. (*continued*)

Factors related to milieu	Potential user	Spouse
	abilities by inconsistently asking for repetition in conversation	
Cognition	Basically unimpaired	
Literacy	Reading comprehension at the paragraph level Written expression at the word level	
Technology	Minimally experienced with computers for employment purposes Prefers not to use computers	Experienced with computers for work purposes Likes to use computers
Needs	Great desire to talk as she used to talk Desire to resume family responsibilities	
Intervention history	Prolonged outpatient therapy focusing only on speech options as targets of intervention AAC introduced 3 years post-onset as a last resort Owns a simple digitized voice-output device (six-message capability) that she chooses not to use	

Factors related to technology	User priorities	Partner priorities
	Speech that sounds like she used to Easy to use Portable	Inexpensive

Carla is not fully aware of her language comprehension deficits, she does not like computers, and she has no strong desire to return to work outside the home. Her husband, Andy, stressed by their financial status, is often too busy with his job to concern himself with his wife's disabilities. He believes that her communication skills are adequate to meet their daily needs.

Carla participates in several therapies, but Andy does not get involved with these activities. For Carla, therapy focused on regaining speech as the primary intervention goal and continued in this fashion for 3 years, despite limited progress. When she was persuaded to purchase an inexpensive AAC device, she did not experience benefits, and it ended up unused in a closet. The failure of AAC intervention may be related to Carla's personality, the expertise of the clinician, the timing of the introduction of AAC, and how much effort was expended in therapy focusing exclusively on speech goals. For a variety of reasons, Carla and Andy reject AAC at this time.

Profile 3   The third profile concerns Janice, a 55-year-old woman with ALS. This profile evolves from a state of initial rejection of AAC by both partner and user to eventual acceptance by the user (see Table 5). Janice's primary caregiver was her younger brother, Tom, who left his job as a construction worker to care for Janice in his home. While Janice lived with her brother, he received financial compensation through Supplemental Security Income checks. Because he was being subsidized, Tom was able to leave his job as a construction worker to care for Janice full time.

Janice was involved in an outpatient treatment clinic for 6 months. During all clinic visits, Tom insisted on sitting by Janice's side, refusing any request by a professional to speak to Janice without him present. He answered for Janice frequently and often corrected or elaborated on her yes-or-no responses. When the speech-language pathologist discussed various AAC options with Janice and Tom, Tom rejected AAC immediately, stating that "she doesn't need any of that stuff because I understand her fine." When it was suggested that Janice might benefit from AAC in conversations with people other than Tom, he responded that "she doesn't talk to anyone but me." Tom resisted all attempts by the intervention staff for Janice to see the speech-language pathologist without him, apparently worried that he might lose control over her care. The speech-language pathologist suspected that Janice's opinions on AAC were different than her brother's but was unable to discuss the issue with Janice without Tom present.

When Janice's condition deteriorated and she required constant ventilation, she entered a nursing facility. At that time, Tom was forced to return to work, and his visits to Janice became infrequent. On admission, staff at the nursing facility called a speech-language pathologist for immediate consultation to address Janice's communication needs. Janice was eager to consider AAC at this time. A yes-or-no communication system and the use of low-technology AAC strategies (i.e., communication boards and laser pointer) were established. At the time of this analysis, Janice struggles with the computer-based system EZ Keys. It is possible that her ability to use a high-technology system has been impeded by the fact that she was unable to learn the system when she retained some limb movement. At this time, she is forced to access the

Table 5.   Profile 3: Change in acceptance over time
Potential user: Janice, previously employed as a secretary
Significant other: Tom, her brother, recently quit job as construction worker
Course and severity of disease: bulbar amyotrophic lateral sclerosis (ALS)
Time postonset: 2 years

Factors related to milieu	Potential user	Brother
Partners	Never married No family other than her brother Has one close friend from work setting	Divorced twice Visited his sister infrequently once she was placed in nursing facility
Environment	Speech is unintelligible to unfamiliar listeners Leaves home only for doctor's appointments While living with her brother, received no services	Serves as Janice's only communication partner
Funding	Eligible for Medicaid	Quit job to care for sister, receiving financial reimbursement for her care
Attitude	Has had minimal exposure to people with disabilities Does not really understand what AAC is	Has had minimal exposure to people with disabilities Does not really understand what AAC is
Personality	Compliant Eager to please Has become progressively more passive since her diagnosis	Frightened of new experiences Is determined to "take charge" of situation since his sister has been in his care
Age	55 years old	48 years old
Communication status	Spoken output limited to vocalics Comprehension unimpaired	
Language	Unimpaired	Understands his sister's vocalic yes-or-no responses
Cognition	Basically unimpaired	
Literacy	Reading and writing skills that reflect college education	Reading and writing adequate to pass high school equivalency test
Technology	Has limited experience with computer technology	Has no experience with computer technology

(continued)

Table 5.   (*continued*)

Factors related to milieu	Potential user	Brother
Needs	Needs to communicate with medical staff Needs to communicate with occasional visitors	
Intervention history	Was exposed to AAC in outpatient treatment as speech skills deteriorated (four visits in 6 months) Appeared interested in AAC but unwilling to express interest in front of her brother After transfer to nursing facility, speech-language pathologist was called for communication consult	Unwilling to consider either low-technology or high-technology AAC options Claimed he understood his sister's dysarthric speech without difficulty

computer through the use of a vision key, a system based on eye movement. One might hypothesize that she would have been more successful had computer software been introduced when she had minimal movement adequate for switch access at an alternate site. When questioned, Janice confirms that she depended entirely on her brother when she lived with him and that she was unwilling to contradict his wishes regarding communication strategies. At this time, Janice is no longer able to phonate volitionally and uses a variety of low-technology AAC strategies to communicate within the nursing facility.

DIRECTIONS FOR FUTURE RESEARCH

By adapting the Matching Person and Technology (MPT) model from the field of assistive technology, we have developed the AAC Acceptance Model to begin to explain the acceptance of AAC by adults with acquired communication disorders (Scherer, 1993). The AAC Acceptance Model organizes factors under three branches—milieu, person, and technology. As we stated previously, the model contains many assumptions yet to be tested. These include the assumptions that 1) older adults are less accepting of AAC than younger people, 2) people with technological/computer background are more accepting of AAC than those without such background, and 3) AAC is less likely to be accepted when the possibility for recovery of natural speech exists.

Based on this model, an assessment tool measuring the factors leading to acceptance in potential AAC users and partners needs to be developed and validated. Determining the relative weight of these factors across patient–partner pairs may be a goal of future research. Patterns characteristic of acceptance or rejection of AAC may emerge from such research. Researchers can then begin to predict which users are most likely to accept AAC. Such a tool already exists in the wider field of assistive technology: *The Assistive Technology Device Predisposition Assessment* (*ATD PA*; Scherer & McKee, 1989) was developed from data based on assistive technology users and nonusers. It is a survey that includes questions about the consumer's temperament, psychosocial resources, views of disability, and expectations of specific technology.

We are particularly interested in the evaluation of partner and user attitudes toward AAC and how these attitudes contribute to acceptance. There are no assessment tools that accomplish these goals. In an effort to address this need, one may turn to Lasker's qualitative findings (1997) from focus-group discussions with the observers on the basis of their written questionnaire responses. These discussions yielded certain "content themes" related to attitudes about AAC (e.g., comfort, willingness, effectiveness). On the basis of these content themes, it may be possible to develop a tool to assess user and partner attitude accurately (and how partner attitude may influence the acceptance of AAC by the user). Questions arise as to whether attitudes toward AAC change over time and, if so, what factors influence these changes. Additional topics for future study might include whether AAC influences the rate of deterioration or recovery in acquired communication disorders, how partner attitudes influence user acceptance of AAC, and exactly which components of initial exposure to technology have the greatest impact on future AAC acceptance.

CONCLUDING REMARKS

This chapter has highlighted the complex issues surrounding AAC acceptance and has provided several directions for future research in this area. User acceptance is crucial for individuals with acquired disorders because it can influence the emphasis and appropriateness of the communication treatment program. If clinicians could predict which users/partners might accept or reject AAC, they could then tailor the program to best meet their needs and preferences in a timely way. This is particularly important in a health care climate that stresses functional outcomes with maximum cost effectiveness.

REFERENCES

Bedrosian, J.L., Hoag, L.A., Calculator, S.N., & Molineux, B. (1992). Variables influencing perceptions of the communicative competence of an adult augmentative and alternative communication system user. *Journal of Speech and Hearing Research, 35*, 1105–1113.

Bedrosian, J.L., Hoag, L.A., Johnson, D., & Calculator, S.N. (1998). Communicative competence as perceived by adults with severe speech impairments associated with cerebral palsy. *Journal of Speech, Language, and Hearing Research, 41*, 667–675.

Carlson, K., Hux, K., & Beukelman, D. (1994). Comprehension of synthetic speech by individuals with aphasia. *Journal of Medical Speech-Language Pathology, 2*, 105–111.

Carlson, N.R., & Buskist, W. (1997). *Psychology: The science of behavior.* Needham Heights, MA: Allyn & Bacon.

Caudrey, D.J., & Seeger, B.R. (1983). Rehabilitation engineering service evaluation: A follow-up survey of device effectiveness and patient acceptance. *Rehabilitation Literature, 44*(3–4), 80–85.

Code, C., Hemsley, G., & Herrmann, M. (1999). The emotional impact of aphasia. *Seminars in Speech and Language, 20*(1), 19–31.

Crabtree, M., Mirenda, P., & Beukelman, D. (1990). Age and gender preferences for synthetic and natural speech. *Augmentative and Alternative Communication, 6*, 256–261.

Culp, D., & Carlisle, M. (1988). *PACT: Partners in augmentative communication training.* Tucson, AZ: Communication Skill Builders.

Cushman, L.A., & Scherer, M.J. (1996). Measuring the relationship of assistive technology use, functional status over time, and consumer-therapist perceptions of ATs. *Assistive Technology, 8*, 103–109.

Dowden, P. (1999). Lesson 2C: The impact of current communication skills on intervention. In P. Dowden & K. Yorkston, *SPHSC 453: Communication augmentation for non-speaking individuals* [On-line course offering]. Seattle: University of Washington Education Outreach.

Eysenck, H.J. (1967). *The biological basis of personality.* Springfield, IL: Charles C Thomas.

Fox, L.E., & Fried-Oken, M. (1996). AAC aphasiology: Partnership for future research. *Augmentative and Alternative Communication, 12*, 257–271.

Fried-Oken, M., Howard, J.M., & Stewart, S.R. (1991). Feedback on AAC intervention from adults who are temporarily unable to speak. *Augmentative and Alternative Communication, 2*, 38–44.

Garrett, K.L., & Beukelman, D.R. (1995). Changes in the interaction patterns of an individual with severe aphasia given three types of partner support. *Clinical Aphasiology, 23*, 237–251.

Garrett, K.L., Beukelman, D.R., & Low-Morrow, D. (1989). A comprehensive augmentative communication system for an adult with Broca's aphasia. *Augmentative and Alternative Communication, 5*, 55–61.

Geiger, C. (1990). The utilization of assistive devices by patients discharged from an acute rehabilitation setting. *Physical and Occupational Therapy in Geriatrics, 9*(1), 3–25.

Gitlin, L.N., Luborsky, M.R., & Schemm, R.L. (1998). Emerging concerns of older stroke patients about assistive device use. *Gerontologist, 38*(2), 169–189.

Gorenflo, C.W., & Gorenflo, D.W. (1991). The effects of information and augmentative communication technique on attitudes toward nonspeaking individuals. *Journal of Speech and Hearing Research, 34*, 19–26.

Gorenflo, C.W., Gorenflo, D.W., & Santer, S.A. (1994). Effects of synthetic voice output on attitudes toward the augmented communicator. *Journal of Speech and Hearing Research, 37*, 64–68.

Greenwald, A.G., Brock, T.C., & Ostrom, T.M. (1968). *Psychological foundations of attitudes.* San Diego: Academic Press.

Higginbotham, D.J., & Scally, C. (1997). Aging and assistive technology: A critique. In R. Lubinski & D.J. Higginbotham (Eds.), *Communication technologies for the elderly: Vision, hearing, and speech* (pp. 23–39). San Diego: Singular Publishing Group.

Hoag, L.A., & Bedrosian, J.L. (1992). Effects of speech output type, message length, and reauditorization on perceptions of the communicative competence of an adult AAC user. *Journal of Speech and Hearing Research, 35*, 1363–1366.

Hoag, L., Bedrosian, J.L., Johnson, D., & Molineux, B. (1994). Variables affecting perceptions of social aspects of the communicative competence of an adult AAC user. *Augmentative and Alternative Communication, 10*, 129–137.

Kraat, A. (1985). *Communication interaction between aided and natural speakers: A state of the art report.* Toronto: Canada Rehabilitation Council for the Disabled.

Lasker, J. (1997). *Effects of storytelling mode on partners' communicative ratings of an adult with aphasia.* Unpublished doctoral dissertation, University of Nebraska–Lincoln.

Lasker, J., & Beukelman, D.R. (1999). Peers' perceptions of storytelling by an adult with aphasia. *Aphasiology, 13*(9–11), 857–869.

Light, J. (1988). Interaction involving individuals using augmentative and alternative communication systems: State of the art and future directions. *Augmentative and Alternative Communication, 4*(2), 66–82.

Light, J., Beer, D., Buchert, L., Casey, E., DiMarco, R., & Dolan, K. (1995, December). *The effect of grammatical completeness on the communicative competence of students who use AAC.* Poster session presented at the annual convention of the American Speech-Language-Hearing Association (ASHA), Orlando, FL.

Light, J.C., & Binger, C. (1998). *Building communicative competence with individuals who use augmentative and alternative communication.* Baltimore: Paul H. Brookes Publishing Co.

Light, J., Binger, C., Agate, T., & Ramsay, K. (1999). Teaching partner-focused questions to individuals who use augmentative and alternative communication to enhance their communicative competence. *Journal of Speech, Language, and Hearing Research, 42*, 241–255.

Light, J., Binger, C., Corbett, M.B., Gathercole, M., Greiner, N., & Seich, A. (1995, December). *The effect of turn taking on the communicative competence of students who use AAC.* Poster presented at the annual convention of the American Speech-Language-Hearing Association (ASHA), Orlando, FL.

Light, J., Binger, C., Dilg, H., & Livelsberger, B. (1996). *Use of an introduction strategy to enhance communicative competence.* Paper presented at the biennial conference of the International Society for Augmentative and Alternative Communication (ISAAC), Vancouver, Canada.

Light, J., Corbett, M.B., Gullapalli, G., & Lepkowski, S. (1995, December). *Other orientation and communicative competence of AAC users.* Poster presented at the annual convention of the American Speech-Language-Hearing Association (ASHA), Orlando, FL.

McNaughton, D., & Light, J. (1989). Teaching facilitators to support the communication skills of an adult with severe cognitive disabilities: A case study. *Augmentative and Alternative Communication, 5,* 35–41.

Mirenda, P., Eicher, D., & Beukelman, D. (1989). Synthetic and natural speech preferences of male and female listeners in four age groups. *Journal of Speech and Hearing Research, 32,* 175–183.

Pervin, L.A., & John, O.P. (1997). *Personality: Theory and research.* New York: John Wiley & Sons.

Phillips, B., & Zhao, H. (1993). Predictors of assistive technology abandonment. *Assistive Technology, 5,* 36–45.

Pippin, K., & Fernie, G.B. (1997). Designing devices that are acceptable to the frail elderly: A new understanding based upon how older people perceive a walker. *Technology and Disability, 7,* 93–102.

Scherer, M.J. (1993). What we know about women's technology use, avoidance, and abandonment. *Women and Therapy, 14*(3–4), 117–132.

Scherer, M.J., & Galvin, J.C. (1994). Matching people with technology. *Rehabilitation Management, 9,* 128–130.

Scherer, M.J., & McKee, B.G. (1989). *The assistive technology device predisposition assessment (ATD PA).* Rochester, NY: Author.

Starratt, C., & Peterson, L. (1997). Personality and normal aging. In P. Nussbaum (Ed.), *Handbook of neuropsychology and aging* (pp. 15–31). New York: Plenum Press.

Vash, C.L. (1983). Psychological aspects of rehabilitation engineering. In *Technology for independent living* (Vol. II, pp. 48–59). Washington, DC: American Association for the Advancement of Science.

Wessels, R.D., Willems, C.G., & de White, L.P. (1996). How to select a method to evaluate usability of assistive devices. *Journal of Rehabilitation Sciences, 9*(2), 53–57.

Wright, B.A. (1983). *Physical disability: A psychosocial approach.* New York: HarperCollins.

Yorkston, K.M., Miller, R.M., & Strand, E.A. (1995). *Management of speech and swallowing in degenerative diseases.* Tucson, AZ: Communication Skill Builders.

6

Rebuilding Communicative Competence and Self-Determination

Janice C. Light
Maija Gulens

*It was March 1995 and John was no longer eating enough to maintain his weight.
... I decided to talk with John about PEG (feeding) tubes. ... "John, have you
thought about the benefits of getting a feeding tube?" John looked me in the eye
and crossed his arms violently. I continued to talk to him. He continued to cross
his arms violently. I was very upset, near tears. But I stopped talking and started
to think about it. What do I not understand? The guy is brilliant. He has always
been very opinionated. He is obviously very opinionated about this. Looks like the
communications problem is mine. At which point, I started to laugh. I said, "OK,
I get it. You don't want to talk about this." Thumbs up! I felt much better.
I had done everything I could do and he had clearly made up his mind. I vowed
that I would try to be a better listener from that point on. (Goeddel, 1998, pp.
60–61)*

This passage was written by the spouse of a man with amyotrophic lateral sclerosis (ALS). It poignantly illustrates two of the most critical
issues for any person with an acquired neurogenic or neuromuscular
disability: communicative competence and self-determination. *Communicative competence* is the "quality or state of being functionally adequate
in daily communication and of having sufficient knowledge, judgment,
and skills to communicate effectively" (Light, 1989, p. 138). People who
are competent communicators are able to effectively fulfill daily

137

communication goals, such as expressing needs and wants, exchanging information, developing social closeness with others, and fulfilling social etiquette routines (Light, 1997). *Self-determination* is defined as deciding one's own fate or course of action without compulsion from others (*The American Heritage Dictionary of the English Language*, 1992). Self-determined people act as the primary causal agents in their lives; they make choices and decisions without interference from others (Wehmeyer, 1996).

Communicative competence and self-determination are at the core of our existence as human beings. Together they allow us to define who we are, what dreams we have, how these dreams are realized (or not), and what connections and relationships we build with others. Communicative competence and self-determination are fundamental to the quality of our lives. They underlie the essence of our humanity.

There is growing recognition of the importance of communicative competence and self-determination in the fields of augmentative and alternative communication (AAC) and special education, but discussions of these issues have focused primarily on children and young adults with congenital disabilities (e.g., Fried-Oken, Bersani, Anctil, & Staeheley, 1998; Light & Binger, 1998; Sands & Wehmeyer, 1996). To date, much less attention has been given to the challenges of rebuilding communicative competence and self-determination with adults who have acquired neurologic and neuromuscular disabilities. Thus, this chapter has three main objectives: 1) to identify basic issues underlying the attainment of communicative competence and self-determination for individuals with acquired disabilities who require AAC; 2) to review what is known about rebuilding communicative competence and self-determination with individuals with acquired disabilities; and 3) to highlight what is *not* known and thus to suggest future research directions to advance the field.

OVERVIEW OF COMMUNICATIVE
COMPETENCE AND SELF-DETERMINATION

Communicative competence and self-determination are separate constructs, but they are highly interdependent (M. Fried-Oken & H. Bersani, personal communication, August, 1998). People cannot be fully self-determined without being competent communicators. In other words, people cannot act as the primary causal agents in their lives without being able to communicate effectively with others to make their decisions and choices known and understood. Similarly, people cannot become competent communicators without being self-determined. In order to attain communicative competence, people must be able to decide what they want to achieve within their interactions, plan how to achieve these goals, and act to achieve them. They must be able to act autonomously.

Both communicative competence and self-determination are learned; they are not innate. Communicative competence and self-determination are built over time through social experiences. In fact, a significant amount of learning is required to become a competent communicator and a self-determined person. The journey to attain communicative competence and self-determination requires many years of experience as a communicator and a decision-maker. The process begins in infancy and continues through childhood and adolescence to adulthood.

Adults with acquired neurogenic and neuromuscular disabilities, because they are *adults*, typically were communicatively competent and self-determined prior to the onset of their disabilities. Indeed, for most adults without disabilities, communicative competence and self-determination are firmly established; they are typically taken for granted. The sudden onset, for example, of a traumatic brain injury (TBI) or stroke or the onset of a degenerative neurological disorder such as ALS can result in motor, sensory-perceptual, cognitive, and/or language impairments so significant that the individual's communicative competence and self-determination are seriously affected. Communicative competence and self-determination rest on the individual's knowledge, judgment, and skills in a variety of interrelated domains. As a result, these abilities are both vulnerable: The loss of function in any of the domains may negatively affect an individual's communicative competence and self-determination.

Communicative competence and self-determination are not absolute constructs; rather, they are context-dependent. Adults with acquired disabilities may be communicatively competent and self-determined within some situations but not in others because of different environmental demands, constraints, opportunities, and adaptations. Although communicative competence and self-determination depend, to a great extent, on the individual's knowledge, judgment, and skills, an individual's communicative competence and self-determination can be enhanced or impeded by the actions of others and by the practices of society as a whole. The onset of an acquired neurogenic or neuromuscular disability can negatively affect how others perceive an individual and how society treats the individual. This sudden change in social status and others' perceptions can alter an individual's access to life experiences and to opportunities to communicate and make decisions.

The onset of an acquired neurogenic or neuromuscular disability can affect an individual's communicative competence and self-determination in two ways: 1) by affecting the individual's knowledge, judgment, skills, and motivation to be a competent communicator and a self-determined person and 2) by affecting others' perceptions of the individual and thus limiting opportunities for the individual to communicate and make decisions. In order to better understand the impact of acquired neurogenic and neuromuscular disabilities on communicative competence and self-determination, let's consider each of these constructs in more detail.

COMMUNICATIVE COMPETENCE

Light proposed that communicative competence is the "quality or state of being *functionally adequate* in daily communication, of having *sufficient knowledge, judgment, and skills* to communicate effectively with others" (1989, p. 138, italics added). Three principles were highlighted in this definition: 1) functionality of communication, 2) adequacy of communication, and 3) sufficiency of knowledge, judgment, and skills to communicate effectively. Each of these principles is next considered in relation to people with acquired disabilities who require AAC.

Functionality of Communication

Functional communication implies utility within the demands of daily living (Light, 1989). Communication demands vary significantly across individuals based on each individual's personal interests and goals, partner characteristics, and environmental factors. For example, communication demands for a man with aphasia who is married, has two adolescent children, works as a manager for a large company, and serves as a lay preacher with his church will vary significantly from those for a man with aphasia who is retired, lives in a nursing home, and has few visitors.

Communicative competence means that people are able to attain their communication goals. Light (1988) proposed that adults typically have four main goals in their communicative interactions—to express needs and wants, develop social closeness, exchange information, and fulfill social etiquette routines. (See Table 1 for a summary of these four communication goals, their characteristics, and examples of these types of interactions for adults generally and for adults with acquired disabilities specifically.)

Expression of Needs and Wants   One basic reason that people communicate is to express their needs and wants, specifically to regulate someone else's behavior as a means to obtain desired objects or actions or to reject undesirable objects or actions (Light, 1988). Adults

Table 1.   Characteristics of the four main communication goals

	Communication goals			
Characteristics	Expression of needs and wants	Social closeness	Information exchange	Social etiquette
Goal of the interaction	To regulate the behavior of others to fulfill needs/wants (Light, 1988)	To establish and develop personal relationships (Light, 1988)	To obtain information and/or impart information (Light, 1988)	To conform to social conventions of politeness (Light, 1988)
Focus of the interaction	Desired object or action (Light, 1988)	Interpersonal relationships (Light, 1988)	Information (Light, 1988)	Social convention (Light, 1988)
Partners	Familiar or unfamiliar (Light, 1988)	Usually familiar (Light, 1988)	Familiar or unfamiliar (Light, 1988)	Usually unfamiliar or acquaintances (Light, 1988)
Primary communication demands	Emphasis on initiating the interaction and indicating the desired object or action	Emphasis on maintaining the interaction and establishing social bonds	Emphasis on developing the topic (i.e., the information)	Emphasis on fulfilling designated turns politely
Examples of interactions for adults generally	Commercial transactions, expressions of preference, requests for assistance	Social interactions with spouse, children, and other relatives; friends	Exchange of information in education, work, or community environments	Greetings and brief social exchanges with service people, colleagues, and so forth
Examples of interactions unique to adults with acquired disabilities	Expressions of needs and wants related to comfort, daily care, physical well-being, medical issues/ interventions	Healing conversation, interactions to rebuild relationships with family and friends	Exchange of information with professionals about prognosis, treatment, and so forth; advocacy work	Not applicable

who do not have disabilities are usually independent in all activities of daily living (ADL). As a result, expressions of needs and wants play a less significant role in their lives. For these adults, interactions to express needs and wants typically focus on commercial interactions (e.g., ordering food in a restaurant, ordering clothes from a catalog over the telephone, negotiating the price of a new car), expressions of preferences (e.g., asking for a favorite dessert), or requests for assistance (e.g., asking for a ride home after work, asking someone to babysit). Many individuals with acquired neurogenic and neuromuscular disabilities may need to communicate to express these same types of needs and wants.

However, some individuals with acquired disabilities, especially people who have significant motor impairments, may have additional needs and wants to communicate to ensure their comfort, daily care, and physical well-being. For these individuals, expressions of needs and wants may play a more dominant role in daily interactions. For example, Kathy Neill, the wife of a man with ALS, wrote this account describing the importance of expressions of needs and wants for her husband:

> You want to scratch your nose and can't because the hand will not reach the nose. Your glasses are dirty and you can't clean them.... You are always wanting something: "Move my foot," "Pull me up in the wheelchair," "Put me on the potty chair," "Clean my glasses," "My leg needs to be moved again," "Fix me an ice cream float," "Fix the pillow," "The neck brace needs to be tightened again." (1998, p. 26)

The focus in these interactions to express needs and wants is not on the people, but rather on the desired object or action (Light, 1988). Once the object or action is attained (or rejected if it is undesirable), the communication usually ends. In general, these interactions are fairly predictable. They are typically quite short, and the linguistic demands are minimal.

Some of the needs and wants expressed by individuals who have acquired disabilities are of critical importance. For example, Molly Franco, a woman who had ALS, described one of her most significant needs and wants in the late stages of her life:

> I have typed up a form making it clear that I do not wish to be placed on a ventilator should I be in a position of not being able to breathe naturally. I think it covers everything and I would need to have it with me in case I couldn't write, "NO THANKS." (1998, p. 168)

Here, Franco described a communication goal of the highest priority. This goal demands extreme precision of communication; there can be no mistake.

As is evident in Franco's account, expressions of needs and wants are of critical importance to the realization of self-determination. It is through these types of interactions that people make their choices and decisions known and exert control over their lives. (See the section called "Self-Determination" for further discussion of choice making and decision making.)

Social Closeness   A second reason that people communicate is to establish, maintain, and develop social relationships (Light, 1988). These interactions contrast sharply with those to express needs and wants. In social closeness interactions, the focus is on the participants and their relationship (Light, 1988). The interaction itself is what is important. According to Light (1997), interactions to build social closeness may take on various forms; they may involve extended conversation or minimal linguistic content—a smile, eye contact, a shared laugh. Social closeness interactions are "at the very roots of a person's sense of self" (Sarno, 1991, p. 499). Beth O'Brien, the mother of a young man who had a TBI, shared the following reflection about the critical importance of social closeness interactions for her son: "The most difficult part of John's injury for both of us has been his terrible loneliness. He yearns for the companionship of other young people, for the activities that are important for anyone his age" (1987, p. 425).

Because interactions to develop social closeness are so fundamental to the quality of our lives, they carry a special significance for adults with acquired disabilities. Some of these individuals may be facing death; others may have experienced a severe trauma that has changed their lives dramatically. As a result, these individuals may feel an acute need to communicate with others to share their experiences and their hopes and fears. Jaffe described these interactions as "healing conversations" (1981, p. 253). Morrie Schwartz, a man with ALS, wrote the following description of the fundamental importance of interactions for social closeness in his life:

> I have a loving family and many loving friends.... They come regularly, and we talk about what's going on in the world, what's going on with us spiritually, we exchange our loving feelings. We cry with each other. We talk about how meaningful we've been to each other; we touch and hold each other. (1996, p. 121)

The onset of neurogenic and neuromuscular disabilities, whether sudden or gradual, effects fundamental changes in people (Beukelman & Yorkston, 1991). As a result of these changes, the most significant interpersonal relationships in the lives of individuals with acquired disabilities also changed irrevocably. For example, Le Dorze and Brassard (1995) investigated the changes in interpersonal relationships experienced by individuals with aphasia and their families and friends. The participants who had aphasia identified the fundamental changes in their interpersonal relationships following their stroke, including disruption of family relationships, friction with their spouse, misunderstanding by their spouse, loss of authority over children, fewer contacts with brothers and sisters, loss of friends, and anxiety when meeting strangers or when making new friends (Le Dorze & Brassard, 1995). Their relatives and friends reported changes in their interpersonal relationships with the individuals who had aphasia, including changed perceptions of the person with aphasia, role changes, changes in intimacy, changes in household habits, heightened responsibilities (e.g., managing finances, providing medical care, providing assistance with ADLs), and loss of friends (Le Dorze & Brassard, 1995).

Jean-Dominique Bauby, a 43-year-old man who had a brain-stem stroke, reflected on the fundamental changes he experienced in his relationships with his wife, his children, his friends, and his work associates as a result of his stroke; he explained that all the certainties of his former relationships collapsed and his "nearest and dearest" became "strangers" (1997, p. 56). Finding ways to communicate effectively to rebuild close relationships is a priority for most adults with acquired disabilities and their families and friends. The mother of Nate, who has TBI as a result of a motorcycle accident, described this need as follows: "I know it is Nate and I love him, but he doesn't look like Nate, talk like Nate, or act like Nate anymore" (N. McAllister, personal communication, August 1988). This mother described how important it was for her to get to know her son again and build a new relationship with him.

For adults with acquired disabilities, interactions for social closeness are critical to the quality of their lives. Too often these communication goals are neglected in AAC interventions (Light, 1997). For example, Light (1997) recounted the story of a young woman who had severe physical and communication disabilities resulting from a brain tumor. She was married and had a young son. Initially, AAC interventions had focused on providing her with the means to communicate basic needs and wants (e.g., food, personal care items); she rejected these systems, and so did her family. Expressing basic needs and wants was *not* a priority for her; rather, her greatest priority was to reestablish the most important relationships in her life—her relationships with her husband, her son, her parents, and her friends. The initial AAC interventions failed because they did not provide her with a means to meet her most important communication goal—developing social closeness.

For many adults with acquired disabilities, the loss of access to communication to maintain personal bonds is far more devastating than the loss of access to communication to exchange information or to express needs and wants (Lyon, 1998). A number of researchers have proposed interventions to facilitate social closeness for adults with acquired disabilities. For example, Lasker and Beukelman (1998) and Waller and Newell (1997) investigated the use of augmented storytelling as a means for adults with aphasia to maintain social interactions with others. Fox and Fried-Oken (1998) described the role of a stroke club in facilitating social interactions for people with aphasia.

Interactions to develop social closeness are critical not only to the development of satisfying interpersonal relationships but also to the realization of self-determination. Social closeness interactions allow people to find the support and affirmation necessary to help them define their dreams, set goals, make decisions, and solve problems in order to enhance the quality of their lives. These social support systems are critical to all adults but may be especially important to those who have significant neurological impairments, for they may require significant social support to resume control over their lives (Turnbull et al., 1996; Ylvisaker & Feeney, 1996). (See the section called "Self-Determination" for further discussion of social and cognitive supports for self-determination.)

Exchanging Information   A third reason that people communicate is to acquire information from others or to share information with others (Light, 1988). In these interactions, the focus is on the information (see Table 1). These types of interactions are of central importance in educational and vocational environments. The importance of information exchange in the lives of adults with acquired disabilities varies greatly depending on the nature of their disabilities and their lifestyles. For example, some young adults with acquired disabilities may elect to reenter the work force or return to school after the onset of their disability; these adults face significant demands for information exchange in their educational and vocational environments. In contrast, many older individuals may have retired from their jobs and may communicate with others primarily for social purposes. Interactions for information exchange may be less central in their lives.

In general, interactions to exchange information impose complex linguistic demands. These interactions can be lengthy. The range of topics can be varied, and an individual's vocabulary needs can be diverse. The content and accuracy of the communication is very important; as a result, there is a low tolerance for communication breakdown in these types of interactions.

Ironically, the onset of acquired neurogenic and neuromuscular disabilities imposes new demands for effective information exchange as individuals attempt to learn about their disabilities, prognosis, treatment options, resources, and funding. This information exchange with professionals is critical to the realization of self-determination, for it determines whether or not adults with acquired disabilities have the necessary information to make informed choices and decisions. In fact, effective information exchange is the cornerstone of "informed" consent (Gillis, 1996). Unfortunately, this information exchange often is not facilitated effectively by the professionals involved (O'Brien, 1987). (See the section called "Self-Determination" for further discussion of these issues.)

Some adults with acquired disabilities may elect to assume advocacy roles following the onset of their disabilities. They may serve as mentors to others with similar disabilities through informal interactions or peer support groups. When adults with acquired disabilities assume advocacy roles, they face significant new demands for effective information exchange. They must be able to ask appropriate questions and provide key disability-related information as well as offer encouragement and support.

Fulfilling Social Etiquette Routines   The fourth reason that people communicate is to fulfill social etiquette expectations. These interactions include greeting a passerby or chatting briefly with the cashier in a store. In these interactions, the focus is on fulfilling the required turns to be polite (Light, 1988). Often these turns are fulfilled automatically, without much thought or real communicative intent (e.g., "Have a nice day!"). According to Light (1988), these interactions are usually brief and are often with acquaintances or strangers. As a result, these interactions are important for adults with acquired disabilities only if they maintain an active community-based life style in which they encounter many people. Some adults with acquired disabilities (e.g., those with ALS) may use their homes as their central base and may not venture out to interact with strangers; their primary interactions may be with family, friends, and familiar caregivers (Beukelman & Mirenda, 1998). As a result, they may have limited need or desire to participate in social etiquette interactions. In contrast, some adults with acquired disabilities may maintain very active lives within their communities and may frequently engage in social etiquette interactions. Because these interactions are so limited in scope and are often automatic, they pose limited communicative demands. Therefore, these interactions may serve as a key "reentry" point for some adults with acquired disabilities to facilitate participation in the community.

Summary of Communication Goals   The importance and the nature of the four communication goals change across the life span (D.R. Beukelman, personal communication, August 1987). Whereas young children initially have a very limited range of communication goals, adults have more varied and complex communication goals. The importance and the nature of these communication goals vary across individuals depending on their lifestyle, their disabilities, their partners, and the demands of their environments.

In order to be optimally effective, AAC interventions should be driven by the communication goals of individual clients. Interventions with adults with acquired disabilities may be particularly challenging because of the number and the complexity of their communication goals. Furthermore, some of these communication goals may be highly significant ones that address critical issues of self-determination, including issues of medical treatment, personal relationships, financial affairs, or legal issues.

Future research is required to investigate the range of communication goals and the priorities of adults with acquired disabilities and to determine effective interventions to support these adults in successfully attaining their communication goals. Goal attainment scaling (cf. Kiresuk & Sherman, 1968) may provide a simple and useful methodology to allow researchers to measure individual progress toward unique goals as well as to quantify and aggregate outcomes across individuals. (See Bailey & Simeonsson, 1988; Kiresuk & Sherman, 1968; Malec, Smigielski, & DePompolo, 1991, for further discussion.)

Adequacy of Communication

Communicative competence does *not* imply complete mastery or expertise; rather, it implies an adequate level of communication to meet important communication goals (Light, 1989). Historically, speech-language interventions with adults with acquired disabilities focused primarily on remediating areas of speech-language impairment in isolation. In this approach, intervention was concentrated on efforts to "repair broken parts" (Lyon, 1998, p. 204) and restore typical performance. This approach seldom resulted in the attainment of communicative competence (Fox & Fried-Oken, 1996).

Interventions to build communicative competence with adults with acquired disabilities focus instead on determining techniques and strategies to allow participants to adequately meet important communication goals in daily life (Fox & Fried-Oken, 1996). In this approach, the emphasis is on minimizing the speech or language impairment and on maximizing function and quality of life. In these interventions, various tools may be used (including natural supports and AAC techniques) to enhance competence (Beukelman & Mirenda, 1998). Interventions to build communicative competence focus on building competencies across a variety of domains, not just on remediating speech or language skills in isolation (e.g., Culp & Haynes, 1999; Garrett, Beukelman, & Low-Morrow, 1989).

Sufficiency of Knowledge, Judgment, and Skills to Communicate Effectively

Light (1989) argued that for individuals who require AAC, communicative competence rests on knowledge, judgment, and skills in four interrelated domains: linguistic, operational, social, and strategic. Table 2 provides an overview of these four domains and examples of the skills in each domain. Individuals with acquired disabilities may demonstrate strengths (or difficulties) in any or all of these domains, depending on the nature and severity of their disabilities and their individual

Table 2.   Knowledge, judgement, and skills required to be a competent communicator

Domain	Examples of knowledge, judgment, and skills required
Linguistic	Develop skills in the language spoken by the family and community • Understand the form, content, and use of spoken language used by others • Develop as many expressive skills (form, content, and use) in the spoken language as appropriate Develop skills in the "language" code of the AAC system(s) • Develop lexical knowledge of AAC symbols; express concepts via AAC • Develop semantic-syntactic skills using AAC; combine AAC symbols meaningfully to express more complex relationships
Operational	Produce unaided symbols (e.g., conventional gestures, pantomime, signs) as required. For example, • Plan and produce the required hand shape, position, orientation, and movement to make "thumbs up" gesture • Plan, produce, and sequence body movements to act out the concept "swimming" • Look up to communicate "yes" Operate aided AAC system(s) as required. For example, • Open communication book, turn pages, and locate desired vocabulary • Use row–column scanning with a single switch to select desired item on a computer-based system • Use paper and pen to draw or to write
Social	Develop sociolinguistic skills • Use discourse strategies appropriately (e.g., turn taking, initiating, maintaining, and terminating interactions, maintaining cohesion and coherence) • Use a full range of communicative functions appropriately (e.g., protest, request clarification, provide information, request information) Develop sociorelational skills. For example, • Project a positive self-image • Convey an interest in others • Put partners at ease • Try to communicate even if mistakes are made
Strategic	Use appropriate compensatory strategies to bypass limitations in linguistic, operational, and/or social skills as required. For example, • Use mementos to bypass linguistic limitations and establish topic of conversation • Use partner prediction when communicating with an alphabet board to bypass operational limitations and enhance rate • Use an introduction strategy to bypass social limitations and put partners at ease

Domains are as defined by Light (1989).

characteristics. Depending on the individual pattern of strengths and difficulties, intervention may be required to build linguistic, operational, or social knowledge, judgment, and skills or to develop compensatory strategies to bypass limitations in these domains.

Linguistic Competence   According to Light (1989), the linguistic demands for people who require AAC are twofold: 1) knowing the language(s) of their family and the broader social community and 2) knowing the "language" code(s) of the AAC system(s) required.

Competence in the Language of the Family and the Community   In order to attain communicative competence, adults with acquired disabilities must be able to understand what others communicate to them. Comprehension skills are essential to their effectiveness as listeners in communicative exchanges (Romski & Sevcik, 1996). For some adults with acquired disabilities who require AAC, receptive language skills may be preserved and intervention in this domain may not be required to attain communicative competence. For other adults with acquired disabilities (e.g., adults with global aphasia), receptive language skills may be severely impaired. Intervention may be required to maximize comprehension of spoken language. AAC strategies and techniques may also be required as prostheses to enhance comprehension. For example, augmented input (i.e., AAC used in conjunction with spoken input) may be required to support the receptive language performance of adults with global aphasia (Beukelman, Mirenda, & Garrett, 1998; Wood, Lasker, Siegel-Causey, Beukelman, & Ball, 1998).

In addition to ensuring adequate comprehension, many adults with acquired disabilities should also be encouraged to develop their expressive skills in the language or languages spoken by their family and broader social community. Beukelman (1987) cautioned that too often clinicians erroneously view it as an "either/or" decision when deciding whether to work to restore natural speech and language function or introduce AAC techniques and strategies. "Best practices" suggest that interventions should focus on 1) maximizing natural speech and language function as appropriate and 2) providing AAC to augment natural speech and language as required. Future research is required to evaluate the outcomes of this integrative approach to intervention, including not only its effect on speech and language performance but also its impact on communicative competence, self-determination, quality of life, and consumer satisfaction.

Language Differences   It is important to note that, in some cases, the primary language of the individual with an acquired disability may not coincide with that spoken by the broader social community. For example, Achenbach and Zuskin (personal communication, April 1999) discussed a man with aphasia who required AAC whose first language was German, although the language of his broader social community was English. In situations such as this, careful assessment of the individual's communication goals and priorities will determine whether intervention should focus on more than one language or whether one language should assume precedence because it is the language spoken in the primary communication milieu. Clearly, the linguistic demands imposed on the individual with an acquired disability are multiplied and the intervention challenges are much more complex.

Competence in the "Language" Code of the AAC System(s) The language demands for adults who require AAC are not limited to building receptive and expressive skills in the language(s) of their family and community. Adults who require AAC must also learn the "language" code of their AAC system(s). Specifically, they must develop lexical knowledge and semantic-syntactic knowledge with AAC symbols such as signs, line drawings, Blissymbolics, or written words. Adults with acquired disabilities must learn how to express concepts via AAC symbols and how to combine concepts meaningfully to express more complex relationships.

Some adults with acquired disabilities may rely on AAC symbols that they acquired prior to the onset of their disabilities (e.g., traditional orthography, conventional gestures). However, they may need to learn to use these symbols in new ways (e.g., using traditional orthography for face-to-face conversation rather than in prepared, written communication). Some adults with acquired disabilities, such as those with severe global aphasia, may demonstrate significant impairments in their spelling skills and may not be able to rely on traditional orthography to facilitate their communication. They may not be able to use alphabet or word boards or computer-based communication aids that require spelling. These individuals need to use other types of AAC symbols to enhance their communication (e.g., line drawings, AmerInd, Minspeak codes). These AAC symbols require new learning of the symbol–referent associations.

In their discussion of individuals with severe congenital impairments, Romski and Sevcik (1992) described two different patterns of AAC symbol learning: one for individuals with severe comprehension impairments and the other for individuals with adequate comprehension of spoken language. In the first pattern, individuals who had significant comprehension impairments had to use contextual cues in the environment to learn the relationships between the AAC symbols and real-world referents; learning of AAC symbols was slow. In the second pattern, individuals with functional comprehension skills used their understanding of spoken language as a bridge to establish the relationship between the AAC symbols and the spoken words that they already understood; as a result, learning of AAC symbols was much faster. These two patterns of learning may be relevant to adults with acquired disabilities as well.

There is ample evidence in the literature to indicate that adults with acquired disabilities *can* learn various types of AAC symbols as representations for words and concepts (e.g., Bailey, 1983; Beck & Fritz, 1998; Coelho & Duffy, 1985; Steele, Weinrich, Wertz, Kleczewska, & Carlson, 1989). However, as Kraat (1990) noted, this research had a narrow focus: It investigated whether individuals with acquired disabilities (especially those with severe language impairments) *can* learn certain symbol or sign systems. If the goal is to build communicative competence, then future research should investigate which configurations of AAC techniques and strategies are most effective in allowing adults with acquired disabilities to meet their communication goals, given their residual capabilities and impairments.

Regardless of the AAC systems used, some new learning is required for adults with acquired disabilities to develop an adequate level of competence encoding meaning via AAC symbols. The goal should be to minimize these learning "costs" while maximizing the power of communication (Beukelman, 1991). For those adults who have significant language impairments, new language learning may be difficult and may require significant time and effort. This learning may be especially challenging because there is a distinct asymmetry between the primary channel of input (i.e., natural speech) and the channels of expression (e.g., natural speech and AAC symbols such as gestures, line drawings, photographs, and printed words) (Smith & Grove, 1996). For adults with acquired disabilities, there is also a distinct contrast between the primary channel of expression they used premorbidly (i.e., natural speech) and the channels of expression that they are required to use after the onset of their disabilities (e.g., natural speech, various AAC techniques). These differences no doubt complicate the learning process for many adults with acquired disabilities. Learning the language code of AAC systems may be further complicated because there is limited availability of AAC symbols within the environment and there are few models of effective AAC use.

Operational Competence   As adults with acquired disabilities are introduced to AAC systems to augment their communication, they must develop the operational skills to use these systems accurately, efficiently, and appropriately. *Operational competence* refers to the skills to physically produce unaided AAC symbols (e.g., gestures, pantomime, signs) and the knowledge and skills to technically operate aided AAC systems (e.g., communication books, computer-based voice output communication aids [VOCAs]). (See Table 2 for examples of operational skills.) Although adults with acquired disabilities may have had some experience using conventional gestures, pantomime, writing, drawing, or standard computer systems premorbidly, they will face many new operational requirements as they learn to use AAC to augment their communication in daily interactions.

Currently, many AAC systems impose complex cognitive, linguistic, sensory-perceptual, and motor demands. The complexity of these operational demands may overtax the cognitive resources of adults with acquired disabilities and may leave them with few resources to cope with the linguistic, social, and strategic demands of interactions, thus impairing their communicative competence. Light (1990) called for research and development to forge a new generation of AAC systems that offer tremendous power of communication but that are so simple in their operational requirements that consumers will be able to focus their time and effort on interacting with others, not on learning operational skills. In order to design more appropriate AAC systems, Light (1990) proposed the following strategies: 1) reconceptualize the problem of communication and seek simpler solutions, 2) ensure that designs reflect the cognitive models held by adults with acquired disabilities so that AAC systems "make sense" to them, 3) provide distinct cues within AAC systems to clearly designate operational requirements and support learning, and 4) build in sufficient flexibility so that systems can evolve seamlessly to meet the changing needs and skills of adults with acquired disabilities.

Beukelman and colleagues have established a line of research to ensure that the next generation of AAC systems better reflect the conceptual models of adults with acquired disabilities. As a first step, they are conducting a series of studies to investigate the organizational capabilities and preferences of adults with ALS, aphasia, TBI, and Parkinson's disease (e.g., Beukelman, Hustad, & Ball, 1998; Hux, Rankin, Beukelman, & Hahn, 1993). Results of these studies will provide empirically based design specifications for the next generation of AAC systems so that the organization of language within these new AAC systems (e.g., alphabetic, taxonomic, schematic) is congruent with the language organization strategies of adults with acquired disabilities. Research is required to extend this line of research and to identify the most effective and efficient protocols for teaching operational skills to adults with acquired disabilities. This research will result in improved AAC systems and instructional protocols that reduce the "cost" of learning AAC for adults with acquired disabilities.

Social Competence　According to Light (1989), the development of linguistic and operational competencies is not sufficient to attain communicative competence; rather, adults with acquired disabilities must also learn how to *use* these linguistic and operational competencies in social interactions. In other words, they must demonstrate social competencies as well. Light (1989) proposed that there are two types of social competencies required to attain communicative competence: sociolinguistic skills and sociorelational skills (see Table 2). Sociolinguistic skills refer to the pragmatic aspects of communication, including the use of appropriate discourse strategies and the use of a range of communicative functions.

Sociorelational skills are knowledge, judgment, and skills in the development of interpersonal relationships. Light (1988) suggested that the following sociorelational skills may enhance the communicative competence of people who use AAC: a positive self-image, an interest in others, a desire to communicate, active participation in interactions, responsiveness to partners, and the ability to put partners at ease. Rubin (1975) and Savignon (1983) discussed the importance of sociorelational skills for second-language learners. They highlighted skills that they believed enhanced the communicative competence of second-language learners: a strong drive to communicate, the willingness to make mistakes in order to communicate, and self-assuredness or what Savignon (1983) referred to as *communicative confidence*. These sociorelational skills may also be important for adults with acquired disabilities who are attempting to rebuild their communicative competence using AAC.

Adults with acquired disabilities have extensive histories that include many experiences in social interactions. Premorbidly, they knew and understood the rules of communicative interactions and the social dynamics of interpersonal relationships. For some adults with acquired disabilities, these sociolinguistic and sociorelational skills may be preserved after the onset of their disability. In fact, they may be able to draw on their social skills to put partners at ease in communicative interactions and overcome linguistic and operational deficits. For example, Light (1997) described a man with Broca's aphasia, Bob, who demonstrated strong sociolinguistic and sociorelational skills. He knew the turn-taking rules of interactions and the rules of topic initiation, maintenance, and termination; most important, he had a strong drive to communicate with others, a genuine interest in others, the willingness to try (and make mistakes if necessary), and the ability to put others at ease in interactions. Bob used these strengths in the social domain (along with a variety of AAC techniques and strategies) to overcome significant expressive language deficits and achieve his most important communication goal—to participate as a lay preacher at his church.

Some adults with acquired disabilities may experience difficulties with sociolinguistic or sociorelational skills and may require intervention to build their competencies in this domain. For example, Brockway (1991) noted that many individuals with TBI may demonstrate socially inappropriate behavior. This was the case for Jim, one of the six participants in the study conducted by Light, Binger, Agate, and Ramsay (1999) to teach individuals who use AAC to ask partner-focused questions. Jim was a 35-year-old man who had experienced TBI at age 20. He understood the turn-taking structure of conversation, but he typically dominated the interaction by talking about himself and his problems. He did not demonstrate an interest in his partners and had few friends. Intervention focused on teaching Jim to use natural speech and AAC to ask partner-focused questions. Results indicated that Jim successfully learned to ask partner-focused questions spontaneously in naturally occurring contexts, generalized this social skill to new partners and contexts, and maintained its use for at least 2 months postintervention. In social validation interviews, Jim, his family, and personal care attendants indicated that Jim interacted more frequently with other people and for longer periods of time as a result of the intervention. Jim and his partners also reported greater satisfaction with the quality of their interactions postintervention. The intervention served to strengthen Jim's social skills and thereby enhanced his communicative competence.

Strategic Competence   Many adults with acquired disabilities who require AAC face significant limitations in their linguistic, operational, and social competencies because of the nature of their cognitive, linguistic, motor, and sensory-perceptual impairments. They must learn compensatory strategies to bypass these functional limitations and to maximize their communication effectiveness. For example, some adults with severe motor impairments who use alphabet boards to communicate may rely on partner prediction to bypass their limitations in operational skills and accelerate their rate of communication. Some adults with significant language impairments may rely on mementos (e.g., a ticket stub, an ad from the newspaper, a photograph) to help them establish topics of conversation and contexts for interaction (see Garrett et al., 1989, for an example of a 74-year-old man with Broca's aphasia who used various mementos to supplement his communication book and enhance his communication). Many adults with acquired disabilities may require an introduction strategy to describe how they communicate and tell unfamiliar partners what to do to facilitate interactions (see Light & Binger, 1998, for an example of a 35-year-old man with TBI who used introduction strategies to put new partners at ease in face-to-face conversations and over the telephone). The compensatory strategies may be long-term strategies used by adults with acquired disabilities to bypass permanent linguistic, operational, and social impairments that are resistant to remediation, or they may be short-term strategies that are used until linguistic, operational, and social skills recover or develop further.

Holland (1982) highlighted the importance of strategic competence for adults with acquired disabilities. She studied 40 adults with aphasia who had severe linguistic deficits in daily interactions. She found that despite their severe linguistic deficits, these adults were successful in their communicative attempts more often than not. She concluded that these adults were able to preserve their communicative competence (at least in some situations) through the use of functional strategies that compensated for significant linguistic deficits.

Sometimes, adults with acquired disabilities may themselves generate an effective repertoire of compensatory strategies to bypass limitations to their linguistic, operational, or social skills; sometimes, family members may contribute useful strategies to the pool as well. Adults with acquired disabilities have rich life experiences from which to draw in developing their repertoire of compensatory strategies. However, few adults with acquired disabilities or their families have any preparation or training in AAC prior to the onset of their disability. As a result, most require intervention to determine which strategies will be most effective for them and how to use these strategies in their daily lives. Ironically, adults with acquired disabilities must develop their repertoire of strategies with limited access, if any, to models of effective communication via AAC. Peer support groups may serve a key role as a conduit for adults with acquired disabilities to share effective strategies with others (Fox & Fried-Oken, 1998; Holland, 1998; O'Brien, 1987). Systematic research is required to document the range of compensatory strategies used by adults with acquired disabilities to circumvent linguistic, operational, and social limitations successfully and to attain communicative competence.

Integration of Linguistic, Operational, Social, and Strategic Competencies   In summary, adults with acquired disabilities must learn to integrate a wide array of skills in order to rebuild their communicative competence. This array of skills includes linguistic and operational skills (i.e., skills in the "tools" of communication) as well as social and strategic skills (i.e., skills in functional interaction). Some of the skills required by adults with acquired disabilities to be competent communicators are the same skills that are required by adults without disabilities (e.g., receptive language skills in the spoken language of the social community, sociolinguistic skills to initiate conversation and to maintain topics appropriately). Depending on the nature of the acquired disability, these skills may remain intact (e.g., as in the case of the receptive language skills of an individual with ALS), or they may be significantly impaired (e.g., as in the case of the receptive language skills of an individual with severe global aphasia). In the former case, no concerted intervention in this particular domain may be required to rebuild the individual's communicative competence, whereas, in the latter case, intervention may clearly be required to rebuild skills in the affected skill domain or to teach strategies to overcome the skill limitations.

Some of the skills required by individuals who use AAC to achieve communicative competence are unique to that group (Light, 1989). These skills include operational skills in the use of AAC systems, skills in the "language code" of the AAC systems, and compensatory strategies to bypass skill limitations in other domains. All of these skills require *new* learning on the part of adults with acquired disabilities.

Rebuilding communicative competence does not rely on a single skill or strategy. Rather, the attainment of communicative competence depends on the *integration* of knowledge, judgment, and skills in linguistic, operational, social, and strategic domains (Light, 1989). To date, the specific constellations of linguistic, operational, social, and strategic skills required to attain communicative competence are not known. Light (1997) suggested that different individuals may use different constellations of linguistic, operational, social, and strategic skills to attain communicative competence. Personality, gender, age, and individual patterns of strengths and deficits may all affect which specific skills contribute to the attainment of communicative competence. Future research is required to investigate the effect of different constellations of skills on the communicative competence of adults with acquired disabilities.

Intervention goals to build knowledge, judgment, and skills in linguistic, operational, social, and strategic domains should be selected on an individual basis with a clear understanding of the individual's strengths, limitations, values, life goals, and priorities (Light, 1997). Ultimately, these interventions should allow adults with acquired disabilities to achieve their most important communication goals, develop significant social relationships, gain greater control of their lives, and realize their self-determination.

SELF-DETERMINATION

According to Wehmeyer, *self-determination* refers to "acting as the primary causal agent in one's life and making choices and decisions free from undue external influence or interference" (1996, p. 24). Self-determination is essential to personal satisfaction and a high quality of life. There are four principles that are fundamental to self-determination:

1) the individual acts autonomously; 2) the behaviors are self-regulated; 3) the person acts in a self-realizing manner; and 4) the person initiates and responds to events in a psychologically empowered manner (Wehmeyer, 1996). Each of these principles is considered as it relates to adults with acquired disabilities.

Autonomy is the development of personal control over one's life (Lewis & Taymans, 1992). Autonomy should not be confused with independence. It does not necessarily mean doing things independently; it means having control over what is being done. This distinction is particularly important for many adults who have acquired disabilities, especially those with severe motor impairments. These individuals may be completely dependent on others in all ADLs, but they may still act autonomously if they exert personal control over important aspects of their lives. In order to exert personal control, adults with acquired disabilities must have the motivation to be in control and the communication skills to convey their wishes to others effectively. Morrie Schwartz, a man with ALS, wrote of the distinction between autonomy and physical independence:

> I have become more and more dependent as my disease has progressed. I am being wheeled around to get everywhere. I am fed, bathed, taken to the john. A whole host of things I did independently and took for granted as being part of my physical self are now done for me by other people. Although I am dependent, I have an independent mind, mature emotions, and I use my independence to keep my essential self going. (1996, p. 73)

It is not enough that people act autonomously; they need to do so in an organized, self-regulated manner in order to be fully self-determined. According to Wehmeyer (1996), *self-regulation* enables people to examine their environments, consider their own knowledge and skills, decide how to act, and make appropriate plans. Self-regulation includes self-management strategies, goal setting, and problem-solving strategies (Wehmeyer, 1996). Some adults with acquired disabilities may act in a self-regulated manner, but others may be impulsive and may require intervention to assist them in learning to regulate their own behaviors (Brockway, 1991).

People who are self-determined are also *self-realizing* (Wehmeyer, 1996). In other words, they have comprehensive and accurate knowledge of themselves, and they capitalize on this knowledge to act effectively (Wehmeyer, Agran, & Hughes, 1998). They know what they want to achieve, what their own strengths and limitations are, and how best to use their skills to achieve their desired outcomes.

Wehmeyer (1992) emphasized that self-determination requires not only abilities but also the right attitude. *Psychological empowerment* is the term Wehmeyer used to describe the attitude or motivation component of self-determination. The motivation to be self-determined refers to the "intrinsic desire, energy, and positive anticipation of the future that result in an openness to learn, undertake challenges, and solve problems" (Turnbull et al., 1996, p. 238). Some adults with acquired disabilities may be highly motivated to maintain their self-determination; they may be psychologically empowered. Others may experience significant depression. The depression may be an organic effect of the damage to the brain, a psychological reaction to the resulting disability or loss of function, or a result of a preexisting condition (Brockway, 1991). Whatever the cause, depression may interfere with people's motivation to be self-determined, for it may result in decreased desire and energy as well as negative feelings about the future and long-term outcomes. People are unlikely to act in a self-determined way unless they believe that it is worthwhile to do so.

Knowledge, Judgment, and Skills to Attain Self-Determination

As with communicative competence, self-determination rests on the integration of knowledge, judgment, and skills in several interrelated domains. Doll, Sands, Wehmeyer, and Palmer (1996) argued that in order to attain self-determination and to act in an autonomous, self-regulated, self-realizing, and psychologically empowered manner, people need to have skills in the following domains: 1) self-awareness, self-knowledge, and self-evaluation; 2) choice making and decision making; 3) metarepresentation; and 4) goal setting and attainment. Table 3 provides an overview of these four domains and examples of skills required in each domain. Let's consider each of these skill domains as it relates to adults with acquired neurogenic and neuromuscular disabilities and their realization as self-determined people.

Self-Awareness, Self-Knowledge, and Self-Evaluation   If people are to act in self-determined ways, they must 1) understand their individual strengths and weaknesses (i.e., self-awareness), 2) know how to use these unique attributes to enhance their quality of life (i.e., self-knowledge), and 3) evaluate their own actions and outcomes clearly (i.e., self-evaluation) (Doll et al., 1996; Wehmeyer, 1996). They must be able to find ways to approach tasks that capitalize on their own strengths and circumvent functional limitations. They must adjust their approaches as necessary based on their success (or failure). Self-awareness, self-knowledge, and self-evaluation rely heavily on metacognitive skills. Individuals not only must act but also must be able to reflect on their actions and the resulting outcomes (Doll et al., 1996).

The onset of acquired neurogenic and neuromuscular disabilities, whether sudden (as in the case of TBI or cerebral vascular accident [CVA]) or more gradual (as in the case of degenerative disorders), inevitably challenges a person's self-awareness, self-knowledge, and self-evaluation. Adults with acquired disabilities may have difficulties with any or all three of these skills depending on the nature of their disabilities and individual characteristics.

Some individuals whose cognitive functioning is impaired may have difficulty recognizing changes in their own skill levels and may demonstrate a general lack of self-awareness. For example, Brockway (1991) noted that many people demonstrate unrealistic self-appraisal and a lack of awareness of their own skills and impairments as a result of TBI. This was the case for Jim, a 35-year-old man who had sustained TBI in a motor vehicle accident at the age of 20 (see Light & Binger, 1998). He had attention and short-term memory problems and demonstrated a significant lack of self-awareness. He was not employed; he had no previous work experience and few marketable job skills. He

Table 3.   Knowledge, judgment, and skills required to be a self-determined person

Domain	Examples of knowledge, judgment, and skills required
Self-awareness, self-knowledge, and self-evaluation	Understand personal strengths and weaknesses Know how to use these attributes to enhance quality of life Evaluate actions and outcomes clearly Adjust self-awareness and self-knowledge accordingly
Choice making and decision making	Indicate an unforced selection between two or more alternatives, communicate basic choices Communicate more complex choices, preferences, and opinions Make important decisions • Generate options • Anticipate consequences • Understand potential risks and benefits • Assess probability of consequences occurring • Identify best course of action • Have rational reasons for the decision made
Metarepresentation	Think about and understand others' actions, feelings, and intentions Evaluate how own actions will affect others Assess social situations, decide what to do and say Evaluate social consequences of decisions
Goal setting and attainment	Set goals that are challenging but realistic Plan and pursue course of action that is appropriate and produces desired outcome Monitor progress toward goals Evaluate outcomes Adjust goal and/or plan of action accordingly

Domain categories are as outlined by Doll, Sands, Wehmeyer, and Palmer (1996).

expressed a strong interest in securing employment, but he was adamant that he wanted his first job to be a high-level job with the government in the defense department. Jim had difficulty understanding his strengths and limitations, evaluating his performance, and using his self-awareness and evaluation to determine appropriate employment goals.

In other cases, adults with acquired disabilities may have preserved their metacognitive skills sufficiently to be able to reflect on their performance and evaluate outcomes, but they may set unrealistic standards of achievement based on their premorbid status. This was the case with Paul, a man in his forties who had aphasia as a result of a stroke (J. McCarthy, personal communication, September, 1997). Prior to his stroke, Paul had been a manager with a construction firm and had been a recreational sailor; he had had a very active social life. After his stroke, he consistently compared his performance with his past capabilities prior to the stroke. As a result, he underestimated his strengths significantly and concluded that he was "incompetent." He was unwilling to attempt many tasks that he could have completed successfully. Paul did not believe that he had the capacity to act successfully and autonomously. He required intervention to support him in developing more realistic self-evaluation skills.

Finally, some adults with acquired disabilities may have a well-developed understanding of their strengths and limitations (i.e., self-awareness), but they may have limited knowledge of how to use these unique attributes to enhance their quality of life (i.e., self-knowledge). Most adults with acquired disabilities have limited, if any, preparation for their experience with significant disabilities. As a result, they may not know how to use their residual strengths to achieve their goals and how to develop compensatory strategies to bypass functional limitations. Self-help groups or mentoring programs conducted by people with similar disabilities who have successfully overcome many challenges and have developed effective compensatory strategies may be useful techniques to build greater self-knowledge in people with acquired disabilities. The power of peer support groups to affirm the self-worth of people with disabilities and extend their self-knowledge is illustrated in the case study of RR, a man with aphasia (Holland, 1998). Holland noted that, despite the efficacy of the communication intervention provided, RR emphasized that "he did not begin to recover until he met other people who had aphasia" (1998, p. 63). These interactions with others who have similar disabilities served to reaffirm self-worth, extend self-awareness and self-knowledge, and enhance motivation to attain self-determination. Future research is required to investigate the efficacy of peer support groups and other interventions to develop the self-awareness, self-knowledge, and self-evaluation skills of people with acquired disabilities.

Choice Making and Decision Making   Self-determination requires more than self-awareness, self-knowledge, and self-evaluation; it also requires that people be able to make appropriate choices and decisions (Doll et al., 1996). At a basic level, these choices may include deciding which clothes to wear, what food to eat, or what recreation activities to pursue. In order to communicate a basic choice, the individual must be able to reliably indicate an uncoerced selection between two or more alternatives. This selection can be indicated by vocalizing, gesturing, or eye pointing toward the desired item, or it may be communicated via communication boards, books, or computer-based technologies.

Most individuals with acquired disabilities, even those with the most severe disabilities, are able to communicate basic choices to others, although they may require partner support to do so. Beukelman and colleagues (1998) described the following strategies to support adults with profound cognitive and linguistic disorders in communicating basic choices: 1) partners provide opportunities for the adult to communicate choices within familiar daily routines; 2) partners use visual cues to mark the choices available and to support comprehension of oral language (e.g., holding up clothing items, offering food items, showing pictures of possible birthday gifts from a catalog); and 3) the adult indicates the desired choice by pointing, nodding, reaching for the item, vocalizing, or showing changes in facial expression. Some people who have severe neurological impairments may remain Basic Choice communicators (Beukelman et al., 1998). Other adults who have experienced CVA or TBI may function as basic choice communicators during the early stages of their recovery, but may develop more complex choice-making and decision-making skills over time as they recover.

Garrett and Beukelman (1992, 1995) described a written-choice strategy to allow people who require AAC to communicate more complex choices, preferences, and opinions. In the written-choice strategy, the partner generates a list of written word choices pertinent to the conversation, and the adult who requires AAC participates by pointing to the choices and thus communicating his or her preferences, thoughts, and opinions. For example, if the conversation is about the upcoming election, the partner might ask the adult which candidate he or she likes and then generate a list of the candidates' names, and the adult can express his or her opinion by pointing to the preferred candidate's name. (See Garrett & Beukelman, 1992, 1995, for further discussion of the written-choice strategy.)

At a more complex level, adults with acquired disabilities may face critical decisions about living arrangements, employment, finances, personal relationships, and medical care or rehabilitation. Keith Sunbeam, a man with ALS, wrote the following account that illustrates how important it was to him to be able to make autonomous decisions after the onset of his disability:

> I do believe in euthanasia, once I reach a point where I feel I can no longer tolerate my existence. I would like to be able to make one last decision. When and how to die is not a privilege everyone gets to make. (1998, p. 216)

As decisions become more complex, they require more elaborated cognitive skills and communication skills. In order to make appropriate decisions, individuals who require AAC must be able to generate alternative courses of action, anticipate the consequences of each of these options, understand the potential risks and benefits, assess the probability of these consequences occurring, identify the best course of action, and have rational reasons for the decision made (Wehmeyer, 1998). Obviously, this type of complex decision making requires higher-order cognitive processes. Some adults with acquired disabilities may have unimpaired cognitive processes and may be fully capable of making complex decisions independently.

Others may have some level of cognitive impairment and may require support or assistance with more complex decision making. For example, Ylvisaker and Feeney (1996) described Joe, a man who had sustained a TBI in a motorcycle accident at age 24. He had significant impairment in his cognitive functioning, especially his executive system. As a result, he had difficulty with making realistic decisions, problem solving, predicting the outcomes and consequences of his actions, and considering alternative courses of action. Ylvisaker and Feeney (1996) described the use of "supported cognition" to build Joe's decision-making skills and support his self-determination. This intervention involved regular brainstorming and problem-solving sessions with Joe in which the partner guided Joe through the decision-making process by asking him a series of questions (e.g., What do you really want to accomplish? What can you do to get there? What is standing in your way? What help do you need to accomplish your goal?). The partner did *not* provide solutions or make decisions for Joe; the partner simply provided scaffolding support to assist Joe in the decision-making process.

In addition to the supported cognition intervention described by Ylvisaker and Feeney (1996), the literature also suggests several other interventions that may be effective techniques to provide support in rebuilding decision-making skills. These interventions were developed for adolescents and adults with congenital disabilities, but they may be adapted to meet the needs of adults with acquired disabilities who require support in this domain. For example, Wehmeyer (1998) described an instructional program used to support adolescents and young adults with disabilities in goal setting and decision making. In this program, participants learn how to complete a five-step decision-making process (i.e., define the problem, outline the options, identify the outcome of each option, take action, and get excited) and then practice applying the steps to make decisions that are relevant in their lives. Light, McNaughton, and colleagues (1999) developed an instructional program, available on the Internet, to teach effective communication skills, collaborative decision-making and problem-solving skills, and access to disability-related information for adults who require AAC; research to evaluate the efficacy of this instructional program is being conducted. Light, McNaughton, and colleagues (1999) are also involved in a research study to investigate the efficacy of a mentoring program available on the Internet as a technique to build effective problem-solving and decision-making skills with adolescents and young adults who require AAC. In this program, adolescents and young adults who require AAC are paired with older individuals who also use AAC and who have successfully attained key personal, social, educational, and vocational goals. These adults serve as mentors and interact on a regular basis via electronic mail with the adolescents and young adults to provide encouragement and to provide support with collaborative goal setting and problem solving.

As noted previously, most of the programs described were developed to meet the needs of adolescents and adults who use AAC who have congenital disabilities. Unfortunately, there have been few attempts to modify these types of interventions to meet the needs of adults with acquired disabilities. One reason for the lack of attention to these types of interventions for adults with acquired disabilities may be the perceived lack of "fit" of these types of interventions within traditional medical and rehabilitation programs. Research is required to develop effective interventions to meet the needs of adults with acquired disabilities and to evaluate their efficacy in rebuilding self-determination.

Metarepresentation   If people are going to make appropriate decisions, they must be able to think about others and understand their perspectives (Doll et al., 1996). They must be able to understand others' actions, feelings, and intentions and must be able to evaluate how their own actions will affect others (Doll et al., 1996). In other words, they must have effective metarepresentation skills (Doll et al., 1996). Metarepresentation skills allow people to assess social situations and then decide what to do or say. They are critical to effective decision making and problem solving. People without well-developed metarepresentation skills typically assume that others see things as they themselves do and that others act as they would. This erroneous assumption is especially problematic in social problem-solving situations, for it leads people to misjudge the probable consequences of their actions.

Adults with acquired disabilities who do not have significant cognitive impairments may retain adequate metarepresentation skills for effective problem solving to support their self-determination. However, adults who have significant cognitive impairments may have particular difficulty with the metacognitive functions required to understand and take into account others' perspectives. These difficulties may be aggravated by their significant communication impairments, which may limit the effectiveness of their social interactions with others and may restrict their access to essential information about others' feelings, intentions, and reactions.

Many adults with acquired disabilities, especially those who have TBI, may also have significant impairments to their working memory (Honsinger & Yorkston, 1991). As a result, they may have difficulty with retaining memory and processing the wide range of information required for social problem solving (e.g., the proposed act or decision, the other people involved, their personalities and values, their anticipated reactions, consequences of these reactions). This was the case for Jim, a 35-year-old man who had sustained a TBI at the age of 20 (Light, Binger, et al., 1999). Jim reported that social isolation was one of his most significant problems. He complained that his old friends avoided him and that he had difficulty in making new friends. However, he had significant difficulties with the metarepresentation skills required to solve this social problem. He blamed others for his social isolation. He had difficulty with understanding others' actions, feelings, and intentions, and evaluating how his own actions affected others.

Various interventions may be applicable to build metarepresentation skills with adults who have acquired disabilities, including 1) supported cognition, in which others provide the external scaffolding to support social problem solving and metarepresentation, 2) specific interventions to teach metarepresentation skills and social problem-solving strategies using role plays, and 3) interventions to provide external structures or cues to support working memory function in social problem solving (e.g., memory notebooks or cards listing questions to consider in social problem solving). Research is urgently required to develop, implement, and evaluate the efficacy of these types of interventions for adults with acquired disabilities.

Goal Setting and Attainment   People who are self-determined are purposeful: They define goals, make plans, and act in a purposeful way to achieve these goals (Doll et al., 1996). Effective goal setting is inextricably linked to the other skill domains discussed earlier: self-awareness, self-knowledge, and self-evaluation; decision making; and metarepresentation skills. Effective goal setting requires people to 1) set goals that are challenging but realistic, 2) plan an appropriate course of action to attain the desired outcomes, 3) monitor progress toward desired goals, 4) evaluate outcomes, and 5) adjust goals and plans of action according to these outcomes (Mithaug, 1996; Wehmeyer, 1996). People who are not adept at goal setting and attainment typically set their expectations too low or too high, fail to develop appropriate plans to meet their goals or expectations, and fail to adjust their expectations or their course of action if they do not attain their goals (Mithaug, 1996).

Goal attainment is affected by the individual's skills and the effort or the intensity of the individual's desire to achieve the goal (Wehmeyer, 1996). In some situations, luck or other external forces also play a role in determining goal attainment (Doll et al., 1996). People who are self-determined understand the interplay of these three factors (i.e., skill, effort, and luck) in goal attainment and are able to plan accordingly. People who are not self-determined often believe that their success (or failure) results only from luck or from some other external force beyond their control (Mithaug, 1996).

People who are self-determined are not always successful. In fact, goal-oriented behavior can result in three possible outcomes: 1) the desired outcome, 2) unintended outcomes, or 3) no outcome (Wehmeyer, 1996). Each of these possible outcomes may or may not turn out to be beneficial, depending on the appropriateness of the goal and environmental factors. It is important to note that failure to meet a goal can be a rich learning experience, provided the individual has the skills and the support to evaluate the outcome and to adjust goals and plans accordingly.

Goals set by adults with acquired disabilities may or may not correspond to those set by the professionals providing services. For example, Wertz (1998) described a 37-year-old man with aphasia, Doug. Wertz's goals as Doug's speech-language pathologist were to increase Doug's speech-sound production and to develop his functional communication through gesture, writing, and drawing to as great an extent as possible. Doug's goals were to improve his communication to the point where he could reenter his social circle and "hang out with the guys," tinker with his car, and watch television. Once Doug had met his goals, he terminated therapy, although he had not yet attained his "therapy" goals.

Integration of Skills to Build Self-Determination   In summary, adults with acquired disabilities must integrate skills from a variety of domains in order to rebuild their self-determination: self-awareness, self-knowledge, and self-evaluation; choice making and decision making; metarepresentation; and goal setting and attainment. Depending on the nature of the disability, some of these skills may be preserved and others may be significantly impaired. In the latter case, intervention is required to rebuild the skills or to identify compensatory strategies to bypass the skill limitations. Research is urgently required to investigate the efficacy of various interventions designed to teach these skills to adults with acquired disabilities in order to rebuild their self-determination.

INFLUENCE OF PARTNERS AND SOCIETY

So far the discussion has focused on the knowledge, judgment, and skills required by individuals who have acquired disabilities to rebuild their communicative competence and self-determination. This discussion has been predicated on the assumption that these individuals have the *opportunity* to be competent communicators and self-determined individuals. Unfortunately, for many individuals with acquired disabilities who require AAC, this is not the case. Instead, they are frequently preempted from opportunities to communicate and make decisions by family members, friends, medical personnel, rehabilitation professionals, and society generally. Without opportunities to communicate and make decisions in their daily lives, the knowledge, judgment, and skills possessed by these individuals may serve limited function. "Ability is of little account without opportunity" (Napoleon Bonaparte, as cited in Wehmeyer, 1998). One cannot be a competent communicator unless one has the opportunity to communicate. One cannot be self-determined unless one has the opportunity to make decisions and choices in daily life. Let's consider the impact of partners and other environmental factors on communicative competence and self-determination in turn.

Impact of Environmental Factors on Communicative Competence

Beukelman and Mirenda (1988) argued that in order to be maximally effective, AAC interventions must be two-pronged. They must focus not only on the individuals who have severe communication disabilities but also on the significant others in these individuals' lives and on society generally. Intervention with the individuals who require AAC ensures that they have the knowledge, judgment, and skills required to communicate effectively. Intervention with the significant others and with society generally ensures that individuals who use AAC have the *opportunity* to communicate. Beukelman and Mirenda (1998) summarized five major types of opportunity barriers that may restrict opportunities for communication by adults with acquired disabilities: policy, practice, attitude, knowledge, and skill barriers. Table 4 provides definitions of these opportunity barriers, examples of opportunity barriers to communicative competence and self-determination, and examples of interventions to overcome these barriers.

Policy and Practice Barriers   Adults with acquired disabilities confront numerous policy and practice barriers (e.g., legislation, regulations, procedures, conventions) that limit their opportunities to attain communicative competence, including 1) limitations on the availability of AAC services, 2) limitations on the quality of AAC services due to the paucity of trained professionals, 3) funding restrictions to support these services, 4) funding restrictions to support the purchase of AAC technologies, 5) eligibility requirements restricting who receives services and for how long, and 6) limited-use policies (i.e., restrictions on the use of AAC systems) in some medical settings or nursing homes. These policy and practice barriers serve to limit access to effective AAC services and AAC systems, thus restricting the opportunities that adults with acquired disabilities have to rebuild their communicative competence.

Intervention to address policy and practice barriers requires public education and concerted advocacy with government organizations and institutional administrations. Organized advocacy groups for adults with acquired disabilities who require AAC are limited in number, perhaps because of the significant communication difficulties experienced by these individuals and perhaps because of competing priorities in their lives. In some cases, legal action may be required to dismantle policy and practice barriers.

Attitude Barriers   Some opportunity barriers occur not because of the policies or practices of agencies or institutions but because of the attitudes of individuals (see Table 4). Attitude barriers may occur with professionals, family, or friends. Jean-Dominique Bauby, a 43-year-old man who had a brain-stem stroke, wrote the following description of the impact of the attitudes of medical professionals on his communication opportunities: "The hospital staff are of two kinds: the majority, who would not dream of leaving the room without first attempting to

Table 4. Opportunity barriers to rebuilding communicative competence and self-determination for adults with acquired disabilities

Type of barrier	Definition	Examples of barriers to communicative competence	Examples of barriers to self-determination	Examples of interventions to overcome opportunity barriers
Policy barriers	Legislative or regulatory decisions that limit opportunities	Funding restrictions on AAC systems or AAC services; Eligibility requirements set by funding agencies that restrict who receives services and for how long; Limited use policies for AAC systems in medical settings or nursing homes	Traditional medical model of service delivery in which medical personnel are the "experts" and the "patient's" decision making and involvement in care are limited	Advocacy and lobbying of institutions to change policies; Political action/lobbying to change legislation; Legal action
Practice barriers	Procedures or conventions (not actual written policies) in a family, workplace, medical center, and so forth that limit opportunities	Lack of appropriate AAC services available; Limited-use practices in hospitals or nursing homes	Limited access to information required to make appropriate decisions regarding care; Cursory opportunities for "informed consent"	Education of administrative personnel to ensure change in practices; Education of staff to support system change; Public awareness activities
Attitude barriers	Beliefs and attitudes of another person that limit opportunities	Reduced expectations for participation and communication by adults who use AAC; Limited attention to communication attempts by adults who use AAC	Perceptions of "incompetence" that result in withholding information and preempting adult who uses AAC from important decision making	Education of family members, co-workers, and friends to address negative attitudes; Education of professionals; Public awareness activities/information dissemination
Knowledge barriers	Another person's lack of knowledge or information that limits opportunities	Lack of knowledge of availability of AAC services; Lack of knowledge of AAC systems	Another person's lack of knowledge of AAC systems that limits his/her understanding of choices and decisions made by the individual	Information dissemination in user-friendly formats; Training in AAC system operation, maintenance, and development
Skill barriers	Another person's lack of skills that limits opportunities	Communication partners who preempt opportunities for communication, chain questions, provide inappropriate language input, fail to request confirmation, and so forth.	Communication partners who do not present choices to individual who uses AAC in an appropriate manner; Communication partners who do not provide scaffolding for supported goal setting and decision making when required	Partner training in interaction skills and support strategies on an individual or small-group basis; Use of an introduction strategy by the individual who uses AAC to explain to partners what they should do

Definitions are from Beukelman and Mirenda (1998).

decipher my SOS messages; and the less conscientious minority, who make their getaway pretending not to notice my distress signals" (1997, p. 40).

Concerted education is required when attitude barriers are encountered among rehabilitation and medical professionals. Bryen (as cited in Blackstone, 1999) described proactive educational activities conducted by Temple University's Institute on Disabilities for medical, dental, and law school students as well as professionals working for law enforcement agencies, the judicial system, and victim services. According to Bryen, outcomes of these workshops (co-taught by consumers who use AAC and professionals) were very positive: Post-intervention, workshop participants reported greater awareness of AAC and greater comfort interacting with people who require AAC. When educational efforts such as these are unsuccessful in changing the attitudes of professionals, administrative intervention may be required.

Frequently, attitude barriers are more subtle than those described by Bauby (1997); however, they may still affect communication opportunities negatively. For example, Neill described her own experiences with her husband, who had ALS, and the attitude barriers that they encountered with family and friends:

> Your friends and some family members do not come to see you because they do not like to see you this way. They all say that they want to remember you the way you used to be, but they don't understand that the mind still needs the conversation and friends and family around. (1998, p. 25)

Education of family and friends may be required to change their attitudes and increase opportunities for communication. Research is required to investigate the most effective techniques for changing attitudes toward adults with acquired disabilities.

Knowledge and Skill Barriers   Even when partners (e.g., family, friends, nursing staff) are willing to communicate with adults with acquired disabilities, they may lack the knowledge and skills to do so effectively (see Table 4). Bauby wrote the following description of the impact of knowledge and skill barriers on his communication using an alphabet board with partner-assisted scanning:

> It is a simple enough system. You read off the alphabet (ESA version, not ABC) until, with a blink of my eye, I stop you at the letter to be noted. ... That, at least, is the theory. In reality, all does not go well for some visitors. Because of nervousness, impatience, or obtuseness, performances vary in the handling of the ... [AAC system]. Crossword fans and Scrabble players have a head start. Girls manage better than boys. By dint of practice some of them know the ... [system] by heart and no longer even turn to our special notebook.... Nervous visitors come most quickly to grief. They reel off

the alphabet tonelessly at top speed, jotting down letters almost at random; and then, seeing the meaningless result, exclaim, "I'm an idiot!" (1997, pp. 20–21)

Knowledge and skill barriers are reduced when partners are competent with the required AAC systems and provide the necessary scaffolding support to facilitate effective communication. Partner strategies reported to facilitate communication with adults with acquired disabilities include

- Knowing how to use the AAC systems
- Using a written-choice communication strategy
- Asking appropriate questions
- Modeling AAC to encourage use
- Giving topic cues through appropriate resource materials
- Responding to comprehension problems by repeating, slowing down, simplifying, or using AAC
- Waiting and giving adequate processing time
- Providing feedback and requesting confirmation (e.g., Collier, 2000; Garrett & Beukelman, 1992, 1995; Kagan & Gailey, 1993; Ladtkow & Culp, 1992; Light & Binger, 1998; Lyon, 1998; Wood et al., 1998)

Future research is required to determine which of these strategies are most beneficial for which adults with acquired disabilities and to investigate which instructional techniques are most effective for teaching these strategies to which partners.

Impact of Environmental Factors on Self-Determination

The rebuilding of self-determination by individuals who have acquired disabilities is dependent not only on their own knowledge, judgment, and skills but also on the *opportunities* available to them to make decisions and act as the causal agents in their own lives. Environmental factors play a critical role in the self-determination process. Some environmental factors may facilitate self-determination, but others may serve as barriers (Abery & Stancliffe, 1996). As with communicative competence, environmental factors that affect self-determination may be related to policy, practice, attitudes, knowledge, and skills (see Table 4).

Policy and Practice Barriers   The self-determination of adults with acquired disabilities is influenced not only by the actions of their immediate partners but also by the policies and practices of society and social institutions (Abery & Stancliffe, 1996). Decisions and events at this level may affect individuals with acquired disabilities directly or indirectly (Abery & Stancliffe, 1996). For example, the structure and practices of traditional medical, rehabilitation, and long-term care facilities may limit the autonomy and decision making of adults with acquired disabilities. Agich (1993) and Porter (1994) argued that the traditional roles of medical and rehabilitation professionals as the dominant experts relegate "patients" to passive roles in which they are expected to be compliant and follow the doctor's orders. Porter called for reforms in these traditional practices to promote egalitarian interaction so that adults with acquired disabilities would have the knowledge, confidence, and opportunity to make autonomous and informed decisions about the nature of their care.

In theory, informed consent is the cornerstone of all medical and rehabilitation treatment. In practice, most adults with acquired disabilities are poorly informed of their options and are given only cursory opportunities to consent to the planned course of treatment (or not). Gillis (1996) cautioned that a signature on a form does not constitute informed consent. Instead, informed consent requires an ongoing dialogue in which 1) the individual is provided with information that he or she can easily understand about the planned goals and course of treatment, alternative treatments, and the anticipated risks and benefits of each option; 2) the individual has the opportunity to ask questions and have these questions answered; and 3) the individual makes a choice without undue external influence or interference (Agich, 1993). "The basic principle underlying informed consent is an individual's right to autonomy or self-determination" (Gillis, 1996, p. 259). Exercising this right requires effective communication between adults with acquired disabilities and service providers.

Unfortunately, many adults with acquired disabilities may never even be offered the opportunity to make decisions about the course of their treatment as they may be considered ineligible for AAC services and other rehabilitation services. Gillis (1996) pointed out the irony: In Western society, in which where equal rights are valued, all should have equal access to rehabilitation services and benefits; however, in practice, rehabilitation services are not the right of all individuals as determined by limitation or eligibility criteria. Achenbach and Cogburn (personal communication, July 1999) described a man who had severe aphasia that illustrates this problem. He had the need and the desire for AAC services to enhance his communicative competence; however, funding agencies questioned his ability to benefit from these services. He had no immediate family able to advocate for him. He had significant difficulties with negotiating the complex service delivery and funding system and advocating for himself because of his severe communication disability. In cases such as this, AAC professionals may be called upon to fulfill advocacy roles as well as their more traditional service provision roles.

Unfortunately, few AAC professionals receive any training as advocates within their pre-professional training programs.

On a more positive note, the importance of self-determination for individuals with disabilities is recognized in federal legislation in the United States. The Technology-Related Assistance for Individuals with Disabilities Act of 1988 (PL 100-407) calls for the provision of "consumer-responsive" services for individuals with disabilities—services that respond to the needs identified as priorities by the individuals receiving the services themselves.

Attitude Barriers   Not all barriers to self-determination are the result of policies and practices. Some barriers result from the attitudes of other people—professionals, family members, and friends (see Table 4). One attitude barrier commonly encountered by adults with acquired disabilities occurs when others perceive them as "incompetent." Adults with severe communication disabilities are particularly vulnerable to such perceptions, for judgments of competence are typically based on a person's ability to express ideas, thoughts, and opinions effectively. When medical and rehabilitation professionals perceive adults with acquired disabilities as incompetent, they may withhold critical information about treatment and may preempt opportunities for decision making. Gillis (1996) cautioned that declaring a person incompetent is a legal act, not a judgment call on the part of clinicians or family.

Jean-Dominique Bauby wrote the following description of the devastating impact of attitude barriers on his opportunities to make informed choices and decisions about his medical treatment:

> When I came to that late-January morning, the hospital ophthalmologist was leaning over me and sewing my right eyelid shut with a needle and thread, just as if he were darning a sock. Irrational terror swept over me. ... He barked out: 'Six months!" I fired off a series of questioning signals with my working eye, but this man—who spent his days peering into people's pupils—was apparently unable to interpret a simple look. ... He was the very model of the couldn't-care-less doctor: arrogant, brusque, sarcastic. ... Disinclined to chat with normal patients, he turned thoroughly evasive in dealing with ghosts of my ilk, apparently incapable of finding words to offer the slightest explanation. (1997, pp. 53–54)

Sometimes the decisions made by adults with acquired disabilities may be contrary to the recommendations of medical and rehabilitation professionals. These situations can be very difficult for the professionals involved who may feel strongly that they are acting in the adults' best interest. Wertz wrote the following account of this type of dilemma in a case description of communication intervention for Doug, who has aphasia:

Treatment ended before I thought it would. The progress Doug made in our two months together prompted me to urge continued treatment. I was more excited about Doug's progress than he was, and he was more satisfied with his progress than I was. About halfway through our second month, Doug indicated he was ready to go home. He had passed a driving test, qualified for disability income, and achieved sufficient communicative ability for his purposes. His plan was to become a person rather that a patient. That was his right, and he exercised it. (1998, p. 31)

In this account, Wertz clearly recognized Doug's right to self-determination, although he did not agree that Doug's decision was the correct decision. Wehmeyer (1996) cautioned that self-determination does not guarantee that all decisions will be good ones or that all outcomes will be positive. However, these mistakes and failures serve as critical learning opportunities for adults with acquired disabilities to build the knowledge, judgment, and skills required to strengthen their self-determination.

Knowledge and Skill Barriers   Even when partners are willing to provide adults with acquired neurogenic and neuromuscular disabilities with the opportunity to make autonomous decisions, these partners (e.g., family, friends, medical and rehabilitation professionals) may lack the knowledge and skills to facilitate this process effectively (see Table 4). As a first step, partners need to be able to communicate effectively with adults with acquired disabilities so that they can present choices in ways that are easily understood and so that they can understand the choices and decisions that are communicated to them. Where knowledge or skill barriers impede the communicative competence of adults with acquired disabilities, these obstacles also have a negative impact on opportunities for self-determination.

In addition, some adults with neurological impairments may require support from facilitators (i.e., the significant others in their lives) to solve problems, set goals, and make informed decisions. Current views suggest that competence is not necessarily an all-or-nothing matter (Gillis, 1996). Rather, some adults with acquired disabilities may be competent to make decisions independently in some domains, but they may require support to make decisions in other domains. For example, Ylvisaker and Feeney (1996) documented the story of Joe, the young man who had experienced TBI at age 24. Joe was able to make basic choices and decisions independently. However, he required scaffolding support from partners to set important goals, make realistic plans, and solve difficult problems. Partners were trained to provide "supported cognition" by asking Joe key questions to guide him through the goal-setting and problem-solving processes. These partners did *not* provide Joe with advice or make decisions for him; rather, they helped him think through the issues in a systematic manner (Ylvisaker & Feeney, 1996).

It is challenging for facilitators to understand the capabilities of their relatives or friends who have acquired disabilities and to know when supports are required (or not). According to Brockway (1991), families (and friends) typically have difficulty with responding appropriately to individuals with TBIs: "At one extreme, the family may reinforce inappropriate behavior and increase dependency; at the other extreme, the family may inappropriately expect the individual to resume preinjury roles and responsibilities fully" (p. 52)

Partners require training to learn when and how to provide cognitive supports and environmental adaptations (as required) in order to effectively support adults with acquired disabilities in rebuilding their self-determination. Turnbull and colleagues argued that a responsive context is critical if adults with disabilities are to attain self-determination:

> A responsive context consists of environments in which opportunities are available for enjoyable and reciprocal relationships, nonjudgmental and informative feedback, a reasonable degree of successive challenges, negotiation of reasonable and constructive limits, open and honest communication, facilitating but not controlling support, and celebratory affirmations of progress. (1996, p. 238)

CONCLUSIONS

Communicative competence and self-determination are essential for adults with acquired neurogenic and neuromuscular disabilities to maximize the quality of their lives. Rebuilding communicative competence and self-determination requires three fundamental components: 1) adults with acquired disabilities must have the *opportunity* to communicate with others and make informed decisions and choices; 2) they must *believe* that they *can* communicate and act autonomously and that it is worthwhile to do so; and 3) they must have the *knowledge, judgment, and skills* to do so effectively (Turnbull et al., 1996). For some adults with acquired disabilities, all three of these components may be in place and only minimal intervention to rebuild communicative competence and self-determination is required. However, for most adults with acquired disabilities, significant intervention may be required to address one or more of these fundamental components—the opportunity; motivation; and knowledge, judgment, and skills or a combination of these.

The current literature is defined by a critical lack of research to address issues of communicative competence and self-determination with adults who have acquired disabilities. Research is urgently required to

- Identify the knowledge, judgment, and skills required for adults with acquired disabilities to rebuild their communicative competence and self-determination
- Investigate the efficacy of interventions to rebuild this knowledge, judgment, and skills and to teach compensatory strategies to bypass functional limitations
- Determine effective techniques to foster motivation to rebuild communicative competence and self-determination
- Identify current policy, practice, attitude, knowledge and skill barriers that impede communicative competence and self-determination
- Investigate the efficacy of interventions to address these opportunity barriers and ensure that the necessary environmental adaptations are in place to support adults with acquired disabilities in attaining communicative competence and self-determination

This research will lay the empirical foundation to ensure that adults with acquired neurogenic and neuromuscular disabilities have the opportunity; the motivation; and the knowledge, judgment, and skills required to become competent communicators and self-determined people.

REFERENCES

Abery, B., & Stancliffe, R. (1996). The ecology of self-determination. In D. Sands & M. Wehmeyer (Eds.), *Self-determination across the life span* (pp. 111–146). Baltimore: Paul. H. Brookes Publishing Co.

Agich, G.J. (1993). *Autonomy and long-term care*. New York: Oxford University Press.

The American heritage dictionary of the English language (3rd ed.). (1992). Boston: Houghton Mifflin Co.

Bailey, D.B., & Simeonsson, R. (1988). Investigation of use of GAS to evaluate individual progress of clients with severe and profound mental retardation. *Mental Retardation, 26,* 289–295.

Bailey, S. (1983). Blissymbolics and aphasia therapy: A case study. In C. Code & D. Muller (Eds.), *Aphasia therapy* (pp. 178–186). London: Edward Arnold.

Bauby, J-D. (1997). *The diving bell and the butterfly* (Jeremy Leggatt, Trans.). New York: Alfred A. Knopf.

Beck, A.R., & Fritz, H. (1998). Can people who have aphasia learn iconic codes? *Augmentative and Alternative Communication, 14,* 184–196.

Beukelman, D.R. (1987). When you have a hammer, everything looks like a nail. *Augmentative and Alternative Communication, 3,* 94–95.

Beukelman, D.R. (1991). Magic and cost of communicative competence. *Augmentative and Alternative Communication, 7,* 2–10.

Beukelman, D.R., Hustad, K., & Ball, L. (1998). The study of organizational strategies for adult AAC users. In F. DeRuyter (Ed.), *AAC-RERC: Engineering advances for communication enhancement in the new millenium*. Grant proposal submitted to and funded by the National Institute on Disability and Rehabilitation Research, Washington, DC.

Beukelman, D.R., & Mirenda, P. (1988). Communication options for persons who cannot speak: Assessment and evaluation. In C.A. Coston (Ed.), *Proceedings of the National Planners Conference on Assistive Device Service Delivery* (pp. 151–165). Washington, DC: Rehabilitation Engineering and Assistive Technology Association, Association for the Advancement of Rehabilitation Technology.

Beukelman, D.R., & Mirenda, P. (1998). *Augmentative and alternative communication: Management of severe communication disorders in children and adults*. (2nd ed.). Baltimore: Paul H. Brookes Publishing Co.

Beukelman, D.R., & Mirenda, P. (with Garrett K.L.) (1998). Adults with severe aphasia. In D.R. Beukelman & P. Mirenda (Eds.), *Augmentative and alternative communication: Management of severe communication disorders in children and adults*. (2nd ed., pp. 465–499). Baltimore: Paul H. Brookes Publishing Co.

Beukelman, D.R., & Yorkston, K. (1991). Traumatic brain injury changes the way we live. In *Communication disorders following traumatic brain injury: Management of cognitive, language, and motor impairments*. (pp. 1–14). Austin, TX: PRO-ED.

Blackstone, S. (1999). Communication partners. *Augmentative Communication News, 12*(1–2), 2–6.

Brockway, J. (1991). Psychosocial disturbances after head injury. In D.R. Beukelman & K. Yorkston (Eds.), *Communication disorders following traumatic brain injury: Management of cognitive, language, and motor impairments*. (pp. 47–55). Austin, TX: PRO-ED.

Coelho, C.A., & Duffy, R.J. (1985). Communicative use of signs in aphasia: Is acquisition enough? *Clinical Aphasiology, 15*, 222–228.

Collier, B. (2000). *Communicating matters: A training guide for personal attendants working with consumers who have enhanced communication needs*. Baltimore: Paul H. Brookes Publishing Co.

Culp, D., & Haynes, S. (1999). *Augmentative technique training for aphasic individuals: Project summary (Phases I & II)*. Unpublished research report, Callier Center for Communication Disorders, University of Texas, Dallas.

Doll, B., Sands, D., Wehmeyer, M., & Palmer, S. (1996). Promoting the development and acquisition of self-determined behavior. In D. Sands & M. Wehmeyer (Eds.), *Self-determination across the life span*. (pp. 65–90). Baltimore: Paul H. Brookes Publishing Co.

Fox, L., & Fried-Oken, M. (1996). AAC aphasiology: Partnership for future research. *Augmentative and Alternative Communication, 12*, 257–271.

Fox, L., & Fried-Oken, M. (1998). Coping with aphasia: AAC communication opportunities in a stroke club. In *Proceedings of the Biennial Conference of the International Society for Augmentative and Alternative Communication (ISAAC)* (pp. 14–15). Toronto: ISAAC.

Franco, M. (1998). Molly's story. In D. Feigenbaum (Ed.), *Journeys with ALS: Personal tales of courage and coping with Lou Gehrig's disease* (pp. 155–169). Virginia Beach: DLRC Press.

Fried-Oken, M., Bersani, H., Anctil, T., & Staehely, J. (1998). Beyond "best clinical judgement": Self-determination and augmentative communication. In *Proceedings of the biennial conference of the International Society for Augmentative and Alternative Communication (ISAAC)* (pp. 34–35). Toronto: ISAAC.

Garrett, K.L., & Beukelman, D.R. (1992). Augmentative communication approaches for persons with severe aphasia. In K. Yorkston (Ed.), *Augmentative communication in the medical setting* (pp. 245–338). Tucson, AZ: Communication Skill Builders.

Garrett, K.L., & Beukelman, D.R. (1995). Changes in the interaction patterns of an individual with severe aphasia given three types of partner support. *Clinical Aphasiology, 23,* 237–251.

Garrett, K.L., Beukelman, D.R., & Low-Morrow, D. (1989). A comprehensive augmentative communication system for an adult with Broca's aphasia. *Augmentative and Alternative Communication, 5,* 55–61.

Gillis, R.J. (1996). Ethical and legal considerations. In R.J. Gillis (Ed.), *Traumatic brain injury: Rehabilitation for speech-language pathologists* (pp. 255–284). Boston: Butterworth-Heinemann.

Goeddel, K. (1998). John's story. In D. Feigenbaum (Ed.), *Journeys with ALS: Personal tales of courage and coping with Lou Gehrig's disease* (pp. 50–65). Virginia Beach: DLRC Press.

Holland, A.L. (1982). Observing functional communication of aphasic adults. *Journal of Speech and Hearing Disorders, 47,* 50–56.

Holland, A.L. (1998). A strategy for improving oral naming in an individual with a phonological access impairment. In A.L. Holland & N. Helm-Estabrooks (Eds.), *Approaches to the treatment of aphasia* (pp. 39–68). San Diego: Singular Publishing Group.

Honsinger, M.J., & Yorkston, K. (1991). Compensation for memory and related disorders following traumatic brain injury. In D. Beukelman & K. Yorkston (Eds.), *Communication disorders following traumatic brain injury: Management of cognitive, language, and motor impairments* (pp. 103–121). Austin, TX: PRO-ED.

Hux, K., Rankin, J., Beukelman, D., & Hahn, D. (1993). Alternative procedure to evaluate semantic classification. *Augmentative and Alternative Communication, 9,* 119–125.

Jaffe, J. (1981). The psychiatrist's approach to managing the aphasic patient. *Seminars in Speech, Language, and Hearing, 2,* 249–258.

Kagan, A., & Gailey, G.F. (1993). Functional is not enough: Training conversation partners for aphasic adults. In A.L. Holland & M.M. Forbes (Eds.), *Aphasia treatment: World perspectives* (pp. 199–226). San Diego: Singular Publishing Group.

Kiresuk, T., & Sherman, R. (1968). Goal attainment scaling: A general method for evaluating comprehensive community health programs. *Community Mental Health Journal, 4,* 443–453.

Kraat, A.W. (1990). Augmentative and alternative communication: Does it have a future in aphasia rehabilitation? *Aphasiology, 4,* 321–338.

Ladtkow, M., & Culp, D., (1992). Augmentative communication with the traumatically brain injured population. In K. Yorkston (Ed.), *Augmentative communication in the medical setting* (pp. 149–243). Tucson, AZ: Communication Skill Builders.

Lasker, J., & Beukelman, D. (1998). Partners' perceptions of augmented storytelling by an adult with aphasia. In *Proceedings of the biennial conference of the International Society for Augmentative and Alternative Communication (ISAAC)* (pp. 18–19). Toronto: ISAAC.

Le Dorze, G., & Brassard, C. (1995). A description of the consequences of aphasia on aphasic persons and their relatives and friends, based on the WHO model of chronic diseases. *Aphasiology, 9,* 239–255.

Lewis, K., & Taymans, J.M. (1992). An examination of autonomous functioning skills of adolescents with learning disabilities. *Career Development for Exceptional Individuals, 15*, 37–46.

Light, J.A. (1988). Interaction involving individuals using augmentative and alternative communication systems: State of the art and future directions. *Augmentative and Alternative Communication, 4*, 66–82.

Light, J.A. (1989). Toward a definition of communicative competence for individuals using augmentative and alternative communication. *Augmentative and Alternative Communication, 5*, 137–144.

Light, J.A. (1990). A vision of simplicity for augmentative communication systems. In B. Mineo (Ed.), *Augmentative and alternative communication in the next decade: Visions conference proceedings* (pp. 30–35). Wilmington: University of Delaware, Applied Sciences and Engineering Laboratories, and A.I. DuPont Institute.

Light, J.A. (1997). "Communication is the essence of human life": Reflections on communicative competence. *Augmentative and Alternative Communication, 13*, 61–70.

Light, J.A., & Binger, C. (1998). *Building communicative competence with individuals who use augmentative and alternative communication*. Baltimore: Paul H. Brookes Publishing Co.

Light, J.A., Binger, C., Agate, T., & Ramsay, K. (1999). Teaching partner-focused questions to individuals who use AAC to enhance their communicative competence. *Journal of Speech, Language, and Hearing Research, 42*, 241–255.

Light, J.A., McNaughton, D., Gulens, M., Krezman, C., Williams, M., & Cohen, K. (1999). *The mentor program for individuals who use AAC*. Unpublished manuscript, Pennsylvania State University, University Park.

Lyon, J.G. (1998). Treating real-life functionality in a couple coping with severe aphasia. In A.L. Holland & N. Helm-Estabrooks (Eds.), *Approaches to the treatment of aphasia* (pp. 203–240). San Diego: Singular Publishing Group.

Malec, J., Smigielski, J., & DePompolo, R. (1991). Goal attainment scaling and outcome measurement in postacute brain injury rehabilitation. *Archives of Physical Medicine, 72*, 138–143.

Mithaug, D. (1996). The optimal prospects principle: A theoretical basis for rethinking instructional practices for self-determination. In D. Sands & M. Wehmeyer (Eds.), *Self-determination across the life span* (pp. 147–165). Baltimore: Paul. H. Brookes Publishing Co.

Neill, G. (1998). Garland's story. In D. Feigenbaum (Ed.), *Journeys with ALS: Personal tales of courage and coping with Lou Gehrig's disease* (pp. 25–29). Virginia Beach: DLRC Press.

O'Brien, B. (1987). A letter to professionals who work with head injured people. In M. Ylvisaker & E.M. Gobble (Eds.), *Community re-entry for head injured adults* (pp. 421–430). Boston: College-Hill.

Porter, S. (1994). New nursing: The road to freedom? *Journal of Advanced Nursing, 20*, 269–274.

Romski, M.A., & Sevcik, R. (1992). Developing augmented language in children with severe mental retardation. In S.F. Warren & J. Reichle (Eds.), *Communication and language intervention series: Vol. 1. Causes and effects in communication and language intervention* (pp. 113–130). Baltimore: Paul H. Brookes Publishing Co.

Romski, M.A., & Sevcik, R. (1996). *Breaking the speech barrier: Language development through augmented means*. Baltimore: Paul H. Brookes Publishing Co.

Rubin, J. (1975). What the "good language learner" can teach us. *TESOL Quarterly, 9*, 41–50.

Sands, D., & Wehmeyer, M. (Eds.). (1996). *Self-determination across the life span.* Baltimore: Paul H. Brookes Publishing Co.

Sarno, J.E. (1991). The psychological and social sequelae of aphasia. In M.T. Sarno, (Ed.), *Acquired aphasia* (pp. 499–517). San Diego: Academic Press.

Savignon, S. (1983). *Communicative competence: Theory and classroom practice.* Reading, MA: Addison Wesley Longman.

Schwartz, M. (1996). *Morrie: In his own words.* New York: Walker & Co.

Smith, M., & Grove, N. (1996, August). *Input/output asymmetries: Implications for language development in AAC.* Paper presented at the biennial conference of the International Society for Augmentative and Alternative Communication (ISAAC), Vancouver, British Columbia, Canada.

Steele, R.D., Weinrich, M., Wertz, R.T., Kleczewska, M.K., & Carlson, G.S. (1989). Computer-based visual communication in aphasia. *Neuropsychologia, 27,* 409–426.

Sunbeam, K. (1998). Keith's story. In D. Feigenbaum (Ed.), *Journeys with ALS: Personal tales of courage and coping with Lou Gehrig's disease* (pp. 213–216). Virginia Beach: DLRC Press.

Technology Related Assistance for Individuals with Disabilities Act of 1988, PL 100–407, 29 U.S.C. §§ 2201 *et seq.*

Turnbull, A., Blue-Banning, M., Longan Anderson, E., Turnbull, H., Seaton, K., & Dinas, P. (1996). Enhancing self-determination through group action planning. In D. Sands & M. Wehmeyer (Eds.), *Self-determination across the life span* (pp. 237–256). Baltimore: Paul. H. Brookes Publishing Co.

Waller, A., & Newell, A.F. (1997). Towards a narrative-based augmentative communication system. *European Journal of Disorders of Communication, 32,* 289–306.

Wehmeyer, M. (1992). Self-determination and the education of students with mental retardation. *Education and Training in Mental Retardation, 27,* 302–314.

Wehmeyer, M. (1996). Self-determination as an educational outcome. In D. Sands & M. Wehmeyer (Eds.), *Self-determination across the life span* (pp. 17–36). Baltimore: Paul. H. Brookes Publishing Co.

Wehmeyer, M. (1998, November). *Self-determination and individuals with disabilities: An introduction and overview.* Paper presented at the American Speech-Language-Hearing Association (ASHA) annual convention, San Antonio, TX.

Wehmeyer, M., Agran, M., & Hughes, C. (1998). *Teaching self-determination to students with disabilities.* Baltimore: Paul. H. Brookes Publishing Co.

Wertz, R.T. (1998). A case of aphasia, apraxia of speech, and apraxia of phonation. In A.L. Holland & N. Helm-Estabrooks (Eds.), *Approaches to the treatment of aphasia* (pp. 11–38). San Diego: Singular Publishing Group.

Wood, L., Lasker, J., Siegel-Causey, E., Beukelman, D., & Ball, L. (1998). Input framework for augmentative and alternative communication. *Augmentative and Alternative Communication, 14,* 261–267.

Ylvisaker, M., & Feeney, T.J. (1996). Executive functions after traumatic brain injury: Supported cognition and self-advocacy. *Seminars in Speech and Language, 17,* 217–232.

Part Two

7

AAC for Individuals with Amyotrophic Lateral Sclerosis

Pamela Mathy
Kathryn M. Yorkston
Michelle L. Gutmann

Amyotrophic lateral sclerosis (ALS) is a disease with no known cause or cure. Individuals with ALS experience a series of losses. The first is the loss of control over one's fate. One individual shortly after diagnosis expressed this loss of control by saying, "I've always taken such good care of myself. So, what on earth did I do to deserve this?" The second loss is the loss of control of the body and its movements. Profound weakness robs individuals with ALS of the control of their arms, legs, and speech muscles. The final loss involves the loss of communication. It can be described as a loss of control, in which *control* is defined as contacting, influencing, and directing those in one's personal and social network. Unfortunately, little can be done about the first two of these losses, the loss of control over fate and the loss of motor function. However, speech-language pathologists who work with individuals with ALS share a strong conviction that the loss of communication in ALS is not inevitable and that augmentative and alternative communication (AAC) strategies can preserve this critical function even in the face of profound motor deterioration.

> *It is possible to live a productive and happy life with ALS if you do not lose yourself.*
>
> —Kim, 1989, p. 345

This chapter reviews the state of practice related to AAC intervention for individuals with ALS. Because service delivery in this population is provided within the framework of medical management, a variety of issues with implications for communication are also addressed, including the nature of the disease, respiratory issues, and communication and cognition. A system of staging of dysarthria and a classification of augmentative techniques according to communication needs is presented along with data related to patterns of use of technology. Finally, intervention is described from the broad perspective of how individuals with ALS and their families cope with the disease, including the role of hope in the intervention process.

NATURE OF AMYOTROPHIC LATERAL SCLEROSIS

ALS is the most common among a group of motor neuron diseases, representing 80% of cases of people with motor neuron diseases (Caroscio, Mulvihill, Sterling, & Abrams, 1987). Other motor neuron diseases include progressive bulbar palsy (characterized by flaccid weakness of the bulbar musculature), primary progressive muscular (i.e., spinal) atrophy (characterized by weakness and wasting of the extremities), and primary lateral sclerosis (characterized by spastic weakness of the trunk and extremities). ALS is a rapidly progressive degenerative disease of unknown etiology involving the motor neurons of both the brain and spinal cord. The signs and symptoms are generally divided into two areas—bulbar functions and spinal functions. The bulbar symptoms are those associated with speech and swallowing, and the spinal symptoms are associated with changes in arm and leg function.

Neuropathology

Since 1990, tremendous advances have been made in the understanding of the neuropathology of ALS. Several theories exist regarding the pathogenesis of ALS, including glutamate excitotoxicity, free radical oxidative stress, neurofilament accumulation, and autoimmunity (Jackson & Bryan, 1998). The pathophysiologic mechanisms underlying ALS have been described as complex, multifactorial, and interrelated (Eisen & Krieger, 1993). For example, the excitotoxicity theory suggests that glutamate, the primary excitatory neurotransmitter in the central nervous system (CNS), accumulates to toxic concentrations at synapses and causes neurons to die (Bensimon, Lacomblez, & Meininger, 1994). Rothstein, Martin, and Kuncl (1992) demonstrated defective glutamate transport activity in the motor areas of the spinal cords of individuals with ALS. These advances are critical because they have spawned a series of clinical trials of drugs such as antiexcitotoxic agents, antioxidants, immunosuppressants, and neurotrophic factors (Louvel, Hugon, & Doble, 1997). Riluzole, an antiglutamate agent, marks the beginning of pharmacotherapy for patients with ALS. Results of a double-blind, placebo-controlled clinical trial offered some promise, especially for the group with bulbar symptoms (Bensimon et al., 1994; Riviere, Meininger, Zeisser, & Munsat, 1998). Although only 35% of individuals with bulbar onset who were given the placebo were alive after 1 year, 73% of similar individuals on riluzole survived for 1 year. If a single medication is not sufficient to alter the disease course dramatically, the trend is to investigate drug combinations to determine potential additive or synergistic benefits (Mitsumoto, 1997).

A valid, controlled trial is a real expression of hope.
—Clawson, Rothstein, & Kuncl, 1993

Diagnosing Amyotrophic Lateral Sclerosis

There are no laboratory tests or neuroimaging studies that directly confirm the diagnosis of ALS. The diagnosis of ALS is based primarily on clinical findings and electrodiagnosis (Rowland, 1998). The most common symptom is weakness, with about one fourth of people reporting bulbar weakness with changes in both speech and swallowing ability. As the disease progresses, both upper motor neurons (UMN) and lower motor neurons (LMN) typically become involved. The symptoms of ALS are generally classified by site of involvement (i.e., UMN, LMN) and by the regions of involvement (i.e., brain stem, cervical, thoracic, or lumbosacral spinal cord levels). Although bulbar changes are of obvious importance to speech, AAC specialists must also be aware of spinal symptoms because of their impact on handwriting, typing, and mobility. UMN involvement affects neurons from the cortex to the anterior horn cells of the spinal cord, resulting in weakness, increased tone, spasticity without muscle wasting, hyperreflexia, plantar extensor response, or clonus. LMN involvement affects neurons from the anterior horn cells to the muscles and is responsible for a different pattern of symptoms, including weakness, flaccid muscle tone with muscle wasting or atrophy, hyporeflexia, plantarflexor response, and fasciculation. The World Federation of Neurology has established criteria for the diagnosis of ALS (World Federation of Neurology, Research Group on Neuromuscular Disease, 1994). The diagnosis of ALS requires the *presence* of LMN degeneration by clinical electrophysiologic or neuropathologic examination, signs of UMN degeneration by clinical examination, and progressive spread of signs within a region or to other regions. These features, together with the *absence* of evidence of other disorders, lead to the diagnosis.

Natural Progression of Amyotrophic Lateral Sclerosis

Rate of progression of symptoms is important in planning AAC interventions. ALS is considered a relentlessly and rapidly progressive disease. Although many individuals with ALS live for more than 5 years after its onset, the majority do not. The rate of deterioration is strikingly linear (Armon & Moses, 1998; Caroscio et al., 1987; Pradas et al., 1993). However, in as many of 25% of individuals with ALS, rates of progression may plateau near the end of the disease course. Individuals who plateau in the end stage frequently experience the need for AAC services. The need for AAC services may also increase with the use of respiratory devices, such as bimodal positive airway pressure (BiPAP), timely placement of percutaneous endoscopic gastrostomy (PEG), and combinations of new drug interventions, all of which prolong survival (Eisen & Calne, 1992).

Riviere and colleages classified the overall severity of ALS based on the ability of the individual to speak, to ambulate, and to perform upper extremity activities of daily living (ADLS):

State 1 (mild)
- Recently diagnosed
- Mild deficit in only 1 of 3 regions (i.e., speech, arm, and leg)
- Functionally independent in speech, upper extremity activities of daily living, and ambulation

State 2 (moderate)
- Mild deficit in all 3 regions OR
- Moderate to severe deficit in 1 region, while the other 2 regions are normal or mildly affected

State 3 (severe)
- Needs assistance in 2 or 3 regions

- Speech is dysarthric and/or patient needs assistance to walk and/or needs assistance with upper extremity activities of daily living

State 4 (terminal):

- Nonfunctional use of at least 2 regions and moderate or non-functional use of the third region (1998, p. 527)

These health states have been used in clinical trials in which the goal of drug treatment is to maintain individuals with ALS in early states of health.

Symptoms in an affected region appear to progress at similar rates. In other words, correlations were found between deterioration rates in arm and legs (Pradas et al., 1993) and between speech and swallowing function (Yorkston, Strand, Miller, Hillel, & Smith, 1993). Symptoms typically start in one location, for example, the arms or legs, then spread to other locations. The spread of symptoms of ALS appears to be a function of the distance from the original site of pathology. For example, the spread to different areas within the spinal cord is faster than the spread from the spinal cord to the bulbar region. The time for spread from the arms to the brain stem is shorter than that from the legs to the brain stem. Although the mechanism that underlies this spread is unclear, evidence suggests that it relates to distance between the neural segments (Brooks, 1991).

Survival duration can be predicted on the basis of a number of related factors. Studies suggest that the older the person is at onset of symptoms, the shorter the person's survival time (Eisen, Schulzer, Mac-Neil, Pant, & Mak, 1993). Furthermore, the 5-year survival rate of people with initial spinal symptoms is three times better than that of people with initial bulbar symptoms (Rosen, 1978). Because decline in pulmonary function is closely correlated with increased likelihood of death, respiratory status is an important predictor of survival (Ringel et al., 1993). Finally, psychological well-being has also been shown to influence survival (McDonald, Wiedenfeld, Hillel, Carpenter, & Walter, 1994).

RESPIRATORY ISSUES AND COMMUNICATION

Changes in respiratory status are common in ALS and may affect the ability to communicate. This section contains a description of respiratory problems commonly encountered in individuals with ALS, along with a description of technology for their management. Also addressed are issues that individuals with ALS who opt for mechanical ventilation and their families face.

Characteristics of Respiratory
Problems in Amyotrophic Lateral Sclerosis

Understanding the respiratory problems associated with ALS is important for the long-term planning of communication management. The muscles of respiration are weakened and eventually paralyzed as ALS progresses. Failure of the respiratory system is the most common cause of death in ALS (Braun, 1987; Schiffman & Belsh, 1993). Respiratory risk is especially high for individuals with bulbar symptoms. They may experience the cumulative effect of respiratory and swallowing problems that may lead to a nonproductive cough and failure to protect the lungs from aspiration. Although difficulty with breathing typically is not one of the first symptoms to appear in ALS, many individuals with ALS show evidence of respiratory muscle weakness, including the inability to take a deep breath, a weak cough, low vocal loudness, and shallow breathing (Cazzolli & Oppenheimer, 1998). Studies suggest that 86% of individuals had respiratory impairment, but only 7% complained of respiratory symptoms (Schiffman & Belsh, 1993). The typical rate of decline in vital capacity was reported to be 3.5% per month among the 36 individuals whom Schiffman and Belsh studied. Taken together, these studies suggest that monitoring of respiratory status should begin early and be a regular part of management.

Decline in respiratory status must be anticipated in ALS, regardless of whether the initial pattern of impairment involves the bulbar or the spinal musculature. Although individuals with initial bulbar symptoms experience respiratory decline earlier than those with initial spinal symptoms, the respiratory status of individuals with initial spinal symptoms must also be carefully monitored. Knowledge of the changes in respiratory status is necessary for the adequate timing of speech and swallowing intervention for a number of reasons. First, poor respiratory support exaggerates the oral movement problems of individuals with bulbar symptoms and contributes to vocal changes in individuals with spinal symptoms (Yorkston, Strand, & Miller, 1996). Second, respiratory decline must be considered in the management of swallowing disorders. Optimal timing of surgical placement of feeding tubes is dependent not only on swallowing status but also on respiratory status (Miller et al., 1999; Strand, Miller, Yorkston, & Hillel, 1996). Finally, knowledge of an individual's respiratory status is crucial for the timing of education regarding ventilatory support and the AAC issues that frequently are associated mechanical ventilation.

Technology for Management of Respiratory Problems

A variety of life-prolonging technologies are available to individuals with respiratory failure associated with ALS. Information about these technologies is of great interest. When asked what type of information they wished to have, individuals with ALS ranked information about ventilation as most important (Silverstein et al., 1991). Topics of greatest interest were kinds of ventilation, nursing care with ventilators, and insurance coverage for this technology. Because many of the respiratory devices used affect communication, they are briefly reviewed here. A more complete description of ventilation (Bach, 1998; Kapadia, 1998) and communication options for individuals who use ventilators (Dikeman & Kazanddjian, 1995) can be found elsewhere.

Noninvasive Devices   A variety of noninvasive respiratory supports are available, including intermittent positive pressure ventilation by mouth, by nose, or by both. The BiPAP system is perhaps the most commonly used noninvasive respiratory support device for individuals with ALS (Pinto, Evangelista, Carvalho, Alves, & Sales Luis, 1995). The system is small, lightweight, portable, and easy to maintain. It is capable of delivering two different levels of pressure: one pressure during inspiration and a lower pressure during expiration. Studies suggest that use of noninvasive respiratory support prolongs the lives of individuals with ALS; however, tolerance for such a device requires some strength of the bulbar musculature (Aboussousan, Khan, Meeker, Stelmack, & Misumoto, 1997; Bach, 1995). Devices to assist coughing are also available (Hanayama, Ishikawa, & Bach, 1997). These devices supply a large tidal volume via positive pressure followed by a rapid negative pressure. This rapid change in pressure mimics a forceful cough and aids in clearing pulmonary secretions.

Invasive Devices   Ventilation via tracheostomy is an option selected by some with severe respiratory impairment. Such intervention is considered invasive but provides a small, secure connection to the airway when bulbar impairment makes noninvasive ventilation difficult. Because air is delivered via a surgical opening in the neck, the face is free of masks, headgear, and straps that are associated with many of the noninvasive devices. If there are no preexisting speech problems, speaking can continue via tracheostomy-speech devices such as the Passy-Muir valve (Manzano et al., 1993). Individuals with ALS may survive for extended periods of time when using such devices (Cazzolli & Oppenheimer, 1996).

Studies describe the long-term outcomes of mechanical ventilation in ALS. Moss and colleague followed 75 individuals with ALS receiving long-term ventilation (Moss et al., 1996). Nearly three quarters

(72%) lived at home. Results suggested that home-based mechanical ventilation was less costly and associated with greater patient satisfaction than was institution-based intervention. The cost of home-based intervention was estimated to be more than $150,000 per year in the early 1990s (Moss et al., 1993).

Effects of Mechanical Ventilation on Communication

Both invasive and noninvasive mechanical ventilation affect communication. Those who use noninvasive devices during the day must communicate while wearing face or nose masks. These masks change the quality of speech production even when bulbar impairment is not present. Ventilation via tracheostomy can dramatically affect many aspects of communication. There is a growing body of literature related to the experience of ventilator dependency. Although many of these studies do not focus on individuals with ALS, both the research methodology and the issues related to communication that emerged are pertinent.

A variety of research methods have been employed. For example, a quasi-experimental study was conducted in which a group of individuals who received presurgery instruction in the use of communication boards were compared with a control group who relied on the experience and creativity of the nurse to provide a method of communication during the postsurgical intubation period (Stovsky, Rudy, & Dragonnette, 1988). Results indicated that the group who used a communication system that was planned prior to surgery had higher patient satisfaction scores than the control group. The experimental and control groups were no different in terms of nurse satisfaction.

Other studies rely on patient report (Viner, 1985) or qualitative research methods (Gries & Fernsler, 1988; Hafsteinsfottir, 1996; Menzel, 1997). The experience of communication has been studied from both the perspective of the nurse (Ashworth, 1980; Berghom-Engberg & Haljamae, 1993) and of the patient (Ashworth, 1980; Jablonski, 1994; Menzel, 1997, 1998). For example, Jablonski (1994) conducted in-depth interviews with 12 people who had been mechanically ventilated. Many verbalized feelings of frustration, helplessness, and resignation regarding their inability to communicate. They believed that health care providers acted as communication gatekeepers, limiting patients to whatever material the health care provider offered as communication aids. The individuals interviewed found that their gestures, written messages and physical symptoms were initially interpreted as apprehension, and the health care provider would respond by telling the person to relax or by giving sedatives.

Interviews with nurses also suggest some negative experiences (Ashworth, 1980). Nurses interviewed indicated that they were uncomfortable caring for an individual with a ventilator because of their frustration, embarrassment, or concern for the patient. The majority of the interactions were initiated by nurses and were "short-term informative," that is, for the purpose of telling the patient what the nurse was going to do. The majority of communication methods used by patients were patient-initiated, or methods that the patient could use without assistance from the nurse, including, for example, gestures or mouthing words.

Although, for the most part, research has focused on temporary experiences with mechanical ventilation, the picture that emerges is a troubling one. It depicts frustration and lack of communication from both the perspective of the health care provider and the individual receiving the care. Menzel argued for the need for communication-related research in this field of nursing (Menzel, 1994). This research would be based on the current evidence that 1) traditional means of communication are not effective, 2) different communication methods appear to serve different functions, and 3) communication needs may vary during the course of the ventilation experience. This type of research would benefit not only individuals who temporarily require a ventilator because of an acute medical condition but also individuals who use mechanical ventilation on a long-term basis because of neuro-muscular disease.

The Decision to Live Beyond Respiratory Failure

Mechanical ventilation, both invasive and noninvasive, may be an effective means of prolonging the survival of individuals with ALS (Sherman & Paz, 1994). Individuals with tracheostomy survived respiratory failure much longer than did individuals with noninvasive ventilation (Winterhooler, Erbguth, Hecht, & Neunderfer, 1998). Unfortunately, ventilator support does not prevent or slow the progression of neurologic impairment. Arms and legs continue to weaken, and bulbar function continues to decline. Because of this increasing impairment, tracheostomized individuals are more often depressed, and their families complain more about the burden of care.

Only a minority of individuals with ALS require, request, and receive ventilatory support (Goldblatt & Greenlaw, 1989; Moss et al., 1993; Winterhooler et al., 1998). From 5% to 20% of individuals with ALS select mechanical ventilation following advanced planning (Oppenheimer, 1997). Clinical experience suggests that this proportion may be increasing, at least at major centers, because of the increasing feasibility of home ventilation, the increasing number of people who opt for noninvasive ventilatory support, and the increasing potential to maintain communication via AAC devices.

Studies have described individuals who opt for mechanical ventilation. Some studies described the physical characteristics of these individuals. Hayashi and colleagues studied the level of cranial nerve
involvement in a series of 18 individuals with ALS who were sustained
on mechanical ventilation. Results indicated that these individuals
tended to have severe impairments. Nearly 90% had no functional
swallow. Lip, tongue, and jaw function were at least partially impaired
in two thirds of the cases. Although eye movement tended to be the
most preserved of the bulbar functions studied, approximately half
had partial impairment in this area.

Other studies have investigated the psychological status of individuals who select mechanical ventilation (McDonald, Hillel, &
Wiedenfeld, 1996). McDonald and her colleagues found no significant
differences in sociodemographic makeup, depression, hopelessness,
overall quality of life, or psychological well-being in a group of individuals who were supported by ventilators as opposed to other individuals with ALS. The group supported on ventilators had a more
internal locus of control for their health care. In other words, they
highly valued their ability to make their own decisions.

The quality of life of individuals with ALS who required ventilators has also been examined. Effective communication has been associated with better quality of life and the ability to live in the community
(Bach, 1993). Other studies have suggested that although individuals
on mechanical ventilation had severe limitation of daily activities as
measured by a quality-of-life scale designed for the ALS population,
their self-reported quality of life was satisfactory (Gelinas, O'Connor, &
Miller, 1998). However, caregivers were heavily burdened, and outside
activities were severely limited. Still another indicator of quality of life
for people who are on ventilation is the question, "Would you chose
ventilation if you were to make the decision again?" Nearly 90% of
individuals receiving mechanical ventilation indicated that they would
make the same decision again (Kaub-Wittemer, von Steinbchel, Wasner,
& Borasio, 1998). Caregivers were not as enthusiastic about mechanical
ventilation. Only 80% of caregivers would advise the individual to
choose it again. And only a minority of caregivers (20%) would choose
ventilation for themselves in a similar situation.

Many factors must be considered when making decisions about
mechanical ventilation, including quality of life, severity of disability,
availability of ventilation by means of nasal mask, possible admission
to a long-term care facility, ability to discontinue use of mechanical
ventilation, desire to live, concern for family members' emotional
health, and concern for care demands placed on families (Young, Marshall, & Anderson, 1994). Because of the complexity of the decision,

planning is necessary to avoid decision making in a crisis. The goals of this planning include the prevention of unwanted ventilation, delivery of optimal palliative care, and recognition of the individual's right to withdraw consent to an invasive procedure (Borasio & Voltz, 1997, 1998). Many individuals are reluctant to prolong life when, in their judgment, the quality of life with such intervention is not acceptable. Most individuals with ALS receiving long-term mechanical ventilation want to stop it under certain circumstances (Moss et al., 1996). The process of planning care in advance requires the communication of preferences to family and health care providers. Thus, adequate AAC systems are mandatory.

COGNITION

The classic view of ALS suggests that it is a disease involving only the UMN and the LMN. Thus, the clinical features are restricted to changes in motor function. This classic view that ALS spares cognitive and memory function has recently come under critical review. Isolated instances of dementia associated with ALS have been reported since the disease was first described by Charcot in the 1860s (Montgomery & Erickson, 1987). Epidemiologic studies suggest that dementia appears to occur in 1%–2% of sporadic cases (Montgomery & Erickson, 1987) and in approximately 15% of familial cases (Hudson, 1981). However, studies reporting the results of neuropsychological testing suggest a higher prevalence of cognitive change. More than one third of individuals (35.6%) with ALS displayed evidence of *clinically significant impairment*, defined as performing at or below the 5th percentile on at least two of eight neuropsychological tests (Massman, Kreiter, Jankovic, & Doody, 1996).

Montgomery and Erickson (1987) suggested that epidemiologic figures may represent an underestimation for a number of reasons. First, specialty centers from which the majority of statistics arise usually serve outpatients and typically exclude individuals with very advanced or rapidly progressing disease. Second, few clinical protocols include testing with sufficiently sensitive neuropsychological instruments to detect subtle cognitive changes in the presence of overwhelming motor impairment. Finally, compromised cognition may be misinterpreted as depression or withdrawal due to motor dysfunction.

Neuropathology of Cognitive Decline

The underlying mechanism for the cognitive disruptions seen in ALS is of great interest. One explanation is that dementia with ALS represents a chance co-occurrence of ALS with another degenerative disease that affects cognitive function, that is, the co-occurrence of ALS and Alzheimer's disease. This explanation is unlikely because the brains of individuals who have ALS with dementia do not always exhibit the neuropathologic features associated with Alzheimer's disease (e.g., neurofibrillary tangles, senile plaques) (Montgomery & Erickson, 1987). Another explanation is that ALS is characterized by multisystem involvement, particularly of the frontal lobes. It has been suggested that there is a continuum of cognitive disability in individuals with ALS corresponding to the pathologic process in the frontal lobes ranging from normality to significant impairment (Abe et al., 1997). The evidence for this suggestion comes from a variety of neuroimaging studies including positron emission tomography (Abrahams et al., 1996; Abrahams et al., 1995; Kew, Goldstein, et al., 1993; Kew, Leigh, et al., 1993; Ludolph et al., 1992; Tanaka et al., 1993) and magnetic resonance imaging (Frank, Haas, Heinze, Stark, & Munte, 1997).

Further evidence for multisystem degeneration comes from studies of the neuropathology of individuals who have survived considerably beyond the point of respiratory failure (Sasaki, Tsutsumi, Yamane, Sakuma, & Maruyama, 1992; Takahashi et al., 1993). In these individuals, ALS has progressed to include a wide variety of neural areas, including the reticular formation, cerebellar cortex, dentate and red nuclei, thalamus, and the mamillary body. Significant subclinical deterioration of the sensory nerve function may also occur in ALS (Gregory, Mills, & Donaghy, 1993).

Correlates of Cognitive Change

Cognitive changes can occur at any stage of the disorder. In six sporadic cases of ALS and dementia, the age of onset for ALS was very similar to the age of onset of dementia, and memory change was an early behavioral indicator (Horoupian et al., 1984; Wikstrom, Paetau, Palo, Stand, & Roger, 1983). Cases have also been reported in which cognitive changes preceded the motor changes (Cavalleri & DeRenzi, 1994). Still others suggest that cognitive change comes late in the course of the disease. Individuals with advanced disease, particularly those with respiratory complications, subjectively experience loss of attention, cognition, and memory (Montgomery & Erickson, 1987).

Potential for cognitive change is of particular concern in AAC management. These changes are prominently associated with a bulbar form of ALS with eventual UMN involvement reported in nearly all cases (Montgomery & Erickson, 1987). There is a significant negative correlation between UMN symptoms and tests of mental status (Iwasaki, Kinoshita, Ikeda, Takamiya, & Shiojima, 1990). Both dysarthria and greater severity of motor symptoms place individuals with ALS at greater risk for cognitive changes (Massman, Sims, et al., 1996). Dementia with ALS may be a distinct clinical entity whose disease classification is poorly understood (Caselli et al., 1993). It has been suggested that it should be classified as one of the frontal lobe degenerative dementias in a grouping that also contains Pick's disease and progressive aphasia (Brun & Passant, 1996; Talbot et al., 1995). More detailed discussions of frontal lobe dementia and motor neuron disease can be found elsewhere (Neary & Snowden, 1996; Neary et al., 1998; Neary et al., 1990).

Neuropsychologic Testing

In an excellent review of cognitive function in ALS, Strong, Grace, Orange, and Leeper (1996) reported a number of studies suggesting that cognitive changes can be described in individuals with ALS. These changes are different from the pattern characteristic of Alzheimer's disease and are consistent with frontal lobe involvement (Abrahams et al., 1997; Gallassi et al., 1989; Kew, Goldstein, et al., 1993; Kew, Leigh, et al., 1993; Ludolph et al., 1992; Peavy, Herzog, Rubin, & Mesulam, 1992). Deficits were identified in tasks requiring sustained attention and the ability to shift from one topic to another. Confrontation naming, verbal fluency, insight, and judgment also were extensively impaired (Peavy et al., 1992). Only one study found no evidence of cognitive deficits in ALS, according to Strong and colleagues (1996). However, it should be noted that this study (Poloni, Capitani, Mazzini, & Ceroni, 1986) included only individuals in the first 14 months of illness and did not use tests thought to be sensitive to frontal lobe dysfunction. Despite the new neuropathologic and neuropsychologic findings, Strong and colleagues revealed that researchers still do not know whether these pathological changes are of clinical significance in individuals with ALS.

Language Function

The language capability of individuals with ALS is also of critical interest to the AAC field. Unfortunately, little systematic work has been reported in this area other than a comparison of the language of individuals with ALS and frontal dementia with those of individuals with Pick's disease, another disease with fronto-anterior temporal lobe neuropathology (Strong et al., 1996). Individuals with Pick's disease often exhibit early language deterioration. With progression, these individuals generally retain access to semantic information but may become echolalic or mute.

Studies of the language impairments in ALS are complicated by the presence of dysarthria that may in itself influence language production.

The relationship between spontaneous language production and dysarthria was examined in nine speakers with ALS (Wilkinson, Yorkston, Strand, & Rogers, 1995). Speech samples were recorded at two points as the dysarthria became more severe (on average, sentence intelligibility decreased from 91% to 79%). Results of this study indicated that individuals with ALS adopted an "economy of wording" strategy that was characterized by fewer words, shortened grammatical units that were at times incomplete, and a reduction in mazes (e.g., false starts, fillers, asides to the examiner). Measures of the number of concepts communicated and vocabulary were not different for individuals with ALS when compared with the control group. The telegraphic language strategy seen in some individuals with ALS may have been a response to increasingly effortful speech or to the slowed speaking rates associated with dysarthria. However, it may also reflect subtle language changes such as those associated with aggramatism in aphasia.

SPEECH CHARACTERISTICS

The speech of individuals with ALS has been classified as a mixed dysarthria with components of both spasticity and flaccidity (Duffy, 1995). Many of the perceptual features are present in both spastic and flaccid dysarthria. For example, imprecise consonants, hypernasality, and harsh voice quality are found in both types of dysarthria. Low pitch, reduced stress, and strained-strangled voice quality are found in spastic dysarthria, yet audible inspiration and nasal emission are found in flaccid dysarthria. As the disease progresses, the symptoms associated with the flaccidity, including muscle wasting and atrophy, predominate.

Individuals with ALS demonstrate impairment in all components of the speech mechanism. A moderate to strong relationship between the speech impairment (i.e., changes in muscle tone, weakness, and range and rate of movement) and measure of function such as speech intelligibility has been found in speakers with ALS (Yorkston, Strand, & Hume, 1998). A number of studies are available that focus on impairment in each of the components of the speech production mechanism, including respiratory function (Hillel, Yorkston, & Miller, 1989; Putnam & Hixon, 1984) and laryngeal function (Aronson, Ramig, Winholtz, & Silber, 1992; Kent et al., 1994; Strand, Buder, Yorkston, & Ramig, 1994). Because impairment in tongue function is so common in ALS, lingual impairment has been studied at length (DePaul, Abbs, Caligiuri, Gracco, & Brooks, 1988; DePaul, Waclawik, Abbs, & Brooks, 1998; Dworkin & Aronson, 1986; Kent et al., 1990, 1992; Weismer, Martin, Kent, & Kent, 1992). In summary, speech of individuals with ALS is characterized by differences in voice quality, nasality, and consonant production. Although considerable variability exists from speaker to speaker, results of a 1999 study by Klasner, Yorkston, and Strand suggested that the pattern of perceptual prominency that is established early in the disease tends to be preserved as the progression occurs.

Staging of Dysarthria

Information about the rate of symptom progression is important in AAC intervention. Results of a study tracking the progression of dysarthria in 44 individuals with ALS indicated that rapid decline of speech function is not inevitable. However, it occurs frequently enough that sound clinical practice dictates early preparation for the potential loss of speech (Yorkston et al., 1993). Although some individuals progress slowly, others progress rapidly to the need for AAC (Yorkston, Miller, & Strand, 1995). The following stages describe a typical progression of the speech course in individuals with ALS:

Stage 1: No Detectable Speech Disorder

- Speech of individuals with a spinal presentation of ALS sounds normal.
- Speaker notices no change in function.
- Listeners note no changes in speaking rate, precision, or loudness.

Stage 2: Obvious Speech Disorder with Intelligible Speech

- Changes in speech are apparent.
- Changes may be more pronounced with stress or fatigue.
- Most speakers compensate unconsciously for articulatory or respiratory impairment by decreasing their speaking rate and the length of their breath groups.
- Speech at this stage remains easy to understand, although voice quality may be harsh or breathy and mild articulatory problems may be present.

Stage 3: Reduction in Speech Intelligibility

- Speaking rate, articulation, and resonance are impaired and may make speech difficult to understand, depending on the communication environment.
- Individuals can and do modify their speech production (Kennedy, Strand, & Yorkston, 1994).
- Helpful strategies include maintaining a slow speaking rate, conserving energy, increasing the precision of speech

production, and developing strategies to resolve communication breakdowns.

- Some speakers may begin to use AAC techniques to resolve breakdowns. When speaking rate is 50% or less, AAC assessment and intervention should be initiated.

Stage 4: Natural Speech Supplemented with Augmentative Communication

- Speech must be combined with AAC approaches (Kazandjian, 1997).
- Natural speech may be limited to highly predictable messages, such as responses to questions or greetings.
- The speaker may supplement natural speech by writing key words or by pointing to the first letter of each word as he or she speaks.
- Intervention for speakers at this stage may include alphabet supplementation, changing communication modes for different situations, an alerting signal for gaining attention, augmented telephone communication, and portable writing systems (Hustad, 1999).

Stage 5: No Useful Speech

- Speakers with advanced bulbar ALS lose speech function.
- Some individuals at this stage may vocalize for emotional expression or with extreme effort but do not produce understandable speech.
- Intervention for speakers at this stage may include establishing a reliable yes-or-no system, eye-gaze systems, communication systems for speakers dependent on ventilators, and integrated, multipurpose AAC systems.

Classification of Augmentative Communication Needs

Because there is considerable variability in rate and pattern of progression across individuals, the best approach to clinical decision making in ALS is to consider not just speech decline but also decline in upper- and lower-extremity functioning. For example, an individual who seems to have minimal speech deterioration but reduced upper extremity functioning may need information on how to adapt his or her computer to meet written communication needs. Six groups, each reflecting different augmentative communication needs, have been identified (Yorkston et al., 1993).

Group 1: Adequate Speech and Adequate Hand Function   This group comprises individuals in Stage 1 (i.e., no detectable speech disorder) through Stage 3 (i.e., reduction in speech intelligibility) of speech progression. Thus, speech is generally functional but behavior modifications (e.g., slowed speaking rate, frequent repetitions) are necessary. Hand functioning is also adequate in that individuals accomplish self-help tasks with minimal assistance. The AAC specialist is unlikely to encounter individuals in this category unless they are served in a multidisciplinary clinic setting. This is unfortunate because individuals with ALS and their families often have questions and fears regarding how they will manage these individuals' impending loss of speech.

Communication intervention for this group includes monitoring the impairment as well as introduction to AAC approaches. Baseline measurements of the impairment of the speech production mechanism as well as hand and leg function are obtained to assist the timing of future interventions. Measurements may include rapid alternating movements of articulators, velopharyngeal sufficiency, voice, speaking rate, and vital capacity. Measures of hand function for written communication and keyboard access may be obtained in collaboration with the occupational therapist. Intervention may also focus on maintenance of activity, including development of strategies for managing. Use of portable amplification systems for demanding speaking situations may also be considered. Prosthetic devices such as palatal lifts may be considered for some individuals with velopharyngeal insufficiency. Strategies for maintaining comprehensibility may also be introduced (Yorkston, Strand, & Kennedy, 1996). These include setting the topic, developing effective conversational repair strategies, and using alphabet supplementation.

Group 2: Adequate Speech and Poor Hand Function   For this group, speech continues to be functional, but hand functioning to support written communication is severely impaired. The speech assessment and intervention goals described for the previous group are also applicable to this group. Because of loss of hand functioning, needs for written communication should be addressed as well. With the increase in use of computers, many individuals may already be using or may have access to a computer for personal use or employment use. If the individual is already using a computer, software and hardware for adapting it to meet his or her access needs should be evaluated. The individual's future speech augmentation needs should be considered in choosing written communication augmentation software.

Considerations with respect to written communication, or the prescription of a system for written communication, should include

- Familiarity with computers
- Desire to learn technology for writing
- Daily writing needs: personal communication, business correspondence educational needs, and so forth
- Current needs and adaptability of systems being demonstrated in terms of alternate access (e.g., scanning, optical pointers, voice input)
- Whether this system might serve as an integrated (or multipurpose) system
- What technical support is available? (This is an important consideration for the successful implementation of either a dedicated writing system or an integrated system.)
- Does the person need or want a stationary system or a portable system?
- What software should be considered?

Software is a pivotal issue the importance of which cannot be stressed enough. In fact, it is software exploration that should drive decisions about system hardware. Knowledge and familiarity with a range of mainstream productivity tools, as well as software that supports alternate access (e.g., on-screen keyboards) and provides rate enhancement features (e.g., sticky keys, abbreviation expansion, word prediction), is essential to effective software selection.

The growth of the Internet and the use of e-mail should also be taken into account when considering written communication. In a study by Mathy (1996), 12 individuals who use AAC systems received instruction in the use of e-mail and other Internet services. Following the training period, all reported that they used e-mail at least once per week. Furthermore, all indicated that they preferred e-mail to the telephone for telecommunication purposes. One participant stated the following:

> As for comments about experiences using on-line services, I really enjoy e-mail. I feel on par with others as long as I can compose off-line and then send. It's a good feeling. For a time when writing and reading mail received, it's as though I don't have this terrible disease. (L.L., personal communication, June 1995)

What is clear from this excerpt is that individuals whose social network has been limited by ALS may, in fact, derive significant psychological benefit from access to online communication. It is the contention of many clinicians that early discussion of AAC options, including access to on-line communication, may defer and, in some cases, alleviate the social isolation often associated with ALS.

Another reason to encourage the consideration of written communication augmentation with this group is that the same technology will eventually support spoken communication. Understandably, it is difficult for individuals with ALS and their families to face the potential loss of speech. Some put off considering AAC intervention until their speech is no longer functional. The authors have found that individuals who begin with augmentation for written communication make a smoother transition to speech augmentation. Moreover, it is easier for an individual to learn to use an AAC device and access technique when he or she can still use speech to ask questions, indicate preferences, and so forth.

Computer adaptations for augmenting written communication begin with software that support various forms of keyboard adaptation or alternate keyboard access. All Macintosh and Microsoft Windows operating systems furnish standard keyboard adjustments, such as toggle shift and control functions, adjustments in repeat rate, and adjustments in keyboard acceptance time. Such adjustments used in conjunction with a keyguard and a stylus or hand splint may provide an inexpensive means for the individual with ALS to prolong use of the typical keyboard. Keyboard adaptations include modifications to standard keyboards to allow the user continued use of the standard keyboard for as long as possible. Modifications can range from minor positioning or angling of the keyboard to supporting the user's forearms and elbows. These supports allow the user's hands to be suspended so that direct selection of keys is accomplished with relative ease. When upper-extremity function deteriorates to the point where use of the standard keyboard is no longer viable, methods of alternate access should be explored.

Individuals who lack the range of motion and stamina to use an adapted keyboard can use a mouse or a trackball to access an on-screen keyboard. For individuals who lack functional hand use, access methods requiring minimal motor movement, such as single-switch scanning, are commonly used. At times, control of head movement remains reliable longer than use of upper or lower extremities. Because the ocular muscles are not usually affected until late in the disease process, there has been an increasing interest in eye-movement access systems by individuals with ALS and their advocates. With these systems, a camera focused on the pupil is calibrated to the user's eye movements as he or she looks at items on the "keyboard." These selections, often determined by dwell time or by detection of ocular movements, are sent to the computer program.

For the individuals with ALS, a writing system chosen carefully can support written communication needs throughout the course of their disease. It may also provide a basis for an integrated system, which would fulfill both face-to-face and written communication needs. The need for learning a dedicated (i.e., developed primarily for spoken communication) voice output communication system as a face-to-face system would be eliminated with an integrated multipurpose system. However, the need for low-technology (i.e., those that involve some form of chart and a means by which to access it) backup communication becomes even more important as the dependence on a single system to meet all communication needs rises. Should any technical problems curtail use of the integrated multipurpose system in the absence of low-technology backup, all means of communicative output for the user would be disrupted. Team involvement in all phases of assessment and implementation of a writing system is essential to ensure its initial and ongoing success. Assessment for the physical aspects of written communication should be done jointly by a speech-language pathologist and an occupational therapist who is knowledgeable about assistive technology. The input of a rehabilitation engineer or technologist may be valuable as well in this regard.

Group 3: Poor Speech, Adequate Hand Functioning, and Adequate Mobility   *Poor speech functioning* is defined as speech that is so distorted that it must be supplemented with AAC techniques. Intervention considerations for individuals in this group must take into account the need for portability because often these individuals are ambulatory despite marked communication problems. The majority of individuals in this group prefer using handwriting to supplement speech in face-to-face conversation. For individuals who have some residual natural speech, alphabet supplementation may also be effective for general conversation with familiar partners. With this technique, the individual points to the first letter of each word as she or he speaks. In addition to providing the listener with the additional cue of the first letter, the user must slow the rate of speech and say one word at a time. Typically, alphabet supplementation is initiated when repairing a communication breakdown. That is, when the spoken message is not understood, the message is repeated using alphabet supplementation. Although individuals generally learn alphabet supplementation in a short demonstration, some individuals have had difficulty with mastering it. This may be because of cognitive impairments. As discussed previously, some individuals with ALS have shown impairments in executive functioning. Although alphabet supplementation is a low-technology strategy, successful use requires coordination of speech with locating the first letter of the word as well as monitoring listener understanding as the message is constructed. Impaired executive functioning reduces the ability to coordinate simultaneously multiple components of a task or activity.

The writing tools used for conversation should also be considered. Many individuals find dry erase boards and markers or magic slates less fatiguing and more convenient than pencil or pen and paper. It is also helpful to place an alphabet board on the back along with an explanation of why and how the individual uses these tools. This can assist the individual to train unfamiliar partners regarding his or her communication strategies. Because they are independent in self-care and mobility, it is common for individuals in this group to spend time at home alone. In these cases, the need for a method of telecommunication arises. If the individual or the family already owns a personal computer, a simple, inexpensive solution is adding a talking word processor. This can be used with a telephone program on the computer or in conjunction with a speaker telephone. A dedicated AAC device can also be used with a speaker telephone. Some individuals who cannot speak choose not to use speech output devices. These individuals may opt to use a fax machine for telecommunication with their families and a tape recorder and loop tapes for emergency messages. Another nonspeech telecommunication tool is a telecommunication device for the deaf (TDD). Most states have toll-free relay operators who verbally transfer spoken and TDD messages for callers and receivers.

Group 4: Poor Speech, Adequate Hand Functioning, and Poor Mobility   Individuals in Group 4 use devices such as wheelchairs for mobility and require AAC systems for interaction. Although individuals at the upper end of this group are still able to achieve independent mobility for short distances (e.g., around the house) with the use of an assistive device (e.g., cane, walker), they often use a wheelchair for longer distances. AAC intervention needs for this group are similar to those for Group 3. If the person uses a wheelchair, the size and weight of the device is not as critical because it can be mounted on the wheelchair. It is important to keep in mind, however, that many individuals with ALS use their wheelchairs only for longer-distance mobility. Therefore, decisions about AAC device mounting systems must be made with full knowledge of the different environments in which an individual with ALS needs to use the communication system.

Group 5: Poor Speech, Poor Hand Functioning, and Good Mobility For individuals in Group 5, the greatest challenge is providing strategies for speech augmentation. Not only does poor hand functioning limit the ability to carry a device, it also prevents the individual from manipulating the device to set it up for communication. Therefore, unassisted strategies (i.e., methods that do not involve any form of electronic device or chart) or low-technology strategies (e.g., partner-assisted auditory scanning, partner-assisted manual scanning and light-technology optical pointing with a head-mounted laser) are most likely to be feasible in locations outside the home. For partner-assisted manual scanning, the partner holds an alphabet, word, or message display in front of the user and systematically scans selections until the user indicates that the desired element has been reached. This process is repeated until the message is complete. With partner-assisted auditory scanning, the partner verbally lists the elements (i.e., alphabet or a predetermined list of options) until the user indicates that the desired element has been reached. The process is repeated until the message is complete. In order to enhance the rate of this iterative process, it is often helpful for the conversation partner to segment the alphabet in some measure. Popular options for segmentation of the alphabet in partner-assisted scanning include halving or quartering the alphabet or somewhat more arbitrary divisions such as *A* to *G*, *H* to *L*, *M* to *R*, *S* to *Z*. In order to support individuals using scanning in home or work environments, a comprehensive AAC assessment with an occupational therapist is essential to ensure that all options have been explored.

Group 6: Poor Speech, Poor Hand Functioning, and Poor Mobility If individuals in this group have been followed on a regular basis by an ALS clinical team, they should already be using a variety of low-technology and high-technology (i.e., those that use electronic devices) AAC aids and techniques to supplement spoken and written communication. Unfortunately, individuals with ALS and their families who are not receiving regular follow-along support may not seek out the assistance of a speech-language pathologist with expertise in AAC until they are at the later stage of the disease process. These individuals can be very challenging to service providers.

It is essential that individuals in this group are provided with reliable unassisted and low-technology strategies, such as partner-assisted auditory and visual scanning and optical pointing, if possible. They should also be evaluated to determine their ability and desire to use high-technology aids as well. The success of high-technology devices (especially multipurpose devices) with this group depends on their prior experience with technology, their desire to remain an active communicator, and the quality of training and support provided.

Patterns of Use of Augmentative Communication Aids and Techniques

A variety of AAC aids ranging from inexpensive, low-technology, alphabet boards to high-technology systems costing thousands of dollars have been used by people with ALS. Yet, there is a paucity of information in the literature regarding how these communication methods are employed to meet communicative needs. Evidence regarding the use and effectiveness of AAC aids and techniques is needed to provide support for third-party funding. Such information may assist manufacturers of AAC devices to improve their products in terms of meeting the unique communication needs of this group. Finally, information on use and effectiveness of AAC aids and devices could be used to improve clinical service delivery.

Access to Augmentative Communication Management Services and Information   Information regarding augmentative communication is available to individuals with ALS and their families through a variety of resources, such as multidisciplinary specialty clinics, advocacy agencies (Amyotrophic Lateral Sclerosis Association [ALSA], Muscular Dystrophy Association [MDA]), support groups, and the web. As discussed previously, those served in multidisciplinary, specialty clinic environments are more likely to receive routine communicative management based on the staging of the disease process. To date, however, there are no large-scale demographic studies indicating the proportion of individuals with ALS whose care is managed through multidisciplinary clinics versus those whose care is managed by private physicians. Advocacy agencies such as ALSA and MDA provide informational literature that includes descriptions of AAC devices. Some maintain lending libraries where individuals can check out devices to use as long as they need them. Often their inventories are not large enough to accommodate the demand, however. Support groups sponsored by ALSA and MDA are an excellent resource because individuals with ALS and their families can obtain firsthand information regarding successful (and unsuccessful) AAC interventions. The web offers a medium through which individuals with ALS can research AAC interventions at their own pace. In addition to agency-sponsored web pages, a number of individuals with ALS have developed personal web resource pages. A sampling of agency-sponsored and personal web pages is presented in the resource section at the end of this chapter.

Although individuals with ALS have access to communicative intervention resources, some choose not to use them, and many use them only in the end stages of the disease process. Albert, Bene, Murphy, and Rowland (1998) conducted a 2-year study of the use of palliative care by 121 individuals with ALS receiving services at a MDA or ALS clinic in a large midwestern medical center. At the end of the study, there were two groups: Group 1 included 41 patients who had died during the 2-year period; Group 2 included 80 patients who were still living. There were significant differences between the groups regarding the use of speech-language therapy and wheelchairs. Of the subjects in Group 1, 61% had used speech therapy services and 58.5% acquired a wheelchair before their deaths. In Group 2, 38.8% of the subjects used speech therapy and 35.0% acquired a wheelchair during the 2-year study period. Gutmann and Gryfe (1996) evaluated trends in use of AAC systems for 126 individuals with ALS receiving services from an assistive technology clinic in Toronto during a 16-month period. They found that, on average, 27% of individuals elected not to pursue AAC intervention.

Augmentative Communication Usage Patterns   Mathy (1996) studied AAC usage patterns of 36 individuals with ALS who were followed for communicative services by the speech pathology department within a medical center between May 1988 and July 1996 (Mathy, 1996). Information gathered included age at time of the initial AAC evaluation, gender, initial symptom presentation (i.e., bulbar or spinal), AAC methods used, and the duration of use of AAC. Information was also gathered regarding which augmentative method subjects typically used for particular communicative activities.

Table 1 contains demographic information about the 36 participating individuals. A review of this table suggests that subjects with initial spinal symptoms were typically younger at the time of the initial AAC evaluation, and they used their AAC aids and techniques for a longer duration than the subjects with initial bulbar symptoms did. It should be noted that 3 of the 36 individuals, (2 with initial bulbar symptoms, 1 with initial spinal symptoms) chose not to pursue high-technology AAC interventions. Of the 33 individuals who used a range of augmentative communication devices, 24 individuals (12 with initial bulbar symptoms and 12 with initial spinal symptoms) were interviewed during follow-up intervention visits to obtain information regarding their patterns of use of AAC methods. None of these individuals had functional speech at the time of data collection. All subjects with initial spinal symptoms were in Group 6—poor speech, poor hand functioning, and poor mobility. The majority of subjects with initial bulbar symptoms were in Group 3—poor speech, adequate hand functioning, and adequate mobility. The remainder were in Group 4—poor speech, adequate hand functioning, and poor mobility.

Table 1.   Summary of demographic information on 36 individuals with ALS who received AAC evaluations

	Men	Women	Mean age at initial evaluation	Age range at initial evaluation	Mean duration of use[1, 2]	Range of duration of use[1, 2]
Spinal	14	6	49.9	36.1–69.9	1.8	0.1–6.1
Bulbar	3	13	60.7	35.9–78.9	0.8	0.1–2.9
Overall	17	19	54.5	35.9–78.9	1.2	0.1–6.1

[1] N=33.
[2] in years.

Table 2.　AAC methods used by 12 individuals with spinal symptoms

Gender	Dependent auditory scanning	Facial expression	Yes-or-no question	Yes-or-no hierarchy	Coded eye-blink	Alphabet board	Call buzzer	Multipurpose device
F		X	X	X		PDVS	X	X
M	X	X	X		X	PDVS	X	X
M	X	X	X				X	X
F		X	X	X		PDVS	X	X
F	X	X	X		X	PDVS	X	X
M		X	X		X		X	X
M	X	X	X				X	X
M		X	X			PDVS	X	X
M		X	X			ODS	X	X
M		X	X	X		PDVS	X	X
M	X	X	X			PDVS	X	X
M		X	X			PDVS	X	X

PDVS = Makes selections using partner-dependent visual scanning.
ODS = Makes selections using optical direct selection (laser pointer mounted on a cap).

Tables 2 and 3 contain information about the AAC methods used by individuals with spinal and bulbar symptoms, respectively. Individuals with initial spinal symptoms used more partner-dependent techniques (i.e., partner-dependent auditory scanning, partner-dependent visual scanning, responses to yes-or-no questions, yes-or-no hierarchy, or coded eye blinks) than those in the initial bulbar symptom group whose only partner-dependent technique was response to yes-or-no questions. This finding is obviously the result of differences in upper-extremity functioning. Individuals in the bulbar group were able to make use of

Table 3.　AAC methods used by 12 individuals with bulbar symptoms

Gender	Facial expression/ manual gestures	Yes-or-no questions	Hand-writing	Alphabet board	Multipurpose device	Dedicated device
F	X	X	X	X	X	
M	X	X	X		X	
F	X	X	X		X	X
F	X	X	X		X	
F	X	X	X			X
M	X	X	X	X	X	
F	X	X	X			X
F	X	X	X		X	
F	X	X	X		X	
F	X	X	X			X
F	X	X	X			X
F	X	X	X		X	

natural gestures and handwriting—methods that are familiar and efficient in a variety of situations with trained as well as untrained listeners.

For individuals with spinal symptoms, trained partners resulted in increased communicative efficiency. This was particularly evident with the three subjects who used coded eye-blink strategies. One used eye blinks (i.e., short, long) to send Morse code messages, and the other two used idiosyncratic "eye codes" to represent high-frequency words, vowels, and consonants (e.g., a wink to stand for *I*). Only partners who were trained to interpret these communication signals could understand them. With unfamiliar partners, these three subjects used partner-dependent visual or auditory scanning or their multipurpose devices. The rate of communication in conversation was fastest with familiar partners who could interpret their eye-blink codes.

Regarding high-technology methods, those with spinal symptoms chose exclusively multipurpose devices, whereas subjects in the bulbar group used a mixture of dedicated and multipurpose devices. Dedicated devices were favored by some of the subjects with bulbar presentation because they were smaller and easier to carry than a notebook computer–based multipurpose device. Caution should be used when interpreting these results, especially as related to the selection of high-technology devices. All of the individuals received intervention at the same center. Furthermore, the center's pool of loaner devices contained many more multipurpose device units than dedicated devices. Some individuals (especially those with bulbar presentation) may have chosen dedicated devices had funding been available.

Those with initial spinal symptoms generally chose unassisted or low-technology methods to communicate in conversation and for quick needs or wants. They most often chose high-technology methods for the rest of their communicative activities (see Table 4). These individuals

Table 4.   Category Of AAC method used most of the time in communicative activitiies by 12 individuals with spinal symptoms of amyotrophic lateral sclerosis (ALS)

Kind of communication	Level of method	Number of subjects
Stories	High technology	12
Written communication	High technology	12
In-depth information	High technology	12
Telephone	Unassisted	1
	High technology	4
	Does not participate	7
Quick needs	Unassisted	12
Detailed needs	Unassisted	1
	High technology	11
Conversation	Unassisted	5
	Low technology	4
	High technology	3

and their families particularly stressed the superiority of high-technology multipurpose devices for communicating detailed needs and wants. In contrast with immediate needs (e.g., "Wipe my mouth") that can often be communicated with eye gaze (e.g., a look at the wash cloth used for wiping the mouth), or a few words, detailed needs require a few sentences to communicate effectively. Communicating a lengthy message using partner-dependent low-technology or unassisted strategies can be extremely taxing and frustrating for the AAC user and partner. High-technology, multipurpose devices allow the user to construct detailed messages independently that can be printed or saved to display for communication partners as required.

As would be expected based on the differences in upper-extremity functioning and mobility, a very different pattern of AAC method use emerged for the bulbar group (see Table 5). All of the individuals in this group used handwriting for quick, basic needs and wants, and the majority of them used handwriting for face-to-face conversation. Half of this group relied on handwriting for all communicative activities except talking on the telephone. Moreover, for 7 of the 12, the need to use the telephone was the primary reason for pursuing an AAC evaluation. Three lived alone, and the others were typically at home alone during the day while their spouses were working. In communicative activities requiring greater verbal output—communicating detailed needs, providing detailed information and telling stories, written correspondence—half of the bulbar group reported that they used their high-technology methods most of the time, and half primarily relied on handwriting. Subjects who used high-technology devices for these activities did so because typing was less fatiguing.

Table 5.   Category of AAC method used most of the time in communicative activities by 12 individuals with bulbar symptoms of amyotrophic lateral sclerosis

Kind of communication	Level of method	Number of subjects
Stories	Handwriting	6
	High technology	6
Written communication	Handwriting	6
	High technology	6
Detailed information	Handwriting	6
	High technology	6
Telephone	High technology	7
	Does not participate	5
Quick needs	Handwriting	12
Detailed needs	Handwriting	6
	High technology	6
Conversation	Handwriting	10
	High technology	2

As part of an ongoing study, Pamela Mathy is recruiting individuals with ALS who are competent users of AAC to complete a detailed outcomes questionnaire. Thus far, a total of six individuals have completed the questionnaire, five with initial spinal symptoms and one with initial bulbar symptoms. All six used a multipurpose device as their high-technology method of choice at the time of the completion of the questionnaire. The overall breakdown of AAC methods by communicative activity is shown in Figure 1. Although preliminary, initial results suggest that subjects in this study tended to use their unassisted and low-technology methods for communicating in conversation and to indicate quick needs and wants, and their high-technology methods for communicating detailed needs and wants, written communication, and stories.

Familiarity with a communication partner had a distinct influence on the selection of augmentative communication method. As seen in Figure 2, when subjects communicated quick needs or wants or participated in conversation with familiar partners, they predominately relied on their unassisted and low-technology strategies. Conversely, high-technology methods dominated when engaging in conversation or conveying quick needs or wants to unfamiliar partners. It can be inferred from these findings that if their high-technology methods were not available, these individuals would be less likely and less able to engage in conversations or indicate their needs with unfamiliar partners. This underscores the importance of training medical personnel and care providers who work with people who have ALS in the effective use of unassisted and low-technology strategies as well as high-technology

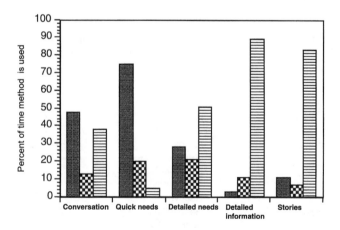

Figure 1.   Mean percentage of AAC method use by communicative activity. (■ = Unassisted; ▨ = Low-tech; ▤ = High-tech)

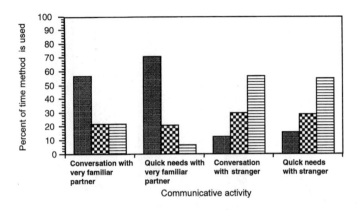

Figure 2.   Use of AAC methods by partner familiarity (*N* = 6). (■ = Unassisted; ▨ = Low-tech; ▤ = High-tech)

strategies. Participants' choice of AAC methods varied by physical position (e.g., wheelchair, conventional seating, bed) and location (e.g., car or van, home, community). Unassisted methods and low-technology methods were used in all positions and locations, whereas high-technology methods were used in fewer positions and were not used outside the home.

Gender Preferences for Augmentative Communication Methods In a retrospective review of data for 126 people with ALS (61 men and 65 women), clear patterns of preferences emerged with respect to the type and nature of AAC intervention (Gutmann, 1999). Identifiable patterns of preferences emerged along gender lines. Specifically, women preferred voice output systems almost twice as often as did men (49% of women and 26% of men), and women tended to be more accepting of communication displays or low-technology options almost three times as much as did men (20% of women; 6% of men). For men, the profile was such that they preferred high-technology writing systems almost three times more often than did women (22.9% of men; 7.6% of women), and men preferred integrated systems more than twice as much as did women (12% of men and 4.5% of women). Almost an equivalent number of men (27.8%) and women (26%) did not wish any AAC intervention according to information available upon chart review.

User Satisfaction with Augmentative Communication and Effect on Quality of Life Figure 3 contains information about satisfaction with AAC methods as reported by the six participants in the outcomes questionnaire described earlier. Note that these individuals reported generally a high level of satisfaction with their collection of AAC methods. With the exception of conversation, all ratings ranged from 5 to 7

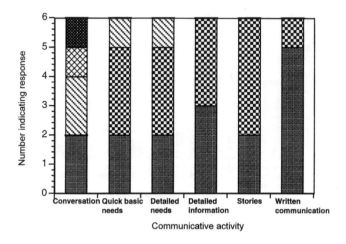

Figure 3.   Satisfaction with AAC methods by communicative activity (N=6). (▦ = 7 [Very satisfied]; ▨ = 6; ◨ = 5; ▨ = 4 [Neutral]; ▩ = 3; ■ = 2; ⬚ = 1 [Very dissatisfied])

on a 7-point scale, with 1 being the least satisfied and 7 being most satisfied. Subjects expressed the highest level of satisfaction with their methods for written communication, yet they rated their collection of AAC methods to be the least satisfactory for meeting their communicative needs in conversation. The divergence in ratings between conversation and written communication activities appears to reflect the ability of individuals' AAC methods to meet the inherent demands of these activities. Written communication is a solitary task that proceeds at one's own pace. However, conversation is a rapid exchange of ideas, opinions, and information between at least two people. It is likely that individuals' poorer evaluation of their AAC methods for use in conversation reflects the fact that the field has yet to overcome the severe reduction in word-per-minute rate imposed.

There have been no studies evaluating the effect of AAC intervention on the quality of life of individuals with ALS; however, the body of anecdotal evidence for this conclusion continues to build. As part of a study of the extent of survival of 89 people (49 men and 40 women) with ALS receiving ventilatory support, Bach (1993) examined the effects of providing AAC support on disposition. Although maintenance of effective communication did not appear to affect survival, it had a positive effect on individuals remaining in the community (receiving care in their own homes). Furthermore, anecdotal evidence (i.e., patient comments) from the 24 subjects in the study who used "computer-assisted" communication appeared to demonstrate a substantial improvement in quality of life. In the following section, the loss of communication and the acceptance of assistive technology is placed in the larger context of coping with ALS and all of the changes that this disease brings about.

COPING WITH AMYOTROPHIC LATERAL SCLEROSIS

ALS involves many losses: job, income, position in society, strength, muscle coordination, energy, independence, ability to communicate verbally, relationships with loved ones and others, sexuality, secure future, ability to eat, swallow, and even breathe—loss of almost everything a person has gained in life (Kim, 1989, p. 342).

Coping with these losses is a challenge that individuals with ALS, their families, and intervention teams face. The losses are continuous and require a constant process of adapting to one loss before another presents itself. The losses associated with ALS have been described as predictable crises points when difficult decisions must be made by the individual and the family (Baumann, 1991).

Consider the following case example of a 42-year-old woman with ALS who came to the clinic 2 months after being diagnosed. The changes in speech that she had been experiencing for 6 months had brought her to a neurologist, who diagnosed her ALS. These changes also necessitated taking a disability leave from her job. She enjoyed her work and relinquishing her job was a loss both socially and psychologically. During her second clinic visit, 4 months postdiagnosis, a discussion of the placement of a feeding tube was necessary because of the progression of bulbar symptoms. During this discussion, she commented that she did not wish to "give in" to the disease and that she would do her best to maintain the target fluid and caloric intake that we had suggested for her. At the next visit, she had maintained her weight but was devoting most of her day to this activity. She indicated that she was ready for an alternate route for eating and drinking. By this time, her natural speech was difficult to understand, and her handwriting was becoming slow and laborious. When AAC technology was suggested, she indicated that she wanted "to talk and not have another badge of disability." Two months later, when even her daughter was unable to understand her, she was willing to schedule an appointment with the Assistive Technology Clinic to explore various AAC options. This case illustrates a rapid series of losses, first of future plans because of the diagnosis, then of work, of the ability to eat, and finally of the ability to communicate with family members. Each of these losses is a painful reminder of deterioration that must be acknowledged, mourned, and managed. Issues of how individuals with ALS manage their lives have been addressed from the perspectives of both the insider (i.e., the individual living with ALS and his or her personal network) and the literature related to the psychosocial aspects of the disease. These two perspectives are described in the following sections.

The Insider's Perspective

The insider's perspective takes the point of view of the individual living with the disease and asks the question, What is it like to live with and in spite of the disease? (Peters, 1996). One rich source of such information about the lived experiences of people with ALS comes from the literary genre sometimes called *pathography*, in which individuals write personal accounts of their experiences (Kent, 1998). A number of excellent examples of such writing exists in which individuals describe their experiences of ALS (Albom, 1997; Malcolm, 1987; Rabin, 1985; Schwartz, 1996). For example, the story of Emily Bauer is recounted in a book by Andrew Malcolm called *This Far and No More* (1987). Malcolm was a journalist investigating issues of patient autonomy and medical decision making. He presented these issues in the framework of Emily's story. She was a clinical psychologist in her late thirties with a young family when the diagnosis of ALS was made. She had always kept a diary and continued to do so throughout the course of the disease, first by writing, then by dictating, then by having someone lipread, and finally by using a single-switch scanning AAC system with printed output. In a medical crisis, she was placed on a ventilator but later used her AAC system to persistently request that the ventilator be removed.

Although the story deals with the broad topic of medical ethics, speech-language pathologists will see in it the pivotal role that communication plays in Emily's story and how issues of communication cannot be easily separated from other psychosocial aspects of the disease. For example, Emily wrote the following entry in her diary when she first noticed speech changes:

> I was trying to think of what could keep my life meaningful.... I think I'll record some stories for the children, as well as the scrapbooks. I should do the activities involving speech first. I'm terrified that will go soon. Yesterday, I realized I can't move my tongue side to side very quickly. (Malcolm, 1987, p. 44)

Later when she was hospitalized and on a ventilator, she was given an electrolarynx for communication. She describes her 4-year-old daughter's reaction to this device in the following way:

> I was hoping Ali would be interested in talking to me with my new machine. But when she came in, she was very afraid of it. She put her hands over her ears and shook her head. Please God, is there some way to help them not be so frightened of it—of me? (Malcolm, 1987, p. 107)

Later, Emily was describing her written interaction with physicians when she wrote,

I have spent much of the morning printing notes to doctors. Communication is so tedious and difficult. I try to be direct, but even my written communications are responded to as selectively as if they were ambiguous Rorschach cards. (Malcolm, 1987, p. 148)

Thus, Emily's story depicts a woman who is acutely aware of her increasing speech impairment. The consequence of the impairment, when viewed from her perspective, relates to her inability to play the communicative roles she chooses—that is, the role of mother and the role of patient attempting to direct important parts of the management of her condition.

The insider perspective has also been examined through the analysis of in-depth interviews with individuals with ALS. Cobb and Hamera (1986) interviewed two women with ALS at 2-month intervals throughout the course of their disease. The first participant was a 54-year-old retired woman with grown children and a husband with emphysema. During the first and second interviews, she described how the emotional lability and uncontrollable laughing and crying that are frequently associated with ALS caused her to curtail social activities and to isolate herself from friends. As her dysarthria worsened, she saw friends as changing from being "kind" to being nervous around her and "shying away," not wanting to be alone with her as her speech continued to decline. She was also annoyed with friends who expressed their anxiety by talking compulsively. This informant also commented on the role of assistive devices offered to her to help maintain function. She believed that these devices would hasten the loss of function. By the third interview, her opposition to assistive technology was clearly related to her self-image when she stated, "It's not me." The authors propose that the devices may have been symbolic of her illness. Any assistive device not specifically linked to her illness (e.g., electric toothbrush, speaker telephone) did not challenge her self-image, but those related to the illness (e.g. wheelchair, suction equipment) were rejected. She saw the devices as helpful to her caregivers rather than to herself and resented her lack of control over selecting them. She also rejected simple communication systems and expressed dislike of using an alphabet board to communicate by stating, " I prefer to *talk*!" This rejection came at a time when her speech was, by then, almost totally unintelligible.

The second participant was a 51-year-old woman with two grown children. During the initial interviews, she recognized her symptoms and associated them with the loss of functioning. She was frustrated with her dysarthria and labeled herself as having a lazy tongue. During subsequent interviews, she expressed a decreasing satisfaction in social interaction that was presumed to be related to her increasing difficulty in being understood when she spoke. Unlike the first participant, this woman did not reject assistive technology. Rather, she approached assistive devices in a practical manner; if they worked, she used them and seemed to appreciate them. Despite this acceptance, she did not credit the rehabilitation service providers as being helpful. For the most part, she believed that commercial devices were not adjusted for the user, were too costly, or did not work. She felt that the devices altered or built by her husband worked well for her, and she viewed his efforts in a positive light.

The role of the caregiver in the process of psychosocial adaptation to chronic disability is an important one. Tolerating the uncertainty of living with a chronic illness has long been of interest to social scientists (Wiener & Dodd, 1993). A variety of factors contribute to caregiver strain, including the amount of direct care, negative lifestyle changes, predictability of the disease, help from others, and disease severity (Archbold & Stewart, 1990; Archbold et al., 1995). Caregiver strains may result in depression, decreased physical health, and increased acute care utilization. In a survey of 24 individuals with ALS receiving nonhospice home care, the burden placed on family caregivers was examined. Results indicated caregivers spent a median of 11 hours per day caring for the person with ALS, despite having care assistance. Nearly half the caregivers studied reported feeling physically and psychologically unwell. The role of AAC in preventing or minimizing caregiver burden has not been studied.

Analysis of qualitative interviews with individuals with ALS and their families may suggest a number of pessimistic themes: feelings of helplessness and powerlessness, fears of becoming totally dependent on others, and the loss of friends with its associated social isolation (Leach & Delfiner, 1989). Other interviews have focused on gains that emerge from coping with the disease. From an analysis of in-depth interviews with 13 people who were coping well with ALS, several positive themes emerged. These include the development of wisdom and the vital importance of interpersonal relationships (Young & McNicoll, 1998). Although some of these themes related to communication, the impact of AAC intervention on the psychosocial aspects of life has largely been ignored.

Psychosocial Aspects

The fields of rehabilitation counseling and psychology have long been interested both clinically and theoretically in how people adapt to disability. Psychosocial adaptation may involve the gradual process of accommodating oneself to a variety of changes—in one's body, self-concept, and person–environment interactions. Because successful rehabilitation efforts often depend on utilizing an individual's coping skills, understanding these adaptation strategies is critical. Psychosocial adaptation in ALS has been investigated from a theoretical point of view (Hewson, 1997) and with a variety of empirical studies. Early studies using batteries of psychological tests indicated that individuals with ALS had a high degree of internality or the belief in personal control of life events. Results of one study of only 10 individuals with ALS were interpreted to suggest that individuals with ALS tend to avoid asking for help (Brown & Mueller, 1970). Somewhat later studies modified these conclusions and reported that internality may be a function of the duration of the disability (Houpt, Gould, & Norris, 1977). Individuals early and very late in the course of the disease may exhibit a more external locus of control, thus relying more on a physician's advice, existential fatalism, and religious faith. Both clinical impression and research literature suggest that individuals with ALS wish to make their own decisions about a variety of issues including ventilation (Moss et al., 1996; Silverstein et al., 1991), assisted suicide (Ganzini, Johnston, McFarland, Tolle, & Lee, 1998), living at home (Moore, 1993), use of assistive technology (Cobb & Hamera, 1986), and communication options (Gutmann, 1999). In their summary of the psychosocial aspects of ALS, Livneh and Antonak (1997) concluded that only limited inferences can be drawn from the existing literature. Most of the studies are small and represent a nonrandom sample of the population. Furthermore, researchers often fail to consider aspects of premorbid status (e.g., personality attribute, family support) that may influence adaptation. Finally, Livneh and Antonak pointed out a conspicuous lack of research using longitudinal designs to trace temporal changes in psychosocial adaptation as the disease progresses.

Everyone is broken by life, but some people become strong in the broken places.
—*Ernest Hemingway as cited in Wiener & Dodd, 1993, p. 28*

The topic of the psychological status of individuals with ALS has also been addressed. In fact, psychological status is strongly related to outcomes in ALS. In a longitudinal study of 144 individuals with ALS, the survival curves for those who were in the group with high psychological well-being were significantly different from those in the group with low psychological well-being (McDonald et al., 1994). Not surprisingly, studies indicate that psychological distress as measured with a questionnaire is widespread among individuals with ALS at all stages of the disease (Hunter, Robinson, & Neilson, 1993). However, the severity of the functional limitations explains only a small part of the variance in the relationship between psychological distress and severity of ALS. Like psychological distress, depression is not uncommon in people with ALS. Studies suggest that it occurs at about the rate in motor neuron disease as in other degenerative neurological conditions, such as multiple sclerosis (Tedman, Young, & Williams, 1997). As in the case of psychological distress, the severity of depression is only weakly associated with the severity of the physical disability.

In the clinical setting, it is important to distinguish depression, chronic sorrow, and emotional lability. Depression is characterized by pessimism and hopelessness coupled with decreased motivation, drive, and an inability to enjoy life. Chronic sorrow, however, is a term denoting the grief experienced from continual loss during the experience of an illness or a disability (Olshansky, 1962). It is a sadness that is permanent, periodic, and triggered by milestones or events, such as the loss of future plans and restricted social life (Hainsworth, 1994, 1996; Lindgren, 1996). Like depression, chronic sorrow has a component of sadness, but there is no loss of self; rather, the individual experiences a cyclical sadness associated with loss. Although depression is marked by the inability to enjoy things, chronic sorrow is not. Emotional lability is quite different. The term literally means an unsteadiness of emotions in which individuals experience bouts of laughter and crying that are not in proportion to the stimuli (Gallagher, 1989). Lability is not typically considered a psychological impairment. Rather, it is consistent with bilateral corticobulbar lesions that result in loss of pyramidal tract inhibitory control over the behavioral-expressive responses of an emotion (Montgomery & Erickson, 1987).

Role of Hope in the Intervention Process

Hope consists of a collection of feelings and thoughts centering on the belief that there are solutions to needs and problems (Lange, 1978). It is an inner quality of life and one of the most valuable, private, and powerful resources of a human being (Kim, 1989). Kim suggested that hope plays a powerful role in coping with ALS because

> One has to exercise the most creative of all human potentials to find meaning in suffering. It is extremely difficult work, for it requires one to change oneself (when one can no longer change one's fate as in the case of ALS), to rise above and to grow beyond oneself. (p. 344)

In fact, individuals with ALS see maintenance of hope as an important role of care providers (Beisecker, Cobb, & Ziegler, 1988). When hope is defined as "desire with the expectation of fulfillment," it may serve as a framework upon which intervention can be built. For example, in the field of AAC intervention, hope may be encouraged by developing a "wish list" of communication activities. Listening to the wishes and hopes of the individual with ALS and those in the personal network and helping to achieve those wishes is at the heart of AAC intervention. One grandmother with ALS wished to tell family stories to her young grandchildren. Because her natural speech was somewhat difficult to understand, she used a family picture album to tell them the story of how she lived in London during the bombings of World War II. She used the album of pictures, letters, and memorabilia as an AAC device to supplement her highly distorted speech. Maintenance of social contact with her grandchildren was a realistic wish that was at least in part fulfilled by a simple AAC technique.

Curing refers to practices which are efficacious from the point of view of biomedical science, while healing refers to practices that are efficacious from the point of view of the person experiencing the illness.
—Cobb & Hamera, 1986, p. 642

OUTLOOK FOR THE FUTURE

In this chapter, we review the current state of practice in AAC for individuals with ALS. From this review, it is clear that there are many reasons for hope, including, for example, progress in understanding the basic nature of the disease and the first careful studies documenting the benefit of drug intervention. We begin by discussing some possible directions of future research related to AAC. First, issues related to maintenance of communication should be studied within the framework of medical management. Understanding the impact of new drug interventions on the progression of dysarthria is an important topic for investigation. Practice parameters developed from evidence-based reviews of the literature are becoming common in many fields of medicine. In 1999, the Quality Standards Subcommittee of the American Academy of Neurology published an initial set of practice parameters for the care of individuals with ALS (Miller et al., 1999). Five important areas were addressed, including breaking the news to patients and families, nutrition and feeding tube placements, respiratory insufficiency and mechanical ventilation, management of emotional lability, and palliative care. Unfortunately, issues related to communication, such as the timing of AAC intervention, were not addressed in the initial practice parameters but certainly deserve future investigation. As individuals with ALS live beyond respiratory failure, the need to provide effective means of communication is particularly critical.

The research literature focusing on cognitive issues associated with ALS points to a series of important next steps. For the field of AAC, these next steps might include answers to a number of questions. How does cognitive functioning change over time in ALS? For the most part, the studies of cognition reported here are cross-sectional rather than longitudinal studies of groups of individuals. What is the relationship between motor impairment and cognitive impairment? Motor impairment is thought to decline in a linear fashion. Does the cognitive impairment exhibit a similar pattern of decline? Do the differences identified in neuropsychological testing make a difference in functional activities? For example, how do cognitive changes affect the ability to learn to use AAC systems? What assessment tasks free of extensive motor demands can be used to screen cognition in individuals with advanced ALS who are considering communication with AAC strategies? Does the individual with ALS report any changes in cognition? For the most part, the studies reviewed here were quantitative examinations of differences in performance. Qualitative methods in which individuals with ALS could be interviewed in depth may help to clarify what the insider is experiencing.

The topic of how AAC services are provided to individuals with ALS also warrants investigation. For example, how can information and services be provided in a "just in time" fashion? In other words, just when it is needed, not too early and not too late. What features of AAC systems are preferred by individuals with ALS and their families? What service delivery models are most appropriate in this population?

Finally, advances in technology will continue to enhance augmentative communication systems. Next-generation AAC devices will allow effective and efficient access even in the face of profound lack of movement. For example, as seen on *60 Minutes,* eye-controlled access devices for written and spoken communication such as VisionKey are becoming portable and monetarily feasible:

Wallace (voiceover):   Dr. Howard Hornstein still finds life enriching, though most of us would find it terrifying. Because of ALS, all he can move are his eyes, but he can type with his right eye by pointing his pupil toward specific letters on a visual keyboard attached to his right lens and a voice synthesizer speaks what he's written. We sent him questions in advance to give him time to type his answers.

Dr. Hornstein (through computer translator):   Although at this time I have no movement except for my eyes and breathe by means of a ventilator, technology is my salvation.

(*Choosing Life*: A *60 Minutes* transcript, Broadcast on Sunday, February 28, 1999, at 7:00 P.M.)

Going beyond the necessity for physical movement, access techniques that use neurophysiological responses to control cursor movements on a computer screen are being developed, and their efficacy for individuals with ALS is being assessed (Birbaumer et al., 1999; Kubler et al., 1999). Until such access strategies become part of routine practice, however, an immediate challenge for researchers and clinicians is to determine the characteristics of the individual and his or her support system required to receive maximal benefit from these cutting-edge technologies.

Another, ever-present challenge is funding. ALS typically strikes in mid- to late life, yet Medicare, the nation's federal health services funding program for older adults and individuals receiving Social Security Disability Insurance, does not routinely cover AAC devices. As this book goes to press, Medicare's guidelines for covering AAC devices are in flux. For more information regarding this issue, please visit the Brookes Publishing web site (www.brookespublishing.com/aac.htm).

REFERENCES

Abe, K., Jujimura, H., Yoyooka, K., Sakoda, S., Yorifuji, S., & Yanagihara, T. (1997). Cognitive function in amyotrophic lateral sclerosis. *Journal of Neurological Sciences, 148*(1), 95–100.

Aboussousan, L.S., Khan, S.U., Meeker, D.P., Stelmack, K., & Misumoto, H. (1997). Effect of noninvasive positive-pressure ventilation on survival in amyotrophic lateral sclerosis. *Annals of Internal Medicine, 127*(6), 450–453.

Abrahams, S., Goldstein, L.H., Al Chalabi, A., Pickering, A., Morris, R.G., Passingham, R.E., Brooks, D.J., & Leigh, P.N. (1997). Relation between cognitive dysfunction and pseudobulbar palsy in amyotrophic lateral sclerosis. *Journal of Neurology, Neurosurgery, and Psychiatry, 62*(5), 464–472.

Abrahams, S., Goldstein, L.H., Brooks, D.J., Lloyd, C.M., Frith, C.D., & Leigh, P.N. (1996). Frontal lobe dysfunction in amyotrophic lateral sclerosis: A PET study. *Brain, 119,* 2105–2120.

Abrahams, S., Leigh, P.N., Kew, J.J., Goldstein, L.H., Lloyd, C.M., & Brooks, D.J. (1995). A positron emission tomography study of frontal lobe function (verbal fluency) in amyotrophic lateral sclerosis. *Journal of the Neurological Sciences, 129,* 44–46.

Albert, S.M., Bene, M.D., Murphy, P., & Rowland, L.P. (1998). *Prospective study of palliative care in ALS: Determinants of choice and timing of therapies* [On-line]. Available: www.alsmndalliance.org/newsymp.htm

Albom, M. (1997). *Tuesdays with Morrie*. New York: Bantam Doubleday Dell.

Archbold, P.G., & Stewart, B.J. (1990). Mutuality and preparedness as predictors of caregiver role strain. *Research in Nursing & Health, 13*(6), 375–384.

Archbold, P.G., Stewart, B.J., Miller, L.L., Harvath, T.A., Greenlick, M.R., VanBuren, L., Kirschling, J.M., Valanis, B.G., Brody, K.K., Schook, J.E., & Hagan,

J.M. (1995). The PREP system of nursing interventions: A pilot test with families caring for older members . . . preparedness (PR), enrichment (E), and predictability (P). *Research in Nursing & Health, 18*(1), 3–16.

Armon, C., & Moses, D. (1998). Linear estimates of rates of disease progression as predictors of survival in patients with ALS entering clinical trials. *Journal of the Neurological Sciences, 160*(Suppl. 1), S37–S41.

Aronson, A.E., Ramig, L.O., Winholtz, W.S., & Silber, S.R. (1992). Rapid voice tremor, or "flutter," in amyotrophic lateral sclerosis. *Annals of Otology, Rhinology and Laryngology, 101*(6), 511–518.

Ashworth, P. (1980). *Care to communicate.* London: Whitefriars Press.

Bach, J. (1995). Amyotrophic lateral sclerosis: Predictors for prolongation of life by noninvasive respiratory aids. *Archives of Physical Medicine and Rehabilitation, 76,* 828–832.

Bach, J.R. (1993). Amyotrophic lateral sclerosis: Communication status and survival with ventilatory support. *American Journal of Physical Medicine and Rehabilitation, 72,* 343–349.

Bach, J.R. (1998). Rehabilitation of the patient with respiratory dysfunction. In J. DeLisa (Ed.), *Rehabilitation medicine: Principles and practice* (3rd ed., pp. 1359–1384). Philadelphia: Lippincott, Williams & Wilkins.

Baumann, A. (1991). ALS—decision making under uncertainty: A positive approach. *Axone, 13*(2), 41–44.

Beisecker, A.E., Cobb, A.K., & Ziegler, D.K. (1988). Patients' perspectives of the role of care providers in amyotrophic lateral sclerosis. *Archives of Neurology, 45,* 553–556.

Bensimon, G., Lacomblez, L., & Meininger, V. (1994). A controlled trial of riluzole in amyotrophic lateral sclerosis. *New England Journal of Medicine, 330*(9), 585–591.

Berghom-Engberg, I., & Haljamae, H. (1993). The communication process with ventilator patients in the ICU as perceived by the nursing staff. *Intensive and Critical Care Nursing, 9*(1), 40–47.

Birbaumer, N.G., Hinteberger, T., Iversen, I., Kotchoibey, B., Kubler, A., Perelmouter, J., Taub, E., & Flor, H. (1999). A spelling device for the paralysed. *Nature, 398*(6725), 297–298.

Borasio, G.D., & Voltz, R. (1997). Palliative care in amyotrophic lateral sclerosis. *Journal of Neurology, 244,* S11–S17.

Borasio, G.D., & Voltz, R. (1998). Discontinuation of mechanical ventilation in patients with amyotrophic lateral sclerosis. *Journal of Neurology, 245*(11), 717–722.

Braun, S.R. (1987). Respiratory systems in amyotrophic lateral sclerosis. *Neurologic Clinics, 5*(1), 9–31.

Brooks, B.R. (1991). The role of axonal transport in neurodegenerative disease spread: Meta-analysis of experimental and clinical poliomyelitis compared with amyotrophic lateral sclerosis. *Canadian Journal of Neurological Sciences, 18*(Suppl.), 435–438.

Brown, W.A., & Mueller, P.S. (1970). Psychological function in individuals with amyotrophic lateral sclerosis (ALS). *Psychosomatic Medicine, 32*(2), 141–152.

Brun, A., & Passant, U. (1996). Frontal lobe degeneration of non-Alzheimer type. Structural characteristics, diagnostic criteria and relation to the frontotemporal dementias. *Acta Neurologica Scandinavica, 168*(Suppl.), 28–30.

Caroscio, J.T., Mulvihill, M.N., Sterling, R., & Abrams, B. (1987). Amyotrophic lateral sclerosis: Its natural history. *Neurologic Clinics, 5*(1), 1–8.

Caselli, R.J., Windebank, A.J., Petersen, R.C., Komori, T., Parisi, J.E., Okazaki, H., Kokmen, E., Iverson, R., Dinapoli, R.P., Graff-Radford, N.R., et al. (1993). Rapidly progressive aphasic dementia and motor neuron disease. *Annals of Neurology, 33*(2), 200–207.

Cavalleri, F., & DeRenzi, E. (1994). Amyotrophic lateral sclerosis with dementia. *Acta Neurologica Scandinavica, 89*, 391–394.

Cazzolli, P.A., & Oppenheimer, E.A. (1996). Home mechanical ventilation for amyotrophic lateral sclerosis: Nasal compared to tracheostomy-intermittent positive pressure ventilation. *Journal of the Neurological Sciences, 139*, 123–128.

Cazzolli, P.A., & Oppenheimer, E.A. (1998, November). *Prediction of respiratory failure in amyotrophic lateral sclerosis: Decision making for mechanical ventilation or palliative care.* Paper presented at the Ninth International Symposium of the International Alliance on ALS/MND, Munich, Germany.

Clawson, L.L., Rothstein, J.D., & Kuncl, R.W. (1993). Amyotrophic lateral sclerosis. In R.T. Johnson (Ed.), *Current therapy in neuologic disease* (Vol. 4, pp. 286–295). Philadelphia: B.C. Decker.

Cobb, A.K., & Hamera, E. (1986). Illness experience in a chronic disease—ALS. *Social Science and Medicine, 23*(7), 641–650.

DePaul, R., Abbs, J.H., Caligiuri, M.P., Gracco, V.L., & Brooks, B.R. (1988). Hypoglossal, trigeminal, and facial motoneuron involvement in amyotrophic lateral sclerosis. *Neurology, 38*, 281–283.

DePaul, R., Waclawik, A.J., Abbs, J.H., & Brooks, B.R. (1998). Histopathological characteristics in lingual muscle tissue in ALS: Perspectives on the natural history of the disease. In M.P. Cannito, K.M. Yorkston, & D.R. Beukelman (Eds.), *Neuromotor speech disorders: Nature, assessment, and management* (pp. 69–84). Baltimore: Paul H. Brookes Publishing Co.

Dikeman, K., & Kazanddjian, M. (1995). *Communication and swallowing management of tracheostomized and ventilator-dependent adults.* San Diego: Singular Publishing Co.

Duffy, J.R. (1995). *Motor speech disorders: Substrates, differential diagnosis, and management.* St. Louis: Mosby.

Dworkin, J., & Aronson, A. (1986). Tongue strength and alternate motion rates in normal and dysarthric subjects. *Journal of Communication Disorders, 19*, 115–132.

Eisen, A., & Calne, D. (1992). Amyotrophic lateral sclerosis, Parkinson's disease and Alzheimer's disease: Phylogenetic disorders of the human neocortex sharing many characteristics. *Canadian Journal of Neurological Sciences, 19*(1), 117–123.

Eisen, A., & Krieger, C. (1993). Pathogenic mechanism in sporadic amyotrophic lateral sclerosis. *Canadian Journal of Neurologic Sciences, 20*(4), 286–296.

Eisen, A., Schulzer, M., MacNeil, M., Pant, B., & Mak, E. (1993). Duration of amyotrophic lateral sclerosis is age dependent. *Muscle and Nerve, 16*(1), 27–32.

Frank, B., Haas, J., Heinze, H.J., Stark, E., & Munte, T.F. (1997). Relation of neuropsychological and magnetic resonance findings in amyotrophic lateral sclerosis: Evidence for subgroups. *Clinical Neurology and Neurosurgery, 99*(2), 79–86.

Gallagher, J.P. (1989). Pathologic laughter and crying in ALS: A search for their origin. *Acta Neurologica Scandinavica, 80*(2), 114–117.

Gallassi, R., Montagna, P., Morreale, A., Lorusso, A., Tinuper, P., Daidone, R., & Lugaresi, E. (1989). Neuropsycholgoical, electroencephalogram and brain computed tomography findings in motor neuron disease. *European Neurology, 29,* 115–120.

Ganzini, L., Johnston, W.S., McFarland, B.H., Tolle, S.W., & Lee, M.A. (1998). Attitudes of patients with amyotrophic lateral sclerosis and their care givers toward assisted suicide. *New England Journal of Medicine, 339*(14), 967–973.

Gelinas, D.F., O'Connor, P., & Miller, R.G. (1998). Quality of life for ventilator-dependent ALS patients and their caregivers. *Journal of Neurological Sciences, 160*(Suppl. 1), S134–136.

Goldblatt, D., & Greenlaw, J. (1989). Starting and stopping the ventilator for patients with amyotrophic lateral sclerosis. *Neurologic Clinics, 7*(4), 789–806.

Gregory, R., Mills, K., & Donaghy, M. (1993). Progressive sensory nerve dysfunction in amyotrophic lateral sclerosis: A prospective clinical and neurological study. *Journal of Neurology, 240*(5), 309–314.

Gries, M.L., & Fernsler, J. (1988). Patient perceptions of the mechanical ventilation experience: Focus on critical care. *Focus on Critical Care, 15,* 52–59.

Gutmann, M. (1999, November). *The communication continuum in ALS: Client preferences and communicative competence.* Paper presented at the annual convention of the American Speech Language Hearing Association (ASHA), San Francisco.

Gutmann, M.L., & Gryfe, P. (1996, August). *The communication continuum in ALS: Critical paths and client preferences.* Proceedings of the seventh biennial conference of the International Society for Augmentative and Alternative Communication (ISAAC), Vancouver, British Columbia, Canada.

Hafsteinsfottir, T.B. (1996). Patient's experience of communication during the respirator treatment period. *Intensive and Critical Care Nursing, 12*(5), 261–271.

Hainsworth, M.A. (1994). Living with multiple sclerosis: The experience of chronic sorrow. *Journal of Neuroscience Nursing, 26*(4), 237–240.

Hainsworth, M.A. (1996). Helping spouses with chronic sorrow related to multiple sclerosis. *Journal of Psychosocial Nursing and Mental Health Services, 34*(6), 36–40.

Hanayama, K., Ishikawa, Y., & Bach, J.R. (1997). Amyotrophic lateral sclerosis: Successful treatment of mucous plugging by mechanical insufflation-exsufflation. *American Journal of Physical Medicine and Rehabilitation, 76*(4), 338–339.

Hewson, D. (1997). Coping with loss of ability: "Good grief" or episodic stress response? *Social Science and Medicine, 44*(8), 1129–1139.

Hillel, A.D., Yorkston, K.M., & Miller, R.M. (1989). Use of phonation time to estimate vital capacity in amyotrophic lateral sclerosis. *Archives of Physical Medicine and Rehabilitation, 70,* 618–620.

Horoupian, D.S., Thal, L., Katzman, R., Terry, R.D., Davies, P., Hirano, A., DeTeresa, R., Fuld, P.S., Petito, C., & Blass, J. (1984). Dementia and motor neuron disease: Morphometric, biochemical and Golgi studies. *Annals of Neurology, 16,* 305–313.

Houpt, J.L., Gould, B.S., & Norris, F.H. (1977). Psychological characteristics of patients with amyotrophic lateral sclerosis (ALS). *Psychosomatic Medicine, 39,* 299–303.

Hudson, A.J. (1981). Amyotrophic lateral sclerosis and its association with dementia, parkinsonism, and other neurologic disorders: A review. *Brain, 104*(2), 217–247.

Hunter, M.D., Robinson, I.C., & Neilson, S. (1993). The functional and psychological status of patients with amyotrophic lateral sclerosis: Some implications for rehabilitation. *Disability and Rehabilitation, 15*(3), 119–126.

Hustad, K. (1999). Optimizing communicative effectiveness. In K.M. Yorkston, D.R. Beukelman, E.A. Strand, & K.R. Bell (Eds.), *Management of motor speech disorders in children and adults* (pp. 483–542). Austin, TX: PRO-ED.

Iwasaki, Y., Kinoshita, M., Ikeda, K., Takamiya, K., & Shiojima, T. (1990). Neuropsychological dysfunction in amyotrophic lateral sclerosis: Relation to motor abilities. *International Journal of Neuroscience, 54*(2), 191–195.

Jablonski, R.S. (1994). The experience of being mechanically ventilated. *Qualitative Health Research, 4*(2), 186–207.

Jackson, C.E., & Bryan, W.W. (1998). Amyotrophic lateral sclerosis. *Seminars in Neurology, 18*(1), 27–39.

Kapadia, F. (1998). Mechanical ventilation: Simplifying the terminology. *Postgraduate Medical Journal, 74*(872), 330–335.

Kaub-Wittemer, D., von Steinbchel, N., Wasner, M., & Borasio, G.D. (1998, November). *A cross-sectional study of the quality of life of ventilated ALS patients and their caregivers in Germany.* Paper presented at the Ninth International Symposium of the International Alliance on ALS/MND, Munich, Germany.

Kazandjian, M.S. (1997). *Communication and swallowing solutions for the ALS/MND Community.* San Diego: Singular Publishing Group.

Kennedy, M.R.T., Strand, E.A., & Yorkston, K.M. (1994). Selected acoustic changes in the verbal repairs of dysarthric speakers. *Journal of Medical Speech-Language Pathology, 2*(4), 263–280.

Kent, J.F., Kent, R.D., Rosenbek, J.C., Weismer, G., Martin, R., Sufit, R., & Brooks, B.R. (1992). Quantitative description of the dysarthria in women with amyotrophic lateral sclerosis. *Journal of Speech and Hearing Research, 35,* 723–733.

Kent, R.D. (1998). Insights from memoirs of illness and disability. *Asha, 40*(3), 22–25.

Kent, R.D., Hyang-Hee, K., Weismer, G., Kent, J.F., Rosenbek, J.C., Brooks, B.R., & Workinger, M. (1994). Laryngeal dysfunction in neurological disease: Amyotrophic lateral sclerosis, Parkinson disease, and stroke. *Journal of Medical Speech-Language Pathology, 2*(3), 157–176.

Kent, R.D., Kent, J.F., Weismer, G., Sufit, R.L., Rosenbek, J.C., Martin, R.E., & Brooks, B.R. (1990). Impairment of speech intelligibility in men with amyotrophic lateral sclerosis. *Journal of Speech and Hearing Disorders, 55*(4), 721–728.

Kew, J.J., Goldstein, L.H., Leigh, P.N., Abrahams, S., Cograve, N., Passingham, R.E., Frackowiak, R.S., & Brooks, D.J. (1993). The relationship between abnormalities of cognitive function and cerebral activation in amyotrophic lateral sclerosis: A neuropsychological and positron emission tomography study. *Brain, 116,* 1399–1423.

Kew, J.J., Leigh, P.N., Playford, E.D., Passingham, R.E., Goldstein, L.H., Frackowiak, R.S., & Brooks, D.J. (1993). Cortical function in amyotrophic lateral sclerosis: A positron emission tomography study. *Brain, 116*(Pt. 3), 655–680.

Kim, T. (1989). Hope as a mode of coping in amyotrophic lateral sclerosis. *Journal of Neuroscience Nursing, 21*(6), 342–347.

Klasner, E.R., Yorkston, K.M., & Strand, E.A. (1999). Patterns of perceptual features in speakers with ALS: Prominence and intelligibility considerations. *Journal of Medical Speech-Language Pathology, 7*(2), 117–126.

Kubler, A., Kotchoubey, B., Hinterberger, T., Ghanayim, N., Perelmouter, J., Schauer, M., Fritsch, C., Taub, E., & Birbaumer, N. (1999). The thought translation device: A neurophysiological approach to communication in total paralysis. *Experimental Brain Research, 124*(2), 223–232.

Lange, S.P. (1978). Hope. In C.E. Carlson & B. Blackwell (Eds.), *Behavioral concepts and nursing intervention* (pp. 287–299). Philadelphia: Lippincott, Williams & Wilkins.

Leach, C.F., & Delfiner, J.S. (1989). Approaches to loss and bereavement in amyotrophic lateral sclerosis. In S.C. Klagsbrun (Ed.), *Preventive psychiatry: Early intervention and situational crisis management* (pp. 201–211). Philadelphia: Charles Press.

Lindgren, C. (1996). Chronic sorrow in persons with Parkinson's and their spouses. *Scholarly Inquiry for Nursing Practice, 10*(4), 351–370.

Livneh, H., & Antonak, R.F. (1997). *Psychosocial adaptation to chronic illness and disability.* Gaithersburg, MD: Aspen Publishers.

Louvel, E., Hugon, J., & Doble, A. (1997). Therapeutic advances in amyotrophic lateral sclerosis. *Trends in Pharmacological Sciences, 18*(6), 196–203.

Ludolph, A.C., Langen, K.J., Regard, M., Herzog, H., Kemper, B., Kuwert, T., Bottger, I.G., & Feinendegen, L. (1992). Frontal lobe function in amyotrophic lateral sclerosis: A neuropsychologic and positron emission tomography study. *Acta Neurologica Scandivavica, 85*(2), 81–89.

Malcolm, A. (1987). *This far and no more.* New York: Times Books.

Manzano, J.L., Lubillo, S., Henriquez, D., Martin, J.C., Perez, M.C., & Wilson, D.J. (1993). Verbal communication of ventilator-dependent patients. *Critical Care Medicine, 21*(4), 512–517.

Massman, P.J., Kreiter, K.T., Jankovic, J., & Doody, R.S. (1996). Neuropsychological functioning in cortical-basal ganglionic degeneration: Differentiation from Alzheimer's disease. *Neurology, 46,* 720–726.

Massman, P.J., Sims, J., Cook, N., Haverkamp, L.J., Appel, V., & Appel, S.H. (1996). Prevalence and correlates of neuropsychological deficits in amyotrophic lateral sclerosis. *Journal of Neurology, Neurosurgery and Psychiatry, 61,* 450–455.

Mathy, P. (1996, August). *Use of electronic communication by addult AAC users.* Paper presented at the seventh biennial conference of the International Society of Augmentative and Alternative Communication, Vancouver, British Columbia, Canada.

McDonald, E.R., Hillel, A., & Wiedenfeld, S.A. (1996). Evaluation of the psychological status of ventilatory-supported patients with ALS/MND. *Palliative Medicine, 10*(1), 35–41.

McDonald, E.R., Wiedenfeld, S.A., Hillel, A., Carpenter, C.L., & Walter, R.A. (1994). Survival in amyotrophic lateral sclerosis: The role of psychological factors. *Archives of Neurology, 51*(1), 17–23.

Menzel, L. (1994). Need for communication-related research in mechanically ventilated patients. *American Journal of Critical Care, 3*(3), 165–167.

Menzel, L.K. (1997). A comparison of patients' communication-related responses during intubation and after extubation. *Heart and Lung, 26*(5), 363–371.

Menzel, L.K. (1998). Factors related to the emotional responses of intubated patients to being unable to speak. *Heart and Lung, 27*(4), 245–252.

Miller, R.G., Rosenberg, J.A., Gelinas, D.F., Mitsumoto, H., Newman, D., Dufit, R., Borasio, G.D., Bradley, W.G., Bromberg, M.B., Brooks, B.R., Kasarskis, E.J., Munsat, T.L., Oppenheimer, E.A., & the ALS Practice Parameters Task Force. (1999). Practice parameter: The care of the patient with amyotrophic lateral sclerosis (an evidence-based review): Report of the Quality Standards Subcommittee of the American Academy of Neurology. *Neurology, 52,* 1311–1323.

Mitsumoto, H. (1997). Riluzole—What is its impact in our treatment and understanding of amyotrophic lateral sclerosis? *Annals of Pharmacotherapy, 31*(6), 779–781.

Montgomery, G.K., & Erickson, L.M. (1987). Neuropsychological perspectives in amyotrophic lateral sclerosis. *Neurologic Clinics, 5*(1), 61–81.

Moore, M.K. (1993). Dying at home: A way of maintaining control for the person with ALS/MND. *Palliative Medicine, 7*(Suppl. 4), 65–68.

Moss, A.H., Casey, P., Stocking, C.B., Roos, R.P., Brooks, B.R., & Siegler, M. (1993). Home ventilation for amyotrophic lateral sclerosis patients: Outcomes, costs, and patient, family and physician attitudes. *Neurology, 43*(2), 438–443.

Moss, A.H., Oppenheimer, E.A., Casey, P., Cazzolii, P.A., Roos, R.P., Stocking, C.B., & Siegler, M. (1996). Patients with amyotrophic lateral sclerosis receiving long-term mechanical ventilation: Advance care planning and outcomes. *Chest, 110*(1), 249–255.

Neary, D., & Snowden, J. (1996). Fronto-temporal dementia: Nosology, neuorpsychology, and neuropathology. *Brain and Cognition, 31,* 2.

Neary, D., Snowden, J.S., Gustafson, L., Passant, U., Stuss, D., Black, S., Freedman, M., Kertesz, A., Robert, P.H., Albert, M., Boone, K., Miller, B.L., Cummings, J., & Benson, D.F. (1998). Frontotemporal lobar degeneration: A consensus of clinical diagnoistic criteria. *Neurology, 51*(6), 1546–1554.

Neary, D., Snowden, J.S., Mann, D.M.A., Northern, B., Goulding, P.J., & MacDermott, N. (1990). Frontal lobe dementia and motor neuron disease. *Journal of Neurology, Neurosurgery, and Psychiatry, 53,* 23–32.

Olshansky, S. (1962). Chronic sorrow: A response to having a mentally defective child. *Social Casework, 43,* 191–193.

Oppenheimer, E.A. (1997). *Living with ALS: Adapting to breathing changes.* Woodland Hills, CA: ALS Association.

Peavy, G.M., Herzog, A.G., Rubin, N.P., & Mesulam, M.M. (1992). Neuropsychological aspects of dementia of motor neuron disease: A report of two cases. *Neurology, 42*(5), 1004–1008.

Peters, D.J. (1996). Disablement observed, addressed, and experienced: Integrating subjective experience into disablement models. *Disability and Rehabilitation, 18,* 593–603.

Pinto, A.C., Evangelista, T., Carvalho, M., Alves, M.A., & Sales Luis, M.L. (1995). Respiratory assistance with a non-invasive ventilator (BiPAP) in MND/ALS patients: Survival rates in a controlled trial. *Journal of the Neurological Sciences, 129,* 19–26.

Poloni, M., Capitani, E., Mazzini, L., & Ceroni, M. (1986). Neuropsychological measures in amyotrophic lateral sclerosis and their relationship with CT scan-assessed cerbral atrophy. *Acta Neurologica Scandivavica, 74*(4), 257–260.

Pradas, J., Finison, L., Andres, P.L., Thornell, B., Hollander, D., & Munsat, T.L. (1993). The natural history of amyotrophic lateral sclerosis and the use of natural history control in therapeutic trails. *Neurology, 43*(4), 751–755.

Putnam, A.H.B., & Hixon, T. (1984). Respiratory kinematics in speakers with motor neuron disease. In M.R. McNeil, J.C. Rosenbek, & A.E. Aronson (Eds.), *The dysarthrias: Physiology, acoustics, perception, management* (pp. 37–68). San Diego: College-Hill.

Rabin, R. (1985). *Six parts love: One family's battle with Lou Gehrig's disease.* New York: Charles Scribner's Sons.

Ringel, S.P., Murphy, J.R., Alderson, M.K., Bryan, W., England, J.D., Miller, R.G., Petajan, J.H., Smith, S.A., Roelofs, R.I., Ziter, F., et al. (1993). The natural history of amyotrophic lateral sclerosis. *Neurology, 43*(7), 1316–1322.

Riviere, M., Meininger, V., Zeisser, P., & Munsat, T. (1998). An analysis of extended survival in patients with amyotrophic lateral sclerosis treated with riluzole. *Archives of Neurology, 55,* 526–528.

Rosen, A. (1978). Amyotrophic lateral sclerosis: Clinical features and prognosis. *Archives of Neurology, 35,* 638–642.

Rothstein, J.D., Martin, L., & Kuncl, R.W. (1992). Decreased glutamate transport by the brain and spinal cord in amyotrophic lateral sclerosis. *New England Journal of Medicine, 326*(22), 1464–1493.

Rowland, L.P. (1998). Diagnsois of amyotrophic lateral sclerosis. *Journal of the Neurologic Sciences, 160*(Suppl. 1), S6–24.

Sasaki, S., Tsutsumi, Y., Yamane, K., Sakuma, H., & Maruyama, S. (1992). Sporadic amyotrophic lateral sclerosis with extensive neurological involvement. *Acta Neuropathologica Scandivavica, 84*(2), 211–215.

Schiffman, P.L., & Belsh, J.M. (1993). Pulmonary function at diagnosis of amyotrophic lateral sclerosis: Rate of deterioration. *Chest, 103*(2), 508–513.

Schwartz, M. (1996). *Letting go: Morrie's reflections on living while dying.* New York: Dell.

Sherman, M.S., & Paz, H.L. (1994). Review of respiratory care of the patient with amyotrophic lateral sclerosis. *Respiration, 61*(2), 61–67.

Silverstein, M.D., Stocking, C.B., Antel, J.P., Beckwith, J., Roos, R.P., & Siegler, M. (1991). Amyotrophic lateral sclerosis and life-sustaining therapy: Patients' desires for information, participation in decision making, and life-sustaining therapy. *Mayo Clinic Proceedings, 66,* 906–913.

Stovsky, B., Rudy, E., & Dragonnette, P. (1988). Comparison of two types of communication methods used after cardiac surgery with patients with endotracheal tubes. *Heart and Lung, 17,* 281–293.

Strand, E.A., Buder, E.H., Yorkston, K.M., & Ramig, L.O. (1994). Differential phonatory characteristics of four women with amyotrophic lateral sclerosis. *Journal of Voice, 8*(4), 327–339.

Strand, E.A., Miller, R.M., Yorkston, K.M., & Hillel, A.D. (1996). Management of oral-pharyngeal dysphagia symptoms in amyotrophic lateral sclerosis. *Dysphagia, 11,* 129–139.

Strong, M.J., Grace, G.M., Orange, J.B., & Leeper, H.A. (1996). Cognition, language and speech in ALS: A review. *Journal of Clinical and Experimental Neuropsychology, 18*(2), 291–303.

Takahashi, H., Oyanagi, K., Ikuta, F., Tanaka, M., Yuasa, T., & Miyatake, T. (1993). Widespread multiple system degeneration in a patient with familial amyotophic lateral sclerosis. *Journal of the Neurological Sciences, 120*(1), 15–21.

Talbot, P.R., Goulding, P.J., Lloyd, J.J., Snowden, J.S., Neary, D., & Tests, H.J. (1995). Inter-relation between classic motor neuron disease and frontotemporal dementia: Neuropsychological and single photon emission computed tomography study. *Journal of Neurology, Neurosurgery, and Psychiatry, 58,* 541–547.

Tanaka, M., Kondo, S., Irai, S., Sun, X., Yamagishi, T., & Okamoto, K. (1993). Cerebral blood flow and oxygen metabolism in progressive dementia associated with amyotrophic lateral sclerosis. *Journal of the Neurological Sciences, 120*(1), 22–28.

Tedman, B.M., Young, C.A., & Williams, I.R. (1997). Assessment of depression in patients with motor neuron disease and other neurologically disabling illness. *Journal of Neurologic Science, 152*(Suppl. 1), S75–79.

Viner, E.D. (1985). Life at the other end of the endotracheal tube: A physician's personal view of critical illness. *Progressive Critical Care Medicine, 2,* 3–13.

Weismer, G., Martin, R., Kent, R.D., & Kent, J.F. (1992). Formant trajectory characteristics of males with amyotrophic lateral sclerosis. *Journal of the Acoustics Society of America, 91*(2), 1058–1098.

Wiener, C.L., & Dodd, M.J. (1993). Coping amid uncertainty: An illness trajectory perspective. *Scholarly Inquiry for Nursing Practice, 7*(1), 17–31.

Wikstrom, J., Paetau, A., Palo, J., Sul Kara, R., & Haltia, M.. (1983). Classic amyotrophic lateral sclerosis with dementia. *Archives of Neurology, 39,* 681–683.

Wilkinson, C., Yorkston, K.M., Strand, E.A., & Rogers, M. (1995). Features of spontaneous language in speakers with amyotrophic lateral sclerosis and dysarthria. *American Journal of Speech-Language Pathology, 4*(4), 139–142.

Winterhooler, M., Erbguth, F., Hecht, M., & Neunderfer, B. (1998, November). *Home ventilation in patients with amyotrophic lateral sclerosis: A comparison of invasive and non-invasive ventilation techniques.* Paper presented at the Ninth International Symposium of the International Alliance on ALS/MND, Munich, Germany.

World Federation of Neurology Research Group on Neuromuscular Disease. (1994). El Escorial World Federation of Neurology criteria for the diagnosis of amyotrophic lateral sclerosis. *Journal of the Neurological Sciences, 124*(Suppl.), 96–107.

Yorkston, K.M., Miller, R.M., & Strand, E.A. (1995). *Management of speech and swallowing disorders in degenerative disease.* Tucson, AZ: Communication Skill Builders.

Yorkston, K.M., Strand, E., Miller, R., Hillel, A., & Smith, K. (1993). Speech deterioration in amyotrophic lateral sclerosis: Implications for the timing of intervention. *Journal of Medical Speech/Language Pathology, 1*(1), 35–46.

Yorkston, K.M., Strand, E.A., & Hume, J. (1998). The relationship between motor function and speech function in amyotrophic lateral sclerosis. In M. Cannito, K.M. Yorkston, & D.R. Beukelman (Eds.), *Neuromotor speech disorders: Nature, assessment, and management* (pp. 85–98). Baltimore: Paul H. Brookes Publishing Co.

Yorkston, K.M., Strand, E.A., & Kennedy, M.R.T. (1996). Comprehensibility of dysarthric speech: Implications for assessment and treatment planning. *American Journal of Speech-Language Pathology, 5*(1), 55–66.

Yorkston, K.M., Strand, E.A., & Miller, R.M. (1996). Progression of respiratory symptoms in amyotrophic lateral sclerosis: Implications for speech function. In D.A. Robin, K.M. Yorkston, & D.R. Beukelman (Eds.), *Disorders of motor speech: Assessment, treatment, and clinical characterization* (pp. 193–204). Baltimore: Paul H. Brookes Publishing Co.

Young, J.M., Marshall, C.L., & Anderson, E.J. (1994). Amyotrophic lateral sclerosis patients' perspectives on use of mechanical ventilation. *Health and Social Work, 19*(4), 253–260.

Young, J.M., & McNicoll, P. (1998). Against all odds: Positive life experiences of people with advanced amyotrophic lateral sclerosis. *Health and Social Work, 23*(1), 35–43.

Resources

Amyotrophic Lateral Sclerosis Association (ALSA)

Web site address: http://www.alsa.org/

The mission of ALSA is to promote awareness and understanding of ALS. The organization's web site provides up-to-date information on the latest developments in ALS research, education, health care, and patient advocacy. It also contains many links to other information about ALS on the web.

Al's ALS Resource Page

Web site address: http://members.aa.net/~dusta/AARP.htm

This web page has been developed and is maintained by Al Pickens, who is himself one of the Partners with ALS (PALS). This site contains resources that Al Pickens has found useful in understanding and coping with ALS in his own life. He has made the site as physically accessible as possible to accommodate users whose physical abilities have been affected by ALS. The site is updated continuously, and Al welcomes comments and suggestions.

The ALS March of Faces

Web site address: http://www.siscom.net/~alsmof/

Like the ALSA, the ALS March of Faces is a patient/caregiver founded, governed, and operated organization dedicated to increasing public awareness of ALS and to promoting and advocating issues that are of benefit or concern to PALS. The ALS March of Faces was founded by PALS Kyle Hahn and his caregiver, Terry Frank. Kyle was diagnosed with ALS in November 1995. This web page contains many useful links. Of particular interest are links to free AAC software and free computer access software.

ALS Digest

To subscribe, to unsubscribe, or to contribute notes to *ALS Digest*, please send e-mail to bro@huey.met.fsu.edu (Bob Broedel). Back issues of the *ALS Digest* are available on-line at: http://www.brunel.ac.uk/~hssrsdn/alsig/

The *ALS Digest* was originated by Bob Broedel to serve as a resource for the worldwide ALS community, including ALS patients, ALS researchers, ALS support/discussion groups, and ALS clinics. Others interested in ALS are welcome to join. This e-mail publication is published (approximately) weekly. It should be noted that the information on this site is not peer reviewed.

Muscular Dystrophy Association

Web site address: http://mdausa.org/

The Muscular Dystrophy Association (MDA) is a nonprofit organization that provides many services to individuals with neuromuscular disorders. Unlike the organizations that are devoted strictly to ALS, MDA maintains information and provides clinics for individuals who have about 40 different neuromuscular diseases. Its web page contains a searchable database of more than 230 MDA-sponsored clinics throughout the United States and numerous publications, including MDA's *Quest Magazine* and the *ALS Newsletter*.

The ALS Survival Guide

Web site address: http://www.lougehrigsdisease.net/

The ALS Survival Guide has been developed and is maintained by Doug Eshleman, a PALS who was diagnosed with ALS in August 1997. He created the web site in October 1998. Doug says, "The disease has taught me about life. Dying brings forth living." In addition to containing an extensive library of information on ALS, a personal diary of Doug's life with ALS, and many useful links to other information about ALS on the web, Doug's page contains articles by experts in managing symptoms of ALS, such as pharmacy, occupational therapy, AAC, respiratory therapy, and so forth.

8

AAC for Huntington Disease and Parkinson's Disease

Planning for Change

Estelle R. Klasner
Kathryn M. Yorkston

The man lurching toward you holding out an unsteady hand in greeting is your next client. As you introduce yourself, he rocks back, looking as if he is about to fall. Then he shifts his weight from one foot to the other. He frequently brushes back his hair in an unconscious gesture and puts his hands on his hips. He constantly walks toward and away from you. You are so distracted by his continuous movements that you need to ask him to repeat his name and awkwardly reach out to steady him. When he repeats his name, his voice sounds as if he is being strangled, and the next phrase sounds as though he has run out of air. The walk down to the office is endless. You hope he doesn't tumble down the hall and wish you had never agreed to see this person. You wonder what to do and how to begin the process of developing an augmentative communication plan for him.

This description of a first encounter with an individual diagnosed with Huntington disease illustrates some of the challenges that augmentative and alternative communication (AAC) specialists who serve individuals with movement disorders face. Speech production is made up of finely composed and delicately coordinated movements. This orchestration is accomplished through the integration of many neural systems. One of the most important of these systems is the extrapyramidal system, which includes the basal ganglia. The term *movement disorders* in the field of neurology often refers to a group of diseases affecting the extrapyramidal system. Movement disorders are classified as either hyperkinetic (i.e., excessive abnormal involuntary movement as in Huntington disease) or hypokinetic (i.e., paucity of or lack of movement as in Parkinson's disease). These diseases illustrate what happens when the extrapyramidal or indirect nervous system cannot exert its influence of speech production.

This chapter focuses on 1) movement disorders, including Huntington disease and Parkinson's disease, and their impact on communication; 2) the lived experience of individuals with these diseases and how the diseases change the lives of these individuals, their families and friends, and others in their personal and community networks; and 3) AAC intervention at various stages of these diseases.

HUNTINGTON DISEASE

Huntington disease, an inherited illness, is a classic example of a movement disorder. Progressive motor disturbances, cognitive impairments, and psychological changes significantly affect an individual's ability to communicate. Frequently, the person becomes nonverbal by the end stages of the disease (Folstein, 1990). The complex and unpredictable nature of speech and language difficulties associated with Huntington disease make communication assessment and intervention challenging endeavors for the person, his or her family, and the communication specialist. The nature, symptoms, and impact of Huntington disease on daily life for the person with the illness and his or her family must be well understood in order to provide reasonable and appropriate communication evaluation and treatment.

This section reviews the genetic, neuropathological, and clinical features of Huntington disease, including the movement, cognitive, and emotional changes that occur, and the impact that these changes have on communication. In addition, the effects of living with Huntington disease and the resulting alterations that occur in communication with family, friends, and community are discussed. Finally, the application of AAC interventions at various stages of the disease process is addressed.

Characteristics of Huntington Disease

The prevalence of Huntington disease has been estimated to be between 3 and 7 individuals per 100,000, with a lower rate occurring in Asian and African populations than in Caucasian populations (Nance,

1998). The typical age of onset of Huntington disease symptoms is between 35 and 42 years, with a disease duration of approximately 15–17 years. A juvenile onset (i.e., onset before age 20) and a late onset (i.e., after age 55) have also been documented. Evidence has indicated that symptoms tend to start at an earlier age in successive generations (Quinn & Schrag, 1998).

Genetic Aspects Huntington disease is an autosomal dominant, adult-onset, progressive, and hereditary disorder (Folstein, 1990). The gene responsible for Huntington disease is located on the short arm of chromosome 4, with the abnormality resulting from variable expansions of normally occurring trinucleotide amino acid sequences. Because of its genetic dominance, only one defective gene is required for an individual to be affected (Haddad, Santoro, & Cummings, 1997). Thus, each individual who is part of a family with a history of Huntington disease has a 50% chance of becoming affected because the genetic dominance pattern does not skip a generation—every generation is affected.

Since the discovery of the genetic marker in 1983 and the subsequent identification of the gene for Huntington disease in 1993, individuals have had the option of undergoing predictive testing to ascertain whether the disease will affect them. Being appreciative of the significance of the genetic aspects of the disease is important for the communication specialist. Family members are often well aware of the decline of communication skills that is part of Huntington disease. The previous exposure of the individual with Huntington disease and his or her communication partner to the loss of communication skills in others who have been affected by Huntington disease will greatly influence current acceptance of speech-language services. If services have not been effective in the past with other individuals, the person may be reluctant to be involved with the treatment suggested. Communication interaction and problem-solving skills within a family are likely to be affected by the presence of Huntington disease. Family members must make constant adjustments to continue communicating and functioning within the context of Huntington disease.

The psychological impact of being in a family with an identified inherited illness for which there is no cure cannot be overestimated. The genetic nature of Huntington disease places a tremendous strain on family members. Living with the "risk" of developing a disease that has devastating consequences is a continual issue that family members cope with. The decision of whether to proceed with predictive testing is extremely difficult. If the person decides to have predictive testing, emotional effects accompany both positive and negative results. (Codori & Brandt, 1994; Kessler, 1993, 1994; Quaid & Wesson, 1995).

The range of emotional reactions includes guilt, depression, sadness, relief, hopelessness, and an increased risk of suicide.

Neuropathologic Aspects   Huntington disease results in selective neurodegeneration of the basal ganglia, specifically the caudate nucleus, putamen, and globus pallidus (Albin, 1995). Basal ganglia structures are linked to cortical structures, including frontal and temporal lobes, and are also linked to one another by a series of internal neuronal loops. Huntington disease affects internal communication within the basal ganglia and external communication with those structures linked to the basal ganglia. This interference results in significant motor, cognitive, and emotional dysfunction. As neurons become damaged, the delicate balance of neurotransmitters required to maintain efficient and accurate communication with the cortical and subcortical regions is also disrupted. The imbalance of both inhibitory and excitatory neurotransmitters results in the clinical features typically associated with Huntington disease (Mello & Villares, 1995). Both projection neurons and interneurons are vulnerable to the disease. It appears that there is a temporal sequential atrophy of neurons. In other words, neurons appear to be affected in a sequential order; that is, not all neurons are susceptible at the same point in the disease, which accounts for the varied presentation of symptoms as the disease progresses (Albin, 1995).

Although it is clear that the basal ganglia is the brain structure most affected by Huntington disease, little is known about the relationship between brain atrophy and demonstration of the disease symptoms. Research has indicated that although most who are affected with Huntington disease show bilateral symmetrical atrophy of the basal ganglia, there is great variability in the amount of atrophy. About 20% of those with symptomatic Huntington disease show little to no atrophy of brain tissue. These cortical differences may in part explain the wide variability in the clinical presentation of the disease (Vonsattel & DiFigila, 1998).

Clinical Characteristics   Huntington disease can be characterized as a triad of clinical components, including motor, cognitive, and emotional characteristics (Folstein, 1990). The interaction of these sets of symptoms is responsible for the clinical features of Huntington disease. Each component and its impact on the implementation of AAC is discussed in this chapter so that the reader may gain a full understanding of the relative contribution of individual symptoms to the overall disease presentation and how a variety of impairments can affect the use of AAC.

Motor Component   Motor disturbances associated with Huntington disease are the result of the damage to the basal ganglia and the connecting neuronal circuits to other subcortical and cortical regions. Two types of motor disturbances have been described: involuntary movements and abnormal voluntary movements. The most obvious motor dysfunction associated with Huntington disease is chorea, the involuntary, unpredictable, jerky movements that can randomly affect any skeletal muscle (Hallett, 1993). These movements that may appear repetitive and stereotypical are, in fact, irregular and arrhythmic. Although individuals with Huntington disease report the consequences of abnormal voluntary movements, they rarely list involuntary movements as a significant problem. Involuntary movements have been shown to be unrelated to functional decline (Feigin et al., 1995). Snowden, Crauford, Griffiths, and Neary (1998) found that individuals with Huntington disease do not physiologically experience the involuntary movements. The internal feedback mechanism required to be aware of these movements is dysfunctional. It is this lack of feedback that is responsible for the unawareness of the involuntary movements rather than cognitive or psychological impairments.

In addition to the presence of involuntary movements, voluntary movements are also affected by the disorder. The abnormality of voluntary movements has been determined to be more detrimental to maintaining independent functioning than the involuntary movements (Nance, 1998). Voluntary movement impairments include akinesia (i.e., the inability to initiate movement), bradykinesia (i.e., a slowing and inability to initiate, maintain, or perform voluntary movement sequences) and hypokinesia (a reduction of movement) (Folstein, 1990; Nance, 1998; Phillips et al., 1996). The presence of hypokinesia, when investigated longitudinally, has been found to interfere with the maintenance of independent functioning to a much larger extent than the presence of involuntary movements or cognitive losses (van Vugt, van Hilten, & Roos, 1996).

Internal timing cues provided by the basal ganglia are disturbed in Huntington disease, leading to more variable, slower, and less precise movement patterns (Phillips et al., 1996). Slower reaction times and movement times have also been documented, reflecting the presence of akinesia. Studies have also indicated that impairments in reaction and movement times are correlated with cognitive and functional decline (Girotti, Marano, Soliveri, Geminiani, & Seigliano, 1988; Rothlind, Blysma, Peyer, Folstein, & Brandt, 1993). Bradykinesia is particularly evident during later stages of disease progression and often becomes the primary motor symptom as episodes of involuntary movement decrease (Thompson et al., 1988). Impairments in initiation of movement as well as more variability and less precision in motor movements are some of the consequences of bradykinesia. Bradykinesia has a notably major effect on the ability to perform sequential movement patterns (Shannon, 1996). More time is required to complete activities that require a sequential movement pattern. These movement difficulties have a tremendous influence on the successful use of AAC devices. For example, if a letter board is being used, the affected person may have trouble initiating pointing movements toward letters and will require more time to spell out a sequence of letters to form a word. The extra time required calls for extra effort on the part of the communication partner to remember the sequence of letters over a period of time and to wait for the word to be spelled out.

Change in handwriting is also evident in people with Huntington disease because of both involuntary movements and voluntary movement impairments. Extra strokes and inadequate or excessive pressure during writing most frequently result in macrographia; however, micrographia has also been observed (Phillips, Bradshaw, Chiu, & Bradshaw, 1994). Initially, writing may be employed as an augmentative means of communication before communication becomes severely compromised as the disease advances.

Many of the communication symptoms associated with Huntington disease are a consequence of the involuntary movements and the voluntary movement abnormalities. Although hyperkinetic dysarthria is the most common motor speech disturbance, other movement impairments also contribute to impaired communication abilities. Specifically, oculomotor disturbances typically associated with Huntington disease have a negative impact on communication. These include inability to sustain eye contact, visual tracking difficulty, and initiation of eye contact (Quinn & Schrag, 1998). This is extremely important to take into account when considering the use of AAC systems. Scanning devices may not be an option because of the type of visual difficulties that occur with Huntington disease. If visual disturbances are present, individuals will not be able to achieve the precise eye movements that a scanning device requires, such as visual scanning to the correct space on a board, or they may not be able to sustain eye contact long enough on the appropriate item in order to communicate a message. These disturbances also make it difficult to establish and maintain eye contact during communication interactions. Loss of face-to-face communication does not allow the individual with Huntington disease to recognize nonverbal communication signals (e.g., facial expressions) and creates a distance among communicators (Seidman-Carlson & Wells, 1998). Associated with the inability to read the facial expression of others, involuntary movements may also affect the oral facial area, making it difficult, if not impossible, for the person with Huntington disease to assume the facial expression to match the verbal message. This mismatch may also lead to many communicative misinterpretations (Snowden et al., 1998).

Motor disturbances, most specifically the involuntary movements, have been the target of many pharmacological treatments. Neuroleptic medications have most often been prescribed in an attempt to control the interference of involuntary movements on daily functioning (Shale & Tanner, 1996). Studies have found, however, that the use of neuroleptic medications prescribed to control involuntary movements worsened hypokinesia but did little to control involuntary movements (van Vugt et al., 1996). Because involuntary movements do not significantly interfere with independent functioning and the increase in voluntary movement disturbances does affect daily functioning, neuroleptic medications must be used with extreme caution, and the overall effects of the medication must be considered carefully (Snowden et al., 1998; Thompson et al., 1988)

Cognitive Component   In addition to motor disturbances, cognitive functioning is significantly affected in Huntington disease. The cognitive impairments specifically associated with Huntington disease have been classified as subcortical dementia (Folstein, 1990; Haddad, Santoro, & Cummings, 1997; Huber, Shuttleworth, Paulson, Bellchambers, & Clapp, 1986; Zakzanis, 1998). Generally, the area of neuronal loss responsible for cognitive impairments lies in the subcortical regions of the brain, the basal ganglia. The connections among subcortical structures and cortical structures may also be affected, causing further cognitive loss. Because cognitive impairments greatly compromise the ability to communicate effectively, it is important for the communication specialist to be aware of the extent and dynamic nature of cognitive disturbances when suggesting communication intervention strategies. Communication systems and strategies must be flexible enough to accommodate changing cognitive abilities as the disease progresses. A generalized cognitive slowing compromises the ability to initiate conversations, and there is a gradual, marked decrease in verbal communication. Decreases in conversational initiation do not allow the person with Huntington disease to engage others in communicative interaction. Affected individuals tend to use short, simple sentences and phrases that are predictable and that only address the most basic needs. It also becomes a challenge for the person with Huntington disease to maintain specific topics and introduce new topics of conversation. Diminishing content in conversation becomes apparent as the disease progresses (Podoll, Caspary, Lange, & Noth, 1988). Cognitive slowing also interferes with the ability to follow complex directions and impairs the ability to understand abstract language concepts (Morris, 1995; Podoll et al., 1988). Understanding and maintaining newly presented information becomes increasingly challenging, making learning novel skills extremely difficult. Problem-solving abilities, judgment, and reasoning abilities are also affected by the disease and frequently make it impossible for the individual to live independently (Feigin et al., 1995; Morris, 1995; Zakzanis, 1998). These types of cognitive impairments and their impact on the ability to communicate are the result of diffuse subcortical and cortical damage rather than focal lesions that cause specific speech and language impairments, such as aphasia. Cognitive impairments must be accounted for when introducing AAC systems. Optimally, training should occur for the affected person when new learning is still easily accomplished. Partners should be trained in the use of the system and simple modifications that can be made as the person's cognitive skills change.

Memory skills are also affected by subcortical changes. Impairments appear to be a difficulty with retrieval rather than with storage of information. Poor performance has been documented on confrontation naming tasks, latency in item recall, and self-correction strategies (Podoll et al., 1988). The inability to sustain a search for stored information further contributes to memory impairments. Retrieval difficulties have a major effect on recent memory skills (Morris, 1995). There has been some evidence that retrieval of information is facilitated by the use of visual and auditory cuing techniques, as well as other cues, such as relating of the specific item to the individual's personal experiences (Podoll et al., 1988). Cuing systems may be combined with AAC systems to facilitate recall during communication interactions.

Executive functioning impairments have been well documented in Huntington disease and affect communication abilities (Lawrence et al., 1996). Individuals have difficulty planning, organizing, and scheduling activities. The ability to shift sets is strikingly impaired even in the early stages of Huntington disease. Individuals are often able to formulate an initial response to a situation and hold on to that response but are unable to shift behavior as tasks demand. For example, an affected person may be engaged in a conversation when a third person enters and attempts to join in the conversation. The affected person may not easily be able to include the third person and may lose track of the conversation or perseverate on the initial conversation. As the disease progresses, the functioning of individuals with Huntington disease is found to be more impaired than that of individuals with a diagnosis of Alzheimer's disease or Parkinson's disease with comparable dementia ratings. This inability to switch sets leads to perseverative errors (Sprengelmeyer, Lange, & Homberg, 1995). The time required for mental processing of all tasks requiring organizing and planning was found to be significantly longer for those individuals with Huntington disease.

Spatial working memory or the ability to hold onto and apply information to the processing of a related task is also decreased. Difficulties are evident when individuals are asked to continually access information to solve related problems. Although individuals demonstrate the capacity to plan, extensive time and more trials are required. Impairments are also evident when individuals attempt to perform sequential memory tasks (Lange, Sahakian, Quinn, Marsden, & Robbins, 1995; Lawrence et al., 1996). For example, an affected individual may experience a great deal of difficulty with giving directions to a particular location. Giving directions requires that the person be able to hold onto the final destination in working memory while explaining the best way to that point. The holding of one piece of information (i.e., the final destination) while explaining something else (i.e., directions) is extremely difficult for the individual with Huntington disease. Executive functioning abilities are critical in communication interactions. One must be able to process information quickly, hold on to information, and switch sets as the situation demands in order to be a successful communicator. Executive function impairments are in large part responsible for the functional communication disabilities that individuals with Huntington disease experience in the early stages and throughout the disease process.

Another area that affects communication is the loss of the ability to perceive and interpret emotion in the facial expressions of communication partners. Sprengelmeyer and colleagues (1995) found severe impairments in the ability of individuals with Huntington disease to recognize emotions. The most difficult emotion to recognize for this group was disgust. Individuals also had difficulty in differentiating fear from anger. This inability to recognize facial expressions plays a tremendous role in communication breakdown. The individual with Huntington disease may misinterpret the meaning of a statement by misreading the speaker's accompanying facial expression. The communication partner then responds to this misinterpretation, and a cycle of miscommunication is initiated and perpetuated. This can cause significant distress in interpersonal relationships and can socially isolate the person with Huntington disease. The communication specialist must pay special attention to this impairment and alert communication partners as well as the individual and work on the development of a system to compensate for this disturbance.

Emotional Component   Emotional disturbances also occur as a part of the disease process. A low frustration tolerance is commonly an initial emotional change noted by friends and family (Cummings, 1995). Communication interactions can be frustrating because of the extra effort required to compensate for motor and cognitive impairments. This effort, coupled with a low frustration tolerance, often results in avoidance of communication interaction and eventually social isolation. Depression has also been identified as an emotional change that accompanies Huntington disease (Levy et al., 1998). Depression may also decrease the motivation to communicate and to share ideas with others. Reports indicate that depression has been treated successfully with selective serotonin reuptake inhibitor medications (Morris, 1995).

Irritability often associated with Huntington disease can easily escalate into aggression and explosive outbursts directed at the individuals themselves and others around them (Cummings, 1995) These outbursts may be unpredictable and come without warning, which makes others reluctant to engage in communication interactions. The affected individual is certainly aware of the consequences of his or her behavior but often can do little to prevent it.

There is evidence of a higher suicide risk in individuals with Huntington disease than among the general population (Kessler, 1993). Occasionally, suicide has been viewed as a rational choice for people with a diagnosis of Huntington disease. However, the circumstances that surround the suicide often reveal that the choice to commit suicide was impulsive and not well planned (Kessler, 1993).

Individuals with Huntington disease frequently go through an extended period of denial of symptoms (Kessler & Bloch, 1989). This denial can create a great deal of conflict within the family because the affected individual may often refuse help from others or intervention (Kessler & Bloch, 1989). It is important to be available to provide services when the person is ready to accept it, even if intervention may have been more productive earlier in the disease process. Being aware of the emotional changes that frequently accompany Huntington disease and providing a means of expression for the affected individual can be of great assistance to families and friends in coping with the disease. Maintaining communication and knowing what changes to expect often encourages family members to stay connected and be able to separate the effects of the disease from the person. This ability to separate disease from identity allows individuals to cope with Huntington disease with courage and dignity (Kessler, 1993).

In addition to the emotional disturbances caused by cortical changes, emotional reactions to the disease are constantly taking place as the person and his or her family and others witness the inevitable decline that Huntington disease brings. Both types of emotional change may be evident in communication interactions. The communication specialist must be prepared to make appropriate referrals when necessary.

Communication Disorders

The combination of motor, cognitive, and emotional disturbances that accompany Huntington disease has a profound effect on individuals' ability to communicate. The speech characteristics associated with Huntington disease have been described as a hyperkinetic dysarthria with a number of variable dysarthric speech features that affect intelligibility (Yorkston, Beukelman, Strand, & Bell, 1999). Individuals are often unintelligible at the end stages of the disease and, thus, are rarely successful in using natural speech as a means of communication (Yorkston et al., 1999)

All of the physiologic subsystems involved in speech production are affected by the motor dysfunction, with the respiratory system contributing most to the dysarthric features of the disease. Respiratory muscles are most affected by the involuntary movement and voluntary movement disturbances. Movement disturbances may cause forced expiration and inspiration during rest and speaking activities. Because of poor coordination of the respiratory system, individuals with Huntington disease often speak on inhalation rather than on exhalation, making it virtually impossible to sustain speaking or to make any of the necessary respiratory adjustments required for speech production (Duffy, 1995; Yorkston et al., 1999). Phonatory function is also affected in a variety of ways. Brief, random, inappropriate hyperadduction of the vocal folds can produce harsh and/or strained-strangled vocal quality and inappropriate cessation of phonation. Movement disturbances can also cause brief, random, inappropriate abduction of the vocal folds, producing transient breathiness and a reduction of respiratory energy required for speech production (Duffy, 1995).

Both respiratory and phonatory impairment is evident in the expression of prosody (Darley, Aronson, & Brown, 1975; Duffy, 1995). Both prosodic excess and insufficiency have been noted in hyperkinetic dysarthria associated with Huntington disease. This range of prosodic abnormality can be present in one individual and can vary from moment to moment as a reflection of the movement disturbances of the vocal folds. Prolonged intervals, inappropriate silences, and prolonged phonemes, as well as excess and equal stress, are evidence of prosodic excess. Prosodic insufficiency results in monopitch, monoloudness, reduced stress, and short phrasing (Darley et al., 1975). These prosodic disturbances not only affect intelligibility but also may make speech sound so unusual that it is troublesome for the listener to pay attention to the message rather than be distracted by the speech pattern.

Resonatory disturbances that are due to unpredictable or abnormal velopharyngeal movements can produce a hypernasal and/or hyponasal vocal quality. Articulatory skills are also affected because of unexpected and dysfunctional maneuvers of the articulators (i.e., jaw, tongue, and lips). Irregular articulatory breakdown is a common feature of hyperkinetic dysarthria, causing imprecise consonants and vowel distortion (Darley et al., 1975).

Because Huntington disease is a slowly progressive disease, with a duration of 15–17 years, and speech skills can often be affected rather early in the disease process, the individual with the disease may be unable to communicate with others for a prolonged period of time. He or she may be unable to participate in daily activities and decisions about his or her own self-care, rendering the person with little control over his or her own life. It is imperative that communication skills be maintained as much as possible and for as long as possible so that the individual with Huntington disease can continue to participate in daily life and make active contributions to decisions concerning him- or herself and those individuals around him or her.

Because of the variable nature of the dysarthria associated with Huntington disease, listeners often cannot discern the pattern of speech characteristics of an individual with the disease. Each time the person with Huntington disease and his or her partner communicate, a new array of dysarthric speech features can occur, greatly increasing the effort required to speak and to understand the speech signal. This effort required on the part of both partners often causes the individual with Huntington disease to be reluctant to communicate for fear of not knowing what to expect and for fear of not being understood. It also causes the partner to avoid engaging in communication exchanges because of the amount of energy required to understand the most basic of messages and the fear of not being able to understand the person at all. The desire and motivation to communicate is greatly compromised by the profound speech production disturbances for both the individual with Huntington disease and his or her communication partner.

Clinical Decision Making

Huntington disease is not a static condition. Progression of the disease and fluctuation of a variety of symptoms make for a constantly changing presentation. This dynamic aspect of Huntington disease must be taken into account when designing and implementing AAC treatment strategies. No single device will serve the individual with the disease effectively throughout its course. AAC systems must be modified to accommodate changing motor, cognitive, and emotional status. In addition, AAC in the context of Huntington disease must be broadly defined to include any strategy or system that may facilitate the maintenance of communication.

Stage 1: No Detectable Speech Disorder   Individuals who receive a diagnosis of Huntington disease often do not at first have any noticeable speech symptoms. The individual with the disease and his or her communication partners may have noticed an occasional period of unclear speech. The beginnings of cognitive changes may also interfere with communication, resulting in occasional difficulties with completing a thought or processing complex information. Depression and irritability may negatively affect communication at this stage. Handwriting difficulties may begin at this stage as well.

Individuals who rely on excellent communication for their livelihood may benefit from a speech-language consultation. Individuals at this point should be alerted to situations that may bring on communicative lapses, such as fatigue and an excess of responsibilities. Individuals with Huntington disease may want to make others aware of situations that can cause communication breakdown and begin the delegation of responsibilities. A variety of memory aids and organizational tools may assist in maintaining a schedule of daily activities. Those who experience handwriting difficulties at this stage may benefit from portable word-processing systems. The communication specialist can be especially helpful teaching the individual to break down tasks into manageable portions and to use organizational systems to act as external cuing mechanisms.

Stage 2: Obvious Speech Disorder with Intelligible Speech Changes in prosody and respiratory support for speech production are some of the features of dysarthria in Huntington disease. Prosodic alterations vary and result in monopitch, monoloudness, and inappropriate silences between words (Darley et al., 1975). Vocal quality changes also occur, and the voice may be breathy and or strained/strangled depending on whether hypoadduction or hyperadduction of the vocal folds is occurring as a result of motor disturbances. Individuals may attempt to speak on inhalation or experience forced inspiration and/or expiration, which can interfere with the ability to produce speech. They may begin to have trouble being understood on the telephone or in other indirect communication situations, and they may have to limit this type of communication. The individual may also experience orofacial motor disturbances and may begin to have difficulty deciphering facial expressions. Direct speech treatment can be extremely helpful at this stage. Eliminating abnormal respiratory behaviors through a program of awareness and practice of appropriate breath groupings can help to maintain speech intelligibility.

Memory aids may be used on a more frequent basis at this stage than in the previous stages. When fatigued or overwhelmed, the individual may choose to use AAC devices, such as a writing pad or portable word processor, in order to jot down key words or concepts to avoid possible misunderstanding. The communication specialist can be most helpful at this stage by suggesting natural gestures to be used to supplement speech production. For example, circling the thumb and forefinger to indicate approval may prove invaluable in avoiding the misinterpretation of facial expression on the part of both the affected individual and the communication partner. Introducing these types of systems early, when the individual can still acquire new skills, is vital in maintaining communication as the disease progresses. If shifting sets becomes a more obvious difficulty at this stage, the communication specialist may want to assist with the development of a natural or discreet written signaling system to be used by the communication partner as an external cuing device to indicate a shift of topic and to facilitate the affected person's difficulty with this skill. It may also be helpful for the communication partner to become more explicit during conversation and leave nothing to be implied or interpreted. If the individual with Huntington disease is required to participate in an important speaking situation, practice in initiating and reviewing the course of the exchange may assist in maintaining the topic and processing information. Frequent communication partners can also be invited to gently remind the individual with Huntington disease of the procedures necessary to maintain clear and understandable speech.

Stage 3: Reduction in Speech Intelligibility   Unintelligible speech occurs with more frequency at this stage. In addition to prosodic alterations, poor respiratory support for speech, vocal changes, and imprecise articulation can also compromise speech intelligibility. Communication partners may have difficulty with understanding the affected person and may ask for frequent repetition. These repetitions may not be successful because of the underlying unpredictability of the speech movements. In other words, speech production attempts may differ each time but will not be closer to the target utterance. This can be a frustrating experience for both the affected individual and the communication partner. Processing information may also be slowed at this stage, making for uncomfortable silences within conversational exchanges. It must be remembered that the individual with Huntington disease often comprehends a great deal more than he or she is able to express as speech production deteriorates. A variety of topics should continue to be addressed, and the affected individual should be given the opportunity to be a communication participant whenever possible.

The introduction of an assortment of AAC devices tailored to different situations may help to maintain communicative interaction. A cuing board used to keep the person on topic, signal topic changes, and facilitate thinking processes may be one of the most helpful devices.

For example, a cuing board may include a message such as "You have already shared this information" to avoid the unnecessary and often arduous process of repetition of information. Interruption of the individual would also be greatly decreased, which would avoid possible emotional outbursts and interference with communication and processing efforts. This type of board, coupled with an alphabet board or a word board with large spaces to compensate for imprecise pointing gestures, may be used to facilitate communication exchanges. Orienting cues such as "We need more letters to make a word" or "You were talking about your outing" are extremely helpful in assisting the cognitive processes required for combination of letters and words. These extra cues may be all that is necessary to understand the message. Training in the appropriate use of both of these types of boards is highly recommended. The introduction of AAC aids during a communicative crisis is sure to meet with resistance and failure. Distraction should also be minimized at this time to improve the chances of communicative success. Simple strategies, such as having a set time to talk about difficult-to-communicate topics or the reduction of background noise, may significantly improve communication successes. The individual with Huntington disease must be able to trust his or her communication partner and to accept the necessary guidance and help. This trust is based on the belief that the partner values communication and understands that the affected individual has many important things to share.

Stage 4: Natural Speech Supplemented by Augmentative Techniques At this stage, speech has become so severely affected that it can no longer be used as the primary means of communication. Initiation of speech production may take a long time, and, when initiated, the dysarthric features may be so overwhelming that only an occasional word or two can be understood by communication partners. Cognitive impairments may impede the individual's ability to engage in conversation, and he or she may communicate in one- or two-word utterances. There may be periods where speech becomes more intelligible and can be used as the means of communication. However, AAC systems are required more frequently at this stage. If the person was previously introduced to letter, word, and cuing boards, these should continue to be used and expanded or modified as required to meet changing communication needs. Low-technology direct-selection systems, which can frequently be modified to fit the changing needs of the individual, would be most appropriate. The amount of information to be placed on a board needs to be individually determined, as each person's capacity to process and act upon visually presented information varies depending on the disease presentation. The communication partner may have to be proactive in encouraging the use of the AAC system and in making sure it is used before the frustration of not being understood becomes a common occurrence. Continuing to communicate when the person is well rested and in a quiet environment also helps to facilitate communication. If the individual no longer is able to live at home, the care facility must be made aware of the communication interventions that are already in place and must be constantly reminded that although cognitive impairments exist, the person can and should still be provided with as many communication opportunities as possible.

Stage 5: No Functional Speech   By the end stages of Huntington disease, individuals are usually nonverbal. Because of cognitive decline, previously successful AAC systems may no longer be effective. At this stage, it is important to remember the person's likes, dislikes, hobbies, and interests to provide communicative content. The communication partner needs to shoulder the responsibility of keeping the person informed of what is happening around him or her. Small, simple communication devices with common requests or words can still be used with some success and assistance from the communication partner. The maintenance of a yes-or-no system is imperative at this stage of the disease. A system such as a squeeze of the hand or the touch of a colored square is all that is needed to maintain such a yes-or-no system of communication. Communication partners must be trained in the phrasing of interactions and questions to facilitate yes-or-no responses. Extra processing time is also likely to be required, so the communication partner must be vigilant about waiting for a response before posing another question. Keeping communication exchanges short but frequent helps to avoid misunderstandings and make communication a positive experience.

Living with Huntington Disease

Huntington disease has been aptly referred to as a disorder of families (Folstein, 1990). Understanding the life experiences of people with Huntington disease must begin with an appreciation of the numerous ways in which individuals can be influenced by the disease. A person can experience symptoms firsthand, be at risk for the disease, or be a spouse and/or caregiver of an individual with Huntington disease. Huntington disease most often strikes at the time of life when decisions about family, work, and lifestyle are just beginning to be made. A diagnosis of Huntington disease permanently alters any previous plans. Many families cope with more than one person affected by the disease and likely have been experiencing unidentified changes (e.g., irritability, depression, apathy) for several years before the actual diagnosis is made. Many have had previous experience with Huntington disease and have formed opinions about the health care community based on those previous experiences. All of these influences must be acknowledged by the communication specialist in order to establish an effective treatment plan. The communication specialist must be constantly aware of the emotional upheaval and crises that Huntington disease can cause. He or she must also acknowledge the special relationships that may have developed because of the disease and offer to facilitate communication in a way that continues to foster these relationships.

Kessler (1993) referred to the spouse as the "forgotten person" in the family. Yet it is often the spouse who acts as the principal person in the daily care of the individual with Huntington disease. Spouses play a multitude of roles, including decision maker, wage earner, and nurturer, to the extent that their own needs are often neglected. Spouses often experience social isolation, are shunned by other family members, have periods of depression and anxiety, and often feel overwhelmed with all of their responsibilities (Kessler, 1993). It is imperative to maintain communication between the spouse and the person with Huntington disease. This facilitates connections between the couple and allows the individual with Huntington disease to contribute to daily functioning as much as possible. It also allows for the opportunity of joint decision making.

Many families still wish to keep the diagnosis of Huntington disease a secret from friends, other family members, and their community. The need to keep the disease a secret may make it difficult for the family to accept services, or they may ask the communication specialist to maintain the secrecy. Though the maintenance of the secret may not be the best course of treatment, the wishes of the family must be respected. Previous negative experiences, such as the loss of insurance funding, may be the reasons for maintaining secrecy. It is important to be able to work with the family coping with Huntington disease in whatever context that is comfortable for them.

Future Directions

The effects of Huntington disease on daily life and, specifically, on the ability to communicate have yet to be fully explored and understood. Further understanding of the use of cuing systems to facilitate thinking and communication would contribute greatly to the number of techniques available to use with this population. For generations families have been coping and communicating with those who have the disease. An in-depth study of the coping mechanisms used and the strategies developed to maintain communication would be most beneficial in enriching the understanding of this disease process. The attitude of communication partners can play a vital role in the maintenance of communication. An extensive study of the attitudes that communication partners convey to the individual with Huntington disease would help to understand the difference that attitude can make between a successful, ongoing, communicative relationship and one that fails at the first signs of the disease. Awareness of the factors that influence communication partners and that make communication interactions successful or unsuccessful would also be important information to investigate and could have an impact on intervention and training of communication partners for this population. A specific study examining the influence of motor changes on the use of AAC devices could offer valuable information necessary for the appropriate prescription of AAC devices that accommodate for changes in motor function. The individual and the family with Huntington disease present a challenge to the field of speech-language pathology that we have only begun to address.

PARKINSON'S DISEASE

Parkinson's disease is a slowly progressive movement disorder associated with basal ganglia dysfunction affecting 1 in 100 individuals in later life. Although dysarthria is the most common communication problem associated with Parkinson's disease, other problems do exist and may affect AAC intervention. Therefore, communication is broadly defined here to include not only speech production but also both verbal and nonverbal communication, writing, and communication in the context of natural interactive situations. Although evidence-based practice guidelines are not available for AAC intervention in Parkinson's disease, the field has something to offer individuals with this disorder. The following sections set the framework for this intervention.

Characteristics of Parkinson's Disease

Parkinson's disease is a common, slowly progressive disease of the central nervous system, specifically the basal ganglia. The pathology of parkinsonism is associated with the loss of dopaminergic neurons in the basal ganglia (especially the *substantia nigra*) and brain stem. It is a disease of late middle age and beyond. The essential problem in Parkinson's disease is the inability to automatically execute learned motor plans (Marsden, 1984). The hallmark features or classic triad of the motor impairments are resting tremor, bradykinesia, and rigidity. Communication disorders are common, often beginning with a decrease in facial expression or nonverbal gesture, at times progressing to decrease in vocal loudness, and later progressing to severe hypokinetic dysarthria characterized by changes in speaking rate, articulatory precision, and speech intelligibility. Because the movement disorders are critical to understanding the motor speech and communication disorders in Parkinson's disease, the following section reviews the pathophysiology, symptoms associated with these movement disorders, pharmacologic management, and the impact of these factors on communication and AAC intervention.

Movement Disorders and Treatment

The movement disorder in Parkinson's disease arises from an imbalance among dopamine-activated and acetylcholine-activated neurons of the corpus striatum, in other words, an imbalance between excitatory and inhibitory striatal influences. Thus, it is a disorder of the basal ganglia, affecting motor control. Jain and Kirshblum described the role of the basal ganglia in movement and their relationship to the cerebral cortex as follows:

> The cerebral cortex plans the movement, and the basal ganglia, via their connections with the thalamus and cortex, are involved in influencing the direction, course, and amplitude of these movements. Thus, this system provides the postural support necessary for execution of voluntary movements and may be involved in the initiation of such movements. (1998, p. 1035)

More recently, the basal ganglia has been said to bind input to output in the executive forebrain (Brown & Marsden, 1998). This focused attention provides the automatic links among voluntary effort, sensory input, and the calling up and operation of a sequence of motor programs or thoughts. Brown and Marsden suggested that the basal ganglia play a major role in facilitating this important aspect of neural processing and may allow movements to come together as one action.

The movement disorders in Parkinson's disease are characterized by a constellation of symptoms including a resting tremor with a frequency of 3–6 Hertz that may involve hands, limbs, and trunk and is suppressed by activity or sleep; rigidity (i.e., increased tone of both agonist and antagonist muscle groups); bradykinesia (i.e., paucity of movement); and postural instability (i.e., a flexed or stooped posture that the patient is unable to correct, often associated with a tendency to fall to one side or backwards). Of these symptoms, bradykinesia has the most profound impact on communication.

Bradykinesia is literally translated as slowness of movement but is more appropriately thought of as an inability to initiate or to perform voluntary movement sequences. Patients with bradykinesia describe the problem as one of no longer being able to depend on their automatic pilot but rather needing manual control. Other individuals describe even simple sequences of everyday movements as campaigns of voluntary control in which each element of the sequence needs to be considered and executed. When a movement is initiated, it is often performed more rapidly than normal and with rapid fatigue and decrease in the scale of the movement. Gait may become more and more rapid, degenerating into a shuffle (known as *festination*). Speech syllables can also exhibit festination.

Many of the communication symptoms of parkinsonism are a consequence of bradykinesia. For example, the number of automatic movements is decreased, including eye blinking, eye movements, expressive gestures of the hands, expressive facial gestures, handwriting, and perhaps swallowing of saliva. Many of these movements are fundamental to typical communication interaction. Norberg and Athlin (1987) studied the interaction among individuals with severe Parkinson's disease and their caregivers during mealtimes. During these interactions, as in other conversational interactions, partners need to coordinate their actions. A synchronous "dance" develops between successful partners in which one partner sends clear cues and the other is sensitive to them, interprets them correctly, and responds with clear cues to which the first partner is sensitive, and so forth (Norberg & Athlin, 1987). The loss of automatic movements disrupts the synchronous interaction. Individuals with Parkinson's disease react slowly and in a deliberate way. Actions that should be automatic need to be performed voluntarily, and actions that should be simultaneous need to be performed consecutively. Thus, even when dysarthria is not present or is not severe, communication can be disrupted by symptoms associated with Parkinson's disease. When the dysarthria is severe, bradykinesia and rigidity may disrupt successful use of AAC devices.

The movement disorders associated with Parkinson's disease are typically managed using a wide variety of drugs, such as Sinemet (a combination of levodopa and carbidopa) (Duvoisin, 1991). Although about a quarter of patients appear to have a good response to long-term drug use (Marsden, 1994), many experience unwanted side effects that can also influence communication. With the passage of time, many individuals experience fluctuations in their response to drugs. Initially, these are called end-of-dose deterioration and are defined as fluctuations in motor disability related to the timing of levodopa intake. With extended drug treatment, they become more severe and are referred to as the *on–off effect*, defined as sudden unpredictable fluctuations in motor disability unrelated to the timing of levodopa intake. These sudden changes in motor ability may affect both the production of natural speech (Caligiuri, 1989) and the use of AAC devices (Lang, 1983). Some individuals with severe on–off effects may use different AAC systems at different points in their fluctuating drug cycles.

Another side effect of long-term levodopa treatment is the development of dyskinesia. Dyskenesia typically described in terms of when it occur in the drug cycle. For example, *peak-dose* dyskinesia may occur when the drug is at its maximum dose and includes choreic, ballistic, or stereotyped involuntary movements. When severe, these unpredictable, involuntary movements may interfere with the use of AAC devices. When less severe, they call attention to themselves, may be perceived as unsightly, and are distracting in communication interactions. For example, an individual with Parkinson's disease may have a masklike, expressionless face in combination with large, involuntary movements of the head, neck, and limbs during periods of peak-dose dyskinesia. Although long-term levodopa treatment continues to help some symptoms of the disease, other disabilities such as postural imbalance and speech disorders may begin to emerge late in the disease and may not be highly responsive to medications.

Associated Disorders   Parkinson's disease is often associated with several other disorders, including depression, cognitive disorders, language disorders, and micrographia.

Depression   Depression, characterized by pessimism and hopelessness, decreased motivation and drive, and increased concern with health, is common in Parkinson's disease (Gotham & Marsden, 1986). Depression can affect social interaction and communication. Estimates of the occurrence of significant depression in the parkinsonian population vary widely; the prevalence of depression among people with Parkinson's disease in one large survey was 47% (Dooneief et al., 1992; Mayeux, Williams, Stern, & Cote, 1984). Depression in people with Parkinson's disease is usually mild to moderate in intensity. The specific origin of the depression is unclear. On the one hand, it may be a reactive depression in which the individual with Parkinson's disease is responding to fears associated with a potentially disabling disease. A mild to moderate degree of depression may be expected in anyone who has a chronic disabling condition. On the other hand, the depression may be endogenous, reflecting some neurochemical aspects of the disease. The depression may also be the result of other factors, such as aging. Because depression is common in old age, its occurrence in Parkinson's disease may be coincidental. Diagnosis of depression, especially in early stages, is made somewhat difficult because of parkinsonian symptoms such as a masklike, expressionless face and changes in cognition. Medication has been shown to be successful in alleviating some of the symptoms of depression (Mayeux, 1990)

Cognitive Disorders   Although the primary impairment associated with Parkinson's disease is motor impairment, a variety of cognitive impairments have been identified. Because these impairments influence a speaker's ability to use AAC systems, those who manage the communication needs of individuals with Parkinson's disease must be aware of potential impairments in these areas. Exact estimates of the frequency and type of cognitive impairment is made difficult by a number of features characteristic of Parkinson's disease, such as age, the progression of the disease, and the co-occurrence of depression. The picture is also clouded by the generalized slowness of movement that limits performance on some measures of cognition. In fact, in early reports, the term *bradyphrenia* was used to suggest a parallel between the slowness of movement (bradykinesia) and slowness of thinking. However, studies suggest that the slowing of thought often reported in Parkinson's disease does not necessarily accompany bradykinesia and thus may be related to dopaminergic dysfunction (Rafal, Posner, Walker, & Friedrich, 1984). Other studies suggest that bradyphrenia is an impairment of attention and vigilance unique to Parkinson's disease and may be associated with an alteration in norepinephrine metabolism (Mayeux, Stern, Sano, Cote, & Williams, 1987).

Despite difficulty in obtaining precise incidence figures, there is consensus that a substantial number of individuals with the disease experience changes in cognition. Conservative estimates suggest that about 15% of individuals with Parkinson's disease meet the criteria for dementia as described by the *Diagnostic and Statistical Manual of Mental Disorders, Fourth Edition* (DSM-IV; American Psychiatric Association, 1994; Levin, Tomer, & Rey, 1992). A higher proportion exhibit milder or highly focal cognitive impairments. Studies using psychological assessment techniques report much higher rates, with an incidence of intellectual impairment approaching 70% (Cummings, 1988). A growing body of evidence supports the existence of more than one type of dementia in Parkinson's disease. Cummings and Bensen (1984) suggested two types of dementia. The first is a subcortical dementia characterized by slowing, forgetfulness, depression, and impaired cognition. The second is a cortical dementia with features more typical of Alzheimer's disease.

The principal features of cognitive impairment in Parkinson's disease include impairments in executive function, visuospatial function, and memory. Executive function has been described as a heterogeneous group of skills involved in the anticipation, planning, initiation, and monitoring of goal-directed behaviors (Levin, Llabre, & Weiner, 1989). The function requires the use of feedback to modify behavior and concept formulation as well as set shifting. Executive function is frequently tested with the Wisconsin Card Sorting Test (Heaton, 1981), a task of concept formulation and set shifting (Levin et al., 1989) that uses controlled word association tasks, also known as verbal fluency tasks (Cools, van den Berckess, & Hortink, 1984; Dalrymple, Kalders, Jones, & Watson, 1994; Levin et al., 1989). Because executive function represents a heterogeneous group of skills, the relationships between executive function and other cognitive skills is complex (Owen et al., 1993). In fact, inflexibility of thought, a hallmark feature of executive dysfunction, may account for many of the visuospatial, memory, language, and perceptual impairments seen in Parkinson's disease (Bondi, Kaszniak, Bayles, & Vance, 1993; Levin et al., 1989).

Executive function is fundamental to the use of many AAC systems. Consider the simple example of an individual with Parkinson's disease learning to use an alphabet supplementation technique whereby the speaker points to the first letter of each word as the word is spoken. The speaker's next actions are always dependent upon the responses of the listener. If the listener has understood, then the speaker continues. If not, the speaker must shift into a sequence of breakdown resolution activities—that is, repeating the word, giving feedback to the listener, and perhaps spelling the word if it is not understood after repetition. Thus, even this simple technique involves considerable set shifting and continuous integration of input and may be deceptively difficult for an individual with Parkinson's disease and impairments in executive function.

Visuospatial dysfunction in Parkinson's disease has been focused on the following areas (Levin, 1990): visual analysis and synthesis, facial recognition, judgment of direction, orientation and distance, and constructional praxis and spatial attention. Studies suggest that these skills change over time but that the decline in visuospatial skills is independent of dementia (Levin et al., 1991; Owen et al., 1993). Use of many AAC systems can be described as being fundamentally a visuomotor task. Consider the visual demands of both word/alphabet boards and displays of many high-technology AAC systems. It is particularly challenging for management of these systems that the visuospatial impairments are most prominent in later stages of the disease when the need for AAC systems is most urgent.

Memory impairments involving episodic memory, paired associate learning, auditory verbal learning, and visual reproduction of geometric designs are well documented in Parkinson's disease (Levin et al., 1992). Although a complete review of memory impairments in Parkinson's disease is beyond the scope of this chapter, some aspects of memory that are particularly pertinent to learning AAC systems are briefly described. Procedural memory, or knowing how to do things, is especially important in AAC intervention and is impaired in Parkinson's disease. Impairments have been described as difficulty in both learning and making that learning automatic (Allain, Lieruy, Quemener, & Thoma, 1995; Thomas, Reymann, Lieury, & Allain, 1996). No studies of Parkinson's disease have focused on learning to use electronic communication systems. However, the perceptual motor tasks involved in learning mouse control while looking at a computer screen have been investigated (Thomas, Laurent, Foyatier, & Laporte, 1996). Although during the first session the performance of individuals with Parkinson's disease did not differ from that of controls, on subsequent trials, they learned eight times less well than controls. The authors suggest that success in procedural tasks for this group seemed to depend on the capacity to initiate the response. Those who manage the AAC needs of individuals with Parkinson's disease must be aware these types of learning difficulties when planning intervention.

Language Disorders   Although aphasia is not characteristic of Parkinson's disease, changes in language function are present and have received increasing attention (Bayles, 1990; Beatty & Monson, 1989; Grossman et al., 1991; Lieberman, Friedman, & Feldman, 1990; Lieberman et al., 1992). Clinical understanding of potential language impairments in Parkinson's disease is complicated by cognition impairments, including executive dysfunction and memory, and by the motor aspects of speech production, including altered speech prosody. Evidence exists that individuals with Parkinson's disease differ from peers who function typically on a number of language-related measures, including comprehension of complex commands (Cummings, Darkins, Mendez, Hill, & Benson, 1988), sentence processing (Grossman et al., 1991; Grossman, Carvell, Stern, Gollomp, & Hurtig, 1992), production of written sentences (Small, Lyons, & Kemper, 1997), and syntactic complexity in spontaneous speech (Illes, 1989; Illes, Metter, Hanson, & Iritani, 1988). The changes in language seen in Parkinson's disease may have an impact on AAC systems that depend on the production of written language.

Micrographia   The presence of small handwriting, known as micrographia, is a hallmark characteristic of Parkinson's disease. In fact, the item "I am having trouble writing or typing" was agreed with by 75% of individuals with Parkinson's disease in a study by Longstreth, Nelson, Linde, and Munoz (1992). Micrographia may interfere with use of handwriting as an AAC approach or as a breakdown resolution strategy. Some studies suggest that handwriting is improved with levodopa (Poluha, Teulings, & Brookshire, 1998) and behavioral intervention involving external cues (Oliveira, Gurd, Nixon, Marshall, & Passingham, 1997).

Communication Disorders   The prevalence of communication disorders among people with Parkinson's disease is high. Most of the prevalence information, however, is related to dysarthria. Logemann, Fisher, Boskes, and Blonsky (1978) studied 200 speakers with parkinsonism and reported that 89% exhibited laryngeal problems and 45% demonstrated articulatory problems. In self-reports, individuals with Parkinson's disease also note a high incidence of dysarthria. In a survey of 230 people with Parkinson's disease, 70% reported that their speech or voice was worse than it was prior to disease onset (Hartelius & Svensson, 1994). Several of the most common problems these individuals reported were related to the voice: weak voice (61% reporting this problem), hoarse voice (32%), and monotonous voice (17%). Other common problems were imprecise articulation (36%) and difficulties getting started (27%) (Hartelius & Svensson, 1994). Although the prevalence of communication problems in Parkinson's disease is high, the disorders are frequently not severe enough to prevent the use of natural speech in many or all communication situations. Dysarthria is typically not associated with the early stage of the disease; rather, it develops late in the course of the disease (Metter & Hanson, 1991).

Although dysarthria associated with Parkinson's disease has perhaps received more research attention than any of the dysarthrias, it is beyond the scope of this chapter to review the impairment of the various speech subsystems or the perceptual and acoustic characteristics of the hypokinetic dysarthria association with Parkinson's disease. Comprehensive references can be found elsewhere (Adams, 1997; Duffy, 1995; Yorkston et al., 1999). Rather, our discussion focuses on the staging of the functional limitations associated with dysarthria (Yorkston et al., 1999) and the AAC approaches that may be appropriate at each stage.

Clinical Decision Making

The speech and language impairments associated with Parkinson's disease decline as the disease progresses. This change in skills must always be considered when planning for AAC. Systems should serve current needs but also be flexible enough to adapt to changing needs. AAC cannot be system-dependent but must encompass any external strategies to enhance communication abilities.

Stage 1: No Detectable Speech Disorder   Early in the disease, individuals with Parkinson's disease have received the diagnosis but often do not yet exhibit speech symptoms. Individuals who participate in highly demanding communication activities (e.g., trial attorneys, ministers, teachers) may be referred to a speech-language pathologist for consultation. At times, AAC approaches such as an amplification system are appropriate for these individuals, especially in demanding public speaking situations. Speakers should be made aware that they might not personally be as sensitive to the onset of speech problems as their listeners. Therefore, they may need to seek the feedback of others closely associated with them to monitor the appearance of symptoms that would warrant AAC intervention. Some individuals with Parkinson's disease and micrographia may benefit from typing systems for notetaking and letter writing. Finally, some individuals with Parkinson's disease experience the loss of facial expression before speech itself is affected. These individuals may benefit from learning to voluntarily use nonverbal gestures in interactive situations. The losses of a spontaneous smile and other gestures have an important impact on conservation interaction. Furthermore, the individual with Parkinson's disease may not be aware of the negative impact unless it is made explicit by their communication partners. For example, the use of a thumbs-up gesture or a voluntary smile may need to be substituted for a spontaneous smile in response to a joke.

Stage 2: Obvious Speech Disorder with Intelligible Speech Changes in the voice are typically the first speech features to be observed in individuals with Parkinson's disease. The vocal features associated with this stage of parkinsonian dysarthria include reduced loudness, breathy or weak voice, reduced pitch variability, and an unsteady, hoarse, or rough voice (Ramig, 1992). Speech treatment focusing on learning to calibrate the appropriate level of effort when speaking and on being sensitive to the partner's feedback may be useful (Ramig, Pawlas, & Countryman, 1995; Yorkston et al., 1999). At this stage, devices such as amplifiers and delayed auditory feedback units to enhance loudness and slow rate (Adams, 1994, 1997; Hanson & Metter, 1983) may be used for everyday communication rather than for special situations as outlined in Stage 1. Because individuals with Parkinson's disease are typically not sensitive to the extent of their own speech difficulties, they may be ineffective in shifting sets and adopting differing communication styles in different situations. Therefore, frequent communication partners begin to play an active role at this stage, to signal the speaker with Parkinson's disease when to use clear speech, voluntary gestures, or devices such as amplifiers.

Stage 3: Reduction in Speech Intelligibility A reduction in speech intelligibility in certain situations is a key feature distinguishing this stage from the previous one. Frequent communication partners may complain that they need to ask the speaker with Parkinson's disease to repeat or to speak up. In addition to the voice changes mentioned earlier, dysarthria in this stage is typically characterized by imprecise articulation. The range of oral movements may be limited, and speakers may fail to reach articulatory targets. Some speakers may pause longer than is typical or may pause at unusual locations within an utterance. Other speakers may begin to use excessively rapid rates or rushes of rapid speech.

AAC intervention at this stage may involve some of the devices used in previous stages. In addition, techniques to resolve communication breakdowns are appropriate. These may include notepads, alphabet or word boards (Hustad, 1999), and pacing boards (Helm, 1979). Both the speaker and the caregivers should be counseled regarding barriers to effective communication. For example, caregivers should be aware that forgetting to speak up when talking on the telephone is not sign a of stubbornness or a generalized memory or cognitive problem. Rather, it is more likely the result of a combination of features of Parkinson's disease, including failure to appreciate the extent of the speech problem, difficulty with shifting sets from one speaking situation to another, difficulty in doing two things at a time (e.g., talking and thinking about how to talk clearly), and so forth. Also, the speaker with Parkinson's disease should be aware that partners' reminders about speech are not nagging but rather are direct and explicit feedback aimed at improving the communicative interaction.

Stage 4: Natural Speech Supplemented by Augmentative Techniques   In Stage 4, natural speech is no longer a functional means of communication for individuals with Parkinson's disease. Speech features may include difficulty with initiating voicing and short rushes of poorly articulated speech. Once speech is initiated, the speaker may freeze in mid-utterance and be unable to continue. Language production may be sparse, perhaps because of associated cognitive problems. Speech performance may noticeably worsen in off periods as compared with on periods.

During this stage, treatment may focus on the supplementation of natural speech with AAC approaches such as alphabet supplementation. In this procedure, the speaker points to the first letter of each word as the word is spoken. This technique controls speaking rate and provides the listener with additional information. Case reports are available that suggest that alphabet supplementation increased the comprehensibility of a speaker with severe hypokinetic dysarthria secondary to Parkinson's disease by 27% at the word level and by 57% at the sentence level (Schumacher & Rosenbek, 1986). Because of problems in self-perception of communication difficulties, the caregiver needs to take an active role in use of any AAC device. At this stage, the environment can be viewed as a type of assistive technology that compensates for disease-related loss (Steinfeld, 1997). For example, the environment may be designed to facilitate communication with quiet, well-lighted settings for face-to-face interactions. In addition to serving as a communication device, the physical world structures and organizes the social relationships of older people, especially those in sheltered living environments, and must be considered as part of AAC intervention.

Stage 5: No Functional Speech   A small percentage of individuals with Parkinson's disease lose all functional speech. When such a severe speech disorder is present, AAC intervention is required. Given the overall motor control impairment and the relatively frequent cognitive impairments late in the disease, complex AAC interventions are very difficult to institute and must be individualized. Typically, these individuals do not use multifunctional AAC devices but rather use systems that require letter-by-letter typing with print or speech output. Partner support to structure communicative interaction is critical at this stage.

Lived Experience of Parkinson's Disease

Lived experience is a term used in the qualitative research literature to denote the perspective of the insider regarding the process of disablement (Peters, 1996a, 1996b). What is it like to live with and in spite of Parkinson's disease? Taking the insider's perspective places emphasis on the environmental and social contexts of communication and is particularly critical in AAC intervention in Parkinson's disease. Many factors may contribute to the decrease in quality of life for individuals with Parkinson's disease, including restrictions in mobility, falls, emotional disorders, social embarrassment, isolation, sleep disturbances, dyskinesia, and fluctuations (Martinez-Martin, 1998). Although some of these factors are clearly associated with the level of physical disability, other psychosocial factors are also related to well-being, such as self-esteem, coping styles, and social supports (MacCarthy & Brown, 1989).

Understanding the life experiences of people with Parkinson's disease must begin with an appreciation of the demographics of the disease. Parkinson's disease is a disorder of older adults, with incidence peaking between the sixth and eighth decade of life. Men and women are equally affected (Hanson & Metter, 1983; Jain & Kirshblum, 1998; MacCarthy & Brown, 1989). Most individuals with Parkinson's disease live in the community with family and are often retired. In a study conducted in Great Britain, slight less than one quarter (22%) of individuals with Parkinson's disease resided in a hospital or in residential facilities (Harris, 1971). One third (33%) lived in the community but were experiencing disability. The remainder (45%) were living in the community without substantial disability. Because of the long-term nature of Parkinson's disease, the care management process may span the remaining lives of both the caregiver and the care receiver.

Caregiver   There is growing appreciation that the individual with Parkinson's disease and the caregiver must be considered as a unit in order to understand the effects of a chronic illness such as Parkinson's disease (Speer, 1993; Wallhagen & Brod, 1997). This patient–caregiver team is also the unit that must be considered in AAC intervention. As the chronic illness progresses, caregivers change how they manage their lives. The time and energy spent in managing this chronic illness becomes more troublesome for caregivers as their care receiver's course of illness progresses and physical functioning declines. Studies suggest that the primary reason for admitting an individual with long-term disabilities to a nursing home is that there is no family member to care for the individual in the home, or if one was previously present, circumstances have altered the availability of that family member (Berry & Murphy, 1995).

Caregiver burden also increases over time. *Burden* has been defined as the extent to which caregivers perceive their emotional or physical health, social life, and financial status as suffering as a result of caring for their relative (Zarit, Todd, & Zarit, 1986) Burden is not linearly or directly related to the severity of impairment. Some studies suggest that the relationship between severity of impairment and caregiver burden is complex. Factors contributing to this complex relationship are not completely understood, although comprehensive models of caregiving and stress have been proposed (Pearlin, Mullan, Semple, & Skaff, 1990). Carter and colleagues (1998) reported questionnaire data from spouses of individuals with Parkinson's disease. These data provide a caregiver perspective as the disease progresses and provide insights into the important role of communication and how that changes over time. Frustration with communication problems is present at all levels of the disease. It becomes prominent in the middle stages of the disease, probably before dysarthria and changes in speech intelligibility have arisen. Furthermore, it is rated as one of the higher variables in later stages of the disease.

Communication from the Insider's Perspective   The communication disorders associated with Parkinson's disease have been viewed largely from the perspective of outsider observations (i.e., those individuals without the disease). The insider's perception of the communication problems has received much less attention, either from the perspective of the individual with Parkinson's disease or the individual's caregivers. Communication has been examined as part of a larger study of disease symptoms (Abudi, Bar-Tal, Ziv, & Fish, 1997). In general, mental and psychosocial symptoms are perceived by individuals with Parkinson's disease as higher in frequency and severity than problems in performing activities of daily living. Somewhat surprisingly, communication problems are reported very frequently. In the study conducted by Abudi and colleagues, for example, under the category of motor symptoms, writing difficulties were reported by 69% of those sampled. The only motor symptom that was reported more frequently was tremor/dyskinesia. Under the category of psychosocial symptoms, social interaction difficulties were the most frequently reported (68%). Communication (i.e., verbal) difficulties were reported by 55% of individuals, thus ranking higher than shame, depression, anxiety, or frustration. Abudi and colleagues described the psychosocial and communication problems experienced by individuals with Parkinson's disease as impressive and summarized them as follows:

> Patients' appearances tend to make strangers feel that they have some mental impairment, and so they treat them inappropriately. This is a source of distress for the patient and his/her family. Since the lack of affect in speech and the problems of articulation interfere with communication, the patient often feels alone and alienated. (1997, p. 57)

Many features of communication that affect AAC change over time. Communication becomes more difficult because of increasing dysarthria and writing problems. Dependency on others increases; intellectual functioning declines. A progressive withdrawal from interpersonal relationships occurs. All of these factors influence the lived experiences of people with Parkinson's disease and their ability to adapt to the disease.

Directions for the Future

This section contains reflections about what researchers need to know before AAC services for individuals with Parkinson's disease can be improved. For the most part, these research directions involve asking questions about individuals with Parkinson's disease, their skills, and their communication needs. The following areas of inquiry are appropriate: 1) attitudes of people with Parkinson's disease, family members, caregivers, and peers; 2) learnability of AAC devices in light of the cognitive decline prevalent in this population; 3) integration of AAC and residual natural speech; and 4) interface and message organization issues for this population (i.e., age, social contexts, cognitive issues). As is characteristic in the field of AAC, reflections on future direction must also include new technology. What new technologies might be particularly useful for people with Parkinson's disease? Consider, for example, incorporating a speech-loudness feedback function into AAC technology. This would allow the individuals with Parkinson's disease to monitor the intensity of their natural residual speech, a task that the literature and clinical experience suggest is very difficult for them.

MODELS OF CARE

In the beginning of this chapter, we describe a clinician's first encounter with an individual with Huntington disease in order to illustrate some of the issues that service providers face. Throughout the chapter, information is presented about movement disorders that has implications for the management of severe communication disorders. This information included the characteristics of the underlying motor impairment, concomitant problems, such as cognition, and a variety of psychosocial issues brought about by the degenerative trajectory of the disease. We close this chapter by providing the reader with several models arising from various fields. These models provide a framework for identifying critical issues and understanding the possible interaction among these issues. Thus, the models provide a way of structuring and organizing the service delivery process for these individuals.

The first, a model of palliative care, comes from the field of medicine. The World Health Organization (WHO) has defined palliative care as follows:

> The active total care of patients whose disease is not responsive to curative treatment, where the control of pain, of other symptoms, and of psychological, social, and spiritual problems is paramount, and where the goal is the achievement of the best quality of life for patients and their families. (1980, p. 12)

For conditions such as Huntington disease, palliative care starts at the time of diagnosis and can co-exist with other types of care. Because maintenance of optimum communication is critical to quality of life, AAC management is central to palliative care. The model of palliative care helps to define the role of the communication specialist, especially at the end stages of the disease.

The second model, the participation model, comes directly from the field of AAC (Beukelman & Mirenda, 1998). This model provides a systematic process for conducting AAC assessments and designing intervention programs. The key components of this model include identifying participation patterns and communication needs (e.g., How does the individual with Parkinson's disease use natural speech, with gesture?), assessing barriers to opportunity (e.g., If the individual with Huntington disease lives in an extended care facility, what are the practices and attitudes toward communication?), and assessing barriers to access (e.g., Does the individual with Parkinson's disease have the motor and cognitive capabilities to learn to effectively use AAC devices?).

The third model, the model of caring, comes from the field of nursing. Providing AAC services to the family with movement disorders calls for an awareness of caring for the person and his or her family at several levels. Swanson (1991) described the caring process as knowing, being with, doing for, enabling, and maintaining belief. Although this process has not been applied to the area of communication disorders, the model is well suited to describing some factors critical in AAC management. *Knowing* as part of the caring process includes the capability to be able to express understanding of the plight of people with Huntington disease and the family's experience of their family member's disease. This overt expression of the communication specialist's interpretation of the disease experience provides the framework for open and honest communication throughout the treatment process. The presence of Huntington disease heavily affects the family's ability to be involved in services. At times, coping with the disease is so overwhelming that the person and his or her family members may not be able to take an active role in therapy. If services cannot be accepted at the time they are offered, the family should have the assurance that the communication specialist will be available when the time is right for the family to engage in therapy. It indicates to the person and his or her family that the communication specialist is willing to *be with* the family and understands that nonparticipation in therapy does not mean a disinterest in maintaining communication. This acceptance also prevents burdening the family with unrealistic therapy demands.

The *doing for* stage of the caring process sets the stage for the type of intervention to be offered. Intervention needs to focus on the provision of communication facilitation that is designed to meet the needs of the individual. In other words, communication services should enable the individual to participate in daily life as much as possible as if he or she were independent in communication. This requires that the communication specialist be knowledgeable in the services and technology available and how to gain access to them. He or she must also be able to explain these services in such a way that the family can make an informed choice. *Enabling* the family calls for a positive attitude when presenting treatment strategies and the willingness to incorporate the family's wisdom into therapeutic practices. In the face of deterioration of communication skills, the imparting of a realistic optimism will facilitate the person's transition from phase to phase of the disease and provide ways to cope with declining communicative abilities. This means providing service to the family throughout the illness. The family and the person with the disability may require services most at the end stages of the disease, when communication abilities are significantly decreased, to maintain a connection, however tenuous. Continuing to treat the person at this stage also validates the belief that the person's thoughts and ideas continue to be significant and important and need to be shared in whatever way possible. The person and his or her family have then been supported and appropriately cared for throughout the disease process. This is essential not only for the person but also for all at-risk individuals who may be seeking care at a future point. Believing that the communication specialist sincerely cares about the person and the process they are experiencing can only facilitate therapeutic suggestions.

REFERENCES

Abudi, S., Bar-Tal, Y., Ziv, L., & Fish, M. (1997). Parkinson's disease symptoms: Patients' perceptions. *Journal of Advanced Nursing, 25,* 54–59.

Adams, S.G. (1994). Accelerating speech in a case of hypokinetic dysarthria: Descriptions and treatment. In J.A. Till, K.M. Yorkston, & D.R. Beukelman (Eds.), *Motor speech disorders: Advances in assessment and treatment* (pp. 213–228). Baltimore: Paul H. Brookes Publishing Co.

Adams, S.G. (1997). Hypokinetic dysarthria in Parkinson's disease. In M.R. McNeil (Ed.), *Clinical management of sensorimotor speech disorders* (pp. 261–286). New York: Thieme Medical Publishers.

Albin, R.L. (1995). Selective neurodegeneration in Huntington's disease. *Annals of Neurology, 38*(6), 835–836.

Allain, H., Lieruy, A., Quemener, V., & Thoma, V. (1995). Procedural memory and Parkinson's disease. *Dementia, 6*(3), 174–178.

American Psychiatric Association (APA). (1994). *Diagnostic and statistical manual of mental disorders* (4th ed.). Washington, DC: Author.

Bayles, K.A. (1990). Language and Parkinson disease. *Alzheimer Disease and Associated Disorders, 4*(3), 171–180.

Beatty, W.W., & Monson, N. (1989). Lexical processing in Parkinson's disease and multiple sclerosis. *Journal of Geriatric Psychiatry and Neurology, 2,* 145–152.

Berry, R.A., & Murphy, J.F. (1995). Well-being of caregivers of spouses with Parkinson's disease. *Clinical Nursing Research, 4*(4), 373–386.

Beukelman, D.R., & Mirenda, P. (1998). *Augmentative and alternative communication: Management of severe communication disorders in children and adults* (2nd ed.). Baltimore: Paul H. Brookes Publishing Co.

Bondi, M.W., Kaszniak, A.W., Bayles, K.A., & Vance, K.T. (1993). Contributions of frontal system dysfunction to memory and perceptual abilities in Parkinson's disease. *Neuropsychology, 7*(1), 89–102.

Brown, P., & Marsden, C.D. (1998). What do the basal ganglia do? *Lancet, 351,* 1801–1804.

Caligiuri, M.P. (1989). Short-term fluctuations in orofacial motor control in Parkinson's disease. In K.M. Yorkston & D.R. Beukelman (Eds.), *Recent advances in clinical dysarthria* (pp. 184–207). Austin, TX: PRO-ED.

Carter, J.H., Stewart, B.J., Archbold, P.G., Inoue, I., Jaglin, J., Lannon, M., Rost-Ruffner, E., Tennis, M., McDermott, M.P., Amyot, D., Barter, R., Cornelious, L., Demong, C., Dobson, J., Duff, J., & Erickson, J. (1998). Living with a person who has Parkinson's disease: The spouse's perspective by stage of the disease. *Movement Disorders, 13*(1), 20–28.

Codori, A.M., & Brandt, J. (1994). Psychological costs and benefits of predictive testing for Huntington's disease. *American Journal of Medical Genetics, 54,* 174–184.

Cools, A.R., van den Berckess, J.H.L., & Hortink, M.W.I. (1984). Cognitive and motor shifting aptitude disorder in Parkinson's disease. *Journal of Neurology, Neurosurgery, and Psychiatry, 47,* 443–453.

Cummings, J.L. (1995). Behavioral and psychiatric symptoms associated with Huntington's disease. *Advances in Neurology, 65,* 179–186.

Cummings, J.L. (1988). Intellectual impairment in Parkinson's disease: Clinical, pathologic, and biochemical correlates. *Journal of Geriatric Psychiatry and Neurology, 1,* 24–36.

Cummings, J.L., & Bensen, F. (1984). Subcortical dementia: Review of an emerging concept. *Archives of Neurology, 14,* 874–87.

Cummings, J.L., Darkins, A., Mendez, M., Hill, M.A., & Benson, D.F. (1988). Alzheimer's disease and Parkinson's disease: Comparison of speech and language alterations. *Neurology, 38,* 680–684.

Dalrymple, A.J.C., Kalders, A.S., Jones, R.D., & Watson, R.W. (1994). A central executive deficit in patients with Parkinson's disease. *Journal of Neurology, Neurosurgery and Psychiatry, 57*(3), 360–367.

Darley, F.L., Aronson, A.E., & Brown, J.R. (1975). *Motor speech disorders.* Philadelphia: W.B. Saunders.

Dooneief, G., Mirabello, E., Bell, K., Marder, K., Stern, Y., & Mayeux, R. (1992). An estimate of the incidence of depression in idiopathic Parkinson's disease. *Archives of Neurology, 49,* 305–307.

Duffy, J.R. (1995). *Motor speech disorders, substrates, differential diagnosis, and management.* St. Louis, MO: Mosby.

Duvoisin, R.C. (1991). *Parkinson's disease: A guide for patient and family* (3rd ed.). New York: Raven Press.

Feigin, A., Kierbutz, K., Bordwell, K., Como, P., Steingberg, K., Sotack, J., Zimmerman, C., Hickey, C., Orme, C., & Shoulson, I. (1995). Functional decline in Huntington's disease. *Movement Disorders, 10,* 211–214.

Folstein, S.E. (1990). *Huntington disease: A disorder of families.* Baltimore: The Johns Hopkins University Press.

Girotti, F., Marano, R., Soliveri, P., Geminiani, G., & Seigliano, G. (1988). Relationship between motor and cognitive disorders in Huntington's disease. *Journal of Neurology, 235,* 454–457.

Gotham, A.M., Brown, R.G., & Marsden, C.D. (1986). Depression in Parkinson's disease: A quantitative and qualitative analysis. *Journal of Neurology, Neurosurgery and Psychiatry, 46,* 381–389.

Grossman, M., Carvell, S., Stern, M.B., Gollomp, S., & Hurtig, H.I. (1992). Sentence comprehension in Parkinson's disease: The role of attention and memory. *Brain and Language, 42,* 347–384.

Grossman, M., Carvell, S., Gollomp, S., Stern, M.B., Vernon, G., & Hurtig, H.I. (1991). Sentence comprehension and praxia deficits in Parkinson's disease. *Brain and Language, 41,* 1620–1626.

Haddad, M., Santoro, M., & Cummings, J.L. (1997). Huntington disease. *Psychiatric Clinics of North America, 20*(4), 791–807.

Hallett, M. (1993). Physiology of basal ganglia disorders: An overview. *Canadian Journal of Neurological Sciences, 20*(3), 177–183.

Hanson, W., & Metter, E. (1983). DAF speech rate modification in Parkinson's disease: A report of two cases. In W. Berry (Ed.), *Clinical dysarthria* (pp. 231–254). Austin, TX: PRO-ED.

Harris, A.I. (1971). *Handicapped and impaired in Great Britain.* London: Her Majesty's Stationery Office.

Hartelius, L., & Svensson, P. (1994). Speech and swallowing symptoms associated with Parkinson's disease and multiple sclerosis: A survey. *Phoniatrica et Logopaedica, 46,* 9–17.

Heaton, R.K. (1981). *The Wisconsin Card Sorting Test* (WCST) *manual.* Odessa, FL: Psychological Assessment Resources.

Helm, N. (1979). Management of palilalla with a pacing board. *Journal of Speech and Hearing Disorders, 44,* 350–353.

Huber, S.J., Shuttleworth, E.C., Paulson, G.W., Bellchambers, M.J.G., & Clapp, L. (1986). Cortical versus subcortical dementia. *Archives of Neurology, 43,* 392–394.

Hustad, K. (1999). Optimizing communicative effectiveness. In K.M. Yorkston, D.R. Beukelman, E.A. Strand, & K.R. Bell (Eds.), *Management of motor speech disorders in children and adults* (pp. 483–542). Austin, TX: PRO-ED.

Illes, J. (1989). Neurolinguistic features of spontaneous language production dissociate three forms of neurodegenerative disease: Alzheimer's, Huntington's, and Parkinson's. *Brain and Language, 37*(4), 628–642.

Illes, J., Metter, E.J., Hanson, W.R., & Iritani, S. (1988). Language production in Parkinson's disease: Acoustic and linguistic considerations. *Brain and Language, 33,* 146–160.

Jain, S.S., & Kirshblum, S.C. (1998). Parkinson's disease and other movement disorders. In J.A. DeLisa & B.M. Gans (Eds.), *Rehabilitation medicine: Principles and practices* (3rd ed., pp. 1035–1056). Philadelphia: Lippincott, Williams & Wilkins.

Kessler, S. (1993). The spouse in the Huntington disease family. *Family Systems Medicine, 11*(2), 191–199.

Kessler, S. (1994). Predictive testing for Huntington's disease: A psychologist's view. *American Journal of Medical Genetics, 54,* 161–166.

Kessler, S., & Bloch, M. (1989). Social system responses to Huntington disease. *Family Process, 28,* 59–68.

Lang, A.E. (1983). The "pacing board" in selected speech disorders of Parkinson's disease. *Journal of Neurology, Neurosurgery, and Psychiatry, 46,* 789–791.

Lange, K.W., Sahakian, B.J., Quinn, N.P., Marsden, C.D., & Robbins, T.W. (1995). Comparison of executive and visuospatial memory function in Huntington's disease and dementia of the Alzheimer's type matched for degree of dementia. *Journal of Neurology, Neurosurgery, and Psychiatry, 58*(5), 598–606.

Lawrence, A.D., Sahakian, B.J., Hodges, J.R., Rosser, A.E., Lange, K.W., & Robbins, T.W. (1996). Executive and mnemonic functions in early Huntington's disease. *Brain, 119,* 1633–1645.

Levin, B.E. (1990). Spatial cognition in Parkinson's disease. *Alzheimer Disease and Associated Disorders, 4,* 161–170.

Levin, B.E., Llabre, M.M., Reisman, S., Weiner, W.J., Sanchez-Ramos, J., Singer, C., & Brown, M.C. (1991). Visuspatial impairment in Parkinson's disease. *Neurology, 41,* 365–369.

Levin, B.E., Llabre, M., & Weiner, W. (1989). Cognitive impairments associated with early Parkinson's disease. *Neurology, 39,* 557–561.

Levin, B.E., Tomer, R., & Rey, G.J. (1992). Cognitive impairments in Parkinson's disease. *Neurological Clinics, 10*(2), 471–481.

Levy, M.L., Cummings, J.L., Fairbanks, L.A., Masterman, D., Miller, B.L., & Craig, A.H. (1998). Apathy is not depression. *Journal of Neuropsychiatry, 10*(3), 314–319.

Lieberman, P., Friedman, J., & Feldman, L. (1990). Syntax comprehension deficits in Parkinson's disease. *Journal of Nervous and Mental Disorders, 178,* 360–365.

Lieberman, P., Kako, E., Friedman, J., Tajchman, G., Feldman, L.S., & Jiminez, E.B. (1992). Speech production, syntax comprehension, and cognitive deficits in Parkinson's disease. *Brain and Language, 43*(2), 169–189.

Logemann, J.A., Fisher, H.B., Boskes, B., & Blonsky, E. (1978). Frequency and co-occurence of vocal tract dysfunction in the speech of a large sample of Parkinson patients. *Journal of Speech and Hearing Disorders, 43,* 47–57.

Longstreth, W., Nelson, L., Linde, M., & Munoz, D. (1992). Utility of sickness impact profile in Parkinson's disease. *Journal of Geriatric Psychiatry and Neurology, 5*(3), 142–148.

MacCarthy, B., & Brown, R. (1989). Psychosocial factors in Parkinson's disease. *British Journal of Clinical Psychology, 28,* 41–52.

Marsden, C.D. (1984). The pathophysiology of movement disorders. *Neurologic Clinics, 2,* 435–459.

Marsden, C.D. (1994). Parkinson's disease. *Journal of Neurology, Neurosurgery, and Psychiatry, 57*(6), 672–681.

Martinez-Martin, P. (1998). An introduction to the concept of "quality of life in Parkinson's disease." *Journal of Neurology, 245*(Suppl. 1), S2–S6.

Mayeux, R. (1990). Depression in the patient with Parkinson's disease. *Journal of Clinical Psychiatry, 51* (Suppl.), 20–23.

Mayeux, R., Stern, Y., Sano, M., Cote, L., & Williams, J.B. (1987). Clinical and biochemical correlates of bradyphrenia in Parkinson's disease. *Neurology, 37*(7), 1130–1134.

Mayeux, R., Williams, J.B.W., Stern, Y., & Cote, L. (1984). Depression and Parkinson's disease. In R.G. Hassler & J.F. Christ (Eds.), *Advances in neurology* (Vol. 40, pp. 241–251). New York: Raven Press.

Mello, L., & Villares, J. (1995). Neuroanatomy of the basal ganglia. *Psychiatric Clinics of North America, 20*(4), 691–704.

Metter, E.J., & Hanson, W.R. (1991). Dysarthria in progressive supranuclear palsy. In C.A. Moore, K.M. Yorkston, & D.R. Beukelman (Eds.), *Dysarthria and apraxia of speech: Perspectives on management* (pp. 127–136). Baltimore: Paul H. Brookes Publishing Co.

Morris, M. (1995). Dementia and cognitive changes in Huntington's disease. *Advances in Neurology, 65,* 187–200.

Nance, M.A. (1998). Huntington disease: Clinical genetic and social aspects. *Journal of Geriatric Psychiatry and Neurology, 11,* 61–70.

Norberg, A., & Athlin, E. (1987). The interaction between the parkinsonian patient and his caregiver during feeding: A theoretical model. *Journal of Advanced Nursing, 12*(5), 545–550.

Oliveira, R.M., Gurd, J.M., Nixon, P., Marshall, J.C., & Passingham, R.E. (1997). Micrographia in Parkinson's disease: The effects of providing external cues. *Journal of Neurology, Neurosurgery and Psychiatry, 63,* 429–433.

Owen, A.M., Beksinska, M., James, M., Leigh, P.N., Summers, B.A., Marsden, C.D., Quinee, N.P., Sahakian, B.J., & Robbins, T.W. (1993). Visuospatial memory deficits at different stages of Parkinson's disease. *Neuropsychologia, 31*(7), 627–644.

Pearlin, L.I., Mullan, J.T., Semple, S.J., & Skaff, M.M. (1990). Caregiving and the stress process: An overview of concepts and their measures. *Gerontologist, 30*(5), 580–581.

Peters, D.J. (1996a). Disablement observed, addressed, and experienced: Integrating subjective experience into disablement models. *Disability and Rehabilitation, 18,* 593–603.

Peters, D.J. (1996b). Qualitative inquiry: Expanding rehabilitation medicine's research repertoire: A commentary. *American Journal of Physical Medicine and Rehabilitation, 75,* 144–148.

Phillips, J.G., Bradshaw, J.L., Chiu, E., & Bradshaw, J.A. (1994). Characteristics of handwriting of patients with Huntington's disease. *Movement Disorders, 9*(5), 521–530.

Phillips, J.G., Bradshaw, J.L., Chiu, E., Teasdale, N., Iansek, R., & Bradshaw, J.A. (1996). Bradykinesia and movement precision in Huntington's disease. *Neuropsychologia, 34*(12), 1241–1245.

Podoll, K., Caspary, P., Lange, H.W., & Noth, J. (1988). Language functions in Huntington's disease. *Brain, 111,* 1475–1503.

Poluha, P.C., Teulings, H.L., & Brookshire, R.H. (1998). Handwriting and speech changes across the levodopa cycle in Parkinson's disease. *Acta Psychologica, 100,* 71–84.

Quaid, K.A., & Wesson, M.K. (1995). Exploration of the effects of predictive testing for Huntington disease on intimate relationships. *American Journal of Medical Genetics, 57,* 46–51.

Quinn, N., & Schrag, A. (1998). Huntington's disease and other choreas. *Journal of Neurology, 245,* 709–716.

Rafal, R.D., Posner, M.I., Walker, J.A., & Friedrich, F.J. (1984). Cognition and the basal ganglia: Separating mental and motor components of performance in Parkinson's disease. *Brain, 107,* 1083–1094.

Ramig, L.O. (1992). The role of phonation in speech intelligibility: A review and preliminary data from patient with Parkinson's disease. In R.D. Kent (Ed.), *Intelligibility in speech disorders: Theory, measurement and management* (pp. 119–156). Amsterdam: John Benjamins.

Ramig, L.O., Pawlas, A.A., & Countryman, S. (1995). *The Lee Silverman voice treatment.* Iowa City, IA: National Center for Voice and Speech.

Rothlind, J.C., Blysma, F.W., Peyer, C., Folstein, S.E., & Brandt, J. (1993). Cognitive and motor correlates of everyday functioning in early Huntington's disease. *Journal of Nervous and Mental Disease, 181*(3), 194–199.

Schumacher, J., & Rosenbek, J. (1986). Behavioral treatment of hypokinetic dysarthria: Further investigation of aided speech. *Asha, 28,* 145.

Seidman-Carlson, R., & Wells, D.L. (1998). The ability to comprehend affective communication in individuals with Huntington disease. *Journal of Gerontological Nursing, 24*(12), 16–23.

Shale, H., & Tanner, C. (1996). Pharmacological options for the management of dyskinesias. *Drugs, 52*(6), 849–869.

Shannon, K. (1996). Chorea. *Current Opinion in Neurology, 9,* 298–302.

Small, J.A., Lyons, K., & Kemper, S. (1997). Grammatical abilities in Parkinson's disease: Evidence form written sentences. *Neuropsychologia, 35*(12), 1571–1576.

Snowden, J.S., Craufurd, D., Griffiths, H.L., & Neary, D. (1998). Awareness of involuntary movements in Huntington disease. *Archives of Neurology, 55,* 801–805.

Speer, D.C. (1993). Predicting Parkinson's disease patient and caregiver adjustment: Preliminary findings. *Behavior, Health, and Aging, 3*(3), 139–146.

Sprengelmeyer, R., Lange, H., & Homberg, V. (1995). The pattern of attentional deficits in Huntington's disease. *Brain, 118,* 145–152.

Steinfeld, E. (1997). Architecture as a communication medium. In R. Lubinski & D.J. Higginbotham (Eds.), *Communication technologies for the elderly: Vision, hearing, and speech* (pp. 262–294). San Diego: Singular Publishing Group.

Swanson, K.M. (1991). Empirical development of a middle range theory of caring. *Nursing Research, 40*(3), 161–166.

Thomas, A.C., Laurent, B., Foyatier, M.N., & Laporte, S. (1996). Procedural memory: Computer learning in control subjects and in Parkinson's disease patients. *Behavioral Neurology, 9,* 127–134.

Thomas, V., Reymann, J.M., Lieury, A., & Allain, H. (1996). Assessment of procedural memory in Parkinson's disease. *Progress in Neuro-Psychopharmacology and Biological Psychiatry, 20*(4), 641–650.

Thompson, P. D., Berardelli, A., Rothwell, J.C., Day, B.L., Dick, J.P.R., Benecke, R., & Marsden, C.D. (1988). The coexistence of bradykinesia and chorea in Huntington's disease and its implications for theories of basal ganglia control of movement. *Brain, 111,* 223–244.

van Vugt, J.P.P., van Hilten, B.J., & Roos, R.A.C. (1996). Hypokinesia in Huntington's disease. *Movement Disorders, 11*(4), 384–388.

Vonsattel, J.P., & DiFigila, M. (1998). Huntington disease. *Journal of Neuropathology and Experimental Neurology, 57,* 369–384.

Wallhagen, M.I., & Brod, M. (1997). Perceived control and well-being in Parkinson's disease. *Western Journal of Nursing Research, 19*(1), 11–31.

World Health Organization (WHO). (1980). *International classification of impairments, activities and handicaps.* Geneva: Author.

Yorkston, K.M., Beukelman, D.R., Strand, E.A., & Bell, K.R. (1999). *Management of motor speech disorders in children and adults.* Austin, TX: PRO-ED.

Zakzanis, K. (1998). The subcortical dementias of Huntington's disease. *Journal of Clinical and Experimental Neuropsychology, 20*(4), 565–578.

Zarit, S.H., Todd, P.A., & Zarit, J.M. (1986). Subjective burden of husbands and wives as caregivers: A longitudinal study. *Gerontologist, 26*(3), 260–266.

9

AAC and Traumatic Brain Injury

Influence of Cognition on System Design and Use

Molly Doyle
Mary R.T. Kennedy
Ginta Jausalaitis
Barbara Phillips

People with a traumatic brain injury (TBI) may experience such severe neurogenic communication disorders that they are unable to meet their communication needs through natural speech alone. Many individuals use augmentative and alternative communication (AAC) systems sometime during the recovery process. In most cases, AAC systems are used on a temporary basis while attempts are made to establish functional speech, though sometimes more permanent AAC systems are required. Some individuals supplement their speech with AAC strategies, and others communicate nearly all of their messages via AAC (Beukelman & Mirenda, 1992, 1998; DeRuyter & Donoghue, 1989; DeRuyter & Kennedy, 1991; Dongilli, Hakel, & Beukelman, 1992; Ladtkow & Culp, 1992). In this chapter, we review the neuropathology of TBI, discuss the cognitive impairments and behavior issues that are commonly associated with TBI, present a theoretical framework that assists in the rehabilitation of individuals with TBI using AAC systems, and discuss the influence of cognition on the selection, design, and use of AAC systems.

NEUROPATHOLOGY OF TRAUMATIC BRAIN INJURY

TBI is an insult to the brain caused by an external blow to the head, resulting in limitations in cognitive, language, visual, physical, and/or behavioral functioning (Long Island Head Injury Association, 1999). It is the leading cause of death or disability for individuals in the United States who are younger than 45 years in age. An estimated 2 million individuals sustain TBIs each year. Of those, approximately 500,000 individuals require hospitalization, rehabilitation, or both, and 70,000–90,000 develop impairments so severe that independent living is affected (Long Island Head Injury Association, 1999).

First, a distinction should be made between congenital and acquired brain injury (ABI). A congenital brain injury occurs prior to or during birth, whereas an ABI occurs after birth. Specifically, there are two classifications of ABI: nontraumatic and traumatic. Nontraumatic ABIs can be caused by cerebrovascular accidents (i.e., strokes), sudden changes in oxygen supply (i.e., hypoxia or anoxia), intracranial infections, tumors, metabolic disorders, and toxicity. TBIs are broadly classified as open or closed. An open TBI occurs when the skull is penetrated or partially removed, exposing brain tissue or forcing skull fragments into brain tissue. The result is a localized injury to brain tissue occurring in the vicinity of the blow. Closed brain injury occurs when an external force is applied to the skull, without penetration into brain tissue. The sudden rotation and acceleration/deceleration of the brain within the skull results in diffuse brain tissue damage. Some areas of the brain are more susceptible to damage than others following TBI because of the presence of the bony shelves within the skull. For example, the frontal and temporal lobes are frequently damaged because of their location near the sharp edges of the inside of the skull.

The neuropathologic changes related to TBI can be classified into two major groups, primary and secondary. Primary injury occurs as a direct result of the mechanical forces at the time of the trauma. Examples of primary injury include various cranial neuropathies, vascular injury, scalp injury, and a number of hemorrhagic lesions to be discussed further in this chapter. Secondary TBI usually occurs as a result of the brain's response to injury. Causes of secondary TBI include hypoxia or anoxia, electrolyte disturbances, seizures, elevated intracranial pressure, and systemic complications, to name a few. Cerebral edema due to loss of cerebral autoregulation is the most common secondary injury. Other secondary lesions include infection, infarction, and subacute cranial nerve injury.

Subdural hematomas most commonly occur from the traumatic disruption of the bridging veins, located between the brain and the inner layer of the dura. Lack of dural attachments sometimes allow subdural hematomas to spread over large cortical areas. This lack of flow impedance explains why subdural hematomas may become quite large before exhibiting any clinical manifestations. In individuals with generous subdural spaces, often secondary to brain atrophy, subdural hematomas are not uncommon, owing to the fragility of the stretched veins. These patients may be asymptomatic, however, because of the large area available to the expanding hemorrhage. Subdural hematomas can be classified as acute, subacute, and chronic.

Epidural hematomas most often result from middle meningeal artery injury, leading to rapid accumulation of arterial blood between outer dural layer and the inner skull. The classic presentation is that of a brief loss of consciousness after which a patient awakens and may look well. Subsequently, the patient's neurologic status deteriorates as the hematoma enlarges within its confined space. Some studies have shown, however, that this classic epidural hematoma may occur in fewer than 30% of people who experience hematomas (Gallagher & Browder, 1968).

Diffuse axonal injury has been described as *white matter shearing injury*. The term refers to the axonal disruption and vascular shearing that occur as a result of rotational acceleration/deceleration forces. This type of injury is usually the result of motor vehicle accidents rather than blunt head trauma or falls. These lesions may be small and may be better visualized on a magnetic resonance imaging (MRI) scan rather than on a computed tomography (CT) scan. Diffuse axonal injury occurs most frequently in the brain stem, corpus callosum, and subcortical white matter. Clinically, a person may exhibit a variety of conditions, including coma, motor weakness, spasticity, cranial neuropathies, and impaired cognition.

Contusions are hemorrhages, which are most often limited to the cerebral gyri, especially in regions where the brain is in close contact with roughened surfaces of the inner skull table. The orbitofrontal and temporal lobes are the most common sites, although any lobe may be affected. Contusions tend to improve as the edema subsides. Cerebral hematomas are hemorrhages within the brain parenchyma and generally have a poorer prognosis than contusions. Hematomas are the most common cause of death in patients who experienced a lucid period after their injury (Reilly, Graham, Adams, & Jennett, 1975). In patients who are unconscious after their injuries, diffuse axonal injury is generally found (Gennarelli et al., 1982).

COMMUNICATION DISORDERS ASSOCIATED WITH TBI

There are three categories of communication impairment following TBI: cognitive-communication disorders, specific language impairment, and motor speech disorders. Cognitive-communication disorders reflect underlying cognitive impairment and are behaviorally manifested as distractibility and confusion, for example. The processes, ranging from alertness to higher-level executive function, are described later in the chapter and have been summarized elsewhere (Kennedy & DeRuyter, 1991; Rosenthal, Griffith, Kreutzer, & Pentland, 1999). Impairments in these processes directly affect the use of language. For example, the verbal output of an individual with attention and memory impairments may be described as confused, disorganized, and tangential. Specific language impairment (i.e., damage to specific language-processing areas of the brain), specifically aphasia or subclinical aphasia, have been reported in individuals following individuals with TBI (Sarno, Buonaguvro, & Levita, 1986). Impairments in word retrieval, word fluency, and sentence formulation significantly affect verbal expression. Motor speech disorders also cause communication disorders in individuals with TBI (Yorkston & Beukelman, 1991). Researchers report that approximately one third of individuals with TBI have dysarthria. Sarno and colleagues (1986) found that 34% of 124 individuals exhibited dysarthria ranging from mild articulatory imprecision to unintelligible speech. In all cases, the dysarthria occurred in conjunction with subclinical aphasia. Apraxia is less common in TBI. Clinicians have noted apraxia in isolation or in conjunction with dysarthria; however, little has been documented in the literature.

Cognitive, linguistic, and motor speech disorders can coexist or occur independently in TBI. These areas may recover at varying rates. Cognitive and language skills may improve while speech production remains severely dysarthric or apraxic. In those cases, AAC devices are usually considered as temporary measures until natural speech reemerges. However, AAC is also indicated for patients with such severe cognitive impairment that it is difficult to assess the severity of language or motor speech impairments, let alone the extent to which these impairments contribute to the individual's overall communication competency.

Recovery of Speech

The majority of individuals with TBI recover functional speech so that AAC is no longer needed or is used only to augment speech in specific situations or with certain partners. Ladtkow and Culp (1992) followed 138 individuals with TBI. Twenty-nine (21%) were considered "nonspeaking" at some point in the recovery process. Of these 29, 16 (55%) regained functional speech. Dongilli and colleagues (1992) followed 27 individuals who were unable to speak upon admission to an inpatient rehabilitation program. Sixteen of these individuals (59%) became functional speakers. Of the 11 who did not gain functional speech by discharge, 1 attained functional speech 24 months after the injury and another was making significant gains toward natural speech 48 months after the injury. Doyle and Nance (1993) followed 44 children with TBI, ages 5–17, who were unable to speak upon admission to inpatient rehabilitation. Thirty-seven (84%) recovered functional speech, and thirty (81%) did so within 3 months after injury. These studies provide evidence of a relationship between cognitive recovery and emergence of functional speech. Adults who regained speech did so by the middle stage of recovery or at level of cognitive functioning (LOCF) V (i.e., confused, inappropriate, and nonagitated) or LOCF VI (i.e., confused, appropriate) (Hagan, 1984; Hagan, Malkamus, & Durham, 1979) (see Table 1). There have been cases where individuals recovered speech several years after injury (Light, Beesley, & Collier, 1988; Workinger & Netsell, 1988). In these cases, individuals made the transition through multiple AAC systems before reacquiring speech. Review of case studies that describe types of AAC systems and strategies used by individuals with TBI are provided in the literature (Beukelman & Mirenda, 1998; DeRuyter & Donoghue, 1989; DeRuyter & Kennedy, 1991; Ladtkow & Culp, 1992).

Types of AAC Systems

The purpose of AAC intervention and the type of system used is influenced by the severity of the injury, the stage of recovery (i.e., early, middle, late), and the LOCF. In the early stages of recovery, with individuals at lower levels (LOCF II–III), intervention focuses on establishing a reliable response modality for purposes of assessment, choice making, and beginnings of a yes-or-no system. In the middle phase of recovery (LOCF IV–V), individuals may use a range of simple AAC techniques to convey basic needs and participate in therapy. Techniques include yes-or-no responses; gestures; picture, word, or alphabet boards; and in some cases, simple voice output devices. Boards and devices are often limited to a single display with a limited number of message choices. These systems are still considered temporary because individuals at this stage may recover speech or may continue to experience improvements in cognitive, language, and motor abilities and therefore need the system modified to accommodate these changes. During this phase, individuals need structure and cues in order to use systems effectively in basic communication interactions. It is only in the later phases (LOCF VI–VIII) that permanent AAC solutions may be considered for individuals who remain severely dysarthric or apraxic and have plateaued in terms of cognitive recovery. Communication notebooks, alphabet boards with words/phrases, and voice output devices are implemented at this stage. Individuals can learn to use

Table 1.   Levels of cognitive functioning and associated language behaviors

General behaviors	Language behaviors
I. No Response Patient appears to be in a deep sleep and is completely unresponsive to any stimuli.	Receptively and expressively: No evidence of processing or verbal or gestural expression.
II. Generalized Response Patient reacts inconsistently and non-purposefully to stimuli in a nonspecific manner. Responses are limited and often the same, regardless of stimuli presented. Responses may be physiologic changes, gross body movements, or vocalization.	Receptively and expressively: No evidence of processing or verbal or gestural expression.
III. Localized Response Patient reacts specifically, but inconsistently, to stimuli. Responses are directly related to the type of stimulus presented. May follow simple commands such as "Close your eyes," or "Squeeze my hand" in an inconsistent, delayed manner.	Language begins to emerge. Receptively: Patient progresses from localizing to processing and following simple commands that elicit automatic responses in a delayed and inconsistent manner. Limited reading emerges. Expressively: Automatic verbal and gestural responses emerge in response to direct elicitation. Negative head nods emerge before positive head nods. Utterances are single words serving as "holophrastic" responses.
IV. Confused-Agitated Behavior seems bizarre and non-purposeful relative to immediate environment. Does not discriminate among persons or objects; is unable to cooperate directly with treatment efforts; verbalizations are frequently incoherent or inappropriate to the environment, and confabulation may be present. Gross attention to environment is very short, and selective attention is often non-existent. Patient lacks short-term recall.	Severe disruption of frontal-temporal lobes with the resultant confusion apparent. Receptively: Marked disruption in auditory and visual processing, including inability to order phonemic events, monitor rate, and attend to, retain, categorize, and associate stimuli. Disinhibition interferes with comprehension and ability to inhibit responses to self-generated mental activity. Expressively: Marked disruption of phonologic, semantic, syntactic, and suprasegmental features. Output appears bizarre, unrelated to environment, and incoherent. Literal, verbal, and neologistic paraphrasias appear with disturbance of logicosequential features and incompleteness of thought. Monitoring of pitch, rate, intensity, and suprasegmentals is severely impaired.
V. Confused, Inappropriate, Nonagitated Patient is able to respond to simple commands fairly consistently. However, with increased complexity of commands or lack of any external structure,	Linguistic fluctuations are in accordance with the degree of external structure and familiarity predictability of linguistic events. Receptively: Processing has improved,

Table 1.   (continued)

General behaviors	Language behaviors
responses are nonpurposeful, random, or fragmented. Has gross attention to the environment but is highly distractible and lacks ability to focus attention on a specific task; with structure, may be able to converse on a social-automatic level for short periods; verbalization is often inappropriate and confabulatory; memory is severely impaired; often shows inappropriate use of subjects. Individual may perform previously learned tasks with structure but is unable to learn new information.	with increased ability to retain temporal order of phonemic events, but semantic and syntactic confusions persist. Only phrases or short sentences are retained. Rate, accuracy, and quality remain significantly reduced. Expressively: Persistence of phonologic, semantic, syntactic, and prosodic processes. Disturbances in logicosequential features result in irrelevances, incompleteness, tangents, circumlocutions, and confabulations. Literal paraphrasias subside, while neologisms and verbal paraphasias continue. Utterances may be expansive or telegraphic, depending on inhibition-disinhibition factors. Responses are stimulus bound. Word retrieval deficits are characterized by delays, generalizations, descriptions, semantic associations, or circumlocutions. Disruptions in syntactic features are present beyond concrete levels of expression or with increased length of output. Written output is severely limited. Gestures are incomplete.
VI. Confused-Appropriate Patient shows goal-directed behavior but depends on external output for direction; follows simple directions consistently and shows carryover for relearned tasks with little or no carryover for new tasks; responses may be incorrect because of memory problems but appropriate tothe situation; past memories show more depth and detail than recent memory.	Receptively: Processing remains delayed, with difficulty in retaining, analyzing, and synthesizing. Auditory processing is present for compound sentences, while reading comprehension is present for simple sentences. Self-monitoring capacity emerges. Expressively: Internal confusion-disorganization is reflected in expression, but appropriateness is maintained. Language is confused relative to impaired new learning and displaced temporal and situational contexts, but confabulation is no longer present. Social-automatic conversation is intact but remains but remains stimulus bound. Tangential and irrelevant responses are present only in open-ended situations requiring referential language. Neologisms are extinguished, with literal paraphasias present only in conjunction with an apraxia. Word retrieval errors occur in conversation but seldom in confrontation naming. Length of utterance reflects inhibitory-initiation mechanisms. Written and gestural expression increases. Prosodic features reflect the "voice of confusion," characterized by monopitch, monostress, and monoloudness.

(continued)

Table 1.   (continued)

General behaviors	Language behaviors
VII. Automatic-Appropriate Patient appears appropriate and oriented within hospital and home settings and goes through daily routine automatically, but is frequently robotlike with minimal-to-absent confusion; has shallow recall of activities; shows carryover for new learning but at a decreased rate; with structure, is able to initiate social or recreational activities; judgment remains impaired.	Linguistic behaviors appear "normal" within familiar, predictable, structured settings, but features, organize, integrate input, order, and retain detail. Expressively: Automatic level of language is apparent in referential communication. Reasoning is concrete and self-oriented. Expression becomes tangential and irrelevant when abstract linguistic concepts are attempted. Word retrieval errors are minimal. Length of utterances approximately normal. Writing is disorganized and simple at a paragraph level. Prosodic features may remain aberrant. Pragmatic features of ritualizing and referencing are present, while other components remain disrupted.
VIII. Purposeful and Appropriate Patient is able to recall and integrate past and recent events and is aware of and responsive to the environment, shows carryover for new learning and needs no supervision once activities are learned; may continue to show a decreased ability relative to premorbid abilities in language, abstract reasoning, tolerance for stress, and judgment in emergencies or unusual circumstances.	Language capacities may fall within normal limits. Otherwise, problems persist in competitive situations and in response to fatigue, stress, and emotionally characterized in reduced effectiveness, efficiency, and quality of performance. Receptively: Rate of processing remains remains limited at paragraph level but improved with use of retrieval-organization reduced but unremarkable on testing. Retention span strategies. Analysis, organization, and integration are reduced in rate and quality. Expressively: Syntactic and semantic features fall within normal limits, while verbal reasoning and abstraction may fall below premorbid level. Prosodic features are essentially normal. Pragmatic features of referencing, presuppositions, topic maintenance, turn taking, and use of paralinguistic features in context remain impaired.

From Hagen, C. (1984). Language disorders in head trauma. In A. Holland (Ed.), *Language disorders in adults* (pp. 257–258). Austin, TX: PRO-ED; adapted by permission.

encoding and other acceleration strategies but require practice in using strategies in order to be effective. Electronic voice output devices are recommended for permanent use only if an individual accepts and uses the system. This requires the individual to have insight and recognize the need and benefit of an AAC device. For individuals without adequate insight, voice output devices can be provided for trial in an attempt to demonstrate to the person the benefit of such a system.

The remainder of this chapter focuses on describing the assessment and AAC decision-making process for individuals with TBI who have profound speech impairments, as well as various cognitive-communication deficits. The cognitive demands of different AAC components are also discussed. The information presented can be applied to individuals with other types of ABIs who experience severe communication disorders and who exhibit cognition-based communication disorders that are also candidates for AAC (e.g., anoxia, encephalitis, tumors). Although the specific deficits and recovery patterns of nontraumatic ABI may differ from TBI, many of the AAC assessment and intervention procedures discussed here can be applied across clinical populations.

RELATIONSHIP BETWEEN COGNITIVE-COMMUNICATION DISORDERS AND AAC MANAGEMENT AFTER TBI

Individuals who are unable to meet their daily communication needs through natural speech as a result of TBI are unique from other "nonspeakers" and require a specialized approach to assessment and treatment. Individuals with acute injuries need a temporary system established immediately in order to convey basic needs and participate in ongoing evaluations.

Cognitive Recovery and Type of AAC System

There appears to be a relationship between the survivor's cognitive/behavioral status and the type and design of the AAC system to be used. DeRuyter and Kennedy (1991) found a direct relationship between the primary type of AAC system used and the individual's LOCF. At lower LOCFs, simple systems were used and as cognition improved, more complex systems were used by individuals with TBI (Carlisle & Culp, 1988; DeRuyter & Kennedy, 1991; Fried-Oken & Doyle, 1992). For example, individuals functioning at LOCF III may rely on choices or a yes-or-no system as a primary system, whereas those at LOCF V use picture- or word-based systems. AAC systems are changed as functional status improves; changes in the areas of vision, perception, cognition, language, and motor control may occur quickly, so systems are redesigned to accommodate these changes. Readers are referred to Fried-Oken and Doyle (1992) for discussion of system expansion strategies based on LOCF and system type. The purpose of communication also changes as cognition improves. At lower levels, individuals communicate basic wants and needs, whereas at higher levels the primary purposes of communication is to share information and maintain social closeness (DeRuyter, Becker, & Doyle, 1987; DeRuyter & Kennedy, 1991).

To promote functional AAC use, involvement of an interdisciplinary team is critical. The team establishes the system and throughout all stages of recovery systematically upgrades it to accommodate for changes in status and needs. Team members also provide the structure, training, and support that individuals need when using the system during therapy and other daily activities. Instruction throughout the day is critical, given the individuals' deficits in new learning and generalization. The social support system is an integral component of the rehabilitation team. Their early involvement can enhance learning and generalization of AAC use by providing opportunities for the person with TBI to communicate and by reinforcing the use of the system.

Unique to the individual with TBI is the use of AAC in cognitive retraining. Context- or topic-specific miniboards may be developed to target specific cognitive processes. For instance, a board may be designed to help with recall of orientation information and therapy schedules. Using AAC as a tool for cognitive retraining or remediation is common practice; however, formal data demonstrating its effectiveness is lacking. (Refer to Chapters 4 and 12 for additional discussion of these issues.)

Specific Cognitive Disorders that Influence AAC Management
Attention is a group of processes that includes arousal, focused, selective, alternating, divided, and sustained attention (for review, see Sohlberg & Mateer, 1989). Attention is distributed and mediated neuroanatomically by the reticular activating system and the connections among the frontal lobes and subcortical structures, temporal lobes, and the hippocampus. These areas are frequently damaged after a TBI and represent a group of impairments commonly associated with damage to these brain regions. Individuals with TBI may demonstrate difficulty with staying awake and with consciously increasing their level of alertness, orienting to stimuli, attending to relevant information while ignoring irrelevant information, alternating attention between activities, paying attention to two different types of information at the same time, or staying focused on an activity for a designated period of time. As a result, individuals with TBI are slower at performing tasks that require controlled attention (Gronwall & Wrighton, 1974; Van Zomeren & Deelman, 1978). The nature and severity of the attentional impairments affects AAC use in different ways. At a basic level, an individual may not be able to sustain attention long enough to fully compose a message. Another individual may have difficulty with using multiple AAC strategies, such as spelling and word prediction, because of difficulty with shifting attention between strategies.

Visual perception involves the interpretation of incoming stimuli by comparing it with one's knowledge stored in working memory.

Visual perception deficits have received much attention in the research literature and are categorized as primary and secondary deficits after TBI. Primary deficits include visual field cuts, visuospatial neglects, and visual figure–ground disturbances. Secondary deficits are due to generalized cognitive impairment and include difficulties with various forms of visual attention. To accommodate primary perceptual deficits, AAC displays may be positioned in the optimal visual field. Displays may be simplified, in terms of number and complexity of messages, to accommodate for secondary perceptual deficits.

Memory deficits are the most frequently identified group of symptoms reported by researchers, clinicians, survivors, and families of survivors following a TBI (for review, see Goldstein & Levin, 1995; Jacobs, 1988). Memory and learning impairments typically associated with TBI include deficits of working memory and learning new information, including events that have occurred since the injury (i.e., episodic memory), and remembering what needs to be done in the future (i.e., prospective memory) (Gronwall & Wrighton, 1981; Wilson, 1995). After conceptualizing memory as short-term and long-term started in the 1960s (Atkinson & Shiffrin, 1968, 1971), the notions of a working memory and a central executive system proved to be more clinically valid for the types of memory impairments following brain injury (Baddeley, 1984). Working memory includes an articulatory rehearsal process (associated with the left temporal region of the brain) and a visuospatial sketchpad (associated with the right temporal-parietal region of the brain) and is modulated by the central executive system by directing attention via the frontal lobes.

The memory disorders associated with TBI are not homogeneous. Depending on the relative contribution of both diffuse and focal brain damage, survivors can demonstrate various types of memory impairments with a wide range of severity. Although the results of empirical research have supported the claim that a disruption in working memory is the underlying basis for memory impairments after TBI, there are several types that have been identified (Baddeley, Wilson, & Watts, 1995). Attention-based memory impairments are the result of reductions in the allocation of attention resources and distribution of attention, which in turn affects working memory processing (Sohlberg & Mateer, 1989). Reductions in encoding have also been identified in this population. Impairments of this type are the result of selection of inefficient strategies or the absence of strategies (Gasquoine, 1991). Some individuals with TBI cannot transfer information into their long-term memory (i.e., knowledge base), and others have lost the capacity to store new information (Haut & Shutty, 1992). Finally, many individuals with TBI experience difficulty with retrieving information from long-term memory for use in working memory and may retrieve it slowly (Blachstein, Vakil, & Hoffien, 1993).

Another clinically useful way to examine memory disorders after TBI is to identify the kinds of information that is remembered and learned. These include declarative information (i.e., semantic, episodic) and nondeclarative information (i.e., procedures, conditioning, priming, nonassociative learning) (Squire, 1992). Individuals with TBI have the most difficulty with remembering recent events; remembering facts, people, and details associated with the event (i.e., episodic memory); and remembering future events (i.e., prospective memory) (Wilson, 1995). Individuals with TBI have difficulty on an everyday basis with remembering details of events throughout the day, names and faces, and future appointments and tasks they must accomplish sometime in the future. They also have difficulty with using external and internal compensatory strategies (e.g., written checklists, rehearsal strategies).

Clinical researchers have been able to identify various types of learning after TBI. Millis and Ricker (1994) identified four kinds of learners after TBI: active, passive, disorganized, and deficient. Haut and Shutty (1992) classified learning problems after TBI. The results from their investigation indicated that there are individuals with TBI who have no learning problems, those who experience difficulty during the acquisition phase of learning, and those who can acquire new information but are delayed in recall and experience serious interference effects. In addition, researchers have found that individuals with TBI do not use learning strategies efficiently, which can eventually interfere with recall (Blachstein et al., 1993; Paniak, Shore, & Rourke, 1989).

The individual with TBI who is a candidate for AAC may have difficulty with any or all of the memory deficits described in this chapter. For individuals with severe communication disorders who are in a heightened state of confusion and posttraumatic amnesia (PTA), keeping systems as simple as possible may actually reduce confusion (or at least not increase confusion). For example, limiting the number of messages and using high-frequency vocabulary allows the individual to attend to visual stimuli rather than be distracted by rapid changes in environmental stimuli. Some individuals may not be able to remember the steps necessary to retrieve messages (i.e., procedural memory). Others may be unable to retain messages in working memory sufficiently in order to formulate them using their AAC, especially if formulation takes several minutes. To compensate for these deficits, procedural steps, vocabulary, and phrases can be displayed as constant reminders to the AAC user with memory deficits (Light & Lindsay, 1991).

Metacognition is the foundation on which executive decisions are made. Metacognition is the thinking and monitoring of one's own cognition, including awareness of deficits and behavior; self-monitoring prior, during, and after performing an activity; and beliefs one has about mental operations (Flavell, 1979; Nelson & Narens, 1990). Executive functions are the spontaneous adjustments in behavior that a person makes in response to information generated by metacognition (Butterfield & Belmont, 1977). For example, upon approaching a colleague to discuss an important topic, I notice that she continues to work at her desk while I begin the conversation. I interpret this behavior to indicate that this is not the best time to discuss this topic and change my original plan (of having a long discussion) to accommodate the constraints of the situation. (I state the issue quickly and concisely.) Individuals with TBI have difficulty with monitoring situations quickly and monitoring their own performance (while it is occurring) and are slow to make adjustments that fit the situation.

Use of AAC strategies to expedite communication and minimize communication breakdown requires astute metacognitive and executive function capabilities. These kinds of deficits make it difficult for AAC users to determine the optimal communication modality and shift effectively between modalities depending on the topic, environment, and partner. For example, when ordering from a menu in a noisy restaurant, pointing to the item on the menu is more efficient than spelling out HAMBURGER on the AAC system. Shortening messages, establishing topic, and other similar strategies are critical for maximizing communication in a natural environment. Proper use of these strategies is dependent upon the individual's understanding his or her limitations with communication, recognizing his or her role in a conversational exchange, seeing that a breakdown is occurring, and then selecting and using the appropriate combination of strategies to minimize the breakdown.

Pragmatic deficits are commonly associated with individuals with TBI and result in social isolation. Although it is a commonly held assumption that the cognitive/language deficits are the underlying basis for pragmatic deficits in this population, there is little empirical evidence to support this claim. Regardless, it seems clinically intuitive that difficulty with monitoring subtle changes in the communication partners, settings, and goals would have an effect on the ability to make quick, spontaneous adjustments in communication situations.

Both verbal and nonverbal pragmatic deficits have been documented in the literature (for review, see Hartley, 1995; Kennedy & DeRuyter, 1991). The communication of some individuals with TBI is described as being impaired and perseverative in content (e.g., few words, topics, ideas), yet others' is described as verbose, disorganized, and tangential (Coelho, Liles, & Duffy, 1991; McDonald & Pearce, 1995; Milton, Prutting, & Binder, 1984). Some individuals are described as reluctant to communicate even when it is their "turn," yet others talk excessively (without yielding their turn) and interrupt to take a turn (Hartley & Jensen, 1992). AAC users may have pragmatic deficits that mimic the speaking population. Unfortunately, when using an AAC system, the user's attention is momentarily diverted from the communication partner, further reducing the chances that subtle changes in the conversational direction and feedback from the partner will be noticed. Without noticing these changes, the AAC user with TBI will not consistently have information they need to make quick decisions about adjusting the communication message.

AAC INTERVENTION USING A CHRONIC DISEASE MODEL

As a clinical group, individuals with TBI experience a wide range of cognitive-communication deficits, in addition to language and motor deficits, that influence the design and use of AAC within the rehabilitation setting and in more natural communication environments (DeRuyter & Kennedy, 1991). Cognitive deficits in attention, visual perception, memory and learning, pragmatics, metacognition, and executive function can directly or indirectly influence the functional capabilities during rehabilitation and everyday communication. A useful framework that organizes assessment and intervention for the individual with TBI who cannot speak is the World Health Organization (WHO) model of chronic disease that was revised by the Institute of Medicine and the National Center for Medical Rehabilitation and Research (Institute of Medicine, 1991). Deficits are categorized into five parameters: *pathophysiologic changes* occur as the result of tissue damage or death; *impairments* are considered a loss of function as a result of pathophysiologic damage; *functional limitations* are decreases in the ability to perform during isolated activities; *disabilities* are reductions in performance during activities within the naturally occurring contextual environment; and *societal limitations* are changes in one's role within society due to rules or barriers. The model has been applied to various adult neurogenic communication disorders, including cognitive-communication and motor-speech deficits following TBI (for comprehensive review, see Yorkston & Kennedy, 1999). An application of this model to AAC users who have TBI and cannot speak is presented in Table 2. Each parameter is described in the following discussion. The following discussion focuses on AAC intervention with recognition that for this population improving cognitive, language, and motor speech abilities is also a critical aspect of a therapy plan.

Table 2. The revised World Health Organization (WHO) Model of Chronic Disease applied to the assessment and treatment of AAC users with TBI who cannot speak

	Definition	Level of deficit	Examples of assessment targets	Examples of approaches to intervention
Pathophysiology	Interruption or interference of normal physiological and developmental processes or structures	Damage to cells in cortical, subcortical, and brainstem regions of the central nervous system (CNS)	Evidence of damage using radiographic, imaging and electroencephalographic diagnostic techniques	Pharmologic intervention to reduce spasticity and to improve memory
Impairment	Loss and/or abnormality of cognitive, emotional, physiological, or anatomical structure or function, including losses and pain	Reduced components of cognitive, memory, language, motor-speech, motor skills, metacognition, and executive functions directly and indirectly associated with trauma	Orienting to visual stimuli in environment; divided and alternating attention for visual scanning; visual perception for determining background, size, and location of stimuli; memory for procedures; retrieval of vocabulary; self-monitoring and error detection; isolated movement of extremities	Sensory stimulation to improve arousal and alertness; attention process training; encoding strategies to improve storage; self-cues to improve retrieval; drill and rehearsal strategies; scanning and selection techniques; word retrieval of vocabulary; learning procedures for using the AAC system; language therapy
Functional limitation	Restriction or lack of ability to perform an action or activity as compared with preinjury performance; results from impairment	Decreased performance in communication (e.g., reading, listening, producing AAC output) as direct or indirect result of impairments	Examine effectiveness, efficiency, and effort when using AAC strategies; access to and selection of vocabulary, organization of messages. Identify AAC system that allows for least amount of effort by user. Specific communication tasks assessed within therapeutic setting; amount of time it takes to create a message, getting partners' attention, responding to direct questions, and so forth.	Practice AAC procedures errorlessly; train vocabulary selection and message organization; teach strategies that improve efficiency in creating messages and delivering them; practice responding and delivering communication messages (responding to questions, creating narratives, describing feelings and emotions, initiating social activities to facilitate organized messages

(continued)

285

Table 2. (continued)

	Definition	Level of deficit	Examples of assessment targets	Examples of approaches to intervention
Disability	Inability or limitation in performing socially defined activities and roles within a social and physical environment as a result of internal or external factors and their interplay	Reduced ability to use AAC system in various natural communication environments, for various purposes and goals, and with various communication partners	Examine effectiveness, efficiency, and effort when using AAC system in natural communication situations that vary in environmental contraints, communication goals and purposes, and types and number of partners	Therapy activities to improve self-monitoring and interpreting feedback from partners; engage in various kinds of interactions (e.g., discussing topics, meeting someone for the first time, asking health-related questions) that require the AAC user to make adjustments in conversational style, topic, and vocabulary. Practice greetings; pre-program information user has "forgotten" in the past; train user to identify information he or she is likely to forget and train him or her to store information in the system
Societal limitation	Restriction attributable to social policy or barriers (structural or attitudinal) that limit fulfillment of roles or deny access to services or opportunities	Social role changes due to environmental, social, or situational barriers, rules, and laws	Determine family's, employer's and/or school's expectations for making a transition with an AAC system; determine barriers in community that will affect access to social services; identify physical accommodations needed in home/school/work to facilitate highest level of independence	Address home, work, school, community (i.e., people, environments) to bring about change and facilitate removal of social, physical, and attidudinal barriers. This may include educating family, employers, school administrators, and public policy makers. Changes in institutional policy are optimal goals.

From Yorkston, K.M., & Kennedy, M.R.T. (1999). Treatment approaches in communication disorders. In M. Rosenthal, E.R. Griffith, J.S. Kreutzer, & B. Pentland (Eds.), *Rehabilitation of the adult and child with traumatic brain injury* (pp. 286–287). Philadelphia: F.A. Davis; adapted by permission.

Impairments

Impairments are component deficits in cognition, memory, language, and motor speech. By far, the majority of theoretical and clinical research into the communication disorders following TBI has been conducted on impairments (Yorkston & Kennedy, 1999). Many resources on impairments after TBI are available to interested readers (e.g., Kennedy & DeRuyter, 1991; Rosenthal et al., 1999; Sohlberg & Mateer, 1989). Impairments that can have an effect on the design, selection, and training in AAC use for individuals with TBI are discussed next.

Assessing Impairments   For the survivor of TBI who does not speak, assessing impairments has a dual purpose. First, the underlying cognitive-communication, language, motor-speech, and other physical deficits must be carefully identified in order to create a rehabilitation plan that will facilitate improvement. Improvement in the underlying processes is critical in order to maximize independent use of AAC systems. Second, assessment results at the impairment level provide important initial information on where to begin designing AAC systems. For someone with fluctuating alertness and inconsistent responses (comparable to Level III using Rancho's LOCF system), assessment at the impairment level needs to include various forms of attention, object discrimination, localization, and identification of volitional motor responses. Based on these results, the speech-language pathologist, with input from the occupational therapist, would determine the most suitable type of communication methods (e.g., object choices, yes-or-no selection) and begin to identify how AAC should be implemented. For example, if the optimal motor response is eye pointing, then choices would need to be presented with the correct orientation (i.e., vertically, horizontally) in the optimal visual field. Similarly identifying visual perceptual deficits provides useful information for the configuration of the AAC display and its positioning.

For someone who is experiencing PTA and is unable to remember declarative forms of information on a day-to-day basis, assessment of various types of memory functioning is critical to the selection and design of an AAC system. For example, some forms of procedural learning are preserved after TBI, even in individuals with severe forms of amnesia. The extent to which a survivor is able to retain new procedures defines the extent to which the survivor will retain procedures for implementing an AAC system. If the survivor of TBI cannot retain new procedures, then the AAC system should be kept simple, using procedures that rely on old learning (e.g., head nods, spelling, pointing) with explicit instructions visible at all times.

Remediating Impairments   When specific components of cognition, memory, language, motor speech functions, and other physical abilities "are believed to be directly amenable to intervention, the speech-language pathologist engages the TBI survivor in exercises and activities specifically designed to reduce the impairment" (Yorkston & Kennedy, 1999, p. 289). This basic assumption is held for survivors who are verbal communicators as well as for those who are not. The goals of a therapy program aimed at impairments is to facilitate improvement in the underlying process, which then generalizes to contextually appropriate communication tasks and situations. This approach is not task-specific. Several examples of treating impairments in individuals with TBI who do not speak are discussed next.

Treating impairments in individuals who are unable to speak differs from treating those with functional natural speech in that additional impairments must be addressed. Motor speech impairments are often addressed at the same time that other cognitive and language processes are being formally treated. In addition, improving physical ability will eventually enhance access to an AAC system and usually begins at the impairment level (e.g., range of motion exercises, serial casting programs, surgical intervention). Pharmacologic intervention to bring about changes in muscle tone (e.g., spasticity) is an example of intervention at the pathophysiological level.

For survivors who use AAC and demonstrate serious attention impairments, treatment activities include hierarchically graded auditory and visual tasks of increasing difficulty. An example of such a program is the Attention Process Training Program (Sohlberg & Mateer, 1989). Although some adaptation is required for individuals with severe motor and motor speech deficits, improvement in some aspects of attention have been documented in survivors without severe motor speech impairments.

The nature of activities designed to improve memory depends on the type of memory impairment that is present (e.g., attention-based, encoding, retention, retrieval, short-term, long-term, semantic knowledge, procedural). Various programs to improve short-term memory have been found to be somewhat efficacious, although efficacy does not appear to generalize to different tasks or stimuli (Malec & Questad, 1983).

For someone with TBI who uses AAC, treating the impairment focuses on teaching the mechanics of the AAC system in addition to treating the underlying deficits that influence system use. For the survivor using a communication board, tasks designed to improve visual scanning and identifying stimuli (e.g., pictures, letters, words, phrases) of increasing complexity and amount should be used. Treatment activities that include identifying messages and retrieving vocabulary are prerequisites to using most dedicated AAC systems. Teaching the steps or procedures for using devices is necessary before the system can be used successfully for communication (e.g., turning devices on and off, remembering steps involved in scanning, operating the function keys on a device, creating and storing frequently used messages). Although addressing underlying impairments in the AAC user should improve these processes, it cannot be assumed that these changes will automatically result in improvement in functional limitations or disabilities (Yorkston & Kennedy, 1999).

Functional Limitations

As a direct or indirect result of combinations of impairments, functional limitations are "the behavioral manifestation of cognitive-language deficits within a category of activities or actions" (Yorkston & Kennedy, 1999, p. 289). Three aspects of functional communication must now be considered: effectiveness (e.g., message accuracy), efficiency (e.g., speed, organization, length of message), and effort (i.e., amount of concentration or "work" needed).

Assessing Functional Limitations   For individuals with TBI who are verbal communicators, many standardized tests are available to evaluate memory, cognition, auditory comprehension, verbal expression, motor speech production, reading, and writing. Many of these tests can be modified to evaluate these same limitations in AAC users. However, prior to becoming competent in the use of an AAC system in natural communication situations, the individual should first be competent at using the system within the structured therapy setting during structured communication tasks.

The individual's AAC competency can be determined by evaluating the effectiveness of the interaction, the efficiency of the message, and the effort required to deliver the message (Kennedy, 1997). The effectiveness of an interaction is determined by the accuracy of messages conveyed in the interaction (predetermined by the interaction goal). For example, if a survivor responds inaccurately to a question because of memory limitations or incorrect word choice, then the response is ineffective. The efficiency with which a message is conveyed is determined by the speed of delivery as well as the overall organization and length of the message. The pragmatic disorders associated with TBI described previously in this chapter can occur regardless of speaking status. For example, someone with TBI may demonstrate disorganization and tangentiality when responding to open-ended questions (i.e., inefficient), but another survivor may communicate so little information that the response is incomplete (i.e., inaccurate). Determining the amount of effort that is required to communicate effectively and efficiently is an important part of assessment, especially for the AAC user with TBI. Because the capacity to modulate attention is frequently compromised after TBI, those who use alternative means to communicate have to allocate additional attention resources to gain access to a new system and to respond by using it. Various assessment activities are recommended to determine the individual's capacity to attend to several aspects of communication at the same time. By starting with simple communication tasks, such as answering closed and open questions using the AAC system, and progressing to complex communication tasks, such as using the AAC system to answer questions when distractions are present (e.g. radio playing in the background), the speech-language pathologist can examine the relationship between effort, effectiveness, and efficiency.

Remediating Functional Limitations   Basic competence in the use of an AAC system is imperative before an individual is expected to be successful at using it in natural communication situations. Treatment plans aimed at functional limitations should provide sufficient practice within a structured therapy environment, so that failure in natural situations is minimized. Therapy goals of improving effectiveness and efficiency while reducing effort should be incorporated into various AAC activities.

Two key research findings provide evidence for the need for errorless, repetitive practice using an AAC system. First, individuals with TBI are more likely than are people who have not experienced brain injury to recall their errors or mistakes instead of the corrected response (Baddeley & Wilson, 1994). Second, individuals with TBI require four times as much practice to learn the same amount of information as do people without brain injury (Wilson, Baddeley, Evans, & Shiel, 1994). Therefore, the importance of therapeutic practice that is error-free needs to be emphasized (Wilson, 1995). Accessing phrases, creating organized messages, operating AAC systems quickly, using acceleration strategies, using strategies to shorten repaired messages, and learning to repeat only misinterpreted portions of messages are examples of AAC therapy tasks that can be practiced through repetitive drill work with goals aimed at being effective, efficient, and effortless. Additional examples of intervention activities for functional limitations are identified in Table 2.

Disabilities

According to the revised WHO model of chronic disease, a disability is a reduction in an ability within its natural context. Because many individuals with TBI have difficulty with attending to all aspects of a situation simultaneously, do not consistently monitor themselves, do not always respond to external feedback, and are slow to make "online" adjustments during interactions, addressing communication disabilities is a critical part of the rehabilitation process.

Managing Disabilities   Effectiveness, efficiency, and effort of various AAC communication activities can be evaluated by observing and documenting performance in "real-life" situations. Systematically varying communication environments (e.g., quiet therapy room versus a noisy gymnasium), communication partners (e.g., number of partners, talkative versus quiet partners, employers versus peers), and communication goals (e.g., introducing oneself, getting acquainted, discussing current events) allows the speech-language pathologist to identify the AAC user's communication competency.

Intervention at the disability level is not dependent on the severity of cognitive-communication deficits. For example, for someone with TBI who has fluctuating alertness and inconsistent responses, intervention would be focused on providing opportunities to make choices during daily routines. Treatment could be carried out by caregivers who have been trained by the speech-language pathologist. For AAC users who have TBI with residual metacognitive and executive function deficits, treatment would focus on the use of compensatory strategies and monitoring partner cues in their natural communication environments.

In additional, therapists can identify naturally occurring barriers that may interfere with AAC users' progress toward becoming competent in certain situations. For example, when calling on the telephone to inquire about changes in the bus schedule, the AAC user must be well prepared to deliver a quick and efficient question. For AAC users who cannot respond quickly, preprogrammed messages are very useful when initiating conversations such as this. Use of strategies "online" to expedite message production and minimize communication breakdowns is the focus of intervention at the level of disability.

ROLE OF COGNITION IN THE DESIGN AND USE OF AAC

Given that there are excellent resources on AAC assessment and intervention with TBI (Beukelman & Mirenda, 1992, 1998; DeRuyter & Kennedy, 1991; Ladtkow & Culp, 1992), the remainder of this chapter focuses on cognitive demands of different AAC components and how cognition influences the design and use of AAC. Researchers have investigated the cognitive, perceptual, and motor requirements of some AAC components. The areas of focus have been physical access (e.g., direct selection versus scanning) and message production/retrieval (e.g., encoding, prediction); however, little of this research has involved people with TBI. This section reviews these areas, along with other AAC components, as they relate to individuals with TBI who do not speak. The interrelationship among perception, cognition, language, and motor control in the design and use of systems is highlighted. The need for clinical research is stressed.

Configuration of AAC Display

The configuration or design of an AAC display is determined by visual acuity and perception, motor control, and cognitive status. Displays can be designed to accommodate deficits in these areas. Proper design often requires task analysis.

Visual Acuity and Perception   Usually conducted by an occupational therapist, a vision screening helps determine the size and type of symbol and the configuration and positioning of a display. Primary perceptual problems in TBI can be accommodated, for instance, by positioning the communication board in the intact visual field. Although an individual's acuity may be adequate to discriminate a particular symbol size (e.g., 1-inch pictures), any secondary deficits, such as visual attention, along with general confusion may warrant use of large pictures with minimal detail in a field of fewer choices.

Motor Control and Means of Access   Motor control screening is typically conducted by an occupational or physical therapist. The purpose of the screening is to determine the optimal means of access for AAC and to obtain information regarding the physical layout of a communication display.

All AAC users, regardless of their disorder's etiology, need AAC access to be transparent (i.e., they do not have to think about how to select a message) in order to focus on message production and interaction with a partner. This is particularly important with individuals with TBI, who have difficulty with alternating attention between activities or attending to two activities simultaneously. The individual with TBI is more successful when tasks are automatic, familiar, and capitalize on old learning. Direct access is inherently more concrete than scanning because scanning involves completing a series of steps in order to select a message (Beukelman & Mirenda, 1998; Harris, 1982; Harris & Vanderhaiden, 1980; Piché & Reichle, 1991; Ratcliff, 1994). Successfully completing these steps involves various types of attention, sequencing, memory, visual processing, and executive functions (e.g., timing, anticipating and adjusting motor responses, making corrections). Some researchers question the differing cognitive requirements of direct selection and scanning and urge further research in this area (Mizuko & Essez, 1991).

Given that adults with TBI recover enough motor function to rely on direct selection, scanning may be used as a temporary means of access (DeRuyter & LaFontaine, 1987). During this time, scanning can be altered to accommodate deficits in attention, processing, motor planning, and timing. How to simplify scanning is determined by task analysis; however, in general, some accommodations may include slowing the scan rate, simplifying the scan pattern, enlarging the text or symbols, minimizing the amount of visual information on the display and providing auditory feedback. It is important to realize that in some cases accommodating deficits or weaknesses in one area may merely shift or even increase the cognitive load to another area. For example, when scanning, turning on auditory prompts to label messages may reduce the need to maintain visual focus on the display. Visual attention and processing demands may be decreased, but the individual must also attend to auditory cues. This may hinder performance in individuals who have difficulty attending to multiple stimuli simultaneously (i.e., auditory, visual) or who are distracted by auditory cues and do not consistently redirect themselves to the task. In clinical settings, it is common practice to reduce the number of items on a display to accommodate the user's vision and motor skills. Additional displays may be needed to provide the individual with sufficient vocabulary. The vision and motor demands have been reduced by potentially increasing the cognitive and linguistic demands. These adjustments are common in clinical practice, but implications of such changes need to be quantified with further research.

Another component of the motor screening is to determine the physical layout of the display, specifically the optimal size of the display and of the cells. The physical layout is optimal when it allows the individual to retrieve messages accurately and with minimal effort. The size of the display and the individual cells directly influence the number of messages that can be included or presented at one time. The ability to physically access a display of 20–30 cells, for example, does not mean the individual can use the same number of messages for functional interaction. At a minimum, the cognitive components of attention and visual processing influence the number of messages the individual can use functionally. For individuals who experience confusion, displays with fewer choices may be indicated. Individual boards for certain topics or activities may be used rather than using one system that contains all relevant vocabulary.

Symbol Use and Message Formulation

The speech-language pathologist is responsible for assessing which type of symbol the individual can use to generate and retrieve messages. The symbol hierarchy ranges from actual objects to the alphabet (i.e., concrete to abstract). Standard practice is to begin assessment at the highest symbolic level that the individual understands. Components of symbol assessment include identification, categorization, association, and sequencing. Performance on these tasks influences how vocabulary is organized and retrieved (in a system) and which encoding technique or combination of techniques is optimal. Vocabulary may be categorized by function (e.g., food, places, clothing), by event or schema (e.g., activities in therapy, items on the menu at McDonald's), or by part of speech (e.g., nouns, verbs). Research with individuals with typical functioning found that recall was more accurate for vocabulary grouped by schema versus vocabulary grouped by function (Rabinowitz & Mandler, 1983). In assessment, the speech-language pathologist determines which categorical system is easiest for the individual. Clinical experience indicates that for individuals with TBI, organizing messages according to function or event is preferred over parts of speech because these categories are more concrete, contain specific and relevant vocabulary, and provide more structure. Further research quantifying these findings is needed.

Association is the ability to use a single symbol to represent a variety of concepts (e.g., *car* can mean *car, go, leave,* or *drive*). Symbols are combined to generate or retrieve messages (*I* plus *go* plus *home*), or a series of multimeaning icons are sequenced to retrieve words and phrases (i.e., Minspeak). Abstract association and sequencing are critical for individuals who are illiterate and have extensive or novel communication needs. For adults with TBI who were literate prior to their injury, spelling often reemerges with alertness and cognition. The majority of these individuals can rely on a spelling-based system (Fried-Oken & Doyle, 1992) if they require an AAC system. However, before this point, some individuals may be using word- or picture-based systems. AAC users with TBI tend to be concrete and literal; combining words or pictures may be difficult because of decreases in attention, organization, memory, and mental flexibility (Fried-Oken & Doyle, 1992). Displays with single pictures, words, or phrases representing highly relevant needs allow individuals to convey information quickly and accurately.

Messages can be generated or retrieved by sequencing icons on a fixed display or by accessing several individual displays that have vocabulary organized by topic, activity, or function. The latter is commonly referred to as *dynamic display;* by pressing a symbol representing a category, the display changes and is replaced with vocabulary pertaining to that category. Dynamic display systems are sometimes considered for individuals whose vision, motor skills, or cognition limit the number of items that can be presented on one screen. Individuals who are literate may use a dynamic display system with pages programmed with frequently used messages. The keyboard is merely one of the pages they use.

Before providing this type of system to any individual, it is critical to assess the individual's skills and set up the displays accordingly. Results of the assessment indicate the type, size, and number of symbols that can be presented on one display; how to organize or categorize symbols; the number of displays the individual can use functionally; and how to link displays in a manner logical to the individual user. It is important to recognize that vision, motor skills, cognition, and language all influence the design. At a minimum, the cognitive demands of retrieving vocabulary from multiple displays requires attention, categorization, association, sequencing, memory (both working and procedural), new learning, and some degree of problem solving. Sustained attention, sequencing, and working memory are required to press the correct keys to formulate the message; linking from one display to another requires shifting attention, sequencing, and memory. Remembering locations of messages allows faster retrieval.

Simple problem solving is required when an individual gets "lost" and needs to navigate a series of pages in order to locate a particular page or message. Again, if displays are set up based on how the individual organizes information, then navigation will be easier. Task analysis helps customize the displays to accommodate the individual's deficits and to maximize communication. Some general suggestions to minimize the impact of cognitive impairment are as follows:

- Start with a few functional displays.
- Limit the number of message choices on each display.
- Organize the vocabulary and link the displays based on what makes most sense to the user.
- Keep the steps to access a page to one or two key hits.

Spelling-Based Systems   As indicated previously, the majority of adults with TBI eventually are candidates for a spelling-based system. The literature indicates that a fourth- to sixth-grade spelling level is required in order to rely on spelling as a primary means of communication. For individuals who only need to augment their speech in certain contexts (e.g., giving partners initial letter cues, spelling out part of a message), spelling skills at a lower level would suffice. Individuals may demonstrate spelling at the appropriate grade level but what is often overlooked is the cognitive demands required to use spelling as an effective strategy (Fried-Oken & Doyle, 1992). Individuals need sufficient attention to focus long enough to formulate and deliver the message, retain the message (to be spelled), visually search for and then select the appropriate letter, sequence the letters and words in the correct order, and monitor performance to ensure letters are not skipped or misinterpreted, and, if so, make the necessary corrections. The cognitive load is further increased for individuals with motor impairments where pointing is slow and laborious (Light & Lindsay, 1991). Furthermore, individuals with TBI who also exhibit language impairment (specifically difficulties with word retrieval and sentence formulation), the use of spelling as an effective strategy is further compromised.

In an effort to speed up communication with individuals who are spelling, partners often anticipate the intended word or message once they see the first few letters of the word. For example, if the topic is what to order at McDonalds, the user spells *sh*, and the partner guesses *shake*. Although this may help the partner, it does not necessarily increase the communication rate for the AAC user, particularly if there is more to the message. This involves recognizing that the partner guessed, stopping the AAC user's spelling momentarily, acknowledging the partner and giving feedback, remembering the next word in the message, and then mentally shifting to formulate that word. Because of these cognitive demands, some individuals find it easier and more automatic to complete each word and not be interrupted. Through task analysis, the system can be designed or strategies can be identified to help minimize the impact of these deficits. Some general suggestions are as follows:

- Consider arranging letters alphabetically because this may be more automatic and familiar than the usual QWERTY layout, particularly for individuals with no typing or computer experience.
- Use large fonts.
- Highlight key letters or vowels to help the individual scan, search, and locate target letters.
- Provide the individual with visual feedback (e.g., the partner writes down each letter as the person spells) to help retention (Light & Lindsay, 1991; Light, Lindsay, Siegel, & Parnes, 1990).
- Give the individual sufficient time to prepare the message.
- Minimize environmental distractions initially.

Message Production and Retrieval Strategies for Literate AAC Users A variety of strategies are available to help message production and retrieval in literate AAC users. Extensive research has been done on these strategies, which are sometimes referred to as *rate enhancement* or *acceleration techniques*. There is general consensus among AAC service providers and researchers that these techniques do save keystrokes but do not automatically increase communication rate, owing to the cognitive, linguistic, and visual-motor demands of these techniques. (Levine, Horstmann, & Kirsch, 1992; Venkatagiri, 1994, 1995). The following section reviews strategies as they apply to individuals with TBI who use AAC.

Strategies to help message production and retrieval include providing stored words or phrases (on the AAC display), message encoding, and lexical prediction. Words and phrases representing frequent messages, such as social greetings or people's names, are often included on an alphabet system. The objective is to increase the individual's rate of communication by having him or her point to the word or phrase rather than spelling out these messages. Some individuals with TBI tend to spell out *all* messages, even those that are written out on the display. This is because of the cognitive and linguistic demands of using words and phrases in combination with spelling (DeRuyter & Kennedy, 1991; Fried-Oken & Doyle, 1992). Shifting attention between strategies (i.e., from spell or indicate to words) and knowing when to shift can be problematic. Individuals need to retain their messages, remember that messages are listed on the display, scan the messages, determine if the word they need is listed, point to the word, and then resume spelling. With structure and training, some individuals can learn to use these strategies. Initially, the system needs to be simplified. Over time, these strategies can gradually be introduced:

- Start with a few functional highly occurring words or phrases
- Select messages that represent specific needs or thoughts. Set up the system so that spelling and stored words and phrases are two distinct strategies so that the system does not require the individual to shift between spelling and the word list to prepare a message. Gradually upgrade the system and provide instruction in using both strategies.
- Keep the messages on the same display as the alphabet (assuming vision, motor, and processing permit) to avoid the need to manage multiple displays.

Message Encoding   Encoding involves sequencing a series of symbols or signals to retrieve a word or a sentence. The most common types of encoding include iconic, letter, alphanumeric, and Morse code. Many individuals who use or who are candidates for iconic encoding or Minspeak rely on spelling to varying degrees for some of their communication needs. Given that the cognitive and linguistic demands of icon encoding were discussed previously, the focus here is on letter encoding. Alphanumeric and Morse code are less commonly used with TBI and are discussed elsewhere (Beukelman & Mirenda, 1998).

Letter Encoding   There are two types of letter-encoding strategies: salient letter and letter category. In salient letter, the initial letters of the most important content words in the message are used to represent the code. For instance, "I'm ready to go home" may be coded as GH. With letter category, messages are organized according to categories. The first letter of the code represents the category, and second and subsequent letters represent a key word in the message. For instance, the messages "I'd like a Coke, I'd like some milk, and I'd like some water" may all start with the letter D for drink, as this is the category, followed by the first letter of the name of the drink, such as C for Coke. Therefore, the code DC would represent "I'd like a Coke." Both strategies require basic understanding of traditional orthography (i.e., letter recognition), association, and memory. Letter category also requires categorization skills. Musselwhite and St. Louis (1988) speculated that accurate recall of salient letter codes is dependent on the individual retaining the exact syntactic form of the message. However, Light and Lindsay (1992) found that some individuals shorten messages to the most salient words and use the abbreviated message to recall the appropriate codes. For example, "I'm ready to go home" is condensed to "go home" and coded "GH." Given that the codes are an abbreviated message, the demands on memory and recall are reduced (Light & Lindsay, 1992). Light also found that the accuracy of recall for salient letter exceeded letter category for subjects with "functional literacy" (i.e., second grade and above); however, for individuals with literacy skills at or below the first-grade level, recall accuracy was comparable, with both methods exceeding recall of iconic codes. Regardless of encoding strategy, individuals were more accurate at retrieving codes for concrete messages than for abstract messages (Light & Lindsay, 1992). Clinical assessment will determine which letter-encoding strategy is optimal, the approximate number of encoded messages the individual can use functionally, and which strategies will facilitate recall (e.g., written cue card that lists codes and corresponding messages, abbreviating messages first and then assigning codes). In general, among individuals with TBI, the simpler and more concrete the encoding strategy, the better. Personalizing the codes may assist with retrieval provided that clinicians assist the individual in identifying the salient words within messages, shortening the messages accordingly and overall, and developing and using a consistent encoding structure or model. These findings are based on the authors' clinical experience. Research in this area is indicated.

Lexical Prediction   In addition to letter encoding, lexical prediction can be used to help in the formulation of novel messages. Lexical or word prediction is a "dynamic retrieval process in which options offered to the AAC user change based on the portion of the message that has already been formulated" (Beukelman & Mirenda, 1998, p. 81). Word prediction is typically recommended as a feature of an AAC system for individuals with slow physical access and adequate word retrieval, sentence formulation, spelling, and reading comprehension skills. Given the amount of information published in the area of word prediction and rate enhancement, this section briefly summarizes prediction techniques and reviews the cognitive and linguistic demands of these techniques and their use with AAC users with TBI. The most common types of prediction are word completion and "next word." Phrase or sentence prediction is offered in some software programs and electronic communication devices. With word completion, the initial letter of a word is typed, and a list of the most frequently occurring words that start with that letter appears on the screen; if the intended word is not listed, the individual resumes typing until the word appears in the list. To select the predicted word, the individual types the letter corresponding to that word in the list. In "next word" prediction, items listed are based on syntactical or grammatical rules. Prediction programs are designed to learn the user's vocabulary and include these items, based on most frequently used items, in the word list. Software programs or electronic devices with phrase and sentence prediction rely on algorithms for predicting language units longer than single words. AAC clinicians and researchers recognize that although word prediction may save keystrokes, it does not necessarily enhance communication rate owing to linguistic, cognitive, and perceptual motor demands. (Horstmann & Levine, 1990; Koester & Levine, 1994a; Levine, Horstmann, & Kirsch, 1992; Venkatagiri, 1993).

As indicated, effective use of word prediction requires spelling and reading skills. In addition, the cognitive requirements include alternating attention and mental flexibility (i.e., shifting between the word list and the alphabet array), procedural and working memory (i.e., remembering the steps required to access a word from the list and retaining message long enough), and some executive functions, such as self-monitoring and self-correction. Clearly, generating messages through spelling and word prediction is a highly dynamic process. Given that the word list constantly changes depending on what the individual inputs, a level of automaticity can not be achieved. Should the assessment indicate that word prediction may be an effective technique for the survivor of TBI, clinicians may consider introducing the technique gradually, providing practice opportunities and using the following strategies in order to minimize the cognitive demands:

- Keep the word prediction list short (e.g., five words) (Newell et al., 1992; Venkatagiri, 1994).
- Keep the list vertical (easier to scan and process) versus horizontal (Newell et al., 1992).
- Set up the display so the text or message being formulated is visible and is not covered by the word list.

FUTURE DIRECTIONS

The 1990s saw significant advances in AAC technology for individuals with severe communication impairments. Devices are getting smaller and more powerful, and they perform a variety of functions. Speech-language pathologists and other rehabilitation professionals are increasingly aware of the benefits of AAC for people with TBI and are incorporating AAC into treatment plans for individuals at all stages of recovery. However, there are still many areas that require clinical research to

- Identify or develop interfaces and message organization/ retrieval strategies that provide access to sufficient vocabulary while minimizing the cognitive demands on attention, memory, and new learning
- Develop assessment procedures to measure more effectively the cognitive capabilities of people with TBI as these abilities affect AAC interventions
- Document the impairment of various cognitive limitations on AAC use
- Clarify the staging of AAC interventions over the course of recovery in TBI
- Develop an outcome database on which evidence-based practice guidelines can be developed for the people with TBI who experience severe cognitive-communication disorders
- Develop efficient intervention strategies and programs to teach communication partners to support AAC interventions for people with TBI who experience severe communication disorders

Research in these areas will help improve the AAC services provided to people with TBI.

REFERENCES

Atkinson, R.C., & Shiffrin, R.M. (1968). Human memory: A proposed system and its control processes. In W.K. Spence & J.T. Spence (Eds.), *The psychology of learning and motivation: Vol. 2. Advances in research and theory* (pp. 89–195). San Diego: Academic Press.

Atkinson, R.C., & Shiffrin, R.M. (1971). The control of short-term memory. *Scientific American, 225,* 2–10.

Baddeley, A.D. (1984). *Working memory.* London: Oxford University Press.

Baddeley, A.D., & Wilson, B.A. (1994). When implicit learning fails: Amnesia and the problem of error elimination. *Neuropsychologia, 32*(1), 53–68.

Baddeley, A.D., Wilson, B.A., & Watts, F.N. (Eds.). (1995). *Handbook of memory disorders.* New York: John Wiley & Sons.

Beukelman, D.R., & Mirenda, P. (1998). *Augmentative and alternative communication: Management of severe communication disorders in children and adults* (2nd ed.). Baltimore: Paul H. Brookes Publishing Co.

Blachstein, H., Vakil, E., & Hoffien, D. (1993). Impaired learning in patients with closed-head injuries: An analysis of components of the acquisition process. *Neuropsychology, 7*(4), 530–535.

Butterfield, E.C., & Belmont, J.M. (1977). Assessing and improving the executive cognitive functions of mentally retarded people. *Psychology of mental retardation* (pp. 277–318). New York: Bialer and Sternlicht, Psychological Dimensions.

Carlisle, M., & Culp, D.M. (1988, October). *Evolutionary stages in augmentation for brain-injured patients: Clinical framework.* Paper presented at the biennial meeting of the International Society for Augmentative and Alternative Communication (ISAAC), Anahiem, CA.

Coehlo, C.A., Liles, B.Z., & Duffy, R.J. (1991). Analysis of conversational discourse in head-injured adults. *Journal of Head Trauma Rehabilitation, 6*(2), 92–99.

DeRuyter, F., & Donoghue, K.A. (1989) Communication and traumatic brain injury: A case study. *Augmentative and Alternative Communication, 5,* 49–54.

DeRuyter, F., & Kennedy, M.R. (1991). Management of augmentative communication in brain injury. In D.R. Beukelman & K.M. Yorkston (Eds.), *Communication disorders following traumatic brain injury: Management of cognitive, language and motor impairments* (pp. 317–365). Austin, TX: PRO-ED.

DeRuyter, F., Becker, M., & Doyle, M. (1987, November). *Assessment and intervention strategies for the nonspeaking brain injured.* Short course presented to the American Speech-Language-Hearing Association (ASHA) annual conference, New Orleans, LA.

DeRuyter, F., & LaFontaine, L. (1987). The nonspeaking brain injured: A clinical demographic database report. *Augmentative and Alternative Communication, 3,* 18–25.

Dongilli, P., Hakel, M., & Beukelman, D.R. (1992). Recovery of functional speech following traumatic brain injury. *Journal of Head Trauma Rehabilitation, 7,* 91–101.

Doyle, M., & Nance, T. (1993, November). *Recovery of speech and the use of AAC by children with TBI.* Poster session presented at American Speech and Hearing Association (ASHA) annual conference, Seattle.

Flavell, J.H. (1979). Metacognition and cognitive monitoring: A new area of cognitive development inquiry. *American Psychologist, 34,* 906–911.

Fried-Oken, M., & Doyle, M. (1992). Language representation for the augmentative and alternative communication of adults with traumatic brain injury. *Journal of Head Trauma Rehabilitation, 7*(3), 59–69.

Gallagher, J.P., & Browder, E.J. (1968). Extradural hematoma: Experience with 167 patients. *Journal of Neurosurgery, 29*(1), 1–12.

Gasquoine, P.G.(1991). Learning in post-traumatic amnesia following extremely severe closed head injury. *Brain Injury, 5*(2), 169–175.

Gennarelli, T.A., Thibault, L.E., Adams, J.H., Graham, D.I., Thompson, C.J., & Marcincin, R.P. (1982). Diffuse axonal in jury and traumatic coma in the primate. *Annals of Neurology, 12*(6), 564–574.

Goldstein, F.C., & Levin, H.S. (1995). Posttraumatic and anterograde amnesia. In A.D. Baddeley, B.A. Wilson, & F.N. Watts (Eds.), *Handbook of memory disorders* (pp. 187–209). New York: John Wiley & Sons.

Gronwall, D., & Wrighton, P. (1974). Delayed recovery of intellectual function after minor head injury. *Lancet, 2*, 95–97.

Gronwall, D., & Wrighton, P. (1981). Memory and information processing capacity after closed head injury. *Journal of Neurology, Neurosurgery, and Psychiatry, 44*, 889–894.

Hagan, C. (1984). Language disorders in head trauma. In A. Holland (Ed.), *Language disorders in adults* (pp. 257–258). Austin, TX: PRO-ED.

Hagan, C., Malkamus D., & Durham, P. (1979). *Rehabilitation of the head injured adult: Comprehensive physical management.* Downey, CA: Professional Staff Association of Rancho Los Amigos Medical Center.

Harris, D. (1982). Communicative interaction processes involving nonvocal physically handicapped children. *Topic in Language Disorders, 2*, 21–32.

Harris, D., & Vanderhaiden, G. (1980). Augmentative communication techniques. In R.L. Schiefelbusch (Ed.), *Nonspeech language and communication: Analysis and intervention* (pp. 259–301). Baltimore: University Park Press.

Hartley, L.L. (1995). *Cognitive-communicative abilities following brain injury.* San Diego: Singular Publishing Group.

Hartley, L.L., & Jensen, P.J. (1992). Three discourse profiles of closed-head-injury speakers: Theoretical and clinical implications. *Brain Injury, 6*(3), 271–281.

Haut, M., & Shutty, M.S. (1992). Patterns of verbal learning after closed head injury. *Neuropsychology, 6*(1), 51–58.

Horstmann, H.M., & Levine, S.P. (1990). Modeling of user performance with computer access and alternative communication systems for handicapped people. *Augmentative and Alternative Communication, 6*, 231–241.

Institute of Medicine. (1991). *Disability in America: Toward a national agenda for prevention.* Washington, DC: National Academy Press.

Jacobs, H.E. (1988). The Los Angeles head injury survey: Procedures and initial findings. *Archives of Physical Medicine and Rehabilitation, 68*, 425–431.

Kennedy, M., & DeRuyter, F. (1991). Cognitive and language bases for communication disorders. In D. Beukelman & K. Yorkston (Eds.), *Communication disorders following traumatic brain injury: Management of cognitive, language, and motor impairments* (pp. 124–190). Austin, TX: PRO-ED.

Kennedy, M.R. (1997). *Management of cognitive-communicative disorders in survivors of traumatic brain injury.* Chicago: Rehabilitation Institute of Chicago.

Koester, H.H., & Levine, S.P. (1994, June). Qualitative indicators of cognitive load during use of word prediction system. *Proceedings of the RESNA 17th annual conference* (pp. 118–120). Washington, DC: RESNA Press.

Ladtkow, M., & Culp, D. (1992). Augmentative communication with traumatic brain injury. In K. Yorkston (Ed.), *AAC in the medical setting* (pp. 139–243). Tucson, AZ: Communication Skill Builders.

Levine, S.P., Horstmann, H.M., & Kirsch, N.L. (1992). Performance considerations for people with cognitive impairment in accessing assistive technologies. *Journal of Head Trauma Rehabilitation, 7*, 46–58.

Light, J., Beesley, M., & Collier, B. (1988). Transition through multiple augmentative and alternative communication systems: A three-year case study of a head-injured adolescent. *Augmentative and Alternative Communication, 4*, 2–14.

Light, J., & Lindsay, P. (1991). Cognitive science and augmentative and alternative communication. *Augmentative and Alternative Communication, 7*(3), 186–203.

Light, J., & Lindsay, P. (1992). Message-encoding techniques for augmentative communication systems: The recall performances of adults with severe speech impairments. *Journal of Speech and Hearing Research, 35,* 853–864.

Light, J., Lindsay, P., Siegel, L., & Parnes, P. (1990). The effects of message encoding techniques on recall by literate adults using AAC systems. *Augmentative and Alternative Communication, 6,* 184–201.

Long Island Head Injury Association. (1999). *Facts about head injury* [On-Line]. Available: www.lihia.org/statistics.html/

Malec, J., & Questad, K. (1983). Rehabilitation of memory after craniocerebral trauma. *Archives of Physical Medicine and Rehabilitation Medicine, 64,* 436–438.

McDonald, S., & Pearce, S. (1995). The dice game: A new test of pragmatic language skills after closed-head injury. *Brain Injury, 9*(3), 255–271.

Millis, S.R., & Ricker, J.H. (1994). Verbal learning patterns in moderate and severe traumatic brain injury. *Journal of Clinical and Experimental Neuropsychology, 16*(4), 498–507.

Milton, S.B., Prutting, C.A., & Binder, G.M. (1984). Appraisal of communicative competence in head injured adults. In R.H. Brookshire (Ed.), *Clinical aphasiology conference proceedings* (pp. 114–123). Minneapolis, MN: BRK Publishers.

Mizuko, M., & Essez, J. (1991). The effect of direct selection and circular scanning on visual sequential recall. *Journal of Speech and Hearing Research, 34,* 43–48.

Musselwhite, C., & St. Louis, K. (1988). *Communication programming for persons with severe handicaps: Vocal and augmentative strategies.* Boston: Little,Brown.

Nelson, T.O., & Narens, L. (1990). Metamemory: A theoretical framework and new findings. *Psychology of Learning and Motivation, 26,* 125–141.

Newell, A., Arnott, J., Booth, L., Beattie, W., Brophy, B., & Ricketts, I. (1992). Effect of the "PAL" word prediction system on the quality and quantity of text generation. *Augmentative and Alternative Communication, 8*(4), 304–311.

Paniak, C.E., Shore, D.L., & Rourke, B.P. (1989). Recovery of memory after severe closed head injury: Dissociations in recovery of memory parameters and predictors of outcome. *Journal of Clinical and Experimental Neuropsychology, 11*(5), 631–644.

Piché, L., & Reichle, J. (1991). Teaching scanning selection techniques. In J. Reichle, J. York, & J. Sigafoos (Eds.), *Implementing augmentative and alternative communication: Strategies for learners with severe disabilities* (pp. 257–274). Baltimore: Paul H. Brookes Publishing Co.

Rabinowitz, M., & Mandler, J. (1983). Organization of information retrieval. *Journal of Experimental Psychology: Learning, Memory, and Cognition, 9,* 430–439.

Ratcliff, A. (1994). Comparison on relative demands implicated in direct selection and scanning: Considerations from normal children. *Augmentative and Alternative Communication, 10*(2), 67–74.

Reilly, P.L., Graham, D.I., Adams, J.H., & Jennett, B. (1975). Patients with head injury who talk and die. *Lancet, 2*(7931), 375–377.

Rosenthal, M., Griffith, E.L., Kreuter, J.S., & Pentland, B. (Eds.). (1999). *Rehabilitation of the adult and child with traumatic brain injury.* Philadelphia: F.A. Davis.

Sarno, M., Buonaguvro, A., & Levita, E. (1986). Characteristics of verbal impairment in closed head injured patients. *Archives of Physical Medicine and Rehabilitation, 67,* 400–405.

Sohlberg, M.M., & Mateer, C.A. (1989). *Introduction to cognitive rehabilitation.* New York: Guilford Press.

Squire, L.R. (1992). Declarative and nondeclarative memory: Multiple brain systems supporting learning and memory. *Journal of Cognitive Neuroscience, 4,* 232–243.

Venkatagiri, H.S. (1993). Efficacy of lexical prediction as a communication acceleration technique. *Augmentative and Alternative Communication, 9,* 161–167.

Venkatagiri, H.S. (1994). Effect of window size on rate of communication in a lexical prediction AAC system. *Augmentative and Alternative Communication, 10*(2), 105–112.

Venkatagiri, H.S. (1995). Techniques for enhancing communication productivity in AAC: A review of research. *American Journal of Speech-Language Pathology, 4,* 36–45.

Van Zomeren, A.H., & Deelman, B.G. (1978). Long-term recovery of visual reaction time after closed head injury. *Journal of Neurology, Neurosurgery, and Psychiatry, 41,* 452–457.

Wilson, B.A. (1995). Management and remediation of memory problems in brain-injured adults. In A.D. Baddeley, B.A. Wilson, & F.N. Watts (Eds.), *Handbook of memory disorders* (pp. 451–479). New York: John Wiley & Son.

Wilson, B.A., Baddeley, A.D., Evans, J.J., & Shiel, A. (Eds.). (1994). Errorless learning in the rehabilitation of memory-impaired people. *Neuropsychological Rehabilitation, 4,* 307–326.

Workinger, M., & Netsell, R. (1988). *Restoration of intelligible speech 13 years post–head injury.* Unpublished manuscript, Boys Town National Communication Institute, Omaha, NE.

Yorkston, K.M., & Beukelman, D.R. (1991). Motor speech disorders. In D.R. Beukelman & K. Yorkston (Eds.), *Communication disorders following traumatic brain injury: Management of cognitive, language, and motor impairments* (pp. 251–315). Austin, TX: PRO-ED.

Yorkston, K.M., & Kennedy, M.R.T. (1999). Treatment approaches in communication disorders. In M. Rosenthal, E.R. Griffith, J.S. Kreutzer, & B. Pentland (Eds.), *Rehabilitation of the adult and child with traumatic brain injury* (pp. 284–296). Philadelphia: F.A. Davis.

10

Proactive Management of Primary Progressive Aphasia

Margaret A. Rogers
Julia M. King
Nancy B. Alarcon

The gradual deterioration of language in the context of degenerative disease has been reported for more than 100 years (Dejerine & Serieux, 1897; Pick, 1892, 1904; Rosenfeld, 1909). Historically viewed as an atypical presentation of dementia, primary progressive aphasia (PPA) was eventually recognized as a distinct clinical entity (Mesulam, 1982). Although the most common symptom of dementia is deterioration of memory function (particularly in Alzheimer's disease [AD]), PPA is characterized by the gradual deterioration of language abilities in the context of preserved memory, judgment, insight, visuospatial skills, and overall comportment at least until the terminal stages of the disease (Mesulam, 1987). Mesulam and Weintraub (1992) distinguished PPA from other degenerative neurologic conditions such as AD by its gradual progression of language dysfunction in the absence of more widespread cognitive or behavioral disturbances for a period of at least 2 years. There are reports of individuals with AD (Pogacar & Williams, 1984), Pick disease (Graff-Radford et al., 1990; Scheltens, Ravid, & Kamphorst, 1994), and Creutzfeldt-Jakob disease (Mandell, Alexander, & Carpenter, 1989; Shuttleworth, Yates, & Paltan-Ortiz, 1985) who initially presented with progressive aphasia. After a 2-year history of isolated language symptoms, some individuals diagnosed with PPA eventually exhibit more widespread cognitive involvement consistent with a diagnosis of dementia (i.e., deterioration in two or more cognitive areas such as memory, personality changes, and the ability to independently carry out *activities of daily living* [ADL] due to cognitive as opposed to physical impairments). Estimates vary concerning the percentage of individuals who, after initially presenting with a 2-year history of isolated language dissolution, eventually exhibit widespread cognitive involvement. These estimates range from 30% to 50% (Duffy & Petersen, 1992; Mesulam & Weintraub, 1992; Rogers & Alarcon, 1999). Thus, it is likely that between 50% and 70% of individuals diagnosed with PPA experience only the consequences of declining speech, language, and communication for many years. These individuals continue to drive, manage their own finances, and (in all respects other than speech, language, and communication) maintain baseline levels of performance on repeated testing over many years (e.g., 20 years in Kempler et al., 1990; 11 years in Schwartz, De Bleser, Poeck, & Weis, 1998; 11 years in Thompson, Ballard, Tait, Weintraub, & Mesulam, 1997; 9 years in Mazzoni, Pollera-Orsucci, & Giraldi, 1996).

This chapter focuses on an approach to assist individuals with PPA and their families to make proactive adjustments concerning how they communicate and, in some respects, structure their lives. This approach, labeled *proactive management,* was designed to minimize the activity limitations and participation restrictions that ensue from declining speech and language. The intervention approach for individuals with PPA described in this chapter is guided by the premise that, as speech and language functioning decline, the communicative competency of the individual with PPA can be maintained. The label *proactive management* was chosen to convey the idea that the intervention goals are formulated and implemented in anticipation of future declines so that the individual with PPA is prepared to maximize communication competency at every stage, despite the relentless deterioration of speech and language (Rogers & Alarcon, 1998a). Maximizing communication competency in the context of progressive aphasia requires early intervention focused on the development and training of augmentative and alternative communication (AAC). Once an individual can no longer gain access to phonologic and orthographic information, parse syntactic structures, or retain sentence-length material in working memory, it is arguably too late to begin teaching the individual and the indivudaul's family to use many AAC options effectively. If, however, during the early stages of decline, individuals and their families participate in the development and generalization training of AAC approaches, then the independence and safety of the individual, as well as the quality of communicative interactions, will be optimized during the later stages of decline. Although research concerning AAC acquisition and generalization in PPA has not yet been directed toward investigating whether earlier training is more effective than later training, a positive correlation between receptive language ability and learning an AAC symbol system (e.g., Blissymbols) in nonprogressive aphasia has been demonstrated (Lane & Samples, 1981; Sawyer-Woods, 1987). The finding that aphasia severity predicts success at learning an AAC symbol system is in agreement with the assumption that the earlier that AAC is introduced during the course of PPA, the more likely that it will be successfully acquired and generalized. It is central to proactive management that AAC strategies and systems be incorporated into the individual's communication repertoire long before the individual becomes an entirely nonverbal communicator.

Minimizing the activity limitations and participation restrictions in PPA requires a three-pronged strategy of intervention: education, AAC training, and family/partner intervention. The speech-language pathologist is the principal health care professional responsible for assisting individuals with PPA, in part because there is presently no medical intervention available that can cure or decelerate the disease's progression. Furthermore, the consequences of the disease primarily, if not exclusively, affect the domain of communication. This chapter can be a practical resource for speech-language pathologists and others working with individuals with PPA to help the development and implementation of communication strategies and systems so that individuals with PPA are able to communicate optimally at every stage of the disease.

FLUENCY DIMENSION

One of the most controversial questions is whether PPA is simply a precursor to global dementia or is a distinct diagnostic entity. Some researchers have argued that the progressive language disturbance differs from dementia only with respect to the duration of isolated language symptoms before global cognitive impairments become manifest (e.g., Foster & Chase, 1983; Gorden & Selnes, 1984; Kirshner, Webb, Kelly, & Wells, 1984; Mandell et al., 1989; Pogacar & Williams, 1984; Shuttleworth et al., 1985). However, many cases have been documented in which global cognitive dysfunction was not present 9 years postonset (Green, Morris, Sandson, McKeel, & Miller, 1990; Mesulam & Weintraub, 1992; Scholten, Kneebone, Denson, Field, & Blumbergs, 1995), 14 years postonset (Mendez & Zander, 1991), and even 20 years postonset (Kempler et al., 1990). Mesulam (1982) suggested waiting

5 years after the onset of symptoms before trying to predict the course of cognitive involvement. However, there is no indication from the literature that individuals are less likely to develop dementia if they have already passed the 5-year benchmark (Rogers & Alarcon, 1999). Researchers have attempted to identify clinical symptoms that could serve as reliable predictors of eventual cognitive status. The profile of speech and language dysfunction has been investigated as a prognostic indicator of whether an individual is likely to develop generalized dementia.

The hypothesis that a language profile consistent with fluent aphasia, as opposed to nonfluent aphasia, predicts a course of earlier cognitive decline has been investigated through case study (e.g., Snowden, Neary, Mann, Goulding, & Testa, 1992) and systematic review of the literature (Duffy & Petersen, 1992; Mesulam & Weintraub, 1992; Rogers & Alarcon, 1999). The fluency dimension in aphasia refers to a dichotomous classification based on the nature of the spoken language disturbance. Individuals with fluent aphasia produce speech at typical-to-fast rates, with typical-to-long phrase length and few, if any, phonological speech errors (e.g., Beland & Paradis, 1997; Tyler, Moss, Patterson, & Hodges, 1997). Verbal output in fluent aphasia is characterized as loggorheic and neologistic, and it tends to be empty (i.e., devoid of meaningful content). Disturbances of auditory comprehension and anomia were primary symptoms in most cases of fluent PPA reviewed by Rogers and Alarcon (1999). Hodges and Patterson (1996) found these to be the primary presenting complaints in the fluent PPA individuals, whom they labeled with *semantic dementia*.

A nonfluent profile is characterized by effortful speech, sparse output with decreased phrase length, phonological disorder, infrequent use of grammatical markers, and disturbed prosody and is frequently associated with an apraxia of speech (AOS). Auditory comprehension, although affected, has been generally observed to deteriorate later than expressive language skills (Hodges & Patterson, 1996; Rogers & Alarcon, 1998a). Nonfluent spontaneous speech and the production of phonemic paraphasias in naming have been proposed as important characteristics distinguishing PPA from progressive aphasia in AD (Mesulam & Weintraub, 1992; Schwartz et al., 1998; Weintraub, Rubin, & Mesulam, 1990). However, the language disorder evinced by individuals with PPA rarely fits neatly and unambiguously into the fluency typology (Mesulam, 1987). Snowden and colleagues (1992) described a group of individuals with PPA who exhibited expressive and receptive disruptions of phonology and semantics. Beland and Ska reported an individual with PPA who presented with "a syntactic deficit as a Broca's ... auditory comprehension deficits of the Wernicke's aphasia type ... and phonemic approximations as found in conduction aphasia" (1992, p. 358). Though there is no accepted classification for individuals exhibiting this profile, the term *mixed aphasia* has been applied (e.g., Snowden et al., 1992). Although reliable classification of aphasia in PPA into the fluent/nonfluent dichotomy has not been firmly established, the hypothesis that individuals with a fluent profile are more likely to develop generalized cognitive involvement than those with a nonfluent profile has received much attention (e.g., Duffy & Petersen, 1992; Rogers & Alarcon, 1999; Snowden et al., 1992; Weintraub et al., 1990).

In a study of 16 individuals with PPA over an 8-year period, Snowden and colleagues (1992) investigated the relationship between language profile and eventual cognitive status. Five individuals exhibited a nonfluent profile, six exhibited a fluent profile, and five exhibited a mixed fluent/nonfluent profile. Snowden reported that only the fluent and mixed groups developed nonlanguage symptoms. Five of the individuals in the fluent group developed an associative agnosia characterized by an inability to recognize the meaning or significance of objects, despite intact perceptual abilities (i.e., copying and matching performance remained intact). All five of the individuals in the mixed group developed alterations in personality and comportment. None of the individuals in the nonfluent group exhibited symptoms of more widespread cognitive decline. Their finding that only the individuals with a nonfluent PPA exhibited isolated language dissolution over the 8-year period was interpreted as supporting the hypothesis that the course of cognitive involvement may vary with aphasia subtype.

The hypothesis that the profile of language impairment may predict the course of generalized cognitive involvement also has been examined through systematic review of the literature. Duffy and Petersen (1992) reviewed 28 reports (1977–1990) describing 54 individuals with PPA. Approximately half of the 54 individuals developed generalized dementia, but none of the 12 cases identified with nonfluent profiles evidenced generalized cognitive involvement. This finding was interpreted as supporting the hypothesis that a nonfluent profile may predict a longer duration of isolated language symptoms or, perhaps, a lower probability of developing widespread cognitive involvement. Mesulam and Weintraub (1992) reviewed 63 cases of PPA. The average duration of isolated language symptoms was 5.2 years, including six individuals who exhibited isolated language symptoms for more than 10 years. They reported that, compared with either probable or pathologically confirmed AD, the PPA group contained more males, a higher incidence of onset before age 65, and a greater incidence of nonfluent aphasia. A nonfluent profile was never observed among the

AD group, whereas the distribution of fluent and nonfluent profiles in the PPA group was balanced (48% fluent; 44% nonfluent). According to Mesulam and Weintraub (1992), not all individuals with probable AD exhibit aphasic disturbances, but those who do exhibit only the fluent aphasia subtype.

Rogers and Alarcon (1999) reviewed 57 articles that contained reports of 147 cases of individuals with relatively isolated deterioration of speech and language for at least 2 years. In this review of the PPA literature published between 1982 and 1998, information was collected concerning the variety of speech and language symptoms present in this population, the relationship of speech-language dysfunction to eventual cognitive status, and the distribution of concomitant nonlinguistic sequelae. This review revealed that there is quite a heterogeneity of clinical features associated with PPA both within and across aphasia subtypes. Table 1 lists the concomitant symptoms obtained from all the articles reviewed, regardless of aphasia typology, including motor, psychological-emotional, speech-language, as well as cognitive and sensory sequelae.

The review by Rogers and Alarcon included 37 cases of fluent PPA, 88 cases of nonfluent PPA, and 22 cases in which the type of aphasia was indeterminate. Among the individuals with fluent PPA, 27% exhibited clinical symptoms of dementia. Among the nonfluent PPA group, 37% were reported to develop generalized dementia. Of the 22 individuals with an undetermined type of aphasia, 73% exhibited clinical symptoms of dementia. The average duration of isolated language symptoms among the 77 individuals who developed generalized dementia was 5 years (6.6 years in fluent PPA, 4.3 years in nonfluent PPA, and 3.7 years among those with an undetermined type of aphasia). The data obtained from this review did not support the hypothesis that individuals with a nonfluent profile are less likely to develop generalized cognitive involvement than those with a fluent profile. Furthermore, the data did not support the hypothesis that a nonfluent profile predicts a longer duration of isolated language symptoms. Despite the unequal number of cases in each of the fluency groups and the possibility that there may be considerable bias to publish reports of individuals with PPA not exhibiting generalized dementia, it does not appear that the fluency profile is a reliable predictor of eventual cognitive status. However, the classification of language symptoms in PPA according to the fluency dimension remains useful for the purposes of management planning, especially with respect to selecting and teaching communication strategies and systems.

Table 1. Concomitant symptoms reported in association with primary progressive aphasia

Motor	Psychological and emotional	Speech and language	Cognitive and sensory
Abnormal reflexes	Compulsive eating and walking	Aggramaticism	Acalculia
Akinetic rigidity	Depression	Alexia	Amusia
Bilateral upper-limb dystonia	Emotional lability	Anomia	Dressing apraxia
Bradykinesia	Inappropriate jocularity	Apraxia of speech	Hemianopia
Bulbar palsy	Nocturnal restlessness	Dysarthria	Hypesthsia
Dysphagia	Paranoia	Dysgraphia	Impaired executive functioning
Epilepsy	Personality changes	Dysprosodia	Impaired nonverbal functions
Essential tremor	Violent behaviors	Echolalia and palilalia	Impaired verbal memory
Impaired bimanual praxis		Hoarse vocal quality	Perseverative behavior
Incontinence		Impaired articulatory agility	Poor recall
Limb apraxia		Impaired auditory comprehension	Prosopagnosia
Motor impersistence		Impaired repetition	Short-term memory deficits
Myoclonus		Impaired spelling	Visual agnosia
Oral dyskinesia		Impaired syntax	
Oral-facial apraxia		Mutism	
Progressive right hemiparesis		Neologisms	
Right-sided facial paresis		Phonemic paraphrasias	
Truncal apraxia		Pure word deafness	
		Reduced mean length of utterance	
		Semantic paraphrasias	
		Slow speaking rate	
		Staccato speech	
		Stuttering	
		Telegraphic speech	
		Verbal hesitancy and long pauses	

Adapted from Rogers and Alarcon (1999).

IN THE BEGINNING

The initial symptoms of PPA vary from individual to individual, but anomia is the most commonly reported in individuals with both fluent and nonfluent PPA (Mesulam, 1987; Rogers & Alarcon, 1999). McNeil described the anomia experienced by an individual at the onset of PPA as "trouble thinking of or remembering specific words when talking or writing" (1998, p. 47). Another early symptom, particularly in nonfluent PPA, is slow, hesitant speech frequently punctuated by long pauses and filler words (e.g., "um" and "uh"). Although this may represent simply one of many manifestations of anomia, it also portends the formulation difficulties that later render these individuals' communcation telegraphic (i.e., reduced mean length of utterance consisting primarily of content words). Other individuals with nonfluent PPA are initially bothered by a marked increase in speech errors (Rogers & Alarcon, 1998a). At first, the sound errors do not differ in kind but in frequency from those produced by typical speakers; however, later the sound exchanges, substitutions, and distortions begin to resemble the phonemic paraphasias and apraxic errors commonly observed among individuals with Broca's aphasia. The initial symptom of progressive speech apraxia also has been reported by Hart, Beach, and Taylor (1997). Impaired access to phonologic form is frequently associated with later-emerging spelling difficulties, though partial access to initial letters and syllable structure may be retained for many years (Rogers & Alarcon, 1998a, 1999). Difficulties with phonologic encoding have also been reported in cases of fluent PPA. Tyler and colleagues (1997) described the anomic difficulties of one individual with fluent PPA as impaired mapping between the semantic lexicon and output phonology. More typically, individuals who eventually exhibit fluent PPA initially complain of difficulties with understanding spoken language (Hodges & Patterson, 1996), whereas individuals with nonfluent PPA typically exhibit preserved language comprehension in the early stages (Karbe, Kertesz, & Polk, 1993).

Diagnosis

The diagnosis of PPA is generally made based on a 2-year history of progressive language deterioration that emerges in the absence of any marked disturbance of other cognitive functioning and is not associated with any vascular, neoplastic, metabolic, or infectious disease (Duffy & Petersen, 1992; Mesulam & Weintraub, 1992). In addition to neurological examination, medical assessment typically includes neuroimaging to rule out vascular or neoplastic pathology and neuropsychological testing. The prototypical result of neuroimaging in the first few years postonset is either negative (e.g., Southwood & Chatterjee, 1998) or mild to moderate atrophy of the left perisylvian region (e.g., Mesulam, 1982; Rogers & Alarcon, 1998a; Sinnatanby, Antoun, Freer, Miles, & Hodges, 1996; Turner, Kenyon, Trojanaowski, Gonatas, & Grossman, 1996). If metabolic neuroimaging (e.g., positron emission tomography) is conducted, left perisylvian hypometabolism is typically reported (e.g., Kempler et al., 1990; Mazzoni et al., 1996; McNeil, Small, Masterson, & Fosset, 1995; Parkin, 1993; Philbrick, Rummans, Duffy, Kokmen, & Jack, 1994). Results of neuropsychological assessment typically reveal relative preservation of nonverbal cognitive function (e.g., abstract reasoning, visual short-term memory, visuoperceptual organization) in conjunction with below normal performance on tests requiring verbal processing, such as immediate verbal recall, novel verbal learning, and verbal fluency (e.g., Sapin, Anderson, & Pulaski, 1989; Weintraub et al., 1990). In addition, many studies have reported the presence of nonlinguistic sequelae known to co-occur frequently in nonprogressive aphasia, such as acalculia and apraxia of speech (Rogers & Alarcon, 1999).

Predictably, the clinical diagnosis of PPA is received by individuals and their families with mixed emotions. In our clinical experience, it is not uncommon for the fear and uncertainty to be accompanied by a sense of relief expressed in response to not receiving the diagnosis of AD or another variant of dementia involving widespread cognitive impairments. The individual and family recognize that the clinical course of PPA is somewhat more benign than the widespread cognitive deterioration associated with AD (Mesulam, 1987). There are two unfortunate ironies embedded within this relief. The first is that approximately 30%–50% of all individuals diagnosed with PPA develop more widespread cognitive disturbances within 5 years of diagnosis (Duffy & Petersen, 1992, Mesulam & Weintraub, 1992, Rogers & Alarcon, 1999). The second is that for those individuals with PPA who do remain cognitively intact, the eventual complete decimation of expressive and receptive language functioning renders these individuals communicatively locked-in. The term *communicatively locked-in* is used metaphorically to convey the notion that, despite intact cognition, without any residual language abilities, these individuals may experience a degree of social isolation similar to that experienced by individuals who have lost all motor control.

Disablement

The consequences of PPA can best be described with reference to the World Health Organization (WHO, 1997) model of disablement. The term *disablement* is an umbrella term covering all three dimensions of the WHO model: impairments, activities (formerly disabilities), and participation (formerly handicaps). The 1980 International Classification of Impairments, Disabilities, and Handicaps (ICIDH) has been revised as ICIDH-2 in part to label each of these dimensions using neutral terminology. This classification scheme provides a unified language for describing the consequences of health conditions. The ICIDH-2 does not classify diseases, disorders, and injuries. That is the aim of a complementary classification scheme within the WHO family of classifications that is labeled the International Classification of Diseases (ICD). Rather, ICIDH-2 provides a framework to conceptualize the disablements associated with health conditions, namely the impairments, activity limitations, and participation restrictions.

The term *impairment* refers to abnormalities of body structures and functions, which can be permanent, temporary, or progressive. Examples of impairments include broken legs, aphasia, and secondary depression associated with the onset of the broken leg or aphasia. Negative consequences affecting activities are called *activity limitations*. Activity limitations refer to inabilities or limitations in performing tasks, activities, and roles to levels expected within physical and social contexts. Examples of activity limitations include climbing stairs and running for an individual with a broken leg and understanding and conveying information using spoken and written language for an individual with aphasia. The participation domain is the third classification provided by ICIDH-2. Participation is determined by the interaction of impairments, activity limitations, contextual factors, such as the social and physical environment, and personal factors, such as personality, attitude, and affective state. Participation restrictions are restrictions attributable to either structural or attitudinal barriers that limit the fulfillment of roles or access to opportunities associated with full participation in society. For a person with a broken leg, an example of participation restrictions would be difficulty with participating in work and family responsibilities, and the impairment may temporarily prohibit independent living. For an individual with aphasia, reduced engagement in social interaction, reduced involvement with work and family responsibilities, and in some cases, reduced ability to live independently are examples of participation restrictions. The adjustment of individuals to their impairment, activity limitations, and participation restrictions is not determined simply by the severity of the consequences in any one of these dimensions. The interaction among these three domains is especially important to consider with individuals with progressive health conditions because changes within one domain (e.g., increased severity of the impairment) are likely to affect the status within another domain (e.g., increased activity limitations). Conversely, poor adjustment to language deterioration can increase activity limitations and also restrict the individual's participation in social interactions, which can exacerbate or cause depression (e.g., increased severity of impairment). Thus, periodic assessment of each of the three domains of disablement is warranted throughout the course of the disease.

PROACTIVE MANAGEMENT

Assessment

The purpose of assessment in the context of planning proactive management for individuals with PPA differs somewhat from the goals of assessment for nonprogressive aphasia. When the nature and severity of aphasia is either going to improve or remain unchanged, the goal of assessment is to determine the scope and severity of the speech-language impairments, ascertain the activity limitations experienced by the individual, determine potential strategies for compensation, and identify the barriers that are restricting the individual's opportunities for communication and participation (Rogers, Alarcon, & Olswang, 2000). Assessment of individuals with PPA in the context of planning proactive management, although also encompassing the previously described goals, is primarily directed toward identifying the present and future communication needs of the individual, the present communicative abilities and self-generated strategies of the individual with PPA, the individual's opportunities for participation and any potential barriers, and the communication partners who are most critical and who might be the most supportive in assisting the individual with PPA to maintain communicative competence. Thus, unlike traditional approaches to the assessment of nonprogressive aphasia, there is less emphasis regarding the nature of the impairment and more attention directed to identifying the individual's communication needs, partners, and environments. This shift is warranted because the impairment in PPA continually changes but the individual's communication needs, partners, and environments remain relatively stable. Furthermore, AAC selection and generalization training require a thorough assessment of these three domains (Wasson, Arvidson, & Lloyd, 1997).

Assessment of communicative functioning for people with PPA is based on both the Communication Needs Model and the Participation Model (Beukelman & Mirenda, 1998). Assessment of the individual's communication needs is conducted with the aim of enhancing and maintaining participation opportunities as well as the individual's independence in the environments in which he or she functions. Light (1988) discussed four purposes of communicative interactions: 1) communication of needs or wants, 2) information transfer, 3) social closeness, and 4) social etiquette. Similarly, communication needs encompass 1) regulating another's behavior to obtain something or to cause something to happen; 2) conveying the content of a message to transfer information; and 3) establishing, maintaining, and developing interpersonal relationships. Thus, although identification of specific vocabulary and strategies to maintain functional communication concerning the person's basic needs (e.g., food, clothing, personal care) is important, it is not sufficient. Communication needs encompass more than basic needs. They include engaging socially, resolving conflicts, expressing emotions, exchanging opinions, telling stories, controlling the social environment, and in essence participating in the full range of human interactions. Unfortunately, as the individual with PPA develops moderate to severe aphasia, the communication challenges that emerge often restrict the range of topics and roles played during exchanges. The increasing frequency of communication breakdowns, especially with emotional, abstract, or open-ended topics, begins to limit communicative interactions to primarily "yes" or "no" forced-choice formats typically revolving around the basic needs of the individual with PPA. Thus, as the aphasia becomes more severe, it is not uncommon for the individual with PPA to adopt the role of the passive respondent, rarely initiating interaction or selecting conversational topics (Rogers & Alarcon, 1998b). Likewise, the communication partners unavoidably assume more responsibility for directing these exchanges. Unfortunately, this can result in the repertoire of communicative exchanges becoming restricted to transferring information about basic needs. These types of exchanges are characterized as *transactions* in that their purpose is primarily to convey specific information. Transaction should not be confused with *interaction*, which is a more complex phenomenon entailing flexibility and creativity of topic evolution and often no identifiable goals other than to engage socially with another person (Rogers et al., 2000). As the severity of the speech-language impairment increases, individuals with PPA begin to participate less in communicative interactions. Unfortunately, if AAC has not been proactively established, communication exchanges become limited prematurely to transactions primarily revolving around basic needs, and thus the broader domain of communication needs ceases to be met.

When assessing individuals with PPA, information should be gathered to assist in making both short- and long-term management decisions. It has been argued that the focus of intervention for individuals with aphasia, progressive or otherwise, should be to reduce activity limitations and to enhance participation and independence (e.g., Rogers et al., 2000). Thus, assessment should be undertaken with the aim of identifying sources of and solutions to activity limitations as well as participation and independence restrictions. Figure 1 depicts assessment domains that are important to include while planning proactive management for progressive aphasia. The figure is divided into three domains: 1) abilities and impairments, 2) activities and limitations, and 3) participation opportunities and restrictions. There are several areas listed within each domain that require consideration. Due to their interrelatedness, abilities, activities, and participation opportunities should be identified and evaluated concurrently with the process of making management decisions.

Assessing the Impairment Domain   Assessment of abilities and impairments in PPA is conducted to identify the individual's current ability to communicate using alternative modalities (e.g., orthographic, symbolic, gestural), the presence of motor, sensory, psychological, and cognitive sequelae (see Table 1), and the status of speech-language function. Although AAC decisions concerning modalities for communication, vocabulary and symbol selection, AAC devices, and generalization training should be made with the individual's eventual impairment status in mind (i.e., severe aphasia), the current constellation of impairments and residual skills provides a starting place for intervention. Because the linguistic impairment will worsen and new sequelae may appear, assessment of abilities and impairments must be ongoing and, ideally, must continue in conjunction with intervention.

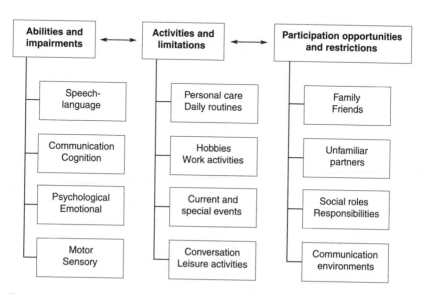

Figure 1.   Assessment areas with each domain of the World Health Organization Model of Disablements.

Rogers and Alarcon (1998a) repeatedly administered a comprehensive battery of speech, language, and cognitive assessments for 4 years to an individual with an 8-year history of nonfluent PPA. One of the goals of this investigation was to determine which measures were most sensitive to the course of decline and changes in the severity of the impairments. The measures that proved to be the most sensitive were those obtained from connected speech (e.g., story retelling, procedural discourse, personal narratives). Repeated administrations of selected subtests from standardized aphasia batteries did not yield evidence of decline that was observed from discourse analyses. It was hypothesized that, unlike level-specific subtests (i.e., subtests that are designed to probe relatively isolated stages of processing, such as word retrieval, apart from syntactic formulation), the requisite simultaneity of processing across levels during connected speech taxes the language-processing system of the individual with PPA. It was concluded from this study that standardized speech-language subtests may lack the sensitivity required to track the slow and complex decline in language function exhibited by individuals with PPA. Subtests tend not to require integrated processing across the multiple levels entailed in spoken language production. Furthermore, it was suggested that the most sensitive indices of language dissolution may be measures obtained from discourse production precisely because this context taxes the speaker's ability to integrate simultaneously semantic, syntactic, phonologic, and motor programming operations. Thus, it may be that the best method to track impairment changes in PPA are measures derived from connected speech (e.g., mean length of utterance, percentage correct information units [Nicholas & Brookshire, 1993], words per minute).

Assessing the Activity Domain   Assessment of activities in PPA is conducted to identify the topics, vocabulary, and content that the individual needs or desires to communicate. The activity limitations associated with aphasia primarily include speaking, understanding spoken language, reading, writing, and, accordingly, a whole host of activities, such as ordering food, asking for directions, and telling jokes. As the linguistic impairment worsens, activities entailing communication are affected. However, inherent to proactive management is the tenet that, with anticipatory implementation of AAC and partner training, declines in the impairment domain do not necessarily have to result in comparable decrements within the activity domain. It is possible to forestall activity limitations in the face of declining speech-language ability by using AAC techniques to compensate.

Assessment of the activity domain entails assessment of communication needs. Many people with PPA, along with the support of their family and friends, can identify their current communication needs.

Thus, a communication needs assessment can be conducted through interview, questionnaire, and observation formats. The categories listed in Figure 1 under the "Activities and limitations" domain provide a list of topics that may be used to help individuals identify topics and vocabulary that address some of their communication needs. During the early stages of the disease progression, information and relevant vocabulary associated with personal care, daily routines, hobbies, and other areas listed under the activities and limitations domain in Figure 1 can be obtained through interview with the individual with PPA. Obtaining information concerning where the person with PPA currently communicates (e.g., a neighbor's house, a hardware store), with whom they usually communicate (e.g., a neighbor, a salesperson), and what sorts of specific information they communicate about (e.g., politics, leisure activities) helps to establish a personalized profile of the individual's communication needs. For intervention programs that begin during the middle to late stages of the disease progression, information may need to be obtained by proxy (i.e., from family members or friends). Regardless of when intervention begins, it is important to identify which communication needs are successfully being met using their current modes of communication and to predict how future declines in language ability will affect that success. In addition, the communication needs that are not being met should be identified. These findings serve as a starting point for intervention. Once AAC strategies and systems have been introduced, observation of how the individual performs in a variety of communication environments (i.e., outside the treatment setting) with a variety of communication partners becomes a necessary component of ongoing assessment to evaluate functionality (Blackstone, 1994). Field-based assessments, such as direct observation, videotaping, and partner observation logs provide ecologically valid methods by which to evaluate and adjust aspects of both the systems and the users (i.e., the individual with PPA and communication partners).

Assessing the Participation Domain   Assessment of participation opportunities and restrictions begins with identifying the communication partners of the individual with PPA. Second, but most important, the clinician must try to evaluate the partner's ability and motivation to support and assist the individual with PPA in developing communicative competency as an AAC user. Light and Binger (1998) used the term *facilitators* to refer to communication partners who actively work with AAC users to foster their communicative competence. As the severity of aphasia increases, the individual with PPA becomes increasingly reliant on the assistance of communication partners for successful message transmission and participation opportunities (Rogers &

Alarcon, 1998a). Although there are instruments, such as the Caregiver Burden Scale (Elmstahl, Malmberg, & Annerstedt, 1996), that might provide indirect estimates of a communication partner's candidacy as a "good" facilitator, presently there are no prescribed methods for directly making these determinations. Nonetheless, assessment of communication partners of AAC users is advocated (Wasson et al., 1997) as their role is critical in providing proactive management in PPA (Rogers & Alarcon, 1998a). The following methods have been suggested: 1) measure communication opportunities provided by the communication partner (National Joint Committee for Communicative Needs of Persons with Severe Disabilities, 1992, as cited by Wasson et al., 1997), 2) determine the percentage of communication acts that facilitate interactions versus the percentage that are nonfacilitatory (Rogers et al., 2000), and 3) determine how much time the communication partner is willing to commit to training (Rogers & Alarcon, 1998b). It may be that the assessment of partners is best accomplished through both interview and observation (Wasson et al., 1997).

Assessment of participation opportunities and restrictions also includes 1) evaluation of how the individual with PPA communicates with familiar and unfamiliar partners, 2) determination of the social roles and responsibilities performed, and 3) identification of the communication environments in which the individual participates. These last areas can also be assessed through observation and interview. Beukelman and Mirenda (1998) recommended the Participation Model as a means of identifying the participation patterns of peers to determine the potential participation patterns for a person with a severe communication impairment. Instead of using peers, adults who have communicated effectively for many years can serve as their own model of participation to determine which social and communication roles have changed since the onset of the progressive language impairment. The identified roles also serve as intervention targets for increasing participation in communicative activities (e.g., a grandmother [social role] who used to read stories [communication role] to her grandchildren is no longer able to read aloud). Adapting the Participation Model by comparing the person's current communication skills and style with premorbid skills and style encourages continued participation in the person's previous communication activities. Discussions concerning the variety of social roles, responsibilities, and social gatherings can be supplemented by daily logs kept by the communication partner. A journal of daily events can provide a rich source of information concerning participation opportunities and restrictions. If, in addition, the communication partner can record information about communication breakdowns and content vocabulary used during communicative exchanges, then the log also can be used as a resource for partner training and communication notebook development.

Intervention

The cornerstone of proactive management is the formulation and implementation of intervention goals in anticipation of future declines (Rogers & Alarcon, 1998a). Proactive management was originally described based on three principles that guided intervention planning for O.D., an individual with an 8-year course of nonfluent PPA. These principles include 1) anticipatory implementation of communication strategies, 2) disability-based intervention focused on early utilization of AAC, and 3) dyad-oriented intervention. These principles were based on the perceptions that 1) speech and language deterioration could not be forestalled, 2) nonverbal modalities were declining less rapidly than speech and language, and 3) O.D.'s wife needed to adjust her approach to communication as much as O.D. needed to adjust his own.

The classification scheme of *AAC Communicators with Aphasia* proposed by Garrett and Beukelman (1992) provides a useful framework to guide intervention planning in PPA. They classified communicators with aphasia using five categories and provided descriptions of the different types of AAC intervention required by each. Table 2 provides a summary of their classification scheme. Each of the five categories corresponds to individuals with aphasia of varying severity and type. For example, individuals with aphasia who fall under the category of *basic-choice communicators* would be considered to have a more severe aphasia than *specific-needs* communicators. The *augmented-input communicator* has significant receptive language impairments, but the *comprehensive communicator* is described as primarily requiring AAC to assist with expressive difficulties. As individuals progress from early to later stages of PPA, their AAC needs change in a manner that can be described within the framework provided by the Garrett and Beukelman classification scheme.

Early Stage Typically, during the early stages of progressive aphasia, individuals continue to use primarily spoken language to communicate. However, the word-finding problems that typify this stage diminish most individuals' confidence concerning their ability to communicate efficiently and reliably, especially with unfamiliar communication partners. According to Garrett and Beukelman's classification scheme, individuals experiencing difficulties with spoken language in circumscribed situations fall under the category of *specific-need communicators*. These individuals need AAC support to convey specific information in specific situations. Examples of AAC support

Table 2.   Classification of AAC communicators with aphasia

Communicators	Nature of impairment	AAC intervention
Specific-need communicators	Mild to moderate impairments, need AAC support in specific situations to facilitate accurate transmission of information	AAC strategies developed for specific situations (communication cards with specific information, tape-recorded messages for phone use); nominal training
Comprehensive communicators	Mild to moderate impairments, participating in a variety of communication contexts	Communicates using a variety of AAC techniques (communication notebooks, voice output devices, photographs, symbols, gestures, orthography, alphabet cards); training directed primarily at individual with aphasia
Augmented-input communicators	Moderate to severe impairment of auditory comprehension, expression better than comprehension	Communication partners trained to use orthography, picture-based symbols, drawing, and gestures to augment speech input to facilitate message comprehension
Controlled-situation communicators	Moderate to severe impairment of spoken language, comprehension better than expression	Provide system to indicate conversation topic; specific vocabulary represented in communication notebooks either with written words or with picture-based symbols; extensive time to develop and accomplish generalization training
Basic-choice communicators	Severe impairment in both expression and reception of spoken language	Provide system to express basic needs, typically using communication board with picture-based symbols; requires training of communication partners to provide prompts and assistance making choices

Adapted from Garrett and Beukelman (1992).

required at this stage include 1) printed material with descriptive information concerning the nature of the individual's language impairment to use with unfamiliar communication partners; 2) printed material with questions prepared in advance to assist the individual with PPA to function in specific situations, such as buying, returning, or ordering merchandise; 3) idiosyncratic gestures conveying "past, present, and future" established to supplement spoken language for individuals experiencing expressive difficulty with temporal morphology; 4) idiosyncratic gestures or manual signs to express antonyms (e.g., yes and no, right and left) to compensate for frequent selection errors in the oral-verbal modality; and 5) communication boards or a set of index cards containing specific vocabulary to enable the individual to continue to participate in group activities, such as card games or sports. Intervention that begins during the early stages of PPA offers a valuable opportunity to introduce AAC in limited contexts using techniques that require little training and produce noticeable improvements with regard to communicative efficiency and effectiveness. Introducing AAC techniques while individuals with PPA are specific-needs communicators enables all involved to become accustomed to communicating in nonspeech modalities gradually. For both the individual with PPA and the communication partners, this gradual introduction can foster acceptance of the need for more comprehensive AAC solutions in the future.

Middle Stage   Individuals with aphasia who would be considered *comprehensive communicators* participate in a variety of communication contexts with varied partners and benefit from using a variety of AAC techniques. Unlike the specific-needs communicator, the comprehensive communicator requires AAC support in most, if not all, communication contexts. Once individuals with PPA, particularly those with nonfluent PPA, begin to experience significant word-finding blocks and syntactic dysfunction, they need to use AAC techniques to continue to participate in a variety of communication contexts. It is the aim of proactive management that an extensive repertoire of AAC techniques should be established prior to the individual's reaching the level of comprehensive communicator. Thus, the transition period between being a specific-needs communicator and a comprehensive communicator is a critical time for the development and training of AAC for individuals with PPA. Table 3 displays a list of AAC techniques that may be useful to establish during this transition period. Because many individuals with PPA function as a comprehensive communicator for many years, fostering successful utilization of a full armament of AAC techniques is arguably one of the most important components of proactive management.

Augmented-input communicators are individuals who experience significant impairment of auditory comprehension and require the assistance of their communication partners to enhance their comprehension. As mentioned previously, one of the first problems noticed by individuals who later receive a diagnosis of fluent PPA is difficulty with auditory comprehension (Hodges & Patterson, 1996; Rogers & Alarcon, 1999). Ideally, intervention includes family/partner training early on for these individuals because augmenting spoken language with, for example, drawings, graphic symbols, orthography, and gestures, diminishes communication breakdowns (Murray, 1998; Rogers &

Alarcon, 1998a). Individuals with fluent PPA should be trained as augmented-input communicators early on, but this category does not apply exclusively to individuals with fluent PPA. Because the symptoms of individuals with nonfluent PPA eventually includes difficulty with auditory comprehension, training their communication partners to use augmented speech is likely to become necessary. Many of the techniques listed in Table 3 can be used by communication partners to enhance comprehension. For example, picture-based symbols and gestures can be used by communication partners to indicate specific referents, orthography may be useful to convey key words and chronicle the content of a conversation, and drawings can be very useful to enhance comprehension of sequential information such as in storytelling or planning itineraries. By using multiple modalities, augmented speech facilitates comprehension. It also decreases the processing demands placed on the individual with PPA because, inevitably, the rate of message transmission will be slower if gestures, writing, and other forms of multimodality communication are used by the communication partner.

Late Stage   The last two categories included in the Garrett and Beukelman classification scheme characterize the severe communication impairments evident during the late stages of PPA. The *controlled-situation communicator* may be able to indicate basic needs by pointing to items but typically does not initiate communication. With prompting, he or she can choose an item or topic from an orthographic list or pictorial array. Sometimes, controlled-situation communicators are able to communicate additional information once the topic has been established. Individuals with PPA who have become controlled-situation communicators may continue to use communication notebooks containing symbols, pictures, and perhaps even words and phrases, especially if the book had been developed and used during earlier stages (Rogers & Alarcon, 1998a). Partner training becomes paramount at this stage because, typically, these individuals do not initiate communication and require much assistance to participate in conversational exchanges. As further deterioration renders these individuals *basic-choice communicators,* severe impairments of comprehension and expression in both typical language modalities (i.e., writing and speaking) greatly limits their ability to communicate even basic needs without significant support from trained communication partners (i.e., facilitators). Accordingly, although involvement of communication partners in the intervention process is helpful in the beginning stages to foster the individual's competency as an AAC user, partner participation in the late stages is critical to maintain communication concerning basic needs and choices.

Table 3. Examples of AAC techniques and devices recommended for use by individuals with primary progressive aphasia and their communication partners

Categories of AAC	Examples within categories	Early stage	Middle stage	Late stage
Gestures	Pointing	Introduce	Maintain	Maintain
	Yes or no headshakes	Introduce	Maintain	Maintain
	Thumbs-up, thumbs-down	Introduce	Maintain	Maintain
	Actions (e.g., stop, good-bye, eat, sleep, come, drink)	Introduce	Maintain	Maintain
	Pantomime	Introduce	Adjust	Maintain
	Idiosyncratic gestures (created by the individual)	Introduce	Adjust	Maintain
	Sign language (particularly iconic signs)	Introduce	Adjust	Maintain
Referential symbols	Line drawings (e.g., basic Rebus, Boardmaker)	Introduce	Adjust	Maintain
	Symbol systems (e.g., Picture Communication Symbols, Blissymbols, PICSYMS)	Introduce	Introduce	Maintain
Voice output communication devices	Dedicated Communication Devices (e.g., DynaMyte, Pegasus, Lingraphica, LightTalker)	Introduce	Introduce	Adjust
	Computer-based communication devices (e.g., EZ Keys, Speaking Dynamically, Speech Thing)	Introduce	Introduce	Adjust
Orthography	Alphabet boards	Introduce	Adjust	Obsolete
	Words paired with symbols	Introduce	Adjust	Maintain
	Phrases/sentences (e.g., questions, requests, greetings, expression of feelings, conversational topics)	Introduce	Adjust	Obsolete
Visual representations	Photographs (family/friends, rooms, stores, objects)	Introduce	Maintain	Maintain
	Maps	Introduce	Maintain	Adjust
	Calendars	Introduce	Maintain	Maintain
	Family trees	Introduce	Maintain	Maintain
	Drawings (e.g., static representations of objects and places, sequential representations of events)	Introduce	Introduce	Adjust
	Visual analog scales (e.g., 5-point scales to indicate strength of feelings or opinion)	Introduce	Introduce	Maintain

The techniques and devices are categorized according to their functional similarities. The last three columns provide timeline information relative to when each technique should be introduced, adjusted, maintained, and/or when it becomes obsolete.

Communication Notebooks   Because of the gradual deterioration of spoken language abilities in individuals with PPA, communication notebooks can be developed gradually, with ample time for planning and field testing before individuals need to rely on them as their primary means of communication. It is for this reason that individuals with PPA may be more successful users of communication notebooks than individuals with nonprogressive forms of aphasia secondary to stroke or other etiologies with sudden onsets. Another consequence of the gradual onset of PPA is that individuals can participate more fully in the development of their notebooks. While experiencing only mild impairments, they can create a book that reflects their own personality and communication needs better than anyone else. These individuals have the opportunity to participate in the creation of a personalized communication tool in advance of its need. They have the opportunity to grow into it, at first using the notebook only in specific situations, then gradually using it more comprehensively. It is for these reasons that communication notebooks should be regarded as an essential communication tool for individuals with PPA, and ideally, development of the notebook should commence during the first encounter.

The creation of a communication notebook that will be used requires planning, work, and a team effort that involves the clinician, the individual with aphasia, and his or her frequent communication partners. Creating a communication notebook can be a daunting task. Mistakenly, clinicians often provide individuals with aphasia with a prefabricated communication notebook stocked with generic vocabulary and icons. It is given to these individuals with the hope that, with little or no training, this unnatural communication tool will be incorporated into the individual's daily activities. Because of the limited amount of time speech-language pathologists can spend with a single individual, the prefabricated communication book offers a seemingly efficient solution to circumvent the spoken language impairments of individuals with aphasia. However, given that the users (both the individual with aphasia and his or her communication partners) have limited opportunities to provide input on the book's content and organization and given that the users are not typically trained regarding how to communicate using the book, it is not surprising that clinicians frequently report that most recipients of prefabricated books rarely use them. An unfortunate consequence of the fact that prefabricated books are seldom used by recipients is that clinicians are abandoning communication notebooks in general. This is tantamount to throwing the baby out with the bathwater because communication notebooks may be the most effective AAC device for individuals with aphasia—progressive or static. Successful incorporation of communication notebooks into an individual's daily communication activities requires, at a minimum, that the users 1) participate in the development of the book, thereby making it personalized; 2) are trained to communicate using the book, thereby making it utilized; and 3) are taught to update the book's content, thereby making it dynamic.

Rule #1: The communication notebook must reflect the person; it must be personalized. The individual with PPA should be encouraged to take the lead role in selecting and customizing the book's content. This may be the most important factor for engendering acceptance of this unnatural tool. The role of the speech-language pathologist is to facilitate content selection and organization in accordance with the individual's communication needs, personal preferences, and skill level. Table 4 outlines key sections and core vocabulary to be used as an initial template for developing a communication notebook. These sections provide a skeleton on which more personalized content can be fleshed out. Lists of sample vocabulary can be given to the individual and family to provide choices for inclusion. Daily logs of conversational topics and activities can be kept to further identify useful vocabulary. It is imperative that pictures, symbols, and photographs be included in addition to traditional orthographic information because the reading skills of individuals with PPA invariably deteriorate. Similarly, the clinician should guide the users to consider how the book will be used to optimize the organizational format. For example, items that are frequently referenced in daily communication might be located at the beginning of the book or of each section. The clinician should assist individuals to identify the organizational format, topics, and vocabulary that reflect the user's personality, activities, and interests.

Rule #2: The communication notebook and opportunities to use it must be available; it must be utilized. As the communication notebook is developing, it is important to increase opportunities to incorporate this tool into daily communication. Initially, time may be devoted to assisting the individual with PPA in learning to locate information within the book with relative efficiency and effectiveness; however, in most cases, the individual's involvement in notebook development mitigates this step. Creating opportunities within and outside the treatment setting reinforces the benefits of using this tool to support communication and therefore should promote generalization. It is informative and useful to ask the individual and the communication partner to converse for approximately 5–10 minutes once per week using whichever modalities they choose while the clinician observes unobtrusively. As stated in Rule #2, the notebook should be available during these conversations, on a table in front of the users. No one is forced to use the book, but because it is available, it is more likely to be

Table 4.   Key sections and core vocabulary of communication notebooks

Person (individual with PPA)

Address, telephone, date of birth
Medications
Emergency contact information
Education history
Work history
Unique personal histories (e.g., travel, life
   events, experiences, awards, hobbies,
   interests)

People

Immediate family
• Names and relationships
• Address and phone
Extended family
Friends
Pets
Personal contacts
• Doctors
• Therapists
Family tree and/or terms for relatives
General list of occupations

Places

List of places he/she regularly visits (i.e., malls,
   stores, parks, towns, cities, states, countries)
List of places he/she might want to refer to
Maps for these locations
Maps for city, state, country, world

Food/Drink

Mealtimes
Types of food preferences
Beverages
Restaurants
Grocery stores

Clothing/Personal Items

Hygiene items
Daily clothing items
• Undergarments
• Outerwear
Prosthetic items (e.g., glasses, dentures,
   hearing aid)

Time

Clock with movable hands
Time vocabulary
Calendar
List of years
Holidays
Seasons
Weather

Numerals

Money words and symbols
Arithmetic functions (e.g., plus, minus)

Emotions/Feelings

Visual analog scale
Word list or iconic symbols

Medical

Doctors (area of specialty, telephone number)
Therapists
Specialists
Body picture
Body parts
Medical terms
Medications

Question Concepts

Who (relative, friend, stranger, occupation)
What (size, shape, color, occupation)
When (past, present, future, refer to time
   section)
Where (home, store, street, city, state)
Why (urgent, necessary, desirable)
How (how much, how long, how many)

Current Events

Sports (teams, favorite players)
Politics (parties, governmental levels)
Leaders (local, national, international)
Celebrities
Televison shows
Movies
Public topics
Vocabulary lists
Personalized list of concepts frequently
   conveyed
Options for verbs, adjectives, and so forth
Occupations, hobby topics, family events

Vocabulary Lists

Personalized lists of concepts frequently
   conveyed
Options for verbs, adjectives, and so forth
Occupations, hobby topics, family events

Additional Materials

Pen, pencil, blank paper
Notebook pockets for brochures, news
   clippings, personal items, business cards,
   photos
Dividers for sections with tab labels
• Label each side of tab
• Consider picture symbol & word labels
Instructions for new communication partners on
   "how to use this book" inside front cover
Activity log or diary
Visitor sign-in log
"Message center" where information can be
   written to communicate among various
   communication partners

used. This method allows the users to discover the utility of the book for themselves without being prompted or nagged. In addition to facilitating generalization, these opportunities allow the clinician to observe how the notebook is being used and to generate recommendations concerning how the book or the interaction style of the dyad might benefit from modifications.

Rule #3: The communication notebook is never finished; it must be dynamic. The communication notebook is a dynamic tool, not a static product. Communication notebook construction is a neverending process. Because communication needs change, conversation topics change, and, with deterioration, the individual's abilities change, the communication notebook must be adapted periodically and updated continually. This may constitute a shift in perspective for clinicians who have become accustomed to prescribing prefabricated books. Similarly, emphasizing the dynamic nature of communication notebooks may seem counterintuitive to many communication partners because typically they want to make neat and complete books in the genre of family photo albums. Communication notebooks should be a little messy, pages should be written on with pen or pencil, sticky notes should be applied liberally, new items should be added, and obsolete ones should be removed.

Transferring responsibility for adapting and updating the notebook from the clinician to the users is a crucial step that is often overlooked. With much emphasis placed on the task of establishing content, clinicians may neglect to adequately train the users to keep the book updated. User involvement early on establishes a critical path. By involving the individual with PPA and his or her communication partners during the early stages of notebook development, their ability to become active participants in expanding and modifying the communication notebook is likely to be enhanced. It should be explicitly stated that the individual with PPA is centrally responsible for his or her own system. However, over the course of PPA, notebook modification becomes increasingly a shared responsibility, with those most closely involved adopting more responsibility during the later stages.

In summary, the following guidelines are recommended to foster acceptance and use of communication notebooks for individuals with PPA:

- Introduce the concept of a communication notebook to the individual and family as soon as possible, emphasizing the utility of the tool as a means to support communication as the individual's aphasia becomes more severe.
- Emphasize the interactive nature of communication by suggesting content that should enhance conversational exchange

and social interaction, not just be the means of transactions of information concerning basic needs.
- Involve the individual and his or her communication partners from the beginning by eliciting their contributions regarding content and organization.
- Establish a functional format for the communication notebook, accounting for issues such as visual acuity, visual attention, and current reading abilities (i.e., single-word and phrase-level comprehension).
- Practice using the notebook with a variety of partners and in a variety of communication environments to assist the users in incorporating this tool into the communication activities of their daily lives.
- Facilitate transferring the responsibility for updating and modifying the notebook from the clinician to the users (i.e., individuals with PPA and their communication partners).

AAC LEADS TO SUCCESSFUL ADAPTATION

The following vignettes are provided to exemplify how two individuals with PPA, despite severe impairments, managed to reduce their activity limitations and participation restrictions. The first vignette describes how an individual with a 10-year history of nonfluent PPA manages to "discuss" rebuilding a mailbox stand with a neighbor who was complete stranger. This individual is referred to as N.A. because he had nonfluent aphasia. At the time that the mailbox story occurred, N.A. was a completely nonvocal comprehensive communicator who also required AAC to comprehend even short, simple utterances. N.A. communicated using a well-developed communication notebook, a DynaVox, and other techniques including drawing and gesturing. The second vignette describes how an individual with a 4-year history of fluent PPA manages to continue participating in a weekly poker game. This individual is referred to as F.A. because he had fluent aphasia. F.A. also required augmented speech and communicated expressively using a well-developed communication notebook, gestures, and AAC strategies designed for specific situations, such as playing poker.

N.A.'s Story

N.A. recently attempted to rebuild the mailbox stand that housed three mailboxes for him and his neighbors. Apparently, he liked a stand that he had spotted just up the street. So, N.A. got in his car with paper, pencil, and communication notebook in hand to seek out building and pricing information from the owner of the mailbox stand. The owner later contacted N.A.'s wife, which is how the story became known. According to the owner, N.A. knocked on his door and immediately offered the neighbor his personal identification card. The card has N.A.'s name and address, provides a brief description of PPA, and describes the nature of his communication impairment. The card also conveys that N.A. has no other cognitive involvement and gives some brief advice about how best to communicate with him. N.A. went on to offer two drawings: one depicting his broken mailbox stand with the street number printed clearly on it, and a second showing a neatly constructed stand with the owner's address. Next to the neatly constructed stand, N.A. wrote "$$$–?" and drew a measuring tape. The man reported that he was initially "caught off guard" because he had never met N.A. before. However, he quickly realized that N.A. was inquiring about his mailbox stand and agreeably followed N.A. when he gestured to walk outside to the stand. Apparently, the two men "discussed" the construction, materials, and approximate cost. N.A. went home with a pad of notes written by the man and proceeded to build the new mailbox stand.

The man called later in the week and spoke with N.A.'s wife. He told her how amazed he was that they had communicated so well and offered to help when N.A. went about building the new stand. N.A.'s wife did not have the heart to tell him that the stand was nearly completed. A couple of weeks later, N.A. brought pictures of the new mailbox stand to language group and, using a white board, he showed the group how he had constructed the stand. Again, N.A. wrote "$$$–?" and, pointing back and forth from the board to each group member, he asked each person to guess what the total cost had been. After everyone had grossly overestimated the cost, he pulled out an index card displaying the amazingly low price of $43 and smiled proudly.

F.A.'s Story

F.A. recently hosted the monthly poker game with his friends. He had not participated in the last 6 months. Prior to the game, F.A.'s wife called the poker players and asked them if they would come play with F.A. because he had learned some new strategies and techniques in therapy that would help him play. The men arrived and were greeted by F.A. holding an index card that said, "I hope you brought lots of money." F.A. gestured to his wife, who told the other players that she would briefly explain the system F.A. would use during the poker game. F.A.'s wife requested that the players not all talk at the same time during the game and showed them how they might use F.A.'s communication book to introduce a topic of conversation (F.A.'s communication book contained a "topics page" that listed topics F.A. enjoyed talking about. They included family, politics, weather, travel, and sports). F.A.'s wife then explained the strategies and techniques F.A. would use during the poker game.

F.A. had index cards that represented the different poker games (e.g., five-card poker, three-card draw was represented by the text "five-card poker, three-card draw" and symbolically underneath the text with the number 5, five cards, a bold slash line, a picture of a person drawing, and the number 3). F.A. used the cards to call the game when he dealt and asked the other players to use the cards to let him know which game they would be playing when someone else was the dealer. Because F.A. had played poker with the same men for years, they used the same rules (e.g., minimum ante, minimum bid, pot limit, number of raises) they had always used (F.A. did have the rules written on index cards if he needed clarification). At one point in the game, another player tried to raise the bid. F.A. held up the rule card that said "Maximum number of raises is five." Everyone laughed and thanked F.A. for making sure no one was breaking the rules.

A communication breakdown did occur during the game between F.A. and the dealer. F.A. got his wife to help identify the information he did not understand, and they made a new rule card at that time. The communication breakdown was repaired, and the game continued. The game was a success by all accounts. F.A. participated in the poker game and even won a few hands.

The men planned next month's game before the evening ended. F.A. turned to the calendar in his communication book and gestured to another player with a pen. He pretended to write in the air with the pen. The player asked F.A. if he would like him to write the time and place of the next game on his calendar. F.A. nodded to affirm the player's request. According to his wife, at the end of that evening, F.A. looked happier than he had in a long time.

Summary of Vignettes

These two individuals with PPA and their stories depict successful adaptation in the face of relentless deterioration. The AAC strategies that they once resisted, slowly became their own and provided them with a means to stay connected, to participate in social interaction. These individuals learned to successfully use any and all modalities to communicate. N.A. used specific-situation techniques such as his personal identification card and the drawings that he had prepared to specifically communicate that he wanted to build a nice, new mailbox stand. He successfully used facial expressions to convey questioning, humor, sadness, and much more. With a combination of reassuring smiles, drawings, and gesturing, he managed to get a total stranger to leave his home and walk out to the mailbox. N.A. was able to tell the whole story to the language group without uttering a single word and without receiving help from anyone. Furthermore, he was able to query each member of the group, thereby involving them. F.A. was able to play poker, to call another player on a rule violation, and laugh with the guys despite a severe impairment of auditory comprehension. He was able to make plans to play again and feel like he belonged. Perhaps the most important accomplishment is that both of these individuals persistently struggled not to allow their severe language impairments to limit their activities or to keep them from participating. These individuals continued to enjoy the activities that gave them pleasure and to interact with family, friends, and even strangers.

CONCLUSIONS

Adaptation to illness and disablement has been defined as the dynamic, mutual accommodation of both the subjective experience of disablement and the external environment (Shontz, 1975, as cited in Livneh & Antonak, 1997). Adaptation is conceptualized as an evolving process leading toward successful adjustment. Accordingly, successful adjustment is viewed as necessitating two separate processes: psychological adjustment and environmental accommodation. The mutual accommodation of the subjective experience and the external environment is clearly depicted by these two individuals' successful striving to combat limitations and restrictions by modifying their approach to communication. Individuals with PPA are faced with the challenge of adapting to a life in which language, communication, and social interaction are continually a struggle. With successful management, hopefully individuals with PPA realize that the relentless decline of speech and language does not have to mean social isolation. As the two individuals in the vignettes demonstrate, negative life experiences can be successfully managed by reducing limitations in the physical and social environment and by participating in and enjoying valued activities. This message is axiomatic and must be explicitly appreciated by clinicians, family members, and most important, by the individual with PPA. All components of proactive management, early utilization of AAC, partner training, and anticipatory implementation of communication strategies are founded in the belief that *negative life experiences can be successfully managed by reducing limitations in the physical and social environment and by participation in and enjoyment of valued activities.*

REFERENCES

Beland, R., & Paradis, C. (1997). Principled syllabic dissolution in a primary progressive aphasia case. *Aphasiology, 11*(12), 1171–1196.

Beland, R., & Ska, B. (1992). Interaction between verbal and gestural language in progressive aphasia: A longitudinal case study. *Brain and Language, 43,* 355–385.

Beukelman, D.R., & Mirenda, P. (1998). Communication options for persons who can not speak: Assessment and evaluation. In C.A. Coston (Ed.), *Proceedings of the National Planners Conference on Assistive Device Service Delivery* (pp. 151–165). Washington, DC: RESNA and the Association for the Advancement of Rehabilitation Technology.

Blackstone, S. (1994). The purpose of AAC assessment. *Augmentative Communication News, 7*(1), 2–3.

Dejerine, J., & Serieux, P. (1897). Un cas de surdite verbale pure termineé par aphasie sensorielle, suivi d'autopsie. *Comptes Rendus des Séances de la Société de Biologie (Paris), 49,* 1074–1077.

Duffy, J.R., & Petersen, R.C. (1992). Major review: primary progressive aphasia. *Aphasiology, 6*(1), 1–13.

Elmstahl, S., Malmberg, B., & Annerstedt, L. (1996). Caregiver's burden of patients 3 years after stroke assessed by a novel caregiver burden scale. *Archives of Physical Medicine and Rehabilitation, 77,* 177–181.

Foster, N.L., & Chase, T.N. (1983). Diffuse involvement in progressive aphasia. *Annals of Neurology, 13*(2), 224–225.

Garrett, K., & Beukelman, D.R. (1992). Augmentative communication approaches for persons with severe aphasia. In K.M. Yorkston (Ed.), *Augmentative communication in the medical setting* (pp. 245–338). Tucson, AZ: Communication Skill Builders.

Gorden, B., & Selnes, O. (1984). Progressive aphasia "without dementia": Evidence of more widespread involvement. *Neurology, 34,* 102.

Graff-Radford, N.R., Damasio, A.R., Hyman, B.T., Hart, M.N., Tranel, D., Damasio, H., Van Hoesen, G.W., & Rezai, K. (1990). Progressive aphasia in a patient with Pick's disease: A neuropsychological, radiologic, and anatomic study. *Neurology, 40,* 620–626.

Green, J., Morris, J.C., Sandson, J., McKeel, D.W., & Miller, J.W. (1990). Progressive aphasia: A precursor of global dementia? *Neurology, 40,* 423–429.

Hart, R.P., Beach, W.A., & Taylor, J.R. (1997). A case of progressive apraxia of speech and non-fluent aphasia. *Aphasiology, 11*(1), 73–82.

Hodges, J.R., & Patterson, K. (1996). Nonfluent progressive aphasia and semantic dementia: A comparative neuropsychological study. *Journal of the International Neuropsychological Society, 2,* 511–524.

Karbe, H., Kertesz, A., & Polk, M. (1993). Profiles of language impairment in primary progressive aphasia. *Archives of Neurolology, 50,* 193–200.

Kempler, D., Metter, E.J., Riege, W.H., Jackson, C.A., Benson, D.F., & Hanson, W.R. (1990). Slowly progressive aphasia: Three cases with language, memory, CT, and PET data. *Journal of Neurology, Neurosurgery, and Psychiatry, 53,* 987–993.

Kirshner, H.S., Webb, W.G, Kelly, M.P., & Wells, C.E. (1984). Language disturbance: An initial symptom of cortical degeneration and dementia. *Archives of Neurology, 41,* 491–496.

Lane, V.W., & Samples, J.M. (1981). Facilitating communication skills in adult aphasics: Application of Blissymbols in a group setting. *Journal of Communication Disorders, 14,* 157–167.

Light, J.C. (1988). Interaction involving individuals using augmentative and alternative communication systems: State of the art and future directions. *Augmentative and Alternative Communication, 4*, 66–82.

Light, J.C., & Binger, C. (1998). *Building communicative competence with individuals who use augmentative and alternative communication.* Baltimore: Paul H. Brookes Publishing Co.

Livneh, H., & Antonak, R.F. (1997). *Psychosocial adaptation to chronic illness and disability.* Gaithersburg, MD: Aspen Publishers.

Mandell, A.M., Alexander, M.P., & Carpenter, S. (1989). Creutzfeldt-Jakob disease presenting as isolated aphasia. *Neurology, 39*, 55–58.

Mazzoni, M., Pollera-Orsucci, M., & Giraldi, C. (1996). Primary progressive aphasia: Description of a clinical case with nine years of follow-up. *Italian Journal of Neurological Sciences, 17*(2), 161–165.

McNeil, M.R. (1998). The case of the lawyer's lugubrious language: Dysarthrias plus primary progressive aphasia or dysarthria plus dementia? *Seminars in Speech and Language, 19*(1), 49–58.

McNeil, M.R., Small, S.L., Masterson, R.J., & Fossett, T.R.D. (1995). Behavioral and pharmacological treatment of lexical-semantic deficits in a single patient with primary progressive aphasia. *American Journal of Speech-Language Pathology, 4*, 76–87.

Mendez, M.F., & Zander, B.A. (1991). Dementia presenting with aphasia: Clinical characteristics. *Journal of Neurology, Neurosurgery, and Psychiatry, 34*, 542–545.

Mesulam, M.M. (1982). Slowly progressive aphasia without generalized dementia. *Annals of Neurology, 11*(6), 592–598.

Mesulam, M.M. (1987). Editorial: Primary progressive aphasia: Differentiation from Alzheimer's disease. *Annals of Neurology, 22*(4), 533–534.

Mesulam, M.M., & Weintraub, S. (1992). Spectrum of primary progressive aphasia. In M.N. Rossor (Ed.), *Bailliere's clinical neurology: Vol. 1. Unusual dementias* (pp. 583–609). London: Bailliere Tindall.

Murray, L.L. (1998). Longitudinal treatment of primary progressive aphasia: A case study. *Aphasiology, 12*(7/8), 651–672.

Nicholas, L.E., & Brookshire, R.H. (1993). A system for quantifing the informativeness and efficiency of the connected speech of adults with aphasia. *Journal of Speech and Hearing Research, 36*(2), 338–345.

Parkin, A.J. (1993). Progressive aphasia without dementia: A clinical and cognitive neuropsychological analysis. *Brain and Language, 44*, 201–220.

Philbrick, K.L., Rummans, T.A., Duffy, J.R., Kokmen, E., & Jack, C.R., Jr. (1994). Primary progressive aphasia: an uncommon masquerader in psychiatric disorders. *Psychosomatics, 35*, 138–141.

Pick, A. (1892). Uber die Beziehungen der senilen Hirnatrophie zur Aphasie. *Prager Medizinishe Wochenschrift, 17*, 165–167.

Pick, A. (1904). Zur Symptomatologie der linksseitigen Schlafenlappenatrophie. *Monatsschrift jür Psychiatre und Neurologie, 16*, 378–388.

Pogacar, M.L., & Williams, R.S. (1984). Alzheimer's disease presenting as slowly progressive aphasia. *Rhode Island Medical Journal, 67*, 181–185.

Rogers, M.A., & Alarcon, N.B. (1998a). Dissolution of spoken language in primary progressive aphasia. *Aphasiology, 12*(7/8), 635–650.

Rogers, M.A., & Alarcon, N.B. (1998b, November). *Primary progressive aphasia: Case studies and a demographic overview.* Paper presented at the American Speech-Language-Hearing Association (ASHA) annual convention, San Antonio, TX.

Rogers, M.A., & Alarcon, N.B. (1999). Characteristics and management of primary progressive aphasia. *Neurophysiology and Neurogenic Speech and Language Disorders Newsletter, 9*(4), 12–26.

Rogers, M.A., Alarcon, N.B., & Olswang, L.B. (2000). Aphasia management considered in the context of the WHO model of disablements. In I.R. Odderson & E.M. Halar (Eds.), *Physical medicine and rehabilitation clinics in North America* (pp. 907–923). Philadelphia: W.B. Saunders Co.

Rosenfeld, M. (1909). Die partielle Grosshirnatrophie. *Journal of Psychology and Neurology, 14,* 115–130.

Sapin, L.R., Anderson, F.H., & Pulaski, P.D. (1989). Progressive aphasia without dementia: Further documentation. *Annals of Neurology, 25*(4), 411–413.

Sawyer-Woods, L. (1987). Symbolic function in a severe non-verbal aphasic. *Aphasiology, 1,* 287–290.

Scheltens, P., Ravid, R., & Kamphorst, W. (1994). Pathologic finding in a case of primary progressive aphasia. *Neurology, 44,* 279–282.

Scholten, I.M., Kneebone, A.C., Denson, L.A., Field, C.D., & Blumbergs, P. (1995). Primary progressive aphasia: Serial linguistic, neuropsychological and radiological findings with neuropathological results. *Aphasiology, 9*(5), 495–516.

Schwartz, M.F., De Bleser, R., Poeck, K., & Weis, J. (1998). A case of primary progressive aphasia: A 14-year follow-up study with neuropathological findings. *Brain, 121*(pt. 1), 115–126.

Shontz, F.C. (1975). *The psychological aspects of physical illness and disability.* New York: Macmillan.

Shuttleworth, E.C., Yates, A.J., & Paltan-Ortiz, J.D. (1985). Creutzfeldt-Jacob disease presenting as progressive aphasia. *Journal of the National Medical Association, 77*(8), 649–656.

Sinnatanby, R., Antoun, N.A., Freer, C.E.L., Miles, K.A., & Hodges, J.R. (1996). Neuroradiological findings in primary progressive aphasia: CT, MRI, and cerebral perfusion SPECT. *Neuroradiology, 38,* 232–238.

Snowden, J.S., Neary, D., Mann, D.M.A., Goulding, P.J., & Testa, H.J. (1992). Progressive language disorder due to lobar atrophy. *Annals of Neurology, 31*(2), 174–183.

Southwood, M.H., & Chatterjee, A. (1998). Phonological and articulatory disturbances in a case of primary progressive aphasia. *Aphasiology, 12*(2), 161–178.

Thompson, C.K., Ballard, K.J., Tait, M.E., Weintraub, S., & Mesulam, M. (1997). Patterns of language decline in non-fluent primary progressive aphasia. *Aphasiology, 11*(4), 297–321.

Turner, R.S., Kenyon, L.C., Trojanaowski, J.Q., Gonatas, N., & Grossman, M. (1996). Clinical, neuroimaging, and pathologic features of progressive nonfluent aphasia. *Annals of Neurology, 39*(2), 166–173.

Tyler, L.K., Moss, H.F., Patterson, K., & Hodges, J. (1997). The gradual deterioration of syntax and semantics in a patient with progressive aphasia. *Brain and Language, 56,* 426–476.

Wasson, C.A., Arvidson, H.H., & Lloyd, L.L. (1997). AAC assessment process. In L. L. Lloyd, D.R. Fuller, & H.H. Arvidson (Eds.), *Augmentative and alternative communication: A handbook of principles and practices* (pp. 169–198). Needham Heights, MA: Allyn & Bacon.

Weintraub, S., Rubin, N., & Mesulam, M. (1990). Primary progressive aphasia: Longitudinal course, neuropsychological profile, and language features. *Archives of Neurology, 47,* 1329–1335.

World Health Organization (WHO). *International classification of impairments, activities, and handicaps* (9th rev.). Geneva: Author.

World Health Organization (WHO). *(1997). ICIDH-2 International classification of impairments, activities, and participation* [On-line]. Available http://www.who.int/ msa/mnh/ems/icidh/index/html

11

AAC and Aphasia

Cognitive-Linguistic Considerations

Kathryn L. Garrett
Mikael D.Z. Kimelman

Aphasia is a communication disorder that is typically acquired in a sudden manner by linguistically sophisticated adults. The neurologic injuries that cause aphasia are most frequently the result of a vascular accident (i.e., stroke) or injury to the left hemisphere of the brain. Aphasia is characterized by inefficient verbal symbolic manipulations in conjunction with language use (McNeil, 1983). Chapey (1986) further defined aphasia as an acquired impairment of the cognitive processes that underlie language as well as an impairment of language itself. Most aphasiologists concur that aphasia is manifested across all of the communication modalities—speaking, listening, reading, and writing (Chapey, 1986; Darley, 1982; Schuell, Jenkins, & Jimenez-Pabon, 1964). However, aphasia does not present as a uniform syndrome. Depending on individual characteristics, people with aphasia can have relatively greater difficulty with comprehending the linguistic signal, retrieving semantic concepts and lexical labels, syntactically encoding thoughts to represent meaning, or producing the phonologic and motor sequences of the speech stream.

In colloquial terms, people with aphasia must work hard to communicate. Their ability to decode and encode language "short-circuits," and these neurologic disruptions interfere with the transmission of ideas and meanings. People with aphasia cannot consistently send or receive adequate linguistic signals, and this inability, in turn, can diminish their ability to participate in information-laden communication interactions. Although aphasia is typically attributed to breakdowns in linguistic processing (Goodglass & Kaplan, 1983; Wepman & Jones, 1961), it may also, in some part, be a result of inefficient information processing (McNeil & Kimelman, 1986). Aphasia has also been associated with the following cognitive challenges: difficulties with communicating propositional versus nonpropositional information (Goodglass, 1993; Jackson, 1878); relatively greater impairment of controlled versus automatic processing (Stark, 1988); a reduced ability to process analytic, time-dependent, and sequential functions (Bradshaw & Sherlock, 1982); decreased ability to focus on details or features (Cohen & Woll, 1981); and a reduction in the efficient action and interaction of memory, convergent and divergent thinking, and evaluative thinking (Chapey, 1983).

HISTORIC INTERVENTION APPROACHES FOR APHASIA

Speech-language pathologists have a relatively brief but rich history of providing rehabilitation to people with aphasia. Traditionally, speech-language therapy has focused on the restoration of expressive and receptive language processes for people with aphasia (Lyon, 1992; Simmons-Mackie, 1998). The efficacy of these restoration approaches has been well documented for many individuals with mild and moderate aphasia (Horner, Loverso, & Gonzalez Rothi, 1994; Robey, 1994). However, Porch (1981) observed that approximately half of all adults with aphasia who were treated with a linguistic stimulation/restoration approach continued to be highly restricted in their ability to communicate in everyday conversational exchanges. Nicholas and Helm-Estabrooks (1990) similarly suggested that the restoration of speech is not realistic for many individuals with aphasia. They advocated a shift in therapy goals from talking to communicating through alternative modalities when appropriate.

Concurrently, aphasiologists have begun to address the social context, functional needs, interactional dynamics and hidden competencies of all communicators with aphasia (Fitch-West, 1983; Kagan, 1998; Lyon, 1992; Simmons-Mackie & Damico, 1995). As Kagan (1998) noted in a description of her intervention program, Supported Conversation for Adults with Aphasia (SCA), aphasia therapy techniques should acknowledge and reveal the communicative competence that is masked by aphasia. One of the ways in which clinicians have attempted to unmask the underlying communicative competence of individuals with severe aphasia is through augmentative and alternative communication (AAC) strategies. Hux, Beukelman, and Garrett (1994) proposed that many individuals with aphasia are "candidates" for AAC strategies because they do not regain sufficient natural speech for communication of basic needs or because their speech is inadequate or inefficient in certain situations.

CAN PEOPLE WITH APHASIA
USE AAC STRATEGIES SUCCESSFULLY?

AAC systems have been used successfully by many individuals whose severe motor impairments prevent them from speaking or writing independently (Beukelman & Mirenda, 1998). However, for people with aphasia, AAC design and implementation issues appear to be different from those for people with motor impairments or even cognitive developmental disabilities. Kraat (1990) suggested, in a review of the then current literature in AAC and aphasia, that clinicians encountered many challenges in their efforts to devise functional AAC systems for people with aphasia. She observed that it appeared as if people with aphasia "did not think to turn to these alternative forms, could not shift strategies to use them, or somehow could not integrate them into real communication contexts" (Kraat, 1990, p. 324).

Thus, the linguistic and cognitive processing patterns unique to aphasia may prevent a simple application of the AAC interventions developed for individuals with motor access challenges. The purpose of this chapter is therefore to analyze some of the cognitive-linguistic demands of AAC strategies for communicators with aphasia. Information presented in this chapter is intended to provide a bridge between what is known about the cognitive-linguistic abilities of individuals with aphasia, the AAC process, and potential clinical interventions.

Early research in the area of AAC and aphasia attempted to develop alternative symbol communication systems specifically for people with limited verbal expression skills as a result of aphasia. Glass, Gazzaniga, and Premack (1975) asked seven adults with global aphasia to arrange word-equivalent paper symbols in sentence order. Two of them could construct subject-verb-object strings by the end of the study, although the other five adults had more limited productions. The researchers presented no data on generalization to spontaneous communication situations. Bailey (1983) and Johannsen-Horbach, Cegla, Mager, and Schempp (1985) used Blissymbolics (Bliss, 1965) with individuals with aphasia who do not speak. Bailey's patient mastered a 200-word Blissymbol chart and then developed functional writing skills. The latter group of investigators also developed communication boards for four individuals with global aphasia. One of

these individuals reportedly used the board to communicate functionally in all situations; the others used it to supplement their verbal expression, to respond in single words, or unsuccessfully. Weinrich, Steele,
Carlson, and Kleczewska (1989) developed a computerized version of a
visual-symbol communication board, and an individual with global
aphasia demonstrated some success in communicating trained syntactical forms with it. In the majority of these and other clinical research
efforts, some of the individuals with severe aphasia learned to access a
repertoire of referents for common or personal words. However, few
participants used their AAC systems and strategies to communicate
immediate needs or thoughts outside the clinic. Even fewer participants
learned to combine referents with pivot words to create complex propo-
sitions. The difficulties appeared to parallel the disturbances seen in the
spoken language of these communicators with aphasia.

Later studies focused on the manner in which people with aphasia
were taught to use AAC interventions. Bellaire, Georges, and Thompson's (1991) intervention study used a low-technology, or noncomput-
erized, communication system with two individuals with aphasia who
could neither speak nor write. The participants learned to request basic
items (e.g., coffee, cookies) and to communicate personal information
(e.g., name, occupation) by pointing to pictures on a communication
board. The participants were able to complete the task with direct clinical instruction but did not generalize this behavior to untrained messages until the twenty-third session. Both individuals eventually used
their boards to communicate five target messages after an additional
period of naturalistic communication training. This study by Bellaire
showed that although carryover of adaptive communication strategies
is possible in severe aphasia, it requires extensive time and message-
specific training in the target natural context.

Yanak and Light (1991) also described a situation in which a 38-
year-old man with severely limited speech in conjunction with Broca's
aphasia learned to communicate in social situations by pointing to
stored messages in a communication wallet during 6 weeks of intensive therapy. Yanak and Light reported that he generalized use of these
messages to community situations only after participating in an additional 6 weeks of role playing and practice in actual community situations. Garrett, Beukelman, and Low-Morrow (1989) reported on the
outcomes of a multimodal AAC intervention with a man who had
Broca's aphasia. They stated that in addition to assisting this individual to compile each customized component of the system, the largest
proportion of training time was spent on teaching him to use his strategies appropriately and effectively in actual communication situations.

Purdy, Duffy, and Coelho (1994) investigated whether individuals with aphasia could use 20 learned black-and-white symbols (i.e., line drawings) during a referential communication task (e.g., picture description) and while conversing about common daily activities following training. They also measured the frequency with which the individuals spontaneously switched between modalities when initial communication attempts failed. Results showed that participants spontaneously and correctly used 53% of the available 33 trained symbols on a referential communication task; usage increased by 23% with a cue. In structured conversation, spontaneous symbol use averaged 49% and increased by an additional 34% when cued. However, subjects switched to the alternate modalities only 41% of the time in conversation and only 37% of the time in the referential communication task when an opportunity arose.

The data from the preceding investigations suggest that individuals with severe aphasia seem to have a preliminary ability to use nonverbal visual symbols to communicate concepts in structured situations. However, without contextual training, few of the subjects generalized alternate symbol communication to real-life contexts. It is also apparent that when generalization occurred, it was in response to situation-specific, intensive training. The study by Purdy and colleagues (1994) also suggested that it might not be immediately intuitive to people with aphasia to choose an alternate modality when verbal communication is insufficient.

BASIC PREMISES ABOUT AAC LEARNING AND APHASIA

The authors of this chapter propose three primary reasons for the apparent challenges in assisting people with aphasia to use AAC strategies. First, in most situations, an adequate match has not been made between the communicator's spectrum of abilities and needs and the particular cognitive and linguistic skills required to use a specific AAC strategy effectively. Light and Lindsay (1991) noted that many interventionists may have a limited understanding of the cognitive and linguistic demands that AAC imposes on communicators. Thus, clinical practitioners may not thoroughly evaluate the user's requirements for using various alternative symbol systems or modalities. If AAC interventions such as alphabet boards, communication notebooks, computers, or voice output communication aids (VOCA) are disseminated without adequate consideration, they are almost certainly to be discarded if they are too difficult for the communicator with aphasia to use (DeRuyter, Kennedy, Doyle, & Donaghue, 1990).

The second premise pertains to the challenge of learning AAC strategies after a lifetime of relatively effortless use of natural communication skills. Reacquiring communication ability after the onset of aphasia is an imposing task at best. Before injury, communicators gain access to their internal, dynamic language matrix without giving much conscious attention to the communication process. After injury, the automaticity of communication is disrupted. The components of natural communication strategies (e.g., listening, retrieving words, encoding words syntactically, selecting appropriate phonological processes, programming motor movements) often must be reacquired in an effortful, conscious manner. AAC strategies often are equally, if not more, challenging for the individual with aphasia, perhaps in part because they are entirely new forms of communication. Communicators using AAC systems must shift from their internal language system to an externally represented set of symbols. As adult communicators without impairment, they seldom considered going to an external reservoir of symbols to communicate their ideas.

Third, few communicators are taught to use AAC strategies in integrative situations that demand strategic, on-the-spot implementation. People with aphasia are seldom taught to recognize when to use an adaptive communication strategy, much less how to use the system in an actual interaction. Even when communicators with aphasia learn to use the basic components of their AAC systems in a controlled situation, they often break down when facing the complexities of real-life communication scenarios. To move forward in the clinical application of AAC for people with aphasia, practitioners must be able to consider each of these premises and manage their potential limitations.

A BRIEF SUMMARY OF THE
COGNITIVE PROCESSES UNDERLYING APHASIA

When considering the cognitive processing needs of individuals using AAC strategies, an information-processing approach may be highly informative. Theoretically, information-processing impairments are intrinsic to all people with aphasia (McNeil, 1983). For individuals with severe aphasia, information-processing impairments may, in fact, constitute the largest portion of their communication impairment. Attentional, perceptual, and memory challenges may be particularly evident when people with severe aphasia engage in new learning with an AAC strategy or technique. These cognitive variables are described in more detail in the next sections.

Perceptual Processing

People with aphasia may experience breakdowns at one of the earliest stages of cognitive processing: perception. Perceptual deficits may consist of visual field cuts or processing breakdowns, such as neglect. Chronic neglect is typically thought to be the consequence of right parietal lobe lesions, although it can be due to lesions in other cortical areas, including the left hemisphere (Mesulam, 1981). When implementing strategies for people with severe aphasia, perceptual processing breakdowns may go unrecognized. Visual perceptual processing problems can present as difficulty with attending to items used in an AAC application (e.g., call button, sections of a communication board or AAC device) or even in recognizing the presence of communicative partners.

Memory

The memory skills of people with aphasia have been investigated from many perspectives (Barba, Frasson, Manotvan, Gallo, & Denes, 1996; Haarmann, Just, & Carpenter, 1997; Kolk & Hartsuiker, 1999; Ostergaard & Meudell, 1984). Although long-term memory impairments do not appear to pose significant problems, short-term memory processes appear to be impaired in many people with aphasia. This phenomenon was first observed by Schuell (1965) who described breakdowns during the encoding and storage stages of working memory. In addition, encoding, decoding, and access to semantic/lexical memories may also be impaired in aphasia. However, researchers have not yet been able to determine whether short-term memory impairments are actually primary impairments or the secondary consequences of resource capacity and allocation impairments (Haarmann et al., 1997; Just & Carpenter, 1992).

Attention

Attention in its myriad forms is a primary factor in any communicative interaction. For the individual with severe aphasia who must communicate basic needs, even fundamental levels of alertness and attention may be difficult to achieve. When engaging in interactions, people with aphasia must have the ability to focus attention and then sustain their attention over even relatively short periods of time. Work on the role of prosody in auditory comprehension has suggested that people with severe aphasia may benefit proportionally more than individuals with mild aphasia from extralinguistic cues. These cues may help them focus on relevant linguistic stimuli (Kimelman, 1999). However, it should be noted that the value of general alerting cues for people with aphasia has not yet been confirmed in empirical investigations (Loverso & Prescott, 1981).

Resource Capacity and Allocation

It has been increasingly suggested that people with aphasia have impaired resource capacity, impaired resource allocation abilities, or both (Haarmann et al., 1997; McNeil & Kimelman, 1986; McNeil, Odell, & Tseng, 1991; Peach, Newhoff, & Rubin, 1993). Basic knowledge about resource capacity and allocation models may assist in understanding why people with aphasia sometimes experience behavioral break-downs in dynamic versus structured communication situations (Friedman & Polson, 1981; Haarmann et al., 1997; Kahneman, 1973). For those unfamiliar with the concept of resource allocation, it is analogous to the economics of a fixed income, on which many of these individuals live. People with fixed incomes receive the same amount of money (i.e., resources or capacity) each month to pay rent, buy groceries, pay utility bills, purchase transportation, pay taxes, pay for amenities and entertainment, and pay for the upkeep and replacement of clothing, furniture, and other possessions. These everyday functions are some-what analogous to the homeostatic maintenance of motor functions, perception, attention, memory, semantics, syntax, pragmatics, and other cognitive-linguistic skills. If the amount of money available each month is permanently cut (i.e., resource capacity is reduced) or if an individual's ability to appropriately manage finances is diminished (i.e., resource allocation is impaired), or both, significant problems will occur. Sometimes people choose to pay part of each bill. Alternatively, some bills may be overpaid and others underpaid or totally ignored.

Similarly, in aphasia, communication becomes compromised when the cognitive system tries to process information with fewer resources or incorrectly allocated resources. Impairments of perceptual processing, attention, and memory have a negative influence on the overall integrity of an individual's communication system. For example, when people with aphasia attempt to communicate verbally when others are talking in the background, they may have more difficulty because they must filter out the competing conversational voices. Alternatively, the individual with aphasia may be completely success-ful at producing the same communication act in a structured speech practice session. Performance variability is frequently evident as people with aphasia encounter complex communication demands in real-life situations. It may in fact be one of the primary hallmarks of aphasia (McNeil, 1983).

COGNITIVE-LINGUISTIC DEMANDS OF
EVERYDAY COMMUNICATION SITUATIONS

Why do many people with aphasia have difficulty with using AAC systems as a primary method of communication? First, it is instructive to analyze the potential processing demands when people with aphasia attempt to communicate in various contexts using typical (non-AAC) communication modalities.

Situation #1: Communicating Basic Needs (Blanket)

Communicator:	[finds call light, activates, waits for nurse]
Nurse:	[some time later] Did someone call me?
Communicator:	Help.
Nurse:	Sure!
Communicator:	[grabs own arm, then points to blanket]
Nurse:	Oh, you're cold. Let me help you with that blanket.
Communicator:	Thank you.

Even in this minimally complex communication situation, an extraordinary number of communication skills are needed:

1. **Self-awareness** and the **ability to identify a physiologic need.** In addition, the communicator has to acknowledge that another's skills are required to resolve the need.

2. The ability to generate an **action plan** to decide who would meet the need and how this need would be accomplished (calling for help, stating the need).

3. The ability to generate a **conceptual representation** of how the need could be met (vision of blanket in drawer, feeling of blanket).

4. **Attentiveness to the environment**—auditorily (listening for a nurse), visually (watching for a nurse) and selectively (filtering out other activities). The communicator must also sustain attention until the need is met.

5. The ability to **identify an expressive modality** to signal for help: speech (e.g., ability to coordinate the motor/vocal/automatic language system to say "help" or "nurse" or to groan), gesture (e.g., ability to reach out for nurse, ability to point to area of need), or an AAC system if necessary (e.g., board, device, call button).

6. **Allocation of enough attention and memory resources** to recall the need or message during the time period required for the nurse to arrive. The communicator must persist and try again if the first effort to get help does not pay off and must retain the original idea and action plan despite distractions or the passage of time.

7. Adequate **semantic mapping/translation skills** to retrieve and encode the spoken word or gestural representation for "blanket," order and sequence semantic concepts (i.e., syntax) to express more complex relationships (e.g., where, who) or to add appropriate pragmatic spin to the request (e.g., politeness, urgency).

8. Sufficient **pragmatic and linguistic comprehension** processes to determine whether the partner has received the message accurately.

9. The **metacommunicative ability** to try again, to revise the content of message, or to try an alternative strategy if necessary.

Unlike the individual in Situation #1, many people with aphasia cannot consistently communicate basic needs, even in a familiar context such as a hospital or a nursing home. Sometimes it is because they cannot initiate the act of gaining attention. At other times, they are unable to retrieve the words to communicate the specific idea. The individual can also forget the message while waiting for a partner to appear. Or, sometimes, the person with aphasia cannot process the multiple steps required to express the need through natural or AAC modalities.

When additional demands are applied to the communication situation, the communicator must retrieve and manipulate even more information. The following scenario represents a more extended conversation in which a person with severe aphasia attempts to answer personal questions.

Situation #2: Basic Conversation with a Communicator Who Has Aphasia: Autobiographical Questions

Communicator:	[no initiation]
Partner:	So, tell me about yourself.
Communicator:	[vague head nodding]
Partner:	Do you have any kids?
Communicator:	[tapping fingers, counting off number of children. Partner does not understand]
Partner:	Do you like it here?

Communicator:	[facial expression indicating frustration, head nod/shake unclear]
Partner:	Where are you from?
Communicator:	[points toward window, then toward door]
Partner:	I didn't understand. Maybe you can tell me what you did for a living?
Communicator:	[shakes head, unable to answer]

In this frustrating interaction (for both the person with aphasia and the communication partner), the informational demands of the interaction are so challenging that the communicator cannot retrieve any meaningful information or channel it through a communication modality.

Following are three additional cognitive linguistic demands required in this extended conversation:

1. The ability to **comprehend complex linguistic input**
2. The ability to access, autobiographical information in episodically stored **long-term memory**
3. The ability to **semantically map and encode complex information,** often combinations of semantic concepts that are displaced across space and time and that involve multiple relationships with other people, objects, and events

The next situation illustrates the additional demands created when multiple communication partners have an interactive discussion about a contemporary topic. For this topic, "going to the movies," the information is not as overlearned as in the situation involving autobiographical questions. Another supposition of dynamic conversation is that all conversation partners are expected to participate somewhat equally in the interaction by initiating and responding in a timely manner.

Situation #3: Complex Conversation Between Participants Who Do Not Have Aphasia: Discussing the Movies

Partner #1:	Did you go see that new movie everyone is talking about?
Partner #2:	Which one do you mean?
Partner #1:	Oh, the one about tornadoes with all of the special effects.
Partner #3:	Yeah, have you seen it?

Partner #1:   Yes, but it was really stupid.

Partner #3:   Why?

Partner #1:   The plot wasn't very believable.

Partner #2:   Were the special effects any good?

Partner #1:   Well, it might be worth seeing for that but I'd rec-
ommend renting the video instead.

This type of interaction illustrates an everyday conversation that is co-constructed on a moment-by-moment basis by all participants. Although conversing in this manner seems effortless to experienced communicators who do not have aphasia, equal participation in this type of interaction would require a monumental effort by a person with severe aphasia. Requisite skills include

1. The cognitive ability to **move beyond self** (i.e., egocentric focus) and discuss topics of shared relevance (i.e., other/world focus)

2. The ability to **initiate a topic or subtopic**

3. An ability to **semantically map and translate question forms and highly specific concepts in a timely, dynamic manner** (i.e., to keep up with the conversation)

4. **Pragmatic awareness** of the appropriateness of the conversational information; the amount of the partner's prior knowledge, time constraints, turn-taking rules, and so forth; and the ability to make adjustments in the interaction as needed

5. **Advanced discourse skills** to open the conversation, develop a story line, manipulate language for humor and irony, and use available context

These illustrations may clarify some of the processes in which people with aphasia must engage to communicate during ordinary interactions. The essential issue is that people with aphasia, even if they use AAC, must still engage in these processing steps; AAC does not make the communication process any easier. In fact, AAC strategies and technologies add several cognitive and linguistic demands to any of the preceding scenarios. A description of these demands follows.

Additional Cognitive-Linguistic Demands Imposed by AAC Systems

By definition, aphasia affects each of the levels of processing that AAC systems require. For example, locating written or pictured messages in a book or an electronic device requires individuals to translate symbols that are much more novel than natural speech. They must learn the meanings and internal representations of unfamiliar symbols, such as line drawings or other symbols. When multiple symbols are used, people with aphasia must also learn to search an array, search multiple arrays or levels, and possibly combine symbols to represent complex meanings. Most individuals with aphasia, even those with relatively good comprehension, would have difficulty with these tasks. If a message encoding strategy is used, such as numeric encoding (e.g., N1 = "I need to go to the bathroom"), then the person with aphasia must store, associate, and then recall these encoded representations. Even spelling, a more "natural" communication skill, is a type of encoding that requires selection and sequencing of arbitrary symbols to represent sounds and meanings. Because successful spelling requires many repetitions of this procedure, it is often extremely difficult for people with aphasia to spell an entire word or phrase. Thus, providing some people with aphasia with an alphabet board, typewriter, or computer keyboard may be more frustrating than therapeutic.

People with aphasia who use the type of AAC strategy that stores a number of messages on one or more levels may not have sufficient working memory or attentional capacity to complete the steps involved in accessing the messages. At times, the demands are such that communicators forget their intent or lose their partner's interest before they can convey their idea. In addition, if communicators with aphasia are using a high-technology system, they may have to learn new operational skills, such as turning the device on and off, locating messages stored on invisible levels, using flowchart operational menus, keyboarding, and charging the device. Complex visual displays may also challenge people who have visual processing deficits. Individuals with hemiplegia may have challenges carrying, holding, or accessing a system with their nondominant hand.

Finally, individuals with aphasia also must have the metacognitive skills to introduce their novel communication strategies to unfamiliar partners. They also have to know how to use their strategies in a dynamic manner, for example, using natural strategies such as speech and writing when able and then shifting to an AAC strategy during communication breakdowns.

Cognitive-Linguistic Demands of Specific AAC Strategies   In addition to the general challenges already presented, specific AAC strategies place other cognitive-linguistic demands on the communicator. Refer to Table 1 for additional information on these characteristics.

Yes-or-No Communication Board   This common AAC strategy requires none of the sequential processing skills needed to operate complex systems. However, it is a deceptively demanding task for people with aphasia. The binary choices of "yes" or "no," although seemingly simple to comprehend and produce, are vulnerable to the inefficient, variable, and imprecise processing that are characteristic in aphasia. First, many individuals with severe aphasia cannot manage the first cognitive step—to think of turning to the strategy when unable to clearly communicate "yes" or "no" through speech or head nods. Second, individuals with aphasia frequently misunderstand one element of their partner's message and then answer incorrectly. Or, third,

Table 1.   Characteristics of aphasia that can affect AAC strategy use

Characteristic of aphasia	Affected skills
Decreased awareness of cause and effect	Ability to understand that AAC or natural strategy can convey meaning or influence an event/behavior
Syntactic encoding difficulties	Symbol combining for message retrieval, ability to encode complex messages
Word retrieval/semantic breakdowns	Ability to comprehend and associate meanings to alternate symbol forms, message-encoding skills
Auditory comprehension difficulties	Ability to comprehend partner's message, ability to understand synthesized speech on high-technology devices
Reading comprehension difficulties	Ability to comprehend displays/symbols containing written words
Reduced ideational skills	Ability to formulate a novel message or select a prestored message that is appropriate for a specific communication context
Memory (long- and short-term) impairments	Ability to search multiple levels for messages, ability to retain ideas and persevere until message is communicated, ability to recall operational procedures for a system
Spelling/phonological processing impairments	Ability to generate novel messages on a spelling-based system, ability to retrieve alphabetically encoded messages
Hemiplegia, limb apraxia	Ability to physically access and transport a system
Visual field cuts, neglect, and other visual disturbances	Ability to see all or part of a visual display
Multiprocess reasoning	Ability to think of next operational and/or linguistic step in a dynamic conversation, ability to use multiple modalities
Metacommunication	Ability to assess adequacy of communication act (AAC or natural modalities), ability to repair communication efforts, ability to select most appropriate modality
New procedural learning	Ability to learn operational procedures for low- or high-technology communication systems

during the encoding of yes-or-no, they can slip down the incorrect output channel, nodding "yes" when they mean "no," and thereafter shift the communication sequence into an irresolvable series of misunderstandings. Fourth, partners may have difficulty with understanding the nuances of a communicator's "yes" and "no" responses, such as when a communicator's "no" means "No, I didn't do that," instead of "No, that's not a good question," "I don't know," or "Sort of yes, sort of no." Communication breakdowns then result. Although some individuals may benefit from having "yes," "no," "maybe," or "I don't know" available in graphic form, many others continue to misprocess during a yes-or-no question exchange even with a yes-or-no board or device. It is therefore important to evaluate whether yes-or-no answer cards should be a cornerstone of an AAC intervention package for each communicator with aphasia.

Buzzer/Call Light   Clinicians often choose to implement a needs-based communication system for individuals with severe aphasia, especially those who are in a hospital or care facility. They often design picture- or word-based boards representing physical needs (e.g., blanket, drink, bathroom) for these individuals. Many individuals with aphasia severe enough to warrant a needs-based AAC intervention also have difficulty in gaining a caregiver's attention, and activating a call signal is often a critical component of a needs-based communication system in a hospital or care facility. However, it is important to assess whether an individual with aphasia can initiate the thoughts and actions necessary to call for attention with an external aid such as a buzzer or call light. At times, it may be necessary to explicitly instruct a person with aphasia to use a call buzzer using direct instruction (e.g., "Call if you want to use the bathroom"), models, physical prompts, natural contingencies (e.g., the nurse arrives within a short time according to a prearranged plan), and multiple opportunities to practice in the actual needs context.

Communication Board   Like yes-or-no boards, simple communication boards representing basic needs are often one of the first external communication aids introduced to people with aphasia. Some individuals with mild aphasia may have no difficulty discriminating among the visual choices on the board and may independently turn to this alternate form of communication without requiring external cues. However, these individuals are also the most likely to obtain the desired item independently or to request the item with residual speech or gestures. The most obvious beneficiaries of a needs board are communicators with severe aphasia. However, clinicians must carefully assess whether these individuals have the necessary cognitive and linguistic prerequisites for representational communication before crafting a board and placing it on the individual's dresser or taping it to the wheelchair tray. As when teaching someone to use a call light, it may be helpful to use integrative instructional strategies if the expectation is that the individual will independently use a picture board to communicate needs. These strategies are discussed in the section on AAC training strategy.

Written-Choice Conversation   The written-choice conversational technique (Garrett, 1993; Garrett & Beukelman, 1995) requires facilitators to generate word choices representing answers to conversational questions for the communicator with aphasia. People with aphasia answer by pointing to the choices to convey their opinions and preferences, as shown in Figure 1. Because the field of choices is selected and presented by the communication partner, communicators with aphasia do not have to initiate or retrieve specific semantic terms themselves—they simply have to conceptualize their answer and recognize the corresponding word choices. This strategy therefore may help extend the content and quality of interactions among people with aphasia and their communication partners without increasing the cognitive load for the communicator with aphasia.

Simple Voice Output Communication Aid   Some limited message capacity devices with digitized VOCA (e.g., Digivox by Sunrise Medical Systems; AlphaTalker by Prentke-Romich, Inc.; TechSpeak by Adaptive Communication Consultants, Inc.) can be used for communication situations in which a specific spoken message is required or desired (e.g., telephone calls, telling stories). Messages are typically represented with printed words or symbols on paper overlays; the number of message choices most often ranges from 8 to 32. This type of system allows an entire idea or proposition to be "recorded" on each activation cell; the communicator does not have to sequence symbols to activate an entire message (although this symbol sequencing is possible in some devices such as the AlphaTalker). On this type of system, all desired messages can be displayed at one time; therefore, the demands on the communicator's visual memory are minimal. However, visual scanning and discrimination skills may be taxed instead. Communicators receive instant feedback via the voice output when activating the touch panel underneath each printed message, and this may help them to learn message location and meaning if their visual or reading skills are compromised. Because of their relative communicative power but minimal demands on memory and encoding, simple VOCAs lend themselves to use in specific communication contexts. People with aphasia reportedly have used these devices to share news in face-to-face conversations (Garrett, 1995), to participate in card games (Stuart, 1995), and in telephone conversations (Garrett & Beukelman, 1992).

Symbol Sequencing High-Technology Systems   Some high-technology systems (e.g., Liberator by Minspeak, Talking Screen by Words+, Inc., Lingraphica) allow communicators to access many messages by recalling and activating icon, or picture symbol, sequences. For example, symbols representing a person and a car in sequence might mean "Let's go for a drive." Often, icons can be interpreted in multiple ways, depending on the cognitive flexibility of the communicator and the

---

Partner: Are you following the elections?

Communicator: [nods "yes"]

Partner: What party do you vote for?

Communicator: [shrugs, does not respond]

Partner: [Writes and says aloud]
                  Are you....
                  • Democrat
                  • Republican
                  • Independent
                  • Libertarian
                  • Communist

Communicator: [Laughs, points to "Democrat"]

Partner: Oh, you're a Democrat! What are the chances
                  they'll re-elect a Democrat after all that business
                  last year? [draws a 5-point scale] Very good, so-so,
                  or no way

Communicator: [points to "1—no way"]

                  No way   So-so   Very Good
                  ←——/——/——/——/——/——→
                     1   2   3   4   5

Partner: Well, I'm voting Republican, so I hope you're right!

Figure 1. Sample written-choice conversation.

particular contextual associations that can be derived for each symbol. Although several investigators (Koul & Harding, 1998; Thorburn, Newhoff, & Rubin, 1995; Weinrich, McCall, Weber, Thomas, & Thornburg, 1995) found that some communicators with aphasia are indeed able to learn associations for iconic symbols, no data have yet been reported on the ability of individuals with aphasia to use an iconic-symbol, high-technology systems in functional, dynamic situations. The cognitive-linguistic demands may overwhelm most communicators who have aphasia in the throes of fast-paced, real-life interactions—simultaneously operating a high-technology system, listening to the communication partner, composing a thought, and recalling a large number of relatively arbitrary semantic associations may be overwhelming unless communicators are specifically taught to manage these demands.

Multilevel High-Technology Systems   Some high-technology systems (e.g., Vanguard by Prentke-Romich, Inc., DynaVox by Sunrise Medical Systems, Inc.) allow communicators to access large quantities of messages by storing them on hidden levels, or electronic layers. Users typically open a new array of messages or symbols by touching an ordinate type symbol that represents the new category of messages (e.g., transportation, my life). A dynamic screen allows new layers of visually represented messages to appear at a single touch or activation. The advantage to this type of system is that many hundreds of messages can be represented visually on an individual basis, yet the hidden leveling allows for compact access in comparison to paper overlay systems. For people with compromised visual memory and semantic retrieval systems, however, the sheer size of the available vocabulary can be taxing. In addition, "out of sight" can equal "out of mind," meaning some communicators with aphasia simply cannot recall where messages are stored. However, with extensive training during situation-specific use, some communicators with aphasia reportedly have used this type of system successfully for activities such as storytelling and limited conversational interactions (Fried-Oken, 1995; King & Beukelman, personal communication, September 1996).

Multimodal Communication Systems   Several reports have described the implementation of multimodal communication systems for adults with aphasia (Beukelman, Yorkston, & Dowden, 1985; Garrett et al., 1989; Yanak & Light, 1991). In these interventions, clinicians conducted a careful needs and capabilities assessment (Beukelman & Mirenda, 1998). Then the messages that communicators needed to use in specific contexts were matched to available residual modalities (e.g., gestures, speech). Information that could not be communicated through these channels was represented in some manner in an external communication aid (e.g., communication notebook, VOCA, communication wallet). The general principles that guided the selection of these external aids centered on their ease of use. Systems were selected because they were portable, represented messages in an easily interpretable form, were concisely organized, and idiosyncratic. In short, the cognitive-linguistic demands were minimized for the user.

In addition, each of the intervention reports just described also included a description of an environmentally based instruction phase. Each communicator needed to spend time in target communication contexts practicing how to use their various communication modes. Scripts, role playing, and cuing were used to enhance the individuals' communication abilities. All authors reported that this phase was critical to the success of the overall intervention. Additional information on instructional strategies is presented in the following section.

Possible Methods of Embedding Cognitive-Linguistic Support into AAC Strategy Training

Although AAC systems may not easily replace the damaged cognitive-linguistic systems of the person with severe aphasia, some selective applications of AAC technologies and strategies have reportedly helped increase the quality and functionality of interactions. Stuart (1995) described the use of a limited message AAC device to assist an older man with aphasia during card playing. Fried-Oken (1995) and S. Stuart (personal communication, April 1994) reported that communicators with aphasia successfully used digitized-voice limited-message AAC systems during storytelling activities with communicators with aphasia. Garrett and Beukelman (1992) also described novel ways of using technology. For example, in one intervention, partners typed messages on a notebook computer to augment the comprehension of a family member with severe auditory processing problems associated with aphasia. In another, a man with aphasia placed bets at a horse race using a list of essential phrases (e.g., "Trifecta," "Double my bet!").

The most problematic group of individuals with regard to use of AAC strategies may be people with moderately severe co-existing apraxia of speech and aphasia. Many of these communicators display a tremendous desire to communicate, a relatively large receptive vocabulary and language-processing capacity, and limited verbal output. These individuals, also known as *comprehensive communicators* (Garrett & Beukelman, 1992), often wish to communicate specific ideas at the rate and quantity that they were accustomed to before aphasia. Another challenging group consists of those people with good environmental and social awareness but poor language skills. Garrett (1996) noted that this group, the *controlled-situation* communicators

(Garrett & Beukelman, 1992), have great difficulty with accessing the right message at the right time in unstructured contexts. Following are some preliminary thoughts on how interventionists can begin the process of tailoring AAC strategies to match the cognitive-linguistic strengths of these individuals.

General Principles   Clinicians should take advantage of the extensive residual world knowledge that most adult communicators with aphasia possess (Garrett & Beukelman, 1992; McNeil & Kimelman, 1986). Rather than focus solely on needs or on abstract vocabulary, people with aphasia may communicate more successfully if personally relevant topics are selected. In addition, communicators may generalize their AAC learning more readily if strategies are introduced as part of "real-life" interactions and conversations from the very beginning of the therapeutic process, rather than save these types of therapy activities until shortly before the individual is discharged from therapy.

Clinicians may also wish to avoid strategies that are at the heart of the disability of aphasia. For example, expecting a person who has syntactic encoding problems (e.g., Broca's aphasia) to combine verb symbols to communicate an event sequence may put an unmanageable burden on the person's syntactic formulation skills. Similarly, asking individuals with severe aphasia to use a typing keyboard or multilevel symbol system to access vocabulary would probably be beyond their linguistic skills. Garrett and Beukelman (1992) and Garrett (1996) described a system for matching communicators to specific strategies. Regardless of the type of assessment protocol used, it is extremely important to match communicators' skills to the demands of the AAC intervention.

Access Issues   In general, it is important to keep physical access demands to a minimum for the person with aphasia. In practical terms, this may mean avoiding systems with certain features that hamper accessibility. People who are hemiplegic and ambulatory may not be able to carry a device that is larger than a wallet or that weighs more than a pound because of the threat to balance. Instead, it may be useful to develop multiple systems—a small, portable low-technology communication wallet or notebook when the communicator is going to walk and a larger, heavier high-technology system for use at a stationary location in the home. It is important to ask communicators about where and how they will be using their system and attend to all physical access issues before initiating an AAC intervention.

Information Storage and Access   At times, communicators with aphasia may demonstrate the need for a large number of messages. However, because of memory or visual constraints, they may not be able to sift through this available repertoire of messages in an effective manner. It may be helpful to keep in mind that the more steps that are involved in accessing information, the more likely it is that the individual will forget the purpose of the interaction or the target message or word. Therefore, the first principle of information storage is to assess how many steps an individual with aphasia is able to execute before forgetting the target message. The Multimodal Communication Screening Tool (Garrett, 1997a, 1997b; Garrett & Beukelman, 1998) may help the clinician to measure this ability in a more standardized manner. This tool assesses whether people with aphasia can identify pictures of nouns and actions by name or concept, search multiple pages for messages, identify written phrases needed to conduct a pharmacy transaction, and answer "where" questions by pointing to a map or the first letter of the location's name.

In terms of specific system modifications, it may be helpful to minimize any need for the individual to access messages via a menu system. Rather than use keyboard commands to access messages, touch screen access may be a more effective method. However, for communicators who cannot recall the location of stored messages, a paper storage system (e.g., notebook, communication board, wallet) may be more appropriate than a "hidden page" dynamic screen system because the individual can always resort to a manual search for the desired information. In addition, in low-technology systems such as notebooks, key information can always be indexed with tabs or dividers for easier access.

Information storage always represents a balance among message availability, cognitive complexity, and visual density. Having an adequate number of messages available may crowd the display, and the communicator then cannot quickly scan the information for the target icon or message. In general, it is important to avoid crowding a display. For people with visual field cuts, vertical displays or colored borders may be of assistance. For individuals who have minimal cognitive ability to sort through choices and initiate a message, plus a concomitant visual field cut, the written choice conversation strategy (Garrett & Beukelman, 1995) may be the most effective.

Visual/Symbolic Representation   Cognitively mismatched visual representations of message meanings lead to unsuccessful system use by communicators with aphasia. The following are some ways in which visual representations can be enhanced to decrease the cognitive processing demands for communicators with aphasia:

- Use visual linkages and associations where appropriate (e.g., arrows, color coding).
- Provide idiosyncratic symbol enhancements to locate a message (e.g., coupon tab for grocery store page).

- Use graphic timelines to represent episodic information (e.g., life events).
- Use graphic scales to represent qualitative information (e.g., how much, how long, how good).
- Provide circular displays for clock time and seasons.
- Use photographs representing scenes or connected events to augment storytelling vocabulary or to evoke concepts and ideas—it may not be necessary to use only single object representations.
- Encourage the communicator with aphasia to choose or edit the location of symbols and messages.
- Keep symbols in the same locations.
- Evaluate the communicator's ability to understand abstract symbol representations (e.g., lightning bolt symbol for "fast") before including them on a display.

After a level of representation has been selected to match the communicator's capabilities, information must then be organized in a complete display for different kinds of systems (e.g., multipage, multilevel, single message, symbol sequencing systems). This may be a particularly important consideration for individuals with less severe aphasia who use multimodal communication systems containing a large number of vocabulary items and messages. However, little research exists on the best means of visually representing and organizing various kinds of messages for people with aphasia. In lieu of more substantial guidelines from controlled investigations, the following methods for organizing visual symbols may be possibilities for individual communicators:

- Visual-spatial: maps, family trees, and scales for qualitative concepts
- Categorical lists: may work best for names, places, and items related to needs
- Chronological/episodic: may work for life stories
- Alphabetical order: for concepts, items, and names
- Preferential order: favorite topics, friends, stories, and jokes
- Environmental/topical: all phrases necessary for communicating in a specific situation or conversation contained on one page

Vocabulary and Message Selection   Sigafoos and York (1991) described vocabulary selection as an analysis of demands and opportunities in specific environments. Vocabulary and message selection does not attempt to replace all language forms but rather targets words and phrases the individual needs to accomplish functional tasks and to participate in meaningful interactions. This process, also termed an ecological inventory, accomplishes the twofold task of reducing cognitive-linguistic demands (by narrowing the field of possible messages) and deriving relevant vocabulary and messages for the adult with aphasia's communication system. Following are specific procedures related to vocabulary and message selection:

- Carefully inventory the communication needs of the person with aphasia by interviewing the individual and significant others.
- To identify specific vocabulary, it may be useful to divide messages into four purposes of communication described by Light (1988): needs, social closeness, information transfer, and social etiquette.
- Task-analyze the individual's environments for messages needed to complete specific activities. Consider the entire sequence of communication acts needed to participate in the activity. For example, if an individual wishes to go to the horse races and place bets, the following terms may be needed: "Exacta," "Trifecta," "Stretch him out," "Needs a new jockey," "Retire that horse," "I hit the jackpot!"
- Inventory situations that would allow individuals with aphasia to participate in communication activities relevant to their peer group (Stuart, 1995): storytelling about the good old days, telling funny anecdotes, giving advice to children, sharing opinions about politics, bragging, and commenting and exclaiming during an activity (e.g., hollering "Strike" while watching bowlers).

Cognitive Processing Issues   A clinician's rule-of-thumb should be to minimize the amount of information the person with aphasia has to process at any given time. The following suggestions provide preliminary guidelines:

- Use holophrastic (i.e., all-in-one) messages versus requiring individuals to combine symbols.
- Teach communicators to use one overlay or page successfully before proceeding to additional pages.
- Assess an individual's potential to become a multimodal, strategic "searcher of information." If the communicators with aphasia cannot recall where information is stored, consider providing them with a tangible, externalized system so that they can physically search (e.g., wallet versus computer)

and recognize the message rather than having to recall its exact location.

- If the individual does not initiate communication, consider shifting to a strategy in which the partner initiates the communication act and constrains the amount of semantic processing that is needed (e.g., written choice conversation; see Garrett & Beukelman, 1992, 1995).
- Gradually introduce multimodal components, and teach each component to mastery in actual communication situations (e.g., a "teach/edit as you go" approach) rather than overwhelm the communicator with all components at once.
- Provide external reminders (e.g., cue cards) regarding which modality is most appropriate in a given situation.
- Avoid taxing the spelling skills of the person with aphasia, but provide access to spelling for opportunities when it may work, especially for automatic messages such as names of family members or sports teams.
- Provide explicit feedback regarding the communicator's success, ability to maintain listeners' interest, or efficiency as appropriate. Develop feedback loops to the individual's own metacognitive system whenever possible.
- Provide context for communication activities requiring displaced thinking (i.e., removed in time, space, or perspective), such as props for discussions about gardening, scrapbooks for storytelling, headlines for conversations about current events.
- Encourage communication partners to summarize what they have understood by writing key words on a flowchart or in sequence.

Instructional Issues/Developing Integrated Communication Skills
Yanak and Light (1991) stated that if the focal point of AAC intervention is to improve interaction, then opportunities for interactions must become integral parts of the treatment process. It is important to teach communicators to *use* their strategies in meaningful contexts from the beginning of the therapeutic process rather than at the conclusion of the therapy program. Specific teaching techniques include developing scripts for conversations or transactions in the community, role playing these interactions, videotaping the communicators and reviewing their performance, or providing "on-the-spot" cuing.

When first teaching the person with aphasia to switch to an alternate modality, it may also be beneficial to include communication acts that the individual can do automatically rather than expect volitional, generative speech acts. For example, begin with "introduction scripts," in which people with aphasia can access overlearned, familiar information about themselves in their AAC system. Or, teach people with aphasia how to greet others and explain their communication strategy with a simple VOCA at the beginning of a telephone interaction. This is also a good opportunity to gradually introduce them to operational skills, such as turning on the telephone's speaker and the VOCA.

A primary treatment objective should be to assist people with aphasia to become metacommunicative, or conscious about the effectiveness of their own communication and the comprehension of their conversational partner. Encourage communicators to plan ahead for specific interactions by asking, "What strategy would you use?" Challenge them to evaluate their effectiveness by asking, "How well did you do? What could you have done better?" It may also be important to prepare the communicator with aphasia to deal with the demands of everyday interactions in a structured, progressive manner. In the therapeutic setting, a clinician can tax the communicator with additional discourse demands, such as simulating when a partner does not understand, interrupts, requests more information, or adds information that was not included in the practiced script.

Finally, it is often good practice to involve family and other important communication partners in practiced exchanges with AAC strategies early in the intervention process. Clinicians can take advantage of natural opportunities to communicate that occur in conjunction with family activities, such as talking to grandchildren about failing grades, giving advice to a daughter before her wedding, or asking about an upcoming move to a new home.

R.H.'s Story   The following case report illustrates many of the cognitive challenges that people with aphasia may face when learning to use AAC strategies. However, the authors acknowledge that some components of the following intervention may not be supported in health care reimbursement schemes. Research needs to determine whether these skills can be acquired more efficiently using modifications of this intervention.

R.H. was a well-educated businessman who sustained a massive thrombotic stroke in the region of the middle cerebral artery when he was in his late sixties. For 2 years following his stroke, he did not speak as a result of severe aphasia and co-existing apraxia of speech. Expressive output consisted mainly of repetitive stereotypies (e.g., "nu-nu-nu") and occasional instances of automatic speech. Receptive language skills were moderately impaired although much improved within highly contextual situations. R.H. could sign his name in automatic contexts but demonstrated no other generative writing ability. Reading was a strength; he demonstrated an ability to comprehend 60%–70% of factual information in short, highly contextual paragraphs. Single-word reading comprehension was less accurate. Testing with the Western Aphasia Battery (Kertesz, 1982) yielded an aphasia quotient of 13.5 of 100 possible points. R.H. was not ambulatory except for very short distances during transfers. He continued to live at home with his wife and received assistance from caregivers for approximately 16 hours per day.

Phase I: Group Communication Therapy   One-and-a-half years following the onset of aphasia, R.H. attended the authors' university outpatient clinic, where he participated in weekly group therapy sessions for 1 year. During that time, treatment focused on increasing R.H.'s ability to interact with other group participants through verbal and nonverbal means. R.H. increased his ability to take turns and ask questions by gesturing to others, answering yes-and-no with an upturned and downturned thumb or by nodding and shaking his head. He also successfully participated in topical conversations about current events by pointing to written word and phrase choices generated by communication partners. The clinician attempted to introduce a communication notebook that contained family information, yes-or-no cards, and customized messages for thematic group activities. However, after 1 year of participation in weekly group therapy (i.e., 2.5 years postonset), R.H. still did not attempt to use this system during communication opportunities unless cued or prompted.

Despite R.H.'s limited success with using an external means of communication, he demonstrated consistent increases in his ability to participate in group interactions by gesturing and vocalizing "what?" and "no." He increased the frequency with which he reached for other group member's written notes or tangible topic setters, such as photographs, apparently in an effort to sustain a topic or comment. He also showed a gradually improving ability to locate key information in printed articles that were discussed by the group, and often answered the question more rapidly than did other participants by pointing to words embedded in the text. General awareness of group routines appeared improved, and he frequently protested by vocalizing loudly when routines were violated. However, he began to refuse to attempt verbal communication. When queried with written choices, R.H. indicated that speech was too difficult and that he no longer wished to try imitating words.

Phase II: Assessment   Because R.H. showed continued interest and awareness of group communication activities, a second attempt at developing an appropriate AAC system was initiated. The clinicians theorized that a stored information-focused set of VOCA messages would allow R.H. to share more specific information in topical discussions about personal events or news stories. The following assessment tasks were implemented: 1) a thorough Aphasia Needs Assessment (Garrett &

Beukelman, 1998), in which the clinicians catalogued situations and messages that R.H. and his family determined were of primary importance, and 2) a Multimodal Communication Screening Test for Aphasia (Garrett & Beukelman, 1998). This latter tool assesses whether people with aphasia can identify pictures of nouns and actions by name or concept, search multiple pages for messages, identify written phrases needed to cònduct a pharmacy transaction, and answer "where" questions by pointing to a map or to the first letter of the location's name. R.H. located approximately 60% of target concepts when presented individually or in a simple sequence. He also searched multiple pages given minimal cues or suggestions. He was not able to identify how to represent a complex concept with a series of symbols and did not point to the first letter to communicate locations or personal names. On the basis of this information, the intervention team, including family members and R.H., decided to try using a limited-message VOCA in structured therapy activities.

Phase III: VOCA Intervention   R.H. was first introduced to a VOCA in group therapy. The VOCA, a six-level digitized voice output device, was programmed with a set of 10–15 familiar conversational messages on a single level. Messages consisted of a greeting (e.g., "Hello"), conversational question (e.g., "How are you?"), choice for responses (e.g., "good," "so-so," and "bad"), and three to four topical messages pertaining to a personal event or a current event. They were graphically represented with key words on a single 32-message color-coded paper display. R.H. reviewed the messages with his clinician prior to each group session using a situational-question drill format (e.g., "How would you say...?") and contextual cues and props. During group conversational interactions, the clinician provided a variable amount of cuing to prompt R.H. to participate with his VOCA when conversational opportunities arose. Initial observations during this phase of the intervention were as follows:

- R.H. frequently initiated questions and comments without prompting.
- R.H. typically accessed a series of related messages without stopping for a conversational partner's response. For example, he told about gambling trips by activating four sentence-length messages in a row. Although each message was relevant and appropriate, this sometimes interfered with conversational interaction, particularly during the opening sequence when partners wished to answer or ask follow-up questions.
- R.H. appeared to visually search the display for messages. He correctly located message areas about 60% of the time, such as

those devoted to conversational questions versus those pertaining to news. However, he made frequent errors when
attempting to answer questions with a field of semantically
similar messages (e.g., "good," "so-so," "bad," "daughter,"
"son").

- R.H. frequently interrupted others' conversational attempts
  by activating messages randomly, apparently in an attempt to
  regain the conversational floor.
- Other group members responded positively to R.H.'s VOCA
  communication efforts, often applauding when he initiated a
  conversation or responding contingently to his message.

Phase IV: Instruction in Conversational Use of the VOCA   For 3
weeks, R.H. participated in twice weekly individual instructional sessions that focused on using the VOCA in a more appropriate conversational manner. At the beginning of each session, the clinician reviewed
four written instructions with him: 1) Start the conversation using your
machine; 2) ask questions or share your news; 3) then wait for her to
answer, and listen to what she says; and 4) then pick a good answer—
no guessing. The clinician then practiced conversing with R.H., stopping when he randomly activated messages or did not wait for a
response. The clinician also told him when a message was confusing,
and R.H. was then encouraged to select a more appropriate response.
The final two instructional sessions were videotaped. Analysis
revealed that conversational pausing had improved to 75% accuracy
and that R.H. selected messages with 70% accuracy. He continued to
use the system during subsequent clinical activities while potential for
long-term use of the VOCA was further evaluated.

Phase V: Multilevel High-Technology System   R.H. continued to
receive speech-language therapy into a second year. He and his wife
expressed an interest in pursuing more advanced AAC technology to
increase his communication options in other environments. The clinical team decided to investigate the usefulness of a multilevel dynamic
screen communication system with internal programming capability
for several reasons: 1) R.H.'s wife and caregiver expressed concern that
changing paper overlays would be too confusing, and the team then
hypothesized that single key access to a different message level might
be beneficial; 2) it was thought that a combination of picture symbol
and text representation might increase R.H.'s ability to locate messages
with more accuracy and timeliness; 3) size and arrangement of symbols
could be customized more easily; and 4) voice output appeared to benefit R.H. in two ways—it provided feedback regarding his message
selection, and the inherent power of voice output messages helped him
gain the attention of a communication partner. Concerns included

1) R.H.'s ability to recall symbol/message locations that were stored on "invisible" pages within the dynamic screen system, 2) R.H.'s ability to use the system in a conversational manner, and 3) R.H.'s ability to comprehend synthesized speech messages.

During the initial system trial, four pages were designed. Each page contained 9–15 messages. All messages were represented with written text, representational symbols, or a combination of the two. Pages were color coded; each symbol was then embedded in a background color corresponding to the page color. This also aided in improving figure–ground contrast. Pages included R.H.'s "conversation and news" page, "about R.H" page (i.e., personal history page), a "numbers" page, and a "needs" page. Pages added in the next 4 weeks included a "Jeopardy!" game page, a "drugstore" page, a "telephone call" page, and a "stock market" page. R.H. was instructed in the following sequence: 1) review individual symbols through situational question drills, 2) practice using scripted role play with the clinician, and 3) practice interacting in group activities or with a novel partner.

After 4 weeks of intervention, R.H. showed both abilities and challenges when communicating with the multilevel communication device. He demonstrated frequent semantic confusions when choosing between items that had some conceptual similarity (e.g., light bulb and battery). He also appeared to have some difficulty searching for items in the upper-right quadrant of the display, which the clinicians theorized was perhaps due to a residual visual field cut. To manage these challenges, several changes in message options and instructional strategies were made. Within each page, messages that appeared to be semantically related were either deleted or reorganized. On several occasions, additional contextual information was added to the output message to clarify the symbol. For example, the spoken message "bad" on the conversational page was enhanced to say, "I feel really awful today." In addition, during the instructional review at the beginning of each session, the clinician used props to enhance the situational context for each message. For example, to teach R.H. to communicate the message, "I need a refill on my prescription," she placed an empty pill bottle on the table and then said, "Oh no, looks like you're out of medication. What message would work to get more?" To compensate for the visual field cut, a bright orange guide strip was affixed to the right side of the device's visual display; R.H. was then cued to "look all the way to the right until you see the orange stripe."

R.H. also demonstrated some initial difficulties with recalling the location of five "hidden" pages stored on alternate levels. However, given repeated opportunities to access pages to communicate and cues to attend to the color of the page symbol, he demonstrated approximately

70% success at locating pages after six sessions of instruction with only minimal to intermittent cuing. R.H. also continued to require instruction to purposefully choose appropriate messages instead of randomly activating them in an apparent effort to gain or maintain the conversational floor. The clinicians hypothesized that part of this randomness was a result of the cognitive demands of selecting vocabulary from a set of messages that was not visually structured to support a natural conversational flow. Choosing questions and answers from various parts of the screen on a turn-by-turn basis appeared to overload R.H.'s cognitive and semantic processing abilities. Therefore, each screen was designed in the following manner: Each topic was segmented into two or three subtopics, and, within each of these subtopics, messages were sequenced vertically according to conversational order (see Figure 2).

During the 2 weeks following this cognitive-semantic simplification of the message display, R.H. showed noticeably more rapid and accurate conversational turns. He purposefully selected conversational subtopics, and then could select multiple concepts using a visual–sequential strategy rather than through semantic skills alone.

After 12 sessions of clinical instruction and practice with the multilevel communication system, R.H. participated in four conversations and two group role plays. In each of these communication activities, he showed good ability to initiate questions, comment, share several items of news in a sequence, clarify a message, confirm messages by saying "yes" or "no," and, in general, interact with others in a mutually participatory manner. Initial observations suggest that with the continued implementation of the cognitive and linguistic modifications described earlier, as well as ongoing contextual instruction and role playing, R.H. will be able to use the system to participate more fully in a number of important communication activities.

SUMMARY

The purpose of this review of cognitive-linguistic challenges inherent in AAC strategies is not to warn clinicians away from trying to implement AAC with communicators who have aphasia. Instead, the message is that it is critical to match strategies to the individual's needs and skills. Many intervention "failures" may have occurred because clinicians expected people with significant cognitive-linguistic challenges to master a complex, novel piece of technology and use it in a manner similar to when they communicated by speaking. To illustrate, if an individual shows only basic environmental awareness, it is inappropriate to select a high-technology system that requires sequential

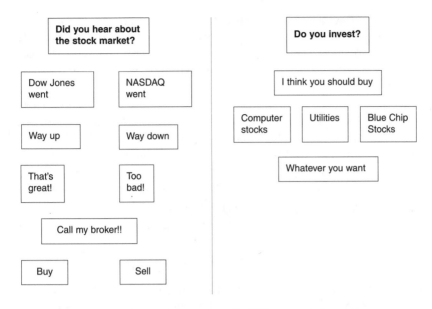

Figure 2.   Sample story-order message arrangement for R.H.'s communication system.

cognitive operations (e.g., spelling, combining words). Clinicians and researchers need to continue to discuss and research successful system designs and teaching strategies. Perhaps more functional communication successes can be achieved if clinicians revisit instructional approaches for technology and consider teaching AAC skills within personally relevant communication activities based on real-life contexts and needs. Communicators with aphasia will ultimately teach clinicians what works, and clinicians must continue to observe and listen to their individual successes to construct a more comprehensive and logical intervention philosophy for AAC and aphasia in general.

Directions for Future Research

Clearly, the fields of AAC and aphasia need to continue the process of analyzing the demands of communication strategies for individuals with aphasia. It is our hope that the preceding discussion assists in germinating these lines of investigation and research. Specific research questions might include

1. How many operational steps can people with aphasia complete before forgetting a target message?
2. How efficiently do people with aphasia communicate target messages that vary across a continuum of abstraction?

3. How do communicators with aphasia compare in their ability to search and access messages represented on tangible display systems (e.g., notebooks, communication devices with paper overlays) and dynamic screen/hidden message pages?

4. How do different message representations and symbol sets (e.g., key words, phrases, representative picture symbols, pictures or photographs of entire scenarios, videotapes) affect a communicator's ability to access information in meaningful situations?

5. What types of teaching strategies assist people with aphasia to communicate messages in real-life contexts?

6. What are the long-term AAC use patterns among communicators with aphasia?

7. How does skilled AAC use affect functional outcomes?

Ultimately, the final goal of all interventions in aphasia is to address the needs of the whole person and to acknowledge that, as a communicator, he or she has a rich history of experiences and feelings to share. It is our hope that continuing analyses of the demands imposed by AAC strategies ultimately allow people with aphasia to express these experiences and feelings more successfully and to participate more fully in meaningful life activities.

REFERENCES

Bailey, S. (1983). Blissymbolics and aphasia therapy: A case study. In C. Code & D. Muller (Eds.), *Aphasia therapy* (pp. 178–186). London: Edward Arnold.

Barba, G.D., Frasson, E., Mantovan, M.C., Gallo, A., & Denes, G. (1996). Semantic and episodic memory in aphasia. *Neuropsychologica, 34,* 361–367.

Bellaire, K., Georges, J., & Thompson, C. (1991). Establishing functional communication board use for nonverbal aphasic subjects. In T.E. Prescott (Ed.), *Clinical aphasiology* (pp. 219–227). Austin, TX: PRO-ED.

Beukelman, D., & Mirenda, P. (1998). *Augmentative and alternative communication: Management of severe communication disorders in children and adults* (2nd ed.). Baltimore: Paul H. Brookes Publishing Co.

Beukelman, D., Yorkston, K., & Dowden, P. (1985) *Communication augmentation: A casebook of clinical management.* San Diego: College-Hill.

Bliss, C.K. (1965). *Symantography: Blissymbolics.* Sydney: Semantography Publishers.

Bradshaw, J.L., & Sherlock, D. (1982). Bugs and faces in the two visual fields: The analytic/holistic processing dichotomy and task sequencing. *Cortex, 17,* 211–226.

Chapey, R. (1983). Language-based cognitive abilities in adult aphasia: Rationale for intervention. *Journal of Communication Disorders, 16,* 405–424.

Chapey, R. (1986). An introduction to language intervention strategies in adult aphasia. In R. Chapey (Ed.), *Language intervention strategies in adult aphasia.* Philadelphia: Lippincott, Williams & Wilkins.

Cohen, R., & Woll, G. (1981). Facets of analytical processing in aphasia: A picture ordering task. *Cortex, 17,* 557–569.

Darley, F. (1982). *Aphasia.* Philadelphia: W.B. Saunders.

DeRuyter, F., Kennedy, M., Doyle, M., & Donoghue, K. (1990, May). *Augmentative communication and stroke rehabilitation: Who is doing what and do the data tell the whole story?* Invited presentation to the National Stroke Rehabilitation Conference, Boston.

Fitch-West, J. (1983). Aphasia: Cognitive considerations. *Topics in Language Disorders, 3,* 49–66.

Fried-Oken, M. (1995). Story telling as an augmentative communication approach for a man with severe apraxia of speech and expressive aphasia. *Augmentative and Alternative Communication, 4,* 3–4.

Friedman, A., & Polson, M.C. (1981). The hemispheres as independent processing systems: Limited capacity processing and cerebral specialization. *Journal of Experimental Psychology: Human Perceptual Performance, 7,* 1031–1058.

Garrett, K. (1993). *Changes in the conversational participation of individuals with severe aphasia given three types of partner support.* Unpublished doctoral dissertation, University of Nebraska–Lincoln.

Garrett, K. (1995). Expanding expressive communication options for a person with severe aphasia. *ASHA Special Interest Division 12 Newsletter: Augmentative and Alternative Communication, 4,* 5–7.

Garrett, K. (1996, August). *AAC Interventions and aphasia: Cognitive-linguistic considerations.* Miniseminar presented at the International Society for Augmentative and Alternative Communication (ISAAC) Biennial Convention, Vancouver, British Columbia, Canada.

Garrett, K. (1997a). *Multimodal communication screening task for persons with aphasia: Booklet* [On-line]. Available http://aac.unl.edu/asm/main.html

Garrett, K. (1997b). *Multimodal communication screening task for persons with aphasia: Score sheet* [On-line]. Available http://aac.unl.edu/score/html

Garrett, K., & Beukelman, D.R. (1992). Augmentative communication approaches for persons with severe aphasia. In K. Yorkston (Ed.), *Augmentative communication in the medical setting* (pp. 245–337). Tucson, AZ: Communication Skill Builders.

Garrett, K., & Beukelman, D.R. (1995). Changes in the interaction patterns of an individual with severe aphasia given three types of partner support. In M. Lemme (Ed.), *Clinical aphasiology* (pp. 237–251). Austin, TX: PRO-ED.

Garrett, K., & Beukelman, D.R. (1998). Adults with severe aphasia. In D.R. Beukelman & P. Mirenda (Eds.), *Augmentative and alternative communication: Management of severe communication disorders in children and adults* (2nd ed., pp. 465–499). Baltimore: Paul H. Brookes Publishing Co.

Garrett, K., Beukelman, D.R., & Low-Morrow, D. (1989). A comprehensive augmentative communication system for an adult with Broca's aphasia. *Augmentative and Alternative Communication, 5,* 55–61.

Glass, A., Gazzaniga, M., & Premack, D. (1975). Artificial language training in global aphasics. *Neuropsychologia, 11,* 95–103.

Goodglass, H. (1993). *Understanding aphasia.* San Diego: Academic Press.

Goodglass, H., & Kaplan, E. (1983). *The assessment of aphasia and related disorders* (2nd ed.). Philadelphia: Lea & Febiger.

Haarmann, H.J., Just, M.A., & Carpenter, P.A. (1997). Aphasic sentence comprehension as a resource deficit: A computational approach. *Brain and Language, 59*, 76–120.

Horner, J., Loverso, F., & Gonzalez Rothi, L. (1994). Models of aphasia treatment. In R. Chapey (Ed.), *Language intervention strategies in adult aphasia* (pp. 135–145). Philadelphia: Lippincott, Williams & Wilkins.

Hux, K., Beukelman, D., & Garrett, K. (1994). In R. Chapey (Ed.), *Language intervention strategies in adult aphasia* (pp. 338–357). Philadelphia: Lippincott, Williams & Wilkins.

Jackson, H. (1878). On affections of speech from disease of the brain. *Brain, 1*, 304–330.

Johannsen-Horbach, H., Cegla, B., Mager, V., & Schempp, B. (1985). Treatment of global aphasia with a nonverbal communication system. *Brain and Language, 24*, 74–82.

Just, M.A., & Carpenter, P.A. (1992). A capacity theory of comprehension: Individual differences in working memory. *Psychological Review, 99*, 122–149.

Kagan, A. (1998). Supported conversation for adults with aphasia: Methods and resources for training conversation partners. *Aphasiology, 12*, 816–830.

Kahneman, D. (1973). *Attention and effort.* Upper Saddle River, NJ: Prentice-Hall.

Kahneman, D., & Triesman, A. (1984). Changing views of attention and automaticity. In R. Parasuraman & D.R. Davies (Eds.), *Varieties of attention* (pp. 29–61). Orlando, FL: Academic Press.

Kertesz, A. (1982). *Western Aphasia Battery.* New York: Grune & Stratton.

Kimelman, M.D.Z. (1999, June). *Memory load, prosody, and auditory comprehension in aphasia.* Paper presented at the Annual Clinical Aphasiology Conference, Key West, FL.

Kolk, H., & Hartsuiker, R.J. (1999). Aphasia, prefrontal dysfunction, and the use of word-order strategies. *Behavioral and Brain Sciences, 22*, 103–104.

Kraat, A. (1990). Augmentative and alternative communication: Does it have a future in aphasia rehabilitation? *Aphasiology, 4*, 321–338.

Koul, R., & Harding. R. (1998). Identification and production of graphic symbols by individuals with aphasia: Efficacy of a software application. *Augmentative and Alternative Communication, 14*, 11–23.

Light, J. (1988). Interaction involving individuals using augmentative and alternative communication systems: State of the art and future directions. *Augmentative and Alternative Communication, 4*, 66–82.

Light, J., & Lindsay, P. (1991). Cognitive science and augmentative and alternative communication. *Augmentative and Alternative Communication, 7*, 186–203.

Lyon, J. (1992). Communication use and participation in life for adults with aphasia in natural settings: The scope of the problem. *American Journal of Speech-Language Pathology, 1*, 7–14.

Loverso, F.L., & Prescott, T. E. (1981). The effect of alerting signals on left brain damaged (aphasic) and normal subjects accuracy and response time to visual stimuli. In R.H. Brookshire (Ed.), *Clinical aphasiology conference proceedings* (pp. 55–67). Minneapolis, MN: BRK Publishers.

McNeil, M.R. (1983). Aphasia: Neurologic considerations. *Topics in Language Disorders, 3*, 1–19.

McNeil, M.R., & Kimelman, M.D.Z. (1986). Toward an integrative information-processing structure of auditory comprehension and processing in adult aphasia. *Seminars in Speech and Language, 7*, 123–146.

McNeil, M.R., Odell, K., & Tseng, C.H. (1991). Toward the integration of resource allocation into a general model of aphasia. In T. Prescott (Ed.), *Clinical aphasiology* (pp. 21–39). Austin, TX: PRO-ED.

Mesulam, M.M. (1981). A cortical network for directed attention and unilateral neglect. *Annals of Neurology, 10,* 309–325.

Navon, D., & Gopher, D. (1979). On the economy of the human processing system. *Psychological Review, 56,* 214–255.

Nicholas, M., & Helm-Estabrooks, N. (1990). Aphasia. *Seminars in Speech and Language: The Efficacy of Speech-Language Pathology Intervention, 11,* 135–144.

Ostergaard, A.L., & Meudell, P.R. (1984). Immediate memory span, recognition memory for subspan series of words, and serial position effects in recognition memory for supraspan series of verbal and nonverbal items in Broca's and Wernicke's aphasia. *Brain and Language, 22,* 1–13.

Peach, R.K., Newhoff, M., & Rubin, S.S. (1993). Attention in aphasia as revealed by event-related potentials: A preliminary study. In M.L. Lemme (Ed.), *Clinical aphasiology* (pp. 345–356). Austin, TX: PRO-ED.

Porch, B. (1981). *Porch Index of Communicative Ability* (3rd ed.). Palo Alto, CA: Consulting Psychologists Press.

Purdy, M., Duffy, R., & Coelho, C. (1994). An investigation of the communicative use of trained symbols following multimodality training. *Clinical Aphasiology, 22,* 345–356.

Robey, R. (1994). The efficacy of treatment for aphasic persons: A meta-analysis. *Brain and Language, 47,* 582–608.

Schuell, H. (1965). *The Minnesota Test for Differential Diagnosis of Aphasia.* Minneapolis: University of Minnesota Press.

Schuell, H., Jenkins, J., & Jimenez-Pabon, E. (1964). *Aphasia in adults.* New York: Harper Medical Division.

Sigafoos, J., & York, J. (1991). Using ecological inventories to promote functional communication. In J. Reichle, J. York, & J. Sigafoos (Eds.), *Implementing augmentative and alternative communication* (pp. 61–70). Baltimore: Paul H. Brookes Publishing Co.

Simmons-Mackie, N.N. (1998). In support of supported conversation for adults with aphasia. *Aphasiology, 12,* 831–838.

Simmons-Mackie, N.N., & Damico, J.S. (1995). Communicative competence in aphasia: Evidence from compensatory strategies. In M.L. Lemme (Ed.), *Clinical aphasiology* (pp. 95–106). Austin, TX: PRO-ED.

Stark, J. (1988). Aspects of automatic versus controlled processing, monitoring, metalinguistic tasks, and related phenomena in aphasia. In W. Dressler & J. Stark (Eds.), *Linguistic analyses of aphasic language* (pp. 179–242). New York: Springer-Verlag.

Stuart, S. (1995). Expanding communicative participation using augmentative and alternative communication within a game playing activity for a man with severe aphasia. *Augmentative and Alternative Communication, 4,* 9–11.

Thorburn, L., Newhoff, M., & Rubin, S. (1995). Ability of subjects with aphasia to visually analyze written language, pantomime, and iconographic symbols. *American Journal of Speech-Language Pathology, 4,* 174–179.

Weinrich, M., McCall, D., Weber, C., Thomas, K., & Thornburg, L. (1995). Training on an iconic communication system for severe aphasia can improve natural language production. *Aphasiology, 9,* 343–364.

Weinrich, M., Steele, R., Carlson, G., & Kleczewska, M. (1989). Processing of visual syntax in a globally aphasic patient. *Brain and Language, 36,* 391–405.

Wepman, J., & Jones, L. (1961). *Studies in aphasia: An approach to testing. The Language Modalities Test for Aphasia.* Chicago: Education-Industry Service.

Yanak, K., & Light, J. (1991). Use of augmentative communication with persons with Broca's aphasia: A case study. *National Student Speech-Language-Hearing Association Journal, 19,* 27–34.

12

AAC and Dementia

Melanie Fried-Oken
Marie T. Rau
Barry S. Oken

In 1994, Franklin Silverman wrote a letter to the editor of *Augmentative and Alternative Communication* asking if augmentative and alternative communication (AAC) clinicians could help people with dementia. He described an initial survey he had conducted in which he sent a questionnaire to 100 certified speech-language pathologists working in medical settings, asking them if and how they provide AAC treatment to adults with dementia. Four of twenty-eight respondents indicated that AAC had helped their clients to some degree. Silverman challenged the AAC field to systematically explore the possibility of introducing AAC to adults with dementia. We take on this challenge in the following discussion. Our confidence is supported by Blackstone's (1996) suggestion that, as a group, AAC consumers, researchers, service providers, advocates, payers, educators, and manufacturers do, indeed, have the capability to respond to the challenges faced by older adults who have severe communication impairments.

This chapter is divided into two parts. First, we define and describe diagnosis, symptomatology, and medical management issues associated with dementia. Considerable attention is paid to the communication impairments seen in progressive dementia. Second, with the basic clinical observations in place, we direct the reader to questions that have not yet been explored by the AAC community for people with dementia. This chapter is a collaborative effort among experts from three clinical fields: a leading clinician in adult AAC issues, an expert in communication impairments associated with dementia and a behavioral neurologist. Together, we use our different perspectives to reflect on clinical issues in this unexplored AAC area.

MEDICAL DIAGNOSIS
AND MANAGEMENT OF ADULTS WITH DEMENTIA

Dementia is a medical syndrome characterized by an acquired, chronic cognitive impairment (Cummings & Benson, 1992). The cognitive impairment must encompass impairments in at least two of the commonly assessed domains: memory, language, attention, visuospatial function, praxis, and executive or frontal lobe functions. Change in social-emotional behavior and personality is considered an additional domain. Memory is required to be one of the impairments in the *Diagnostic and Statistical Manual of Mental Disorders, Fourth Edition,* (DSM-IV; American Psychiatric Association, 1994) criteria for dementia. However, some people may not have memory impairments as part of the early cognitive changes, even though they are diagnosed with dementia. Frontal lobe dementia and vascular dementia fall into the category of neurodegenerative disease. The inclusion of impairments in at least two cognitive domains helps differentiate dementia from more specific syndromes, such as amnesia or aphasia syndromes, which have different, although partially overlapping, etiologies. The dementia syndrome needs to be differentiated from delirium, the acute syndrome of altered cognition usually associated with fluctuations in the level of arousal. Dementia is acquired; that is, the cognitive impairments represent a decline from prior level of functioning. This differentiates the syndrome from mental retardation and other developmental central nervous system (CNS) disorders. In fact, people with mental retardation may develop a dementing syndrome (Zigman, Schupf, Haveman, & Silverman, 1997). The DSM-IV dementia criteria also require there to be a significant impairment in social or occupational functioning, described as *activities of daily living* (ADL). This is an important criterion because neuropsychological testing of healthy older adults may reveal declines in many aspects of cognitive functioning independent of any overt disease. However, some people seek medical opinions very early in the course of a dementing illness when cognitive impairments may be relatively obvious but there is no decline in ADL or social function. Another important consideration in the differential diagnosis of dementia is the worried well—healthy older adults who are concerned about their cognitive functioning but perform within typical range for age and education on formal cognitive testing.

Dementia is an extremely common syndrome. The prevalence is age-dependent, increasing from about 1% at age 65 to almost 50% at age 90 (Jorm & Jolley, 1998). Given that the 85-years-and-older age group is the fastest-growing segment of the population, the prevalence of dementia will increase significantly in the 21st century (assuming that no scientific breakthroughs delay or prevent the onset of dementia). The cost of taking care of this number of people with dementia is enormous. In addition to the personal toll and the public health care costs of dementia, there is a major impact on the family and the primary caregiver, including higher levels of stress, depression, and mortality.

Differential Diagnosis of Dementia

There has been an attempt to categorize the various dementing syndromes into cortical and subcortical dementia (Cummings & Benson, 1984). Although this categorization is not perfect, grouping specific diseases into clusters can be helpful. It is important to realize that the terms *cortical dementia* and *subcortical dementia* help the clinician think about the clinical aspects of the dementia syndrome but may not be specific to lesion localization. *Cortical dementia* produces typical cortical syndromes of amnesia, aphasia, apraxia, and agnosia. Alzheimer's disease (AD) is considered a typical cortical dementia syndrome. The pathology is mostly in the cortex, although there may be some changes in subcortical gray matter as well. Other typical cortical dementia syndromes include Pick's disease and frontotemporal degeneration. *Subcortical dementia* is associated with significant slowness (both in reaction time and latencies to respond to questions) and by prominent impairments in attention as well as additional impairments in motor and gait function. The first description of subcortical dementia was related to progressive supranuclear palsy (PSP), a neurodegenerative disease in which most of the pathology is actually in the brain stem (Albert, Feldman, & Willis, 1974). Other conditions that produce subcortical dementia include AIDS (acquired immunodeficiency syndrome), encephalopathy, multiple sclerosis, and depression. Mixed types of dementia, in which the primary pathology can be either cortical or subcortical, include traumatic brain injury (TBI) and vascular dementia.

There are dozens of causes of dementia (Cummings & Benson, 1992; Tatemichi, Sacktor, & Mayeux, 1994; Whitehouse, 1993). The most common cause in the United States is AD, which accounts for 50% of new cases of dementia (Terry, Katzman, & Bick, 1994). Although most cases are sporadic, several genes are known to produce AD. In addition, essentially all people with Down syndrome develop the neuropathologic changes of AD by age 40, with many developing a clinical dementia syndrome after age 40 (Wisniewski, Wisniewski, & Wen, 1985). Vascular dementia is the second most common syndrome and is caused by large infarcts or by small, lacunar infarcts that primarily involve the deep white and gray matter (Tatemichi et al., 1994). The infarcts may be symptomatic, producing an acute hemiplegia, or relatively asymptomatic and silent. Infarcts in certain critical locations such as the genu of the internal capsule are more likely to produce a global dementia syndrome than strokes in other locations.

There are other, less common neurodegenerative diseases that cause dementia (Tatemichi et al., 1994), only some of which are mentioned here. Frontotemporal degeneration and Pick's disease usually present with dementing symptoms of frontal lobe dysfunction. Primary progressive aphasia and speech apraxia are clinical syndromes with variable pathologies. Several syndromes are associated with movement disorders. Individuals with longstanding idiopathic Parkinson's disease (PD) may develop dementia during the course of their illness (see Chapter 11). In diffuse Lewy body disease, Lewy bodies (the characteristic pathology of PD) are located throughout the cortex rather than being confined to the brain stem as in PD. PSP primarily affects subcortical structures and causes parkinsonism as well as a disorder of eye movements. Corticobasal degeneration often presents with an initial apraxia but is commonly associated with dementia. Creutzfeldt-Jakob disease (CJD) is a rapidly progressive dementing syndrome usually associated with myoclonus caused by an infectious protein particle or prion that, fortunately, is not easily transmitted. Huntington disease is an autosomal dominant genetic disorder that causes significant behavioral and cognitive changes in addition to the movement disorder (see Chapter 11).

Other medical causes of dementia include medications, such as CNS active drugs (e.g., benzodiazepines, neuroleptics, other sedative-hypnotics), depression, hypothyroidism, vitamin B_{12} deficiency, normal pressure hydrocephalus, CNS tumors, chronic CNS infections (e.g., syphilis, HIV [human immunodeficiency virus]), encephalopathy, electrolyte disturbances, certain heavy metals and industrial toxins, CNS trauma, anoxic encephalopathy, and certain organ failures with systemic symptoms (e.g., renal and hepatic failure, markedly reduced cardiac output).

Clinical Symptomology of Dementia

Although memory loss is the most common symptom of dementia, other cognitive domains are affected and may even be affected prior to memory (see, e.g., Cronin-Golomb, Corkin, & Rosen, 1993).

Memory Domain   Memory dysfunction is common to most of the dementing syndromes. Although there are many types of memory, an impairment in declarative memory or what Squire (1994) called *episodic memory* is usually the earliest manifestation of AD. The memory impairments are presumably related to pathology in the hippocampal memory system. The memory disorder affects the ability to learn new information, events, and their details but does not initially affect previously acquired memories (e.g., general knowledge, personal events from the remote past). The inability to learn new information affects material in all domains (e.g., verbal and visual) and, although of variable severity, affects the ability to learn how to use AAC strategies and devices.

Another memory system affected in the course of progressive dementing disease is *working memory,* the ability to maintain thoughts in mind for brief periods of time, such as looking up a telephone number and remembering the number until dialing the telephone. The term was used by Baddeley (1992b) to refer to the multiple operations that go on simultaneously in consciousness as we attempt to remember incoming information, synthesize this information, form intentions based on the information, and decide on a course of action. Engaging in a conversation, for example, requires an intact working memory system. Working memory is an aspect of short-term memory, and information in working memory is not necessarily stored in longer-term memory. Working memory impairments are less common early in AD as compared with the subcortical dementias. These impairments in the ability to hold information in mind for a few seconds are independent of the hippocampal memory system and cause impairments in processing long sentences. Although working memory may be considered part of attention, other impairments in attention may produce functional problems secondary to an inability to focus attention or avoid distracting stimuli, inability to sustain attention, and inability to shift attention. Environmental changes to address some of these impairments might produce improved function in individuals with dementia.

Semantic memory, or the memory for concepts and world knowledge, is an aspect of working memory and is dependent on the cortical sensory association areas of the brain. There is evidence that the apparent loss of semantic memory in individuals with AD may, in fact, represent impaired *access* to conceptual knowledge when more difficult tasks are used to tap semantic knowledge (Bayles, Tomoeda, Kaszniak, & Trosset, 1991). Associated with semantic memory is *lexical memory,* or memory for words and language. Another important memory system is *procedural memory,* or memory for skills, habits, and motor learning. The ability to ride a bicycle, ski, or play the piano is dependent on procedural memory.

In AD, there is a usual sequence of memory system deterioration. Episodic memory is affected early in the course of the disease, followed by working memory. Semantic memory and lexical memory are more resistant and tend to be affected later in the disease process, although procedural memory may be spared until quite late in the course of the disease.

Visuospatial Domain   Visuospatial impairments may occur as the earliest symptoms in individuals with pathology beginning in the parieto-occipital regions. Early complaints may center around inability to integrate visual information or visual agnosia, searching for objects, or reaching for objects. One individual, for example, complained of an inability to read signs while driving but could read the signs after stopping. Individuals with AD or CJD may experience this type of impairment. Focal sensory processing impairments such as hemi-anopia or hemi-inattention may be seen with strokes and also rarely with AD.

Frontal Lobe Domain   Impairments in frontal lobe functions, of which attention could be considered one, are commonly seen in Pick's disease and frontotemporal degeneration but may also be seen in AD. These frontal lobe impairments include apathy, social disinhibition, decreased social closeness, aggression, poor judgment, and inability to plan behavior. A person's insight into their cognitive impairment is variable but is usually impaired in most dementias. Thus, family members are more aware of the impairment than the individual is. This lack of insight may contribute to worse performance (e.g., while driving). Early in the course of the disease, many people with progressive dementia may have intact judgment and be able to make medical and fiscal decisions; at some point in the disease this is no longer possible.

Motor Processing Domain   Many people with dementia syndromes have atypical motor processing that may produce difficulty with communication in addition to the cognitive dysfunction. Apraxia is a common early symptom in corticobasal degeneration. Extrapyramidal signs such as bradykinesia, rigidity, and tremor are always present in individuals with PD and dementia, often present in Lewy body disease, and sometimes present with individuals with AD and individuals with vascular dementia. Myoclonus is part of the clinical diagnosis of CJD but also may be seen in AD. Prominent apraxia is seen in corticobasal ganglia degeneration and may be seen in AD and vascular dementia.

Language and Communication Domain   There is, indeed, a rich research base from which to describe the communication characteristics of people with dementia. AD is not only the most commonly diagnosed type of dementia but also has been the most frequently studied in terms of its effects on communication. For that reason, our discussion refers primarily to studies of the disruption of communication in AD, but is applicable to other dementing conditions as well.

From the evidence available, one can view the deterioration of language functions in AD as following generally predictable patterns that correspond to the early, middle, and later stages of the illness (Bayles & Tomoeda, 1995, 1998b; Bayles, Tomoeda & Trosset, 1992; Ripich, 1991). We use Bayles and Tomoeda's (1998b) descriptions of early-, middle-, and late-stage communication impairments, as well as residual cognitive-linguistic strengths or abilities to discuss the usefulness of AAC with this population of individuals. These researchers have summarized the results of their testing of hundreds of individuals with a probable diagnosis of AD.

Early-Stage Communication Impairments/Residual Abilities People with mild or early-stage AD experience somewhat diminished reading comprehension abilities, especially for longer material or material that requires making inferences. They have difficulty with composing letters and make uncharacteristic spelling errors in writing. Mild word-retrieval problems, somewhat reduced verbal output, and "forgetting what I want to say" are observed in expressive language. The word-finding difficulties of people with mild dementia have been well documented (Flicker, Ferris, Crook, & Bartus, 1987; Henderson, Mack, Freed, Kempler, & Andersen, 1990; Kirshner, Webb, & Kelly, 1984). Other researchers have provided evidence that discourse abilities may be among the earliest communication skills to be affected by AD. Chapman, Ulatowska, King, Johnson, and McIntire (1995), for example, found qualitative differences in the discourse coherence of people diagnosed with probable early AD and older individuals without dementia. Ripich (1994) also described breakdowns in discourse cohesion and coherence in early-stage dementia. It has been documented that, compaired with age- and education-matched controls, people with early-stage dementia have additional pragmatic impairments, such as poor topic maintenance, briefer but more frequent conversational turns, and more frequent requests for confirmation and clarification (Ripich & Terrell, 1988). In an investigation of conversational repair behaviors in individuals with AD, Orange, Lubinski, and Higginbotham (1996) found that people with early-stage dementia produced more requests for repairs than their family-member conversational partners.

In addition to linguistic problems, related impairments that may be present at this stage include distractibility and difficulty with concentrating, some confusion, disorientation in time, and difficulty with instrumental activities of daily living (IADLs), such as managing finances, housekeeping, and managing medications. At this stage, however, grammar and syntax are very much intact. Individuals with mild impairments can express their needs without assistance, converse, generate examples, describe objects and feelings, comprehend language, and answer multiple-choice and yes-or-no questions.

Middle-Stage Communication Impairments/Residual Abilities   In the middle stages of AD, an individual may show poor comprehension of written material and poor writing skills. There is noticeably reduced verbal output, and the person has difficulty with expressing a series of related ideas and staying "on track" in conversations. Several studies (Chenery & Murdoch, 1994; Mentis, Briggs-Whittaker, & Gramigna, 1995; Orange et al., 1996; Ripich & Terrell, 1988; Tomoeda & Bayles, 1993; Ulatowska et al., 1988; Watson, Chenery, & Carter, 1999) have examined the pragmatic impairments of heterogeneous (in terms of stage or severity level) groups of people with AD. These studies, although generally having very small numbers of individuals, have helped to describe the pragmatic bases for communication breakdown in dementia. Pragmatic problems noted have included reduced ability to change the topic of conversation and still maintain discourse flow; difficulty in contributing actively to the propositional development of a topic; breakdown in discourse cohesion and coherence (usually related to lack of appropriate referents); and omission of information related to setting, a complicating action, and a resolution when providing narratives for sequential pictures.

At this stage, more obvious related cognitive impairments are observed. The person affected is disoriented with regard to both time and place, is highly distractible, and has difficulty with handling more complex ADLs, such as dressing. There are a number of communication-related strengths, however, that can still be utilized to facilitate communication in the middle stages. The person with dementia still exhibits intact, or relatively intact, use of grammar and syntax; reads and comprehends single words; expresses his or her needs with some assistance from the communication partner; follows two-stage commands; and understands or benefits from gestural input to augment verbal information. Individuals in the middle stages of dementia can demonstrate good recognition memory for information that they cannot freely recall.

Late-Stage Residual Communication Abilities   Despite severe deterioration in the ability to generate relevant language and the loss of the ability to function independently, people with late-stage dementia may still produce some meaningful words and be able to read single words aloud. They may respond appropriately to questions and exhibit some of the social aspects of communication, such as responding to greetings. Despite a very limited attention span, they may attend to pleasant stimuli for a period of time. It is important to appreciate that language knowledge and conceptual knowledge may be well preserved until late in the course of the disease. This topic is discussed further in the next section.

The question of what underlies the communicative behaviors of people with dementia has been studied extensively. The current state of knowledge indicates that the primary reason for deterioration of communicative functions as dementia progresses is "serious, malignant memory deficits" (Bayles & Tomoeda, 1998b). Although earlier work in this area attributed the communicative disruptions seen in progressive dementia to deterioration of semantic memory (Chertkow & Bub, 1990; Huff, Corkin, & Growdon, 1986), more recent evidence suggests that the memory system most dramatically affected early in the disease is episodic memory, the long-term memory system discussed previously.

Dementia Assessment

The assessment of people with dementia focuses on several areas. A thorough history, a cognitive screening and more in-depth neuropsychological testing as needed, a general neurological examination, and screening laboratory tests, including a neuroimaging study, should be part of every dementia assessment. At every step in the assessment, it is important to differentiate between common age-related changes in neurologic function and pathologic changes relevant to the dementia diagnosis (Albert & Knoefel, 1994). Common age-related changes in vision and hearing (Kline & Scialfa, 1996) may produce some symptoms that can be confused with dementia, and, furthermore, these age-related changes need to be taken into account when considering AAC.

The first general area is the history. The clinician should probe into the acuteness of onset (vascular dementia is more likely to be of abrupt onset, but AD has an insidious onset). The history is important in determining to what extent the cognitive impairment is producing functional impairment. Several ADL scales can be used to determine functional impairment (Fillenbaum, 1988; Galasko et al., 1997). Questions regarding personal hygiene and eating should be posed, though these functions are usually unimpaired early in AD. Other clinical probes include the following: Does the person get lost while driving? Is he or she still able to manage a checkbook and pay monthly bills? Does he or she remember important appointments or conversations? The history also needs to probe for symptoms suggestive of the two most common reversible causes of dementia: depression and medications.

The second general area of assessment is the cognitive evaluation (for more detail, see Cummings & Benson, 1992). The evaluation can be relatively abbreviated. The Mini-Mental State Exam (MMSE) (Folstein, Folstein, & McHugh, 1975) is commonly used. Scores that fall below 24 on a scale of 0–30 show evidence of definite impairment. Unfortunately, the MMSE is not sensitive to frontal lobe functions or to very early-stage dementia. Other screening cognitive instruments that are commonly used include the Blessed Information-Memory-Concentration Test (Blessed, Tomlinson, & Roth, 1968), the Neurobehavioral Cognitive Status Exam (Kiernan, Mueller, Langston, & Van Dyke, 1987) and the Alzheimer Disease Assessment Scale–Cognitive subscale (Rosen, Mohs, & Davis, 1984). In general, the cognitive screening should include probes into all of the previously noted domains that are potentially impaired. Particular emphasis should be placed on new learning (e.g., learning a word list). With certain individuals, a fuller formal neuropsychological evaluation may be necessary. This is when a complete communication battery may be given as well. On the basis of the history, functional status and cognitive evaluation an overall severity score can be given (e.g., the Clinical Dementia Rating Scale; Hughes, Berg, Danziger, Coben, & Martin, 1982).

The next step in the assessment is the general neurological examination (Mayo Clinic Foundation, 1998). This is necessary to determine if there are neurological changes in addition to the cognitive change that may point to certain diagnoses such as the presence of PD, hemiparesis, or myoclonus.

The final part of the initial dementia assessment includes some screening laboratory tests to exclude reversible causes of dementia (e.g., hypothyroidism). A neuroimaging study (computed topography [CT] or magnetic resonance imaging [MRI] scan) is recommended to further improve the diagnostic accuracy by looking for evidence of strokes, normal pressure hydrocephalus, or even the rare brain tumor presenting with dementia.

Medical Management

The medical management of dementia is limited, but there are medications that affect cognitive function and functional status. The most established of these are acetylcholinesterase inhibitors, drugs that increase the amount of acetylcholine in the brain. Acetylcholine is decreased in brains of people with AD, and cholinesterase inhibitors increase cognitive performance in individuals with AD by small amounts, relative to individuals treated with a placebo (Davis et al., 1992; Rogers, Farlow, Doody, Mohs, & Friedhoff, 1998). The improvements may be more noticeable in certain behavioral symptoms, such as apathy, relative to improvements in memory (Cummings & Kaufer, 1996). Extracts of Ginkgo biloba leaf have also produced small improvements in cognitive functioning among individuals with AD, compared with placebo (Oken, Storzbach, & Kaye, 1998). Data on clinical efficacy of antioxidants, estrogen, nonsteroidal anti-inflammatory drugs, choline, lecithin, acetylcarnitine, and dehydroepiandrosterorne (DHEA) are limited. However, high-dosage vitamin E is often prescribed because of the single large study suggesting some improvement in outcome, although notably no change in cognitive function (Sano et al., 1997).

Certain behaviors that cause individual or caregiver stress may be targeted by behavioral or pharmacological interventions. Common behavior problems that may need to be treated include aggression and sleep disturbance. Other behaviors, such as wandering, are less easily treated. Much of the management of dementia is directed to the family, environmental adjustments, and caregiver training and is discussed later in the chapter as possible communication treatment options. Legal issues centering around conservatorship, guardianship, and power of attorney for health care decisions should be addressed as well.

RAISING UNANSWERED QUESTIONS

As with any new area of clinical investigation, questions are raised once behaviors are described. Questions about the appropriateness of AAC for people with dementia can be grouped into five main categories: Should we intervene? What is the evidence that AAC approaches are helpful for people with dementia? How should we intervene? When should we intervene? What should we measure?

Should We Intervene?

Before deciding whether to intervene, the evidence that is available on communication intervention for adults with dementia must be examined. On the basis of what is known about the deterioration of memory function in AD and related dementias, there are some basic principles for enhancing communicative functions in these individuals throughout the course of the disease process. Many of the more "classic" communication interventions, indeed, resemble the principles that are applied in AAC treatment.

Bayles and Tomoeda (1998b), in an excellent videotape designed to educate both professional and family caregivers of people with dementia, suggested that these basic principles include reducing demands on episodic memory in communicative interactions; supporting working memory; and evoking positive fact memory, emotion, and action by modifying and manipulating the physical and linguistic environment. They suggested and demonstrated several techniques for supporting working memory, from the obvious one of reducing distractions during communicative interactions to highlighting important information through the use of color, size, and placement cues and the use of both upper- and lower-case letters. Other strategies for supporting working memory, according to these researchers, include being careful to provide information within the individual's immediate or short-term memory span, to "chunk" incoming information into smaller units, to use the person's strongest sensory modality for input, and to keep clearly written or printed instructions and reminders visible. In addition, Bayles and Tomoeda suggested using the person's relatively preserved skills of recognition memory and procedural memory.

Some authors (Bourgeois, 1994; Camp, 1998; Glisky, 1997) have emphasized the importance of using external memory aids, such as memory wallets, memory books, and other visible, tangible cues rather than depending on the individual's increasingly compromised internal memory systems. Camp and his colleagues (1993) further suggested an intervention model that capitalizes on *implicit memory*, which Schacter defined as "an unconscious form of retention that ... is assessed with tasks that do not require conscious recollection of specific episodes" (1992, p. 559). This type of memory does not require cognitive effort or recollection of a specific learning event. Examples of implicit memory processes include priming, the learning of motor skills and habits, and classical conditioning. Implicit memory appears to enable individuals, even those with relatively severe dementia, to successfully perform learned motor skills, such as bowling, or to use procedural memories, such as those involved in making coffee, setting the table, or brushing one's teeth. It has also been used as an explanation for why individuals with dementia respond in much the same way as individuals without dementia respond in research paradigms involving priming, a situation in which prior exposure to an item facilitates later processing of that item or a related item. Such interventions as the use of Montessori-based methods and spaced retrieval strategies, which are discussed in the next section, are based on the assumption that implicit memory is still available to individuals with dementia who cannot consciously remember or retain recently learned information.

Communication treatment for people with dementia is founded on the same functional objectives as AAC treatment. Like dementia treatment, AAC treatment addresses intervention with the environment, the user, and the partner. Communication strategies that augment or supplement an adult's abilities are common to cognitive-communicative treatment and AAC treatment. If we extend the definition of *AAC* to include any tool or strategy that supports, enhances, or augments a person's *cognitive-communication* skills, then there are a number of AAC alternatives and therapeutic principles that have been empirically tested for the adult with dementia. Tools range from wallets, books, voice output communication aids (VOCAs), and verbal prompters to pets, stuffed animals, and toys. Strategies range from visual cues to partner training and environmental changes that support the person's residual skills. Although many of the terms used to describe treatment for people with dementia are not within the AAC vernacular, they imply the same intervention assumptions and techniques. In AAC terms, these principles apply primarily to *augmented input* rather than to *alternative output* for this population. Augmented input is a partner-dependent strategy to supplement verbal input and provide sensory-relevant information to the adult with dementia so that he or she can understand and participate in interactions. The technique is described in detail by Garrett and Beukelman (1992, 1995) and Garrett and York-ston (1997). In conversation, partners write down key words or concepts to provide visual supplementation and additional context to help process information and messages presented to them. In fact, augmented input in the form of written cues was found to help adults with AD reduce the number of inappropriate repetitive verbalizations produced daily (Bourgeois, Burgio, Schulz, Beach, & Palmer, 1997). Another strategy common to both AAC and communication treatment is basic choice communication, as described by Garrett and Beukelman (1992). The basic-choice communicator uses familiar routines and context for some automatic (i.e., implicit memory) level of communication. With this technique, facilitators analyze situations and predict communication choices. Binary concrete choices ("Would you like to see the magazine or the photo album?") are presented to adults who display severely impaired receptive and expressive language. Partners learn to accept consistent forms of accept/reject signals for responses and to pause without talking to provide sufficient time for the adult with language impairments to process and respond. Basic choice communicators require maximal assistance from the partner to express concrete choices. With this strategy, they can participate in clarifying their needs and interacting in familiar social activities (Garrett & Beukelman, 1992).

What Is the Evidence that AAC Approaches Are Helpful for People with Dementia?

Research data that support the notion that AAC interventions may be helpful to people with dementia come from studies of the use of external memory aids (Bourgeois, 1992, 1993, 1994), studies employing Montessori-based activities (Camp, 1998; Camp et al., 1997), and research on the use of toys (e.g., stuffed animals, dolls) with individuals who have dementia (Hopper, Bayles, & Tomoeda, 1998). Most of the research evidence to date, however, comes from what would have to be considered pilot work, as each study uses few participants.

Bourgeois (1992, 1993, 1994) showed that people with mild to moderate AD improved their personal conversations when using individualized memory wallets or books. In the 1992 study, nine adults with mild to moderate dementia and caregiver-trainers participated. Each pair used a memory wallet that consisted of 30 stimuli (i.e., photographs or pictures with accompanying declarative sentences) for three topics that were chosen by family members. The topics related to personal information (e.g., family names, biographical information, daily schedule). Caregiver-trainers (e.g., spouse, adult child, day staff) were taught how to prompt or model wallet use with the adult who has dementia during personal conversation ("Tell me about your day"). Training results indicated that the participants increased the frequency of factual statements and decreased the amount of ambiguous, perseverative, erroneous, or unintelligible utterances produced during personal conversations with familiar partners. The wallets successfully augmented personal conversations for adults with mild to moderate dementia and language impairments. Furthermore, three participants maintained successful use of the wallets at 3, 6, and 30 months after the intervention. In another study, Bourgeois (1993) determined that a memory wallet does affect the conversational content and social discourse behaviors of the trained individuals with dementia when conversing with another individual with dementia. When adults with mild to moderate dementia conversed with other adults with dementia using memory wallets, they increased their conversational responsibility, as measured by total number of utterances in a 5-minute conversation, the number of turns, and the number of utterances per turn in the 5-minute conversations. Furthermore, the participants decreased the number of ambiguous or nonproductive comments and used more on-topic statements. Results were not as favorable for adults with moderate to severe dementia who use AAC. However, secondary benefits were observed in the nursing homes where these studies were conducted. Nursing home staff and therapists began making personalized wallets for other residents and improving attention and responsiveness to all individuals with dementia.

Camp and his colleagues (1993) and Camp and Brush (1999) successfully utilized Montessori-based interventions with individuals with dementia in a variety of settings, including day care and long-term care environments. These researchers maintained that there are parallels among the principles of Montessori-based learning for children and interventions for adults with cognitive impairments. Both Montessori-based activities and cognitive rehabilitation are designed to circumvent impairments or as yet unlearned skills, allow for independent functioning as much as possible, have the individual engage in meaningful activity, and provide feedback and success. Montessori-based activities, according to Camp and colleagues, provide structure and order, immediate feedback, a high probability of success, repetition, and task breakdown as necessary. Proponents of Montessori-based interventions maintain that these techniques are particularly well suited to people with dementia because activities and lessons progress from the simplest level to gradually more complex levels, using previously demonstrated skills or concepts. Camp (1998) described Montessori-based activities as "cognitive prostheses" because they enable individuals with dementia to function at a higher level than they would otherwise. These approaches differ from other suggested interventions for individuals with dementia in that they involve actual manipulation of everyday, familiar materials, effortless or unconscious learning, and highly structured activity formats. Information about the nature and sequencing of the activity are part of the materials used and, according to Camp (1998), the materials function as external memory interventions. These tasks utilize procedural memory (e.g., available skills and habits, motor learning, repetition priming) and foster what Montessori called "unconscious learning."

What is the evidence to support the use of Montessori-based approaches? In a pilot study called the Intergenerational Program (Camp et al., 1997), eight residents of a skilled care unit (SCU) with mild to moderate dementia were paired with preschool children ages 2.5–5 years. After the staff had worked individually with the participants first, the SCU residents presented the Montessori-based activities to the preschoolers. The outcome measures were the number of seconds of "disengagement" (e.g., sleeping, not attending), and the total number of disengagement episodes observed in the residents during 5-minute observation periods at three times of day: early in the morning; in midmorning with and without the children, and in the late morning after the children had gone. Results indicated that there were no episodes of disengagement when the residents were working with the children and significantly fewer episodes of disengagement in the late morning after working with the children.

In another study involving Montessori-based research, Camp and Brush (1999) used a group reading activity and measured two kinds of participant *engagement*. They defined *active engagement* as verbal or motor activity focused on the external environment and *passive engagement* as passive observation of the external environment. Participants were individuals with moderate dementia enrolled in an adult day-care program. The investigators were interested in determining whether Montessori-based activities produce more active than passive engagement compared with regular adult day-care programming. Results indicated that the individuals in the Montessori-based programming consistently spent most of their time actively engaged, with less passive engagement observed in the Montessori activity group than in the control group. Taken together, these results suggest that activities that employ implicit learning and external cues (i.e., the Montessori-based stimuli) result in increased engagement and participation on the part of individuals with dementia.

In contrast to these Montessori-based approaches, interventions that depend on free recall of past memories, such as reminiscence therapy (Berghorn & Schafer, 1987; Woods, 1996), are likely to be less beneficial to people with dementia than to older people who do not have cognitive impairments. Woods (1996), for example, contrasted formal reminiscence therapy and reminiscence work. Reminiscence therapy or life review therapy has an important component of *evaluating* past life events and experiences, usually in a one-to-one setting with the therapist acting as a therapeutic listener. Reminiscence work, which might be very appropriate for people with dementia, has a variety of goals, including increased communication and socialization as well as providing pleasure and entertainment. The use of specific themes or prompts in a relaxed, nonevaluative atmosphere to facilitate recall and recognition memories in people with AD can be considered a form of augmented input. Woods (1996) suggested that, if reminiscence-focused activities are used with individuals who have dementia or with groups, these should focus on more general memories rather than specific events or experiences. Awareness of participants' life stories is also important so that appropriate and timely support can be provided as necessary (e.g., if certain events have traumatic connotations for a particular individual in the group).

Another approach to enhance the communication and participation of individuals with dementia that is being explored in research paradigms is the use of toys, specifically stuffed animals and dolls. Studies that have employed tangible stimuli such as dolls, stuffed animals, and handmade recreational items have consistently found measurable, positive effects on behavior and mood as well as on communication (Bailey, Gilbert, & Herweyer, 1992; Buettner, 1999; Francis & Baly, 1986; Hopper et al., 1998). One rationale that has been suggested for the use of toys is that the presence of tangible stimuli reduces demands on episodic memory and may stimulate recognition memory and recall of past experiences. Tangible stimuli may also provide a shared context for meaningful communication, even in people with severe dementia. Hopper and colleagues (1998), for example, investigated the effect of the presence of a stuffed animal or a doll on the communicative behaviors of four women with AD. Hopper and colleagues hypothesized that having a tangible stimulus present would decrease the demands on free recall of episodic knowledge and stimulate more relevant communication. They found that participants produced more meaningful and relevant statements when a toy stimulus was present, as measured by number of information units. The presence of a stuffed animal or a doll was not associated with an increase in the total number of words produced or the number of verbal initiations for three of the four participants.

Another memory-enhancing strategy that has been found to be effective for people with memory impairment is a technique called *spaced retrieval*. This approach requires the individual to rehearse and successfully recall specific information at gradually increasing time intervals. It is based on principles of errorless learning (Baddeley, 1992a). Camp and McKitrick (1992) have observed that the acquisition of new information using spaced retrieval appears to occur effortlessly. These authors have speculated that spaced retrieval may tap into intact implicit memory systems. What is the evidence that spaced-retrieval techniques can facilitate the recall of information for people with AD? Brush and Camp (1998) used spaced retrieval as a memory intervention for three learning tasks: learning a therapist's name, learning one piece of information that was important to the individual with dementia, and learning a compensatory technique. Their results indicated that this technique enabled the individuals with dementia to learn and use the information functionally. Abrahams and Camp (1993) used spaced retrieval to improve the ability of individuals with dementia to name target common objects. They found that the training resulted in improved recall of the objects' names and generalized from line drawings to actual exemplars of the objects, maintained across several weeks.

Empirical evidence suggests that, for individuals with dementia, there are a number of promising techniques to enhance communication and social interaction. These techniques employ the principles of tapping into intact procedural and implicit memory functions with compensatory strategies and reducing the burden on episodic memory and assisting working memory with the use of external memory aids (Bayles & Tomoeda, 1998a; Camp et al., 1997). Some examples of reports in the literature of successful interventions for people with moderate and severe dementia that employ augmented input and that tap into procedural memories include those of Santo Pietro and Boczko (1998) and Witte (1987).

How Should We Intervene?

Lloyd, Fuller and Arvidson (1997) stressed that AAC is a communication process that uses the basic elements of the human communication model with unique applications, standards, and expectations. In fact, the multimodalities of communication are extended with AAC and are represented on a communication continuum from unaided natural strategies and speech modifications to aided communication with alternative access and high-technology equipment. The question arises, then, as to where on this communication continuum should one intervene for the person with dementia? There are many questions to ask. Consequently, we discuss them in categories of language representation, strategies, devices, and partner training.

Language Representation   Lloyd and Fuller (1986) described a symbol as a static or dynamic representation of a referent that is defined by features. Symbol use is one aspect of language representation. According to Sevcik and colleagues (1991), symbols play two important roles in AAC. Symbols represent a person's internal representations of the environment. They also are the external medium or vehicle for portraying the world to others. For adults with dementia, the AAC specialist must examine the user's internal cognitive and language systems, evaluate his or her access to language through the impaired cognitive processes, make sure that the external symbols are familiar to the user, and place the symbols in a display that can be supported by the environment and communication partners. Furthermore, the evaluation must be conducted repeatedly as the individual becomes more dependent on caregivers and his or her cognitive-communication skills decline.

The symbol hierarchy that is imposed on language representation is critical for this population. The hierarchy travels from the three-dimensional realm of objects and miniatures to two-dimensionality. As soon as clinicians consider presenting symbols to individuals with dementia who, by definition, have impaired learning ability and rely on recognition memory, many questions about representation arise. Unfortunately, there is no evidence to help out with this area of inquiry. And each question that is raised must be asked repeatedly during the process of cognitive-communicative degeneration. Can adults with dementia discriminate among symbols? Can they use symbols as the external representations for their thoughts? Consider the adult with mild dementia who has a cue card above the toilet that reads, "Remember to flush." If he or she can no longer rely on the written text, should pictures be introduced? Or should the picture with the written text be introduced at the beginning to permit incidental learning? Bourgeois'

(1992) research used photographs and pictures with accompanying declarative sentences for adults with mild to moderate dementia. Would results be different if other levels of representation were used? Leseth and Meader (1995) used items from personal events or activities (e.g., business papers, sewing scraps) in an attractive box to reduce agitation. From their case report, one might ask whether concrete items, past experience, or familiarity is needed for symbol use. Can symbols that are not familiar be learned? Are there adult-specific differences in the types of symbols that should be used? One might predict that variables such as iconicity (i.e., the ease of symbol recognition), with descriptors such as *transparency* (i.e., the symbols visually resemble their referents) and *opaqueness* (i.e., the visual relationship to referents is not obvious), will influence use by adults with dementia. Consider Frieda, an 87-year-old woman with mild dementia, who benefits from a communication wallet and has requested pictures for feelings and emotions. How should the abstract concepts of anger, fear, or impatience be represented?

Clinicians know that adults with middle- to late-stage AD still retain single-word reading ability. Should orthography be used as the primary symbol set? Abrahams and Camp (1993) used orthography to successfully teach name recall with spaced retrieval. Clinicians also know that people with cognitive impairments from TBI rely on the overlearning of alphabet for most successful AAC use (Fried-Oken & Doyle, 1992). If one extrapolates from the TBI population to the dementia population and uses the data from the pilot communication research, then the alphabet should be the primary choice for representation.

Clinicians also must consider changes in the message set or symbols as a user's disease progresses (Fried-Oken, 1992). A number of staging questions come to mind if different kinds of symbols are introduced over the course of the dementing process. Longitudinal studies are needed to explore whether adults with early-stage dementia should learn to manipulate a symbol set other than the alphabet. If they can learn to use pictures, for example, can they continue to use them as cognitive, language, visuospatial, and attention skills decline? Perhaps research could provide formulas for the types of symbols that should be introduced at different stages in the dementing illness depending on symptom complex. Consider Betty, who at 93 years old, has mild dementia. She can remember to take her pills as long as a cue card is placed on the kitchen counter close to the bottles and the number of pills is written on each pill bottle. The card says, "Take pills at 10:00." The question arises: If Betty can no longer read the cue card, can she learn to recognize pictures or symbols with the same message? Should there be a symbol on the cue card under the written text? It is our clinical opinion that it is highly unlikely that Betty will be able to learn to read nonorthographic symbols if she cannot read text. At the stage of dementia when she can no longer associate text and the message, her learning ability is questionable. This raises the possibility, however, of whether a spaced retrieval intervention with text and symbols or photographs might be beneficial so that her independent pill-taking would linger.

The issue of language organization is important for this population, as well. Can clinicians map what degree of semantic memory is available to the adult with dementia and whether they can access the lexicon? It is known from the AAC and aphasia research, for example, that adults with aphasia may categorize words differently than cohorts may with no impairment. Is this the case for adults with dementia as well? Because it appears that episodic memory and not semantic memory per se is impaired with AD, can one assume an intact adult lexicon before the acquired disease? If access to the lexicon and not the lexicon itself is impaired, can clinicians teach adults to use devices or strategies to enter their word store? This final inquiry leads us to our next category.

Strategies   A number of AAC strategies are easily incorporated into treatment for the adult with dementia. We have already mentioned basic choice and written-choice communication as two AAC strategies that are used with adults who have aphasia and can be applied with adults with dementia (Garrett & Beukelman, 1992). Techniques that enhance environmental supports and programs for facilitator training are also strategies that are successfully integrated into AAC treatment plans. For adults with language impairments secondary to dementia, AAC also should be considered as a strategy for alternative access to semantic memory.

Within the fields of rehabilitation engineering and AAC, *alternative access* is a term that is synonymous with selection technique (Cook & Hussey, 1995), or the way that a person with disabilities selects among a set of language options for transmission of information. Many early rehabilitation engineering efforts were devoted to understanding the physical characteristics of alternative access. We propose that there is still another meaning of the term *alternative access* for adults with dementia. Instead of focusing on the motor characteristics of message selection or the message set itself, AAC may offer the adult with dementia an alternative entrance into the semantic memory store or lexicon and give the individual another way to access memories, verbal concepts, or words for expression or comprehension. AAC, then, is used as a cognitive alternative access technique rather than as a motor or physical selection technique. The aids that have been presented to adults with dementia (Bourgeois, 1992) can be described well with this new interpretation of alternative access.

Devices   There appears to be a place for aids (e.g., books, toys) within AAC dementia treatment. It is known that types of stuffed animals may improve relevance of statements and initiation and that picture wallets may improve production of personal information during conversations with familiar partners (Bourgeois, 1992). Bayles and Toemoda (1998b) recommended using cue cards that vary in color, size, and letter case (i.e., upper- and lower-case) to highlight important information. Hanley and Lusty (1984) reported increased orientation and functional behaviors in an individual who used diaries and watches.

So far, we have discussed only strategies and nonelectronic devices. Should electronic devices be considered as tools for the person with dementia? Can they be used for alternative cognitive access of old information? Sabelman, Sheredos, Stone, and Mann (1994) pointed out that the goal of devices should be to reduce burdens imposed by disability and to assist the caregiver as well as the recipient of care. They described two device functions that are pertinent to our discussion: first, written and speech devices should be considered for life fulfillment and continued productivity with disability, and second, memory aids and stimulators, such as those that give step-by-step prompting and cuing can be used for people with severe or combined progressive impairments. Garrett and Yorkston (1997) noted that at present, it is impossible to replace faulty memory and reasoning, so clinicians must use AAC technology to help a person with dementia participate in meaningful interaction throughout the states of the disease process. They listed AAC equipment for older adults with cognitive impairments within Light's (1989) scheme of the four purposes of social interaction. Among their suggestions, they mentioned attention-getting devices and emergency call systems, timers and intercoms, memory aids and environmental organizers, VOCAs, visual reminder charts, and scrapbooks.

If communication technology is considered as an option for individuals with dementia, then one must first determine if the device is used for augmented input, as a cognitive alternative access method, or for expressive communication and augmented output. For individuals with primary language impairments, augmented output may be in order. Consider Lillian, a 76-year-old woman with mild word-finding problems, a mild cognitive impairment, and a diagnosis of early-stage dementia secondary to AD. She lives alone in rural Idaho, where she has always enjoyed fishing, hunting, and canning her own food for the winter. Her son and his family live in the closest town, about 20 miles away, and they speak with Lillian on the telephone daily. Lillian has decided that she will live alone in her home as long as possible. As such, she has chosen to use a simple digitized VOCA by her new programmable, large-button speaker telephone. The VOCA, which has eight large, colored buttons, contains emergency medical information and a few questions and greetings to use with her family. According to the family, they feel much more comfortable with Lillian's living alone now that she has some verbal output for the telephone. As her skill levels change, the family will reevaluate her communication needs.

For others, the symptom complex of AD (i.e., limb apraxia, severe frontal lobe impairments) may preclude device use. Sidney, for example, has early-stage dementia and primary symptoms of limb apraxia and memory complaints. He cannot reliably press the buttons on a VOCA for verbal assistance. Instead, his family has placed cue cards around his home with key words written on them for daily reminders.

As in any AAC assessment, the long list of features must be considered before prescription. For the dementia population, these may include access method, display permanence, and type of output. If speech output is considered, the type and intelligibility of speech output (e.g., digitized versus synthesized speech) is a factor, as well as the content of digitized recordings (e.g., speech, familiar environmental sounds), the recording times (e.g., 10 seconds, 30 minutes), and the volume (for adults with age-related hearing impairments). Additional factors include but are not limited to portability, ease of use, physical acceptability, and partner participation. These variables are by no means exhaustive and have been described (Fishman, 1987).

The bottom-line question that emerges from this discussion is: Can a prescriptive formula be developed for clinical AAC intervention for adults with dementia? Perhaps one should consider a clinical formula as a guideline. The formula might include all of the dementia domains (i.e., attention, memory, language, visuospatial skills, praxis, frontal lobe functions) with indications of which symptoms are appearing with the progressive dementia on one side of the equation and the AAC treatment features on the other. Of course, the individualization provided from an environmental assessment would still need to fit into the solution. What might the symptom equation look like? And what would be derived from it?

Individual #1

Intact attention + moderately impaired memory + intact language + intact visuospatial skills + moderately impaired praxis + moderately impaired frontal lobe functions = cue cards placed around familiar environment with written text and black-and-white symbols + partner training in prompting

Individual #2

Mildly impaired attention + moderately impaired memory + mildly impaired language + intact visuospatial skills + intact praxis + mildly impaired frontal lobe functions = communication wallet with photographs and sentences + partner training in conversational prompts and items added to wallet

---

Perhaps algorithms can be developed based on the symptom complex that, together with the needs and environmental assessments, could direct the user, the family, caregivers, therapists, physicians, and payers.

Partner Training   Communication partners in AAC terminology are similar to caregivers in the dementia literature. Although there is not an exact parallel among the terms *caregiver* and *communication partner,* it is implicit that a caregiver, indeed, acts in the role of communication partner for both transmission and reception of information. Both are individuals who interact with the AAC user, either for social communicative purposes only or for providing care during the disease progression. Because of the nature of AD and its related communication deterioration, the dementia literature has focused on caregiver issues quite extensively. Since the 1970s, numerous studies have investigated the impact of dementia on caregivers' well-being (see Haley, 1997, and Rau, 1995, for reviews of this literature). Ory, Hoffman, Yee, Tennstedt, and Schultz (1999) summarized the results of data from the 1996 National Caregiver Survey, in which they found that family caregivers of adults with dementia spend significantly more time providing care than caregivers of adults without dementia. Caregivers of adults with dementia also reported greater effects on employment, caregiver strain, mental and physical health problems, reduced leisure time and time for other family members, and greater family conflict than did caregivers of people without dementia. These results are consistent with previous work and point to the need to tailor programs and services, including communication interventions, to the unique needs of caregivers of adults with dementia.

Another aspect of caregiving in dementia that has been explored is caregiver training focused on communication. Bayles and Tomoeda (1998a), Bourgeois (1994), and Ripich (1994) have described principles and specific training procedures designed to improve communicative interactions between people with dementia and their caregivers. Other investigators have asked whether caregiver interventions improve the cognitive and communicative functioning of these individuals. Quayhagen and Quayhagen (1989) found that participants with dementia in caregiver–participant dyads in the treatment group maintained their level of cognitive functioning over time, and those in the control group declined. In addition, caregivers in the treatment group maintained their self-reported mental health status and subjective burden level over time, but caregivers in the control group reported increased mental health symptoms and burden levels over time. In a replication of this work with 78 community-dwelling dyads (Quayhagen, Quayhagen, Corbeil, Roth, & Rodgers, 1995), participants with dementia in the treatment group improved in cognitive and behavioral performance but returned to their former level of functioning after 9 months. The control group participants declined in functioning, and a third group that received passive activity but not specific dyadic intervention training maintained levels of functioning on cognitive and behavioral measures. In the context of a progressive dementing illness, these are very promising results.

Specific caregiver training issues are beginning to appear within the AAC community. Communication partner training protocols are available that help guide clinicians toward effective AAC partner training (Light & Binger, 1998). Within the gerontology literature, guidebooks that address caregiver roles and responsibilities have been written for families of adults with dementia and often include chapters on communication. The Communication Enhancement Model, as described by Ryan, Meredith, and MacLean (1995), can be used to help caregivers develop improved communication with their vulnerable older adults, including those with dementia, and can offer a research framework to explore the efficacy of AAC strategies for communication partner use. Likewise, Ripich's (1994) seven detailed training modules called FOCUSED might be a paradigm that can be adapted to train partners how to use AAC strategies and devices with the adult with dementia. Like other dementia treatments, FOCUSED embodies many AAC principles in its detailed program. A possible study might include using AAC techniques with the FOCUSED communication strategies for adults with dementia.

One issue that has not yet been addressed by the AAC community is caregiver well-being, retention, and respite. This is yet another area of research that may affect outcomes for the person with dementia who is successfully learning AAC strategies or learning to use devices functionally in the structured environment. Which environmental supports are needed for AAC intervention and success? It is clear that facilitator or partner issues are strategies that must be investigated. As with any degenerative disease, facilitator issues become increasingly important as the dementing illness progresses.

When Should We Intervene?

The issue of timeliness or staging of intervention raises its head for every individual with a degenerative disease, and it is no different for adults with dementia. In fact, many of the AAC questions that we raise apply to adults at different stages of their illnesses. Yorkston, Miller, and Strand (1995), in their clinical text on helping individuals with degenerative disease, stated repeatedly that clinicians should intervene early. For individuals with dementia and severe dysarthria secondary to Huntington disease, for example, Yorkston and colleagues recommended initiating training in AAC approaches early, perhaps before AAC strategies are mandatory and communication becomes frustrating. Early practice of simple communication techniques helps to establish them and develop the indivudual's procedural memory. There is indeed no evidence on when to offer AAC strategies and devices to the adult with dementia or his or her environment and partners, or which changes should be made with the stages of disease. Although information about the progression of AAC options is becoming clearer for individuals with neuromuscular diseases, such as amyotrophic lateral sclerosis, sufficient descriptions of clinical AAC trials with individuals with dementia and their families for prescription still do not exist. Many of the questions raised about language representation can be iterated here. Many of Rau's (1995) suggestions for family staging of intervention can be adapted to AAC strategies and devices as well.

What Should We Measure?

If the empirical data that has been collected to date are used, then a number of measures become apparent. Bourgeois (1992) measured self-prompts during conversations, number of initiations of facts, and number of ambiguous, error, and perseverative utterances when using wallets. Generalization 3, 6, and 30 months after the intervention was considered as well. Sociocommunicative measures from Light's (1989) communicative competence model might be considered for conversation. Camp and colleagues (1997) measured the number of seconds of "disengagement" (e.g., sleeping, not attending) and the total number of disengagement episodes observed in the residents during 5-minute observation periods three times per day with and without intervention. Although these measures may not represent symbolic communication, they certainly are the behaviors that must be in place before symbolic communication can occur. Partner-based measures of satisfaction with conversation, mental health, stress, and perceived burden levels have also been examined. These are pertinent to AAC intervention also. The list of possible intervention outcomes is almost limitless and includes all of the measures that have been described in the AAC and communication literature. We are only at the starting point. It is important that assessment and intervention for the adult with dementia at various stages of the progressive illness include measures that reflect AAC principles for a population of adults and facilitators who have known communicative competence and effectiveness in the past.

REFERENCES

Abrahams, J.P., & Camp, C.J. (1993). Maintenance and generalization of object naming training in anomia associated with degenerative dementia. *Clinical Gerontologist, 12*(3), 57–72.

Albert, M., Feldman, R., & Willis, A. (1974). The "subcortical dementia" of progressive supra nuclear palsy. *Journal of Neurology, Neurosurgery, and Psychiatry, 37,* 121–130.

Albert, M.L., & Knoefel, J.E. (1994). *Clinical neurology of aging* (2nd ed.). New York: Oxford University Press.

American Psychiatric Association (APA). (1994). *Diagnostic and statistical manual of mental disorders* (4th ed.). Washington, DC: Author.

Baddeley, A.D. (1992a). Implicit memory and errorless learning: A link between cognitive theory and neuropsychological rehabilitation? In L.R. Squire & N. Butters (Eds.), *Neuropsychology of memory* (2nd ed., pp. 309–314). New York: Guilford Press.

Baddeley, A.D. (1992b). Working memory. *Science, 253,* 556–559.

Bailey, J., Gilbert, E., & Herweyer, S. (1992, July). To find a soul. *Nursing, 22*(7), 63–64.

Bayles, K.A., & Tomoeda, C.K. (1995). *The ABCs of dementia* (2nd ed.). Phoenix, AZ: Canyonlands Publishing.

Bayles, K.A., & Tomoeda, C.K. (1998a). *Improving the ability of Alzheimer's patients to communicate.* Phoenix, AZ: Canyonlands Publishing.

Bayles, K.A., & Tomoeda, C.K. (1998b). *Understanding the communication problems of Alzheimer's patients* [Videotape]. Phoenix, AZ: Canyonlands Publishing.

Bayles, K.A., Tomoeda, C.K., & Trosset, M.W. (1992). Relation of linguistic communication abilities of Alzheimer's patients to stage of disease. *Brain and Language, 42,* 454–472.

Bayles, K.A., Tomoeda, C.K., Kaszniak, A.W., & Trosset, M.W. (1991). Alzheimer's disease: Effects on semantic memory: Loss of structure or impaired processing? *Journal of Cognitive Neuroscience, 3,* 166–182.

Berghorn, F.J., & Schafer, D.E. (1987). Reminiscence intervention in nursing homes: What and who changes? *International Journal of Aging and Human Development, 24,* 113–127.

Blackstone, S. (1996). The third thirty: Keep on communicating! *Augmentative Communication News, 9*(6), 1–3.

Blessed, G., Tomlinson, B.E., & Roth, M. (1968). The association between quantitative measures of dementia and of senile change in the cerebral grey matter of elderly subjects. *British Journal of Psychiatry, 114,* 797–811.

Bourgeois, M.S. (1992). Evaluating memory wallets in conversations with persons with dementia. *Journal of Speech and Hearing Research, 35,* 1344–1357.

Bourgeois, M.S. (1993). Effects of memory aids on the dyadic conversations of individuals with dementia. *Journal of Applied Behavior Analysis, 26,* 77–87.

Bourgeois, M.S. (1994). Teaching care givers to use memory aids with patients with dementia. *Caregiving in Dementia II: Interventions. Seminars in Speech and Language, 15*(4), 257–322.

Bourgeois, M.S., Burgio, L.D., Schulz, R., Beach, S., & Palmer, B. (1997). Modifying repetitive verbalizations of community-dwelling patients with AD. *Gerontologist, 37*(1), 30–39.

Brush, J.A., & Camp, C.J. (1998a). Using spaced retrieval as an intervention during speech-language therapy. *Clinical Gerontologist, 19,* 51–64.

Brush, J.A., & Camp, C. (1998b). *Using spaced retrieval as a therapeutic technique during the rehabilitative process* [Videotape. Telerounds #45]. Tucson: The National Center for Neurogenic Communication Disorders, University of Arizona.

Buettner, L.L. (1999). Simple pleasures: A multilevel sensoriotor intervention for nursing home residents with dementia. *American Journal of Alzheimer's Disease, 9,* 41–52.

Camp, C.J. (1998). Memory interventions for normal and pathological older adults. *Annual Review of Gerontology and Geriatrics, 18,* 155–189.

Camp, C.J., & Brush, J. (1999). *Montessori-based interventions for persons with dementia* [Videotape. Telerounds #46]. Tucson: National Center for Neurogenic Communication Disorders, University of Arizona.

Camp, C.J., Foss, J.W., Stevens, A.B., Reichard, C.C., McKitrick, L.A., & O'Hanlon, A.M. (1993). Memory training in normal and demented elderly populations: The E-I-E-I-O model. *Experimental Aging Research, 19,* 277–290.

Camp, C.J., Judge, K.S., Bye, C.A., Fox, K.M., Bowden, J., Bell, M., Valencic, K., & Mattern, J.M. (1997). An intergenerational program for persons with dementia using Montessori methods. *Gerontologist, 37,* 688–692.

Camp, C.J., & McKitrick, L.A. (1992). Memory interventions in Alzheimer's-type dementia populations: Methodological and theoretical issues. In R.L.West & J.D. Sinnott (Eds.), *Everyday memory and aging: Current research and methodology* (pp. 86–119). New York: Springer-Verlag.

Chapman, S.B., Ulatowska, H.K., King, K., Johnson, J.K., & McIntire, D.D. (1995). Discourse in early Alzheimer's disease versus normal advanced aging. *American Journal of Speech-Language Pathology, 4,* 124–129.

Chenery, H.J., & Murdoch, B.E. (1994). The production of narrative discourse in response to animations in persons with dementia of the Alzheimer's type: Preliminary findings. *Aphasiology, 8,* 159–171.

Chertkow, H., & Bub, D. (1990). Semantic memory loss in dementia of the Alzheimer's type. *Brain, 113,* 397–417.

Cronin-Golomb, A., Corkin, S., & Rosen, T.J. (1993). Neuropsychological Assessment of Dementia. In P.J. Whitehouse (Ed.), *Dementia* (pp. 130–164). Philadelphia: F.A. Davis.

Cook, A.M., & Hussey, S.M. (1995). *Assistive technologies: Principles and practice.* St. Louis: Mosby.

Cummings, J.L., & Benson, D.F. (1984). Subcortical dementia: Review of an emerging concept. *Archives of Neurology, 41,* 874–879.

Cummings, J.L., & Benson, D.F. (1992). *Dementia: A clinical approach* (2nd ed.). Boston: Butterworth-Heinemann.

Cummings, J.L., & Kaufer, D. (1996). Neuropsychiatric aspects of Alzheimer's disease: the cholinergic hypothesis revisited. *Neurology, 47,* 876–883.

Davis, K.L., Thal, L.J., Gamzu, E.R., Davis, C.S., Woolson, R.F., Gracon, S.I., Drachman, D.A., Schneider, L.S., Whitehouse, P.J., Hoover, T.M., Morris, J.C., Kawas, C.H., Knopman, D.S., Earl, N.L., Kumar, V., Doody, R.S., and the Tacrine Collaborative Study Group. (1992). A double-blind, placebo-controlled multicenter study of tacrine for Alzheimer's disease. *New England Journal of Medicine, 327,* 1253–1259.

Fillenbaum, G. (1988). *Multidimensional functional assessment of older adults: the Duke older Americans resources and services procedures.* Mahwah, NJ: Lawrence Erlbaum Associates.

Fishman, I. (1987). *Electronic communication aids: Selection and use.* Boston: Little, Brown and Co.

Flicker, C., Ferris, S.H., Crook, T., & Bartus, R.T. (1987). Implications of memory and language dysfunction in the naming deficits of senile dementia. *Brain and Language, 31,* 187–200.

Folstein, M.F., Folstein, S.E., & McHugh, P.R. (1975). Mini-mental state. A practical method for grading the cognitive state of patients for the clinician. *Journal of Psychiatric Research, 12,* 189–198.

Francis, G., & Baly, A. (1986). Plush animals: Do they make a difference? *Geriatric Nursing, 74*(9), 140–143.

Fried-Oken, M. (1992). The AAC assessment cube for adults with severe communication disabilities. *Communication Outlook, 14*(1),14–18.

Fried-Oken, M., & Doyle, M. (1992). Language representation for the augmentative and alternative communication of adults with traumatic brain injury. *Journal of Head Trauma Rehabilitation, 7*(3), 59–69.

Galasko, D., Bennett, D., Sano, M., Ernesto, C., Thomas, R., Grundman, M., & Ferris, S. (1997). An inventory to assess activities of daily living for clinical trials in Alzheimer's disease: The Alzheimer's Disease Cooperative Study. *Alzheimer Disease and Associated Disorders, 11*(Suppl. 2), S33–S39.

Garrett, K., & Beukelman, D.R. (1992). Augmentative communication approaches for persons with severe aphasia. In K. Yorkston (Ed.), *Augmentative communication in the medical setting* (pp. 245–338). Tucson, AZ: Communication Skill Builders.

Garrett, K., & Beukelman, D.R. (1995). Changes in the interactional patterns of an individual with severe aphasia given three types of partner support. In M. Lemme (Ed.), *Clinical Aphasiology, 23,* 237–251.

Garrett, K., & Yorkston, K. (1997). Assistive communication technology for elders with cognitive and language disabilities. In R. Lubinski & D.J. Higginbotham (Ed.), *Communication technologies for the elderly: Vision, hearing, and speech* (pp. 203–262). San Diego: Singular Publishing Group.

Glisky, E.L. (1997). Rehabilitation of memory dysfunction. In T.E. Feinberg & M.J. Farah (Eds.), *Behavioral neurology and neuropsychology* (pp. 491–495). New York: McGraw-Hill.

Haley, W.E. (1997). The family caregiver's role in Alzheimer's disease. *Neurology, 48*(Suppl. 6), S25–S29.

Hanley, I.G., & Lusty, K. (1984). Memory aids in reality orientation: A single case study. *Behavior Research Therapy, 22,* 709–712.

Henderson, V.W., Mack, W., Freed, D.M., Kempler, D., & Andersen, E.S. (1990). Naming consistency in Alzheimer's disease. *Brain and Language, 39,* 530–538.

Hopper, T., Bayles, K.A., & Tomoeda, C.K. (1998). Using toys to stimulate communicative function in individuals with Alzheimer's disease. *Journal of Medical Speech-Language Pathology, 6,* 73–80.

Huff, F.J., Corkin, S., & Growdon, J.H. (1986). Semantic impairment and anomia in Alzheimer's disease. *Brain and Language, 34,* 262–278.

Hughes, C.P., Berg, L., Danziger, W.L., Coben, L.A., & Martin, R.L. (1982). A new clinical scale for the staging of dementia. *British Journal of Psychiatry, 140,* 566–572.

Jorm, A.F., & Jolley, D. (1998). The incidence of dementia: A meta-analysis. *Neurology, 51,* 728–733.

Kiernan, R.J., Mueller, J., Langston, J.W., & Van Dyke, C. (1987). The neurobehavioral cognitive status examination: A brief but differentiated approach to cognitive assessment. *Annals of Internal Medicine, 107,* 481–485.

Kirshner, H., Webb, W., & Kelly, M. (1984). The naming disorder of dementia. *Neuropsychologia, 22,* 23–30.

Kline, D.W., & Scialfa, C.T. (1996). Visual and auditory aging. In J.E. Birren & K.W. Schaie (Eds.), *Handbook of the psychology of aging* (pp. 181–203). San Diego: Academic Press.

Leseth, L., & Meader, L. (1995). Utilizing an AAC system to maximize receptive and expressive communication skills of a person with Alzheimer's Disease. *ASHA AAC Special Interest Division Newsletter, 4,* 7–9.

Light, J. (1989). Toward a definition of communicative competence for individuals using augmentative and alternative communication systems. *Augmentative and Alternative Communication, 13,* 61–70.

Light, J., & Binger, K. (1998). *Building communicative competence with adults who use augmentative and alternative communication.* Baltimore: Paul H. Brookes Publishing Co.

Lloyd, L.L., & Fuller, D. (1986). Toward an augmentative and alternative communication communciation system taxonomy: A proposed superordinate classification. *Augmentative and Alternative Communication, 2*(4), 165–171.

Lloyd, L.L., Fuller, D.R., & Arvidson, H.H. (1997). *Augmentative and alternative communication: A handbook of principles and practices.* Needham Heights, MA: Allyn and Bacon.

McKhann, G., Drachman, D., Folstein, M., Katzman, R., Price, D., & Stadlan, E.M. (1984). Clinical diagnosis of Alzheimer's disease: Report of the NINCDS-ADRDA Work Group under the auspices of Department of Health and Human Services Task Force on Alzheimer's disease. *Neurology, 34,* 939–944.

Mentis, M., Briggs-Whittaker, J., & Gramigna, G. D. (1995). Discourse topic management in senile dementia of the Alzheimer type. *Journal of Speech and Hearing Research, 38,* 1054–1066.

Mayo Clinic Foundation. (1998). *Mayo Clinic examinations in neurology* (7th ed.). St. Louis: Mosby.

Oken, B.S., Storzbach, D.M., & Kaye, J.A. (1998). The efficacy of Ginkgo biloba on cognitive function in Alzheimer's disease. *Archives of Neurology, 55,* 1409–1415.

Orange, J.B., Lubinski, R.B., & Higginbotham, D.J. (1996). Conversational repair by individuals with dementia of the Alzheimer's type. *Journal of Speech and Hearing Research, 39,* 881–895.

Ory, M.G., Hoffman, R.R., Yee, J.L., Tennstedt, S., & Schulz, R. (1999). Prevalence and impact of caregiving: A detailed comparison between dementia and nondementia caregivers. *Gerontologist, 39,* 177–185.

Quayhagen, M.P., Quayhagen, M., Corbeil, R., Roth, P.A., & Rodgers, J.A. (1995). A dyadic remediation program for care recipients with dementia. *Nursing Research, 44*(3), 153–159.

Quayhagen, M.P., & Quayhagen, M. (1989). Differential effects of family-based strategies on Alzheimer's disease. *Gerontologist, 29,* 150–155.

Rau, M.T. (1995). Impact on families. In R. Lubinski (Ed.), *Dementia and communication* (pp. 152–167). San Diego: Singular Publishing Group.

Ripich, D.N. (1991). Language and communication in dementia. In D.N. Ripich (Ed.), *Handbook of geriatric communication disorders* (pp. 255–283). Austin, TX: PRO-ED.

Ripich, D.N. (1994). Functional communication with AD patients: A caregiver training program. *Alzheimer Disease and Associated Disorders, 8*(Suppl. 3), 95–109.

Ripich, D.N., & Terrell, B.Y. (1988). Patterns of discourse cohesion and coherence in Alzheimer's disease. *Journal of Speech and Hearing Disorders, 53,* 8–15.

Rogers, S.L., Farlow, M.R., Doody, R.S., Mohs, R., & Friedhoff, L.T. (1998). A 24-week, double-blind placebo-controlled trial of donepezil in patients with Alzheimer's disease. *Neurology, 50,* 136–145.

Rosen, W.G., Mohs, R.C., & Davis, K.L. (1984). A new rating scale for Alzheimer's disease. *American Journal of Psychiatry, 141,* 1356–1364.

Ryan, E.B., Meredith, S.D., & MacLean, M.J. (1995). Changing the way we talk with elders: Promoting health using the communication enhancement model. *International Journal of Aging and Human Development, 41*(2), 89–107.

Sabelman, E.E., Sheredos, C., Stone, J., & Mann, W. (1994). *Opportunities for high technology R&D to fulfill needs of the elderly.* RESNA Proceedings, Arlington, VA: RESNA Press.

Sano, M., Ernesto, C., Thomas, R.G., T., Klauber, M., Schafer, K., Grundman, M., Woodbury, P., Growdon, J., Cotman, C., Pfeiffer, E., Schneider, L., & Thal, L. (1997). A controlled trial of selegiline, alpha-tocopherol, or both as treatment for Alzheimer's disease: The Alzheimer's Disease Cooperative Study. *New England Journal of Medicine, 336*(17), 1216–1222.

Santo Pietro, M.J., & Boczko, F. (1998, May–June). The breakfast club: Results of a study examining the effectiveness of a multi-modality group communication treatment *American Journal of Alzheimer's Disease,* 146–158.

Schacter, D.L. (1992). Understanding implicit memory. *American Psychologist, 47,* 559–569.

Silverman, F.H. (1994). Can AAC help people with dementia? [Letter to the editor]. *Augmentative and Alternative Communication, 10*(1), 60.

Squire, L.R. (1994). Declarative and non-declarative memory: Multiple brain systems supporting learning and memory. In D.L. Schacter & E. Tulving (Eds.), *Memory systems* (pp. 203–232). Cambridge: MIT Press.

Tatemichi, T.K., Sacktor, N., & Mayeux, R. (1994). Dementia associated with cerebrovascular disease, other degenerative diseases, and metabolic disorders. In R.D. Terry (Ed.), *Alzheimer disease* (pp. 123–166). New York: Raven Press.

Terry, R.D., Katzman, R., & Bick, K.L. (Eds.). (1994). *Alzheimer disease.* New York: Raven Press.

Tomoeda, C.K., & Bayles, K.A. (1993). Longitudinal effects of Alzheimer disease on discourse production. *Alzheimer Disease and Associated Disorders, 7,* 223–236.

Ulatowska, H.K., Allard, L., Donnell, A., Bristow, J., Haynes, S.M., Flower, A., & North, A.J. (1988). Discourse performance in subjects with dementia of the Alzheimer's type. In H. Whitaker (Ed.), *Neuropsychological studies I: Vol. 2. Nonfocal brain damage* (pp. 108–131). New York: Springer-Verlag.

Watson, C.M., Chenery, H.J., & Carter, M.S. (1999). An analysis of trouble and repair in the natural conversations of people with dementia of the Alzheimer's type. *Aphasiology, 13*, 195–218.

Whitehouse, P.J. (Ed.). (1993). *Dementia* (Vol. 40). Philadelphia: F.A. Davis.

Wisniewski, K.E., Wisniewski, H.M., & Wen, G.Y. (1985). Occurrence of neuropathological changes and dementia of Alzheimer's disease in Down's syndrome. *Annals of Neurology, 17*, 278–282.

Witte, K. (1987). Discourse and dialogue: Prolonging adult conversation in the Alzheimer patient. *American Journal of Alzheimers Care and Research, 2*, 30–40.

Woods, R.T. (1996). Psychological "therapies" in dementia. In R.T. Woods (Ed.), *Handbook of the clinical psychology of aging* (pp. 575–600). New York: John Wiley & Sons.

Yorkston, K., Miller, R., & Strand, E. (1995). *Management of speech and swallowing in degenerative diseases.* Tucson, AZ: Communication Skill Builders.

Zigman, W., Schupf, N., Haveman, M., & Silverman, W. (1997). The epidemiology of Alzheimer disease in intellectual disability: Results and recommendations from an international conference. *Journal of Intellectual Disability Research, 41*, 76–80.

Index

Page references followed by *t* or *f* indicate tables or figures, respectively.

AAC, *see* Augmentative and alternative communication
AAC Acceptance Model, 110–120, 132
  factors related to acceptance of AAC, 110, 110*t*
  factors related to milieu, 110–112
  factors related to person, 112–118
  factors related to technology, 118–120
AAC Communicators with Aphasia, 321
Abandonment, of AAC devices, 108
Academy of Neurologic Communication Disorders and Sciences, 73–74
Acceleration techniques, 296–297
Access, 358
  alternative, 394–395
  information, 358–359
  means of, 292–293
Acoustic information, signal-dependent, 98
Acquired disorders
  acceptance of AAC by adults with, 107–136
  communication with adults with interventions for, 164
  opportunity barriers for rebuilding, 167, 168*t*
  partner strategies reported to facilitate, 169–170
  features that affect AAC acceptance, 112
  onset of, 139–140
  see also specific disorders
Action plans, 347
Activities
  assessment of, 318–319

International Classification of Impairment, Activities, and Participation level, 60
  limitations on, 314
  Montessori-based, 389–390
Activities of daily living (ADLs), 306, 376
Acute illness, 77
Adaptability, 17
Adaptation, 330–333
Adaptive Communication Consultants, Inc., 354
ADLs, *see* Activities of daily living
Agency for Health Care Policy and Research (AHCPR), 70–71
Agitation, 274–275, 276*t*
AHCPR, *see* Agency for Health Care Policy and Research
Alphabet boards, 206–207, 207*t*
Alphabet supplementation, 49, 84, 100
Alphabetic cues, 88–91, 92*f*, 94–95
AlphaTalker, 354
ALS, *see* Amyotrophic lateral sclerosis
Al's ALS Resource Page, 231
ALS Digest, 232
The ALS March of Faces, 231
The ALS Survival Guide, 232
ALSA, *see* Amyotrophic Lateral Sclerosis Association
Alzheimer Disease Assessment Scale–cognitive subscale, 384
American Psychology Association Task Force on Promotion and Dissemination of Psychological Procedure, 72

American Speech-Language-Hearing
  Association (ASHA), 62
AmerInd, 150
Amyotrophic lateral sclerosis (ALS),
  184–187
  AAC for individuals with, 183–232
  classification of needs for, 198
  individuals evaluated for usage
    patterns, 206, 206t
  methods used by, 209–211, 210f,
    211f
  patterns of use, 204–212
  bulbar symptoms of
    AAC methods used by individu-
      als with, 206–207, 207t
    AAC methods used most by
      individuals with, 209, 209t
    individuals who received AAC
      evaluations, 206, 206t
    linguistic-cognitive capabilities
      and impairments with, 35
  classification of, 186–187
  cognitive decline in, 193–196
    clinically significant impairment,
      193
    correlates of change, 194–195
    neuropathology of, 193–194
  communication interventions in
    hope regarding, 218–219
    staging of, 66
  communication with, 187–193
  coping with, 213–219
  David (example), 4–5, 6t
  diagnosis of, 185–186
  dysarthria in, 196
    staging of, 197
  insider's perspective on, 214–216
  language function in, 195–196
  linguistic-cognitive capabilities
    and impairments in, 35–36
  natural progression of, 186–187
  neuropathology of, 184–185,
    193–194
  neuropsychologic testing in, 195
  outlook for future, 219–221
  psychosocial aspects of, 216–218
  resources, 231–232
  respiratory problems in, 187–193
    characteristics of, 188
    technology for management of,
      188–189

speech in
  characteristics of, 196–212
  staging of, 197–198
spinal symptoms of
  AAC methods used by individu-
    als with, 206–207, 207t
  AAC methods used most by
    individuals with, 208t,
    208–209
  individuals who received AAC
    evaluations, 206, 206t
states of severity
  state 1 (mild), 186
  state 2 (moderate), 186
  state 3 (severe), 186–187
  state 4 (terminal), 187
Amyotrophic Lateral Sclerosis
  Association (ALSA), 205, 231
Aphasia
  AAC Communicators with Aphasia,
    321
  AAC learning with, 343–344
  AAC strategies for, 341–343
    R.H. (example), 363–368, 369f
  assessment of, example, 364–365
  basic conversation with, 348–349
  characteristics that affect AAC
    strategy use, 351, 352t
  classification of AAC communica-
    tors with, 321, 322t
  cognitive-linguistic considerations,
    339–374
  cognitive-linguistic demands,
    347–368
    ways to enhance visual represen-
      tation to decrease, 359–360
  cognitive processing, 344–346,
    361–362
  Derrel (example), 4–5, 6t
    use of communication aids by,
      12–14, 14f, 15, 15f
    use of unambiguous communi-
      cation aid symbols by,
      12–14, 13f
  fluent, 331–332
  Frank (example), 4–5, 6t
  group communication therapy for,
    case report, 364
  historic intervention approaches
    for, 340–341
  instructional issues, 362–368

Jim (example), 4–5, 6*t*
mixed, 309
nonfluent, 330–331
primary progressive (PPA),
  305–337
  AAC for, 330–333
  AAC techniques and devices
    recommended for, 323–324,
    325*t*
  assessment of, 315–321
  communication notebooks for
    individuals with, 326–330
  concomitant symptoms reported
    with, 310, 311*t*
  diagnosis of, 312–313
  disablement associated with,
    313–315
  early stage, 321–323
  fluency dimension, 307–310
  initial symptoms of, 312–315
  intervention in, 321–330
  late stage, 324
  middle stage, 323–324
  N.A. (example), 330–331
  proactive management of,
    306–307, 315–330
  vignettes, 330–333
  psychosocial impact of, 17–19, 18*f*
research on
  future directions, 369–370
  questions for, 369–370
stable moderate
  example user and partner
    acceptance of AAC with,
    125, 126*t*–127*t*
  example user and partner rejec-
    tion of AAC with, 125–130,
    128*t*–129*t*
Supported Conversation for Adults
  with Aphasia (SCA), 340
Voice output communication aids
  and intervention in
  initial observations, 365
  R.H. (example), 365–366
Aphasia Needs Assessment, 365
Appropriateness, 77
Apraxia
  limb, 351, 352*t*
  severe
    user and partner acceptance of
      AAC with, 125, 126*t*–127*t*

user and partner rejection of
  AAC with, 125–130,
  128*t*–129*t*
Archives of Neurology, 74
ASHA, *see* American Speech-
  Language-Hearing Association
Assessment
  of activities, 318–319
  of aphasia, case report, 364–365
  dementia, 383–384
  of impairment, 317–318
  of participation, 319–321
  of primary progressive aphasia,
    315–321
  World Health Organization Model
    of Disablements areas,
    316–317, 317*f*
  see also Evaluation
*The Assistive Technology Device
  Predisposition Assessment (ATD
  PA)*, 133
Assistive Technology Funding and
  Systems Change Project, 221
*ATD PA, see The Assistive Technology
  Device Predisposition Assessment*
Attention
  allocation of resources for, 348
  with aphasia, 345–346
Attention Process Training Program,
  288
Attentiveness to environment, 347
Attitude
  AAC-related questionnaires, 121,
    122*t*
  about AAC, 113
    content themes, 133
    research related to, 120–132
  barriers to communicative compe-
    tence, 167–169, 168*t*
  barriers to self-determination,
    171–173
  components of, 113
  definition of, 113
Attitudes Toward Nonspeaking
  Persons Scale, 121, 122*t*
Auditory comprehension difficulties,
  351, 352*t*
Auditory scanning, dependent,
  206–207, 207*t*
*Augmentative and Alternative
  Communication*, 74

Augmentative and alternative
communication (AAC)
abandonment of, 108
acceptance by adults with acquired
disorders, 107–136
change over time in, 130–132,
131t–132t
future directions for research,
132–133
proposed model for, 110–120
research related to attitudes
relevant to, 120–132
user and partner profiles,
124–132, 126t–127t
for amyotrophic lateral sclerosis,
183–232
for aphasia, 339–374
attitudes toward, 113, 133
avoidance of, 108
with chronic disease model,
284–291
classification of needs for, 198
cognitive disorders that influence,
280–284
cognitive-linguistic demands of,
351–357
decision making in, 55–82
definition of, 386
for dementia, 375–405
example users, 4–5, 6t
gender preferences, 211
for Huntington disease, 233–270
input, 387
integrated model for, 97–100
integrating with natural speech,
49–50, 83–106
linguistic-cognitive capabilities
and impairments of users,
34–39
linguistic demands of, 147
methods used by individuals with
amyotrophic lateral sclerosis,
209–211, 210f, 211f
methods used by individuals with
bulbar and spinal amyotrophic
lateral sclerosis, 206–207, 207t
methods used most by individuals
with bulbar amyotrophic
lateral sclerosis, 209, 209t
methods used most by individuals
with spinal amyotrophic
lateral sclerosis, 208t, 208–209

natural communication strategies
supplemented by, 68
natural speech supplemented by,
198, 247–248, 259–260
needs for
classification of, 198
group 1: adequate speech and
adequate hand functioning,
198–199
group 2: adequate speech and
poor hand functioning,
199–202
group 3: poor speech, adequate
hand functioning, and adequate mobility, 202–203
group 4: poor speech, adequate
hand functioning, and poor
mobility, 203
group 5: poor speech, poor hand
functioning, and good
mobility, 203–204
group 6: poor speech, poor hand
functioning, and poor
mobility, 204
optimal use of, 108
output, 387
for Parkinson's disease, 233–270
for primary progressive aphasia
recommended techniques and
devices, 323–324, 325t
vignettes, 330–333
and quality of life, 211–212
rejection of
categories of, 108
user and partner profiles,
124–132, 128t–129t
training in, 357–368
for traumatic brain injury, 300
usage patterns, 206t, 206–211
user satisfaction, 211–212, 212f
users with aphasia, 321, 322t
users with cognitive impairments,
38–39
users with linguistic impairments,
37–38
users with no linguistic-cognitive
impairments, 35–36
Augmentative and alternative communication (AAC) systems
cognitive-linguistic demands
imposed by, 350–357
design and use of

cognition and, 271–304
role of cognition in, 291–300
strategies for, 152
display configuration, 292–293
dynamic display, 294
features of, 119
"language" code of, 150–151
management services and information, 205–206
message management, 25–54
message production and retrieval strategies, 296–300
multilevel dynamic screen, 366–367
multimodal, 356–357
recommended devices for individuals with primary progressive aphasia, 323–324, 325*t*
sample story-order message arrangement for, 368, 369*f*
spelling-based, 295–296
types of, 275–279, 279–284
Augmented-input communication, 387
Augmented-input communicators, 321, 322*t*, 323–324
Autobiographical questions, 348–349
Autonomy, 156
Avoidance, 108
Awareness
of cause and effect, decreased, 351, 352*t*
of change, 32
pragmatic, 350
self-awareness, 158–160

Basic-choice communication, 387
Basic-choice communicators, 321, 322*t*, 324
Behavior(s)
goal-oriented, 165
language, 274–275, 276*t*–278*t*
Beliefs, personal agency, 12
Blessed Information-Memory-Concentration Test, 384
Blissymbols, 307, 341
Bradyphrenia, 254
Brain and Language, 74
Brain injury, traumatic, 271–304

Care models
caring model, 264–265
for Huntington and Parkinson disease, 263–265
palliative care, 263
participation model, 263–264
Caregivers, 397
burden of, 261
for individuals with Parkinson's disease, 261
relinquishing to, 30
Change, awareness of, 32
Choices
communicating, 161
making, 159*t*, 160–163
Chronic disease, World Health Organization Model, 284–291, 285*t*–286*t*
CINAHL, *see* Cumulative Index to Nursing & Allied Health Literature
Clinical decision making
with Huntington disease, 244–248
individualized subjective judgment, 76
with Parkinson's disease, 257–260
Clinical Dementia Rating Scale, 384
Clinical responsibility, 77
Closeness, social, 42–48
Code-Muller Protocols, 16
Coded eye-blink, 206–207, 207*t*
Cognition
with amyotrophic lateral sclerosis, 193–196
and associated language behaviors, 274–275, 276*t*–278*t*
effects on system design and use, 271–304
role in AAC design and use, 291–300
"supported cognition," 161, 173
Cognitive-communication skills, 386
Cognitive disorders
and AAC management after traumatic brain injury, 279–284
in Parkinson's disease, 254–256
profound, 161
that influence AAC management, 280–284
Cognitive impairments, 38–39
in amyotrophic lateral sclerosis, 193
associated with Huntington disease, 239–241

Cognitive impairments—*continued*
  suggestions to minimize impact of,
    295
Cognitive-linguistic demands
  of AAC strategies, 351–357
  of AAC systems, 350–357
  of communication, 347–368
Cognitive-linguistic support, 357–368
Cognitive processing
  in aphasia, 344–346, 361–362
  suggestions for minimizing,
    361–362
Cognitive prostheses, 389
Cognitive recovery, 279–284
Cohesion, 17
Comments, 41
Communication
  accuracy of, 39–40
  adequacy of, 139, 147
  with adults with acquired disabili-
    ties, 169–170
  basic-choice, 387
  of basic needs, 347–348
  of choices, 161
  cognitive-linguistic demands of,
    347–368
  "computer-assisted," 212
  with dementia, 380–383
  detailed information
AAC methods used by individuals
  with ALS, 209–210, 210f
satisfaction with, 211–212, 212f
  effectiveness of, 101–103
  functional requirements, 39–40
  functionally adequate, 139
  functions of, 139–147
change in, 104
research reviews, 40–53
  goals of, 140, 141t, 146–147
  informed consent requirements,
    171
  from insider's perspective, 261–262
  integrated, 362–368
  knowledge, judgment, and skill
    requirements, 140
  meaningful roles of adults for,
    3–24
  mechanical ventilation and,
    190–191
  message management, 25–54
  modes of, 103
  mutuality model of, 85–87, 86f

natural strategies supplemented
  by augmentative techniques,
    68
  opportunity for, 166, 174
  partner strategies to facilitate,
    169–170
  purposes of, 117, 315–316
  rate of, 39–40
  residual abilities
    early-stage dementia, 381–382
    late-stage dementia, 382–383
    middle-stage dementia, 382
  respiratory issues and, 187–193
  skill requirements, 140
  supplemented, 97, 98f
  timing of, 39–40
Communication aids
  example use of, 12–14, 14f, 15, 15f
  unambiguous symbols, 12–14, 13f
Communication boards
  cognitive-linguistic demands of,
    353–354
  yes-or-no, 351–353
Communication breakdown resolution, 50
Communication disorders
  absence of, 67
  acquired
    adjustment to, 31
    see also Acquired disorders
  associated with Huntington dis-
    ease, 243–244
  associated with Parkinson's
    disease, 257
  associated with traumatic brain
    injury, 273–279
  with intelligible speech, writing,
    and functional reading, 67
  stable or recovering from, 68–69
Communication Enhancement
  Model, 398
Communication environment, 111–112
Communication interventions, *see*
  Intervention(s)
Communication needs, 316
Communication Needs Model, 315
Communication notebooks, 326–330
  dynamic, 329
  guidelines to foster acceptance and
    use of, 329–330
  key sections and core vocabulary
    of, 327, 328t

personalization of, 327
requirements for successful incor-
    poration into daily activities,
    326–327
rules for, 327–330
"topics page," 332–333
Communication partners, 110–111,
    397
acceptance and rejection of AAC
    by, 124–132, 126*t*–127*t*,
    128*t*–129*t*
influence of, 166–174
strategies to facilitate communica-
    tion, 169–170
training, 397–399
use of communication aid symbols
    in response to questions,
    12–14, 13*f*
Communication registers, 51–53
Communication roles
educational and clinical implica-
    tions, 19–21
implications for future research,
    21–22
Communication therapy, group, 364
Communicative competence, 137,
    140–147
acquired disorders and, 139–140
attitude barriers, 167–169
environmental factors and,
    166–170
knowledge, judgment, and skill
    requirements, 147–156, 148*t*,
    174
opportunity barriers to rebuilding,
    167, 168*t*
opportunity for, 166
overview of, 138–156
policy and practice barriers, 167
rebuilding, 137–179
research requirements, 174–175
Communicators
AAC Communicators with Aphasia
    classification scheme, 321
augmented-input, 321, 322*t*,
    323–324
basic-choice, 321, 322*t*, 324
comprehensive, 321, 322*t*, 323, 357
controlled-situation, 321, 322*t*, 324,
    357–358
specific-needs, 321, 322*t*
Community language, 149

Competence
communicative, 137, 140–147
acquired disorders and, 139–140
environmental factors and,
    166–170
opportunity for, 166
overview of, 138–156
rebuilding, 137–179
research requirements, 174–175
integration of, 155–156
in "language" code of (AAC) sys-
    tem(s), 150–151
in language of family and commu-
    nity, 149
linguistic, 147–151
operational, 151–152
social, 152–154
strategic, 154–155
Complex conversations, 349–350
Complex information
comprehension of linguistic input,
    349
encoding of, 349
Comprehension
auditory, difficulties, 351, 352*t*
of complex linguistic input, 349
linguistic, 348
pragmatic, 348
reading, difficulties, 351, 352*t*
Comprehensive communicators, 321,
    322*t*, 323, 357
Computer-assisted communication,
    212
Conceptual representation, 347
Confusion-agitation, 274–275, 276*t*
Consensus
for health services and patient
    management strategies, 64, 64*t*
Consumer involvement, 77
Continuers, 41
Controlled-situation communicators,
    322*t*, 324, 357–358
Conversations
basic, 348–349
complex, 349–350
with familiar partners, 12–14, 13*f*
natural environment, 12–14, 14*f*
satisfaction with, 211–212, 212*f*
with strangers, 210–211, 211*f*
with unfamiliar partners, 12–14, 13*f*
with very familiar partners,
    210–211, 211*f*

Conversations—*continued*
  with voice output communication
    aids, case report, 366
  written-choice, 354, 355*f*
Coping, 213–219
Cost efficacy, 77
Cues
  alphabetic, 88–91, 92*f*, 94–95
  effects on intelligibility of
    dysarthric speech, 91, 92*f*
  on-the-spot cuing, 362
  topic/semantic, 91–94, 92*f*, 94–95
  visual and gestural, 95–97
Cumulative Index to Nursing &
  Allied Health Literature
  (CINAHL), 74

Decision making, 159*t*, 160–163
  in AAC intervention, 55–82
  based on staging of intervention,
    64–69
  clinical
    with Huntington disease,
      244–248
    with Parkinson's disease,
      257–260
  evidence-based, 76–77
  judgments and, 63–75
DECTalk synthesized speech, 87
Dedicated devices, 206–207, 207*t*
Degenerative disease, 66–69
Dementia, 375–405
  AAC for people with
    benefits of, 387–391
    devices, 395–397
    measurement of, 399–400
    questions about, 385–400
    strategies for, 394–395
    timing of intervention, 399
  assessment of, 383–384
  clinical symptomatology of,
    378–383
  cortical, 377
  diagnosis of, 376–385
  differential diagnosis of, 377–378
  early-stage communication impair-
    ments/residual abilities,
    381–382
  intervention in
    methods for, 392–399
    rationale for, 385–387

late-stage residual communication
    abilities, 382–383
  management of adults with,
    376–385
  medical diagnosis of, 376–385
  medical management of, 384–385
  middle-stage communication
    impairments/residual abili-
    ties, 381–382
  semantic, 308
  subcortical, 377
Dependent auditory scanning,
  206–207, 207*t*
Depression
  in Parkinson's disease, 253
  after stroke, 114
Design, AAC system
  cognition and, 271–304
  role of cognition in, 291–300
  strategies for, 152
Detailed information communication
  satisfaction with, 211–212, 212*f*
Devices
  AAC
    dedicated, 206–207, 207*t*
    multipurpose, 206–207, 207*t*
    for people with dementia,
      395–397
    recommended for individuals
      with primary progressive
      aphasia, 323–324, 325*t*
  prosthetic, 33
  respiratory
    invasive, 189
    noninvasive, 189
Difficulty, 33
Digivox, 354
Disability, 31–314
  adaptation to, 330–333
  associated with primary progres-
    sive aphasia, 313–315
  International Classification of
    Impairment, Disability, and
    Handicap level of, 58
  identity transformation by, 28–29
  medical model of, 57
  models of, 57–60
  personal consequences of, 28–30
  and personal goals, 29–30
  and self-presentation to others, 29
  social model of, 57
  and social self, 29–30

with traumatic brain injury, 290–291
World Health Organization Model of Chronic Disease, 284, 286t
World Health Organization Model of Disablements, 57, 316–317, 317f
Disablement, see Disability
Discourse
  advanced skills of, 350
  intelligibility of
    effects of alphabetic and topic cues on, 95
    effects of alphabetic cues on, 91
    effects of topic/semantic cues on, 94
Disorders
  and acceptance of AAC, 112–113
  acquired
    acceptance of AAC by adults with, 107–136
    communication with adults with, 164, 167, 168t, 169–170
    onset of, 139–140
  chronic disease model, 284–291
  levels of, 60
  see also specific disorders
Display, AAC
  configuration of, 292–293
  dynamic, 294
Dynamic communication notebooks, 329
Dynamic display, 294
DynaMyte, 125
DynaVox, 330, 356
Dysarthria, staging of, 197–198
Dysarthric speech
  intelligibility of
    effects of cues on, 91, 92f
    effects of stimulus length on, 87, 88f
  listener processing of, 85–97
Dyskinesia, peak-dose, 253
Dysphagia, 74

EBM, see Evidence-based medicine
"Economy of wording" strategy, 196
Education, 19–21
Efficacy research, 63
Emotional disturbances, 241–242
Emotional experience, 17

Emotional state, 113–115
Empowerment, 157–158
Enabling, 264
Encoding
  coded eye-blink, 206–207, 207t
  of complex information, 349
  eye codes, 208
  key-terminated codes, 36
  "language" code of (AAC) system(s), 150–151
  letter, 298
  message, 297–298
  Morse code, 208, 297
  strategies for, 36
  syntactic, difficulties, 351, 352t
Enduring the self, 30–31
Engagement, 389–390
  active, 389
  passive, 389
Environment
  attentiveness to, 347
  communication, 111–112
Environmental factors
  impact on communicative competence, 166–170
  impact on self-determination, 170–174
  influencing social role performance, 8–19
Episodic care, 77
Episodic memory, 379
Etiquette, social, 141t, 146
Evaluation
  of past life events and experiences, 390
  self-evaluation, 158–160
  see also Assessment
Evidence-based decision making, 76–77
Evidence-based medicine (EBM), 74–75
Evidence-based practice, 73–75
  merits of, 74–75
  steps in, 73–74
Evidence of treatment effectiveness
  class I, 72
  class II, 72
  class III, 72
  for health services and patient management strategies, 64, 64t
  types of, 71
Exchanging information, 145

Expectancy theory, 9
Expressive modality, 347
Eye-blink, coded, 206–207, 207t
Eye codes, 208
EZ Keys, 130

Facial expression, 206–207, 207t
Facilitators, 319
Familiar partners
    conversations with, 210–211, 211f
    quick needs communication with,
        210–211, 211f
Family
    language of, 149
    and social roles, 16–19
Family Systems Model, 17–19, 18f
Festination, 252
FIM, see Functional Independence
    Measure
Fiscal responsibility, 77
Fluency, 307–310
FOCUSED (training modules), 398
Frontal lobe, 380
Functional Assessment of
    Communication Skills in Adults
    (ASHA FACS), 62–63
Functional Independence Measure
    (FIM), 62
Functional limitations, 284
    assessment of, 289–290
    International Classification of
        Impairment, Disability, and
        Handicap level of, 58
    remediation of, 290
    World Health Organization Model
        of Chronic Disease, 285t,
        289–290
Functional speech, loss of, 68

Gender preferences, 211
Generalized response, 274–275, 276t
Gestural cues, 95–97
Gestures
    manual, 206–207, 207t
    recommended for individuals with
        primary progressive aphasia,
        323, 325t
Goal-oriented behavior, 165
Goals
    personal, 29–30

setting and attainment, 159t,
    164–165
Grief, 33
Group communication therapy, 364
Guillain-Barré syndrome, 69

Hand functioning
    adequate
        with adequate speech, 198–199
        with poor speech and adequate
            mobility, 202–203
        with poor speech and poor
            mobility, 203
    poor
        with adequate speech, 199–202
        with poor speech and good
            mobility, 203–204
        with poor speech and poor
            mobility, 204
Handwriting, 206–207, 207t
Health care delivery, 75–77
Health care needs, 49
Health services, 64, 64t
Hemiplegia, 351, 352t
History, intervention, 117–118
Huntington disease, 234–250
    AAC for, 233–270
    characteristics of, 234–242
    clinical characteristics of, 236–242
    clinical decision making with,
        244–248
    cognitive component, 239–241
    communication disorders that
        accompany, 243–244
    emotional component, 241–242
    future directions, 249–250
    genetic aspects, 235–236
    living with, 248–249
    models of care for, 263–265
    motor component, 236–239
    neuropathologic aspects, 236
    stage 1: No detectable speech dis-
        order, 245
    stage 2: Obvious speech disorder
        with intelligible speech,
        245–246
    stage 3: Reduction in speech intel-
        ligibility, 246–247
    stage 4: Natural speech supple-
        mented by augmentative tech-
        niques, 247–248

stage 5: No functional speech, 248
Hybrid model of supplemented communication, 97, 98f

ICIAP, *see* International Classification of Impairment, Activity, and Participation
ICIDH, *see* International Classification of Impairment, Disability, and Handicap
Ideational skills, reduced, 351, 352t
Identity, 28–29
Impairment(s), 314
   assessment of, 287, 317–318
   International Classification of Impairment, Activity, and Participation level of, 60
   International Classification of Impairment, Disability, and Handicap level, 58
   linguistic-cognitive, 34–39
   remediation of, 287–289
   World Health Organization Model of Chronic Disease, 285t, 287–289
Incentive theory, 9
Information
   acoustic, signal-dependent, 98
   augmentative communication, 205–206
   extrinsic, 97–100
   intrinsic, 97–100
   novel, 48
   sources of
      extrinsic, 88–97
      intrinsic, 85–87
   storage and access, 358–359
Information exchange, 141t, 145
Information searchers, 361
Information sharing
   through public speaking, 48–49
   through unique (novel) messages, 48
Informed consent, 145, 171
Injury
   shearing, 273
   traumatic brain, 271–304
Insider's perspective
   on amyotrophic lateral sclerosis, 214–216
   communication from, 261–262

Institutes of Medicine (IOM), 64
Institute on Disabilities (Temple University), 167–168
Instruction, 362–368
   in conversational use of voice output communcation aid, case report, 366
Integrated communication skills, 362–368
Integrated model for augmented communication, 97–100
Intelligibility
   communication intervention for reduction in, 67–68
   discourse
      effects of alphabetic and topic cues on, 95
      effects of alphabetic cues on, 91
      effects of topic/semantic cues on, 94
   of dysarthric speech
      effects of cues on, 91, 92f
      effects of stimulus length on, 87, 88f
   sentence
      effects of alphabetic and topic cues on, 95
      effects of alphabetic cues on, 89–91
      effects of topic/semantic cues on, 93–94
   of speech
      obvious communication disorder with, 67
      obvious speech disorder with, 197, 245–246, 258
      reduction in, 197–198, 258–259
   word
      effects of alphabetic and topic cues on, 95
      effects of alphabetic cues on, 88–89
      effects of topic/semantic cues on, 92–93
Interactions, 316
Intergenerational Program, 389
International Classification of Impairment, Disability, and Handicap (ICIDH), 57, 58–59, 314
   classification levels, 58
   disability or context level, 59
   functional limitation level, 59

International Classification of
    Impairment, Disability, and
    Handicap (ICIDH)—*continued*
  impairment level, 58
  pathophysiology level, 58
  social limitation level, 59
International Classification of
    Impairment Activity and
    Participation (ICIAP), 57, 60
Internet, 52–53, 200
Internet registers, 51, 52–53
Intervention(s)
  AAC, *see* Augmentative and alter-
      native communication
  to build metarepresentation skills,
      164
  considerations for, 3
  in degenerative disease, 66–69
  focus of, 149
  historic approaches for aphasia,
      340–341
  in primary progressive aphasia,
      321–330
  staging of, 66–69
    decisions based on, 64–69
    knowledge bases for, 66
    rationale for, 65–66
    for stable or recovering from
        communication disorders,
        68–69
  voice output communication aid,
      case report, 365–366
Intervention history, 117–118
Invasive devices, 189

*JAMA: Journal of the American Medical
    Association,* 74
Journal of Neuroscience and Nursing, 74
*Journal of Speech, Language, and
    Hearing Research,* 74
Journal of Speech and Hearing Research,
    63
Judgment(s)
  and decision making, 63–75
  required for communicative com-
      petence, 147–156, 148*t*, 174
  required for self-determination,
      158–166, 159*t*

Key-terminated codes, 36
Keyboards, 201

Knowledge
  barriers to communicative compe-
      tence, 168*t*, 169–170
  barriers to self-determination,
      173–174
  as part of caring model, 264
  required for communicative com-
      petence, 147–156, 148*t*, 174
  required for self-determination,
      158–166, 159*t*
  self-knowledge, 158–160
Knowledge base, 57–63

Language
  with dementia, 380–383
  of family and community, 149
  multiple levels of, 87
  representation of, 392–395
Language behaviors, 274–275,
    276*t*–278*t*
"Language" code of AAC system(s),
    150–151
Language comprehension, 348
Language differences, 149
Language disorders, 256
Learning
  AAC, 343–344
  with aphasia, 343–344
  new procedural, 351, 352*t*
  after traumatic brain injury, 282
Letter encoding, 298
Levodopa
  on-off effect with, 252–253
  peak-dose dyskinesia with, 253
Lexical memory, 379
Lexical prediction, 36, 299–300
Liberator, 355
Life review therapy, 390
Limb apraxia, 351, 352*t*
Lindblom's mutuality model of com-
    munication, 85, 86*f*
Lingraphica, 355
Linguistic-cognitive capabilities and
    impairments, 34–39
Linguistic competence, 147–151
  demands for people who require
      AAC, 147
  integration with operational,
      social, and strategic competen-
      cies, 155–156
Linguistic comprehension, 348

Linguistic impairments, 37–38
    language disorders, 256
    profound disorders, 161
Listener processing
    of dysarthric speech, 85–97
    mutuality of speaker-listener inter-
        actions, 85, 86*f*
Literate AAC users, 296–300
Lived experience, 260–262
Localized response, 274–275, 276*t*
Long-term memory, 351, 352*t*

Malignant memory deficits, serious,
    383
Manual gestures, 206–207, 207*t*
Matching Person and Technology
    (MPT) model, 132
McGurk effect, 95–96
MDA, *see* Muscular Dystrophy
    Association
Mechanical ventilation, 190–191
Medicare, 221
Medline, 74
Memory
    allocation of resources for, 348
    in aphasia, 345
    in dementia, 379–380
    episodic, 379
    implicit, 386
    lexical, 379
    long-term, 349, 351, 352*t*
    procedural, 379
    semantic, 379
    serious, malignant deficits, 383
    short-term, 351, 352*t*
    working, 379
Memory-enhancing strategies, 391
Memory impairments, 351, 352*t*
Message management, 25–54
    encoding, 297–298
    formulation, 294–300
    implications for service delivery,
        32–34
    issues related to adjustment to
        acquired communication
        disorders, 31
    production and retrieval
        acceleration techniques for,
        296–297
    rate enhancement, 296–297
    strategies for literate users,
        296–300

sample story-order arrangement,
    368, 369*f*
selection, 360–361
self-preservation and, 28–34
societal factors that influence, 27
technical factors that influence,
    26–27
Messages
    communication breakdown resolu-
        tion, 50
    unique (novel), 48
    urgent, 49
Metacognitive ability, 103
Metacommunication, 348, 351, 352*t*
Metarepresentation, 159*t*, 163–164
Micrographia, 256
Milieu factors, 110–112
Mini-Mental State Exam (MMSE),
    384
Minspeak, 150, 294, 297, 355
Mixed aphasia, 309
MMSE, *see* Mini-Mental State Exam
Mobility
    adequate, with poor speech, and
        adequate hand functioning,
        202–203
    good, with poor speech and poor
        hand functioning, 203–204
    poor, with poor speech, and ade-
        quate hand functioning, 203
    poor, with poor speech, and poor
        hand functioning, 204
Montessori-based activities, 389–390
Morse code, 208, 297
Motivation
    integrated theory of, 11–16
    and social role performance, 8–16
    theories of, 8–9
Motivational systems theory (MST),
    11
    applied to example communica-
        tion aid use, 15, 15*f*
    equation for, 11, 12*f*
Motor control, 292–293
Motor disturbances, 236–239
Motor processing, 380
Movement disorders, 234
    in Parkinson's disease, 251–257
    treatment of, 251–257
MPT model, *see* Matching Person
    and Technology model
MST, *see* Motivational systems theory

Multilevel dynamic screen communication systems, 366–367
Multilevel high-technology systems cognitive-linguistic demands of, 356
R.H. (example), 366–368
Multimodal Communication Screening Tool, 359
Multimodal Communication Screening Tool for Aphasia, 365
Multimodal communication systems, 356–357
Multiprocess reasoning, 351, 352*t*
Multipurpose devices, 206–207, 207*t*
Muscular Dystrophy Association (MDA), 205, 232
Mutuality model of communication, 85–87, 86*f*

National Assistive Technology Advocacy Project, 221
National Caregiver Survey, 397
National Outcomes Measure System (NOMS), 62
Natural communication strategies, 68
Natural environment conversations, 12–14, 14*f*
Natural speech
    integrating with AAC, 49–50, 83–106
    supplemented by augmentative techniques, 198, 247–248, 259–260
Needs and wants
    and acceptance of AAC, 117
    communication of, 347–348
        detailed, 208*t*, 208–209, 209*t*, 209–210, 210*f*, 211–212, 212*f*
        quick, 208*t*, 208–209, 209*t*, 209–210, 210*f*, 210–211, 211*f*, 211–212, 212*f*
    expression of, 140–142, 141*t*
    physiologic, 347
    specific-needs communicators, 321, 322*t*
Negations, 41
Neurobehavioral Cognitive Status Exam, 384
Neuropsychologic testing, 195
Nightingale, Florence, 61
NOMS, *see* National Outcomes Measure System

Nonuse or rejection of AAC
    categories of, 108
    user and partner profiles, 124–132, 128*t*–129*t*
Notebooks, communication, 326–330
Novel information, 48
Novel messages, 48

On-off effect, 252
Opaqueness, 393
Operational competence, 151–152, 155–156
Opportunity, 166
Optimal use, 108
Orthography, 323, 325*t*
Outcomes measures, 60–63

Palliative care
    definition of, 263
    for Huntington and Parkinson's disease, 263
Parkinson's disease, 250–263
    AAC for, 233–270
    areas of inquiry for, 262
    associated disorders, 253–256
    characteristics of, 250–251
    clinical decision making with, 257–260
    communication disorders in, 257
    future directions, 262–263
    lived experience of, 260
    models of care for, 263–265
    movement disorders and treatment in, 251–257
    stage 1: No detectable speech disorder, 257–258
    stage 2: Obvious speech disorder with intelligible speech, 258
    stage 3: Reduction in speech intelligibility, 258–259
    stage 4: Natural speech supplemented by augmentative techniques, 259–260
    stage 5: No functional speech, 260
Participation
    assessment of, 319–321
    International Classification of Impairment, Activity, and Participation level of, 60
Participation Model of care, 263–264, 315, 320

Partners
  acceptance and rejection of AAC
    by, 124–132
  communication, 110–111, 397
  influence of, 166–174
  strategies reported to facilitate
    communication, 169–170
  training, 397–399
  use of communication aid symbols
    in response to questions,
    12–14, 13*f*
  very familiar
    conversations with, 210–211, 211*f*
    quick needs communication
      with, 210–211, 211*f*
Partners in Augmentative
  Communication Training study,
  124
Pathography, 214
Pathophysiology
  International Classification of
    Impairment, Disability, and
    Handicap level of, 58
  World Health Organization Model
    of Chronic Disease, 284, 285*t*
Patient management strategies, 64,
  64*t*
Patient response, 77
Perception studies, 121, 122*t*
Perceptual processing, 345
Personal agency beliefs, 12
Personal care, 49
Personal factors
  and acceptance of AAC, 112–118
  consequences of disability, 28–30
  influencing social role perform-
    ance, 8–19
  self-preservation, 28–34
Personal goals, 29–30
Personality
  and acceptance of AAC, 113–115
  bipolar factors underlying, 114
Personalization of communication
  notebooks, 327
Phonological processing impair-
  ments, 351, 352*t*
Physiologic needs
  identification of, 347
  see also Needs and wants
PL 100-407, *see* Technology-Related
  Assistance for Individuals with
  Disabilities Act of 1988

Policy and practice
  barriers to communicative compe-
    tence, 167, 168*t*
  barriers to self-determination,
    170–171
Positive image, 33
Post-Stroke Rehabilitation Practice
  Guidelines (Agency for Health
  Care Policy and Research), 70–71
PPA, *see* Aphasia, primary progres-
  sive
Practice
  barriers to communicative compe-
    tence, 167, 168*t*
  barriers to self-determination,
    170–171
  evidence-based, 73–75
Practice guidelines, 69–73
  development of, 71–73
    consumer involvement in, 77
    procedures for, 71
    rationale for, 70–71
Pragmatic awareness, 350
Pragmatic comprehension, 348
Prentke-Romich, Inc., 354, 356
Procedural learning, 351, 352*t*
Procedural memory, 379
Programming, internal, 366–367
Prosthetic devices, 33
Psychological empowerment, 157–158
Psychological treatment, 72
Psychosocial impact
  of amyotrophic lateral sclerosis,
    216–218
  of aphasia, 17–19, 18*f*
PsycINFO, 74
Public health, 77
Public speaking, 48–49

Quadriplegia, ventilator-dependent,
  4–5, 6*t*
Quality, 77
Quality of life, 211–212
Questionnaires, 121, 122*t*
Questions
  autobiographical, 348–349
  Yes-or-no, 206–207, 207*t*

Rate enhancement, 296–297
Reading
  functional, 67

Reading—*continued*
  literate AAC users, 296–300
Reading comprehension difficulties,
  351, 352*t*
Reasoning, multiprocess, 351, 352*t*
Referential symbols
  recommended for individuals with
    primary progressive aphasia,
    323, 325*t*
  see also Symbols
Rehabilitation Engineering and
    Assistive Technology Society of
    North America (RESNA), 25
Rejection of AAC
  categories of, 108
  user and partner profiles, 124–132,
    128*t*–129*t*
Reminiscence therapy, 390
Representations
  visual, 323, 325*t*
  visual/symbolic, 359–360
Research
  AAC and aphasia, 369–370
  on acceptance of AAC, 120–132,
    132–133
  communication roles and, 21–22
  communicative competence,
    174–175
  on Internet interactions, 52–53
  Parkinson's disease, 262
  on psychosocial impact of aphasia,
    17–19, 18*f*
  on self-determination, 174–175
  small talk, 42
  storytelling, 47–48
Residual abilities
  early-stage dementia, 381–382
  late-stage dementia, 382–383
  middle-stage dementia, 382
RESNA, *see* Rehabilitation
    Engineering and Assistive
    Technology Society of North
    America
Resource capacity and allocation,
    346, 348
Resources, 231–232
Respiratory devices
  invasive, 189
  noninvasive, 189
Respiratory problems
  in amyotrophic lateral sclerosis,
    188

decision to live beyond failure,
    191–193
  technology for management of,
    188–189
Retrieval of messages
  spaced, 391
  strategies for literate AAC users,
    296–300
Retrieval of words, 351, 352*t*
Routines, social etiquette, 146

Satisfaction, user, 211–212, 212*f*
SCA, *see* Supported Conversation for
    Adults with Aphasia
Screen communication systems, mul-
    tilevel dynamic, 366–367
Searcher of information, 361
Self
  enduring, 30–31
  sense of, 33–34
  social, 29–30
  striving to regain, 31
Self-awareness, 158–160, 159*t*, 347
Self-determination, 138, 156–166
  attitude barriers, 171–173
  definition of, 156–166
  impact of acquired disorder on,
    139–140
  impact of environmental factors
    on, 170–174
  integration of skills to build,
    165–166
  knowledge, judgment, and skills
    required for, 158–166, 159*t*
  knowledge and skill barriers,
    173–174
  opportunities for, 170
  opportunity barriers, 167, 168*t*
  overview of, 138–156
  policy and practice barriers, 170–171
  principles fundamental to, 156
  rebuilding, 137–179
  research requirements, 174–175
Self-evaluation, 158–160, 159*t*
Self-knowledge, 158–160, 159*t*
Self-presentation to others, 29
Self-preservation, 28–34
Self-realization, 157
Self-regulation, 157
Semantic breakdowns, 351, 352*t*
Semantic cues, 91–94

Semantic dementia, 308
Semantic mapping/translation skills, 348
    in basic conversation with communicator who has aphasia, 349
    in complex conversations between participants who do not have aphasia, 350
Semantic memory, 379
Sentence intelligibility
    effects of alphabetic and topic cues on, 95
    effects of alphabetic cues on, 89–91
    effects of topic/semantic cues on, 93–94
Service delivery, 32–34
Sharing, *see* Information sharing
Shearing injury, white matter, 273
Short-term memory, 351, 352*t*
Signal-dependent acoustic information, 98
Skills
    and acceptance of AAC, 116–117
    advanced discourse, 350
    barriers to communicative competence, 168*t*, 169–170
    barriers to self-determination, 173–174
    cognitive-communication, 386
    ideational, 351, 352*t*
    integration of, 165–166
    required for communicative competence, 147–156, 148*t*, 174
    required for self-determination, 158–166, 159*t*
    sociorelational, 153–154
    translation, 348
Slang, 51
Small talk
    research issues, 42
    social closeness through, 40–42
Social closeness, 141*t*, 142–145
    through small talk, 40–42
    through storytelling, 42–48
Social competence, 152–154, 155–156
Social etiquette, 141*t*, 146
Social limitation level (International Classification of Impairment, Disability, and Handicap), 58
Social roles, 5–8
    factors influencing performance, 8–19

families and, 16–19
Social Security Disability Insurance, 221
Social self, 29–30
Societal limitations, 284, 286*t*
Society
    factors that influence message management, 27
    influence of, 166–174
    participation in (International Classification of Impairment, Activity, and Participation level), 60
Sociorelational skills, 153–154
Spaced retrieval, 391
Speaker-listener interactions, 85, 86*f*
Speech
    adequate
        with adequate hand functioning, 198–199
        with poor hand functioning, 199–202
    with amyotrophic lateral sclerosis, 196–212
    DECTalk synthesized, 87
    dysarthric
        intelligibility of, 87, 88*f*, 91, 92*f*
        listener processing of, 85–97
    functional, loss of, 68, 248, 260
    intelligible
        with obvious communication disorder, 67
        with obvious speech disorder, 197, 245–246, 258
        reduction in, 197–198, 246–247, 258–259
    natural
        integrating with AAC, 49–50
        supplemented by augmentative techniques, 198, 247–248, 259–260
    poor
        with adequate hand functioning and adequate mobility, 202–203
        with adequate hand functioning and poor mobility, 203
        with poor hand functioning and good mobility, 203–204
        with poor hand functioning and poor mobility, 204
    recovery of, 274–275

Speech disorders, 197, 245–246, 258
Speech registers, 51–52
Speech supplementation, 49–50
   patterns in use, 100–104
   strategies, 88–97
   types of, 49
Spelling-based systems, 295–296
Spelling/phonological processing
   impairments, 351, 352*t*
Stimulus length, 87, 88*f*
Storage, information, 358–359
Stories
   basic segments of, 44
   culturally common, 43
   expansion segments of, 44
   firsthand, 43
   invented, 43
   official, 42
   satisfaction with, 211–212, 212*f*
   secondhand, 43
   types of, 42–43
Story-order message arrangement,
   368, 369*f*
Storytelling
   research areas, 47–48
   social closeness through, 42–48
Strangers
   conversations with, 210–211, 211*f*
   quick needs communication with,
      210–211, 211*f*
Strategic competence, 154–155,
   155–156
Stroke, 114
Substantia nigra, 250
Subtopic initiation, 350
Sunrise Medical Systems, Inc., 354,
   356
Supplemental Security Income, 130
Supplemented communication, 97, 98*f*
"Supported cognition," 161, 173
Supported Conversation for Adults
   with Aphasia (SCA), 340
Symbol sequencing high-technology
   systems, 355–356
Symbols, 294–300, 359–360
   communication aid, unambiguous,
      12–14, 13*f*
   referential, 323, 325*t*
   visual, 360
Syntactic encoding difficulties, 351,
   352*t*
Synthesized speech, 87

Talk, small, 40–42
Talking Screen, 355
TBI, *see* Traumatic brain injury
Technology
   and acceptance of AAC, 118–120
   factors that influence message
      management, 26–27
   high-technology systems
      multilevel, 356, 366–368
      symbol sequencing, 355–356
   invasive devices, 189
   noninvasive devices, 189
   quality of, 77
   for respiratory problem manage-
      ment, 188–189
Technology-Related Assistance for
   Individuals with Disabilities Act
   of 1988 (PL 100-407), 172
TechSpeak, 354
Temple University, 167–168
Therapy
   effectiveness of, 71
   goals that facilitate new sense of
      self, 33–34
   group communication, 364
   life review, 390
   reminiscence, 390
Timing, 39–40
Topic initiation, 350
Topic/semantic cues, 91–94, 92*f*,
   94–95
Topic supplementation, 49, 84, 100
Training
   AAC strategy, 357–368
   FOCUSED (modules), 398
   partner, 397–399
Transactions, 316
Translation skills, 348, 350
Transparency, 393
Traumatic brain injury (TBI), 271–304
   AAC management after, 279–284
   chronic disease model for,
      284–291, 285*t*–286*t*
   cognitive disorders that influ-
      ence, 280–284
   future directions, 300
   communication disorders associ-
      ated with, 273–279
   disabilities associated with,
      290–291
   functional limitations with, 289–290
      assessment of, 289–290

remediation of, 290
impairments in, 287–289
assessment of, 287
remediation of, 287–289
learning after, 282
neuropathology of, 272–273
staging of intervention for, 65
Treatment effectiveness, 71

Uniform Data System for Medical
Rehabilitation (United States), 62
Urgent messages, 49
User satisfaction, 211–212, 212*f*

Validation, 33
Vanguard, 356
Ventilation, mechanical, 190–191
Ventilator-dependent quadriplegia,
4–5, 6*t*
Vigilance, 30
Vision acuity and perception, 292
Visual and gestural cues, 95–97
Visual disturbances, 351, 352*t*
Visual/symbolic representation(s),
359–360
recommended for individuals with
primary progressive aphasia,
323, 325*t*
symbols, 360
Visuospatial domain, 380
Vocabulary
core, 327, 328*t*
selection of, 360–361
VOCAs, *see* Voice output communication aids
Voice output communication aids
(VOCAs)
in aphasia, case report, 365–366
conversational use of, case report,
366
recommended for individuals with
primary progressive aphasia,
323, 325*t*
simple, 354

Volition, 9–11
Volume-equals-expense equation, 77
Volume-equals-revenue equation, 77

Wants, *see* Needs and wants
Western Aphasia Battery, 364
White matter shearing injury, 273
WHO, *see* World Health
Organization
Wisconsin Card Sorting Test, 255
"Wish list" of communication activi-
ties, 219
Word intelligibility
effects of alphabetic and topic cues
on, 95
effects of alphabetic cues on, 88–89
effects of topic/semantic cues on,
92–93
Word retrieval/semantic break-
downs, 351, 352*t*
Wording, economy of, 196
Words+, Inc., 355
Working memory, 379
World Health Organization (WHO),
57, 263
Model of Chronic Disease, 284,
285*t*–286*t*
Model of Disablements, 316–317,
317*f*
Writing, intelligible, 67
Written Choice Communication
Strategy, 38
Written-choice conversations, 354,
355*f*
Written communication
considerations with respect to,
199–200
satisfaction with, 211–212, 212*f*
system prescription for, 199–200

Yes-or-no communication boards,
351–353
Yes-or-no questions, 206–207, 207*t*

DATE DUE

JUL 1 8 2002			